Praise for *America Between the Wars*

"An indispensable history of the decade preceding 9/11. You can't understand today's American crisis without understanding how we got there. This book tells us, eloquently and compellingly."

—Richard Holbrooke

"This book will likely stand as the definitive work on the politics, people, and ideas involved in the foreign policy debates of the 1990s. It shows how, in the decade before Sept. 11, both Republicans and Democrats, both liberals and conservatives, struggled to come to grips with post–Cold War issues such as the use of military force, the promotion of democracy, and the proper U.S. role in the world. This is a lucidly written history, devoid of rhetoric and full of invaluable information."

—James Mann, author of *Rise of the Vulcans*

"*America Between the Wars* is a deeply researched, well-written account of U.S. foreign policy in the first post–Cold War decade. Authors Chollet and Goldgeier should be commended for being comprehensive and fair-minded. Truly essential reading."

—Douglas Brinkley, professor of history at Rice University and fellow at the James A. Baker III Institute for Public Policy

"Here is an excellent account of how the United States and the world changed from the conclusion of the Cold War to the Al Qaeda attacks of 2001. The history of diplomacy and international affairs are inseparable from the history of politics; but it is extremely difficult to do them all justice in a single book. Derek Chollet and James Goldgeier not only succeed, they succeed in style—and they provide a persuasive and entirely original way of understanding America's role in global affairs during a pivotal dozen years."

—Sean Wilentz, professor of history at Princeton University and author of *The Age of Reagan*

"In *America Between the Wars*, Goldgeier and Chollet examine the decade between the collapse of the Soviet Union and the destruction of the Twin Towers and offer illuminating insights into the forces that have reshaped today's world."

—Henry Kissinger

"This book is a gem of current history, a scrupulously fair and highly readable piece of old-fashioned scholarship. Chollet and Goldgeier, two of the most promising young foreign policy experts, now allow us to argue about the ten-year run up to 9/11 and know what we're talking about."

—Leslie H. Gelb, former *New York Times* columnist
and president emeritus of the Council on Foreign Relations

"Chollet and Goldgeier have written a highly informative, engaging, and accessible account of the period between America's most recent major wars—the Cold War and the War on Terror. In this balanced and well-written story, they argue that 9/11 did not change everything and that in order to analyze America's challenges today, one must understand the foreign policy debates and clashes of the 1990s."

—Lee H. Hamilton, president and director of the
Woodrow Wilson International Center for Scholars and
vice-chair of the 9/11 Commission

America Between the Wars

America Between the Wars

From 11/9 to 9/11

*

The Misunderstood Years
Between the Fall of the Berlin Wall and the
Start of the War on Terror

Derek Chollet and James Goldgeier

*

A Council on Foreign Relations Book

PublicAffairs
New York

The Council on Foreign Relations is an independent, nonpartisan membership organization, think tank, and publisher dedicated to being a resource for its members, government officials, business executives, journalists, educators and students, civic and religious leaders, and other interested citizens in order to help them better understand the world and the foreign policy choices facing the United States and other countries. Founded in 1921, the Council carries out its mission by maintaining a diverse membership, with special programs to promote interest and develop expertise in the next generation of foreign policy leaders; convening meetings at its headquarters in New York and in Washington, DC, and other cities where senior government officials, members of Congress, global leaders, and prominent thinkers come together with Council members to discuss and debate major international issues; supporting a Studies Program that fosters independent research, enabling Council scholars to produce articles, reports, and books and hold roundtables that analyze foreign policy issues and make concrete policy recommendations; publishing Foreign Affairs, the preeminent journal on international affairs and U.S. foreign policy; sponsoring Independent Task Forces that produce reports with both findings and policy prescriptions on the most important foreign policy topics; and providing up-to-date information and analysis about world events and American foreign policy on its website, CFR.org. THE COUNCIL TAKES NO INSTITUTIONAL POSITION ON POLICY ISSUES AND HAS NO AFFILIATION WITH THE U.S. GOVERNMENT. ALL STATEMENTS OF FACT AND EXPRESSIONS OF OPINION CONTAINED IN ITS PUBLICATIONS ARE THE SOLE RESPONSIBILITY OF THE AUTHOR OR AUTHORS.

Book design and composition by Mark McGarry, Texas Type & Book Works
Set in Caslon 540 with Big Caslon display

Library of Congress Cataloging-in-Publication Data
Chollet, Derek H.
America between the wars, 11/9 to 9/11 : the misunderstood years between the fall of the Berlin Wall and the start of the War on Terror / Derek Chollet and James Goldgeier. — 1st ed.
p. cm.
Includes bibliographical references and index.
ISBN 978-1-58648-496-5 (hardcover : alk. paper) 1. United States—Politics and government—1989–
2. United States—Foreign relations—1989– 3. United States—Social conditions—1980– 4. Political culture—United States—History—20th century. 5. Social change—United States—History—20th century. 6. Berlin Wall, Berlin, Germany, 1961–1989. 7. September 11 Terrorist Attacks, 2001—Influence. 8. World politics—1989– I. Goldgeier, James M. II. Title.
E839.5.C475 2008   2008004053
973.928—dc22

FIRST EDITION
10 9 8 7 6 5 4 3 2 1

FOR OUR FUTURE:

Lucas Chollet Hostetter
and
Jeffrey Goldgeier and Brian Goldgeier

Contents

Between the Wars

IN MARCH 1995, more than five years after the Berlin Wall fell and the Cold War ended, the *New York Times'* Week in Review section invited readers to name the era in which they were living. Writer James Atlas opened the contest by opining that the term "post-Cold War era" was "tentative, vague; it lacks authority." He complained that "the tepid label we reflexively invoke these days carries a suggestion of self-doubt. It's as if our own historical moment is somehow after the fact, overshadowed by the more significant era that preceded it." Atlas himself tried to guess which event historians would use to define the period—perhaps "carnage in the Balkans, the rise of Islamic fundamentalism, or the unraveling of European unity."[1]

Reporting readers' answers a few weeks later, the *Times* said the majority of respondents were male and extremely pessimistic. Popular labels included the "Age of Anxiety," "Age of Uncertainty," "Age of Fragmentation," "Age of (Great and Failed) Expectations," and "Age of Disillusion (and Dissolution)." One reader from New York suggested the "Cold War Lite Era"—in tribute, "to all those Bills, Newts, and Phils[2] who want a strong defense but didn't get around to serving, and to all those global skirmishes that are morally appalling and complex but lack a clear embodiment of evil like Hitler or Communism." From Greenwich High School in Connecticut came the

"Era of the New Meanies." And one wag from Santa Monica offered the "Age That Even Historians from Harvard Can't Name."[3]

Five years later, the magazine *Foreign Policy*, a staple of elite reading in Washington, took its own stab at the problem, asking leading lights in the field of international affairs to submit essays naming the new era. Christoph Bertram, a longtime observer of the United States and director of one of Germany's leading think tanks, wrote that those living in the Renaissance or Enlightenment had no idea they lived in such times and suggested we were in the "Era of the Interregnum, an age that cannot last." Author Robert Wright, whose book on globalization, *Nonzero* (connoting a world of possible win-win outcomes), was a favorite of Bill Clinton's, trotted out "Pax Kapital." Wright sheepishly noted that he had suggested the name back in 1989, at the start of the era, but it never stuck. From King's College in Cambridge, Emma Rothschild offered the "Age of Insubordination." We lived, she said, in a "postrevolutionary universe . . . more free of the fear of violent revolution than at any time since the 1790s."[4]

None of these ideas took hold. These authors and others who tried their hand at the name game throughout those years suffered from not knowing what was to come. Events have a way of framing history with beginnings and endings, revealing trends and clarifying moments. These are hard to perceive, except in hindsight. Looking back, we can see that, for many, the era of uncertainty and opportunity that began with the fall of the Berlin Wall on November 9, 1989, or 11/9, ended violently on September 11, 2001, the day known in America simply as 9/11.

For George W. Bush, the world changed completely on that fateful day, and in his second inaugural address, he described the era that people had struggled to comprehend. "After the shipwreck of communism," the president declared on January 20, 2005, "came years of relative quiet, years of repose, years of sabbatical—and then there came a day of fire."

Years of repose, years of sabbatical. The United States, the president asserted, was naively complacent in the 1990s, off duty, asleep at the switch. Its leaders squandered an opportunity to make the world safer. These phrases suggest that different decisions during these years could have not only prevented 9/11 but also created a new global order. "They were not just a comment, but an argument," says Michael Gerson, Bush's acclaimed speechwriter. They "suggest that there was a surface calm amidst a series of emerging existential threats that had not been adequately confronted."[5]

Bush was hardly alone in this new depiction of the past. In the aftermath of 9/11, conservative commentator George Will dubbed the previous decade the "holiday from history." And columnist Frank Rich (no friend of Bush's) also described a country shocked out of a national stupor when planes hit the Twin Towers, awakening Americans from "a frivolous if not decadent decade-long dream, even as it dumps us into an uncertain future we had never bargained for."[6]

Calling them "years of sabbatical" is more than just an effort to describe failures of perspective and policy. It also suggests that as a matter of history, we can ignore them altogether, fast-forwarding through a time that offers no relevance today. That would be a mistake. Just as history did not end on 11/9, it did not begin on 9/11. The challenges confronting America—combating extremist forces determined to spread terror, responding to the violent breakdown of states, stemming the proliferation of weapons of mass destruction, managing the economy in an era of dramatic technological revolution, and choosing when to send young American soldiers, sailors, airmen, and marines to fight—did not start on 9/11. They began when the Cold War ended a decade earlier.

In his popular book, *The World Is Flat*, Thomas Friedman argued that these two dates represent the rival imaginations in today's world: the "creative imagination" of 11/9, in which the power of ideas and hope broke down walls and opened the world, and the "destructive imagination" of 9/11.[7] While both moments are important, as a historical pivot, one matters more. It is the legacy of 11/9—and the uncertainties, hopes, confusion, threats, and opportunities it produced—that we still live with today, as Republicans and Democrats try to define the direction the country should take.

THE BRITISH PHILOSOPHER Isaiah Berlin famously argued that thinkers can be divided into two categories: hedgehogs and foxes. The hedgehogs know one big thing, Berlin observed; they have a theory of how the world works, and they see everything through that lens. The foxes, on the other hand, know many things; they are impressed with the great complexities the world offers, and they have much less confidence that they are right about everything.

For forty years, the makers of American foreign policy focused on knowing one big thing: America's role in the world was to contain the expansion of the Soviet Union. Combating the ideological, military, economic, and political challenge posed by Soviet communism was the central occupation of the American national security establishment. The United States deployed hundreds of thousands of troops in Western Europe, went to war in Korea and Vietnam, and confronted Soviet influence in the Middle East, Africa, and Latin America. Intelligence analysts at the CIA gauged the Kremlin's intentions, regional experts at the State Department worried about Moscow's meddling in places such as Angola and Nicaragua, and the Pentagon devised reams of battle plans to thwart the Red Army. The United States built and deployed thousands of nuclear weapons, and American schoolchildren practiced duck-and-cover drills in case of nuclear war.

The greatest hedgehog of all, Ronald Reagan, took office in January 1981, with the Cold War still raging. Reagan's view was simple: By projecting American strength, freedom would inevitably win out over the deceit and lies of authoritarianism, leaving the Soviets on the ash heap of history. All the United States had to do was show the Kremlin that it was serious about defending its interests. Once Mikhail Gorbachev assumed power in the mid-1980s and began loosening the communist system in the vain hope that it could match America's resurgence, the whole edifice began to unravel. In 1989, communism crumbled in Poland, Czechoslovakia, and East Germany; two years later, the Baltic nations of Latvia, Lithuania, and Estonia broke free from the Soviet grip, and Ukraine voted for independence. In December 1991, the Soviet Union itself disappeared. The unfathomable had occurred, and America now stood alone as the world's dominant superpower.

DESPITE the peaceful demise of America's rival and archenemy, the prevailing mood was one of pessimism. The United States had won, but many felt that the country had lost. One of the early signs of this growing anxiety emerged in 1987, when Yale historian Paul Kennedy's massive tome, *The Rise and Fall of the Great Powers*, shot onto the bestseller list, where it remained for thirty-four weeks. Placing America's challenge in the context of 500 years of world history, Kennedy warned of the "enduring fact" that the "sum total of the United States' global interests and obligations is nowadays far larger than the country's power to defend them all simultaneously."[8] America, it seemed, was a great power on the decline, just like Spain, France, and Britain before it.

Remarkably, even after the West's triumph took shape, Americans' sense of unease deepened. They worried that Germany and Japan would be formidable economic competitors. And many elites feared that absent the Soviet threat, Americans would be unwilling to endure the costs of global leadership.

Thus was born the effort to develop a new foreign policy strategy to guide the country in the post–11/9 era. But the hedgehogs were out of luck. One attempt after another to define and explain the new global order failed miserably amidst the growing complexity of international politics. 11/9 had not simply marked the end of the superpower rivalry, it also signaled the onset of globalization, whose powerful economic forces had undermined communist rule. Readers of the *New York Times* and policy wonks writing for *Foreign Policy* were confused for a reason; it was impossible to create one simple phrase to sum up the purpose of American foreign policy in such a world. "A

sure sign that experts are encountering difficulty with figuring something out is their use of 'post-' as a prefix," observed Richard Haass, a
senior official in the two Bush presidencies that marked the beginning and end of the era from 11/9 to 9/11. "Such a label reveals that
people know only where they have been, not where they are now,
much less where they are heading."[9] Humanitarian crises, ethnic
conflict, the dissolution of states, global economic integration, climate change, and the challenge of nonstate actors all defied easy
description and prescription.

IN MANY WAYS, the 1990s resemble an earlier period in American history. When historians look back on the 1920s and 1930s, they cite a
litany of follies after World War I that enabled America's enemies to
gather and launch World War II: bitter partisanship that prevented
U.S. leadership in global affairs; fantasies that the peace and riches in
the Roaring '20s would last forever; notions that America did not
have to involve itself in events on the other side of the globe and
could maintain an "empire without tears."[10] It is a time now known as
the interwar years—an era that links the choices made at the end of
one global war with the start of another two decades later.

The problem during those years was that with no common threat
to unite them, Americans couldn't come together to define the
national interest. Woodrow Wilson tried to get the country to stay
engaged after World War I, but partisan politics (and his own stub-
bornness) prevented him from achieving his vision. Franklin Roosevelt tried to take stronger action when new threats became
obvious, but the politics of the time limited him. It was the surprise
attack on Pearl Harbor on December 7, 1941, that finally brought the
threat home to America and ushered in a new era of unity. Many have
compared the September 11 attacks with Pearl Harbor, making the
era from 11/9 to 9/11 the "modern interwar years."

The implications of the two interwar periods are, however, very
different. The Pearl Harbor attack discredited a major school of
thought in the American foreign policy debate. After 1941, even

those skeptical of American involvement in the world accepted the need for engagement, and isolationism never regained a place as a major force in American politics (although during the 1990s some would try to revive it). Despite the shock of the 9/11 attacks—and the wide support for invading Afghanistan—a broad policy consensus about the way forward did not form. If anything, the debates between conservatives and liberals about America's role in the world that took shape in the modern interwar years only intensified.

Although 9/11 created the illusion that America's purpose was once again clear—this time combating Islamic extremism rather than fascism or Soviet communism—the questions America grappled with in the first decade after the Cold War remain unanswered. When should the United States use force to solve problems? When does it need to work through the United Nations to ensure legitimacy for its actions? Should it care that others perceive American goals as selfish? Will it promote free trade as jobs move overseas? Should it make democracy promotion a central part of its foreign policy? How much should it care about what happens inside other states? Debates over these issues continue to rage.

As THE EVENTS of the 1990s grow more distant, their history has become more contested. Both sides of the political debate have a stake in how this era is remembered. From the start of her 2008 presidential bid, Senator Hillary Clinton invoked nostalgia for these years—when her husband was in the White House, the American economy was strong, and the United States was perceived abroad as a force for good, widely admired for solving problems—and promised to bring them back. Others, such as former Republican House Speaker Newt Gingrich, called the era the "lost decade," in which great opportunities were missed and new threats gathered force. In significant ways, both are right. The world is not defined by the black and white division of the Cold War, the "with us or against us" approach of Bush's "war on terror," or even the boundlessly positive globalizing future that some associate with the Clinton years. It is more complicated.

The era from 11/9 to 9/11 not only shaped American foreign policy, it also transformed American politics. Republicans and Democrats tangled over the nature of global change and the future U.S. role in the world. Both parties forged their modern identities during the Cold War, and both sought to use their end to remake themselves. Democrats hoped they could finally overcome their reputation after Vietnam as a party weak on national security; Republicans believed the United States should husband its tremendous power by taking on fewer commitments. The debates that raged both between *and* within each party during the 1990s shaped their respective responses to 9/11—and still influence their foreign policy choices.

Epitomizing the struggles over how best to respond to opportunities and threats in the post–11/9 world are America's relations with a country that was little more than a pawn during the Cold War: Iraq. George H. W. Bush hoped to build a new world order around his successful prosecution of the Gulf War in the early 1990s; for eight years Bill Clinton struggled to maintain sanctions on Baghdad and ordered military strikes to constrain Saddam Hussein's ambitions; George W. Bush came into office promising a tougher line toward the Iraqi leader. Although the story of America between the wars takes us from the Balkans to North Korea, from Mexico to Russia, and from inside tense White House meetings to presidential campaigns and the halls of Congress, it invariably—and tragically—returns to the Persian Gulf.

CHAPTER ONE

The Lone Superpower, Adrift

ON NOVEMBER 9, 1989, the sixty-six-mile ugly edifice of concrete and barbed wire that had divided Berlin between East and West suddenly became a place to celebrate. Television screens around the world flickered with stunning scenes of young people standing on the Berlin Wall or chipping away at it with hammers. In a year during which communist regimes throughout Eastern Europe collapsed, 11/9 made clear to all but hard-core skeptics that the four decade–long Cold War struggle between East and West was over. In his diary the next day, George H. W. Bush reflected on the prospect of presiding over such unexpected events. "The big question I ask myself is, how do we capitalize on these changes?" he wrote. "And what does the Soviet Union have to do before we make dramatic changes in our defense structure? The bureaucracy answer will be, do nothing big, and wait to see what happens. But I don't want to miss an opportunity."[1]

Yet many thought the American president did just that. Late that afternoon, Bush held an impromptu press conference in the Oval Office. Reporters were eager to hear the president's reaction to the incredible news from Berlin. Rather than express excitement over the new freedom in Eastern Europe that his eight Cold War predecessors had only dreamed of, Bush chose to project calm. "This is a sort of great victory for our side in the big East-West battle, but you don't seem elated," observed Lesley Stahl, of CBS. "I'm not an emotional kind of guy," Bush replied.[2]

In the days that followed, leading Democrats excoriated Bush for his caution. Former Vice President Walter Mondale used words like "bookkeeper" and "bureaucrat" in condemning the administration's tepid response. Senate Majority Leader George Mitchell urged the president to fly to West Berlin "to acknowledge the tremendous significance of the symbolic destruction of the Berlin Wall and to give voice to the exhilaration felt by all Americans." Tennessee Senator Al Gore, a presidential candidate in 1988 and someone viewed as a likely contender in 1992, added, "We have not yet seen the leadership from the White House, the kind of imagination and boldness that is appropriate to this hour."[3]

The next month, at a meeting with Mikhail Gorbachev on a ship off the coast of Malta, Bush justified his inaction. "There are people in the United States who accuse me of being too cautious," he told the Soviet leader in their private discussion. "It is true I am a prudent man, but I am not a coward, and my administration will seek to avoid doing anything that would damage your position in the world. But I was insistently advised to do something of that sort—to climb the Berlin Wall and to make broad declarations. My administration, however, is avoiding these steps; we are in favor of reserved behavior."[4]

The rush of events during the following year made it hard to maintain that posture. Within a few months, the United States and the Soviet Union began working together with the East and West Germans to reunify their country after forty-five years of division, a process completed in the fall of 1990. The two former superpower foes also concluded a conventional arms control agreement that dramatically reduced the huge deployments of tanks and other heavy military equipment that had created fears of massive war in Europe for decades.

Meanwhile, in August 1990, Saddam Hussein's Iraq, a longtime Soviet client state, invaded its neighbor Kuwait and threatened to dominate the region's oil supplies. How would the superpowers respond? Two episodes from that conflict—one of high diplomacy, the other tragic chaos, both involving U.S. Secretary of State James A. Baker III—defined the hopes and challenges for America's global leadership in what Bush and his national security adviser, Brent Scowcroft, aptly called "A World Transformed."[5]

ON AUGUST 3, 1990, Baker and his Soviet counterpart, Foreign Minister Eduard Shevardnadze, stood side-by-side in the lobby of the Vnukovo II airport outside Moscow to condemn jointly the Iraqi invasion. They announced that their two countries were together demanding a weapons ban against Iraq and declared that they would take their case to the United Nations. An event that just a few years earlier would have sparked a superpower showdown had become a spur to cooperation, serving instead as a head-spinning example of the immediate possibilities of the post–Cold War world.

A shrewd diplomat and experienced political operator, Baker knew instinctively what should be done after Iraq's surprise attack on Kuwait. He saw the opportunity to show the world that when it came to solving problems, the United States and the Soviet Union could work together. A little over a month after the joint foreign ministers statement at the Moscow airport, Bush and Gorbachev issued a declaration of their own, saying that "no peaceful international order is possible if larger states can devour their smaller neighbors."[6] For two countries that had spent decades supporting warring client states on opposite sides of the global chessboard, it was a remarkable turnabout. Bush and Gorbachev believed it would establish an important precedent for future crises, with the great powers working together through international institutions like the United Nations.

If Iraq's invasion had happened only a few years earlier, Baker remarked to Shevardnadze afterward, "this whole crisis would have been put in the context of an East-West competition and confrontation. Then this would have been far more dangerous."

"Let's focus on results," Shevardnadze responded, worried about the task ahead. "It's important to make this thing work."[7]

*

EIGHT MONTHS LATER, in April 1991, Baker witnessed a very different, and far less hopeful, side of the post–11/9 world. Saddam's army had been routed after a punishing, forty-two-day air campaign, followed by 100 hours of fierce ground assault by U.S. and allied forces fighting under a U.N. mandate. But to stay in power after the allied troops had withdrawn, Saddam launched a withering attack against his main internal opponents, the Shia in Iraq's south and the Kurds in its north. These lightly armed rebels proved no match for the Iraqi military, and soon a massive humanitarian crisis erupted. In northern Iraq, hundreds of thousands of Kurdish civilians fled their homes and massed on the mountainous Iraq-Turkey border. Some witnesses reported seeing a column of Kurdish refugees twelve miles long, and observers estimated that 1,000 people were dying each day.

The United States promised to airlift food and medical supplies to the refugees, and on April 8 the secretary of state traveled to the remote border area to get a firsthand look. As his small team approached a hillside, Baker was shocked at what he saw. One of his companions described it as something out of Dante's circles of hell. "Before me, a huge mountain valley teemed with approximately fifty to sixty thousand refugees," Baker recalled. "The desperation and deprivation of the scene was literally unbearable."

Baker spent fewer than fifteen minutes out of his four-wheel-drive vehicle, as his security detail worried about the throngs of people overwhelming them. He immediately returned to his Air Force plane and called his old friend and boss, George Bush. "You have no idea of the human nightmare here," he said, his voice shaking with emotion. "People are dying every day. We've got to do something and do it now. If we don't, literally thousands of people are going to die."

Bush and Baker galvanized the administration into action, and within a week (lightning speed for Washington), the U.S. government had put together a massive assistance package for those suffering in northern Iraq. But it was more than just a supply effort. To ensure the delivery of assistance and to protect the Kurds from future attacks by Saddam's forces, America also announced the creation of "safe havens" around key Kurdish towns in northern Iraq, refugee camps that would be administered by the United Nations and secured by the U.S. military. Known as Operation Provide Comfort, this mission involved as many as 20,000 American troops and was the first humanitarian military effort of the post–Cold War era. Ratcheting up the military pressure further, the United States imposed a "no fly zone" north of the Thirty-Sixth Parallel in Iraq, in which American warplanes worked to prevent Saddam's military from operating aircraft in the area. The U.N. Security Council blessed these efforts by passing a resolution that, for the first time in its history, declared a country's internal repression a threat to international peace and security. In effect, the United States—with United Nations support—prevented Saddam from exercising control over a large swath of his country. [8]

The conflict with Iraq had officially ended just weeks earlier, when the United States–led coalition fulfilled its U.N. mandate to eject Iraq from Kuwait. This was the culmination of the process Baker and Shevardnadze had begun in the Moscow airport eight months earlier. Yet now the American military found itself on the ground in Iraq providing protection and in the air deterring aggression. This mission seemed just as noble, but the end goal far less clear. While the American people and their leaders were celebrating a war won with surprisingly few casualties—and looking back with pride and excitement at the high-tech weaponry they had watched in action live on CNN—the reality on the ground was far different. Marine General Anthony Zinni, one of the top leaders of Operation Provide Comfort who would become an influential four-star commander later in the 1990s, recalled thinking at the time: "Hey, this war ain't over."[9]

These two episodes open a window into two of the most important features of American foreign policy after 11/9. The United States could actively work alongside its former great power rival to enforce international rules, fight wrongs, create opportunities, and save lives. But new humanitarian threats and crises within states would test the limits of international cooperation, causing Washington officials and the public to ask difficult questions about the costs and reach of America's global responsibilities in the world after 11/9.

A Noble Vision

During the twentieth century, Americans hoped for greater global cooperation to solve the world's problems. Such ambitions were most eloquently expressed by President Franklin Delano Roosevelt, whose legacy is enshrined in a quiet memorial tucked away on the edge of the Tidal Basin off the National Mall in Washington. Winding through the simple reminders of the era over which FDR presided—when the country overcame first a depression and then the most horrific war of all time—the park visitor comes upon words etched in stone envisioning a better world. Speaking in the midst of war, Roosevelt had declared, "Unless the peace that follows recognizes that the whole world is one neighborhood and does justice to the whole human race, the germs of another world war will remain as a constant threat to mankind."[10]

Seeking to eliminate major war forever, Roosevelt sought to create an organization through which the world's great powers could enforce the peace. Within months of his death, leaders from around the globe gathered in San Francisco to create the United Nations. Yet by 1947, the Cold War division in Europe had taken shape, and the two leading powers, the United States and the Soviet Union, squared off in a confrontation that lasted four decades. Rather than one world, we had two. And the United Nations, which many hoped would be a parliament of man, became yet another arena for division. With each superpower holding a permanent veto over U.N. Security Council actions—and the Soviet Union casting eighty vetoes in the organization's first decade alone—Roosevelt's dream had no chance of being realized.

WORLD WAR II and the rise and fall of the Cold War coincided with the distinguished career of George H. W. Bush. A decorated naval aviator in the 1940s, he rose through the political ranks to become vice president under Ronald Reagan during the 1980s, and only ten months before the Berlin Wall came down he took the oath of office as America's forty-first president.

In the early 1970s, Bush served as the American representative to the United Nations. This was his first significant foray into the world of international diplomacy, and one in which he thrived. After two terms in Congress, Bush seemed more comfortable in the hushed diplomatic halls of the United Nations than in the rough-and-tumble politics of Capitol Hill. He relished the personal diplomacy that was the lifeblood of the organization. But he also experienced the limits of the United Nations during the Cold War deadlock, witnessing the organization's inability to prevent war between India and Pakistan in 1971 and its failure to confront the terrorists who killed Israeli athletes during the 1972 Summer Olympics in Munich. To Bush, the United Nations was the "light that failed."[11]

Nearly two decades later, Saddam's brazen invasion of Kuwait presented Bush with an opportunity to demonstrate that the United Nations could finally work as FDR intended—to approach the world as one neighborhood with rules that would be enforced. The president knew that the invasion would test the international community, and he later reflected, "I didn't know what to expect." He and others in his administration had been talking privately since the Berlin Wall fell about the possibility of a new era of cooperation in world politics, a new purpose and practice to define the "post–Cold War." The concept they came up with was deceptively simple: a new world order.

"No longer can a dictator count on East-West confrontation to stymie concerted United Nations action against aggression," Bush told a joint session of Congress in September 1990, just a month after Saddam invaded Kuwait. "A new partnership of nations has begun." He added, "We're now in sight of a United Nations that performs as envisioned by its founders."[12]

Leading a country that stood preeminent among the world's powers, a political, military, and economic giant, Bush seemed poised to fulfill Woodrow Wilson and Roosevelt's aspirations for America to be the guarantor of world order through international institutions. "Twice before in this century," he reminded a packed congressional chamber at the conclusion of the 1991 Persian Gulf war, "an entire world was convulsed by war. Twice this century, out of the horrors of war, hope emerged for enduring peace. Twice before, those hopes proved to be a distant dream, beyond the grasp of man. Until now, the world we've known has been a world divided—a world of barbed wire and concrete block, conflict and cold war. Now we can see a new world coming into view, a world in which there is the very real prospect of a new world order."[13]

Bush's faith that the international response to Iraq's invasion of Kuwait could usher in a different global order was not universally shared. Deep political divisions—especially within his own Republican Party—prevented him from pushing forward his ambitious goals. For conservatives, anticommunism had been the glue holding their disparate ideological coalition together. Victory in the Cold War and then the Gulf War would prove more disorienting than exhilarating.

The Iraq Precedent

Bush's exhortations about a new kind of global politics implied more forethought and planning than actually existed. He and his advisers were largely making it up as they went along. During World War I and World War II, Wilson and Roosevelt had each launched major postwar planning efforts—both assumed the wars would end and America would be on the winning side.

The Cold War had been a different kind of struggle; unlike those two "hot" wars, it was a battle of ideologies, proxy conflicts, and diplomatic chess moves. There was also a deceptive permanence to the Cold War, leading many to believe that, like gravity, it was a natural phenomenon that would always exist in international relations. Whether inside the intelligence community or America's best academic institutions, few expected the forty-year struggle to come to a crashing end as suddenly as it did.

This surprise coincided with a presidency that was proudly pragmatic and uncomfortable with conceptualizing. Bush relished solving problems, but he openly admitted his discomfort with what he called the "vision thing." One of his top White House national security officials, Richard Haass, recalls, "I wrote memos, suggested presidential speeches, but Bush wasn't comfortable with grand doctrine. His anti-grandness gene kicked in."[14]

David Gompert, another senior Bush adviser on the National Security Council, argued later that White House officials "spent very little time . . . going through the formality of debate on the fundamental concepts and principles of our policies." When asked about the meaning of Bush's new world order, he added, "I recall on a couple of occasions suggestions were made, why don't we [get] together to talk to thrash around some concepts about what our interests and priorities should be. This just was not an administration, not a group at any level that dealt with concepts in the abstract."[15]

THE IMMEDIATE discussions inside the Bush administration after Saddam's military rolled into Kuwait gave no indication that the United States would soon try to turn this crisis into the conceptual foundation of its post–Cold War foreign policy. After the assault, the U.N. Security Council met throughout the night to condemn the invasion and call for immediate withdrawal. Within hours of the U.N. vote, Bush's national security team gathered at the White House.

The one-hour session was surprisingly subdued, with little outrage expressed about what Saddam had done. Scowcroft recalls that the mood "was 'well, this is a little conflict, we don't much like Kuwait anyway, they're not that friendly with us, they're halfway around the world.' The tone of the meeting was 'how do we adjust to this?'" After this discussion, Scowcroft flew with Bush on a scheduled trip to Aspen, Colorado. On the plane, Scowcroft tried to reverse the tenor of the response. "I remember talking to [the president], and said this is not acceptable. We cannot tolerate this kind of naked aggression."[16]

In Aspen, Bush huddled with visiting British Prime Minister Margaret Thatcher, and his spine stiffened. Speaking with reporters after their session, Britain's Iron Lady referred several times to Security Council measures under Chapter VII of the U.N. Charter, which authorizes military force to restore international peace and security.

Reporters badgered Bush about whether Saddam was the root of the problem and if the United States would seek to remove him from power. Bush pushed such questions aside, making clear the limits on any action the United States would initiate: "I would like to see him withdraw his troops and the restoration of the legal government in Kuwait to the rightful place, and that's the step that should be taken."[17] There would be no discussion then or later in the conflict about overthrowing the Iraqi dictator.

BUSH ADMINISTRATION officials sought to build an international coalition, authorized through the U.N. Security Council, to use "all necessary means" to get Iraq out of Kuwait. Yet true to their personalities and style, they began to sketch a vision more by demonstration and example than by preachy rhetoric and overt conceptualizing.

They saw a chance to stand on principle and strengthen the United Nations, which would be authorizing a military action for the first time since the Korean War. Bush and his team also believed they would show what kind of global power the United States could be. "For years our allies had complained about America's cowboy mentality," Baker later wrote. Building a broad coalition would show that the Americans were mindful of such criticisms. But the administration also understood, Baker explained, that the "threat to use force would be even more credible if formally sanctioned by most of the civilized world."[18]

To marshal this coalition, Bush and his top advisers conducted a whirlwind of personal diplomacy. Baker crisscrossed the globe to meet with every head of state or foreign minister whose country had a seat on the Security Council, as well as the many countries that would contribute troops to the military force. Bush himself worked the phones to make the case, enthusiastically getting involved in drafting the specific language of U.N. resolutions.

Such efforts included painstaking negotiations with great powers, including the Soviet Union and China, but also with smaller countries such as Ivory Coast and Romania. In each instance, American leaders stressed that nothing less than the credibility and legitimacy of the U.N. Security Council was at stake as it sought to protect the rights of smaller countries against larger, more powerful ones. Baker even used this logic in a meeting with his Cuban counterpart on the eve of the U.N. Security Council's vote in November 1990. (Cuba held one of the rotating seats on the Security Council.) Illustrating the administration's determination and willingness to leave no stone unturned to get the widest support possible, this remarkable session was the first time the two sides had met at such a high level in nearly thirty years. Ensuring that the United Nations was an effective institution for peace and security was "perhaps more important . . . for smaller countries," Baker argued. "That is what is at stake here."[19] Although Cuba ended up not supporting the resolution when it passed on November 29—establishing January 15, 1991, as the deadline for Iraq to withdraw from Kuwait—many thought that the Bush administration's exhaustive statecraft, trying to woo even its sworn enemies to its side, would endure as a model for how the United States would lead the world after the Cold War.

At the time, Bush believed he was doing more than merely getting Iraq out of Kuwait. He predicted that after the Gulf War, the United States would succeed not just in reinvigorating the United Nations but in setting a valuable precedent, establishing "principles for acceptable international conduct and the means to enforce them." Looking back, Scowcroft echoes this sentiment. "One of the underlying premises of the Gulf War, I wouldn't say for everybody in the administration but for the president and me, probably for Baker, was to conduct this whole thing in a way that would set a useful pattern for the way to deal with crises in an area of cooperation," he recalled in an interview sixteen years later. "Use the United Nations, don't go farther than the mandate of the United Nations, operate in a way that you earned the trust of the smaller countries of the world. . . . That was fundamentally what we were thinking." This strategy, Scowcroft explained, meant that perhaps "the hopes of the world of 1945 . . . could be realized."[20]

*

YET THE GULF WAR was not a harbinger of the future. It was the last gasp of an international order in which the most pressing security threat was one country invading another. When Bush called on the United Nations to act, he was demanding that the institution do what it had been founded to accomplish: operate as the arbiter in a world of sovereign states, ensuring that aggressors not cross interstate boundaries and swallow up smaller neighbors. That's what Baker and Shevardnadze were standing for when they condemned Iraq's invasion of Kuwait in August 1990.

The conflicts of the 1990s bore little resemblance to those Americans feared during the Cold War, or the Iraqi invasion of Kuwait. As Army General Colin Powell, chairman of the Joint Chiefs of Staff, explained later, "The Gulf War was the war against the Russians we didn't have. There were no trees and no hills, but that's what we were trained to fight. The Iraqis sat there and we kicked the shit out of them."[21]

American military action in the ensuing decade, however, would not feature traditional interstate battles but involvement in ethnic conflicts and civil wars. Saddam's attacks on the Kurds in the wake of the Gulf War, Yugoslavia's explosion into civil war, and Somalia's humanitarian crisis in which hundreds of thousands of people starved to death as warring factions prevented food aid from reaching those who needed it—these were emblematic of the crises of the future. The United States and its allies, who sought to empower an organization designed mainly to protect the independence of states, would find that their reverence for sovereignty stood in the way of achieving international consensus regarding threats that emanated from within states.

In the coming decade, the overriding question was whether the United Nations' leading member, the United States, would allow any leader to hide behind the right to independence and noninterference if he brutalized his own population. And if the United States did decide to act against a nation whose aggression was solely inside its own borders, in what ways should it seek to legitimize its actions?

Would it (and could it) do so under U.N. auspices? Or, as some argued, did the United States have all the legitimacy it needed?

THE U.S. DECISION to work through the United Nations to restore Kuwait's sovereignty also had a less noticed but controversial implication—that of self-imposed limits on American action. To gain support from the international community, the United States would have to curtail its objectives and avoid the temptation to act unilaterally.

With the Cold War ending and the Soviet Union unraveling, the United States could have chosen to accept few constraints on its behavior. America's military, economic, political, and cultural dominance made the world "unipolar," and without a rival, it could seemingly do whatever it wanted. Many believed that it should.

In an influential essay written at the end of 1990 in the journal *Foreign Affairs*, conservative commentator Charles Krauthammer called for the United States to summon the "strength and will to lead a unipolar world, unashamedly laying down the rules of world order and being prepared to enforce them."[22] But Krauthammer's "unipolar moment" triumphalism was alien to Bush. Despite the president's rhetoric about building a world order that was "new," what he was really doing was trying to make an old idea work—Roosevelt's founding vision to manage major questions of war and peace multilaterally through the United Nations. The United States would be a global leader, but to build and maintain consensus, it would have to accept limits; it couldn't just do whatever it wanted. For Bush, who had no desire to build a global colossus (and doubted that the American people would support it), such constraints were acceptable.

The implications were immediate—the most important being the decision not to follow the stunningly quick military victory in 1991 with a march to Baghdad to oust Saddam. At the time, the choice to hold American troops after they ejected Iraqi forces from Kuwait was uncontroversial within the administration. But it would prove to be one of the most consequential and far-reaching decisions of Bush's presidency, shaping the course and content of American foreign policy for the next decade and beyond.

Bush and his advisers were surprised at the speed with which military success came; few fully appreciated how dominant the American military had become in the years since the Vietnam War or how eroded Iraq's capability was after the long war with Iran. In the lead-up to the conflict, they had planned for nearly every contingency but one: what to do if victory came quickly. Lacking a postwar plan, they were left without even a basic understanding—let alone a comprehensive strategy—of what they wanted to demand from Saddam other than staying out of Kuwait.

Events wouldn't wait for the bureaucracy to grind out decisions, and neither would victorious U.S. generals. Army commander Norman Schwarzkopf wanted to negotiate a quick Iraqi surrender. The war had become a slaughter, with retreating Iraqi forces pummeled by superior American firepower. So "Stormin' Norman," who, with his puffed chest and commanding voice, had become a kind of folk hero to many Americans, brought the war to a quick and somewhat anticlimactic end after meeting with a group of Iraqi generals in the middle of the desert.[23]

Saddam never had to sign a surrender document. Having made quick work of Iraq's forces in the field, Bush and his senior team worried what would happen if they demanded that the Iraqi leader formally capitulate and he refused. They had no desire to keep the war going or to occupy the country and face a certain insurgency. Bush later explained, "I do not believe in what I call 'mission creep.'" When Schwarzkopf told Powell he wanted the fighting to stop, Powell turned to Bush and said confidently, "mission accomplished."[24]

Perhaps no member of Bush's war council was more adamant on this point than Defense Secretary Dick Cheney. When asked in April 1991 during a television interview why the U.S. military stopped before going to Baghdad, leaving Saddam in power, Cheney shot back a series of questions: "Once we got to Baghdad, what would we do? Who would we put in power? What kind of government would we have? Would it be a Sunni government, a Shia government, a Kurdish government? . . . Would it be fundamentalist Islamic?" Cheney's bottom line reflected the prevailing view, not just inside the Bush administration, but among most of official Washington and throughout the country: "I do not think the United States wants to have U.S. military forces accept casualties and accept the responsibility of trying to govern Iraq. I think it makes no sense at all."[25] Or, as he added in another interview later that year, "I think that was a quagmire we did not want to get involved in."[26]

Yet the administration's decision to end the conflict when it did was about more than avoiding the potential costs of occupation. They believed that time was on their side, that Saddam had been so sufficiently humiliated and weakened that he would eventually fall. And in any event, they had accomplished their goals. Looking back, Scowcroft recalls that there was no single reason the United States ended the war. "But one of the factors was we had a U.N. mandate to take whatever measures necessary to get the Iraqi troops out of Kuwait. And that was all."[27]

The United States had galvanized the international community to support the reversal of the invasion. If American troops had marched to Baghdad, the United States would have lost such unprecedented unanimity. The Soviets would have been unlikely to stay aboard; the Arabs certainly would not have maintained their support; the Europeans would have gone wobbly. The Bush team was well aware of the precedent its handling of Iraq would set: resisting aggression, limiting goals, showing the United Nations' utility as a problem-solving institution, and working with allies.

"From an American foreign policy making perspective," Bush and Scowcroft later wrote in their memoirs, "we sought to respond in a manner which would win broad domestic support and which could, as far as possible, be applied universally to other crises. . . . Going in and occupying Iraq, thus unilaterally exceeding the United Nations' mandate, would have destroyed the precedent of international response to aggression that we hoped to establish."[28] Ten years later,

U.S. Secretary of Defense Donald Rumsfeld would declare in Afghanistan that "the mission will define the coalition." In 1991, the coalition had defined the mission.

LEADING DEMOCRATS in Congress and elsewhere had largely (and loudly) opposed the war. The Senate vote to authorize it narrowly passed by five votes, with all but ten Senate Democrats in opposition. Based on military estimates floated by experts and retired officers, Democrats had warned of thousands of casualties and called for more time for economic sanctions to work. Some—such as former President Jimmy Carter—even publicly urged the other members of the U.N. Security Council to oppose the United States in the November 1990 use of force resolution. The net result was that Democrats ended up looking foolish for having opposed what turned out to be an extraordinarily easy victory. And worse, they appeared weak, a problem that had bedeviled them since the party had nearly ripped itself apart in 1968.

With the Democrats on the political ropes, many of Bush's Republican allies questioned the wisdom of stopping the conflict so soon. And those few Democrats who supported the war, and even some who didn't, criticized Bush for squandering victory by leaving Saddam in power. Al Gore, a war supporter, warned Bush privately that America's policy in the Persian Gulf "should not be mortgaged to the success of tyranny in Iraq, but we are coming painfully close to that position." Along with others, Gore urged the president to provide more support to the Kurds and Shia who were rising up against Saddam.[29]

Bush refused, which gave his political opponents growing confidence to criticize the decision to stop short of removing the Iraqi dictator. As Bush wrote in his diary at the time, "It hasn't been a clean end."[30] And within Republican circles, a bitter debate ensued. The Persian Gulf War—from the coalition building to the fighting itself—had been one of the most impressive displays of American statecraft and military leadership since World War II. Although many staunchly defended the administration's decision to end the war when it did, others second-guessed it.

The fundamental choices Bush faced—whether U.S. goals should be limited or expansive; what costs it should incur and what risks it should run to meet them; and how much the United States should shape its behavior to address the concerns of others—animated the intense policy disputes of the 1990s, exploding into the open during his eldest son's presidency.

THE MOST SIGNIFICANT foreign policy debates of Bush's term in office occurred within the Republican Party itself. For GOP politicians and policy intellectuals, the end of the Cold War and the collapse of the Soviet empire brought to the surface tensions about the nature of global order, the purpose and use of American power, and what, if anything, was required to ensure its legitimacy. These debates had been largely suppressed within the party by the forty-year struggle against communism.

An early indication of these internal tensions was the reaction to the fall of the Berlin Wall itself. Many Republican stalwarts, like some leading Democrats, saw the events as cause for unapologetic celebration. The Evil Empire was crumbling. They imagined what Reagan might have done with the opportunity—possibly a dramatic move like flying immediately to Berlin to give a soaring speech about victory and the possibilities of freedom. Bush's refusal to, as he put it, "dance on the wall," demonstrated his pragmatism, personal modesty, and recognition of the hard work to come. He believed his response also conveyed an image of the United States that was steady, humble, and closely attuned to the perceptions of others—or an America that acted differently than the Reaganite triumphalism that some clamored for.

Bush's alter ego in this endeavor was Scowcroft. A no-nonsense, frank-talking former Air Force lieutenant general, Scowcroft had the distinction of having served once before as national security adviser, under President Gerald Ford in the 1970s. Scowcroft was a key

member of the foreign policy elite who believed strongly in bipartisanship and the importance of international institutions as a vehicle
for U.S. influence in world affairs. In both disposition and intellect,
he was uncomfortable with policies that he believed led to unnecessary or obnoxious displays of U.S. might.

But articulating a guiding doctrine—explaining global change and
the U.S. role in it—was never one of Scowcroft's strengths. Despite
his doctorate in political science from Columbia University, he was
not a naturally conceptual thinker like former national security advisers Henry Kissinger and Zbigniew Brzezinski. He was, like Bush,
deliberate and cautious, more comfortable with practice than theory.

By the end of 1991, some on Bush's team worried that the
moment to frame the new era was passing. At the State Department, one of Baker's top aides, Dennis Ross, grew increasingly concerned about the administration's inability to articulate a coherent
vision. Ross had been a leading foreign policy adviser on Bush's
successful 1988 campaign for president, and then, as director of the
policy planning staff at the State Department, had become one of
Baker's most trusted aides. He had helped Baker and the president
shepherd Germany's unification and conduct the diplomacy prior to
the Gulf War.

Despite such successes, Ross worried that the Bush administration still could not see how the ground was shifting beneath its feet.
Yugoslavia was spiraling into civil war. Most significantly, the Soviet
Union itself was unraveling. In August 1991, Russian President
Boris Yeltsin stood on a tank to face down a coup against Gorbachev
instigated by Soviet hard-liners. After the coup failed, the Baltic
states—Estonia, Latvia, and Lithuania—achieved international
recognition as sovereign nations, and in December, Ukraine, the
largest Slavic republic after Russia, voted in a referendum for independence.

Ironically, although Bush and Scowcroft hoped the Gulf War
would shape a new global order, the conflict's practical effect made
them less capable to respond to such enormous changes. Ross
believed the war played a major role in the administration's confu-

sion. "I say it first in terms of the military, which had just won one war and didn't want to get into something [Bosnia] that they thought was not winnable" he recalled. "You [also] had a very small circle of people [in the administration], both at the top and then in the immediate second tier in the Gulf War, who, from August [1990] until the end of the war, went through an unbelievably intense, emotional, physical, exhausting experience. There was tremendous anxiety, especially when the Pentagon was making some of the predictions about what the casualties would be. I saw how it weighed on the president. But it wasn't just the president. It was all those who were working on this." When the United States needed new policies to deal with the crises in Yugoslavia and the Soviet Union in the months after the Gulf War ended, Ross explained, "We could not generate the interest at the top because, in a sense, they were spent."[31]

IN THE EFFORT to develop new strategies for a rapidly changing world, the views held by Bush and Scowcroft represented only one wing of the Republican Party. These "realists" focused on dealing with other major powers and pursuing the self-interests of the United States. But they also believed, as had Democratic icons Roosevelt and Harry Truman, that one way to serve American interests was by working with other great powers within international institutions, such as the United Nations. Moreover, they thought the best kind of change occurred gradually, without being forced from the outside. Bush and Scowcroft did not believe the United States should spend a lot of time promoting democracy, particularly in places deemed peripheral to American interests.

Over the course of the 1970s and 1980s, a new breed of Republican had emerged under Reagan, people such as Elliott Abrams, who had served as an assistant secretary of state for human rights in the 1980s, and Paul Wolfowitz, a longtime Republican foreign policy official who was undersecretary for policy in the Bush Pentagon. These policy thinkers believed deeply in ideals, and in the power of America to help other countries achieve political and economic liberty.

Many of these Reagan Republicans were former Democrats who saw Reagan as the true heir to Truman in the effort to support free peoples everywhere. Many had felt at home in the Democratic Party of Truman and John F. Kennedy but had abandoned the political left during the domestic upheavals of the 1960s, the angry struggles over Vietnam, and the failures of the Carter years. They became known as neoconservatives (the prefix signaled their roots on the other side), and they proudly promoted the ideological agenda for freedom associated with their new hero, Republican (and former Democrat) Ronald Reagan.

A few neoconservatives held onto their agenda even after the Soviet Union imploded; in fact, they interpreted the Cold War's end as a validation of their approach, and reason to extend it elsewhere. But for most, the end of the Cold War proved as disorienting as it was for pragmatic realists such as Bush. They perceived the end of the Soviet empire as an excuse to close up shop. Two leading neoconservative intellectuals, Midge Decter and her husband, Norman Podhoretz, had left the Democratic Party and in the early 1980s formed the Committee for the Free World to wage the war of ideas against communism and counter American liberals. But while the fall of the Berlin Wall and the demise of the Soviet Union seemed to vindicate everything neoconservatives stood for—the superiority of American power, its inherent legitimacy, and the willingness to stand forthright against evil—it also took the wind out of their sails.

In May 1990, some 500 people gathered in Washington for a Committee for the Free World conference that proved to be the group's last. A founding board member, Irving Kristol (whose son, William, would help revive the neoconservative movement a few years later), summed up the mood among many in the room. "Communism is over, and that means that anticommunism is over too," he declared. "The function of the United States is not to spread democracy around the world."[32] By the end of that year, the committee went out of business. "It's time to say: We've won, goodbye," Decter said.[33] Jeane Kirkpatrick, another anticommunist stalwart, came to a similar conclusion. Formerly a Democratic supporter of Cold Warriors

Hubert Humphrey and Washington Senator Henry "Scoop" Jackson, Kirkpatrick had joined Reagan's cabinet as the U.S. ambassador to the United Nations, where she took pride in facing down the Soviets in the Security Council. But in the fall of 1990, she argued that the United States could now become "a normal country in a normal time." Such sentiments were also echoed by Nathan Glazer, one of Irving Kristol's collaborators in building neoconservatism as an intellectual force. Glazer said the post–Cold War era was "a time for modesty." America's battle against communism had been an exceptional period in the country's foreign policy, many of the old neoconservatives argued, made necessary only by the unique threat from Soviet communism. It was now time to turn attention to the home front— where they pledged to combat domestic programs such as affirmative action—and that meant more narrow definitions of the national interest abroad.[34]

The Philosopher and the Pugilist

As Republicans searched for new guiding principles, two unlikely individuals, with very different backgrounds and worldviews, emerged to give broader meaning to the immediate post–Cold War debate among conservatives and lend credence to the notion that America, now triumphant, could focus on its problems at home. One was a soft-spoken, unknown academic with a deep interest in European philosophers, who would soon become celebrated as a leading thinker of the time. The other was a bombastic television personality and former Richard Nixon speechwriter, who would become a major force in the 1992 Republican primary campaign for president of the United States.

As communism was crumbling, Francis Fukuyama, then a thirty-six-year-old political scientist at the RAND Corporation, gave a lecture at the University of Chicago, in which he drew on the writings of German philosopher Georg Hegel to argue that a new state of history was at hand. The twentieth century had witnessed the efforts of fascism and communism to challenge liberal democratic capitalism for supremacy, and liberalism had vanquished both. The rise of a new ideological challenge appeared unlikely, and thus the world had finally arrived, ideologically speaking, at the end of history. Reflecting on the moment with a tinge of regret, Fukuyama believed the American people would become bored and soon miss the passionate conflicts of the previous fifty years.

Owen Harries, editor of the *National Interest*, thought the lecture would make a great article. By the time it appeared in the summer of 1989, Fukuyama was deputy director of policy planning at the State Department under Ross. Forty-two years earlier, the diplomat George F. Kennan had penned his famous "X" article from the policy planning office. Writing in *Foreign Affairs*, Kennan had laid out the basis for the strategy of containment that guided American foreign policy for the next four decades. The media devoured Fukuyama's piece, making him famous and hailing him as the next Kennan. A policy journal with a modest circulation of 6,000 soon became a must-read, and on at least one newsstand in the nation's capital was reportedly outselling pornography (it was Washington, after all).[35]

Whatever one thought of the argument, the "end of history" bore only a small resemblance to what Kennan produced. True, Fukuyama, like Kennan, provided a keen analysis of the big issue of the day. In the late 1940s, that issue was Soviet power. For Fukuyama, it was the implications of Soviet collapse and the ideological triumph of the West. But Kennan had provided the outline, if not all the specifics, of a strategy for dealing with the communist threat. As Kennan developed the argument in his other speeches and writings at the time, he insisted that America should keep the Soviet Union from encroaching on core areas of the world, including Western Europe, Northeast Asia, and the Persian Gulf. This defined the strategy to contain Soviet power until it, as Kennan put it, "mellowed" due to its own internal contradictions, as finally happened in the late 1980s.

Fukuyama offered no comparable strategy for managing the end of history. Readers of his article could perhaps surmise that America should support democratization wherever it might take root, or they could conclude that the emergence of market economies and democratic governments was inevitable no matter what the United States did. Those who saw Fukuyama's argument as prescriptive then disagreed on where democracy promotion might be most effective and how to carry it out. But the larger message—the one absorbed by the vast majority who did not read much beyond the essay's title—was that the big challenges were over and that the United States could move on to other things, especially at home. In this sense, Fukuyama's argument was interpreted to be one part victory dance and one part call to inaction.

IF FUKUYAMA was the great new intellectual, Patrick Buchanan aspired to be the hero of the working man and woman. Though born and raised inside the Beltway and a graduate of Georgetown University (where he was third in his class), Buchanan was as proudly unrefined as Fukuyama was wonky. He loved to fight, both literally and figuratively—a skilled pugilist of ideas, he also once got into a scuffle with police after being stopped for speeding. "I was ahead on points," he said later, "until they brought out the sticks."[36] After several years in journalism, Buchanan wrote speeches for President Nixon and later came back to the White House under Reagan, whose anticommunism was music to his ears. "The Cold War was the whole cause of my life," Buchanan recalled years later.[37]

By the early 1990s Buchanan had become a colorful TV personality when he, too, responded to Harries's efforts in the *National Interest* to get leading political and policy figures to enunciate a new vision for America after the Cold War. Buchanan penned a piece that became a harbinger of his campaign slogan when he ran for the Republican nomination for president. He called for "a new nationalism, a new patriotism, a new foreign policy that puts America first and, not only first, but second and third as well."[38]

America first. Buchanan's nostalgia was not for the battles against Hitler and Stalin, it was for the interwar years leading up to World War II, when America firsters sought to keep the country from being drawn into a European war. (Buchanan later wrote that Nazi Germany posed no real threat to the United States.)[39] He called for American troops to come home from their overseas bases now that the United States had defeated communism. Ironically, "Come home, America" had been Democrat George McGovern's slogan in his hapless 1972 campaign for president against Nixon, Buchanan's former boss, during the Vietnam War. McGovern later sent a note to Buchanan expressing pleasure at the use of his old slogan; Buchanan responded that although America could not come home in 1972, it could do so in 1992.[40]

Buchanan challenged what he considered the foreign policy orthodoxy: Forget the East Coast elites arguing for continued American engagement in the world, he said, and don't let Bush talk the country into following the United Nations blindly into some other faraway conflict. He criticized the administration's Iraq policy as promoted by Israel's "amen corner." America won the Cold War, and Buchanan said it was high time for the country to tend to its own business.

As much as any Democrat, Buchanan took aim at the neoconservatives. He had served with many of them in the Reagan administration, when they were united in their fight against the Soviet menace. But it had always been an uneasy partnership, and absent the external threat from Moscow, it blew apart. Buchanan called the neoconservatives, "Ex–Great Society liberals," who "support the welfare state and Big Government. They are pro–civil rights and affirmative action." Worst of all, "many are viscerally hostile to the Old Right, and to any 'America first' foreign policy. They want to use America's wealth to promote 'global democracy' abroad and impose 'democratic values' in our public schools." Neoconservatives, Buchanan thundered, "have taken over the exchequer of a Right that traces its lineage to Robert Taft."[41]

Buchanan was purposely tapping into a long-running debate among conservatives about America's engagement with the world. He was trying to draw a connection to an earlier time when the East Coast internationalists looked down their noses at heartland Republicans such as Senator Robert A. Taft, who argued that America needed to limit its international commitments.[42] Whereas Fukuyama had outlined an optimistic vision of the future as communism was crumbling in 1989, Buchanan had begun to speak to the extraordinary economic anxiety that had engulfed the American public. He decided to carry this banner forward to challenge Bush in the 1992 Republican presidential primaries. Americans may have bought into the notion of the end of history, but in an election year, they were worried about their future. Buchanan saw these people as his voters.

The Agony of Victory

The loss of American self-confidence came at a paradoxical moment. After all, as Charles Krauthammer wrote in the *New Republic* in July 1991, there was "no prospect in the immediate future of any power to rival the United States. This situation is almost unknown in the history of the modern nation-state: 1815 and 1945 come to mind, but even then the preeminent power was faced with at least one rival of roughly equal strength."[43] Scholars were drawing comparisons between America's dominance of world affairs and that of Rome.

Befitting Rome, Washington in June 1991 had been the scene of an extraordinary display of the most efficient military machine ever known. Celebrating the Gulf War victory, 8,000 veterans poured into the nation's capital for a military parade down Constitution Avenue. Americans who served in Vietnam had endured the ugliness of a public that shunned them; these warriors, by contrast, were bathed in adulation. "I think we blew away some joggers and sandblasted a few cars," one Air Force pilot joked after landing his Sikorsky helicopter in the midst of adoring crowds on the National Mall, facing the U.S. Capitol. Nearby were an M1 tank and a Tomahawk missile display. And so was what a reporter described as a new Jeep-like vehicle known as the HMMWV, "the Hummer." Eighty warplanes roared over the parade route, shutting down National Airport. And an estimated 800,000 people jammed the National Mall and surrounding streets to cheer the returning heroes. At the Tomb of the Unknowns at Arlington National Cemetery, Bush said, "There is a new and wonderful feeling in America."[44]

Yet that emotion proved fleeting. For many, the victory was bittersweet—an accomplishment, to be sure, but also a reminder of all that had been neglected. As Krauthammer noted at the time, "The response of Americans to this extraordinary state of international affairs is decidedly unenthusiastic . . . [they] do not enjoy their hegemony. They can rouse themselves for a one-day parade to celebrate the most lopsided military victory since Agincourt, but even that merriment . . . seemed a bit forced."[45]

By the fall of 1991, with the Soviet Union on its deathbed, the public had moved on from the great foreign policy debates that motivated American politics during the Cold War. They wanted a president who could secure their economic future in a world that was changing rapidly thanks to the technological revolution under way. Only a few years before, college students still typed their papers on IBM Selectrics; now the world that Apple cofounder Steve Jobs had envisioned, in which computers were used by individuals and not just large corporations, was starting to emerge. Germany and Japan became economic powerhouses during the 1980s—while the United States spent its resources combating the Soviet Union. The economy went into recession, while the federal budget deficit hit an all-time high. There was a burst of anxiety about the character of American society, as the "culture wars" ignited over whether the country had become self-indulgent and was losing its moral core—be it in education, the arts, or the nature of politics.

At the end of that year, Bush had become politically vulnerable. His 90 percent approval rating in the aftermath of the Gulf War had scared away from the presidential race a number of Democrats who believed he was unbeatable. But the president's pollsters speculated privately about the "Churchill parallel," worrying that Bush could share the same fate as the great British prime minister who was voted out of office in July 1945, just after his triumph in World War II. "Leaders are not necessarily reelected for their foreign policy and wartime successes, even when monumental," one Bush political strategist warned.[46] The notion of a new world order led by the United States, which the president had so proudly proclaimed a year earlier, now appeared to be a major liability.

Politically and intellectually, conservatives were in disarray. Some were angry with Bush for talking more about preserving global order than about promoting freedom, while others sounded more like isolationists, who were surging inside the party for the first time since World War II. As the astute political analyst E. J. Dionne wrote at the time, "The disputes on post–Cold War foreign policy juggled alliances all across the right . . . [and] will take years to play out."[47]

BUSH HAD presided over two extraordinary victories: the end of the Cold War and the Persian Gulf War. But he was unable to translate those momentous achievements into a direction for his country. Intellectuals had coined memorable phrases with the "end of history" and the "unipolar moment," but no one had assumed Kennan's mantle as the country's grand strategist for the post–Cold War era. Buchanan had grabbed attention with his call to put America first, and soon more Republicans became drawn to that old approach from their party's history. The superpower was adrift because the Republican Party that had shaped American national security policy in the latter half of the Cold War was now at sea.

The Democratic campaign of William Jefferson Clinton smelled opportunity. Except for Carter's victory in the aftermath of Watergate, the Democrats had appeared incapable of winning a presidential election, and few imagined that would change anytime soon. But their major foreign policy liability—perceived weakness in the face of the communist challenge—had disappeared.

This opened opportunities to renew the Democratic coalition that had led the party until it shattered over Vietnam. Some of the staunch anticommunist liberals who had abandoned the Democrats in the 1970s were increasingly frustrated that Bush refused to trumpet American values and remained unwilling to articulate a bold vision for America's role in the world. Remarkably, they became receptive to the message they heard from a small-state governor being tarnished as a draft-dodging, McGovernite Democrat—the type who had prompted them to support Republicans for president three elections in a row. Clinton talked about commanding the political "center" and followed his advisers' push to reclaim the strong liberal heritage of Truman and Kennedy. He articulated a foreign policy platform that stressed the need to be tough on human rights and active in promoting democracy. The untested governor from Arkansas was not going to win on his foreign policy prowess, but during the campaign, he laid the groundwork for the Democrats' effort to define America's purpose amidst the confusion of the world after 11/9.

CHAPTER TWO

Democrats Unite

ANTHONY LAKE was not the kind of person one would expect to step up and try to heal the Democratic Party's deep wounds over foreign policy. Soft-spoken, unassuming, and bookish, he felt most at home in the quiet farmland hills of western Massachusetts, where he had spent a decade teaching international relations at a small liberal arts college and raising twenty-eight head of cattle. It was not that he was unfamiliar with Washington's power corridors—he had served in several administrations near the highest levels and once been at the epicenter of a foreign policy establishment melt-down, resigning from Henry Kissinger's White House staff in the early 1970s over the Vietnam War and the U.S. military incursions into Cambodia. Yet those days were far behind him.

During the nearly two decades since Vietnam, the Democrats' attitudes toward national security—opposition to intervention abroad and suspicion of the use of military force—left them out of step with many Americans. Many of the party's brightest foreign policy minds, those such as Lake inspired by the tough liberalism of John F. Kennedy and Hubert Humphrey, spent years in the wilderness. Others—the neoconservatives—abandoned the party altogether, dis-gusted by what they saw as the left's chokehold on Democratic ideol-ogy since the 1960s.

But then the Cold War ended. Just as the peaceful demise of the Soviet Union brought opportunities to reshape America's role in the world, it also opened possibilities for the Democratic Party to regain its footing. The 1992 presidential election would select the first president of the post–Cold War era, and some Democratic leaders saw an opportunity to bring together the party's national security factions through the policies of the young Arkansas governor, Bill Clinton. They believed the Democrats could sketch a new vision for America around the concept of spreading freedom and democracy—and by doing so, reunify the party and define a strategy for America in the world.

"In the 1970s and 1980s, every four years we refought the Vietnam War within the party," Lake said at the time. "Every position a candidate took was a victory for either the conservative wing or the liberal wing. With the end of the Cold War, those ideological arguments are finally over. This means that the center has widened enormously—and we want to keep expanding that middle."[1] His efforts to do so—and in some respects, his ultimate failure—shaped the course of American foreign policy during the 1990s and still echo today in debates about the future of the Democratic Party.

LAKE HAD never intended to get involved in the 1992 campaign or return to government. In 1989, he set out to write a book about the Democrats, foreign policy, and presidential campaigns—to explore, in his words, "why we always screw up."[2] But soon he met Clinton, and after several conversations (mainly about foreign policy, but at least one about herding livestock), Lake signed up to help as the governor's top foreign policy adviser.

At the time, that hardly seemed a promising assignment. At Washington's annual Gridiron dinner in March 1991—a Beltway ritual where politicians and journalists gather to poke fun at themselves—Democratic wise man and former party chairman Robert Strauss acknowledged that his side was in trouble. "Everybody's saying that the Democrats' presidential hopes are so desperate there aren't even any announced candidates. Hell, that already makes it a stronger field than we had last time."[3]

Incumbent President George H. W. Bush had all the credentials—

decorated World War II veteran, envoy to the United Nations and China, director of the CIA, vice president, and now the president who had helped preside over the end of the Cold War. As his eldest son and senior campaign adviser, George W. Bush, cracked to reporters, "Do you think the American people are going to turn to a Democrat *now?*"[4]

Most Democratic political operatives agreed. They figured their main advantage was to make the 1992 election about "the economy, stupid" and use Bush's attention to global affairs as a weapon against him. But Lake and his cohort saw it differently, arguing that Bush had a major foreign policy liability that could unite the Democratic Party for the first time since Vietnam: Bush's policy was bereft of democratic values.

As a realist who cherished pragmatism, Bush emphasized stability and the management of great power relations rather than bold solutions or big ideas. He had close relationships with most of the world's key leaders, whether dictators or democrats, and took great pride in his Rolodex. In many ways, this had served him well as the Cold War was ending.

Yet his approach to the world lacked a sense of mission, and he failed to articulate a foreign policy guided by a moral compass, unlike his lionized predecessor, Ronald Reagan. He took pride in being a capable manager, but that was by definition reactive. It meant waiting for crises to happen. Even his biggest successes—waging the Gulf War and responding to the collapse of communism—were not untarnished: Saddam Hussein still reigned in Iraq, and Bush had clearly shown a greater interest in stability than freedom in the final year of the Soviet Union's existence. He seemed to resist change, giving the impression that he was out of touch. As the *New Republic* editors suggested in September 1991, the administration "has failed to grasp the two essential movements of its world: the growing clamor for democracy and the related impulse for national sovereignty. Its instinct has always been the status quo." This, they wrote, speaks "less of a grip on a 'new world order' than a desperate, befuddled attempt to keep up with new world change."[5]

After the Cold War, the American people were looking for a way forward. But Bush and his team of advisers had made their foreign policy careers in the world left behind. Clinton's campaign mantra was "change versus more of the same," and he promised to be different. He saw himself as a "New Democrat" and had worked hard as head of the Democratic Leadership Council, or DLC, to help build a movement to undo the perceptions that had proved so politically damaging in past presidential elections. People didn't trust Democrats to spend their money wisely, believing them to be too inclined to redistribute resources from people who were working to those who weren't; they questioned whether Democrats shared their moral values and outlook; and they didn't believe that Democrats would keep them safe, either against predators at home or threats abroad.[6]

In foreign affairs, the New Democrats sought to broaden their electoral base through a robust internationalism that would be chastened by the terrible experience of Vietnam but would not be fundamentally altered by it. That meant policies that stressed a strong defense and were rooted in liberal values, with an emphasis on spreading democracy. "This is a theme that brings together conservatives and liberals, and would be an excellent vehicle for solidifying your support from both wings of the party," Lake and his team would remind Clinton late in the 1992 campaign. "It also provides a defining purpose for America's role in the post–Cold War world."[7]

FOR RANK-AND-FILE Democrats, the emphasis on values and democracy was not uncontroversial. Although such themes were part of the proud tradition of Democratic presidents as far back as Woodrow Wilson, many liberals worried that the focus on democracy led to an activist, interventionist foreign policy, which could be especially damaging during an election based largely on domestic issues. Moreover, they associated such rhetoric with Republicans such as Reagan. But the Clinton camp decided to deal with these concerns head-on. Clinton picked Al Gore, a consistent Democratic hawk on national security, as his running mate. Together they criticized the Bush team for allowing Saddam to stay in power after the 1991 war, for coddling the "butchers of Beijing" after the Chinese government's 1989 massacre of prodemocracy activists in Tiananmen Square, and for standing aside while genocide raged in the Balkans. They asserted that America needed to be more engaged in solving the world's problems, not less.

This argument was more than just a useful line of attack against Bush. Some believed it could be a way to breathe life into the Democratic Party's foreign policy. For years, when it came to defining America's role in the world, Democrats seemed to relish squabbling with each other as much as fighting the Republicans. In 1968, riots had broken out at the Democratic convention in Chicago, fueled in part by frustrations over the Vietnam War. Four years later, splits within the party over the size of the defense budget and Vietnam led to George McGovern's humiliating defeat by Richard Nixon. Jimmy Carter had won the presidency in the aftermath of Watergate but four years later was saddled by perceptions of foreign policy weakness and was easily beaten by Reagan. Most troubling about the 1980 defeat was the defection of conservative Democrats, particularly the white, Catholic, blue-collar voters in places like Detroit, Cleveland, Milwaukee, and Pittsburgh, who became known as "Reagan Democrats." Although they were driven mainly by economic anxieties and racial resentment, they also identified more with the tough-sounding conservative hero than with the Democratic president who had appeared helpless in the face of Iranian hostage-taking and the Soviet invasion of Afghanistan. Labor unions, most prominently the AFL-CIO, abandoned the Democrats as Reagan championed the Polish union Solidarity in its struggle against Soviet authoritarianism.

Yet it was not just blue-collar Democrats who left the party; many in the foreign policy elite did, too. These policy intellectuals were appalled by the Democrats' willingness to turn their backs on the vigorous anticommunism and promotion of American values that defined the liberalism of Harry Truman and Dean Acheson. A common joke said the neoconservatives were "liberals who had been mugged by reality." But they didn't quite trust Bush. As Jeane Kirkpatrick put it,

Bush "is closely associated with the traditional Republican Party. That's not a party that's ever been associated with making Democrats feel at home." Prominent neoconservatives were distressed by what they saw as Bush's ineffective policies as regimes in Moscow, Beijing, and Belgrade battled those fighting for freedom, and above all by the fact that Saddam remained in power. Commentator Norman Podhoretz colorfully noted, "The Bush problem is like *coitus interruptus*. Nothing is consummated."[8]

Once the 1992 campaign got under way, the Bush administration seemed devoid of ideas. Pat Buchanan continued to hammer away from Bush's right, shocking the incumbent by taking 37 percent of the vote in the New Hampshire primary. Counseled to stop talking about foreign policy, Bush jettisoned the strongest asset any president has over his potential challengers: his leadership in world affairs. Francis Fukuyama recalls prominent conservatives complaining to him that "Bush was all about foreign policy." Vin Weber, then a leading Republican in the House of Representatives, frowned on the effort to deemphasize Bush's international achievements. "All the people around him told him not to talk about it," Weber recalled. The argument, he explained, was straightforward: "The more you talk about foreign policy, the more you'll alienate people [who] really care about the economy, about education. And Bush is very susceptible to all that because even though he was steeped in a foreign policy background, he comes out of a moderate Republican tradition that says we ought to be attentive to these other concerns and there ought to be a role for government on education and things like that."[9]

As the campaign marched on, the president fell further into political trouble. Bush asked his old friend and top diplomat James Baker to step down as secretary of state to come to the White House to oversee the campaign—a move Baker made painfully and reluctantly. By asking his secretary of state to walk away from high diplomacy and return to the political trenches, Bush signaled that foreign policy would be set aside for the election. Yet the campaign remained listless, with staffers dazed by the possibility that they could actually lose. Bush was in a pitched political battle where it was dangerous to discuss his greatest strength. Baker aide Dennis Ross (who also made the jump to the White House) recalls, "Things seemed on autopilot."[10] The Democrats had an opportunity to fill the vacuum.

The Neo–New Democrats

The self-described New Democrats not only thought democracy promotion and values belonged at the core of a liberal foreign policy, but they also believed the theme could have some modest electoral benefit, by wooing back neoconservatives. During the Carter administration, the neoconservatives had been shut out of high positions. Some blamed Lake, who became the State Department's policy planning director and was perceived to be one of the young "doves" who worked to keep the hard-liners on the outside. But the end of the Cold War eased tensions. "Approaching 1992," Lake reflected later, "my own thinking was that win or lose, one thing we can do in the campaign is get the people who believe in ideas to bring them back in because we are natural allies."[11]

Although Clinton focused mainly on domestic issues, he blessed Lake's efforts to bring these men and women back into the fold. A memo to the Clinton campaign's high command from Stuart Eizenstat, one of Carter's top White House advisers, illustrated the strategy. Titled "Winning Back the Neoconservatives," Eizenstat's memo explained that while they represented a small number of people, they "had influence far out of proportion to their numbers." And, importantly, "They can be won back in 1992, and to do so would be viewed as a major crack in the Republican armor."[12] The foreign policy world is hardly immune to the hand-holding and ego-stroking of retail politics, and Clinton's foreign policy advisers worked through long lunches, phone calls, and quiet meetings to cajole key players onto their side. They carefully reached out to disaffected Reaganites such as Kirkpatrick and frustrated Democratic hawks including Zbigniew Brzezinski, who had supported Bush for president in 1988.

These efforts yielded modest results. A group of prominent neocon-servatives publicly endorsed Clinton for president, creating an open-ing to meld the party back together.

For many, the path to the Clinton camp did not seem like a long journey to travel. They saw him as a different kind of Democrat, unburdened by the party's recent dovish legacy. They admired his passion, willingness to talk about big ideas, and bold assertions of American power and moral authority. "It looked like Clinton would embrace humanitarian values more," explains James Woolsey, a defense expert who served in the Carter administration but also led Bush's effort to negotiate the Soviet military withdrawal from Europe. "I would not have endorsed just any Democrat." Brzezinski echoes this sentiment, explaining that he came around when "I felt that [Clinton] was beginning in his speeches to wrestle with the larger issues that we had to be concerned about, whereas Bush seemed to me to be a spent force, kind of running out of steam."[13]

In a statement issued by the Clinton campaign in October 1992, just before the election, many leading hawks explained their support for an untested, draft-avoiding governor with no national security cre-dentials. "We did not agree with the stand Bill Clinton took toward the Vietnam War as a young man. But that should not disqualify him from the presidency today," read a statement signed by a group of prominent national security experts that included Democrats Penn Kemble and Peter Rosenblatt (who had been leading members of the Coalition for a Democratic Majority, formed after the disastrous 1972 McGovern campaign), former director of the National Security Agency William Odom, former arms control adviser Paul Nitze, and Harvard professor Samuel Huntington. "In fact," the statement argued, "his firm support for the democratic and anticommunist movements in the former Soviet empire and in China make him a distinctly preferable candidate to George Bush, who in modern times has shown himself far too willing to cooperate with dictators, and to turn a blind eye to human rights abuses."[14]

Some Washington insiders found this turn of events shocking. In August, commentator Morton Kondracke observed, "It seems implausible that Bush, a World War II combat veteran, could be out-flanked on the right by a Vietnam draft avoider and former McGover-nite, especially after Bush presided over the U.S. victory over communism, ousted [Panamanian president] Manuel Noriega, devastated the Iraqi war machine, and is on his way toward making peace between the Arabs and Israel. But it is happening."[15]

WOOING THE neoconservatives was about more than getting endorsements—especially because, in terms of attracting voters, such elite support rarely amounts to much. Clinton's team also set out to create an intellectual foundation for his post–Cold War presidency. In December 1991, Clinton began his attack on Bush's foreign policy in a speech at his alma mater, Georgetown University. While emphasizing the importance of dealing first with America's domestic priorities, Clinton articulated a bold strategy of American global engagement. He blamed Bush for the isolationist sentiment brewing in the country. "We can't allow this false choice between domestic policy and foreign policy to hurt our country and our economy," Clinton declared. "Our president has devoted his time and energy to foreign concerns and ignored dire problems here at home. As a result, we're drifting in the longest economic slump since World War II, and, in reaction to that, elements in both parties now want America to respond to the collapse of communism and a crippling recession at home by retreating from the world."

The task, he argued, was to recognize that the world was embracing democracy, and America's national interest rested on supporting that global transformation. Unfortunately, he said, "even as the American Dream is inspiring people around the world, America is on the sidelines, a military giant crippled by economic weakness and an uncertain vision." Clinton outlined a litany of Bush failures. Not only had the president stood by when the Chinese government massacred students in Tiananmen Square in June 1989, but he also eagerly reengaged with the Chinese soon after. He ignored Boris Yeltsin before the August 1991 coup in Moscow and was not doing enough to support democracy in Russia. He did nothing to encourage the Baltic nations and Ukraine in their drive for independence, and left the Kurds to an "awful fate" after the successful campaign in Kuwait. "Having won the Cold War," Clinton concluded, "we must not now lose the peace." Therefore, said the young governor, "What we need to elect in 1992 is not the last president of the twentieth century, but the first president of the twenty-first century."[16]

The following summer, Clinton linked Bush's inaction at home to his failures overseas. In a speech to the Los Angeles World Affairs Council in August 1992, Clinton argued that "foreign and domestic policy are two sides of the same coin. If we're not strong at home, we can't be strong abroad. If we can't compete in the global economy, we'll pay for it at home." Clinton lambasted Bush for failing both to support change in the communist world and to keep America strong economically. "The same president who refused to make changes as American wages fell from first to thirteenth in the world was slow to recognize the changes in Eastern Europe and the former Soviet Union," Clinton said. "The same administration that did nothing as ten million Americans lost their jobs due to tired, old economic policies also stood by as courageous Chinese students were attacked with tanks in Tiananmen Square."[17] The American people, he explained, could not afford a status quo president either at home or abroad.

IN THE POLITICS OF 1992, Clinton found himself in the right place at the right time. The Cold War's end allowed a small-state governor with little international experience to go toe-to-toe with a president possessing an extraordinarily distinguished resume in national security and foreign policy. Perhaps if America had no serious enemies, then American voters had the luxury of voting for a world affairs rookie. Clinton himself was acutely aware that he could win only if the Cold War was seen to be over. "The Cold War distorted our politics, and foreign policy became the obsessive concern of our presidents," historian Arthur Schlesinger Jr. argued at the time. He claimed that the 1990s would be like the 1930s, and domestic politics would dominate. The proper balance between foreign and domestic "is going to return to normal now," he predicted.[18]

Republicans tried to take advantage of Clinton's weaknesses, drawing attention to his questionable draft status during Vietnam and chiding that the food-loving governor learned everything he knew about the world from his frequent stops at the International House of Pancakes. But in a campaign focused on the future and on the domestic economy, such criticisms never gained much traction. Clinton actually used his lack of foreign policy experience as an asset, arguing that when it came to understanding and confronting the transforming world and new global challenges, not being burdened by the past was an advantage. The Clinton team was betting that the more Bush appeared frozen in the face of dramatic global change, the more he seemed tone-deaf to the moment of hope and opportunity, the more attractive a young, fresh, energetic face would be.

The 1992 campaign's unusual dynamics also helped Clinton, as two other major candidates challenged Bush: Buchanan in the primaries, and Texas billionaire Ross Perot, the independent Reform Party candidate, in the general election. Buchanan derided Bush's new world order, which, he noted, "our president has yet to define or defend or explain in detail."[19] He also unloaded on the "crusade for democracy." In a speech to the World Affairs Council in Los Angeles, Buchanan called the idea "utopian" and unrelated to America's national interest, arguing that Americans would never "send their soldiers to fight and die for it." He was particularly incredulous that anyone could believe Middle East elections would produce anything other than forces hostile to the United States. Buchanan harkened back to John Quincy Adams, who as secretary of state had urged America to wish well other nations trying to achieve freedom and independence but felt that the United States should be "champion and vindicator only of her own." Although Buchanan ultimately lost the Republican nomination to Bush, he garnered 25 percent of the primary vote and earned a coveted prime-time speaking slot at the Republican National Convention.

Perot, meanwhile, showed little interest in foreign policy; in fact, he never touched on the subject when accepting the Reform Party's nomination for president at the party convention in Valley Forge, Pennsylvania, that summer. He approached every issue from a business perspective—as a question of maximizing profit and minimizing cost—and wanted America to reap the financial benefits of the Cold War's end. For example, he demanded that U.S. allies in Europe and Asia pay $100 billion for American troops to be stationed there. "Keeping U.S. troops on European soil . . . is akin to a parent leaving a light on in a child's room at night to ward off ghosts," Perot argued in one of his trademark folksy witticisms. "It is hard to justify 'night light' troops at U.S. taxpayer expense."[20]

But the international issue that really energized Perot and his followers was trade. He argued that the result of any free trade agreement with Mexico, which Bush was negotiating, would create a "giant sucking sound" of jobs heading south of the border. Perot carried his message by speaking directly to people through appearances on call-in television shows, particularly CNN's *Larry King Live*. He used live cable television to create a maverick, anti-Washington candidacy in the same way Democratic politician Howard Dean used the Internet twelve years later.

While Perot's can-do attitude made him popular on the stump, and at one point put him atop the national polls, his erratic behavior and mercurial management style left many feeling uneasy with him and undermined his own campaign. By comparison, he made the young Clinton more statesmanlike. And by vociferously championing economic protectionism, Perot actually provided Clinton an opening to promote free trade and thereby capture business-oriented Democratic voters who had been drifting toward the Republican Party.

Taken together, the campaign's major themes were instructive. Clinton's larger focus on the economy, Buchanan's angry populism and embrace of "America first," Perot's skepticism of trade, and Bush's image as caring too much about foreign policy all illustrate a larger point: After the Cold War, many Americans expected the U.S. role in the world to be easier, if not diminished. Regardless of whether they had ever heard of Fukuyama, many accepted the idea that history had ended—and were relieved. Clinton and his team rejected the notion that America could disengage, but they preferred a sense that engagement would be less costly in attention, resources, and national sacrifice than it was during the Cold War. For nearly half a century, the dominant organizing principle for the U.S. government was the struggle with the Soviet Union. Now people were ready for something different.

IN THE LATE summer of 1992, Clinton advisers Sandy Berger, Lake, and Nancy Soderberg urged the candidate to give one more foreign policy speech. They understood that international issues alone were not going to get Clinton elected and by definition were secondary, but they argued that voters still needed to be reassured about the Democrats. Clinton had dedicated a mere 141 words to foreign policy in his 4,000-word acceptance speech at the Democratic National Convention back in July, but the two sentences he did deliver on the subject were about the need "not to coddle tyrants from Baghdad to Beijing," and about championing democracy in places such as Eastern Europe, Southern Africa, Haiti, and Cuba. Berger, Lake, and Soderberg wanted him to revisit these themes in detail before the election to remind voters they could trust in Clinton's leadership. "When they walk into the voting booth," the three advisers wrote in a memo to Clinton, "Americans must be able to visualize you as commander-in-chief. It's a threshold test. You are well-positioned, but you're not there yet."[21]

Clinton took their advice, and just weeks before the election he traveled to Milwaukee to deliver his final foreign policy speech as a candidate. The venue was chosen deliberately because Wisconsin was home to many of those blue-collar voters who had gone Republican in the previous three elections. Community leaders, with roots in places such as Poland, Ukraine, and Estonia, had grown disaffected, as Bush seemed to be caught flat-footed by the burst of freedom in Central and Eastern Europe after 1989 and appeared more comfortable working with the unelected leader of the Soviet Union,

Mikhail Gorbachev. (Clinton beat Bush two to one among Reagan Democrats.)

In a forceful address delivered in Milwaukee's Pabst Theatre, a Gothic structure built for opera, not political drama, Clinton delivered a broadside against Bush's policies and laid out a conceptual framework for America's role in the world. "Mr. Bush's ambivalence about supporting democracy," Clinton said, "and his eagerness to befriend potentates and dictators has shown itself time and again . . . [Bush] simply does not seem at home in the mainstream prodemocracy tradition in American foreign policy." Clinton was now confident he could challenge the sitting president on his greatest strength.

This speech was the culminating effort to make democracy the centerpiece of the Democratic Party's foreign policy. But although it appeared that the activist, hawkish Democrats campaigning with Clinton were taking a page from the neoconservative playbook, there was an important distinction, reflecting the two groups' different understandings of how events in the 1980s led to 11/9. For the neoconservatives, the drama of 1989 demonstrated the power of Reagan's strong stance against communism. By not accepting the permanence of the Cold War, by building the American military, by speaking out for freedom's universal appeal, Reagan had pushed the Soviet empire to collapse. A muscular foreign policy was a prerequisite to American leadership to ensure that democracy would advance around the world.

The Clinton Democrats saw it differently. For them, it was not so much Reagan's policies that had ended the Cold War; it was the inevitable power of globalization, which made life difficult for authoritarian regimes by breaking down barriers and empowering individuals. America should stand up for freedom, these Democrats believed, and the president should enunciate a vision. But the United States should not push too hard. As long as America renewed its strength at home, its leadership in the world would be assured.

These differences would manifest themselves later in the decade in debates about America's role in fostering regime change of autocratic governments. At the time, the differences between the neoconservatives and the Clinton team appeared slight, particularly compared to the ideas of Bush, Buchanan, and Perot. But there were also fundamental disagreements within the Bush administration. Although the White House had not added substance to its rhetoric about a new world order, two competing visions played out elsewhere in the government, as first the Pentagon and then the State Department drafted analyses of the world in 1992—and a strategy for America in it.

Globocop?

In Bush's last few months in office, some in his administration attempted to articulate a way forward for American foreign policy, but those efforts proved too late for the president and in one case raised enough controversy that it actually hurt him. Nonetheless, they were serious attempts to come up with ideas about the new world's threats and opportunities, and about America's leadership role. Within the administration, two camps conveyed very different perspectives— and themes from both still resonate today in policy debates among those in and out of government. These were also the unresolved debates that Clinton would inherit.

The most infamous of these attempts to survey the new international landscape and craft a lasting U.S. post–Cold War strategy came from the Pentagon, where a small, tightly knit group of strategic thinkers working for Dick Cheney drafted a set of policies to guide the United States as the lone superpower. Cheney had not wanted to push to Baghdad in 1991, but that did not mean he was uninterested in projecting American influence. His worldview was very different from that of the rest of the senior Bush team. He was much more skeptical of global cooperation through institutions such as the United Nations, and of the need for the United States to legitimize the use of its power. Throughout the Bush term, the civilian advisers around Cheney considered themselves separate from others inside the government; in fact, they often referred to their colleagues across the Potomac River in other agencies as "the administration," as though they were looking in from the outside and never really part of it. Their vision for the role of American power in the emerging world order was based on a belief that pragmatists such as Baker, Scowcroft, and Bush were short on bold ideas and placed too much faith in the importance of building strong international consensus.

The most coherent exposition of their strategic outlook took form in the initial drafts of the 1992 Defense Planning Guidance. Required by law, this document's bland bureaucratic title did not diminish its importance. It was intended to establish America's international goals and thereby shape the military's budget and planning. Yet given the timing, it was the government's first effort to sketch a comprehensive strategy since the collapse of the Soviet Union. Drafted principally by Undersecretary Paul Wolfowitz's aide Zalmay Khalilzad, the document reflected the collective thinking of Wolfowitz and his staff, including Lewis "Scooter" Libby, Stephen Hadley, and Eric Edelman, a formidable group with significant national security expertise.

A draft was leaked to Patrick Tyler of the *New York Times* in early 1992, presumably by someone in the government who wanted to expose these ideas to wider debate. It laid out very clearly how America should think now that the Cold War was over. "Our first objective," this early draft read, "is to prevent the re-emergence of a new rival, either on the territory of the former Soviet Union or elsewhere, that poses a threat on the order of that posed formerly by the Soviet Union. This is a dominant consideration underlying the new regional defense strategy and requires that we endeavor to prevent any hostile power from dominating a region whose resources would, under consolidated control, be sufficient to generate global power."[22]

Such language was not particularly surprising coming out of the Pentagon—an institution focused on military threats. But the strategy was notable for what it said about America's friends. During the Gulf War, the White House had worked closely with allies including Germany and Japan and touted the collective security role the United Nations might play. The Pentagon contemplated a world in which such countries emerged as potential rivals for regional dominance. "We must account sufficiently for the interests of the advanced industrial nations," it continued, "to discourage them from challenging our leadership or seeking to overturn the established political and economic order." Insisting that the United States could not let its guard down by disarming, the draft Defense Planning Guidance said America "must maintain the mechanisms for deterring potential competitors from even aspiring to a larger regional or global role. An effective reconstitution capability is important here, since it implies that a potential rival could not hope to quickly or easily gain a predominant military position in the world." The United States would hedge against democracy's failure in Russia, buttress the North Atlantic Treaty Organization (NATO), expand partnerships with Central and Eastern European countries, maintain its strength in the Pacific to deter a rising China and defend South Korea and Taiwan, preserve access to oil, and prevent a nuclear arms race between India and Pakistan. Others in Washington might have been thinking in terms of a peace dividend that would accrue with the Cold War's end, but not Cheney's Pentagon.

Denunciation was swift and came from every quarter. Buchanan told reporters the president should disavow the Pentagon draft, saying, "This is a formula for endless American intervention in quarrels and war when no vital interest of the United States is remotely engaged." Democratic Senator Alan Cranston derided it as an attempt to make the United States the "global Big Enchilada." Clinton campaign adviser George Stephanopoulos called it "one more attempt to find an excuse for big budgets instead of downsizing."[23] Even Cheney's administration colleagues walked away from it. Scowcroft says of the Pentagon's exercise, "That was just nutty. I read a draft of it. I thought, 'Cheney, this is just kooky.' It didn't go anywhere further. It was never formally reviewed."[24]

Cheney's staff soon produced a new draft, which was also promptly leaked. Perhaps chastened by the criticism, the Cheney advisers seemed to distance themselves from their earlier emphasis on preventing the rise of new global competitors and allowed a role for the United Nations (which had gone unmentioned the first time). The document, rewritten mainly by Libby, may have had more nuance and sought a more diplomatic approach, but it still left clear that for Cheney, Wolfowitz, and their advisers, international institutions had limits and American power should be expanded: "While the United States cannot become the world's policeman and assume responsibility for solving every international security problem, neither can we allow our critical interests to depend solely on international mechanisms that can be blocked by countries whose interests may be very different than our own."[25] Few thought the Cheney team had really changed its tune. The *Wall Street Journal* editorial page, considered by many as the bulletin board for the conservative movement, reassured its readers not to "believe all those press reports that Defense Secretary Cheney rewrote the guidance after a leak exposed Globocop ambitions."[26]

FOR CHENEY'S Pentagon team, the idea that a strategy for American preeminence should be so shocking was bizarre. Edelman, a talented career foreign-service officer who went on to hold important positions in the Clinton and George W. Bush administrations, asks, "What was the White House afraid of?" Even after dialing back some of the original language for the final version, the basic point still held. The strategy, argues Edelman, "was starker in the classified version, more muted in the public version, but it's all in there in the regional strategy white paper published in January 1993."[27]

Foreign policy pundits later pointed to the similarities between the Defense Planning Guidance and George W. Bush's 2002 National Security Strategy. Brzezinski argued that the 1992 document "planted the intellectual seeds for the policy of unilateralist preemption and prevention that emerged a decade later."[28] James Mann, whose book *The Rise of the Vulcans* gives the authoritative account of the George W. Bush administration's national security team, described the strategy paper as "one of the most significant foreign policy documents of the past half-century," an accurate guide to where U.S. policy was headed.[29] But when the final strategy paper was released publicly in January 1993, few paid attention because the Democrats had won the election. Published during the Clinton transition, just before the Democrats returned to power, the Cheney paper gave a spirited defense of the views the Bush White House had viewed as "nutty." It reiterated that the goal of national security policy was "to preclude the development of a global threat contrary to the interests of the United States" as well as "any hostile power from dominating a region critical to our interests." And although it conceded that "we favor collective action to respond to threats and challenges in this new era," it added that "a collective response will not always be timely and, in the absence of U.S. leadership, may not gel."[30]

UP TO NOW, most accounts end here—with the presumption that had Bush been reelected in 1992, the Defense Planning Guidance would have been the prevailing policy of his second term. But in fact, as Scowcroft's blunt reaction to the document made clear, many inside the Bush administration held a very different worldview. And even though they had run out of time, State Department officials quietly set out to develop a strategy to reflect the other perspective. Perhaps because the Bush team was leaving, they finally were forced to reflect on the foreign policy inheritance they were handing to the new administration.

What they came up with reflected a far more humble view of U.S. power and greater hopes for internationalism. Compared with the Defense Planning Guidance, the State Department effort offered a more complete picture of the complex challenges that would come to dominate the policy debates of the 1990s: threats emanating from disintegrating states, the greater role of international economics, transnational dilemmas, such as weapons proliferation and climate change, and a U.S. domestic environment more skeptical of sacrifice for engagement abroad. Another key difference from the Pentagon effort is that this one was never aired publicly.

The State Department perspective was conveyed in a twenty-two-page secret memo written to Clinton's incoming secretary of state, Warren Christopher, from his predecessor, Lawrence Eagleburger, who took over the State Department in the waning months of the George H. W. Bush administration.[31] One of the most respected career diplomats of his generation, Eagleburger rose through the ranks at Kissinger's side. Considered an old-fashioned internationalist, Eagleburger was widely admired for his straight talk, if not for his dismal health habits (a chronic smoker and asthmatic, he was known to smoke cigarettes while using an inhaler). After serving for three years as Baker's deputy, he became secretary of state when Baker left for the White House in the summer of 1992 to save Bush's foundering campaign.

Although Eagleburger spent only a brief time at the helm at the State Department, he was a formidable presence inside the administration and had close relationships with Bush and Scowcroft. William Burns, an extremely able young career diplomat who was then acting director of the State Department's Policy Planning Staff (and later served in senior State Department posts under George W. Bush) helped write the draft. Eagleburger sent this memo to Christopher in early January 1993, just weeks before the new team took office. Every presidential transition creates piles of paper explaining the current state of policy and the choices ahead, and much of it goes unread. But this strategy memo became a must-read among the incoming Clinton team.

THE CHENEY document and the Eagleburger memo shared the same premise: that in a moment of revolutionary transition, the United States had both historic opportunities to shape a new international order and a sobering collection of problems with which to contend. But Eagleburger outlined a very different vision of American power—more hopeful and optimistic, conveying a greater awareness of the changing landscape of global politics. He foresaw the United States leading through example and inspiration, not fear. Instead of seeking to hold others back or only intimidate, this strategy argued that the United States must work to be "a provider of reassurance and architect of new security arrangements; an aggressive proponent of economic openness; an exemplar and advocate of democratic values; [and] a builder and leader of coalitions to deal with problems in the chaotic post–Cold War world."

Rather than seeing the new world only through the prism of traditional security threats, Eagleburger's paper struck a note familiar to the Clinton team: "The most important global challenge we face is the emergence of an increasingly interdependent and competitive global economy." The memo expressed the widespread view that Germany and Japan would pose major challenges to America's economic position. It also connected the strength of America's role in the world with the health of the U.S. economy, arguing that domestic economic shortcomings "undercut competitiveness . . . they devalue U.S. leadership and, perhaps more importantly, threaten domestic support for strong international engagement."

The memo argued for a foreign policy that employs the "broadest possible definition of security," including economic growth, democratic political values, conflict resolution, and military arrangements as "parts of an integrated whole." It described the threat from the spread of weapons of mass destruction as the "central security challenge of the 1990s" and outlined rising concerns about nontraditional threats, including the environment and the spread of HIV/AIDS.

While the Defense Planning Guidance focused on concerns about potential rival powers or those wishing to constrain U.S. behavior, the Eagleburger memo warned that the United States would be far more consumed by the disintegration of states. "Alongside the globalization of the world economy," it read, "the international political system is tilting schizophrenically toward greater fragmentation." As the Bush team had already experienced in the Balkans, this breakdown would be messy and would pose difficult choices. "The resulting chaos is enough to almost—almost—make one nostalgic for the familiar discipline and order of the Cold War. Our basic stake is in peaceful processes of change rather than clinging blindly to old maps . . . this is going to confront us with the dilemma of whether to take part in limited military interventions in situations which do not directly threaten our interests. . . ."

Addressing the democracy issue head-on, the memo celebrated the potential for the spread of freedom but with an important warning. If democratizing societies "fail to produce the fruits of reform quickly," they might slide into other "isms"—nationalism or religious extremism or some combination. In one sentence, it also warned of a threat from extreme Islamic movements in the Middle East: "In much of the world, including parts that are very important strategically for us, Islamic conservatism remains a potent alternative to democracy as an organizing principle." After all the leak-driven public debate over the Defense Planning Guidance's emphasis on American supremacy, it was unfortunate that the State Department memo's clear statement of the looming threat posed by Islamic extremism remained hidden from view, its significance largely lost.

Like his Defense Department colleagues, Eagleburger argued that the United States would have to maintain a dominant role in world affairs. "For better or worse, people and governments still look to us to make sense of the changes swirling around them and show some initiative and purpose. No one else can do this." But unlike those at the Pentagon, he also suggested a range of new policy tools the incoming team should explore. This included a "concept" for humanitarian intervention, including such practical steps as creating American military units that could be drawn upon for U.N. missions or joint training at U.S. facilities, a more comprehensive nonproliferation strategy, a new foreign aid system, and a massive overhaul of Washington's national security institutions.

The strategy memo focused mainly on challenges abroad, but it recognized that perhaps the most difficult hurdle existed at home. Eagleburger and his State Department colleagues had watched the 1992 presidential campaign unfold and saw Bush go from triumphant world leader to defeated incumbent. They knew this meant hard days ahead for their successors. "You will be tackling all of these challenges at a moment in our history when many Americans will be preoccupied with domestic problems, and when budgetary constraints on the conduct of American foreign policy are

likely to be tighter than at any point in the last half-century," Eagleburger explained to Christopher. "This leaves you and the president
with a very difficult task."

ALTHOUGH HARDLY a complete repudiation of Cheney's defense
strategy, the Eagleburger memo did sketch a far different view of the
purpose and use of U.S. power. Cheney wanted the United States to
remain the preeminent world power by keeping others at bay and
bending the world to its wishes. Eagleburger saw American preeminence as leading by example and inspiring others to join the U.S.-led
order. These competing perspectives certainly reflect differences in
philosophy, but perhaps the most important distinction concerns the
contours of the new global landscape and the constraints of the
American political system. One strategy defined the world largely by
traditional concepts—states and threats. The other considered the
world's complexity and how the very concept of security was evolving. One strategy accepted the limits imposed by political realities;
the other didn't. The Defense Planning Guidance hardly mentions
the American domestic context and the counterpressures on an active
U.S. global role at the end of the Cold War, especially one that
involved major sacrifice. Yet these pressures had been evident during
the presidential campaign, and from Eagleburger's perspective,
addressing them at home was the key to a successful foreign policy.

Had Bush won a second term in office, the competition between
these two strategic perspectives would have been intense and overt.
Instead, for the public, foreign policy dropped out of view. Nonetheless, these perspectives reflected the core debate that would dominate inside-the-Beltway discussions for the rest of the decade.
Remnants of the Pentagon strategy stayed alive in prominent think-
tank reports and articles, serving as a platform from which to critique
the Democrats. And many of the points made in the Eagleburger
memo resurfaced inside the Clinton administration.[32] The Bush team
never answered the fundamental questions raised by these two

strategies—defining the role, responsibilities, and limits of American power, and managing the required costs and sacrifice. Instead, they left them for Clinton to figure out.

The incoming president and his foreign policy team, including his new national security adviser, Tony Lake, had set high expectations during the campaign and articulated a bold set of policies about the U.S. role in the world, for those who were paying attention. But in an election dominated by economic concerns and problems at home— exit polls showed only 8 percent of voters regarded foreign affairs as the central issue—many of these policies were secondary (or even irrelevant) in the Clinton election victory. And since in the three-way race he had garnered only 43 percent of the popular vote—the lowest of any incoming president since Woodrow Wilson in 1912—Clinton's mandate was not exactly overwhelming.

In the heady days of the transition, Clinton's advisers knew their most difficult task would be managing expectations. The foreign policy elites, especially the neoconservatives, anticipated that the new team would dramatically depart from the Bush years, while the American people, and in some ways the president himself, believed foreign policy had somehow gotten easier or simply mattered less. During the Cold War, it was relatively easy to make the case for major sacrifice to accomplish foreign policy goals. But as Eagleburger wrote to Christopher, "It is infinitely harder now." Or, as Clinton confided to an adviser during the campaign: "Well, I guess if I win, then my real troubles begin."

CHAPTER THREE

Wrong Foot Forward

I N NOVEMBER 1992, just weeks after the election, Brent Scowcroft picked up the phone in his West Wing office and called Sandy Berger, one of Bill Clinton's senior campaign foreign policy advisers, who soon would be the number-two man on the National Security Council staff. Scowcroft had unexpected news: The lame-duck Bush administration planned to order 25,000 American troops to Somalia, a destitute country in the Horn of Africa, as part of a U.N. force to provide humanitarian relief. It was an overwhelming use of military power in a place that few Americans could find on a map.

"I'm not asking you; we're going to do this," Scowcroft said. "You don't have to worry about it, because they will be out of there by inauguration day."[1] The idea, he explained, was simply that U.S. troops would deliver food and humanitarian assistance to thousands of starving people. He told Berger the "combat phase" of this mission—known as Operation Restore Hope—could be completed in a matter of weeks, after which U.S. forces could withdraw and turn efforts over to an international contingent of humanitarian workers.

A few days later, in his last Oval Office address, President George H. W. Bush took to the airwaves to explain this policy to the American people. Following a campaign in which he was pilloried for caring more about the outside world than Americans' fortunes at home, Bush was leaving the presidency with one last call for global engagement, tapping into a sense of compassion and responsibility.

"Anarchy prevails," Bush declared, "[and] the people of Somalia, especially the children of Somalia, need our help. We're able to ease their suffering. We must help them live. We must give them hope. America must act. In taking this action, I want to emphasize that I understand the United States alone cannot right the world's wrongs. But we also know that some crises in the world cannot be resolved without American involvement, that American action is often necessary as a catalyst for broader involvement of the community of nations." These were strong words, yet the president tried to reassure the public that the goal was not open-ended. "Our mission has a limited objective," he said, "to open the supply routes, to get the food moving, and to prepare the way for a U.N. peacekeeping force to keep it moving. . . . We will not stay one day longer than is absolutely necessary."

Bush made no mention of a vital national interest. There was none, which is why he had avoided sending troops earlier in the year despite the massive starvation under way. But his military advisers had finally concluded that they could ease the suffering at low cost. As a realist, the president was not inclined to intervene abroad for humanitarian purposes. Bush chose action in Somalia in part to stave off increasing calls to do something about the humanitarian disaster unfolding in Bosnia, where his military feared a quagmire if America decided to intervene.[2]

Bush ordered American troops to Somalia on a voluntary effort to serve a noble cause—one that made a strong statement about the purpose of American power in a unipolar world. "To every sailor, soldier, airman, and marine who is involved in this mission, let me say," said Bush, "you're doing God's work." Within a week, the first group of U.S. Marines landed in Mogadishu, as the world watched the landing live on CNN.

In both its rationale and goals, the Somalia mission should have appealed to the incoming Clinton team: It showed the United States could command the moral high ground and act on principle, deploying military power to serve humanitarian ends; it would save hundreds of thousands of innocent lives; and it involved working with other countries through the United Nations. Ronald Reagan had once said the United Nations could be "a humanitarian glove backed by a steel fist of military force."[3] Just as many had high hopes for the institution after its members came together in the Gulf War to reverse interstate aggression, perhaps now it could demonstrate its new abilities to right wrongs within states.

Yet the new administration was nervous. An inexperienced president and a team of advisers who had spent the Reagan and Bush years outside of government hardly felt organized or confident to handle a complex military situation in a part of the world they knew little about. They understood what the mission could accomplish in the near term but were less confident about how it would end. Clinton himself said at the time that he "never believed" Bush's "optimistic hope" to have the troops out by inauguration day. And as Berger later recalled, "[the Bush administration] went in really with no exit strategy, to open humanitarian corridors. But then what? Once they would leave, the corridors would close and we'd be back to square one."[4]

Getting Stuck in Unfrozen Ground

The transition from one presidency to another is one of Washington's more unusual rituals. In less than three months, from the November election to the January inauguration, the entire top level of government changes hands. Cabinet-level officials come and go, as do the thousands of political appointees who staff government agencies. The jockeying and elbow-throwing can be intense: Career insiders burrow in to hold on to bureaucratic turf, campaign and party loyalists cash in chits and maneuver for position, the hungry press corps fights for gossip about who's up or down, and those who are on their way out work to spin their legacy and scramble to find their next jobs. It's not much of a honeymoon. It is a politically charged moment: the new team tries to prove itself while everyone else looks to pounce on them for any mistakes.

In the confusion and distraction of these twelve weeks, decisions can fall through the cracks, while some that are made may seem small at first but prove to have far-reaching consequences. The world doesn't stop to wait, as the Somalia intervention illustrated; the outgoing team still faces crises and has to make decisions. The new players coming in have to adjust to these new realities, as well as figure out how to translate their campaign promises into policy.

"Presidents do not inherit a clean slate," observes Madeleine Albright. After a career working for Democratic presidential campaigns and as a popular professor at Georgetown University, Albright was put in charge of overseeing the transition at the National Security Council in 1992. During the weeks she spent poring through policy memos and talking with the outgoing Bush team, Albright quickly saw that the new Democratic administration would have to deal with a range of issues that had been largely ignored. It had been twelve years since a Democrat had been in the White House, but it seemed like a lifetime. The inheritance looked daunting. It was not simply Somalia. There was the festering crisis in Bosnia, where unfolding genocide and images of starving people herded into concentration camps reminded Europeans of the 1940s. Closer to home, the elected government of Haiti's Jean-Bertrand Aristide was overthrown in September 1991 by a military junta, and refugees continued to pour onto rickety craft in the Caribbean seeking safe haven on U.S. shores. Bush's policy was to turn them back; in the campaign, Clinton had promised to change course.

Albright saw these challenges as part of a broader trend. The end of the Cold War had "thawed the ground," she explained, and "all the worms were crawling out ... [there were] ethnic conflicts that had been frozen."[5] Soon named America's ambassador to the United Nations, she emerged front and center in all these crises. Taken together, they presented an enormous test for the institution. The United Nations had been at its best in the Gulf War in 1991, authorizing its most powerful member to lead a coalition to reverse an invasion of a nation-state. But the United Nations soon proved incapable of responding to civil war in Yugoslavia, a military coup in Haiti, and the use of food as a weapon in a battle among Somali warlords. Still lurking in the shadows was Saddam Hussein, subject to a U.N. sanctions regime, weapons inspections, and no-fly zones that required continual reinforcement.

ALL OF THIS was unfolding against a backdrop of public disengagement from the world. As the Democrats took office, most Americans were attuned to the news from Somalia, but few ranked that country a top priority. In January, 89 percent of Americans said they were following events in Somalia at least somewhat closely, with 52 percent reporting they were following the operation very closely. But when asked what they considered the most important problem facing the country, fewer than one-half of 1 percent cited Somalia.[6]

Clinton agreed. The new president didn't want to make Somalia or any global issue the center of his attention when he came into office. Although he had attacked Bush for his passivity on democracy and human rights, Clinton knew he had been elected by promising to, as he put it, "focus on the economy like a laser beam," not by embarking on a foreign intervention. Deans of the Democratic foreign policy establishment, including Indiana Congressman and House Foreign Affairs Committee Chairman Lee Hamilton, reminded him that every modern president tries to emphasize his domestic agenda but becomes defined by foreign policy. But Clinton believed, with reason, that the election had been fought and won on domestic issues and argued privately that international issues had come up on the campaign trail only in questions from journalists who cared about foreign affairs.[7] In these early days, the new president convinced himself of something Tony Lake had told him: "If we do a really good job, the public may never know it, because the dogs won't bark."[8]

Yet Clinton had an insatiable curiosity and intellect and was genuinely interested in the world and in a strong American leadership role. What he lacked was a sense of priority and the confidence to lead. He questioned his own abilities to make bold moves, becoming tentative and dependent on his more seasoned advisers—Lake, Secretary of State Warren Christopher, and Secretary of Defense Les Aspin, along with Berger and Albright. He relied on them to keep the proverbial global dogs quiet. This team had plenty of Washington experience and standing. Christopher was deputy secretary of state under Jimmy Carter, and Aspin was the longtime chairman of the House Armed Services Committee. But they developed an uneasy working relationship with each other, and their personalities often did not mesh.

Christopher was seen as the senior statesman of Clinton's cabinet. A cautious and pragmatic lawyer from Los Angeles, he had been a high official in the Johnson and Carter administrations and had led Clinton's vice presidential search and helped oversee his transition into office. Aspin, a defense intellectual and former Wisconsin congressman, was as rumpled and undisciplined as Christopher was careful and organized. Neither had an assertive personality, and combined with Lake's scholarly demeanor, the national security team conveyed a weak image in the early days that stood in stark contrast to Bush's more commanding advisers.

In comparison with the crisp and relatively collegial process led by Scowcroft, Cheney, and Baker, the new administration changed some long-standing practices and paid a price for doing so. It ended the custom of regularly scheduled meetings between the president and his foreign policy team followed since the Harry Truman administration. Clinton was supposed to meet with Lake every day at 7:30 a.m., but those meetings were often postponed because of pressing domestic or political business. The president quickly gave up on the daily intelligence briefings by the CIA director, preferring to read the intelligence himself.

Lake, Christopher, and Aspin gathered weekly for lunch, but that was not a substitute for a presidential meeting. And the sessions they did have with Clinton were not particularly fruitful. They tended to be rambling and unfocused. Many of the experienced hands worried that often more attention was paid to the press strategy and political implications of foreign policy than to the substance. General Colin Powell, the chairman of the Joint Chiefs of Staff, found this new style troubling and not conducive to good decision-making. To Powell, who had participated in thousands of White House national security meetings as a senior official in the Reagan and Bush administrations, these discussions "continued to meander like graduate-student bull sessions or the think-tank seminars in which many of my new colleagues had spent the last twelve years while their party was out of power."[9]

THROUGHOUT the transition and into their first months in office, the Clinton foreign policy team faced two overriding challenges: to manage successfully the inherited front-burner crises such as Somalia, Bosnia, and Haiti, and to avoid being hoisted on the president's campaign pledges. In pronouncements from the campaign trail, Clinton sought to outflank Bush by saying he would be bolder and tougher by, for example, doing more to support Russia in its transition to democracy or standing up to Chinese human-rights violations. Now he had to face the implications of his rhetoric and the trade-offs with domestic priorities that such decisions posed. It was the difficult task that Eagleburger had warned Christopher about in his transition memo.

Campaigning is often about raising expectations, while governing is about lowering them. Clinton and his closest advisers, especially the political gurus, were just starting to grapple with this reality. They had enjoyed whacking Bush on foreign policy during the campaign but were now realizing that their words had consequences. "[W]inning the White House had added retroactive weight to everything we had said before," recalled George Stephanopoulos, one of Clinton's top political advisers. "Promises that were briefly considered and barely noticed during the presidential campaign, we had learned, could set entire worlds in motion."[10] The result was that, as some on the national security team half-joked at the time, their new mission was walking back the president from his campaign commitments.

Wobbly Command

The thorniest promise they had to address only indirectly concerned America's role in the world. It had to do more with civil rights at home—but the firestorm it created raised deep and long-lasting

concerns about Clinton's stewardship as commander-in-chief. In significant ways, the damage done during those early days to one of the
most important relationships for the use of American power—that
between civilian leaders and the military—hung like a cloud over the
rest of the Clinton presidency.

Back in October 1991, early in the presidential campaign, Clinton
had promised that one of his first acts in office would be to end the
ban on gays serving openly in the military. It was one of those pledges
candidates find easy to parcel out to key interest groups or donors
without really considering the consequences of actually implementing it as president. The military brass and rank-and-file were bitterly
opposed to ending the ban, and they told Clinton so after the election. In part, they were using this issue to test the young leader.

But they were also appalled at the amount of time the issue took
up and the sense of priority this conveyed. In the new president's first
meeting with Powell and the Joint Chiefs, all but fifteen minutes of
the two-hour meeting were spent discussing the subject.[11] After flail-
ing around as the issue sucked up most of the oxygen in political
Washington, Clinton announced that his secretary of defense would
find a solution to the problem; by summer the administration finally
cobbled together a compromise that kicked the can down the road—
the "don't ask, don't tell" policy that still stands today (and forced
about 10,000 men and women out of the military over the next
decade). It made no one happy. Clinton's gay and lesbian supporters
felt betrayed. The military saw a commander-in-chief who was indecisive and prone to letting politically correct social issues drive his
national security agenda. And the Clinton team worried that the
whole episode sent the signal that, in the words of adviser John
Podesta, "there was a weak hand on the wheel."[12]

The controversy reflected a larger problem the Clinton administration had in its unsteady relationship with the military. During the
campaign, Bush and his surrogates had repeatedly tried to wound
Clinton by questioning his experience and ability to be commander-
in-chief. They tarred him as a draft dodger during Vietnam (without
drawing attention to the fact that two of Bush's highest officials, Vice

President Dan Quayle and Defense Secretary Cheney, also avoided service in that war) and warned that he would usher in a new era of McGovernite, anti-Pentagon policies. Such charges belied the substance of Clinton's policy proposals and ignored the endorsement of supporters such as Admiral William Crowe, chairman of the Joint Chiefs under Reagan.

Still, raising gays in the military as one of his first initiatives compounded Clinton's problem and seemed only to confirm the unflattering image. Clinton "probably knew more gay people than military people before he came to Washington," one observer said at the time.[13] Another widely discussed episode involved one of the Army's most highly decorated officers, Lieutenant General Barry McCaffrey, who allegedly was insulted by a young White House aide, who said she didn't talk to those in uniform. Regardless of whether the story was true, it became lore at the Pentagon.

When the president paid his first visit to an American warship at sea, the USS *Theodore Roosevelt*, the traveling press reported a level of disrespect unimaginable under Bush. Sailors shared jokes about a protestor throwing a beer at Clinton—"Not to worry, it was a draft beer, so he dodged it"—and mocked his gays-in-the-military policy by declaring their love for each other. One pilot said the president's three-hour visit could count as his military service, since it was "more than he had before." Sometimes it seemed that military men and women were looking for ways to express their nostalgia for the Bush team. A few weeks after the aircraft carrier visit, Cheney returned to the Pentagon to attend a ceremony for a retiring officer. "Welcome back, boss," Powell said as he introduced Cheney at the event. The room erupted into thunderous, sustained applause, with one witness calling the moment both "touching and telling, like striking a match to tinder."[14] From Powell down, the military had not accepted their new commander-in-chief, and they chafed under Secretary of Defense Aspin's notorious disorganization.

Clinton and his advisers were not in denial about any of this; they read the press stories and worried about the implications. The president was particularly preoccupied with Powell, whom he admired greatly and at one point considered moving to head State or Defense. The general cut an unusual figure inside the administration. As the nation's highest ranking military officer he was the most senior holdover from the Bush years, but he intended to step down as chairman when his term expired in the fall. On the surface Clinton and Powell got along very well. Clinton worked hard to stay in Powell's favor, calling him and asking him to stay behind after meetings for private chats. Powell said he spent more time with Clinton than with Reagan or Bush.[15]

Yet the president told his closest advisers he worried the general could undermine him and, after retirement, translate his status as a national hero into that of a very formidable political opponent. There was always a bit of uneasiness between Powell and the Clinton team, with the general feeling like the "skunk at the picnic," while civilian officials were often intimidated by him. Powell clashed with Aspin, and the defense secretary's civilian aides believed the general was a source of troubling press leaks. "We were all new, and Powell seemed like the grown-up," Albright recalled. Since such tensions were hardly hidden, the result was a relationship that, for many observers, illustrated the distance that remained between Democrats and the military years after the Vietnam War had ended.[16]

IN SOME WAYS, the salute said it all. Many interpreted Clinton's struggles with the military as a sign of his uncertainty about the purpose and use of American power itself. And they saw his struggle to learn one of the most basic gestures of leadership—the presidential salute—as a metaphor for his lack of confidence. As Stephanopoulos describes it, each time Clinton put his hand to his head "he seemed to be working out his internal conflicts . . . as if he were being caught at something he wasn't supposed to do."[17] The new president believed in U.S. leadership and was comfortable describing it in soaring rhetoric, but when faced with difficult choices, especially those involving the military, he remained uncertain about the sacrifice involved—and felt oddly out of place making such decisions.

At a moment when the U.S. armed forces had thousands of troops serving in Somalia and would soon contemplate interventions in places like Bosnia and Haiti, such doubts were reason for concern. Military leaders were already wondering how they would do more with less. They faced new challenges at the same time the political pressure to reduce Cold War budget levels grew intense. Americans wanted a "peace dividend," and military leaders worried that they did not have a strong advocate in the White House.

As for the presidential salute, Clinton's political aides heard the snickering and worked to fix it, dispatching Lake to help. Although not a military man, he was assumed to know how to salute because of his days as a diplomat in Vietnam—itself a sign of the distance between the Clinton civilians and the military. Yet while Clinton's gesture got snappier, the underlying problem—conveying a purpose for American power and strong presidential leadership—remained.

WORRYING about salutes and gays in the military was not what Lake had planned on when he assumed the role of Clinton's national security adviser. The position was held by grand strategic thinkers in the 1970s—Henry Kissinger for Richard Nixon and Zbigniew Brzezinski for Carter—but had a relatively low profile ever since. Reagan went through six national security advisers during his eight years in office, two of whom became mired in the Iran-Contra scandal; although Scowcroft was an effective manager, he never aspired to be a big thinker or global player in the Kissinger-Brzezinski mold.

Lake was a man of ideas. He had written books on the Washington bureaucracy after leaving it in 1981, including a detailed account of the Carter administration's difficulties in dealing with Nicaragua in the 1970s. As a scholar, he understood why policies failed, and many of his colleagues—and rivals—believed he had what it took to succeed in one of Washington's toughest jobs.

Barely visible in the early months of the Clinton presidency, Lake decided during the summer of 1993 that the foreign policy team needed to wrest back control of the debate, laying out a new strategic framework for American foreign policy in the post–Cold War world. Having swept into office with hopes of new ideas and bold thinking, the administration quickly became hostage to reality. By any measure, the first few months in office had been brutal. Many of the policies they had criticized the outgoing Bush team on—the raging war in Bosnia and the brewing crisis in Haiti—had changed little. And the president was getting hammered politically. His pollsters worried as his favorability ratings dropped 20 percent in his first two weeks alone. By the end of May, public approval of Clinton stood at 36 percent, the lowest for any postwar president at a comparable point in his first year.[18]

Almost four years after the fall of the Berlin Wall, it still seemed that American foreign policy lacked purpose and that the United States was reacting to events, not guiding them. Lake's predecessor, Scowcroft, criticized the Clintonites for a "peripatetic foreign policy at prey to the whims of the latest balance of forces." Jeane Kirkpatrick, who had been intrigued by Clinton during the campaign even though she was unwilling to switch parties again and endorse him, decried the "collapse of American authority and leadership." The Clinton team suddenly seemed as exhausted of ideas as the Republicans had been only a year earlier.[19]

A series of unforced errors bolstered this perception. In a Washington episode that received far greater importance than intended, many observers seized on remarks by Undersecretary of State Peter Tarnoff contradicting the administration's message of strong U.S. leadership. In comments that were supposed to be off the record (but were uttered in a room full of more than forty journalists), Tarnoff seemed to suggest the United States was a declining power, arguing that it had limited resources and needed to be careful not to become overextended. "We simply don't have the leverage, we don't have the influence, [or] the inclination to use military force," he said. "We don't have the money to bring positive results any time soon." Coming from one of Secretary of State Christopher's closest aides and the former head of the Council on Foreign Relations, Tarnoff's statement carried great weight.[20]

Since the president had not yet made a major pronouncement about his foreign policy principles or priorities, Tarnoff's words filled a conceptual vacuum. Some believed his message unmasked the administration's true beliefs about the ability to sustain U.S. leadership and reflected a desire to cede many global responsibilities to others, arguing that this was a return to the Carter years. In the spring of 1977, Carter's secretary of state, Cyrus Vance, for whom both Christopher and Tarnoff worked, delivered a speech warning that the United States should "always keep in mind the limits of our power and of our wisdom." Whether intentional or not, Tarnoff's words sixteen years later seemed to echo such sentiments.[21]

The White House and Christopher went into a panic over Tarnoff's remarks, disavowing them immediately. Some of Christopher's aides considered firing Tarnoff on the spot, but instead hurriedly rewrote a previously planned speech on Russia to address the issue, inserting the words "lead," "leader," and "leadership" more than twenty times. But the storm of criticism Tarnoff's informal remarks attracted was nearly overwhelming. After less than six months in office, the Clinton team seemed to be losing control of, if not abandoning, its foreign policy. They knew that they needed to do more. The president had to speak to the issue, laying out a clear vision that Americans and the rest of the world could understand.

The Kennan Sweepstakes

Speeches are often more than just the public articulation of policy. They are used in government to drive decisions and focus the bureaucracy. Because they need to say something, speeches become a way to force consensus internally. Lake, Christopher, and U.N. Ambassador Albright were each scheduled to give a speech that, in conjunction with the president's planned appearance at the U.N. General Assembly in late September, could set the agenda and help define the new era. If they could outline a coherent vision for the world and America's role in it, perhaps they would help engender confidence in their policy and build some momentum. What insiders called the "Kennan sweepstakes" was under way.[22]

NEARLY a half-century earlier, George Kennan had been stationed in Moscow as Americans were trying to make sense of the world in the aftermath of World War II. In 1946, he cabled home a missive that became known as the Long Telegram—a tour de force laying out the nature of the emerging Soviet threat. Kennan championed a strategy of containment to keep the Soviets from spreading their power and thereby undermining American interests. Containment guided Democratic and Republican administrations for forty years, as America checked Soviet power around the globe much more ambitiously than Kennan had believed necessary. But as he had predicted, Soviet foreign policy eventually mellowed, as Mikhail Gorbachev abandoned competition with the United States for global supremacy.

Ever since the dramatic events of 1989, the expert journals and op-ed pages had been filled with learned essays on the challenges America faced and the way ahead. In the summer of 1993, *Foreign Affairs* published a new, dark vision of the world from Harvard professor Samuel Huntington. His article was titled "The Clash of Civilizations." The post–Cold War era, Huntington argued, would not see the return of balance-of-power politics among nation-states, as had existed in previous periods. Instead, the fault lines would appear among the major world civilizations. Cultural and religious differences would define the new global chessboard, he warned, and the central axis of the new order would be "the West versus the rest." This would be particularly true in places where the West met the "bloody borders" of the Islamic world—the Balkans, the Middle East, and Central Asia.[23]

Huntington's vision proved controversial among foreign policy specialists, who quarreled with his historical analysis and accused him of overemphasizing ethnic differences. Inside the Clinton administration, Huntington's thesis offered little help. What would be the prescription for American policy in such a world? Actively seeking to combat the other great civilizations? Those working in the U.S. government believed America needed a positive message, not the re-creation of the Cold War's division using culture and religion. So in late August, Lake asked his aide Jeremy Rosner to start drafting a speech that would develop a foreign policy "understandable enough you could put it on a bumper sticker."[24]

Rosner was a young Washington insider who personified the centrist "New Democrat" politics of Bill Clinton. An intense and brilliant political operative, Rosner was only thirty-four but one of the more experienced players in town. He had been a close adviser to Democratic mavericks Gary Hart and Bob Kerrey. Although he had never formally joined the 1992 Clinton campaign, he had played a major role in helping shape its policy agenda, working with Will Marshall, head of the Democratic Leadership Council's Progressive Policy Institute, often described as an "ideas mill" for Clinton. Like Lake, Marshall and Rosner believed in the muscular use of American power to help spread democracy in parts of the world where indigenous reformers were looking for support as they challenged oppressive regimes.

But that was hardly a catchy bumper sticker. So Rosner tried another idea. If the goal in the Cold War was to contain the "red blob" of communism—made famous in maps of Europe and Asia showing the ominous spread of Soviet influence—the central task now was to expand the "blue blob" of democracies through new institutions and policies. It hardly was Kissingerian or the stuff of Kennan, but it was evocative at the time (or at least memorable). Writing the speech for Lake, Rosner coined the term "democratic enlargement," and that proved to be the Kennan sweepstakes winner. At least in the White House, officials agreed that America wouldn't be using its power to keep a rival in check; it would use its power to expand its circle of friends and spread its values.

Lake hoped this would culminate his effort to put democracy and values at the heart of American policy, creating a line from candidate Clinton's words in Milwaukee almost a year earlier to President

Clinton's policies in office. It would answer the critics who claimed Clinton had yet to define a strategy for the post–Cold War era. It could also be a way to build a new consensus for American strategy by reaching out to Republicans. By stressing the importance of values and freedom, the Democrats would be connecting themselves to the legacy of Truman, whose mantle was donned more recently by Reagan. As Lake awkwardly tried to explain it, "I think Mother Teresa and Ronald Reagan were both trying to do the same thing— one helping the helpless, one fighting the Evil Empire . . . you can do both at the same time and not see them as contradictory."[25]

Politics never came easily to Lake, but Rosner was a pro. Squiring Lake around Capitol Hill early in 1993 to meet with leaders of both parties, Rosner introduced his boss to the House Republican minority whip, Georgia Congressman Newt Gingrich. Like Lake, Gingrich was a former academic who relished discussing ideas. Gingrich and Lake hit it off. They were two intellectuals in a town not known for bipartisan big-picture thinking and they promised to stay in touch. While drafting the speech, Rosner sought comments from Gingrich. Gingrich loved the red blob, blue blob theory of foreign policy, and he spent half an hour on the phone with Rosner offering detailed edits for the speech Lake was scheduled to give at Johns Hopkins University in late September 1993.[26]

The day before the speech was delivered, one of Lake's most politically attuned advisers, Nancy Soderberg, suggested that he remove the reference to the blue blob of market democracies. "In the grocery store last night," she wrote to her boss, "I noticed the cover of *Star* magazine featured a blue blob blocking out a witness' face."[26] Perhaps the metaphor wasn't the best one to describe America's new grand strategy—and a forecast of how it would be received.

BEFORE A PACKED auditorium at Johns Hopkins, Lake articulated the new strategy simply. "Throughout the Cold War," he explained, "we contained a global threat to market democracies; now we should

seek to enlarge their reach, particularly in places of special significance to us. The successor to a doctrine of containment must be a
strategy of enlargement—enlargement of the world's free community
of market democracies." Outlining what he called a "pragmatic neo-
Wilsonian" worldview, he chastised the "neo-know-nothings" within
both parties who believed that with the Cold War over, America
could retreat from responsibility. Lake seemed determined to build a
strategy that could ensure that Francis Fukuyama's end of history
might actually come to pass. But he also wanted to demonstrate that
he was pragmatic: "We should act multilaterally where doing so
advances our interests—and we should act unilaterally when that will
serve our purpose."[28]

The words were eloquent, as were those of Clinton the following
week at the United Nations, where he echoed the enlargement
strategy and enunciated his view of the impact of globalization on
world politics. "We cannot solve every problem," the president said,
"but we must and will serve as a fulcrum for change and a pivot
point for peace. In a new era of peril and opportunity, our overriding
purpose must be to expand and strengthen the world's community
of market-based democracies."[29] Meanwhile, Christopher gave his
speech on peace in the Middle East at Columbia University the day
before Lake's. Albright delivered hers two days later at the National
War College, articulating a vision of what she dubbed "assertive
multilateralism." Lake had wanted the whole team to deliver a single message, but he was unable to get his colleagues on board, since
none of them shared his passion to find a single concept to replace
containment.

Albright says of her slogan, "I believed in multilateralism, and I
thought, well, benign multilateralism isn't very interesting." But she
also believed the search for a new doctrine to be merely a public relations device and not very helpful in practical terms: "[Bush's] new
world order didn't work because it sounded so fascistic," she says.
"You couldn't keep talking about the post–Cold War world. It was an
era that was hard to explain to people. It was like being set loose on

the ocean and there wasn't really any charted course. There was an attempt [to come up with a phrase] primarily for the purposes of speeches or testimony."[30]

Judged by that standard, the new team hadn't achieved much. Washington commentators were not impressed. One of the nation's most experienced political observers, Elizabeth Drew, wrote that the efforts in these speeches to explain U.S. policy "fell short . . . and they received little attention." Even Clinton's own address betrayed the goals Lake wanted to achieve. "Clinton's delivery gave away the difference within him [between] domestic or foreign policy issues," Drew described. "He was wooden and projected little self-confidence."[31] William Safire, in his "On Language" column in the *New York Times Magazine,* took aim at the core phrase. "I'm all for a new word to describe America's role in the world," wrote the legendary former Nixon speechwriter, "but somehow 'enlargement' doesn't do it for me. First there is the connotation of swelling: Enlargement of the spleen or the prostate comes to mind. Then we have the photographic sense, with its synonym of 'blowup'; surely that is not what diplomats seek. Mr. Clinton may want to grow the economy, as he says frequently, but are we metaphorically ready to grow democracy?"[32]

Part of the problem was process. The national security team had not mastered the art of the rollout. Delivering the speeches would not be enough; they had to fuel the echo chamber of talking heads and pundits to reinforce their message. As Rosner recalls, "There was not a full-court-press effort on the Hill, in the intellectual community, in the professional foreign policy community" to make a huge splash. "I wish we had been more bold about it as an intellectual project—writing it, but also getting people on the outside to support it."[33] Remarkably, in an interview that appeared in the *New Republic* the day before his speech, Lake downplayed his effort rather than emphasize what he was trying to do. "I'm skeptical about doctrines on immensely complicated and difficult issues [that] have all the answers before you ask the questions," he said.[34] If that was how the national security adviser described the administration's message to journalists, democratic enlargement had little chance of being taken seriously as the successor to containment.

But Lake's comments reflected a fundamental truth. It was folly to try to describe how the United States should approach the world's complexities with one single idea. There was and still is a misplaced nostalgia for the simplicity of the Cold War and containment. Containment was an easy concept to understand because there was one Soviet Union—a single ideological, diplomatic, political, military, and economic power competing with the United States for influence around the globe. Yet the United States still had huge debates over how best—or even whether—it should combat Soviet influence in places such as Vietnam, Central America, and Africa. So absent a single foe, the effort to impose one grand theory on global events proved deeply frustrating—and ultimately fruitless. "Every new administration tries to develop a new strategy," says Kissinger. "The problem is that they never start with an analysis of what the world is, but what they think it should be." Even Kennan, whom everyone in the foreign policy elite hoped to emulate, himself had been dubious during the Cold War of the value of seeking "universal formulae or doctrines in which to clothe or justify particular actions."[35]

One Clinton speechwriter, Daniel Benjamin, compares the failure to find a new phrase to "a toothache that wouldn't go away." Another, Robert Boorstin, found the administration's whole effort to come up with a new bumper sticker to be a distraction. "Our search for the proper rhetoric to define the period in international relations we were living through turned out to be a waste of time. Not every period has the equivalent of Kennan's 'containment.' It wasn't what you were going to call it that was important but what you were going to do."[36]

Looking back, Rosner agrees. He says that whatever possibilities existed in September 1993 for outlining a new vision and rebuilding an intellectual consensus around democratic enlargement equal to that around containment during the Cold War—"died on Sunday, October 3."[37]

Black October

That first Sunday in October was the darkest day for American foreign policy since the triumph of 11/9. It would have been bad enough if the only foreign news that weekend was the dramatic shelling of the Russian parliament that President Boris Yeltsin ordered to rout his political opponents. But then, eighteen American soldiers were killed in a massive firefight in Mogadishu, Somalia, and people back home watched horrifying television images of fallen servicemen dragged through dusty streets. Just when things could hardly get worse, an American military vessel tried to dock in Haiti a week later, but it turned around rather than confront an angry mob on the shore. No one died, but the incident was deeply humiliating.

FOR MOST of that year, the Somalia mission actually seemed like a success. Food was delivered. A semblance of security was established. No Americans lost their lives. After securing the situation, American forces handed over responsibility to the United Nations, which created the largest peacekeeping force in its history, with 28,000 military and 2,800 civilian staff. (Just over 4,000 U.S. troops remained as part of the U.N. force.) It appeared that the Clinton team had fulfilled the mission undertaken by its predecessors. The troops were still there on January 20, but in the spring Clinton welcomed them back in a ceremony on the South Lawn of the White House replete with all the pomp and circumstance the military wanted to see from its commander-in-chief.

But progress in Somalia soon began to unravel, and the administration was back at square one, right where Deputy National Security Adviser Sandy Berger worried it would end up when he first learned that Bush planned to send American soldiers and marines there. That summer, Somali militia fighters attacked and killed U.N. troops, and in response U.N. leaders in Mogadishu issued a warrant for the arrest of militia leader Mohammed Farah Aideed. They asked U.S. forces to help.

Within weeks, the administration authorized an aerial attack on Aideed's headquarters, and the first reports were positive. Desperate for good news, the administration played up this victory, and Clinton touted it during his first prime-time press conference in June. Only CNN and PBS bothered to cover the press conference in full, which many took as a further sign of a diminished presidency. Speaking in the East Room of the White House, the president said, "General Powell has reported to me this afternoon that this operation is over and that it was a success. The United Nations, acting with the United States and other nations, has crippled the forces in Mogadishu of warlord Aideed."[38] In his notes, Lake wrote to himself, "Deprived the Aideed faction of their base of operations." After another meeting, he added, "Op over. Aideed out of business . . . knocked legs out from under Aideed and lieutenants."[39] The jubilation reflected a growing infatuation with air power that had begun during the Gulf War. It offered a means of warfare with no American casualties, which was not always the case when the country put boots on the ground.

The administration's desire to show backbone colored its perception of reality. Despite pronouncements of progress, the situation in Somalia grew worse, as violence escalated and U.S. forces became more deeply involved. The result was a classic conflict spiral: Somali militias launched attacks and then U.N. forces responded, and with each outburst of violence the demands for more firepower grew stronger.

For U.S. forces, the conflict proved far more complex than the high-technology displays and set-piece battles of the Persian Gulf War. Unquestionably outgunned, Aideed's militia used innovative tactics that exposed U.S. military weaknesses that later proved all-too-familiar to Americans in Iraq. In early August, four U.S. soldiers were killed when Aideed's forces exploded a remote-controlled bomb—or what we now call an improvised explosive device, or IED—under their Humvee. In response, U.S. commanders on the ground asked for more troops. Despite fears about the conflict worsening, Pentagon leaders deployed a contingent of U.S. Army Rangers and the elite

Delta Force to find and capture Aideed. (It was not until a few years later that American intelligence officials learned that al-Qaeda operatives were sent to help train the Somali militias.)[40]

With little internal discussion and virtually no public debate, the U.S. mission in Somalia had evolved from one feeding innocents to restoring stability and fighting militias. Writing in the *New York Times,* Albright explained the shift in an attempt to rally public support. She articulated a goal that went far beyond merely defeating the warlords. "More Americans may ask why we should care about the United Nations effort to restore that failed state," she wrote. Citing the U.N. Security Council resolutions calling for disarming the militants to create a secure environment for delivery of humanitarian assistance, she declared, "The decision we must make is whether to pull up stakes and allow Somalia to fall back into the abyss or to stay the course and help lift the country and its people from the category of a failed state into that of an emerging democracy. For Somalia's sake, and ours, we must persevere."[41]

Given the context in which the United States went into Somalia, it was an extraordinary statement. A humanitarian mission originally described as having no relation to the vital national interest was now defined as crucial not just for the Somali people, but also for the United States and the credibility of the United Nations. Albright's statement portrayed a country that didn't even have a government as a potential "emerging democracy." Now American forces were on a manhunt to promote democratic values. It was one thing to make the claim that failed states could affect American national security, a prospect that was not yet well understood; but to suggest that success would mean the emergence of democracy set the bar rather high.

The events in the Somali capital exposed the fact that no military mission was purely humanitarian. Conservative columnist Charles Krauthammer asserted that Somalia destroyed the "fantasy" that foreign policy could be subordinated to morality. "We waded ashore in Somalia to feed the hungry," he wrote in *Time* magazine. "Now our gunships hover over Mogadishu shooting rockets into crowded villas." This demolished what he called "the first post–Cold War mirage" that U.S. national security policy could be subordinated to pure humanitarianism. "Once you go beyond relief to policing, you have to shoot. You can't just feed, you have to stop the thugs."[42] But was stopping such thugs in America's national interest?

In the crush of events, the administration never paused to address that question. Of the thirty-eight formal meetings the Clinton national security team had convened since taking office, not one focused on Somalia.[43] As summer turned to autumn, the president and his top advisers were preoccupied by their effort to develop a new foreign policy theme, their desire to encourage peace between Israel and the Palestinians (symbolized by the historic handshake between Israeli Prime Minister Yitzak Rabin and Palestinian leader Yasir Arafat on the White House's South Lawn), and a major effort in Congress to pass the North American Free Trade Agreement. Yet they understood that new realities were being shaped on the streets of Mogadishu.

In Clinton's U.N. General Assembly speech in late September, he raised some pointed questions about the lessons of Somalia for the future of U.N. peacekeeping. "Is there a real threat to international peace? Does the proposed mission have clear objectives? Can an end point be identified for those who will be asked to participate? How much will the mission cost? From now on, the United Nations should address these and other hard questions for every proposed mission before we vote and before the mission begins."[44] These were all good questions. But the fact that Clinton found reason to outline them for future crises, at the exact moment that thousands of American troops were on the ground in Somalia, seemed to be a tragic acknowledgment that the United States was already in too deep.

ON OCTOBER 3, as U.S. Army Rangers and Delta Force commandos swept into Mogadishu in search of Aideed, the mission went awry. Two U.S. helicopters were shot out of the sky by rocket-launched grenades. In a tremendous battle immortalized in the book and the movie *Black Hawk Down*, eighteen Americans were killed, seventy-three were wounded, and an American pilot was captured.

The Clinton administration went into free fall. For a team that had never been sure-footed in its stewardship of the military, this was a disaster. The tragedy was the greatest loss of life for American forces in a firefight since Vietnam. It was one thing for Americans to see their troops killed and wounded to reverse Saddam's invasion of Kuwait; it was quite another to see soldiers dragged through the streets of a country of questionable interest to the United States. The president felt betrayed by his top team and the intelligence community, whom he blamed for soft-pedaling the threat just days before the raid. He could not believe the United States lacked enough forces in Somalia to rescue the troops. "We're not inflicting pain on these fuckers," he screamed at his aides, as they watched televised images of the captured pilot and of Somalis celebrating around dead American bodies. "I believe in killing people who try to hurt you, and I can't believe that we're being pushed around by these two-bit pricks."[45]

The partisan finger-pointing began immediately. Even though he had initiated the original intervention, Bush made sure everyone knew where to place the blame. "Our mission was to go into Somalia, open the supply lines, then to withdraw and have the United Nations handle the peacekeeping function," he said in a speech. "For reasons I'm not sure of, the mission has been redefined."[46] A firestorm erupted on Capitol Hill. Two days after the Mogadishu disaster, Christopher and Aspin briefed more than 200 members of Congress in the Capitol Rotunda's overheated basement. In the one-and-a-half-hour spectacle, members were astonished that rather than lay out a plan, the two secretaries meekly asked for advice.

As defense secretary, Aspin bore the brunt of the blame. Republican Senator John McCain complained, "I learned nothing I didn't already know. Anyone who watches the local and national news would get more information." Texas Republican Phil Gramm said, "The people who are dragging American bodies don't look very hungry to the people of Texas."[47] Looking back, Gingrich called it the "most dismal performance by a national security official in modern times."[48] It was clear that Aspin's days at the Pentagon were numbered.

In the wake of the crisis, Clinton's national security team scrambled to convene its first formal discussion on Somalia. But the meeting focused on press strategy and how to spin the response, which struck some participants as illustrative of the deeper problem. Lake asked Robert Oakley, the rugged career diplomat who was American envoy to the Somali crisis for several months, to join the meeting. The White House planned to dispatch him to Mogadishu to negotiate the release of the captured pilot. Oakley initially believed it was wrong to go after Aideed, and now he was equally convinced that continuing the hunt was a mistake. But he regretted the chaotic policy process that had led to the crisis: "We had a disconnect between the U.N. and the U.S., and a disconnect between the American civilian and military leadership, as well as between the Bush administration people and the Clinton people. That was obviously a recipe for catastrophe."[49]

Clinton was concerned that continuing the hunt for Aideed against the wishes of Congress would cause lasting damage to his ability to conduct foreign policy. So he announced that he would send more troops to Somalia to stabilize the situation, but all American forces would be withdrawn in six months. He needed to get Somalia off the front page. A *Time*/CNN poll showed that 66 percent of the public agreed with the statement that if the United States did not remove its troops soon, Somalia could become another Vietnam.[50]

BUT THE ADMINISTRATION just couldn't escape trouble. On the heels of Somalia, the Clinton team took an equally clumsy approach to another country whose problems did not threaten U.S. national security but were raising fears about an influx of unwanted immigrants. Haiti had presented a thorny challenge since the start of the administration. Bush first faced the issue after Haiti's military overthrew the country's elected leader, Roman Catholic priest Jean-Bertrand Aristide, in a September 1991 coup. Haitians were setting sail on anything that floated to seek refuge in Florida. Bush's policy was to stop them at sea, and despite Clinton's campaign promise to reverse what he saw as an inhumane policy, he continued the Bush approach. The best way to stop the problem, most believed, was to get Aristide back in power and restore democracy.

In the summer of 1993, the United Nations brokered an accord at Governors Island, New York, that provided for an international peacekeeping force and an October 31 deadline for Aristide to return to Haiti. The United States agreed to send noncombat personnel as part of the 1,200-strong U.N. force, but the deployment was the subject of significant internal disagreement. CIA Director James Woolsey and Secretary of Defense Aspin feared these lightly armed trainers and engineers would be in danger. Christopher, Albright, and Lake argued that the Governors Island agreement must be fulfilled because U.S. credibility was on the line.[51]

Unfortunately, Woolsey and Aspin were right. On October 11, just eight days after the Somalia disaster, the naval ship USS *Harlan County* arrived off the coast of Haiti with a few hundred American and Canadian engineers and medical technicians. Armed mobs on the docks (orchestrated by the junta leaders) began to riot, screaming "Somalia, Somalia," and preventing the ship from docking. After much hand-wringing, with the world watching an American military vessel sitting idly in the waters off Haiti, Clinton had the ship turn around and sail home. Critics were outraged that the administration had allowed the U.S. military to be deterred by a bunch of unarmed thugs. The episode was "a total fuckup," Lake later admitted. "It was our fault. We had sent the ship out with zero military support." Once again, it looked like the president was backing down from a fight.[52]

The Bay of Mogadishu

Just weeks after Clinton first spoke from the dais of the U.N. General Assembly aiming to articulate a bold direction for America in the world, the United States looked confused. It was hard to make a convincing push for big change and confident leadership with an administration that had bungled so badly.

For a young president in his first year, these events were demoralizing. "When I ran for president, I didn't dream that within a year I'd be dealing with what happened in Somalia," Clinton said later. He compared his situation to President John F. Kennedy's after the 1961 Bay of Pigs disaster in Cuba. He, too, felt saddled by decisions made by his predecessor and victimized by his inexperience. But these episodes reinforced Clinton's inclination to believe that foreign policy could only bring bad news. "The battle of Mogadishu haunted me," he admitted in his memoirs. Clinton was seared by his meetings with the families of those injured or killed in Somalia, recalling that after he awarded a posthumous Medal of Honor to one of the fallen, the soldier's father confronted him directly and said that he wasn't fit to be commander-in-chief.[53]

In private conversations with his closest confidants, Clinton lashed out at his seasoned advisers, who were supposed to keep him out of trouble. "I would have handled [Somalia] in a different way if I had more experience . . . I know I would have," he later admitted.[54] He complained that his top team failed to project authority with the media, the Congress, or the military, leaving him hanging alone. He also felt that they failed to articulate a convincing case for American leadership, reinforcing the impression that the presidency was adrift. Clinton took particular aim at Lake's "enlargement" speech. Although he had initially told Lake it was "quite good,"[55] the president clearly was frustrated by the results, telling one adviser that the whole enterprise was "weak, pathetic . . . I just didn't get it; it just didn't grab."

FOR THOSE such as Lake, who had returned to Washington with a sense of hope and possibility, October's events delivered a crushing blow. The end of the Cold War was supposed to have opened new opportunities for America abroad. The bitter politics that had animated the angry debates about American foreign policy since Vietnam were supposed to have ended. Looking back later, Lake said, "It was absolutely the bottom of the [first] four years on national security issues. . . . Clearly we inherited a Somali operation with no end point and no clear purpose, and we didn't make it better."[56]

He expressed his frustration in an interview with the *New York Times*. "We have laid out a vision and strategy," Lake said, taking aim at his critics. "A cacophony of voices without a countervision simply encourages the neo-know-nothing isolationists. I would like to hear the alternative vision, not as part of a competitive game of 'gotcha,' but as part of a serious debate." He argued that the administration had learned from the crises it dealt with, and had done well on other issues.[57]

Lake's frustrations were well-founded. Despite its serious setbacks, the administration had some accomplishments. Clinton went to Japan for a meeting of the group of seven advanced industrialized countries (G7) in July and, while there, reached agreement with the Japanese government on important trade issues. He passed a major aid package for Russia to help that country transition away from its authoritarian past. In the fall, with more Republican votes than Democratic ones, Congress approved the North American Free Trade Agreement.

But Clinton and his team had failed to articulate a new foreign policy direction, and they had significant rebuilding to do. The October debacles seemed to be the result of one misstep after another since inauguration day. Critics from all sides piled on, and the neoconservatives who had been so carefully and successfully cultivated during the campaign turned their backs in disgust.

THAT AUTUMN, after the events in Somalia and Haiti, Lake sat alone at his West Wing desk, in the same office from which Scowcroft had called the Clinton team to say troops were heading to Somalia, and drafted a resignation letter to the president. The last time he had left the White House, during the Nixon years, he had resigned in protest over the U.S. bombing of Cambodia. Then, as now, he was deeply distressed by the controversy surrounding the use of America's military power.

"I confess," he scribbled in longhand on a pad of lined paper, "to a series of constant and growing frustrations—partly at the interagency difficulties in pushing through new approaches as hard times bring out new hesitancies and partly also with a White House that . . . still treats foreign policy as [a] 'wholly owned subsidiary.' What concerns me more is a growing sense that your and my own priorities and philosophy may simply not be the same." He laid out his differences with the president: "I very strongly believe that as you define those priorities in your own mind and then—privately as well as publicly—pursue them with a simple-minded passion, you can, with your extraordinary intelligence and eloquence, have a powerful impact in the world. I also believe that you will not do so if you let your critics or the morning columns define your goals, tactics, and necessary compromises."

Lake made clear that he did not believe Clinton was committed enough to the new theme they had enunciated in September, noting that he knew the president found the phrase "democratic enlargement" to be "aesthetically displeasing." He admitted that "as you say, a part of the problem has been our rhetoric (on issues like Bosnia and Haiti and Russia as well). But I think that there was little in the rhetoric that could not have been redeemed by vigorous, determined pursuit of our goals. And while I have no doubt we agree on the importance of opening markets to American workers and reshaping our military forces, I do not sense the same depth of commitment on issues involving the spread of democracy and human rights or the carnage of foreign civil wars. These last are messy issues that require painful choices. But once involved, we can only resolve them through pragmatic but persistent and, when necessary, forceful action."[58]

Depth of commitment. Painful choices. Forceful action. The post–Cold War world could not be defined by policy speeches alone, however thoughtful. It would require poise, leadership, and the willingness to make difficult decisions that entailed sacrifices. Throughout 1993 and into 1994, Clinton lacked confidence in his abilities to conduct foreign policy and to serve as the nation's commander-in-chief.

In the aftermath of Somalia, Clinton and Lake ruefully reflected about how they missed the Cold War. Although they knew it was an absurd notion—Clinton understood he probably never would have been elected president had the Cold War still raged—it reflected their difficulties and their longing for the supposed simplicity that came before.

The problem was that the president still didn't spend enough time on foreign policy, and he didn't project the passion that he showed for his domestic agenda. He was too uncertain and tentative. The popular comic strip *Doonesbury* depicted Clinton as a waffle. He was slow to learn that seemingly small issues—like Somalia or Haiti—were seen by those at home and abroad as symbolic of his leadership and, importantly, of his ability to be commander-in-chief. At one point, Christopher urged the president to meet with his foreign policy team once a week. Although Clinton agreed—which was quickly leaked to the newspapers to force him to keep his word—the group met only twice over the next two and a half months.[59]

Yet the dilemma went deeper than Clinton's learning curve and the number of times his national security advisers got together. The crises of that autumn exposed the significant baggage the Democratic Party still carried when it came to the conduct of national security policy. The Clinton team wanted to support human rights, promote democracy, and stand for liberal values. It seemed natural for them to want to do something about boat people from Haiti, starving children in Africa, and victims of genocide in Bosnia. But it all came down to a question of means. If the president and his team couldn't frame these problems as important to the national interest, they would convince neither the public nor the military that sending U.S. troops was justified, particularly once Americans started dying.

"Americans are basically isolationist," Clinton said to his advisers in the days after Somalia. "They understand at a basic gut level Henry Kissinger's vital-interest argument. Right now the average American doesn't see our interest threatened to the point where we should sacrifice one American life."[60] The president's challenge was to reconcile this belief with his equally firm conviction that the United States must play an active role in solving problems and helping people abroad. The usual answer was to enlist the help of others by working through international organizations such as the United Nations—the concept Albright tried to capture with "assertive multilateralism." But the Somalia disaster made a mockery of this idea. Instead of a means for collective action, the United Nations came to be seen as a place where U.S. power was manipulated to serve others' ends in places where the nation has few interests. One of the ironies of this period is that for all of the Clinton team's efforts to come up with a new slogan to describe U.S. foreign policy, the only two phrases that proved lasting were those used by opponents to describe failures and warn what not to do: "mission creep" and "nation-building."

For the American military, the Somalia experience reinforced a doctrine Powell made famous: Use decisive force in places where there is a clear U.S. interest and an equally clear way out. "Be careful what you get into," Powell argues. "We have to better understand our national interest."[61] For Washington's political leaders and the general public, the tragedy burned a new set of scars on the American psyche. They believed that any military mission short of self-defense must be highly sensitive to risk and not sustain casualties. The diplomat Richard Holbrooke, who soon played a major role in the Clinton administration in ending the war in Bosnia, described this syndrome as the combined legacy of Vietnam and Somalia, or Vietmalia.[62]

JANUARY 1994 brought an end to a very bad first year in office. Slowly the president regained momentum. Personnel changes helped. For months Clinton contemplated reshuffling his national security team, and on any given day someone's job seemed to be in jeopardy, compounding the sense of weakness and desperation. Lake was asked to stay on despite his frustrations, but the president relieved Aspin of his post at the Defense Department. Powell had retired as scheduled on September 30 (just days before the Mogadishu disaster), and while Clinton considered asking him to replace Christopher at State, the former general settled into private life and began contemplating whether to dive into politics. Powell's successor, Army General John Shalikashvili, proved willing to think creatively about the use of force in the kinds of conflicts that were emerging in the post–Cold War world. Having led the U.S. effort to help the Kurds of northern Iraq in 1991, he had a keen understanding of the changing environment in which military force could be used. Early in 1994, Deputy Secretary of Defense William Perry was promoted to succeed Aspin, and his successful three-year tenure at the helm of the Pentagon ultimately helped the Clinton administration recover from its early missteps with the military.

It would be 1995 before the president came to realize he could handle foreign policy as well as he could oversee bold domestic initiatives, such as welfare reform. As he gained confidence, he became more sure of America's role in the world, and he achieved significant results, particularly in Europe, where he expanded NATO, ended the fighting in Bosnia, and put relations with Russia on a steady course. Yet by that time, Republicans controlled Capitol Hill, and the partisan divide grew even deeper.

To the administration's opponents, its stumbles in Somalia and Haiti, combined with its initial inability to solve Bosnia, forever stained the Clinton team—and Democrats altogether—as incompetent and untrustworthy, particularly in the use of force. Three crises inherited from the Bush administration ended up defining Clinton's foreign policy abilities for the rest of the decade—and to a significant degree, still do today. In response to the perceived ineptitude of the Clinton team and the growing isolationism and drift in the Republican Party, a handful of committed neoconservatives began articulating an alternative agenda for America. With a disastrous first year in office, Clinton had lost the initiative to define the era.

CHAPTER FOUR

Contract and Crisis

A T THE END OF 1993, Dick Cheney was worried. Since leaving the Pentagon, the former defense secretary had spent his time at a conservative think tank, the American Enterprise Institute (AEI), mulling his options, including a possible run for president in 1996. Political insiders gave Cheney the best chance to mount a serious campaign among those in former President George H. W. Bush's top command. Unlike James Baker, whose tenure in the Bush administration ended with a whimper after his return to the White House failed to save the 1992 campaign, or former Vice President Dan Quayle, who always seemed to be the punch line for a joke, Cheney's electoral prospects appeared bright. He personified what everyone admired about the first Bush administration: steadiness, tough-mindedness, and experience. Only Colin Powell received more Beltway buzz, but he kept people wondering whether he was a Republican or a Democrat.

To any Republican aspiring to the White House, President Bill Clinton's struggles should have been reason for optimism. After the Democrat's bruising first year in office, there was much nostalgia for the Bush team. Cheney took advantage of this, using numerous media appearances to criticize the president's record, arguing that Clinton and his advisers lacked "intellectual rigor and tight command and control."[1] Cheney was one of the hottest tickets on the political circuit, traveling to forty-seven states on behalf of Republican candidates. But

Cheney was not optimistic about the national mood or the broader political debate; he saw the world as a dangerous place, and while faulting Clinton's failures, he also worried about how conservatives were responding.

Cheney had some tough medicine for fellow Republicans, and he delivered it in December 1993 as the featured speaker at AEI's fiftieth-anniversary dinner.[2] Addressing an audience of nearly 2,000 conservative luminaries, clad in black-tie and packed into the ballroom of Washington's Sheraton Hotel, Cheney lobbed the usual criticisms against the Democratic administration. He decried the fact that foreign and defense policy had been relegated to the bottom of the public agenda, ripping Clinton's misplaced priorities and lack of leadership. Then he turned to his own party. "Republicans bear part of the responsibility for this state of affairs," he told the room of loyalists. "We are the ones who acquiesced last fall in the Democrats' assertion that the 1992 campaign for the presidency should address domestic issues only," he said, delivering a stinging rebuke to the prevailing wisdom of his former boss's political strategy (some of whose architects sat in the audience before him). That lapse meant more than just losing an election. Cheney believed Republicans' "first failing was in allowing ourselves and the American people to be lulled into a false sense of security. . . . As a result, we've lost our focus, and there is now a lack of understanding of what's at stake."

Echoing the central policies of his Pentagon's Defense Planning Guidance the year before, Cheney argued for higher military spending and a focus on traditional threats, including a potentially resurgent Russia and instability on the Korean peninsula. He made only passing mention of challenges such as Somalia, Haiti, or Bosnia. But more important than such specifics was the larger point he wanted to make: Like Democrats, Republicans had become complacent in allowing the debate about America's role in the world to fade. The remedy, Cheney concluded, was clear: "It is more important than ever that our president be a foreign policy president."

To many in the elite audience of political players and think-tankers, Cheney's words resonated. Yet in the months ahead, only the first part of his message gained traction. Republicans had no problem criticizing Clinton's approach to the world. That part was too easy, as they never had to forge a consensus on their own foreign policy ideas. Conservatives failed to make foreign policy central to their rationale for leadership, in part because they remained divided about the direction it should take, and because they were never convinced that it was a political winner.

Ultimately, Cheney too had doubts about how his message worked politically. He found it hard to raise money and garner much support for his campaign to be a "foreign policy president." By 1995, he decided not to run and left Washington for Texas to become CEO of the energy services company Halliburton. The departure of this Republican heavyweight and admired former defense secretary from the political scene—an exit he thought at the time was permanent—symbolized the prevailing forces inside conservatism during the mid-1990s. The incoherence and uncertainty about America's role in the world was not unique to the Clinton team; it was mirrored by those on the right. Cheney's dilemma was summed up by former Bush official and conservative commentator William Kristol, who in the years to come would emerge as an influential agitator for a more forceful American global role: "Foreign policy is just not on anyone's radar screen right now."[3]

The Contract Republicans

The 1994 Contract with America is a gauge of where conservatives placed U.S. defense and foreign policy among their priorities. It laid out ten policy planks a Republican-led Congress would implement if elected in the 1994 midterm elections. Only one had anything to do with America's national security or its role in the world.

The contract first and foremost was about getting Republicans elected. After four decades of Democratic control of Congress, the Republican House leadership—whose most influential member was minority whip and maverick Georgia Congressman Newt Gingrich

—believed 1994 could be their year. Clinton's approval ratings were in the basement, and Republicans needed a way to nationalize the Congressional election, creating a party platform to rally the electorate.

The brainchild of Gingrich and whiz-kid pollster Frank Luntz, the contract had several virtues: It outlined exactly what Republicans aimed to do and made clear that if they were not successful, they should be held accountable (which is why they decided to call it a contract). It was carefully designed to reach out to disaffected voters, many of whom pulled the lever for Ross Perot in the 1992 presidential election. "To say that the electorate is angry," Luntz argued at the time, "would be like saying that the ocean is wet. Voters in general and our swing voters in particular have simply ceased to believe that anything good can come out of Washington."[4]

More than 350 Republican candidates for Congress signed the contract, which was unveiled in a festive Capitol Hill ceremony and published in a full-page advertisement in *TV Guide* (with a circulation of 14 million) in late September 1994; the ad was designed to be torn out and kept as a scorecard for progress. Each plank of the contract had been extensively researched and poll-tested for maximum political value, with great care given not just to which issues were included but also to how each policy was described. Listed in order from most to least important to swing voters (except for the second most popular, term limits, which was listed last for dramatic effect), the pledges included a balanced budget, tax cuts for families, and legal reform. The national security plank was sixth.

Taken as a whole, the contract belied Gingrich's internationalist worldview. Its focus, as he readily admits, was not the direction America should be taking in the post–Cold War world. "It was a domestic political document," he says emphatically. "There was no foreign policy issue that mattered in that period. It's a little bit like *The Great Gatsby*: a feel-good period with relatively modest threats in which the most powerful nation in the world had near hegemonic superiority."[5]

The national security proposals were designed less as a positive vision for conservatives than as cudgels to pound on the Clinton team's greatest vulnerabilities and create the maximum possible embarrassment. The goal was to tar the Democrats as weak on defense, by calling for more Pentagon spending and a review of military needs. With memories of the Somalia disaster still raw, the contract also addressed concerns about the U.S. relationship with the United Nations, prohibiting U.S. troops from serving under U.N. command (which, despite Republican accusations, had not in fact occurred). It included a push for national missile defense, an acceleration of the timetable for the enlargement of the NATO alliance into the former territory of the Warsaw Pact, and a ban on using the military for anything other than vital national interests.

None of these was expected to be a huge political winner. "Newt said all the time that we didn't put anything in the contract that didn't have 70 percent [support] or more," one of Gingrich's senior advisers, Tony Blankley, later explained. "That was true, except for defense, because in 1994, nobody wanted to spend any more on defense. This was the golden era of the peace dividend."[6]

ALTHOUGH these ideas played a minor role in the contract overall, its themes and policies—hostility to the United Nations, higher defense spending, and pursuit of national missile defense—came to dominate the conservative national security agenda. Less than two years after the end of the Bush administration, the Republicans rallied around a set of policies rooted in a far more pessimistic worldview than the "new world order." They embraced a more limited vision of American power than the Cheney team's Defense Planning Guidance, with less conviction about the changing nature of U.S. security and possibility for international cooperation than was displayed in the Eagleburger memorandum.

Whereas Bush had seen hope and possibility for the United Nations, the new generation of Contract Republicans mainly saw the dangers of entanglement with the organization and sought to restrict cooperation and limit American support, especially for peacekeeping. They were skeptical of using U.S. military force for largely humanitarian purposes, as Bush had done in northern Iraq and Somalia, believing such missions fell outside the bounds of national interests. And unlike such party mandarins as Dick Cheney, the Contract Republicans considered foreign policy a low-priority issue, properly overshadowed by domestic and social priorities, as reflected by the Clinton White House.

As important as any of its details was the snapshot the contract provided of the reaction among Republicans, and increasingly among a majority of Americans, to Clinton's foreign policy as a whole. It cemented the perspective that the president was not up to the job, that he had an unsteady team, and that his confusion and bungling would do great damage to American interests. The political lesson of Bush's loss in the 1992 election, combined with the view of Clinton's incompetence, led Contract Republicans away from the global engagement embraced by many conservative policy elites, including internationalist leaders like Gingrich. Such notions of engagement were dismissed as "Clintonism," as though they were inherently illegitimate.

"It's hard to overstate the vitriolic nature of the Republican reaction to Bill and Hillary Clinton," Gingrich says. "[All] of 1993 and 1994, the Republicans are becoming anti-Clinton and therefore [opposed to American] policy because Clinton is the personification of the policies. It was fairly irrational."[7] The president had been in office for less than half a term, and the Republicans had already adopted a policy of "ABC"—anything but Clinton—that would influence their foreign policy ideas for the next decade.

A Tale of Three Crises

"I'm frustrated," the president said. "I'm spending too much time on mechanics, not enough on grand strategy—and that's for domestic as well as foreign policy." Clinton made this complaint in a number of White House meetings during the first months of 1994, leaving his aides puzzled. True, they were discouraged that they had not been able to articulate an overarching framework for U.S. global leadership that policy elites and the American people found convincing. But the real problem was that the president was paying too *little* attention to the mechanics of conducting foreign policy. David Gergen, the Washington insider who had previously worked for Presidents Richard Nixon, Gerald Ford, and Ronald Reagan, and who had joined Clinton's White House staff to help steady the ship, remarked that Clinton spent a quarter as much time on foreign policy as his predecessors had. All the talk of needing an overarching theme made sense given America's experience during the Cold War, but it also seemed like a way for Clinton to get out of doing the hard work or facing the tough decisions, as though finding the right slogan would be a silver bullet to make his problems go away.

Angered by the criticism of his foreign policy, especially from Republicans, Clinton occasionally also pointed the finger at himself. In a meeting with his national security team in May 1994, he said, "There still needs to be a combination of doing the right things and saying the right things" in addressing the world's problems. But as long as the president and his advisers remained divided and uncertain on the exercise of American power—especially the use of military force in places with no obvious U.S. security interest—it would be difficult to craft a strategy that garnered much support.

Three very different crises that year, in Rwanda, North Korea, and Haiti, offer glimpses of how the administration was learning to grapple with the problems of the era and reveal the possibilities, limits, and sometimes tragic consequences of their actions. In many ways, the Clinton team's performance reinforced their opponents' criticisms that American foreign policy was unmoored, careening from crisis to crisis.

IN APRIL 1994, when Rwanda's government-backed Hutu militias began slaughtering hundreds of thousands of ethnic Tutsis in what the author Samantha Power describes as the "fastest, most efficient killing spree of the twentieth century"—reaching a death toll of at least 800,000 in 100 days—Tony Lake issued a statement calling on Rwanda's Hutu military leaders to "do everything in their power to end the violence immediately." Given what was happening, it was not surprising that a senior U.S. official would make such a tepid demand. But Lake's statement proved to be the only public American attempt to prod the Rwandan government to stop the bloodshed. Neither he nor Clinton ever even bothered to call a meeting to discuss what was happening or to seriously consider if there was anything more the United States could do. Looking back, Lake candidly admitted that this episode, topped by his lackluster and lonely effort at influencing events, was "truly pathetic."[8]

The Rwandan genocide barely registered as an international crisis in Washington, demonstrating the mind-set of the Clinton team during the spring of 1994, and how far Somalia's wake extended. The circumstances in Rwanda were a perfect recipe for American inaction: a fast-moving ethnic conflict inside a small Central African country that few Americans had heard of, a humanitarian mission with a weak U.N. peacekeeping presence, and limited options for the United States other than military intervention. The phrases "nation-building" and "mission creep" flashed like ominous warning signs, and officials worried about even approaching what they called the "Mogadishu line"—or the point at which a mission transforms from helping people in need to assuming full responsibility for implementing security.[9] Instead of weighing actions to stop the slaughter, the State Department dithered over whether to classify what was happening in Rwanda as genocide, which would obligate Washington to act under international law. The result was one of the worst acts of omission ever committed in the history of American foreign policy.

Although few criticized them at the time for their inaction—after all, few Republicans believed the United States should get involved—Clinton and his senior advisers came to lament their inaction. "We were so preoccupied with Bosnia, with the memory of Somalia just six months old, and with opposition in Congress to military deployments in faraway places," Clinton recalled in his memoirs, "that neither I nor anyone on my foreign policy team adequately focused on sending troops to stop the slaughter." During a trip to Rwanda a few years later, Clinton apologized for his inaction and later called the episode one of the greatest regrets of his presidency.[10] For the Clinton team, as well as many rank-and-file Democrats and

Republicans, the failure to deal with Rwanda illustrated the grave humanitarian consequences of American inaction, creating a powerful counterpoint to the legacy of the Black Hawk Down disaster in Somalia. In the years ahead, the memories of Rwanda's horrors shaped but did not end the debate about what risks the United States should take to protect innocents.

As THE STRUGGLE over what to do about humanitarian crises within states simmered, another challenge erupted that U.S. policy-makers would wrestle with for years: the threat of an outlaw state intent on acquiring nuclear weapons. Few recall now—or even noticed then—that in the summer of 1994, the United States stood on the brink of war with North Korea's rogue regime.

The crisis evolved slowly. During the first half of the year, North Korea had steadily provoked the United States and the United Nations over its nuclear program. The Clinton administration unanimously believed an isolated North Korean "hermit kingdom" with nuclear weapons would be dangerous, not just because of the threat to U.S. treaty ally South Korea (where 37,000 U.S. troops were stationed), but because North Korea could decide to sell such weapons to the highest bidder. As North Korea continued to escalate tensions, playing a cat-and-mouse game with U.N. nuclear inspectors and issuing blustery threats, Clinton's military and civilian advisers met in a series of White House sessions to decide what to do. The high stakes created by the possibility of direct military confrontation and the possible spread of nuclear weapons led to disciplined and focused discussions. Moreover, this was the first real crisis involving Clinton's new military team: Defense Secretary William Perry and Joint Chiefs Chairman General John Shalikashvili, who each conveyed a reassuring calmness and sense of purpose.

The choices were not attractive. The Clinton administration wanted to impose economic sanctions, but the North Korean regime said that would be an act of war and threatened to respond with a military attack on South Korea, turning its capital, Seoul, into a "sea of flames." In mid-June, Clinton's advisers planned to deploy more U.S. forces to the region and even considered an "Osirak option," a pre-emptive strike on North Korea's nuclear facilities modeled after the famed 1981 Israeli attack on Iraq's nascent nuclear reactor.

At a White House meeting on June 16, 1994, the threat of war hung in the air. Presenting the military options to the president, Perry compared the situation to the 1914 events that historian Barbara Tuchman described in her book *The Guns of August*, when a series of escalating moves with unintended consequences led to the outbreak of World War I. "Politics is not the art of the possible," the defense secretary said. "Rather it consists of choosing between what is disastrous and what is merely unpalatable." Yet just as military plans were being unfurled and Clinton prepared to approve the troop surge, an unusual diplomatic breakthrough emerged.[11]

Former President Jimmy Carter called the White House after meeting in Pyongyang with North Korea's strongman, Kim Il Sung, to report a deal. Carter had gone to the North Korean capital to try to avert the crisis—and did. Since the United States had no high-level diplomatic relationship with the regime, the Clinton team thought allowing Carter to go as a private citizen (not as a formal envoy) might help. Clinton and his advisers had an uneasy relationship with the former president, finding him sanctimonious and believing that his proclivity toward freelancing might put them in the awkward position of publicly rebuking someone for whom many of them had once worked. Yet Carter promptly announced to the world on CNN that the North Koreans wanted to negotiate a way out of this impasse and freeze their nuclear program—news that was welcomed by the administration, if scoffed at by Republicans. There were a lot of details to be worked out, but the North Koreans had conceded.

This breakthrough led to several months of intense negotiations that resulted in the North Koreans agreeing to halt their program and allow U.N. inspections in exchange for U.S. energy assistance. This "agreed framework," negotiated by diplomat Robert Gallucci, did not eliminate the North Korea threat, but it froze it. The administration's conservative opponents lashed out at the deal, with Arizona

Senator John McCain describing it as "appeasement" and criticizing Clinton for lifting the military pressure too soon. Critics rejected the idea that the North Koreans could be trusted to honor the agreement and were outraged that the United States had agreed to help North Korea develop energy. They saw the agreement as a half-measure at best and therefore a piece of unfinished business. The deal was also seen as further evidence that the president would back down easily. Not many people interpreted the episode as a sign of the administration's emerging diplomatic confidence. Clinton might have averted war, but few gave him much credit because the outcome seemed incomplete and because Carter, whom few associated with a robust foreign policy, had stepped in to save the day.

"HOW MANY body bags is it worth to put Aristide back in Port-au-Prince?" Clinton asked himself aloud in a conversation with a close aide in the summer of 1994. This was yet another new dilemma. Haiti's military junta had prevented the democratically elected president, Jean-Bertrand Aristide, from returning to power. Instability in Haiti hardly compared with the threat of nuclear proliferation, but the island's woes mocked the Clinton team, making its rhetoric on democracy seem empty. For the preceding year, the U.S. approach toward Haiti had been a mix of inaction and quick fixes, a policy of trying to stem the tide of refugees (which still numbered in the tens of thousands) while seeking a way to restore the Haitian president to power without American military intervention. The turnaround of the *Harlan County* the year before remained foremost in the Clinton team's mind, with the president privately expressing regret about how the ship's retreat reinforced the image of humiliating weakness. He and his advisers discussed how they could erase that symbol with one that would demonstrate their confidence and forcefulness.

Moreover, unlike Rwanda, which was half a world away, the Haitian crisis was not one the administration could simply ignore. In late July, it convinced the U.N. Security Council to pass unanimously a resolution authorizing "all necessary means" to restore Aristide to power. Significantly, this was the first resolution in which the United Nations sanctioned military force not to reverse one country's attack on another but to restore a democratically elected leader. Yet just because the administration had received the United Nations' backing did not mean it had decided to use it. The most persuasive advocate for bold action was Vice President Al Gore, among the most hawkish of Clinton's advisers. At the end of August, Gore implored Clinton to stop dithering and set a deadline for the junta to leave or face a full-scale military invasion to return Aristide to power. The vice president argued that obtaining congressional authorization to act was impossible since opposition within both parties was overwhelming, and even if that weren't the case, the administration had all the authority it needed. So he urged Clinton to create a "pivot point" around which military planning could begin.

The president agreed to do so but was extremely worried about the risks. Knowing the polls showed little public support for an invasion, Clinton believed he was "throwing all the dice" by doing this. "I was elected to do a lot of stuff and I think I'm doing it," the president fumed, referring mainly to his domestic achievements, "but now I've got to be prepared to throw it all away for Aristide. . . . This has the capacity to destroy my presidency. . . . How did this happen? We should have waited until after the [1996] elections." His top aides understood the downsides of acting, but they stressed the costs of *not* acting. They argued that this was about more than returning one leader to power—it was about restoring democracy and showing the world that the president was prepared to implement a tough policy. "I guess we'll have something to show those people who say I never do anything unpopular," Clinton declared.[12]

As the president's team planned for a possible military invasion, another surprising (and awkward) opportunity arose to pull a diplomatic rabbit out of a hat. Once again Carter was the magician. The former president had been in contact with the junta leaders in Port-au-Prince and proposed that he undertake a last-ditch effort to get them to leave peacefully. Carter also added a twist: Former Joint Chiefs Chairman Powell and Georgia Senator Sam Nunn would join him on this mission. It was an odd delegation for Clinton to send. All of them had openly criticized his Haiti policy and opposed military action there, and they were critics of his foreign policy in general. None of his advisers was excited about the image of the new Democratic president once again being bailed out by the last one. Nor were they enthusiastic about giving Powell, a possible political opponent in 1996, such a platform. The fact that the president allowed them to go at all reflected, in the words of journalist John Harris, "equal measures of desperation and self-restraint."[13]

On Saturday, September 17, with little time to spare before the deadline for invasion, Carter, Powell, and Nunn arrived in the Haitian capital for their talks. During a dramatic forty-eight hours, Clinton and his team monitored the negotiations from the White House while more than 20,000 U.S. troops prepared to deploy. At the climactic moment on Sunday, Clinton gave the order to launch the invasion just as Carter called to ask for more time. "The planes are on the way!" Defense Secretary Perry told Clinton. "Please tell [the three envoys] to get out of there!" Then, just as the president and his team readied for war, the Haitian junta, having learned that the invasion force was en route, backed down. The planes turned back. The next day U.S. troops arrived in Haiti, not to launch an assault, but to implement a peaceful transition of power and restore order.[14]

By upholding democracy without resorting to military force, the administration's Haiti policy proved a success. A year earlier, rioting Haitians had forced back the *Harlan County;* this time the U.S. military had stared down the Haitian junta, and by mid-October Aristide returned to Port-au-Prince. Yet Clinton did not enjoy any significant boost from this achievement. Like the North Korea deal, the triumph seemed tarnished—as if it were Carter's more than Clinton's. It fueled the charge that Clinton was outsourcing his leadership, and he even worried to aides that it looked like they were "Carterizing" foreign policy.

Clinton still could not shake the impression that he was inexperienced and incompetent. His critics continued to hammer his performance, and some even compared his actions as commander-in-chief with his ill-disciplined personal life (the rumors of which captivated the chattering class). Echoing the views of many in Washington, political journalist Joe Klein observed that Clinton always seemed to be "searching for the policy equivalent of a one-night stand—a risk-free intervention, an action with no negative consequences." Even his Oval Office predecessors expressed alarm. "I am sincerely concerned by his handling of foreign policy," former President Ford confided to a journalist at the time. "I don't think he likes foreign policy. . . . [He] is uncertain, he doesn't look comfortable, he doesn't project strength, and that worries me."[15]

ALTHOUGH the resolution of the Haitian crisis did little to burnish the administration's foreign policy image, it did set an important precedent. Working with U.N. Security Council backing, the United States deployed military force not just to prevent further refugees from fleeing to the United States but also on behalf of democracy. It was Clinton's first successful use of American power in the service of American interests as well as ideals. Although the administration had failed the year before to develop democratic enlargement as an overarching conceptual policy frame, its Haitian triumph might give the effort new life.

Yet the intense debate surrounding what to do about Haiti—and the question about how important restoring democracy there would be—revealed new battle lines between liberals and conservatives. The pressure to do something about Haiti came mostly from the political left, including leading human rights activists and the Congressional Black Caucus. They argued that restoring the democratically elected government, with military force if necessary, was the morally correct thing to do. The political right largely opposed the intervention, asserting that Haitian democracy was of secondary importance to American interests and not worth the life of a single U.S. soldier. From the perspective of the Cold War, the hawks and doves had switched roles. Republicans weren't criticizing Clinton for doing too little in the world—they were beating him up for doing too much. If anything, this reinforced his timidity, as he worried about the political costs of failure.[16]

It is hardly surprising that Americans were confused. Polls showed that while they opposed military intervention in places such as Haiti, they also believed the United States had to play an active leadership role in solving the world's problems. It was hard to reconcile these views without a mission to fulfill, a sense of purpose to uphold, a grand strategy to follow. Absent those, Americans rightly asked whether the United States had an interest in restoring an elected leader in Haiti, or why it would use military force there while doing nothing to stop killing in Rwanda or carnage in the Balkans. They wondered how national security threats such as a nuclear North Korea related to the goal of spreading democracy. Clinton knew that Americans needed what he called a "theory of the case" and was immensely frustrated that he could not find it.

FOUR DAYS after he forced the Haitian junta to buckle, Clinton huddled with his senior foreign policy team in the Cabinet Room, ostensibly to discuss his upcoming speech at the annual meeting of the U.N. General Assembly. The president quickly and unceremoniously dispensed with the draft his speechwriters had prepared, launching into a freewheeling discussion that revealed his frustrations about conducting foreign policy without the Cold War map.[17]

"This is a big yawn," the president groaned. He repeated his oft-expressed complaint about not having an inspiring grand strategy and worried he was "telling a generation that's already bored that their mission is boring ... putting icing on the cake that someone else baked forty years ago!" He believed his administration was squandering its historic opportunity to define the era: "World War I gave way to the new deal but also World War II, which gave way to the Cold War, which gave way to the new world order Bush was talking about, but now everyone's afraid that's going to fall apart." The critics, he lamented, "say that we make it up as we go along, that it's all ad hockery, and we make it up solely on the basis of domestic politics. . . . The perception is, right or wrong, that there is no clear line from principle to action."

A big problem, Clinton argued, was that he was being held to an impossible standard set by false memories of the Cold War. "It was a huge myth that we always knew what we were doing during the Cold War," Clinton said. "And we used the alleged certainty of the Cold War to make massive mistakes. . . . The Cold War was helpful as an organizing principle, but dangerous because every welt on your skin becomes cancer." As the president rolled on, his advisers labored to keep up, alternately trying to console him or help with his brainstorming, encouraging him to "make lemonade" out of the recent intervention in Haiti.

Gore finally spoke in the terms Clinton sought. The Cold War threats—nuclear annihilation and the Soviet menace—made sense to people, but now they felt "in their bones that something is fundamentally different about the context in which we live; palpably, ours is a global civilization. There's now a universal sense that democracy is humankind's chosen form of political organization and that the free market is its chosen form of economic organization. But there are also new threats—proliferation, environmental degradation, nonstate actors, and terrorists." The challenge, the vice president explained, is that "the descent into tribalism and the hell on earth of ethnic conflict leads to the abandonment of hope. The U.S. role is to provide that hope. . . . We've got to say in the context of 1994 what FDR said in 1933, that the only thing we have to fear is fear itself."

The president liked what Gore said. For months Clinton had been captivated by the arguments in an *Atlantic* magazine cover story by Robert Kaplan that warned of growing global chaos spread by environmental damage, poverty, overpopulation, resource scarcities, ethnic conflict, and failed states. To Kaplan, this "coming anarchy" brought a "terrifying array of problems that will define a new threat to our security . . . allowing a post–Cold War foreign policy to emerge inexorably by need rather than by design."[18] In this new world, U.S. interests would be threatened more by weak states than by strong ones. Kaplan believed this worldview should replace George Kennan's containment. Clinton sympathized with this outlook and talked about it often. Looking at Somalia, Bosnia, Rwanda, and Haiti, it did seem that the end of the Cold War had blown the lid off of many problems that had long been unnoticed or ignored. Clinton said Kaplan's analysis would help people "visualize a world in which a few million of us live in such opulence we could all be starring on night-time soaps, and the rest of us look as though we're in one of those Mel Gibson 'Road Warrior' movies," and sent a copy of the article to his top foreign policy advisers and every member of his cabinet.[19]

But as compelling as this chaos theory could be, it was hard to conceive of it as the organizing principle for American foreign policy. Jeremy Rosner, the former national security official who had pushed hard for the democratic enlargement frame a year earlier, was put off by the pessimism of such an apocalyptic argument. He warned that "a change in theme from market democracy to global chaos would be an important (and disturbing) development. . . . Those who are flirting with the chaos doctrine are flirting with disaster."[20] Even if Kaplan's diagnosis was correct, the president understood that he needed to articulate a positive vision. And he still lacked a succinct phrase or idea that would crystallize it. "Our motto should be push back fear, push up hope, and spread confidence," Gore proposed. Clinton still wasn't satisfied. "The operative problem of the moment," he said, "is that a bunch of smart people haven't been able to come up with a slogan. And saying that there are no slogans isn't a slogan either. . . . We can litanize and analyze all we want, but until people can say it in a phrase, we're sunk."

Appearing before the U.N. General Assembly the next week, Clinton repeated many of these themes.[21] He discussed a wide range of new threats—from ethnic conflict and nuclear proliferation to terrorism, HIV/AIDS, and the deteriorating environment. Clinton tried out a new slogan, the "age of hope," and set the challenge in historic terms: "It falls to us to avoid the complacency that followed World War I without the spur of the imminent threat to our security that followed World War II." He repeated his push for democracy promotion—or, as he put it, creating a "coalition for democracy" (although notably he did not utter the word "enlargement" anywhere in the speech), and he called for stronger multilateral institutions, especially the United Nations. Stressing that the United Nations could not veto the American use of force, Clinton outlined an early version of what would become a mantra for his approach to multilateralism. "When our national security interests are threatened," the president said, "we will act with others when we can, but alone if we must. We will use diplomacy when we can, but force if we must."

The rhetoric sounded good, but the words washed over the audience. The "age of hope" vanished into the bumper-sticker dustbin. The day after the speech, most news reports focused only on the president's announcement that the United States would lift economic sanctions against Haiti (as well as the traffic his motorcade created in New York). Clinton had shown some success on North Korea and Haiti, but he still didn't have a phrase to make sense of it all. "People don't understand what we are trying to do," he said in a phone call with historian Arthur Schlesinger Jr. "We need to spell out the framework."[22] Yet time was running out. Within six weeks, the outcome of the November congressional elections made the domestic context for his presidency quite challenging. With Republicans fractured on foreign policy yet ascendant politically, the debate about America's role in the world became even more partisan.

The Neoconservative Crack-Up

The lack of a catchy foreign policy concept was particularly troubling for people who believed in ideas above all else—those who still called themselves neoconservatives. As a group, they were a dwindling breed. During these years, they seemed caught between the Clinton administration's missteps and uncertainties and the Contract Republicans' reflexive anti-Clinton anger and constricted view of America's global role. Neoconservatives were disappointed with Clinton. Some had expected their support to be rewarded with high-profile jobs in the administration, and during the 1992 transition

Clinton told close advisers he very much wanted to include them, especially after their help during his campaign. But only one, James Woolsey, was in, and it was well-known that as CIA director he resided far outside Clinton's inner circle. (He never saw the president alone, and when discussing the administration many years later, Woolsey noticeably referred to the Clinton team as "they," not "we.") Sandy Berger met with a group of neoconservatives at the White House to reassure them that their ideas were important and to try to calm them down. But some were so upset at being snubbed, as they had been by the Carter administration in 1977, that they went public with their gripes, writing about the jobs they should have been asked to fill.[23]

But the neoconservatives' critique of Clinton was not just about their failure to share in the Washington spoils. They were also deeply frustrated by the president's stumbles and efforts to walk back his campaign promises. They believed him preoccupied with secondary issues and plagued by timidity. They deplored Clinton's rescue by their bête noire, Carter. Like Tony Lake, neoconservatives had hoped the Cold War's end would allow Democrats to move beyond their divisions and return to the tough liberalism of the immediate post–World War II years. But they found that Clinton and his team remained temperamentally scarred by Vietnam, in their view yet another group of Democrats afraid to use military force. So while they sympathized with Clinton's idealistic rhetoric and statements about standing up for liberal values and democracy, they knew that absent strong action, such words were meaningless.

Yet as neoconservatives abandoned Clinton, the Republican Party abandoned them. The belief that came to dominate conservatism after the Cold War—that American power had limits and, therefore, the greatest threat was overstretch—left little room for pursuing ambitious, values-driven goals. The collapse of the Soviet Union "sever[ed] the Republican internationalist tradition from Republican nationalism," explains David Frum, who wrote two books on conservatism in the mid-1990s and later wrote speeches for President

George W. Bush. "And it really is no surprise that people who advocated an activist Republican foreign policy had difficulty mobilizing the Republican Party for [nation-building] projects [or] for the building of a complex new global architecture. These ideas, maybe they were good, maybe they were bad, but they in no way tapped nationalist feeling and so they left the Republican Party cold."[24]

For the political right, the answer was to emphasize national sovereignty and a foreign policy rooted in military predominance and unlimited freedom of action. The Contract with America summed up this perspective perfectly: Its national security plank hardly mentions "freedom" or "democracy," instead emphasizing skepticism of the United Nations, promotion of missile defense, and similar policies that would allow as few constraints as possible on U.S. behavior, and even fewer responsibilities. With the political winds on Capitol Hill shifting in such a direction, few neoconservatives stuck around to keep up the fight. One who did was a former Reagan official and budding scholar, Robert Kagan.

KAGAN epitomized the plight of the new generation of neoconservatives. Having served in the Reagan State Department as a speechwriter and specialist on Latin American issues, he believed the Cold War victory represented not just a triumph of American ideals, but also the validation of a way of defending and fighting for them. Rather than seeing America's overwhelming military might as a dwindling asset, Kagan believed that like a muscle, American power needed to be used to stay strong. The end of the Cold War didn't mean that the United States could play a lesser global role. If anything, he thought it bestowed tremendous responsibility on the United States to lead—a responsibility that would at times require sacrifices. Kagan was furious with George H. W. Bush and his team for what he saw as acquiescing in "declinism," the idea, much in fashion among the foreign policy intelligentsia of the late 1980s, that America was a diminished power. Believing the Republicans were out of ideas and Democrats would stand up for American ideals, Kagan voted in 1992 for Clinton.

In 1994, Kagan's convictions left him a lonely man both intellectually and politically. The Democratic president he had voted for proved disappointing, and the administration's inability to project confidence undermined its rhetoric. "The Clinton folks were doing [things] so terribly, who cares about Lake's democratic enlargement?" Kagan recalls. Yet the problem for Kagan was that while the Republican Party was not burdened by the Democrats' post-Vietnam anxieties, even relative internationalists such as McCain and Gingrich complained that the country was overextended. "Clinton couldn't answer the question, 'What are we standing for?'" Kagan's friend and fellow neoconservative Gary Schmitt explains: "[The administration] did things on the world stage even if the intellectual debate wasn't settled. Bob's goal was to close the gap between the practice and a strong vision." Having returned to graduate school at American University to earn a doctorate in diplomatic history, Kagan began publishing articles in policy journals such as *Commentary* in hopes of sparking the debate he believed both liberals and conservatives needed to undertake. [25]

"The Republican Party is less and less recognizable as the party of Ronald Reagan or the George Bush who sent troops to Panama and the Persian Gulf," Kagan asserted in an article published the same month as Clinton's showdown with the Haitian junta. The United States had a long history of military intervention to achieve its idealistic goals, Kagan stressed, and the end of the Cold War meant the "areas of the world where America exerts its influence have expanded, not detracted. . . . So, too, have the burdens of promoting and sustaining a world order." Yet conservatism, Kagan warned, was in the process of denying this, repeating its earlier twentieth-century transformation from the internationalist party of Theodore Roosevelt to the isolationist party of Warren Harding, who had naively promised a "return to normalcy" after the trauma of World War I. Explicitly comparing the moment to the years between the world wars, Kagan argued that while Americans did stay involved in the world during that time, they "tried to enjoy the benefits of such involvement while hoping to avoid its inevitable costs."[26]

The response to Kagan's argument proved revealing. Some liberals embraced his call for bold action and an expansive view of U.S. interests. Madeleine Albright approached him at a Washington restaurant to tell him how much she liked the piece. Yet many conservatives, including several of Kagan's former colleagues in the Reagan administration, were less supportive or even outright hostile. Interestingly, most of his critics were usually identified as neoconservatives, but they attacked him with the more restricted, traditional realist argument that America should act only where its vital national interest was threatened.

Francis Fukuyama, whose "end of history" thesis said American liberal capitalism would now go unchallenged, supported Kagan's argument in the abstract, but saw little reason to intervene in such places as Somalia, Haiti, and Bosnia because they did not affect core American interests. He accurately described Kagan's view of American military power as "use it or lose it," while he characterized his own position as "use it and lose it." If America squandered its power in peripheral areas, he argued, the country would be ill prepared to fight when truly necessary. Therefore, the United States should focus its attention on the state of its domestic affairs until the external environment was threatening. "In my view, Americans should be prepared, when the time comes, to have their young people die for Poland," Fukuyama said, because of the country's historically geostrategic location between Germany and Russia. "I think they will be less inclined to make the proper decision then if their young people have been dying on behalf of unfamiliar causes in places like Sarajevo and Kigali along the way."[27] Similarly, Elliott Abrams, who worked with Kagan in the Reagan administration and would later become a leading national security official under George W. Bush, argued that U.S. troops should not be used for nation-building. Paul Wolfowitz explained that when it came to the use of force, in addition to a sense of interest and of duty, Americans also "need to believe that others are doing their share; and they don't like failure." Thus, he warned that Kagan was wrong to support intervention in Haiti, for example, both because it was peripheral to American interests and because "the chances of success are problematic."[28]

THE COMMON THEME running through these arguments was the same one Clinton officials had been struggling with for months: What kind of U.S. global role would the American people support, and how much sacrifice could they endure? The prevailing wisdom on both questions was: not a lot. Yet Kagan's argument pushed against what he saw as the misplaced belief that the American people were strongly opposed to foreign engagement. The polls, he argued correctly, did not demonstrate this. Americans weren't shying away from bold leadership and international engagement; they simply needed leaders to explain the purpose of their actions. The public would remain supportive as long as things were managed effectively.

Public opinion surveys showed that a majority of Americans consistently supported active U.S. engagement in the world, working through international institutions. Americans were not as isolationist as most members of Congress, officials in the executive branch, and journalists assumed.[29] It was true, as Republican pollsters such as Frank Luntz reported, that the public had downgraded the importance of international issues on the list of problems facing the country.[30] The public didn't want the United States to withdraw from the world—in fact, there was evidence for exactly the opposite. Yet policy elites and politicians in and out of government thought differently.[31] As Kagan explained, "[P]ublic attitudes have been influenced by the rather lackluster debate between a Republican Party warning against 'quagmires' and a Democratic president unable to articulate, much less consistently carry out, a strong and active foreign policy."[32]

Few Republicans were in much of a mood to embrace ambitious foreign policy goals in 1994. Clinton was flat on his back politically, and they wanted to win back control of Congress. At the time, it appeared

to be the end of an intellectual era. In a "eulogy" for neoconservatism,
a founding father of the movement, Norman Podhoretz, explained that
as many conservatives turned back toward isolationism, only a tiny
handful of thinkers "still advocate the expansive Wilsonian interventionism that grew out of the anti-communist passions of the neoconservatives at the height of the Cold War, and that repeatedly trumped the
prudential cautions." Or as astute political observer John Judis pointed
out, neoconservative ideas had become "largely irrelevant to the
[Republican] policy debate. . . . If neoconservatism exists in the 1990s,
it is much the way that the New Left survived into the 1980s—as cultural nostalgia rather than distinct politics."[33]

The Contract Republicans were now the dominant force in the
party. Not yet in control of either Congress or the White House, they
were not burdened with the responsibility of guiding America
through the confused, and confusing, world. When that changed,
Republicans were faced with transforming their ideas for a more limited American global role into law and policy.

The Contract Cometh

On November 9, 1994, Republicans shocked the political world by
winning both houses of Congress. The election hardly hinged on
questions surrounding America's role abroad, but it had profound
implications for foreign policy. If Clinton intended to conduct the
more confident, activist foreign policy that analysts such as Kagan
encouraged, it would now be much harder. Most Republicans had
never accepted Clinton's victory in 1992 and were determined to do
whatever it took to uphold what they viewed as Congress's proper
opposition role. It always burned them that a man Gingrich had
described in the hours after the 1994 election as a "counterculture
McGovernik" had won the White House. Poised to be the first
Republican speaker of the house in four decades, Gingrich felt
empowered by the mandate of the voters. Taking on the airs of a
prime minister, he announced to the country, "I am very prepared to
cooperate with the Clinton administration. I am not prepared to com-

promise."[34] Secretary of Defense Perry caustically notes, "Newt was not open to debate and discussion. He was supremely self-confident and smart, and he wasn't looking for new ideas."[35]

The Contract Republicans scoffed at the notion that America had to be engaged in the world. Many new members proudly declared they did not even possess passports. New Senate Majority Leader Bob Dole had to twist arms to fill seats on the Senate Foreign Relations Committee, which during the Cold War had been a prestigious and coveted assignment for a freshman legislator. Looking back, Gingrich was defensive about the isolationist bent of many of his colleagues, and even himself. "A conservative watching a feckless liberal throw away American money in utterly infantile pursuit of projects that have no hope, it's not isolationism to say that's stupid," he said later. "It's not isolationism to say the U.N.'s corrupt. It's not isolationism to say that the way he's doing Somalia, you're better off not doing it. You have a rejection of incompetence as well as a limitation of activity."[36]

One of Gingrich's closest allies, former Republican Congressman Vin Weber, argues that despite Gingrich's own inclinations to take a more expansive view of global engagement, demonstrated by his support of Tony Lake's democratic enlargement speech in 1993, the new speaker was hemmed in by a truly isolationist rank-and-file. "A lot of these people who came into Congress in the '90s," Weber explains, "would burn incense at the altar of Ronald Reagan, but they were not Reaganites in that sense. They didn't have this vision that [Republican conservative hero Jack] Kemp and Gingrich and the rest of us had of an expansive view of American values. There was a lot more [Patrick] Buchanan in those people than there was Ronald Reagan. Newt found himself leading a party like that."[37]

THE CONTRACT REPUBLICANS entered office with a swagger, eager to show immediately that there was a new dynamic in Washington, not just in politics but in policy. They had committed to pass every item in the contract as legislation, which would force Clinton's hand on such items as peacekeeping and the defense budget. And they set out to convey the image that in foreign policy, the Republicans had returned, and the adults were back in charge.

This message was made clear in early January 1995, when the House International Relations Committee opened its first hearing to evaluate U.S. foreign policy. The lead witness was not Secretary of State Warren Christopher, as would have been customary, but his predecessor, Baker. The committee feted the former official; whatever misgivings Republicans had in 1992 about George H. W. Bush, after two years of Clinton, they were clamoring for what now seemed the steady hand of the previous administration. Speaking in a packed room full of cameras and reporters, Baker had a commanding presence and projected a competence many felt had been lacking during the past two years. Some pictured in their minds what might have been if Bush had won a second term in office. Baker ran through a rote critique of the Clinton policies—mishandling Somalia, flip-flopping on North Korea, bungling into Haiti, and frittering away America's global stature—and outlined what he described as a paradigm of "selective engagement." That sounded sensible to a range of Republicans, from those few who still wanted to engage to those for whom "selective" meant "rare."

Yet most notable about the former secretary of state's testimony was what he said about working with Clinton. Baker was an experienced Washington player and had many scars to show from past partisan battles. But he refused to serve up the red meat the Contract Republicans were hungry for. Instead he pleaded with the new majority to tread carefully. The country needed good relations between the White House and Congress, Baker said, "and fundamental to making that relationship work, it seems to me, is respect for the unique role of the president of the United States. He serves as commander-in-chief. He possesses a constitutional prerogative over the conduct of foreign policy." Baker went on: "Let me be very frank. It will be very, very tempting today for my colleagues on the Republican side to give as good as we got when we occupied the White House and the Democrats controlled the Congress, but I think that would be wrong. Attempts at congressional micromanagement of foreign policy were a bad idea when the Democrats were in control, and they remain a bad idea today."[38] This stern message went largely unheard—further evidence that in many ways, the old guard of Baker and Brent Scowcroft had fallen out of step with the angry political core of the party. Although the Contract Republicans liked statesmen such as Baker who conveyed a sense of seriousness and leadership, they didn't have much appetite for the message of bipartisanship.

A more telling example of their attitude came just a few weeks later, when every member of Clinton's senior national security team—the secretaries of state and defense, national security adviser, U.N. ambassador, and chairman of the Joint Chiefs of Staff—traveled to Capitol Hill to brief Gingrich and the freshman class. No one could recall a meeting quite like it in any administration. It was unusual for these top officials to gather together anywhere outside the White House, let alone with their political opposition in Congress. The Clinton team hoped this private session would be a gesture of cooperation and a way to break the ice. But when they arrived in the Rayburn House Office Building, they found an empty room. Gingrich and his colleagues were tied up in a meeting elsewhere. So they waited. After nearly an hour, the country's top foreign policy and defense officials were told that the speaker's meeting could go on indefinitely. So they left.[39]

For Clinton and his team, this petty humiliation encapsulated the debacle the Republican takeover had wrought. It was as if all the stress and anxiety of the previous two years had crested in a massive wave, threatening to wipe out the Democratic administration. The new political environment shocked them. "I had worked with Republicans before," Defense Secretary Perry recalls. "1994 wasn't just a Republican takeover of Congress; it was the Contract with America takeover of Congress. I had never seen anything like the transformation of 1995."[40] As they had so often before, many questioned whether Clinton needed to shake up his team. Some top aides warned against becoming an "Aztec presidency" by offering up a new victim every time the Washington gods clamored for one. Others wanted to leave. Christopher told Clinton he intended to resign. But when the president failed to convince Powell to be secretary of state, Christopher agreed to stay. The only senior official to go was CIA Director Woolsey, and he was hardly considered sacrificial.

The great unknown was what lesson the president would take from the election. His foreign policy advisers nervously believed the Republican takeover would exacerbate Clinton's fear that world affairs could only cause him political trouble. Before the election, Clinton had told aides he was worried that the attacks on his competence left him vulnerable for his 1996 campaign. After the Republican landslide, he looked like a dead man walking.

Some wondered whether the 1994 Republican takeover would become the political equivalent of Woodrow Wilson's stroke—a terminal paralysis that would incapacitate the Democratic president, energize his partisan enemies, and ultimately damage the national interest. The parallels seemed uncanny: Clinton's Republican opponents on the Hill would try to Wilsonize him, thwarting his woolly-headed ideas about America's global role and opposing his misguided faith in idealistic internationalism, as their forebears had gone after the League of Nations seventy-five years earlier. But there was a crucial difference. Wilson lost the vote on the League because he refused to compromise with his Senate opponents; Clinton's political flexibility would save him. And remarkably, despite its inauspicious start, 1995 proved to be a transformational year for Clinton's presidency. Thanks to his success in ending the war in Bosnia, he began to show the world that even without a new global doctrine, America could act confidently on the world stage under his leadership.

CHAPTER FIVE

Turning Point

"FOREIGN POLICY as social work." These five words summed up exactly what critics thought was wrong with Bill Clinton's approach to the world: He had allowed the country to be sidetracked by the lesser humanitarian concerns of Somalia, Haiti, and Bosnia, squandering the opportunity to confront the big issues. The phrase reinforced the stereotypes many Americans held about Democrats being soft on national security and unsteady when using military power. It was not the image the Clinton team wanted to convey, and it stung.

What was worse, even perplexing, was its source. This wasn't a rhetorical bomb thrown by Newt Gingrich or any of the Contract Republicans. Nor did it come from Dick Cheney or James Baker. The author was a former Clinton adviser, a scholar named Michael Mandelbaum.

After Clinton's election in 1992, many expected that Mandelbaum would get one of the top jobs in the new administration. A widely respected foreign policy specialist and professor at Johns Hopkins University's international relations school in Washington, he had signed on early to the Clinton campaign, working among the core of expert volunteers to assist with briefings and to help write the candidate's position papers and speeches. When the controversy over Clinton's Vietnam draft status erupted during the presidential primaries, Mandelbaum had risen to deliver a spirited defense.[1]

Mandelbaum always showed up in media accounts of Clinton's foreign policy circle—gossipy stories that envious Beltway insiders read
closely to learn who is up and who is down. He was described as one
of the "new generation" of Democratic national security experts who
had not served in the Carter administration. He had known Clinton
casually for decades, having first met him when they were both graduate students in England in the 1960s, and was close personal friends
with several members of the Clinton team.[2]

After the election Mandelbaum was offered the job of policy planning chief at the State Department (the same position George Kennan had held at the beginning of the Cold War). But he turned it
down. Some speculated that he thought the job beneath him, but he
made clear privately that he preferred academia and was uncomfortable with some of the other personnel choices Clinton had made.
Mandelbaum was a realist, focusing less on the spread of ideals and
values than on the traditional measures of influence, such as military
and economic might and relations among the world's great powers.
He believed his views and priorities would be out of step with those
of Clinton's top two officials, Tony Lake and Warren Christopher.

As he watched the Clinton policies unfold from the sidelines,
Mandelbaum's worst fears came true. He winced as the administration stumbled. For months he kept his worries largely quiet, confin-
ing his critiques to the occasional op-ed, regular quotes in the
newspapers, and conversations with former colleagues inside government, though he rebuffed several requests to change his mind and
join them. At one point he even had a private audience with the president in the Oval Office, where he shared his unvarnished thoughts
both on the administration's policy and its personnel, encouraging
Clinton to reshuffle his team, spend more time on foreign policy, and
place greater focus on major countries, such as Russia and Japan,
instead of peripheral parts of the globe.

At some point in 1995, Mandelbaum's disgust grew to the point
that he could no longer hold it back, and he made his break. Perhaps
he was angry and frustrated over the course of events and the fact

that his counsel went unheeded; perhaps he felt betrayed by the policies of a man he had supported and been publicly identified with; perhaps he was spurred by the belief that the newly empowered Republicans in Congress would be a receptive audience. Whatever his reasons, Mandelbaum crafted a broadside indictment of Clinton's approach to the world. It appeared as the lead article in the journal *Foreign Affairs* in early 1996 and became a must-read among foreign policy insiders, because of both the message and the messenger.[3]

Although few of Mandelbaum's criticisms were unique, they had teeth coming from a former insider and trusted confidant. His arguments got personal. He ridiculed Lake for comparing American foreign policy goals to those of Mother Teresa: to help the helpless. In describing the administration's approach as "social work," Mandelbaum coined a term everyone would remember, because it encapsulated everything negative Clinton's opponents believed about his policies.

Administration officials bristled at the salvo. But after stripping away the personal barbs and vitriol, they did not deny having allowed secondary problems to dominate their agenda. They could not dismiss the article as right-wing rhetoric. They saw it as a cry from both the foreign policy establishment and a former friend to fix things. Clinton himself understood this. "We've elevated the brushfire to dominate everything else," he lamented to his aides. "We've allowed our foreign policy to be defined in terms of Haiti and Somalia and Bosnia, rather than the really big ones—Russia, China, Japan, world trade."

Every member of Clinton's foreign policy team shared the president's frustration that smaller events had overshadowed "the really big ones." In fact, amid the cacophony of criticism that exploded over how they handled these crises, Clinton had implemented a strategy, rooted in American ideals and power, to deal with two of the biggest challenges bequeathed by the end of the Cold War: the future stability of Europe and the U.S. relationship with its former adversary, Russia.

Unfinished Business

Clinton believed one of his most important jobs was, as he put it, to "finish the unfinished business of leaving the Cold War behind."[4] That meant ensuring that countries in Europe no longer threatened the national security of the United States. From the perspective of more than a decade later, as Americans worry about dangers emanating from the Middle East and ponder the rising power of two Asian giants, India and China, they think of Europe only as a great place to do business or take a vacation. Indeed, it is difficult to remember that for the better part of two centuries—from the Revolutionary War until the end of the Cold War—European great powers posed the primary overseas threat to American national security. With the fall of the Berlin Wall on 11/9 and the subsequent collapse of the Soviet empire, the United States and its Western European allies had the opportunity to reshape what had been a troubled continent. For American policy-makers, the chance to help Europe overcome its past was tremendously appealing; after all, World War I, World War II, and the Cold War all began there.

At the beginning of his presidency, George H. W. Bush had talked about creating a Europe "whole and free." This became a realistic possibility with the reunification of Germany in 1990 and the peaceful collapse of the Soviet Union a year later. But with the Soviet empire's dissolution came tremendous uncertainty and fears of instability, stoked by the violence that erupted among Serbs, Croats, and Bosnians in the former Yugoslavia. Many American policy-makers worried that ethnic divisions elsewhere in Eastern Europe might lead to similar violence, perhaps between Hungarians and Romanians or Estonians and Russians. They feared that the Soviet Union itself could become a "Yugoslavia with nukes" because strategic nuclear weapons were stationed on territories outside Russia. Some experts foresaw a future in which Europe would devolve into the kind of militarized rivalries and ambitions that had led to the world wars. The scholar John Mearsheimer argued in a much-discussed 1990 *Atlantic* cover story that the United States "would soon miss" the stability granted by the U.S.-Soviet standoff, warning of nuclear proliferation throughout Europe and violent hypernationalism.[5]

Clinton articulated his own vision of a Europe peaceful, undivided, and democratic as he sought to integrate the former communist East into the West. Bush never made it to Berlin, but in 1994 Clinton became the first president to travel there since Ronald Reagan in 1987. Speaking before a raucous crowd of 100,000 Berliners on the eastern side of the Brandenburg Gate, just steps from where Reagan had uttered his famous demand to Gorbachev to "tear down this wall," Clinton heralded the promise of a new Europe where "free markets and prosperity know no borders, where our security is based on building bridges, not walls."[6]

He cast such ambitions as far east as Russia, where President Boris Yeltsin was trying to dismantle an autocratic tradition. But these goals often conflicted, and Clinton had to manage several difficult trade-offs. Folding countries such as Poland and Hungary into the West meant exerting American power in parts of Europe the Russians had long considered their sphere of influence. Finding a way to stop the killing in the former Yugoslavia meant combating the Serbs, who were Russian allies. Furthermore, America's most important Cold War alliance, NATO, still existed even though its primary mission—to defend Western Europe against a Soviet attack—had been rendered moot; keeping it in business angered the Russians. The balancing act required to deal with these sometimes competing goals in Europe required a level of diplomatic creativity and skill that tested Clinton and his team. But their ultimate success on the European continent in the mid-1990s proved to be a turning point for Clinton's presidency, even as critics derided him for misplaced objectives in other corners of the globe.

MANY AMERICANS stopped worrying about Russia when the Soviet Union collapsed on Christmas Day 1991. Even before that momentous event, Russia had moved closer to the West. Soviet leader

Mikhail Gorbachev worked with Presidents Reagan and Bush to reach arms control agreements, end the Soviet war in Afghanistan, and cooperate on Germany's unification, then stood shoulder to shoulder with the United States when Iraq invaded Kuwait. With the splintering of the Soviet Union into fifteen new states, the Red Menace's disappearance was complete.

Yet for Washington policy-makers, new challenges had arisen. Russia possessed tens of thousands of nuclear weapons, and three former Soviet states, Ukraine, Kazakhstan, and Belarus, held strategic nuclear weapons from the Soviet arsenal that were still on hairtrigger alert and were aimed at the United States. These weapons were poorly guarded, and officials in the executive branch and Congress worried about nuclear material falling into the hands of terrorists or rogue states, such as North Korea, Iran, or Iraq. Or perhaps Soviet nuclear scientists, seeking to reap lucrative earnings from their know-how, might help such regimes build their own nuclear arsenals.

Bush had only one year in office after the breakup of the Soviet Union. Although he scored some major successes in managing the end of the Cold War, particularly in arms control and German unification, he had done little to assist Russia's internal transition to a democracy and a market economy. He and advisers such as Scowcroft and Baker were skeptical about what the United States could do until Russia built up its own legal and commercial institutions. They understood that the United States had an interest in steering Russia's transformation the right way, but they had no big ideas on how to do it.

Many criticized Bush for acting as though he wanted to put the brakes on the Soviet transformation. In August 1991, he delivered his famous "Chicken Kiev" speech, warning Ukrainians of "suicidal nationalism." That same month, as the hard-liner coup against Gorbachev unfolded, Bush equivocated, saying, "We're not going to overexcite the American people or the world. . . . We will conduct our diplomacy in a prudent fashion, not driven by excess, not driven by extreme." After the Soviet Union collapsed, Bush responded cautiously to Yeltsin's entreaties for closer relations. At Camp David in

February 1992, Yeltsin asked Bush to announce that America and Russia were now allies rather than merely offer the bland "friendship and partnership." Bush demurred, "We are using this transitional language because we don't want to act like all our problems are solved."[7]

The most bruising (and politically damaging) criticism of Bush's failure to do more came from former President Richard Nixon, who invoked memories of the "Who lost China?" charges that had boosted his own career decades earlier. In the spring of 1992, Nixon argued that Bush's support for democracy in Russia was "pathetically inadequate" and claimed that if the United States failed to help Yeltsin, "the prospects for the next fifty years will turn grim."[8] Clinton had seized on those charges during the campaign, asserting that it was another example of how Bush was out of step with events. Support for Russian reform also became a test case of the arguments Clinton had begun to make about supporting the spread of democracy abroad.

In early 1993, after reading the Eagleburger memo, Secretary of State Christopher sent an annotated copy to Strobe Talbott, the former *Time* magazine journalist and longtime friend of Clinton who had joined the administration as a top adviser on the former Soviet states. (Within a year he was promoted to be Christopher's deputy.) Christopher underlined one key passage to get Talbott's attention: "If reform fails in Russia, it most assuredly will mean the failure of reform throughout the former Soviet empire." In early conversations with his advisers, Clinton understood these stakes immediately. "Russia is the biggest and toughest thing out there," he told Talbott in the weeks before the inauguration. Clinton knew he needed to prevent Russia from "blowing up in our faces" as the former adversary began the huge challenge of developing democracy and a market economy after seven decades of communist rule.[9]

From the moment Clinton took office, his policy toward Russia was framed by one overriding goal: to support the country's evolution into a democratic state, at peace with itself and its neighbors. Clinton and his advisers wanted to help Russia build a market economy, conform to international rules and norms, respect its neighbors, and integrate into the community of democratic nations. As Clinton himself put it in a televised townhall meeting with Russian students during his first presidential trip to Moscow in January 1994, Russia's future depended largely on how it answered three questions: "First, will you continue to work for a genuine market economy, or will you slow down and turn back? Second, will you continue to strengthen and deepen your commitment to democracy, or will you allow it to be restricted? And third, how will you define your role in the world as a great power? Will you define it in yesterday's terms or tomorrow's?"[10]

These questions illuminated the extraordinary shift in America's strategic objectives in the Cold War's wake. Since the end of World War II, the greatest challenge for the United States had been the Soviet Union's strength and influence. Nine presidents, from Harry Truman to Bush, worked to contain the Soviets and, where possible, to roll back their influence. But Clinton's task was exactly the opposite: to ensure that Russia's weakness did not plunge it into a deeper crisis and allow hard-line forces to define Russia's power in Cold War terms or spark an outbreak of violence that could destabilize Europe.

Although Clinton knew the choice would ultimately be Russia's, he and his team believed they had to help steer things in the right direction. From their first months in office, they supported Russian reform with billions in financial assistance, not only from the United States, but from G7 allies and institutions including the International Monetary Fund and the World Bank. As Talbott explained, this support "was not aimed at the recovery of what had been lost. Rather it was intended to help in the creation of what did not exist; it was an investment in a revolution, an attempt to help Russia complete the destruction of one system and the building, virtually *de novo*, of a new one."[11]

Beyond preventing catastrophe, Clinton and his aides saw an opportunity to make Russia a partner in efforts to solve global problems. They wanted to build on the kind of cooperation that Bush and Gorbachev had pioneered. During the Cold War, Americans and Soviets really had only one mutual interest: to keep from blowing themselves up in a nuclear Armageddon. Now, the Clinton team believed, the two sides had an opportunity to work together on a range of issues, such as promoting regional stability and preventing nuclear proliferation.

IN MANY WAYS, Russia proved a significant exception to the uncertainty and tentativeness that dominated Clinton's early approach to foreign policy. Having traveled to the Soviet Union as a student at Oxford University, Clinton had long been fascinated by events there, and he approached the issue with a kind of curiosity and confidence he lacked elsewhere.

Part of the difference was that as massive as Russia's problems were, Clinton felt that he understood them. Unlike the crises in Haiti and Somalia—which were less familiar and harder to relate to American interests—Clinton had a firmer grasp of the consequences of Russia's transformation, both good and bad. He saw the possibilities Russia's future offered and believed the relationship no longer had to be zero-sum, with one country's gain being the other's loss.

Like many presidents, Clinton came to see this in personal terms. For him and others in his administration, supporting Russian reform meant first and foremost supporting Yeltsin. Clinton thought the Yeltsin government remained on a reformist course despite some setbacks and, therefore, deserved his support and engagement. Clinton believed that although Yeltsin was often in ill health and slowed by a drinking problem, the Russian leader fundamentally believed in U.S.-Russian cooperation and valued their strong personal relationship. "Yeltsin drunk is better than most of the alternatives sober" was Clinton's assessment.[12]

Time and again, when difficult problems came up between the two sides, "Bill and Boris" got together to find a solution. Over the course of their eighteen meetings in eight years—almost as many as were held by their Cold War predecessors combined—they made enormous strides in solving problems. For example, they used American assistance to build housing in Russia to help get Red Army troops out of the Baltic countries they had occupied since 1940, and they worked together to help move strategic nuclear weapons from Belarus, Ukraine, and Kazakhstan to Russia, where they could be maintained and dismantled. Whenever Russia had to choose what kinds of policies to pursue, Clinton believed he needed to be there to help, encouraging America's former enemy to integrate into the U.S.-led global order.

The NATO Balancing Act

Clinton's and Yeltsin's problem-solving skills were never more crucial than in dealing with the seemingly irreconcilable differences over NATO. American officials did not want to alienate Yeltsin by giving ammunition to his hard-line opponents—the old Moscow elites who still saw the relationship as one of competition. But they also wanted to achieve goals they considered important for U.S. interests. Throughout the Clinton years, the U.S. policy priority that sparked the harshest exchanges with Russia was NATO expansion.

The North Atlantic Treaty Organization was formed in 1949 by the United States, Canada, and ten European allies to defend Western Europe against a possible Soviet attack. By the end of the Cold War, the alliance had grown to sixteen members. The original treaty left open potential membership for any European country that possessed a democracy, a market economy, a respect for human rights, and an ability to contribute to the defense of its members. Yet with the Soviet Union gone, was the alliance still needed?

The Clinton administration concluded yes, believing NATO would help stabilize the East rather than defend against it. The United States had an interest in helping to construct a wider Europe of open societies and open markets, with states that were not potential problems, but partners. The countries of the former Soviet bloc were no longer adversaries, and the Americans sought a way to anchor them in the West, to give them confidence that success was possible and to encourage liberal political and economic reform. Proponents of NATO enlargement sought to use the prospect of alliance membership as a magnet to pull these fledgling democracies in the right direction and to lift them out of the strategic limbo in which the Cold War's end had left them.

Although the administration's 1993 effort to establish "democratic enlargement" as the replacement for containment failed, expanding NATO to the east became the doctrine's concrete manifestation. Washington officials were quick to point out that although the alliance remained foremost a military organization, the logic for its expansion was to foster political and economic reform and, in a sense, a common identity. The chance to join NATO could connect those who had lived behind the Iron Curtain to the rest of Europe and, by extension, to the United States. With the enlargement of the European Union still years away, the alliance could help knit Europe back together.

Importantly, NATO enlargement garnered significant Republican support. Indiana Senator Richard Lugar was an early proponent, as were some former Bush officials, including Baker. NATO enlargement was also one of the few measures in the national security plank of the Contract with America. It appealed to an odd coalition of Republicans and Democrats. The liberal internationalists in the Clinton administration liked using a multilateral institution to help anchor emerging democracies in the West. Yet it also attracted the support of old-line conservatives, such as Republican Senator Jesse Helms of North Carolina, who had never trusted Russia and wanted the alliance to consolidate the Cold War victory by ensuring Eastern Europe's defense.

While a diverse group supported NATO enlargement, many inside and outside the government did not. Some worried that NATO's strength would be diluted by the inclusion of small European countries. And at a time when the American military was being asked to cut back on personnel and equipment in a post–Cold War drawdown, many military leaders were concerned about extending American security guarantees to what had often been an insecure part of the world.

The greatest challenge the administration faced in the process of expansion was the potential for rupturing relations with Russia. This was tricky business, because Russia was uncomfortable with the very existence of the Cold War alliance, let alone the prospect of its engulfing Moscow's former Warsaw Pact allies. As was often said at the time, NATO was a four-letter word to the Russians.

Although NATO enlargement hardly captivated public attention, it proved to be among the administration's most controversial measures, especially among foreign policy elites. Kennan (who had opposed NATO's formation in 1949) called the alliance's offer of membership to Poland, Hungary, and the Czech Republic "the most fateful error of American policy in the entire post–Cold War era."[13] Other leading figures of the national security establishment, including Georgia Senator Sam Nunn, Cold War hard-liner Paul Nitze, and Eisenhower aide Andrew Goodpaster, opposed enlargement. So did leading academics. Cold War historian John Lewis Gaddis wrote, "I can recall no other moment in my own experience as a practicing historian at which there was less support, within the community of historians, for an announced policy position."[14] Officials throughout the State and Defense departments rejected the idea, most importantly Secretary of Defense William Perry, who briefly considered resigning in late 1994 when the enlargement policy began to move forward.[15] Opponents feared enlargement's effect on Russia, worrying that NATO's efforts to admit former Warsaw Pact states would make the Kremlin feel cornered, revive Cold War antagonisms, and set back Russian domestic reform.

To navigate this process and to answer the critics, the Clinton administration worked to ensure that its approach toward NATO would be what Talbott called "bi-lobal." Efforts to expand NATO and to support Russian reform would go together like the two lobes of a brain. They would be coordinated and, hopefully, mutually supporting. To achieve these difficult and somewhat contradictory objectives, the administration sought to develop a NATO-Russia relationship.

By creating a mechanism for dialogue and consultation, the United States hoped to ameliorate Russia's fears about an expanded

NATO. At a summit in Moscow in May 1995, Clinton convinced Yeltsin to take two important steps: Russia agreed to join NATO's Partnership for Peace program (a kind of halfway house that included other European countries on the road to full membership), and it would begin a formal discussion of ways to enhance the NATO-Russia relationship. For the first time, it seemed that the Russian dimension of NATO expansion was on track. But as the summer of 1995 approached, American officials were very concerned that the festering conflict in Bosnia would upset the delicate balance.

Clinton and his team saw an expanded NATO—with new missions and new members—as the engine to create a Europe peaceful, undivided, and democratic. Yet they feared that the alliance's inability to solve the war in Bosnia raised serious questions about its future. What could NATO do if it could not even take care of a war in its own backyard? As Talbott explained to his colleagues, Bosnia was "a cause for deep skepticism and cynicism about whether NATO had any relevance to the post–Cold War world, other than as a standby defensive alliance against Russia in case it goes bad again." The Bosnian War, he said, "is the beast that could eat not only NATO, but the Russian-American partnership."[16]

High Noon at Dayton

From 1991 to 1995, Bosnia symbolized the chaos that many had feared the end of the Cold War would uncork. As the six constituent republics of Yugoslavia went their separate ways after the collapse of communism, the small republic of Bosnia exploded. In the most ethnically mixed of the former Yugoslav states, the violence involved a shocking level of brutality. Thousands of civilians, mostly Muslims, were driven out of their homes and terrorized. An influential argument at the time again came from writer Robert Kaplan, who opined that such carnage could be explained only as the unleashing of "ancient ethnic hatreds" among Serbs, Muslims, and Croats that the Cold War had kept under wraps. Clinton had read Kaplan's book *Balkan Ghosts*, which left him and many others convinced the United

States should not get involved.[17] Under Presidents Bush and Clinton, America's policy toward Bosnia had captured all the doubts of the new era: Should U.S. lives be spent ending ethnic bloodshed? How much should the United States work with international institutions? How much should America share responsibility with its European partners? And how much should the United States risk in its relationship with Russia to help solve global problems?

When Yugoslavia crumbled in 1991, Secretary of State Baker famously argued that the United States didn't "have a dog in that fight." Scowcroft and Eagleburger had served earlier in their careers in the Balkans, and they argued against intervention, believing America would get bogged down in conflict. The United States stood by as genocide erupted, insisting that the Europeans and the United Nations take the lead. But neither was up to the task. And the killings continued.

During the presidential campaign, Clinton had attacked Bush for his inaction, promising that if elected, he would act forcefully to end the war. Clinton's pledge to use America's political, economic, and military arsenal to punish tyrants and defend innocents had attracted many neoconservative hawks to his camp. But once in office, the president quickly discovered that implementing that rhetoric would be difficult if he did not want to incur significant costs in money, political capital, and perhaps American lives.

Initial efforts proved quite embarrassing. In May 1993, Clinton sent Christopher to Europe to find a way ahead on Bosnia. European officials, who hoped to hear how America might engage, instead greeted a secretary of state who said he was in "listening mode." The administration decided to forgo forceful action, compounding an image of weakness. As one journalist observed at the time, "What the European allies have really wanted from President Clinton is firm leadership."[18]

For the better part of three years, the Bosnia policy hung like a strategic albatross around the administration's neck. National security officials were deeply divided. Some such as Lake, Madeleine Albright, and Richard Holbrooke pushed for bolder intervention.

Others, including Christopher, questioned whether the costs were worth it and suggested that the United States just contain or manage the problem rather than fix it.

Like the debacle in Somalia and the struggles with Haiti, the inability to solve the problems in Bosnia wreaked tremendous damage on the perception of the Clinton foreign policy as a whole. The administration labored for the passage of U.N. Security Council resolutions, pushed for NATO air strikes to enforce them, and worked with its European allies to try to forge a peace settlement. But absent the political will to do more, the end result was always the same. By the summer of 1995, the Bosnian death toll neared 300,000, and more than one million people were refugees. As the conflict worsened, it attracted Islamic extremists, with militants from the Middle East traveling to Bosnia to help defend imperiled Muslims against the Serbs (two of the 9/11 hijackers fought in Bosnia).[19] At home and abroad, Bosnia had come to define weak American leadership; the newly elected French president, Jacques Chirac, observed that the position of leader of the free world was vacant.

At that moment a confluence of events forced Clinton's hand. He knew his policy was unsustainable. But in a decision made with remarkably little understanding of the consequences, Clinton committed U.S. forces to a NATO operation to help a feckless U.N. peacekeeping force withdraw from Bosnia. With the U.N. mission teetering on collapse, the administration realized that, one way or another, American troops would eventually be on the ground. The only question was whether they would be there to witness a failure or enforce an agreement.

Then in July 1995, Serb forces overran the small town of Srebrenica, and with the U.N. peacekeeping troops standing aside, rounded up thousands of Muslim men and boys and massacred them with firing squads. The genocide was the worst war crime in Europe since the Second World War, and it galvanized the United States into action. Having done nothing the year before during the mass killings in Rwanda, the Clinton administration had to act. It pushed through a bold new NATO policy that threatened air strikes if the Serbs continued their attacks. Importantly, the policy cut the United Nations out of the decision chain. Up to that point U.N. officials had to approve targets before an air strike, and this "dual key" had neutered the threat of military action. Within weeks, the Serbs shelled a crowded marketplace in the Bosnian capital, Sarajevo, and NATO unleashed an unrelenting air assault against Serb forces that lasted several weeks.

The bombing coincided with the launch of a new American diplomatic effort to forge a peace settlement. Led by Richard Holbrooke, an indefatigable negotiator who understood the critical relationship between military force and diplomacy, negotiations proceeded at a furious pace. During the course of Holbrooke's efforts, three members of his negotiating team were killed in an accident on a mountain outside Sarajevo. In November, after several months shuttling throughout the region, Holbrooke's delegation brought the warring parties to a secluded Air Force base in Dayton, Ohio. For twenty-one days, the Americans and the Balkan parties argued, screamed, and bargained, finally agreeing to halt the war. By the end of 1995, 60,000 NATO troops—including 20,000 Americans—were on the ground in Bosnia to enforce the settlement.

THE DAYTON AGREEMENT was highly ambitious and risky, complex and imperfect. By ending the Bosnian War, Dayton gave hope to millions who had suffered immense hardship. It also closed one of the most difficult chapters in the history of U.S.-European relations, helped define a new purpose for NATO, and ultimately began to restore the credibility of American leadership.[20]

Dayton gave life to the Clinton administration's strategy for Europe and by affirming the rationale for the alliance, boosted the confidence of NATO enlargement proponents. NATO's air campaign showed it could be a peacemaker, and its commitment to implement the Dayton agreement proved it could be a peace enforcer.

The Clinton team also showed how NATO and Russia could work together to solve problems. The Russians had never been enthusiastic about the alliance's role in Bosnia, especially the use of force against the Serbs. But instead of trying to wall off Moscow from the problem, the Clinton team searched for ways to include the Russians. They believed that if Russia worked alongside NATO to help implement Dayton, it would showcase how the alliance was indeed changing and would demonstrate that enlargement was not inherently anti-Russian. While Holbrooke and his team were trying to end the war, Talbott, Defense Secretary Perry, and NATO's military commander, Army General George Joulwan, worked tirelessly to concoct an arrangement for Russia's inclusion in implementing the peace. The result was an agreement that proved the two "lobes" of the brain—America's approach to NATO and its policy toward Russia—could work together to solve problems and help assuage Russian concerns about the mission of a larger alliance on its doorstep.

THE BOSNIA SUCCESS also revealed that despite the bitter partisanship that fueled so much of the domestic debate about America's role in the world, there could be significant areas of common ground. For example, Republican Senator Bob Dole, a dogged advocate for lifting the arms embargo against the Bosnian Muslims, pushed through the Senate a vote to do so, stimulating Clinton's decision to launch the diplomatic effort.

Perhaps nothing symbolized the potential bipartisanship more than the unusual presence of Richard Perle at the Dayton talks. As one of the leading neoconservatives in Washington, the former Reagan Pentagon official was an outspoken and influential critic of the Clinton administration's approach toward Bosnia and foreign policy in general. Yet the Bosnians asked Perle to come to Dayton as an adviser, and Holbrooke wanted him there to help promote a stronger American role. Perle was not a lawyer, so he asked his longtime friend Douglas Feith (who later served as a top Pentagon official in the George W. Bush administration) to help him review the military parts of the agreement for the Bosnians.[21] Perle had Holbrooke's support, but many others in Washington were deeply troubled by his presence. Lake and others did not trust Perle. "Tell Perle to shove his goddamn changes up his ass," one angry Pentagon official told Holbrooke when he learned what Perle was up to. But at that moment, Perle and Holbrooke, two men who knew how to bulldoze their way through the bureaucracy, were fighting for the same thing—a more robust American military role in implementing a peace agreement to protect the human rights of a Muslim population in Europe—and used each other to get what they wanted.[22]

As a matter of policy, America's course fit within a well-established diplomatic tradition: It challenged the status quo and rejected incrementalism, reflecting an all-or-nothing strategy driven less by concerns about niceties or allied consensus than by the desire to get something done. The approach had a gloss of allied involvement and buy-in, but in the end it was unilateral, rejecting U.N. participation and keeping allies at arm's length. The United States acted first and consulted later. And it was truly "maximalist" not only in means but also in ends: Rather than simply seek a cease-fire between the parties (as most Europeans wanted), the United States sought to create the contours of a new democratic Bosnian state.[23] In substance and style, the leader of the free world was back.

Ending the Bosnian War was a turning point for U.S. foreign policy. The Clinton administration's accomplishment mattered for America's global standing, and it mattered for the president personally. After two years of feeling whipsawed by events, the Dayton success finally gave Clinton the credential of global peacemaker. John Harris, author of the best book on the Clinton presidency, explained that the president "emerged from the fall of 1995 as a vastly more self-confident and commanding leader."[24] In less than six months, he took charge of the U.S.-European relationship, spurred NATO to use overwhelming military force, risked America's prestige on a bold diplomatic gamble, and put his political life on the line. A year before his reelection campaign, he placed 20,000 American military men and women on the ground in a dangerous environment. Clinton finally seemed like a steady commander-in-chief. Many of the air strikes against the Serbs were launched off the decks of the USS *Theodore Roosevelt*—the aircraft carrier whose crew had openly ridiculed Clinton during his visit in early 1993.

For Clinton, this was like the journey traveled by Gary Cooper's character in one of the president's favorite movies, *High Noon*. Clinton often talked about how much he loved the Western, having watched it dozens of times as a child in Arkansas, as well as in the White House. "*High Noon* affected my view of the world because Gary Cooper was scared to death, and he did the right thing anyway," Clinton explained. "It wasn't some macho whoop-de-do—it was a man who saw all the implications of the world in which he lived and decided what he was bound to do and did it, even though he was terrified."[25] This accurately captured Clinton's emotions as the Dayton negotiations unfolded, and he worried about the dangers of deploying troops to Bosnia. "We've got to counter the downside of troops with the upside of peace," he said.[26]

In many respects, the *High Noon* metaphor also characterized America's behavior as a world power midway through the '90s: a worried sheriff trying to round up an uncertain and somewhat helpless global posse.[27] By the end of 1996, after the mission in Bosnia proved successful (and, importantly, brought no American casualties), foreign leaders noticed the administration's new swagger. After meeting with his European counterparts just weeks after Dayton, Christopher reported to Clinton that he found "a palpable feeling of relief that impotence had been replaced by determination, and that the divisions that had haunted us from the beginning of the war ... had been replaced by unity. They grumble that we dominated Dayton, but they really know that it would not have gotten done otherwise."[28]

THIS EXPERIENCE taught Clinton and his team many lessons, several of which still reverberate in America's foreign policy debates today. It showed the United States could use military force to get results. Dayton also demonstrated NATO's importance as a security organization able to move beyond its half-century-old mission of collective defense to help solve conflicts and enforce peace agreements "out of area," or beyond the borders of NATO's members. In its efforts to implement peace, the alliance found its post–Cold War role in the world—one that it carried forward in Afghanistan after 9/11.

Yet the Clinton team still struggled with limiting America's responsibilities. The administration was more comfortable with the exercise of global leadership and more willing to use military force but still had not fully faced down the demons of Somalia. To avoid charges of "mission creep," Clinton's Pentagon planners crafted a narrow set of responsibilities for U.S. military forces in Bosnia. And to ensure that the mission had an "exit strategy," the president pledged that troops would be withdrawn within one year. Most officials knew it was completely unrealistic to expect to achieve Dayton's ambitious objectives in twelve months, but they worried about the implications of an open-ended commitment, especially heading into an election year. "If we did not delimit our involvement, the American people would not tolerate something similar down the road," Sandy Berger explained. "We wanted to show success."[29]

It soon became clear that the arbitrary one-year deadline was unworkable and that to stick to it would only unravel the peace. The exit date also made implementing the agreement harder. "By laying out self-imposed time limits," Holbrooke argued, "the United States only weakened itself." Clinton eventually extended the deadline for one year and then in 1997 finally dropped it altogether. Although the decision was made easier by the fact that not a single American soldier was killed in combat in Bosnia, the administration embraced the idea that the United States should stay until the job was done. As Madeleine Albright put it, "The mission should define the timetable, not the other way around."[30]

On a practical level, the success of implementing Dayton taught a generation of military commanders and soldiers important lessons about how to organize and conduct peace enforcement operations. It was a peacekeeping mission they could be proud of. Mandelbaum criticized these efforts as "social work" just as Condoleezza Rice in the 2000 presidential campaign derided the use of the military to escort children to kindergarten. But the Army general in charge of the troops in Bosnia, William Nash, who years later still proudly displayed on his office wall a picture of Clinton addressing thousands of his soldiers, says his superiors were "ecstatic" about the Army's performance. "It was kind of hard to bitch about success," he says.[31]

As for the Clinton team's approach to international institutions, Bosnia's legacy cemented its reliance on NATO. At the same time, it reinforced deep skepticism about working with the United Nations. Many American officials felt burned by the way other countries used the United Nations as cover to pretend they were doing something to solve a problem. Although neither the president nor his advisers embraced the more paranoid, reflexive anti-U.N. attitudes held by the Contract Republicans, they did become more willing to sidestep the organization and find new ways to work with others or establish legitimacy—and if necessary, to act alone. Perhaps nothing represented this new attitude more than the Clinton team's lonely but successful campaign in the months after Bosnia to deny the United Nations' haughty secretary general, Boutros Boutros-Ghali, the customary second term in office, replacing him with the more amenable Kofi Annan.[32]

The most important lesson learned was that America's failure to lead during the early 1990s contributed to the international community's inability to solve the Bosnia crisis. It took America's bold action in 1995 to stop the war. The top European official involved in the Dayton negotiations, the former Swedish Prime Minister Carl Bildt, reflected that the "simple and fundamental fact" of the Dayton episode was that the "United States was the only player who possessed the ability to employ power as a political instrument and, when forced into action, was also willing to do so."[33] This legacy from Bosnia was easily overlooked in the years to come, when, under a different president, many around the world questioned the purpose of U.S. leadership, chafed at the exercise of American power, or claimed that hard-edged American assertiveness was something new.

*

BOSNIA also gave the Clinton team the confidence to move forward with NATO enlargement, a policy that continued into the next administration. By ensuring the security of Eastern Europe, NATO helped buttress the reforms necessary to allow the former Warsaw Pact countries to join the West. In fact, by 2004, fifteen years after the Berlin Wall fell, most of Central and Eastern Europe had joined both NATO and the European Union and were strong allies of the United States. The NATO policy pursued by the Clinton administration was a major factor in creating the peaceful, undivided, and democratic Europe Presidents Bush and Clinton both promoted.

Some misinterpreted this success. Europe's seemingly unstoppable evolution toward greater political and economic openness and integration created a false impression about America's power to build democracy elsewhere. Eastern Europe bordered the West, and two leading Western institutions, the European Union and NATO, provided powerful incentives and huge amounts of economic and technical assistance to countries that sought to build democracy and a market economy. Nongovernmental organizations were heavily involved in the region, helping reformers on the ground develop civil society. Many who served in the first Bush administration concluded that the spread of democratic values and institutions was mainly a matter of getting rid of evil rulers and toppling their statues. The eventual success of the Central and Eastern Europeans in joining NATO and becoming staunch American allies reinforced this perception. It reemerged during the George W. Bush years in discussions about spreading democracy in the greater Middle East.

CLINTON WORKED hard to make Yeltsin feel comfortable with NATO enlargement. He refused to announce a firm timetable for new members until after Yeltsin was reelected in July 1996 to avoid provoking a political backlash against his friend during the Russian presidential campaign. And over the objections of his own Treasury Department, Clinton promoted Russia's inclusion in the G7, even though Russia at the time had an economy the size of a small European country. The president wanted to make Yeltsin feel more included in the West while NATO was marching east.

Although Yeltsin ultimately accepted NATO's enlargement, the Russian national security establishment never embraced NATO's post–Cold War actions. Many Russians still found it galling that the enduring symbol of the West's victory in the Cold War existed at all— let alone was incorporating former members of the Warsaw Pact. It was the same sentiment that reemerged later in reaction to the war in Kosovo in 1999 (as well as to the 2006 American proposal to deploy an antimissile system in Poland and the Czech Republic). Resentments smoldered in Russia, and they broke into the open when a very different Russian leader, Vladimir Putin, came to power.

In 1996, Clinton and his team had good reason to believe their work with Yeltsin had paid off in their efforts to finish the business of the Cold War. The administration scored a major victory for America's nonproliferation policy by working with Moscow to help remove strategic nuclear weapons from Belarus, Kazakhstan, and Ukraine. In June 1996, Perry stood with his Ukrainian and Russian counterparts at a ceremony in Ukraine and planted sunflower seeds where missiles were once aimed at the United States. The Russians served alongside NATO in the military implementation force in Bosnia. Clinton was getting precisely what he wanted from his Kremlin counterpart: a less threatening Russia willing to work with the United States to help solve problems, particularly in Europe.

CLINTON'S NEWFOUND confidence extended beyond Europe to Asia. The evolution of his policy toward China further helped to put his presidency on solid footing. During the 1992 campaign, Clinton pummeled Bush for coddling the "butchers of Beijing," arguing that the Republicans were too ready to overlook human rights concerns and bring Beijing out of its isolation in the wake of the 1989 Tiananmen Square massacre. Clinton saw China as a key test of the commitment to defend liberal ideals; as Lake said in his 1993 "democratic enlargement" speech, the United States needed an approach toward China that "reflects both our values and our interests."

Managing the tension between values and interests proved difficult. Clinton found himself hemmed in by his pledge to restrict trade with China if it did not improve its human rights. That stand had powerful advocates on Capitol Hill, most prominent among them California Congresswoman and future Democratic House Speaker Nancy Pelosi. But the strategic realities of pursuing a deeper U.S.-China relationship were becoming harder to deny. By the early 1990s, China's economic potential had become clear. It was the fastest-growing economy in the world, and American and European business leaders began traveling there frequently. In 1993, new investment in China was higher than ever before.

Yet relations became increasingly contentious. The administration was angry that the Chinese leadership had berated Secretary of State Christopher during a 1994 visit for supporting Chinese dissidents, while some Chinese blamed the United States for working to prevent Beijing from hosting the 2000 summer Olympics (a charge the administration formally denied). Finally Clinton decided to decouple interests and values and delink human rights from trade. He endured a heap of criticism for the decision, but it marked a turning point because it signaled China's importance to U.S. economic prosperity. This was "a milestone in American foreign policy," author Patrick Tyler observed, "and Clinton never looked back."[34]

While Clinton was seeking to build deeper economic ties with China, the two countries nearly came to blows militarily. In the early 1990s, strategists began to consider seriously the emergence of China as a military challenger and worried about the defense of Taiwan. Since the normalization of relations with China in the Carter administration, the United States had pursued a difficult balancing act: recognizing only one China with Beijing as its capital, but at the same time ensuring that the mainland could not forcibly take over the island of Taiwan. Before becoming president, Clinton knew more about Taiwan than perhaps any other foreign policy issue—having visited four times as Arkansas governor to promote trade—but he did not want unnecessarily to stoke tensions with Beijing. Any sign that Taiwan was seeking greater international recognition made the Chinese nervous, and thus they were furious when the Clinton administration granted Taiwanese President Lee Teng-hui a visa to speak at his alma mater, Cornell University, in June 1995. The Chinese feared Lee was pursuing a strategy for Taiwan's recognition as a sovereign state, and Beijing recalled its ambassador to the United States for "consultation." In the summer, China ratcheted tensions further by firing short-range ballistic missiles near Taiwan.

Although the administration did not support Taiwan's independence, neither would it stand aside as Beijing threatened to take the island forcibly. During the fall and winter, China continued to intimidate Taiwan militarily, massing more than 100,000 troops near the island in Fujian province. Then in early March 1996, in advance of Taiwanese presidential elections, Beijing announced it would conduct live-fire military exercises in the Taiwan strait. This set off alarm bells in Washington. Secretary of State Christopher called it "unnecessarily risky" and "unnecessarily reckless," noting that any aggressive actions against Taiwan could pose "grave consequences."[35]

In response to the escalating Chinese actions, the United States sent the aircraft carrier USS *Independence* from Okinawa toward Taiwan. Believing that this alone was insufficient to impress the Chinese with America's resolve to stand up for Taiwan, Secretary of Defense Perry wanted to send a carrier into the strait to deter Chinese aggression. General John Shalikashvili, chairman of the Joint Chiefs of Staff, thought the risk of accidental war too great. But Perry sought and received presidential approval to send the USS *Nimitz*, which had been patrolling the Persian Gulf to enforce the no-fly-zone against Iraq, to head to a position 100 miles from the strait. This was the largest American naval armada deployed to Southeast Asia since Vietnam, and the Chinese noticed. In the wake of the American actions, China concluded its missile tests early and cut back on its planned sea exercises.[36]

This episode, which Clinton described as an example of "America's power and America's character," marked the first time in almost four decades the United States had used a show of military force to coerce China. Even though Beijing backed down, the administration was not eager for a confrontation and set out to lessen tensions. Officials crafted a policy approach designed to reduce conflict and manage differences, working through sustained diplomatic engagement and establishing an agenda of high-level summits replete with pomp and circumstance. Rather than seeking to isolate or contain or punish China, the Clinton team decided to try to integrate the rising economic and military power into the global community. At home, this policy shift brought a dizzying political role reversal: While the Democrats became the champions of a strong U.S.-China relationship, many voices in the Republican Party began to clamor for a more adversarial approach.[37]

The GOP's Games

By 1996, Clinton's foreign policy was a far cry from what it had been at the end of his first year as president. Christopher said 1995 was "the best year for American foreign policy since the end of the Cold War."[38] Clinton succeeded in promoting a new Europe. He established a solid foundation for relations with Russia. He conveyed to China a seriousness of purpose on Taiwan. Not only did he show greater resolve when dealing with global issues—finally coming to see foreign policy as something that could boost his presidency, not just endanger it—but by expanding NATO, supporting Russia reform, and ending the war in Bosnia, he took positions many Republican leaders supported.

The fact that key Republicans came to his aid left them politically neutralized as the 1996 presidential campaign began. After Dayton, when many Republicans in Congress were ready to oppose the U.S. troop deployment in Bosnia, Senate Majority Leader and presumptive GOP presidential front-runner Dole overruled his political advisers to back Clinton's efforts. "After all, we're in this together," he told journalist Bob Woodward at the time. "And he's the president. Particularly when it's foreign policy, I don't think we ought to be playing games. Some people play games all the time."[39]

Those people were not some minority far removed from power; they were most of the Contract Republicans and many in the conservative establishment. With Republicans controlling Congress, there were structural incentives to oppose the president, even when they agreed with him. The House of Representatives passed a strange Republican resolution supporting the troops going to Bosnia, but not the Clinton administration policy. Clinton was deeply frustrated by the Republicans on the Hill, complaining to other world leaders that it was "the most isolationist Congress since the 1930s."[40] He respected those such as Dole who stood on principle and supported him even when it was not politically advantageous to do so. A World War II veteran, Dole was of a different generation than most of the Contract Republicans, who as a group were younger, more partisan, and less internationalist. Although Clinton often agreed with Gingrich and could work with him, the president remarked to his aides that "there's this monster that he's made in his own party. He's fed everybody's hatred of government so much that . . . it's a lot harder to make government work, including in foreign policy."

But the more Clinton succeeded on the international stage, the more apparent the fissures within conservatism became. Potential candidates with long foreign policy resumes, such as Colin Powell, Cheney, and Baker, opted out of the 1996 presidential race, while the primary campaign of internationalist Republican Senator Richard Lugar ended almost as soon as it began. Firebrands such as Pat Buchanan jumped in—and started to gain momentum.

Buchanan had never really stopped campaigning since his surprise emergence in 1992. If anything, the moment seemed even more propitious for his "America first" message. "I was not isolationist but noninterventionist," Buchanan later claimed.[41] With the Contract Republicans mainly focused on bashing the United Nations and building missile defense, Buchanan offered an economic dimension to the platform. His nationalist, protectionist, anti-immigration stance struck a chord with many Republican voters, who rejected Clinton's willingness to use American power in Bosnia and Haiti. And Buchanan tapped into the anxiety that had been apparent in the country ever since the end of the Cold War and the belief among many on the left and the right that America was in decline. For the right, the culprit was immigration, particularly illegal aliens coming from Latin America and the Caribbean. Buchanan harped on these nativist themes with gusto, playing the part of a demagogue to the hilt.

For a moment he caught fire, defeating Dole in the 1996 New Hampshire primary. This set off a frenzy inside Washington that the front-runner was on the ropes, and not surprisingly caused a lot of hand-wringing abroad. Even if Buchanan disappeared—and he eventually did as Dole rolled up victories in other early-primary states—Republican leaders worried that he represented a powerful enough constituency inside the Republican Party that the establishment would have to lean in his direction.[42]

THIS INWARD TURN was particularly troubling for those conservative insurgents who believed the United States needed to pursue a more vigorous foreign policy. They fretted about the torpor among most Republican politicians—seeing them as stuck in knee-jerk anti-Clintonism—and worried that Buchanan was the only person who seemed to be sparking passion on the Republican campaign trail. Although analysts such as Robert Kagan had had little success influencing the direction of the Contract Republicans, these writers wanted to try to shape the debate of the 1996 presidential race.

Kagan teamed up with his friend William Kristol, the conservative commentator who founded the magazine the *Weekly Standard* in the fall of 1995, and set out to forge a new agenda for America in the world. Kristol's involvement was significant; as former chief of staff to Vice President Dan Quayle and son of neoconservative legend Irving Kristol, he had spent the bulk of the previous three years rallying Republicans against Clinton's domestic policies, especially on health care. He was a one-man policy wrecking crew, churning out memos with analysis and talking points that were faxed throughout the media and conservative establishment, often shaping how Republicans responded to Clinton.

Having served in the Bush administration as the Cold War was ending, Kristol never really thought much about defining a new foreign policy. Like many on the right, he implicitly bought into the end of history idea, figuring world events would naturally evolve in America's favor. Yet by 1995 he had grown worried that Republicans were adrift. A policy maven and partisan warrior, Kristol believed that conservatives needed to give Americans a calling, rallying them around a big, generational project that tapped into their sense of national "greatness." He believed such an effort would also have political payoffs for Republicans, who fared better when foreign policy issues were at the center of the debate.[43]

Like Kagan, Kristol saw conservatives at a crossroads similar to the one they faced in the late 1970s, when Reagan rescued them by articulating a bold and confident vision for American foreign policy, focused on defeating the Soviet threat. They worried that like Democrats, Republicans were too fixated on the limits of U.S. power and influence, with the debate being dominated by either the paranoid isolationism of Buchanan or the cold, self-interested policies of establishment realists, such as Scowcroft. "Republicans were very badly split," Kristol said later.[44]

In this sense, the Republican revolution Gingrich helped usher in was not just about taking power away from Democrats; it was a revolution against the foreign policy traditions that had led conservatives through the Cold War. Kristol and Kagan began calling for a "neo-Reaganite" foreign policy and, in the tradition of Theodore Roosevelt, challenged conservatives to embrace a vision of American "benevolent global hegemony." By cleverly harkening back to these two Republican political icons, they hoped to stir up patriotic fervor, renewing the country's sense of mission and giving conservatism (and the American people) a big idea around which to rally.[45]

Although Kristol and Kagan hewed to a standard hawkish line in their call for more spending on the military and improved missile defense, they tried to cast their message as one of inspiration and optimism, not dark warning. They wanted the United States to be an activist power, intervening to solve problems and spreading liberal ideals. They explicitly rejected as too passive the idea of America as a "city on a hill" and John Quincy Adams's admonition not to seek "monsters to destroy." "The alternative," they asserted, "is to leave monsters on the loose, ravaging and pillaging . . . as Americans stand by and watch." They worried most about perpetuating American weakness and ennui, believing that without a greater sense of mission, the temptation to devote fewer resources to national security would prove too great. (In this sense, their warnings were similar to those Cheney made before he retreated from politics.) Looking to restore the happy warrior pride in America that had been waning since the end of the Cold War, they argued that citizens needed to be more involved in the management of hegemony and called for new ways for people to participate in national service.

Changing a nation's mood is difficult. The conservative activist vision failed to catch on as the 1996 presidential election approached. The cheery imperialism was targeted by both isolationists and conservative realists as too interventionist and too costly.[46] For some Republicans, this outlook seemed too similar to that of the Clinton administration, and Kristol and Kagan's support of Clinton's intervention in Bosnia hardly helped. In the heat of a presidential campaign, the "yes, but" position did not draw sharp enough distinctions.[47]

In time, many of Kristol and Kagan's proposals proved more appealing. Soon both Democrats and Republicans embraced the idea of greater national service, and the George W. Bush administration's preemption doctrine echoed the warning not to leave "monsters on the loose." The biggest difference was the means through which these ideas took root. In the mid-1990s, Kristol and Kagan were trying to draw Americans into a bold global effort through inspiration. In the years that followed, fear proved a more persuasive tool.

The "Bridge" Election

Republicans had no appetite for bold visions in 1996. They sought experience and steadiness in a candidate who could collect all of their competing policy differences—those of Buchananites, Contract Republicans, realists, and the beleaguered neoconservatives—under one big tent. If they wanted a seasoned foreign policy hand to contrast with Clinton, they could do no better than Dole. The Kansan personified the "greatest generation." Seriously wounded in Italy during World War II, he dedicated his life to public service and rose through the Senate to become majority leader. He was an honorable man, though not one with daring ideas. His biography was his most powerful asset, and he used it to espouse the leadership he believed the president lacked. "Let me be the bridge to an America that only the unknowing call myth," Dole declared in his Republican National Convention acceptance speech, alluding to Clinton's emphasis on building a bridge to the twenty-first century. "Let me be the bridge to a time of tranquility, faith, and confidence in action." Such language was intended to link Dole with a revered era in American history—but it merely served as a reminder that Clinton was the candidate of the future.

Dole assembled a national security team deep with Washington experience, headed by former Defense Secretary Donald Rumsfeld (who was the national campaign chairman), Jeane Kirkpatrick, and Paul Wolfowitz. They stressed foreign policy and attacked Clinton with enthusiasm. Yet Dole had a hard time defining how his global agenda would be different from Clinton's. On many issues—intervention in Bosnia, support for Russian reform, NATO expansion, the North American Free Trade Agreement—the two candidates largely agreed.

Taking a page from the Contract Republicans, Dole tried to make an issue of Clinton's approach to the United Nations (on the stump, Dole openly mocked Boutros Boutros-Ghali) and pledged to do more on missile defense. He also said the United States needed to be more "selective" in the use of force around the world. But the Clinton team was leading the effort to oust the U.N. secretary general, had committed to spend $20 billion on missile defense, and had chosen not to act in Rwanda, so Dole's assertions rang hollow. At times, the candidate himself seemed just to be going through the motions, as though he were uninspired by his own message of much of the same, only better. All Dole had left was to charge Clinton with incompetence and weak leadership. Yet here as well, the president's recent successes made the claim an unconvincing cliché, one that might have worked in 1994 but was belied by the reality of 1996.[48]

In the end, Dole's foreign policy of distinction without difference made it difficult for him to mount a serious challenge to the sitting president. Jack Kemp, Dole's vice presidential running mate, recalls thinking Clinton was not "particularly vulnerable on foreign policy." In 1996, Dole gave a speech in Washington blasting Clinton's policy in Asia, calling for a more confrontational stance toward China. But when asked a decade later to explain how a Dole presidency might have differed from Clinton's on China and other foreign policy issues, Kemp could not really say. "We wouldn't have done much differently on China or Japan," he admitted. "We would have wanted a more positive outreach to the Third World, but Clinton was doing that."[49]

THE 1996 election victory was a reaffirmation for Clinton and his team. For the first time since the Reagan years, polls showed that a majority of Americans believed the country was on the right track.[50] So as Clinton's second term began, he seemed poised to achieve a great deal at home and abroad—and more willing to articulate a forceful vision of the U.S. role in the world. He had reason to be proud of his foreign policy. In Europe, he had stopped a war, led NATO in its enlargement to the east, and seen his friend Yeltsin reelected in the face of a communist challenge. In calling for a Europe peaceful, undivided, and democratic and bringing together his policies on NATO, Bosnia, and Russia, Clinton had not promoted a universal doctrine such as containment, but he had shown he could execute a bold strategy.

The same could not be said of the Republicans. For them, 1996 was a humiliating blow. They were soundly beaten by a man whose legitimacy as president they could barely acknowledge and whose record around the world they believed was more a testament to luck than leadership. Dole himself could hardly believe he had lost to a man he thought was not up to the "serious business" of the job.[51] For the hard-core partisans, especially the Contract Republicans, the election was a watershed. Their frustration with Clinton's victory caused them to delve deeper into political scandals. Within two years, all their energy was consumed by Clinton's impeachment.

Yet the election loss also proved to be a turning point for conservative foreign policy elites. Dole's defeat made real the old adage that one could not beat something with nothing. The elites knew they had to do better than Dole's policy, which they conceded looked largely the same as Clinton's on the major issues. Those who had been lonely voices, such as Kristol and Kagan, began to attract more attention. Their sharp criticism of Dole during the campaign and their warning that the party was leaning toward isolationism won them few friends but gained traction in the wake of defeat.[52]

After 1996, the conservative national security agenda underwent a subtle but important shift. During the early 1990s, most conservatives viewed the world as largely benign, thinking the greatest threat to U.S. interests was overextending its power. Those who argued for a more robust global role did so because they worried about U.S. power atrophying. Yet a consensus began to coalesce around the view expressed by Cheney at the end of 1993 in his speech at the American Enterprise Institute: that the world had become more threatening, not less. This theme had the virtue of being believable in a global environment marked by the "coming anarchy" and perhaps a "clash of civilizations," but it was also good politics. It had the potential to reunite the old anticommunists around new dangers. As the decade wore on, the driving force for conservatives' thinking became their focus on vulnerabilities and threats—whether from missiles launched by rogue states, rising powers such as China, or, they began to argue, the gathering storm in Iraq.

CHAPTER SIX

The Indispensable Nation
in a Globalizing World

FOR MANY OBSERVERS, Madeleine Albright personified the new-found confidence and ambition that came to characterize the second Clinton administration's approach to the world.

As U.S. ambassador to the United Nations during the first term, Albright had used her perch in New York to be a consistent and forceful proponent for greater American activism in solving global problems, especially in the Balkans. Born in Czechoslovakia just before World War II, she and her family had fled both the Nazis and the communists. She often referred to herself as a child of Munich, evoking the lessons that taught the costs of appeasing dictators. Albright was an idealist. She believed in promoting liberal values, and seemed more comfortable in expressing them and more willing to advocate for the use of military force than many of her colleagues.

A few months into the administration, Albright had famously confronted Colin Powell about intervening in Bosnia, asking, "What are you saving this superb military for, Colin, if we can't use it?" Powell wrote later, "I thought I would have an aneurysm. . . . American GIs were not toy soldiers to be moved around on some sort of global game board."[1] The revelation of this exchange caused a minor uproar in the national security community, serving as a reminder of the Clinton administration's uneasy relationship with the military. Albright relished noting that when Powell's memoirs revealing the episode were published in September 1995, U.S. war planes were doing exactly as she had advocated—pounding the Serbs in Bosnia, eventually forcing them to the negotiating table. "I felt some vindication," she said. "Maybe he'd want to rewrite that page now."[2]

Albright's experience in New York left her committed to working through institutions such as the United Nations but realistic about their limits—after all, she had spearheaded America's unilateral effort to replace Boutros Boutros-Ghali as secretary general, believing he had not pushed hard enough to reform the world body. As Bill Clinton's second-term secretary of state and the first woman to hold the job, Albright stood poised by the strength of her personality, profile, and ideas to help implement a vision of American power and global responsibility that she often summed up in a single phrase: the "indispensable nation."

This idea is usually associated with Albright, but she did not invent it. Clinton regularly uttered the phrase throughout the 1996 presidential campaign. Always in search of a new idea to describe America's role in the world, Clinton had found these words with the help of his friend and adviser Sidney Blumenthal.[3] For months Clinton peppered his speeches with the phrase, including his 1996 acceptance speech at the Democratic National Convention, and he made it a prominent part of his second inaugural address. "America stands alone as the world's indispensable nation," Clinton said from the Capitol steps in January 1997, reminding his audience that it was the last presidential inaugural of the twentieth century. "The world is no longer divided into two hostile camps; instead, now we are building bonds with nations that once were our adversaries. Growing connections of commerce and culture give us a chance to lift the fortunes and spirits of people. . . . And for the very first time in all of history, more people on this planet live under democracy than dictatorship."

The notion of America as indispensable was not just a turn of phrase coined for the political season. It conveyed both a condition and a mission. First, it was a reality of the international landscape. There were few global problems that could be solved without the

active participation or support of the United States. This was especially true when it came to the range of transnational issues including
nuclear proliferation, climate change, terrorism, and the stability of
the global economy. But second, Clinton and Albright sought to rally
Americans behind an activist global role that entailed responsibility
and, at times, sacrifice. "I used it more in motivating the American
people to make them realize that we couldn't just sit back," Albright
explained years later. "Our well-being depended on being integrated
internationally."[4] In this sense, inspiring Americans to support a bold
global role—to give a sense of purpose and idealism to the country's
actions in the world, lest the American people and their leaders suc-
cumb to the temptation to withdraw—resembled the neoconservative effort to build a new national project.

ALTHOUGH the phrase later became seen as a code word for the unilateral use of American military power, Clinton emphasized the ties
of international commerce. This simple idea—that a healthy global
economy depended on a strong United States, and vice versa—had to
weather fierce political crosswinds. As a New Democrat, Clinton
tried to convince the Democratic Party to embrace globalization. He
argued that America could not afford to adopt protectionism but had
to push for even more openness and integration to succeed economically. Clinton struggled to push his party and the country to view the
profound changes wrought by the technological revolution and
increasing global interdependence not as dangers, but as opportunities. "Indispensable nation" was in part an effort to make the case to
the American people that the health of both the domestic and global
economy depended on U.S. leadership.

     The phrase also conveyed a new mood. As Clinton's second term
began, he finally embraced his role as a foreign policy president; he
told Albright he wanted an "activist" policy. By 1997, Clinton had
become a commanding figure on the global stage and as such trans-
ferred some of the ambitions he had to remake American politics
(although he still had plenty he wanted to do on that front) to reshap-

ing global politics and the international economic system. "The last four years I drove you crazy for what I didn't know," Clinton said, chuckling, to his friend Sandy Berger, who succeeded Tony Lake at the White House as national security adviser. "The next four years I'll drive you crazy for what I do know—and what I now want to do."

HOWEVER WELCOME the president's confidence, it would not make problems easier to solve. In fact, the very idea of America as *the* indispensable nation meant that a whole host of trouble spots could not be ignored. Consider the long list of issues Albright inherited when she replaced Warren Christopher at State, each detailed in nearly fifty secret memos written by the relevant assistant secretaries of state to help her prepare for what was to come. Today, these offer an inside glimpse of where the State Department believed it stood on a wide range of subjects and what its greatest concerns were. From managing nuclear proliferation and the ongoing effort to enlarge NATO, to breathing life into the Middle East peace process and maintaining thousands of American peacekeeping troops in Bosnia and Haiti, to meeting the challenges of Iraq and Iran, dealing with China and India, and getting the necessary resources for foreign assistance, the to-do list facing the indispensable nation's chief diplomat were daunting.[5]

Though the administration looked back on first-term successes in Asia—from shoring up the alliance with Japan to freezing North Korea's nuclear ambitions—"the road ahead engenders sobriety rather than celebration," because of pressure to scale back the U.S. military presence and worries of greater tensions with China. In the Middle East, Iran's "support of terrorism, its efforts to derail the peace process between the Israelis and Palestinians, its pursuit of weapons of mass destruction and the means to deliver them, and its striving to destabilize regional governments" challenged American interests. Yet the U.S. effort to pressure the Tehran regime to change its behavior "has failed . . . [so] we must restrict the regime's capacity to harm our interests." There were questions about the negative effects of the

U.S. military presence in Saudi Arabia (in place since the end of the Gulf War in 1991), including, "Could Saudi Arabia deteriorate like Iran did in 1979?" In Russia, a "vast problem" remained in "securing weapons-usable fissile material and combating nuclear smuggling . . . the key issue is how to develop within the Russian government a commitment to make nuclear security a priority." And across the globe in Latin America, the Clinton team found that despite widening trade and efforts to stabilize Haiti, "we are frequently perceived as insensitive, heavy-handed, [and] uncaring."[6]

Selfishness was a theme that ran through nearly every one of the transition papers. The administration's responses to these challenges were complicated by the fact that there was little congressional tolerance, and in some cases, outright hostility, for an active American role. To many politicians on Capitol Hill, America's leadership seemed entirely dispensable. Several memos addressed the problem directly, using phrases such as "disguised isolationism" and describing perceptions of "rampant U.S. unilateralism." In Congress, the debates often swung from uniformly criticizing the administration's policies to forcing it to use blunt instruments, including economic sanctions. Despite the efforts of Newt Gingrich—who was described in the memo from the State Department's top congressional liaison as "one of the few members with a global and strategic vision of U.S. foreign policy goals"—the attitude in the Republican caucus usually made things harder. "Overall, foreign policy was not a vital issue for most members," the paper read, "and many questioned the need for robust American leadership and engagement in the post–Cold War era." The result was that, as another memo explained, "U.S. influence in the international system has been under severe strain," particularly in institutions such as the United Nations, and in an area at the heart of the president's agenda since the 1992 campaign: the American response to the rapidly changing global economy.[7]

STRENGTHENING America's international economic leadership had been one of the most important goals of Clinton's first term, and the president hoped to build on his early accomplishments in his second. The rationale for this agenda is reflected in another of the transition memos for Albright. "At no time since our colonial period has American prosperity depended more profoundly on effective participation in, and leadership of, the world economy," it read. "Moreover, the crucial foreign policy objectives of the day—integrating Russia and China into Western systems and securing Middle East peace—can be achieved only with the help of international economic institutions such as the IMF, World Bank, and World Trade Organization."[8]

Here too, however, domestic politics intervened—because these issues involved Americans' livelihoods and jobs. "The end of the Cold War has brought a weakening of domestic support for trade liberalization," the State Department memo declared. There were many reasons for this, both historical and political, but Clinton had wagered his popularity by defying this domestic suspicion of trade (especially within his own party) to make it a centerpiece of his presidency. "An overarching task during the second Clinton administration will be to repair and refurbish the international economic system and to rebuild a bipartisan constituency for U.S. leadership in the world economy," the memo to Albright explained.

Of course, the secretary of state would not be the only player in this effort. In fact, she would rarely be the leading one, deferring to her colleagues at Treasury or the office of the U.S. Trade Representative. But the fact that international economic issues were featured so prominently in her briefing papers shows the extent to which they were fused with the more so-called traditional areas of statecraft—and the priority the president placed on making these issues a core part of America's global leadership.

It's the Global Economy, Stupid

From the start, critics attacked Clinton for bending to the political winds and taking polls before taking action. They rightly viewed him as indecisive early in his presidency when it came to the use of force. But these criticisms were unfounded on global economic issues, where Clinton often pursued the unpopular course, taking genuine risks and incurring political costs, especially among important constituencies in the Democratic Party. In his first year in office, he pursued deficit reduction, angering rank-and-file Democrats, and later he pushed a welfare reform program that many conservatives embraced. From the beginning, Clinton believed he had to convince Americans that foreign and domestic policies were inextricably linked in a globalizing world. James Steinberg, Clinton's second-term deputy national security adviser, says quite simply, "Clinton was an anti-realist. He didn't see that there had to be inherent competition among nations. The success of some was not threatening to others. It was their failure that was threatening."[9]

THE GLOBAL ECONOMY was one area of international relations where Clinton did not require much of a learning curve. His close aides later explained that his experiences as Arkansas governor—leading a small agricultural state that depended on trade—gave him a deep understanding of the issues involved. "Knowledge and experience make a difference," his friend and first trade representative, Mickey Kantor, explains. On trade issues, Clinton "was totally confident. In national security policy, he was less so, and he felt that he had to rely more on his advisers."[10]

Whereas the president's first term was marred by sniping about the incompetence or a lack of vision of his foreign policy team, many of the leading figures on the economic side—including Robert Rubin and Lawrence Summers—were widely admired for their brilliance and capable economic stewardship. Rubin had decades of successful experience on Wall Street; Summers was widely considered one of the leading academic economists of his generation. They emerged as two of Clinton's most influential gurus on the global economy. "They were like the neocons have been in [the George W. Bush] administration," explains former Treasury department and National Security Council official Mark Medish. They "were a group wielding disproportionate power because they had an intellectual concept and discipline. Clinton bet his presidency on globalization, and Rubin and Summers were his guys."[11] To ensure that economics remained at the heart of the bureaucracy's decisions and was fully integrated into foreign policy, Clinton had reorganized economic policy-making in the White House and created the National Economic Council as a counterpart to the National Security Council, appointing Rubin as the NEC's first director.

The global economy seemed ripe for the big concept Clinton wanted. For him, the 1992 campaign motto "it's the economy, stupid" did not mean a focus on domestic revitalization for its own sake, but rather signaled that the international environment was transforming fundamentally, with borders mattering less and worker education and skills mattering more.

When Clinton began his run for president in 1991, he carried with him a dog-eared and heavily underlined copy of the book *The Work of Nations*, written by his Oxford and Yale classmate Robert Reich. The book was a manifesto about how the United States must adapt to the changes in the international marketplace by strengthening the skills of its workers. "We are living through a transformation that will rearrange the politics and economics of the coming century," Reich's book boldly began. "There will no longer be *national* products or technologies, no national corporations, no national industries. . . . Each nation's primary political task will be to cope with the centrifugal forces of the global economy which tear at the ties binding citizens together—bestowing even greater wealth on the most skilled and insightful, while consigning the less skilled to a declining standard of living." These ideas found their way into many of Clinton's speeches and informed many of the most important policies of his presidency, such as investing in enhanced worker training to alleviate insecurities, spending more on infrastructure to ensure that the United States remained competitive, and building a global trading system that promoted fairness while preserving openness.[12]

*

CLINTON LOVED talking about the transformative power of globalization. The word itself was just becoming prevalent as he entered office, and leaders and common citizens were only starting to grapple with its implications. The contrast between the 1990s and the Cold War's emphasis on national security was illustrated by *Time* magazine's decision to name three CEOs as persons of the year during the decade: CNN's Ted Turner in 1991, Intel's Andrew Grove in 1997, and Amazon's Jeff Bezos in 1999. The last time a CEO had received that distinction was in 1955, and before that, in the interwar years of 1928 and 1929, when Walter Chrysler and Owen Young (CEO of General Electric) were selected. In the 1920s, scions of manufacturing and cabinet officials such as Herbert Hoover at Commerce and Andrew Mellon at Treasury were dominant figures in American life; in the modern interwar years, leaders of technology companies and officials such as Rubin and Alan Greenspan, chairman of the Federal Reserve, took their turn. In both eras, American trade, investment, and economic policy had a huge impact on the global economy.[13]

In contrast to the Cold War divisions, changes in technologies and markets were breaking down barriers around the world. As Greenspan later wrote, "The defining moment for the world's economies was the fall of the Berlin Wall in 1989, revealing a state of economic ruin behind the iron curtain far beyond the expectations of most knowledgeable Western economists."[14] Economies that had once groaned under planned socialism rushed to join the global marketplace at the same time the information technology revolution was reshaping how people did business. *New York Times* columnist Thomas Friedman, who better than anyone championed globalization in his articles and books, argued that it was an entirely new international system, with "its own unique logic, rules, pressures, and incentives." For Clinton, this presented new demands on American leadership both at home and abroad. "Globalization is not a proposal or policy choice, it is a fact," he said. "But how we respond to it will make all the difference."[15]

*

CLINTON UNDERSTOOD the political challenges his response posed. The Democratic base was still heavily dominated by those who bore the brunt of economic change: labor unions and, to a lesser extent, environmental groups. Clinton had built his 1992 candidacy around his ability to rescue the American economy from George H. W. Bush, who was seen by many people as not caring enough about average workers. But rather than embracing protectionism and isolationism, Clinton argued strongly for active global engagement, believing the country had no choice but to pursue trade liberalization. Casting these goals in the broadest terms, he argued that they were aimed at building "a new structure of opportunity and peace through trade, investment, and commerce."[16]

Clinton learned that trade was easier to support in general than in particular—trade's larger benefits for the economy as a whole would not do much for those individuals who were losing their jobs because it had become cheaper for companies to produce goods elsewhere. During the 1992 campaign, Pat Buchanan and Ross Perot had played into American fears about job losses to argue for higher trade barriers. Clinton took a different path, suggesting that he would promote both free and fair trade, pursuing the agreements the Bush administration was initiating, but doing so only after ensuring that labor and environmental standards were protected. Yet there was hardly a consensus on this inside the Democratic Party—and Clinton believed that one of his tasks as president would be to create one.

The first step was to finish the work that Bush had started. On the national security side, Bush had left his successor nasty and unresolved foreign policy crises, such as Haiti, Somalia, and Bosnia. On the international economic front, where Bush had nearly completed two major trade accords, the problems Clinton faced were largely political—the victories he needed to win were within his own party. The North American Free Trade Agreement (NAFTA), whose purpose was to break down trade barriers with Canada and Mexico, had created fears that American companies would take advantage of cheap labor and head south, leaving workers out of luck and out of jobs. Bush had negotiated and signed the treaty, yet it was left to

Clinton to get it through Congress. Even though Democrats were in control, this would not be an easy sell.

The second agreement Bush had bequeathed was designed to reshape the post–World War II international economic framework, known as the General Agreement on Tariffs and Trade (GATT). The GATT trading system drastically reduced the barriers to trade that had contributed to the Great Depression of the 1930s. Countries had met periodically in what were known as "rounds" to lower trade barriers, dealing with issues such as tariffs on goods and government subsidies for companies. The system's primary achievement was enshrining a set of global rules, ensuring that a GATT member country could not discriminate against others that were in the trading system. A country could not set one level of tariffs for certain member countries and another level for others. Exceptions were made occasionally for some regional organizations, but overall, the system performed largely as its founders intended, dramatically increasing global trade flows and overall wealth in the world.

GATT's chief shortcoming was that it had no real enforcement mechanisms. The new agreement would create the World Trade Organization (WTO): an institution that could review disputes between countries and enforce rulings by allowing sanctions against violators. Although creating a stronger rules-based system sounded sensible, it proved deeply controversial. Many conservatives disliked the proposed WTO for what they saw as encroachments on national sovereignty. They did not want international bureaucrats in Geneva (where the WTO was to be headquartered) telling the United States it needed to change its laws to conform to global rules. Many liberals argued that the trade agreement not only allowed other countries to produce products with cheap labor and without environmental and health and safety standards, but also would enable those countries to argue that American efforts to protect health, safety, and the environment (such as blocking meat imports failing to meet U.S. Food and Drug Administration standards) violated free-trade norms.

Despite such fierce skepticism from both sides of the political spectrum, the Clinton team believed that, taken together, securing congressional approval of NAFTA and completing the negotiations to create the World Trade Organization would be a major step in building a lasting international framework for managing economic globalization. Yet forging these agreements required building a stronger political consensus to support it at home. For Clinton, this meant that his most intense foreign policy showdown in his first year as president was not with another country's leader, but with his Democratic allies in the U.S. Congress.

The First Foreign Policy Victory—NAFTA

In the summer of 1993, White House political advisers weren't enthusiastic about the idea of trying to pass a trade accord. They believed that the last thing the president needed was a confrontation with the labor community (especially when union support was needed on so many other parts of Clinton's domestic agenda). But officials such as trade chief Kantor argued that they could not retreat from the positions they had taken during the 1992 campaign. "If we didn't do NAFTA," he says, "it would look like we were backtracking . . . we would look weak." Secretary of State Christopher echoed this advice, linking success on NAFTA to the administration's broader foreign policy goals. "I was absolutely convinced," Christopher recalled, "that failure to approve NAFTA would not only traumatize our relations with Mexico and undermine our credibility throughout Latin America, but have a profound ripple effect on our ability to lead in all areas of foreign policy."[17]

Other influential foreign policy figures agreed and encouraged Clinton from the outside. Henry Kissinger argued that NAFTA presented the president with an opportunity to do something "defining . . . we live in a world in which the ideological challenge has disintegrated and a new architecture needs to be created, and NAFTA is the first and crucial step in that direction." Economist Paul Krugman explained that the economic benefits and costs of the agreement were exaggerated by both sides and that the principal reason to support the deal was its foreign policy rationale, to strengthen relations with an important neighbor—Mexico. "[This] agreement is not about jobs. It is not even about economic efficiency and growth. It is about doing what we can to help a friendly government succeed," Krugman wrote.[18]

BECAUSE NEGOTIATIONS on the agreement had begun under Ronald Reagan and continued under Bush, congressional Republicans promised Clinton half of the votes needed in the House of Representatives to ensure its passage, leaving him to come up with the rest from Democrats. Republican leaders believed in free trade's benefits to the American business community and the overall health of the economy, and they could have promised more votes. But they did not want to give Clinton a free pass to avoid a battle inside his own ranks.

The fight was bruising. Labor unions in rust-belt states demanded that their representatives vote no. The third-ranking member of the Democratic leadership, Michigan Congressman David Bonior, said three-quarters of the House Democrats stood alongside him in opposition to the agreement. Looking back, Bonior wistfully remarks, "I thought we had a chance to defeat NAFTA. We had a great movement, starting with the base . . . labor, environmental, human rights groups." That fall, Thomas Donahue, secretary-treasurer of the powerful AFL-CIO, noted that while his organization was "not threatening anybody," there would be consequences: "If you vote to ship jobs of our members out of this country, we're not going to support you anymore."[19]

Meanwhile on the right, Buchanan was furious that Republicans were going to bail out Clinton and hand him a major victory. "Can Republicans not see," wrote Buchanan in his trademark take-no-prisoners style, "the immense populist coalition forming up against NAFTA—of blue-collar workers and America firsters, of black laborers and small businesses, of populists and Perotistas?" And he asked his friends on the right, "What has Bill Clinton ever done for the GOP that it should be taking casualties to save his NAFTA treaty—and repair his weakened presidency?"[20]

*

UNIONS AND environmentalists on the left and those who feared the loss of American sovereignty on the right forged a formidable coalition that gathered strength through the 1990s. Countering them were the foreign policy and business elites of both political parties, who believed they were carrying on the great tradition of America in the post–World War II era by building a global capitalist economic order under U.S. leadership. Capturing that image was an event at the White House on September 14, 1993, when Clinton stood with three of his predecessors—Gerald Ford, Jimmy Carter, and Bush—before a roomful of other luminaries to show Democrats and Republicans alike that their leaders were united.

Clinton articulated his vision of how the United States needed to adjust to "an era in which commerce is global and in which money, management, [and] technology are highly mobile." He presented the choice as either embracing the hope that America could adjust to the change or succumbing to the impulse that it should wall itself off in fear. The challenge, Clinton said, stemmed from the inability to stop the economic forces at play. "Nothing we do . . . can change the fact that factories or information can flash across the world, that people can move money around in the blink of an eye," he said. And he suggested much more than one agreement was at stake. If NAFTA were to fail, "We cannot then point the finger at Europe and Japan or anybody else and say . . . why don't you help to create a world economy." Bush, admiring his successor's eloquent disquisition, was moved to say, "Now I understand why he's inside looking out and I'm outside looking in."[21]

Although the congressional fight was a steep uphill struggle, the administration pressed ahead with an intense lobbying campaign. Clinton and his team worked hard to get the support they needed, winning commitments from Mexico that could soften the blow if, for example, the prices dropped for sugar (important in Louisiana) or citrus (critical to Florida). The president had meetings or phone calls with 200 members of Congress, in which he made the strategic case for the deal, especially in terms of solidifying the U.S. role in Latin

America. Many members were persuaded by this logic but admitted that the political forces against the deal were simply too powerful. Some even speculated that if the vote could be conducted by secret ballot, it would pass overwhelmingly. But they did not have that luxury and had to fear the wrath of their constituents. To pass the accord, Clinton could not rely on free-trade logic alone, so he promised specific legislative payoffs to members to secure their votes.

No PERSON did more to stoke the sense of doom about trade than Perot, who parlayed his 1992 independent presidential candidacy into serving as a kind of spokesman against NAFTA. He had famously warned that America would hear a "giant sucking sound" coming from its southern border as jobs vanished into Mexico. Perot maintained a strong national following. The administration believed it needed to confront him head-on. Clinton sent Vice President Al Gore onto Perot's home turf—CNN's *Larry King Live*, the show where Perot had burst onto the political scene with his frequent appearances in 1992—for a ninety-minute, freewheeling debate a week before the vote was scheduled in the House of Representatives.

Gore tirelessly prepared for the debate, even talking to Gingrich (a NAFTA supporter) for advice, and came out swinging. With eleven million Americans watching, the vice president was aggressive and succinct. The defining moment came when Gore pulled out a picture of two oft-derided Republicans from yesteryear, Utah Senator Reed Smoot and Oregon Congressman Willis Hawley, architects of the famous bill in 1930 that raised tariffs to protect the American worker, setting off a spiral of tariff increases around the world that inflamed the Great Depression. Gore said sarcastically to an unsmiling and unthankful Perot, "I framed this so you can put it on your wall if you want to."

Having Gore debate Perot turned out to be a brilliant move. The Texas billionaire was easily provoked, losing his temper, calling the vice president a liar, and saying the NAFTA numbers were "phony."

The immediate polls showed that Gore crushed Perot, whose populist aura was never quite the same.[22]

Thanks to such gambits and Clinton's tireless lobbying, the
House of Representatives approved NAFTA on November 17, 1993,
by a vote of 234–200. Yet, only 102 Democrats voted in favor. In the
Senate, the vote was 61–38, with merely 23 Democrats supporting it.
Clinton's first substantial victory on an issue concerning America's
engagement with the world was made possible only with overwhelming support from Republicans.

White House adviser David Gergen, who had also been a top aide
to Republican presidents, called it the "high-water mark of bipartisanship during Clinton's presidency."[23] Conservatives recognized the
political risks Clinton had taken. "Give Bill Clinton credit for
[NAFTA]," Dick Cheney admitted years later, after his return to the
White House as vice president. "I thought that was something they
did well. I didn't agree with much of what he did, but I thought that
was one of his better policies." Gingrich added, "Here's where Clinton gets less credit than he deserves. At some considerable risk, he
took on his own labor union left and the antitrade right . . . it was a
significant moment in keeping the country moving forward." Even
Bonior, who had led the charge against the agreement in the House
of Representatives, acknowledges that NAFTA "was a big accomplishment for Clinton. It changed the rules for trade and paved the
way for the WTO."[24]

But while the White House celebrated a major legislative triumph, the facts behind the NAFTA victory presented a troubling
reality for Clinton that lasted through the decade. Despite all his
efforts, the president could muster barely more than 100 votes from
his party. The agreement "came at a high price," Clinton recalled,
"dividing our party in Congress and infuriating our strongest supporters in the labor movement."[25] Many blamed NAFTA for suppressing
labor turnout in 1994, thus helping the Republicans gain control of
Congress.[26] The base of the Democratic Party remained deeply suspicious of trade deals, and unions and environmentalists maintained
their opposition. If anything, they were motivated to fight harder.

Clinton's victory "changed dramatically the nature of the Democratic Party," Bonior recalls. "It became another corporate party, which a lot of us don't want."[27]

PASSING NAFTA in 1993—followed by the deal to establish the WTO a year later—turned out to be the apex of the administration's globalization agenda. Going forward, Clinton's administration found itself increasingly on the defensive, even as the American economy began to boom to amazing heights. "There has been a steady erosion of support for trade since NAFTA," says Charlene Barshefsky, who later replaced Kantor as the top U.S. trade official. Clinton reflected several years after NAFTA's passage that when it came to trade, "there's still a war in our party."[28]

There were also growing signs of new alliances on both ends of the political spectrum against greater integration into the global economy. One of the more bizarre examples of this left-right collaboration took place in the months before the November 1994 vote to approve the WTO deal, when consumer advocate Ralph Nader offered to give $10,000 to the favorite charity of any member of Congress who could sign a statement saying he or she had read the agreement and was willing to answer ten questions in public. "I never met anyone—members or staff—who had read the bill," Nader recalls, arguing that those voting yes were merely rubberstamping a trade deal out of reflexive habit. Only one senator, Hank Brown, a conservative Republican from Colorado, took Nader up on the offer. "He called and said, 'I don't want your money, but I want to answer the questions,'" Nader says.[29]

Brown, who said he had studied hundreds of flash cards after reading the 514-page document, took twelve questions from Richard Goodwin, an author and former adviser to the Kennedy brothers. Appropriately for this role, Goodwin had helped uncover the 1950s quiz show scandals as a young congressional investigator (and his efforts had been depicted in a popular movie). The studious senator answered all the questions correctly. Although Nader later lamented that the stunt "got very little coverage," he had made his point. Brown told his colleagues he supported free trade, but after studying the agreement, he feared the creation of a global organization whose rules superseded laws passed by the U.S. Congress.[30]

Despite such concerns among liberals and conservatives, at the time Clinton was on a roll, moving the country forward in its embrace of globalization. But this success proved fleeting. Before the year was out, the president confronted a major economic crisis south of the border, in the very country he promised was a stable and worthwhile partner. The political forces challenging his trade policies at home grew more strident as Clinton applied his notion of an indispensable nation to bailing out Mexico.

"The First Crisis of the Twenty-first Century"

Robert Rubin was on vacation in the Virgin Islands in December 1994, looking for some rest before leaving his position as director of the National Economic Council in the White House to replace Lloyd Bentsen as secretary of the treasury. Yet his short respite was interrupted by a phone call from Lawrence Summers, whom Rubin was promoting to be his deputy. Mexico's currency, the peso, threatened to collapse, Summers said. "I didn't know much about Mexico's economic problems," Rubin recalled in his memoirs, "and I didn't understand why a peso devaluation was urgent enough to interfere with fishing."[31] Although a lot of countries in the world faced economic trouble, Rubin admits, "What I didn't realize was that the problems in Mexico weren't passing problems, they were deep."[32]

Similar to other emerging markets—Russia, Brazil, Chile, South Africa—Mexico sparked the interest of investors who were always looking for new places to diversify their portfolios. But like many countries just starting to build democratic rule and a more open economy, Mexico didn't have the legal and economic structures in place (such as a sound banking system) to reassure investors when times were tough. So to keep foreign investors confident, Mexico pegged its currency to the value of the U.S. dollar. In 1994, a brewing rebellion in Mexico's Chiapas region and the assassination of two leading politicians, including a candidate for president, fed the perception that the country might not be such a good bet. By the end of the year, as the economic crisis spiraled out of control, Mexico was forced to devalue the peso, bringing the country to the brink of ruin. Having borrowed a lot of money when times were good, Mexico was in danger of default.

Mexico was not unique in its problems, but it was America's most important southern neighbor and its third-largest trading partner. An unattended crisis would send shock waves through the global financial community, feed doubts about the wisdom of investing in emerging markets, and possibly spark an influx of illegal immigrants searching for economic opportunity in the United States. Considering such potentially far-reaching consequences, Gingrich aptly called it the "first crisis of the twenty-first century."

THROUGHOUT the NAFTA negotiations, the president sought to reassure Americans about Mexico. Then suddenly, at the end of 1994, its economy teetered on the brink of collapse.

In early January 1995, after Rubin's brief swearing-in ceremony as treasury secretary, he and Summers stayed behind in the Oval Office to talk to Clinton. They warned the president that the Mexican government faced an imminent threat of default. To prevent that from happening, they recommended that he support a "massive, potentially unpopular, and risky intervention: providing billions of dollars to the Mexican government to avoid a collapse in its currency and economy." They had conferred with Federal Reserve Chairman Greenspan earlier that day, and the three agreed they would need at least $25 billion to save Mexico. Rubin later called this the economic corollary to Powell's doctrine of military intervention—"intervening only when American interests are at stake and [doing so] with an overwhelming level of force."[33] Greenspan added that it was "the same principle of market psychology as piling currency in a bank's window to stop a run on the bank," as American banks had done before the 1935 legislation establishing government guarantees on deposits.[34]

The president was in a tough position. His economic advisers sought his approval for a hugely unpopular policy (public opinion polls showed that nearly 80 percent of Americans opposed bailing out the Mexican government) with a stunning price tag. Moreover, coming at exactly the moment that the new Republican majority was taking over the reins of power in Congress, the timing was hardly auspicious. Finally, there were no guarantees for success. Even with a massive American bailout, the Mexican economy might collapse anyway. "If this fails," Berger warned Clinton, "you'll be accused of pissing billions of dollars down a Mexican rathole."[35]

The president understood the risks but decided he needed to make a bold move. He later recalled that the decision was "clearcut." Despite the possibility of failure, he reflected, "we simply couldn't stand aside and let Mexico fail without trying to help. In addition to the economic problems it would cause both for us and for the Mexicans, we would be sending a terrible signal of selfishness and shortsightedness throughout Latin America."[36]

But could he convince Congress to release the necessary funds? Clinton picked up the phone and asked for support from the new Hill leadership: Gingrich, Senate Majority Leader Bob Dole, and the respective Democratic leaders in the House and Senate, Congressman Richard Gephardt and Senator Tom Daschle. They were ready to back him, but their rank-and-file wouldn't hear of it. Gingrich explained later why he couldn't deliver his fellow Republicans. "They didn't believe in it," he said. "They didn't trust Clinton; they didn't trust Rubin. They didn't believe the U.S. should intervene. Some of them were free marketers who didn't believe in an intervention as policy. They thought that the secretary of the treasury is basically bailing out his friends in Wall Street, that they were the ones that would get the money in the end because they'd made all these stupid loans." Yet the House speaker was conscious of the balancing act before him. "The question is whether or not at the very beginning of the first Republican majority in forty years you want to consciously take on the administration and be the people who are willing to see Mexico collapse, and that struck me as just nuts."[37]

Congressional liberals and conservatives were outraged. Given such opposition, it had become increasingly clear that despite the favorable support from the bipartisan leadership and other influential politicians, including the new Texas governor, George W. Bush, Congress would not approve the money. So Treasury officials came up with a plan that would work around Capitol Hill. There was a little-known cache of $35 billion called the Exchange Stabilization Fund (ESF) that could be used by the president without prior approval by Congress. Designed in the 1930s to boost the dollar in emergencies, the ESF had been used several times since the 1970s to help prop up foreign currencies, including Mexico's in 1982, but the sums had never been on this scale and some questioned whether such use was beyond the program's legal intent. This was "stretching the law to the breaking point," Berger later admitted.[38] But the administration bit the bullet and forged ahead, believing it had no alternative. International financial institutions would contribute funds only if the United States led the way. Thus, if America did not step in, no one would.

IN THE DAYS before the deal was finalized, the risks of failure loomed heavily over the Treasury secretary and his colleagues. One evening, Rubin hosted a private dinner just a few blocks north of the White House at the Jefferson Hotel, which was home for the New Yorker during his nearly seven years in the Clinton administration. He invited Berger, White House Chief of Staff Leon Panetta, and his top Treasury team to discuss the lending program one more time before they moved ahead. The United States would be disbursing loan guarantees in $3 billion increments, so it would have a chance to cut its losses if the effort failed. Would the gambit work? Over coffee, Rubin asked his dinner companions what the odds were. One adviser, Dan Zelikow, said the chance of success was one in three. Another, David Lipton, thought more than 50 percent. Summers didn't think they were much better. No one suggested that it would be a slam dunk, but none believed they had a choice.[39]

In late February, Rubin and his Mexican counterparts gathered in the Cash Room at the Treasury Building (the same place where U.S. citizens once traded paper dollars for gold) to formalize the currency stabilization agreement. Yet the markets still dropped. Summers went to Rubin that night, offering to resign. Ridiculous, Rubin said, they all bore responsibility, and he contemplated the fact that if this failed, he himself might be forced to step down after only a few weeks on the job. Rubin walked across the street to the White House and suggested that they could cut their losses, withdraw from the agreement unilaterally, and not release the first $3 billion as scheduled. But Clinton wanted to move ahead. The risks were worth running, he believed, and now America's credibility was on the line.[40]

Fortunately for the administration, within months the plan finally seemed to be working. In addition to receiving the loan guarantees, Mexico carried out an economic reform program with advice from the International Monetary Fund and U.S. Treasury officials. By the end of the year, the country had stabilized. Mexico repaid the loans by January 1997, three years ahead of schedule. The first crisis of the twenty-first century was fixed well before the end of the twentieth.

WITH THE bailout's success, the president not only skirted a massive economic and political disaster, but he also emerged victorious. Clinton's advisers and outsiders alike were impressed with the president's courage and self-assurance. Rubin remembered that Clinton "had been at his best: utterly and determinedly presidential." In his *New York Times* column, Friedman observed, "The Mexican bailout could go down as the least popular, least understood, but most important foreign policy decision of the Clinton presidency." The president had found a way to bypass stiff resistance in Congress and spend billions in American taxpayer money on a risky but worthy venture. "It was a pivotal moment," Senator Daschle recalls, "and a big deal for the administration to seize it." [41]

Although the episode signified Clinton's commitment to using American power—in this case, dollars—to stabilize the global economic order, it also revealed his domestic political weakness. To get NAFTA passed, he had to pull out all the stops and rely mainly on Republican support for the votes he needed. On the Mexico bailout, the opposition even among Republicans proved too great and he had to go around Congress. The erosion of support continued in 1997, after his reelection, when Clinton failed to win congressional approval to renew his "fast track" trade authority, which would have empowered him, as it had other presidents over the previous two decades, to continue to negotiate trade deals not subject to congressional amendment.

The president had shown he could be a capable political operator on globalization issues, but he also needed to be an educator to help prepare Americans (and their politicians) for the economic and social changes global integration would bring. NAFTA was a traditional trade deal brokered by a Republican president, and although passage was not easy, lowering tariff barriers to imports and exports had been an American priority since World War II. Worrying about investments in emerging markets was a new phenomenon for Americans who were only beginning to enter the stock market in a big way. Pension funds no longer depended just on the strength of General Motors and General Electric but on the health of companies located in Chile, Poland, and Mexico, places where fund managers were putting increasing amounts of money. Rubin recalled that when he was working on Wall Street in the 1980s, Mexico's previous financial crisis had barely registered with him; now, because of the rapidity with which capital flowed around the globe, it was the kind of event that jeopardized his career.

The task went beyond creating a new international architecture to mitigate financial crises or negotiating new agreements to lower trade barriers. Clinton had to brace the American people for change—to help them realize the benefits of the global economy while preparing for the difficulties. This was how he had justified the NAFTA and

Mexico deals. But their outcome showed how much work remained. By the mid-1990s, the country was still sorting out the implications of globalization, and as people became more interconnected and the world's economies and societies became more integrated, this was not just a matter of public policy, it was about identity. "Something I need to take on even more," Clinton said in 1996, "is trying to figure out a way to make the American people believe, not just episodically but instinctively, that there's no longer an easy dividing line between foreign policy and domestic policy, that the world we're living in doesn't permit us that luxury anymore."[42]

In many ways, the problem had been laid out in the last lines of the 1991 book by Clinton's friend Reich: "The central question for America in the post-Soviet world—a diverse America, whose economy and culture are rapidly fusing with the economies and cultures of the rest of the globe—is whether it is possible to rediscover our identity, and our mutual responsibility, without creating a new enemy."

"The answer," he wrote, "is far from clear."[43]

Storm Clouds on the Right

Despite the underlying difficulties Clinton faced as he sought to galvanize domestic support for his approach to global trade, his economic policies were succeeding. The financial despair that had dominated the early 1990s—and, in Clinton's words, had made Americans "feel like they're lost in a funhouse" and in a "funk"— had lifted. The markets were up, unemployment was down, and by the end of 1997, White House officials started holding meetings to discuss what only years before had been unthinkable: what they should do with an anticipated budget surplus.[44]

Such news was great for the country but left Republicans in a foul mood. Although few conservatives had given Dole's somnolent presidential campaign much chance of success, most still could not believe Clinton had beaten them again. (Some consoled themselves

that for the second time, Clinton had failed to garner at least 50 percent of the popular vote.) The life of perpetual opposition was not a
good one for the Republican Party, and it brought out its worst tendencies. Perhaps most damaging was in its approach to the world. On
both security and economic issues, conservatives turned inward.
They had grown increasingly skeptical of military interventions and
hardly engaged at all with the ideas behind globalization. In fact, few
conservatives would even utter the buzzword, believing it connoted a
kind of one-worldism identified with Clinton and the elites who
gathered every year in Davos, Switzerland, to ponder the changing
global economy.

Gingrich, who loved thinking about the future and the dramatic
pace of global change as much as Clinton did, was hardly representative of the politicians he was supposed to be leading. Some influential outsiders thought Republican leaders bore some responsibility
for allowing these oppositional tendencies to run out of control. "You
depend on them to keep [latent isolationism] under control, and they
didn't do that very well," says former Republican Congressman Vin
Weber, who remained a close ally to Gingrich. "They allowed their
opposition to Clinton to override their proper leadership roles in
keeping the party from drifting to isolationism and protectionism."
Others, such as conservative journalist David Frum, had more sympathy with the caucus. "When you say we are going to have free trade
with Mexico, and we're going to give your money to Mexico, and
they are all going to come in and take your jobs, and change your
state, why would any Republican voter be for any of that?" he asks.
"When their leadership in Washington did it anyway, it just cut them
off."[45]

These were desperate times for the political right. Among those
former Reagan or Bush officials who hoped to serve a Republican
president again one day, the question was less how to defeat the
Democrats than how to prevent the Republican Party from going
over the political edge. They worried that they would prove unable
to win back a presidency that only a decade before they had believed
they would never lose. So they did what Washington insiders who

find themselves out of power do: They met and plotted, usually over a nice meal.

Seeking to continue the debates about America's global role they had launched through their writings, William Kristol and Robert Kagan convened a series of quiet dinners at the Willard Hotel in downtown Washington during the autumn of 1996, bringing together members of the Republican exile community. The discussions proved fruitful enough that they decided to institutionalize their endeavor, asking their friend Gary Schmitt, a former congressional staffer and Reagan administration official, to help. They believed conservatives needed to get back into the foreign policy ideas business, and they needed a venue to organize meetings and present their work. Since 1993, Kristol had conducted his modern-day pamphleteer effort to shape the Washington debate on health care and domestic issues through a small organization he had founded for a little over $1 million, the Project for the Republican Future. Kristol and his colleagues set out to create a similar organization focused on national security. By the spring of 1997, with funding from several conservative foundations, they opened the doors of their new think tank and gave it a grand title that reflected their ambition: the Project for a New American Century.

MEASURED AGAINST the vast conspiracy theories it spawned years later, the project (or PNAC, as it became known in the acronym-obsessed capital) was a modest affair. With just a handful of paid staffers and a few desks in a nondescript office building on Seventeenth Street in downtown Washington, it hardly looked like the seat of influence. It was more like a virtual club than an organization. Looking back, Francis Fukuyama says that "PNAC was Bill Kristol and his fax machine." Visitors would often be surprised by how underwhelming it all seemed—especially high government officials from abroad, who started to hear about PNAC and came there believing they would find the behind-the-scenes drivers of conservatism. Yet for those involved in PNAC, the surroundings seemed entirely appropriate for where they saw themselves—as outsiders even within their own party, far from power.[46]

To get its message across, PNAC followed the formula that had proven so successful for Kristol on issues such as health care—widely disseminating brief, pithy issue statements that were more digestible for politicians and journalists than typical think-tank tomes. For PNAC's launch in June 1997, the group rounded up a who's who of the conservative national security and political establishment to release a manifesto with twenty-five cosigners, including Cheney, Donald Rumsfeld, Paul Wolfowitz, Lewis "Scooter" Libby, Weber, Dan Quayle, Fukuyama, and Florida Governor Jeb Bush, whom many Republicans saw as the likeliest Bush son to become president. These weren't really neoconservatives—by then the designation had virtually disappeared from the political vernacular—but rather internationalist conservatives who worried about the inward drift within the Republican Party.

They tried to push their policy ideas with their allies in Congress but quickly found that doing so was pointless. "PNAC was not effective on the Hill," recalls Schmitt, who was PNAC's executive director. Instead the project sought to shape the broader Republican debate. In PNAC's founding document, its June 1997 Statement of Principles, the Clinton administration was mentioned only in passing. The main targets were those conservatives who "had not confidently advanced a strategic vision for America's role in the world . . . [and] have allowed differences over tactics to obscure potential agreement on strategic objectives." Building on Kristol and Kagan's efforts to promote a "neo-Reaganite" foreign policy, the principles (crafted primarily by Kagan) called for bold American leadership, by strengthening ties to democratic allies, promoting political and economic freedom, and building an international order "friendly to our security." They warned against the temptation for Americans to "shirk their responsibilities."

By focusing on military instruments of power, the PNAC approach emphasized a different argument—one that, as many commentators have noted, is akin to the logic of the 1992 Defense Planning Guidance. PNAC's was an unapologetic depiction of American strength. Yet the sunny optimism and call to service that Kristol and Kagan tried to spark in their earlier writings—harkening back to the outlook of Ronald Reagan and Teddy Roosevelt—had been stripped away.

This was now a fundamentally darker outlook on the world; the emphasis on national defense meant the country's attention had to return to threats, especially military ones. Most conservatives (and many liberals) had embraced the idea that the end of the Cold War made the international environment safer and, therefore, the danger was that too much American involvement in the world would bring about the country's decline. PNAC's founders sought to bring the conversation back to the threats posed by America's enemies. They asserted that the policies of both the Clinton administration *and* the Contract Republicans—cutting defense spending, deploying military power with uncertainty, or opposing it outright—had left America vulnerable.

IN THIS MOVE toward stressing threats and the need for renewed military strength rather than emphasizing the opportunities created by globalization, PNAC's founders were not alone. They echoed the conclusions of a similar idea-generating effort the Republican Party had sponsored in the mid-1990s under the stewardship of party chairman Haley Barbour and John Bolton, a former Reagan and Bush official who had emerged as another prominent national security thinker on the right, especially on arms-control issues.

The organization they headed, the National Policy Forum, was created in 1993 as the GOP's policy arm and brought together nearly 1,500 conservatives into thirteen "policy councils" to come up with ideas for the party on both foreign and domestic issues. More than 200 people participated on the foreign policy councils, with Cheney and Jeane Kirkpatrick among their leaders. Although the effort proved to be more a means to organize partisan loyalists—and, Democrats claimed, a mechanism through which the Republicans could skirt campaign fund-raising rules with undisclosed donations and foreign financing—it did produce a book of policy proposals in 1996, titled the *Agenda for America*. Although hardly a page-turner, the book provided a further glimpse into conservative policy elites' thinking on America's global role.[47]

With a far more partisan tone than PNAC, the book's six chapters on foreign policy were dominated by worries about military weakness and the looming sense of danger.[48] Of the forum's nine "objectives," all but three concerned projecting military strength or dealing with some kind of menacing threat from other countries. The most significant emphasis was on combating the threat of weapons of mass destruction—a subject hardly mentioned in the 1994 Contract with America or during Dole's presidential campaign. The book described the spread of nuclear, biological, or chemical weapons as "America's biggest challenge of the twenty-first century," and advocated taking "all necessary measures" to prevent proliferation from happening. Mentioning Iraq, Iran, North Korea, Syria, and Libya, it warned that eventually "some or all of these rogue states will obtain missiles that can threaten the U.S. homeland."

To deal with such possibilities, the book broke little new ground, emphasizing missile defense and seeking to revise or discard arms control treaties that it argued were outdated. But the main problem, it asserted, was the Clinton administration's naive faith in global cooperation and its over-reliance on international institutions, especially the United Nations. Because Clinton had allowed America to become weak, the authors said, he had allowed such security threats to grow worse.

Such arguments had served conservatives well during the Cold War, and some hoped there would be political benefits in dusting them off. The idea of a threat was also the kind of big tent under which various factions of the political right could gather. Yet despite their ambitions, the National Policy Forum's leaders, like PNAC's founders, knew that by trying to turn the focus to national security, they were going against the tide—not just inside their own party, but among most Americans as well.

When asked about the significance of the National Policy Forum's emphasis on stopping the proliferation of weapons of mass destruction, Bolton counseled "not to make too much of it." Few conservatives outside the national security community were paying attention, and it was hard to get people motivated. One way to do so was by continuing to talk forcefully about threats and vulnerabilities. As Schmitt explains, the United States "had a rare opportunity in history to use our power with our democratic allies to shape the security environment for us and others. But liberal democracies don't gear into action unless threatened."[49]

Yet what were the dangers? These conservatives were not focused on economic crises in Mexico or the one that would emerge in Asia in 1997. Instead, in its early policy briefs, PNAC stressed the generic challenge of U.S. weakness, especially in defense. By the end of 1997, its members seized on specific security threats, including weapons proliferation, the rise of China, and the menacing problem of Iraq.

AS A RALLYING EFFORT, PNAC's emphasis on fulfilling America's global responsibilities through strong leadership and standing up for democratic ideals could have wide appeal. But the organization's manifestos contained a glaring omission, one standing in stark contrast to the Clinton administration's focus in the mid-1990s. PNAC did not mention any aspect of globalization, for the U.S. economy or its security. If anything, it derided such thinking by criticizing the tendency to pursue the "promise of short-term commercial benefits [that] threaten to override strategic considerations." Instead, PNAC's principles represented a more traditionalist, defense-oriented approach to measuring American power and asserting influence, reminiscent of Republican policies during the Cold War. The signatories reflected this tradition. Despite their deep experience in the defense community, none had the global economic stature Rubin and Summers possessed.

Yet looking back, one finds a certain degree of overlap between

PNAC's broader message and the argument Clinton and Albright were trying to make at that time about America's leadership. Other than the lionizing of Reagan and the demands for drastically higher defense spending, there was a lot about this agenda with which the Clinton team would have agreed. To be sure, there were often significant differences in prescriptions for policy execution. But they found common ground on many policy specifics, such as NATO enlargement and intervention in the Balkans. At a broader level, both were pushing back against the impulse inside the political parties and throughout the country to turn away from the world's problems or to decline responsibility. And both were driven by the belief that because of its tremendous power and ideals, the United States had a unique role to play in the world. "Madeleine's 'indispensable nation' was not so different from what we were saying," Schmitt says.[50]

For Albright and her colleagues, however, it was one thing to assert that the United States was an indispensable nation and quite another to deal with that as an everyday reality. They were faced with organizing American foreign policy around that principle—and dealing with the consequences.

The rest of the world, including several close U.S. allies, did not embrace the indispensable nation idea. There was more chatter in Europe and elsewhere about Washington throwing its weight around. The French started complaining about American "hyperpower," and the German foreign minister accused the United States of "lacking in sensitivity." Albright grew indignant at the criticism, recalling that "some thought the term arrogant, but I didn't intend it that way. . . . I did not mean to suggest that we could simply go it alone." She had used the phrase, as had Clinton, to thwart isolationist tendencies at home, but foreigners heard "indispensable nation" differently.[51]

By the end of 1997, the secretary of state found that the rhetoric was backfiring in a way that made global cooperation harder, and she confided to colleagues her concern that perhaps they had taken the language too far. She remarked that in her previous life as a Georgetown professor, the question would have been a good one to study in a course on political science theory. Yet her current job did not afford such luxuries. In the coming months, Albright and the Clinton team were forced to confront a range of challenges that deepened the sense of threat—especially at the nexus of outlaw states and weapons of mass destruction—and tested the abilities of an American-led international system to meet them.

CHAPTER SEVEN

"Remembering the Past and Imagining the Future"

T HE PRESIDENT sat somberly at his desk in the Oval Office. After a long day of continuous meetings, he took a sip of water and reviewed his remarks one last time. Then the red light atop the camera illuminated, and he looked straight ahead, into the faces of millions watching in America and across the globe: "Good evening. Earlier today, I ordered America's armed forces to strike military and security targets in Iraq. . . . Their mission is to attack Iraq's nuclear, chemical, and biological weapons programs and its military capacity to threaten its neighbors. Their purpose is to protect the national interest of the United States, and indeed the interests of people throughout the Middle East and around the world. Saddam Hussein must not be allowed to threaten his neighbors or the world with nuclear arms, poison gas, or biological weapons."

As the president spoke to the nation during prime time, more than 200 U.S. Tomahawk land attack missiles (known as TLAMs) rained down on buildings in Baghdad and on Iraqi Republican Guard fortifications, and viewers watched live televised images of explosions and antiaircraft fire illuminating the night sky. U.S. Navy jets from the carrier USS *Enterprise*, backed by British Tornado fighters, bombed their targets, as an armada of over twenty American warships in the Persian Gulf readied what military planners promised would be a relentless assault. Ever defiant, the Iraqi leader called on his people to stand strong and "fight the enemies of God, enemies of the nation, and enemies of humanity."

For the third time in seven years, the United States was taking military action against Iraq. The decision had been more than a year in the making and was not uncontroversial—in fact, it sparked tremendous public debate. Some believed it was unnecessary. Others thought it was long overdue. A few loud voices argued that it was a cynical move meant to undermine the president's political opponents. Around the world, some countries decried the move as another example of American militarism and a lone superpower out of control. Instead of leading a broad coalition like that assembled for Desert Storm, the United States entered the conflict largely alone, with its loyal ally, Tony Blair–led Great Britain, by its side. At home and abroad, many worried about the consequences of what using force meant not just for the president's political standing, but also for America's global leadership and its ability to confront other problems.

Yet the president barreled ahead, making clear his certainty. "Heavy as they are, the costs of action must be weighed against the price of inaction," he said. "If Saddam defies the world and we fail to respond, we will face a far greater threat in the future. Saddam will strike again at his neighbors. He will make war on his own people. And mark my words, he will develop weapons of mass destruction. He will deploy them, and he will use them." There was no hesitation in the president's voice.

Considering such bold assertions and the dramatic show of force, many might think this could only have been George W. Bush in March 2003. But it was actually Bill Clinton, more than four years earlier.

THE MOST SUBSTANTIAL American military action in the Gulf since Saddam Hussein's capitulation in 1991, Operation Desert Fox in December 1998 was the culmination of the Clinton administration's confrontation with Iraq. Since Clinton had entered office, Saddam had been a constant irritant for American policy-makers, doing his best to skirt obligations placed on him by United Nations resolutions and to break the will of the fragile international consensus supporting them. The relationship had assumed a predictable rhythm—Iraqi defiance escalating into a diplomatic struggle punctuated by an American military strike. Yet the problem only seemed to grow worse. In six years, Saddam had gone from being defeated and diminished to once again becoming one of the Middle East's dominant figures. Despite being pummeled in Desert Storm, Iraq's army was still the region's largest. As tensions spiraled, most national security experts both inside and outside the U.S. government—as well as those in Europe and elsewhere—became convinced the Iraqi dictator had some kind of weapons of mass destruction (WMD) program and every intention of developing it further. Few doubted the need to contain Saddam's ambitions; the question was whether the danger Iraq posed would ever cease as long as he remained in command.

The struggle over Iraq affected all sides of the American foreign policy debate. For the Clinton administration, it meant accepting that the Iraq problem persisted, despite hopes that Saddam would be overthrown or at least change his behavior after years of economic and political sanctions. For Republicans in Congress and outside the government, it meant no relief from the second-guessing about whether the Gulf War had ended too soon, and continued discussion about how much support they should lend a Democratic president whom they could never accept as commander-in-chief. For supporters of the United Nations, it was a crushing blow to their dreams that the institution could be the steward of a new global order, especially as a way to handle threats like WMD proliferation. And for the growing ranks of those across the political spectrum convinced of the need to remove Saddam from power, the question became not whether the United States should instigate regime change, but when and how.

The journey by which the United States arrived at this point in 1998 set the terms for the bitter debate about Iraq that unfolded five years later. With the benefit of hindsight, after the 2003 invasion and costly U.S. occupation, it is easy to see how the arguments about Iraq have consumed the political discourse and transformed the discussion about America's role in the world. But while these debates have taken on a new intensity, their origins stretch back to the 1990s. What to do about Saddam's ambitions to develop weapons of mass destruction was not a challenge that emerged in the years after 2001; it was a legacy of 1991 and the war that, in many respects, had never ended. This history is essential to understanding both the rationale asserted for the 2003 invasion, as well as the views of those who chose to advocate for and support the George W. Bush administration's actions. It is also a cautionary tale about the capabilities of the United States to perceive, measure, and prepare for a new generation of threats.

The Tit-for-Tat War

In many ways, Operation Desert Fox brought Clinton's Iraq policy full circle from where it had begun in January 1993. In the week before Clinton's inauguration, while most of Washington focused on the transition to the first Democratic administration in twelve years, U.S. military forces stepped up their confrontation with Hussein. On January 13, more than 100 American, British, and French fighters bombed Iraqi air-defense targets; five days later, forty-five TLAMs launched at sea destroyed a factory that had been a key part of Iraq's nuclear program. These attacks were followed by further jet-fighter air strikes the next day. Clinton fully supported these moves by the outgoing Bush team, which was shifting U.S. strategy away from the overwhelming military force used in the Gulf War to a gradual increase in pressure on Iraq through tit-for-tat exchanges.[1]

The justification for these bombings was Saddam's continuing defiance of the numerous strictures the U.N. Security Council had placed on his behavior. Since the Gulf War's end, the Iraqi leader's control over his country had been curtailed by a complex web of Security Council resolutions, backed by crippling economic and political sanctions that were enforced by the United States and its allies. These included forcing the Baghdad regime to fully disclose and dismantle its weapons programs, adhere to comprehensive international inspections, and end the repression of its people, namely the Kurd and Shia populations. American jet fighters protected these people by patrolling roughly 40 percent of the country in no-fly zones, areas in which the Iraqi air force was forbidden to operate. It was unprecedented for the United Nations to place such tight legal constraints on a sitting leader's power, in effect, contesting Iraq's sovereignty and seeking to change the nature of its regime without occupying the country. But this reflected the ambition that the institution could shape the behavior of bad actors and enforce a new international order.

As early as 1991, it had become clear to Washington officials that Iraq's adherence to U.N. rules was unimaginable as long as Saddam remained in power. Acceding to the United Nations' demands would have meant a degree of transparency and loss of control that was completely incompatible with the nature of his tyrannical rule. The Iraqis soon began to thwart the U.N. inspectors, making their jobs difficult (by stranding them at sites or slashing their vehicle tires) or simply impossible (by denying them access to sites). In private conversations with his Gulf War partners, President George H. W. Bush shared his concerns about Saddam's defiance. In July 1992 he told French President François Mitterrand, "We believe Iraq is still concealing dozens of Scud missiles and its biological weapons program, for example. If Iraq is able to preserve its weapons of mass destruction, much of what we worked for and fought for will be undermined."[2]

With each violation, Iraq's behavior was duly noted in a complaint to the U.N. Security Council. At times Saddam egregiously crossed the line—such as by locking inspectors out of a suspected weapons site—and military tensions escalated. But American officials knew that complete cooperation would not be possible so long as Saddam was calling the shots. Just a few months after the Gulf War ended, a top Bush official, Deputy National Security Adviser Robert Gates, said Saddam was "discredited and cannot be redeemed" and that sanctions would be lifted "only when there is a new government." To hasten this process, Bush authorized a covert CIA campaign to "create the conditions" to remove Saddam from power, dedicating as much as $40 million to the program.[3]

*

THIS WAS THE policy the Clinton team inherited, and an early mistake forced the new president to confirm the approach just days before he took office. As a candidate, Clinton had criticized the Bush administration's handling of Iraq—arguing that it had failed to deter Saddam from invading Kuwait in the first place—and decried Bush's policy toward the Kurds in the days immediately after Desert Storm, asserting that the United States had not done enough. Clinton's running mate, Al Gore, had been one of Congress's most vocal critics of Bush's postwar decisions and had stepped up his criticisms during the campaign. In September 1992, Gore delivered a blistering speech detailing a litany of Saddam's atrocities, accusing the Bush team of "appeasement" prior to Iraq's invasion of Kuwait. He said Iraq was pursuing a "sustained, concerted effort" to develop weapons of mass destruction. Given this rhetoric, it was reasonable to expect, as some did, that the incoming team would be tougher on the Iraqi despot than its predecessor had been.

On the same day Bush initiated air strikes, President-elect Clinton, in a wide-ranging interview with the *New York Times*, inadvertently made front-page news by suggesting that it might someday be possible for the United States to have a normal relationship with Saddam. "I am not obsessed with the man," he said. "I always tell everybody I am a Baptist. I believe in death-bed conversions. If he wants a different relationship with the United States and the United Nations, all he has to do is change his behavior." The comments sparked a firestorm of criticism. Clinton's critics saw this as an early sign of his wobbliness, and the next day he recanted the statement. "There is no difference between my policy and the policy of the present administration," the incoming president said.[4]

In the White House, the Democrats continued the three-pronged approach toward Iraq: working to maintain international consensus to enforce the U.N. Security Council resolutions, quietly supporting plots to undermine Saddam's power, and responding to the regime's defiance with selective military attacks. Although dissatisfied, American policy-makers were confident that, for the moment, these policies worked to contain the Iraqi threat. But in the months and years ahead, officials questioned how sustainable containment could be—would their strategy of tit-for-tat exchanges, in which a crisis escalated until Saddam backed down, in fact lead to a lasting solution? Following the January 1993 air strikes, some officials already had their doubts. As the *New York Times* reported, "Some Bush and Clinton aides said there was a danger that if matters continued at this level, Mr. Hussein could eventually dictate the pace of the confrontation and gradually win more sympathy," eroding the international community's will to keep the Iraqi strongman in his box.[5]

IT TOOK less than three months for Clinton to learn firsthand how Saddam liked to drive events. In April 1993, George H. W. Bush joined his family and friends, including James Baker, on a visit to Kuwait to be honored for his leadership during the Gulf War. On the last day of the trip, Kuwaiti officials stopped a plot to assassinate Bush with a massive, 175-pound truck bomb. The suspect was an Iraqi national, and the Kuwaitis soon traced the conspiracy to Baghdad and officials in Iraq's intelligence services. In Washington, Clinton ordered the CIA and FBI to investigate, and in the meantime he began to ponder how to respond to a regime that had just tried to kill his predecessor.

Once the evidence was gathered, Clinton decided that this provocation warranted a tough response. He ordered an air attack, and on June 26, twenty-three American TLAMs flattened the Iraqi intelligence headquarters in Baghdad. Since the strike took place in the middle of the night, few Iraqis were killed. At a time when the administration's relationship with the military was off to a rocky start, this decision stood out as an occasion where the decision-making process worked remarkably well (Colin Powell later told Clinton that it was "great"). Some of the president's political advisers grumbled about the downsides, but Clinton barely wavered. "I felt that we would have been justified in hitting Iraq harder, but Powell made a persuasive case that the attack would deter Iraqi terrorism," Clinton recalled.[6] For the new Democratic team and the military leadership, this was the perfect scenario for the rookie president's first use of American military power—a retaliatory strike in response to a brazen act by a known enemy that risked no U.S. casualties. Few subsequent decisions would be as clear, but Clinton had proved he was willing to use force to send a message to Saddam.

THE EFFORT to keep the Iraqi leader in his box required steady vigilance. For a time he receded from the scene, allowing tensions to simmer, quietly testing the limits of the international community's patience. Because the U.N. Security Council required regular reviews of Iraq's compliance with its resolutions, Saddam's cooperation was watched constantly (so much so, U.N. Ambassador Madeleine Albright observed later, that it was consuming the council's work, making it harder to focus on other issues). Yet soon enough, the Iraqi leader did something that forced a response.[7]

In the fall of 1994, he demanded that the United Nations lift sanctions, and to force the issue he deployed 80,000 troops near the Kuwaiti border. To deter a repeat of Iraq's August 1990 invasion, the Clinton administration reinforced the U.S. military presence in the Gulf with about 50,000 troops, including an aircraft carrier battle group and hundreds of aircraft. This display of American might—known as Operation Vigilant Warrior—forced Saddam to back down, but just to play it safe, the United States kept 5,000 troops in Kuwait. A year later, after the Iraqi leader conducted another surprise troop move, American reinforcements went again to Saudi Arabia, Kuwait, and Jordan.[8]

As a result of these efforts, the United States maintained a sizable force in the Persian Gulf. In addition to the troops in Kuwait and the naval presence, the United States stationed military personnel in Saudi Arabia and Turkey to enforce the no-fly zones over northern and southern Iraq. As many as 20,000 American troops were stationed around Iraq. Although such deployments had been welcomed immediately after Desert Storm, they began to breed resentment, especially in Saudi Arabia. Muslim extremists used the basing of American forces in the land of Islam's holiest sites as a rallying cry to rail against the Saudi kingdom. And soon Americans became the target of attack.

In June 1996, a suicide terrorist detonated a truck bomb at the Khobar Towers, a residential complex for U.S. Air Force personnel in Dhahran, Saudia Arabia. The blast killed nineteen and wounded more than seventy. At the end of that summer, al-Qaeda leader Osama bin Laden issued his first fatwa, calling on all Muslims to join a jihad to expel the United States from Saudi Arabia. The American military presence in the Gulf—although designed to contain Hussein—gave sustenance to those bent on twisting Islam to meet their own agendas; this was, as Zbigniew Brzezinski has described, the "original sin" of U.S. policy in the Middle East after Desert Storm, and it had grave consequences.[9]

Two months after the Khobar Towers bombing, Saddam launched another offensive inside Iraq that forced his fourth confrontation with the Clinton administration in less than four years. This time he attacked the Kurds in the north, as his forces captured a key town and threatened to sweep into the entire Kurdish area. The Kurds were under the protection of the northern no-fly zone, imposed in 1991 by Operation Provide Comfort; Saddam's action also violated the U.N. Security Council Resolution prohibiting him from repressing his people. Clinton's military planners readied another response, although this time they were constrained because neither the Saudis nor the Turks allowed U.S. planes to launch air strikes from their territory. (The Saudis were worried about Islamic extremists in the wake of Khobar, while the Turks were wary of anything that might help the Kurds.) So on September 3, Clinton again ordered a cruise missile strike, sending forty-four TLAMs against air defense targets in southern Iraq.[10]

THIS LATEST military showdown occurred in the middle of Clinton's reelection campaign against Bob Dole and revealed how the domestic politics of the Iraq debate were beginning to change. When Clinton's national security team briefed him on the plans for the TLAM strike, after a campaign rally in his hometown of Little Rock,

Arkansas, he displayed a level of confidence that had been missing years before. He was now more comfortable as commander-in-chief, tackling issues with an enthusiasm that once was reserved mainly for domestic politics. As one account describes the scene, "Clinton became so animated as he debated how to contain Saddam Hussein that he might as well have been talking about how to take away electoral votes from Bob Dole in the South."[11]

For the Republicans, this September 1996 confrontation with Iraq illustrated a different story. Throughout the previous several years, each provocation from Saddam served as a painful reminder that Bush had not taken him out when he had the chance. This left Republican politicians defensive. Most stayed away from the subject, and their party's policy manifestos, including the 1994 Contract with America and the 1996 National Policy Forum's *Agenda for America*, hardly mentioned it. Moreover, the fact that Clinton was essentially continuing the policy he had inherited from his predecessor made his actions hard to condemn. Although on the campaign trail Dole's first response to the September 1996 strike was to criticize Clinton, the senator quickly retreated and said "without hesitation or reservation" that he supported the troops who were enforcing the president's action.[12]

Yet Dole's shift exposed a growing fissure among conservatives that would only become more apparent over time. On one side were those who defended the Bush administration's decision not to overthrow the Iraqi leader and, in a sense, backed Clinton's approach. Brent Scowcroft was perhaps this perspective's most adamant defender. "We recognized that the seemingly attractive goal of getting rid of Saddam would not solve our problems, or even necessarily serve our interests," the former national security adviser wrote in the pages of *Newsweek* a few weeks after the September 1996 raids. By leaving the Iraqi leader in power in 1991, he argued, "we pursued the kind of inelegant, messy alternative that is all too often the only one available in the real world." In this way, Clinton was pursuing the most prudent course. "For the foreseeable future," Scowcroft argued, "a successful and sustainable—if unsatisfying—policy is likely to share the same objectives as the one we have followed since the end of the Gulf War: relegating Saddam to the category of nuisance and preventing him from reemerging as a threat to his neighbors or our vital interests."[13]

As Saddam's defiance continued, the containment strategy began to raise more serious questions. Among its most influential critics was Paul Wolfowitz, an architect of Desert Storm who as a senior Pentagon official had been uncomfortable with the way the Bush administration had handled Iraq after the war, particularly concerning the plight of the Shia and Kurds. Although he had spent the past several years defending Bush's decision not to take down Saddam, his emphasis began to shift to what to do moving forward. Wolfowitz began to get to know Iraqi exiles, including Ahmed Chalabi, who were working with CIA funds (the covert program that Bush had begun continued under Clinton) to try to organize an internal opposition to challenge Saddam. While a top adviser to the Dole campaign, Wolfowitz felt liberated to criticize Clinton's policy. He blasted the administration for allowing the Gulf War coalition to grow weaker and for "betraying" the Kurds by not acting more forcefully, belittling Clinton's "pinprick" attacks. But importantly, he also began to stress the threat from Iraq's unconventional weapons programs, arguing that "Saddam is a convicted killer still in possession of a loaded gun—and it's pointed at us." The only way to deal with such a danger, Wolfowitz asserted, would be to go beyond the containment strategy and confront the Iraqi dictator once and for all.[14]

Few supported Wolfowitz's hawkish line at the time, although it gathered adherents in the coming months. With each of Saddam's provocations, the consensus behind the containment strategy grew weaker, both at home and abroad. This was true among Republicans outside government and on Capitol Hill; it was also the case inside the Clinton administration. It became harder to maintain unity in the U.N. Security Council to keep the pressure on Saddam through economic sanctions as the images of Iraqi suffering combined with the prospects for doing business with Iraq led some countries (especially Russia and France) to question the wisdom of maintaining the embargo. At the same time, new revelations about Iraq's programs to build chemical, biological, and nuclear weapons showed the depth of Saddam's deceptions and proved his willingness to thwart U.N. weapons inspectors, leading some officials to ask whether containment was indeed too passive a policy to deal with such a threat.

As the Clinton team prepared for four more years in office, the Iraq situation was proving immensely frustrating. The United States had fallen into the very trap that some had worried about at the beginning of the administration, with Saddam dictating events by provoking confrontations. Officials knew their policy was flagging, and they were becoming increasingly worried that Saddam was not simply a regional nuisance, but with his weapons programs, a real danger to American national security.

The 1996 transition papers for Albright on Iraq make these frustrations clear: "Our policy of containment is time-consuming, fraught with repeated crises, and costly to maintain in terms of our relationships," one memo reads. "The repeated confrontations with Saddam Hussein's regime and the loss of momentum from the Gulf War have led to containment fatigue within the international community." Another State Department memo explains that the second-term administration therefore needed to devise "a strategy to bolster our Iraq policy . . . we need to determine whether there is more to do to accelerate Saddam's departure, whether more can be done to consolidate the coalition, or whether we can envisage beginning Iraq's rehabilitation." Yet Clinton and his senior advisers remained unsure whether it was worth upsetting other priorities and key allied relationships to confront him. Nearly six years after Desert Storm, U.S. policy was at a crossroads. As one transition memo makes clear, the only certainty was that "in the prevailing international and domestic political environment, Iraq will continue to require regular, high-level attention to maintain our leadership of the coalition."[15]

Slouching toward Overthrow

While American policy-makers deliberated, Saddam stayed true to form and forced the issue. By the autumn of 1997, the Iraqi leader was again placing restrictions on U.N. weapons inspections and demanding that all the American inspectors be kicked off the teams (he claimed they were spies, which the United States denied). Since the U.N. inspections program had been put in place after the Gulf War, its mission—to verify Saddam's disarmament—seemed deceptively simple. Many anticipated that this would require only a few months of work. But as the years went by, a clearer picture emerged of the massive breadth of Iraq's weapons programs at the time of the Gulf War. In 1991, Iraq's WMD capabilities, including a nascent nuclear program, went far beyond what American intelligence analysts had believed the country possessed. Because of the extent of Saddam's efforts to conceal them, the inspectors' work became the flashpoint for Iraq's confrontation with the international community.

Given this history and the intelligence reports they received, the Clinton team became convinced that Iraq had weapons of mass destruction and had every intention of developing more. So they began to ratchet up the pressure. They demanded that U.N. inspectors be allowed free and unfettered access to all Iraqi weapons sites, including those Saddam had tried to declare off-limits. To show his resolve, Clinton ordered another buildup of U.S. military forces in the Gulf. His advisers also worked to make the public case for confrontation. For the first time since the Gulf War, American officials took to the airwaves to try to seize control of the issue, making a strong case about the Iraqi threat—and preparing the ground for a serious showdown.

Their aim was to raise awareness about the dangers of Iraq's WMD capabilities. One of the more gimmicky (but memorable) attempts to do so came when William Cohen, the centrist former Republican senator from Maine who replaced William Perry as Clinton's secretary of defense, went on a Sunday morning television show and held up a five-pound bag of sugar to illustrate the danger posed by the anthrax Saddam declared he had. "If this amount could be spread over a city, let's say the size of Washington, it would destroy at least half of the population." He also held up a small vial that could hold VX nerve agent, explaining that Iraq had produced four tons and that "a single drop will kill you within a few minutes." Cohen went on to catalog the details of Iraq's weapons programs, arguing that "this is a global threat, potentially, that he is seeking to generate."[16]

Such rhetoric and props did get the American people's attention about the Iraqi menace. But that begged the question: What would the United States do about it? Cohen's answers reflected the administration's divisions. He stressed that containment, not regime change, remained the U.S. policy, yet also admitted that the threat would never cease as long as Saddam remained in power. In conversations with her colleagues, Albright fumed about the predicament. "If I could take this regime out, I would," she said. But she also knew that America's options were limited. "I don't want to be trigger-happy, but I don't want to be played for a fool either."

The Clinton team again found itself grappling with the difficult trade-off between maintaining a policy backed by as strong an international consensus as possible and implementing measures to protect America's security interests, even in defiance of prevailing global opinion. As events careened toward a more substantial military clash, many administration officials had a sense of déjà vu from earlier crises, including the interventions in Haiti and Bosnia, which had presented similar choices. But they also saw an important difference. As Strobe Talbott explained at the time to his colleagues, "In those earlier showdowns, we faced similar go/no-go moments of truth . . . but [we] had assembled coalitions that we were fairly confident would hold, and we were pretty sure we'd either force the bad guys out (Haiti) or into a corner where we could control them (Bosnia). I'm not sure either of those conditions obtains here."

No one was contemplating anything like a U.S. invasion of Iraq, but even a stepped-up military action carried risks. The worry was that as tensions escalated and the United States continued to threaten military force, the country would face a choice between humiliation or a Pyrrhic victory. If an attack weakened Saddam but he remained in power, America would be more isolated and on the defensive. Given such a scenario, Talbott asked, "Have we looked sufficiently hard at the downside of what may well end up having to be unilateral American action?"

AMONG A GROWING number of conservatives, the answer to Talbott's question was clear: Even if the United States had to act alone, the costs of inaction far outweighed the costs of action. They agreed with the case the Clinton team was making about the threat Iraq posed. But they believed that Saddam's behavior had already gone too far. They began to speak out more forcefully, saying that the administration had to change course and actively seek Saddam's overthrow, not sit back and wait for it to happen. The Sunday before the secretary of defense went on television with his bag of sugar, Wolfowitz and his former Bush Pentagon colleague Zalmay Khalilzad penned an article in the *Washington Post* with the provocative headline WE MUST LEAD THE WAY IN DEPOSING SADDAM. They criticized Clinton's approach, arguing that one reason the international coalition was splintering was that "our partners do not see U.S. policy leading anywhere." What was needed, they asserted, was a "comprehensive strategy" comprising mainly diplomatic and covert measures to promote a new regime. In that strategy, they stressed, "military action will need to be part, but only a part and not the main part."[17]

The year before, Wolfowitz had been a lonely voice inside Republican circles declaring containment dead and pushing for a tougher line. Now the consensus was moving his way—not just because of events in Iraq and Saddam's unrelenting defiance, but because the issue provided a powerful political weapon with which to bludgeon the Clinton team.[18] Wolfowitz's ties with opposition leaders such as Chalabi had become closer. The Iraqi exiles continued to receive millions in covert CIA funds and established good relations with some Clinton administration officials (including John Hannah, who had been a senior adviser to Warren Christopher at the State Department and later became a top national security aide to Vice President Dick Cheney). But they became frustrated with Clinton's tepid approach and began to forge closer partnerships with Republicans.

Working with Wolfowitz, Richard Perle, and others, they created a sophisticated and vigorous campaign to lobby Capitol Hill and conservative think tanks to force a more confrontational approach.[19] By 1998, those at the Project for a New American Century had embraced the overthrow argument, issuing their first open letter to Clinton on Iraq. Until then, like most conservative policy outlets, the organization had spent little time on the subject. The vast majority of PNAC-sponsored writings concerned issues such as China, NATO enlargement, and the Balkans. But the January 26, 1998, letter was the first of seven letters or "project memoranda" on Iraq that PNAC issued that year alone.

With eighteen signers, including Wolfowitz, Khalilzad, William Kristol, Robert Kagan, Donald Rumsfeld, Richard Perle, Richard Armitage, Robert Zoellick, and former Clinton CIA Director James Woolsey, the PNAC letter has become infamous, considered by some as a kind of Rosetta stone for the events that would unfold during the second Bush administration. Yet the letter very much reflected the moment: It did not dispute the premise outlined by the Clinton team about the threat from Saddam, but like Wolfowitz and Khalilzad's op-ed, it went a step further by declaring containment "dangerously inadequate" and calling on the administration to discard the U.N. inspections effort and instead focus on regime change. The PNACers reprinted the letter in full-page ads in the *New York Times* and *Washington Post* to put additional pressure on Clinton. A small group of signatories also went to the White House to discuss their ideas with Sandy Berger and other Clinton officials.

"IF WE'RE SERIOUS about WMD being the biggest threat to the twenty-first century," the president said to his aides as he considered another buildup of troops in the Gulf, "we've got to be ready to use force." As conservatives plotted on the outside, Clinton and his top advisers spent the first months of 1998 dealing with yet one more Saddam-provoked crisis that threw into question the viability of the U.N. approach. Once again, the Iraqi dictator prevented the inspectors from doing their work, and the Clinton team found the U.N. Security Council deadlocked (mainly because of the opposition of Russia and China, who as permanent members wielded a veto over U.N. actions) about whether it should use military means to compel him to cooperate.

The administration believed it had all the U.N. Security Council justification it needed with the resolutions already on the books. So it worked to rally allies including Britain and France, as well as key Gulf countries, in support of a sustained bombing campaign. The Clinton team still hoped for a diplomatic solution but were worried they would once again fall victim to Saddam's rope-a-dope strategy. In one White House meeting, Gore, who had remained consistently tough on Iraq, explained what he described as the "nightmare" scenario: that Saddam would give them a "phony concession and back off just enough until we are forced into another crisis, and he keeps doing this over and over until we run out of steam." So they decided that if the Iraqi leader would not allow the United Nations access to his weapons sites, the United States would destroy them. "If we're going to do it, we might as well do it big," Clinton said.

The president and his top advisers also stepped up their efforts to convince the American people of the need for a possible military move against Iraq. During the past several years, the Iraqi threat had been diminished in the minds of many Americans. If anything, Saddam had proved to be an adept propagandist, portraying the Iraqi people's suffering under the U.N. economic sanctions regime (he of course did not highlight how he worked to siphon off humanitarian assistance to build opulent palaces for himself). The push to lift Iraqi sanctions had become a popular movement, and while it hardly became a major political force, it became a loud presence among some political activists, on college campuses, and overseas.

IN MID-FEBRUARY 1998, Clinton went to the Pentagon, where the Joint Chiefs of Staff briefed him for forty-five minutes on the war plan for Iraq. It was rare for the commander-in-chief to travel across the

Potomac River for such a session, and Clinton's trip was meant to convey the seriousness of the moment. After his meeting in the secretary of defense's dining room, he delivered a speech to make the case for action. Flanked by his senior military and civilian leaders, Clinton couched the choice they faced on Iraq as one of "remembering the past and imagining the future." Thrusting his pointed finger in the air for emphasis as he detailed the history of Saddam's defiance, he argued that this track record made the threat clear. But what was most remarkable about Clinton's speech was what he said about the future, placing the challenges posed by Iraq within the broader context of the transforming world and the opportunities—and dangers—that came with it.[20]

"This is a time of tremendous promise for America," he told his Pentagon audience and those tuning in live on television and radio.[21] "The superpower confrontation has ended; on every continent democracy is securing for more and more people the basic freedoms we Americans have come to take for granted. Bit by bit the information age is chipping away at the barriers economic, political, and social that once kept people locked in and freedom and prosperity locked out. But for all our promise, all our opportunity, people in this room know very well that this is not a time free from peril, especially as a result of reckless acts of outlaw nations and an unholy axis of terrorists, drug traffickers, and organized international criminals." Describing these "predators of the twenty-first century," Clinton explained that they "feed on the free flow of information and technology . . . and they will be all the more lethal if we allow them to build arsenals of nuclear, chemical, and biological weapons and the missiles to deliver them." The clearest example of this kind of threat, the president asserted, was Saddam's Iraq. "His regime threatens the safety of his people, the stability of his region, and the security of all the rest of us."

In this sense, Clinton was stating that how the United States and its allies handled Iraq would set an important precedent for similar dangers in the future. And in an argument Americans would hear again four years later, the president connected the WMD threat to terrorism. "In the next century," Clinton continued, "the community of nations may see more and more the very kind of threat Iraq poses now—a rogue state with weapons of mass destruction ready to use them or provide them to terrorists, drug traffickers, or organized criminals who travel the world among us unnoticed." Therefore, Clinton asserted, the stakes could not be higher—both in the severity of these threats as well as the potential for greater global cooperation to meet them. He continued: "If we fail to respond today, Saddam and all those who would follow in his footsteps will be emboldened tomorrow by the knowledge that they can act with impunity, even in the face of a clear message from the United Nations Security Council and clear evidence of a weapons of mass destruction program."

"If we look at the past and imagine that future," the president concluded, "we will act as one together. And we still have, God willing, a chance to find a diplomatic resolution to this, and if not, God willing, the chance to do the right thing for our children and grandchildren." By invoking the Almighty, Clinton was putting the onus for a peaceful solution on the Iraqi dictator—and preparing the nation for war.

The Pentagon speech encapsulated many familiar Clinton themes: the opportunities of the globalizing world, from the spread of democracy to the potential for greater cooperation, as well as the dangers that globalization presented, such as the threat from weapons of mass destruction, the menace of rogue states, and nonstate actors such as terrorist groups. But the speech was notable because it was one of the first in which he tied the themes together into a coherent narrative to explain the choices facing the United States and its allies. He did not use the phrase "indispensable nation," but the speech made an important statement about America's global role: It must rally the world behind a problem that no single country could solve alone. His remarks also reflect the constraints on forging a common solution when not everyone believes there is a common problem. If other countries did not agree to confront Saddam—or, to borrow Clinton's words, see the future the same way—he made clear that the United States would act alone. Although the president stopped short of embracing the demands of those calling for Saddam's ouster, he made a compelling case for why the United States needed to take the lead to confront Iraq.

IT WAS ONE thing for Clinton to make such an argument, quite another to get the American people to accept it. This was true even within the president's own political party. Like economic and trade issues, the Iraq debate revealed a deep gulf between the Clinton administration and the political left. Many liberals had opposed the Gulf War and were not enthusiastic about a Democratic reprise. Perhaps no event illustrated this more vividly than a free-for-all town hall meeting Clinton's national security team—Secretary of State Albright, National Security Adviser Berger, and Secretary of Defense Cohen—participated in the day after his Pentagon speech.

They wanted to take their case directly to the American people. So on a chilly day in the Midwest, they ventured out to Ohio State University's St. John Arena, where for ninety minutes they took questions from an audience of 6,000 Americans and tried to explain why the United States might have to use force if diplomacy failed. They had asked CNN to moderate and televise the debate because the network's international audience—estimated that day to be as many as 800 million people in more than 150 countries—was believed to include Saddam, whom they hoped to impress with a show of American unity and resolve. Instead, the Iraqi leader and the rest of the world watched as the gang from Washington was shouted down, hooted, and booed from the get-go.[22]

After a questioner demanded to know why the United States wasn't using force against other human rights violators elsewhere, hecklers repeatedly interrupted Albright as she attempted to respond. "One, two, three, four! We don't want your racist war!" the protesters screamed at the officials onstage. The Washington policymakers were unaccustomed to the rough-and-tumble of politics, and they had completely underestimated the bitterness. Visibly angry, Albright finally blurted out, "I am really surprised that people feel that it is necessary to defend the rights of Saddam Hussein, when we ought to be making sure that he does not use weapons of mass destruction." The secretary of state recalled trading worried looks with her two cabinet colleagues onstage as they asked themselves, "What the hell are we doing here?"

Meanwhile, others in the crowd feared the Clinton team wasn't going to be tough enough. A man wearing a Veterans of Foreign Wars cap rose to say he had lost a son and a nephew in Vietnam and had "stood in the gap" for twenty years proudly wearing an American military uniform himself. "If push comes to shove and Saddam will not back down," he wondered, "are we willing to send the troops in and finish the job or are we going to do it half-assed?" Rather than talk about sending troops, Cohen rambled on about his recent visits to American aircraft carriers and tried to reassure those who did not support major military action, saying, "We do not see the need to carry out a large land campaign in order to try to topple Saddam Hussein."

Albright remembered the raucous event as a "fiasco." When asked about it years later, Berger visibly winced at the memory. But in an interview after the town hall meeting, he tried to put the best spin on the situation. "I don't think for a second," he flatly stated, "that [Saddam] can or should think that 40, 50, 200 people in a room of 6,000 reflect the will of the American people or are in any way going to influence the president of the United States. Ultimately there's only one man who decides, and he decides not based on the polls or on forty screamers, but on our national interest."[23]

Watching this unfold on television from his command headquarters in Tampa, Florida, Marine General Anthony Zinni—who would lead American forces in any attack against Iraq—sat in stunned disbelief. "It was the most stupid political theater I have ever witnessed," he says. Republican Congressman John Boehner (later the Republican leader in the House) said that "this is a matter of global security and international peace, and they turned it into the Oprah Winfrey show." After the debacle, Albright recalled, the mere mention of the words "Ohio State" would shut down anyone inside the administration who came up with a "harebrained scheme" to get their message out.[24]

But for the Clinton team, the lesson of Ohio State was about more than public relations; it illustrated the deep skepticism many Americans still had about a military confrontation with Saddam Hussein. Although public opinion polls showed most Americans would support a military strike, the opposition's intensity could not be dismissed. So Clinton and his advisers were hammered from both sides: the increasingly larger numbers on the right who favored overthrowing Saddam, and those on the left who questioned whether Iraq was really a threat.

LIKE PAST CONFRONTATIONS, the February 1998 crisis abated when Saddam negotiated another agreement with U.N. Secretary General Kofi Annan to allow for some inspections. However, with every deal Saddam cut, the drumbeat to discard retaliatory strikes for the sustained use of force grew louder.

By midyear, the conservative position had hardened further, with influential voices calling for a major military campaign—including American ground forces—to take down the Iraqi regime. In May, PNAC released its second open letter on Iraq, this time urging congressional leaders to pressure Clinton to use American military power to "occupy liberated areas in northern and southern Iraq" and to prepare to use force for regime change. Even Richard Lugar, the well-respected and moderate Republican senator from Indiana, began to argue that "a credible program for the removal of Saddam Hussein [is] going to involve U.S. ground troops in due course. . . . Ultimately, there's likely to have to be some ground action, or at least a credible threat of that, for that regime to change." With a growing political consensus behind overthrow, that autumn Congress passed and Clinton signed the Iraq Liberation Act, codifying the aim of regime change into U.S. law and authorizing nearly $100 million in Pentagon funds to support the Iraqi opposition.[25]

Saddam's acts of defiance continued. In November 1998, he again kicked out U.N. inspectors, forcing the Security Council into another corner. Unable to come up with a common position—the divisions among the five permanent members had rendered the council dysfunctional—the United States teed up another military campaign in the Gulf. This time the administration cocked the trigger, only to stop short after another last-minute concession from Saddam. The American and British planes in the air headed to Iraq were ordered to turn back. Those officials who had argued strongest for using force—especially Gore and Albright—were outraged that the administration had been shown up again and were determined that this be the last time. So when the Iraqi leader reverted to playing games with the weapons inspectors a month later—kicking all of them out of the country for good—the United States launched the mission it had aborted just weeks before, Operation Desert Fox.[26]

THIS CRISIS ERUPTED at an uncomfortable moment for Clinton and all Americans. At home the president was in the fight of his life. The debate about Iraq was overwhelmed by a Washington scandal. The very evening Clinton ordered American forces into combat, December 16, the Republican-controlled House of Representatives was preparing to impeach him over his relationship with White House intern Monica Lewinsky. For days the president had maintained an inhuman pace of meetings, shuttling between his national security team and the lawyers and political advisers plotting his strategy for the inevitable impeachment and Senate trial.

Some top officials worried about the timing of the strikes given impeachment, but Clinton's Pentagon advisers urged him to act. "Our word is at stake," Cohen told the president during a meeting in the White House Situation Room. The defense secretary's advocacy proved critical. As a former Republican senator, he could credibly explain to skeptics that the attacks had nothing to do with politics. "If you don't act here," Cohen said to Clinton, "the next argument will be that you're paralyzed."[27]

Although many Republicans in Congress had been agitating for a military strike and arguing that Clinton was too passive in the face of the Iraq threat, many now argued that his use of force was just some stunt to divert attention away from his troubles at home. "I cannot support this military action in the Persian Gulf at this time," said Republican Senate Majority Leader Trent Lott. "Both the timing and the policy are subject to question." Echoing these remarks, House Majority Leader Dick Armey argued that "the suspicion some people have about the president's motives in this attack is itself a powerful argument for impeachment. After months of lies, the president has given millions of people around the world reason to doubt that he has sent Americans into battle for the right reasons." And Florida Republican Representative Tillie Fowler declared, "It's certainly rather suspicious timing. I think the president is shameless in what he would do to stay in office."[28]

Such rebukes to a commander-in-chief with forces in combat were unusual. They were also politically dangerous, and some, including Lott, later issued statements of support for the troops. But these reactions reflected the depth of conservative hatred for Clinton. Of course, a few leaders did support the president's move. Newt Gingrich proudly recalls that the year before, he had delivered to Clinton a sixteen-page plan detailing how to overthrow Hussein, and he says he spoke to the president about Iraq on the day of the impeachment vote.[29] But the turmoil caused by the presidential scandal far overshadowed the use of force against Iraq.

Purposeful Drift

Desert Fox represented a departure for American policy in several respects. In the previous attacks, targets had included only suspicious weapons facilities—this time most of the targets were directly related to Saddam's command and control over the country, such as military barracks, airfields, and communications centers. These strikes sought not only to fulfill the president's stated objective—degrading Iraq's WMD capacity—but also to debilitate the dictator's hold on power, sending a more powerful message to him and giving hope to his regime's opponents.

But Desert Fox was not being used as a coercive measure to force Saddam to comply with any demands. The administration believed the credibility of the United Nations was being destroyed by Hussein's brazen flouting of Security Council resolutions, but it did not demand that the Iraqi dictator allow the inspectors back in (the administration said only that it would "welcome the return" of the inspectors). The attacks were designed purely to punish and weaken Saddam. Air Force General Joseph Ralston, vice chairman of the Joint Chiefs at the time, recalls that the goal was to set Iraq's WMD programs back at least two years, which was deemed accomplished after four days of strikes.[30]

With this act, the Clinton team brought an end to the policy of trying to disarm Iraq through U.N. inspections. "After the attack we had no way to know how much of the proscribed material had been destroyed," Clinton recalled in his memoirs, "but Iraq's ability to produce and deploy dangerous weapons had plainly been reduced."[31]

IT WAS AN inconclusive finish, leaving the administration with the unsatisfying choice of trying to maintain containment or pushing harder for regime change. Senior military leaders held out the possibility that the United States might have to hit Iraq again in several years, after he rebuilt from the 1998 strikes. Containment could keep the pressure on Saddam and restrict his ability to wield power. But as Berger explained in a December 1998 speech at Stanford University, the Clinton team knew the strategy was not "sustainable in the long run, [because] the longer the standoff continues, the harder it will be to maintain the international support." The policy also carried significant costs, from the threat of Iraq producing weapons of mass destruction, to the suffering of the Iraqi people and the fraying of relations between the United States and its allies. Even worse, Berger explained, containment created a "false perception of a conflict between Muslims and the United States." For all these reasons, the Clinton team concluded that Saddam had to go. As the president himself said publicly after Desert Fox, "so long as Saddam remains in power he will remain a threat to his people, the region, and the world," and the best way to end that threat was for "Iraq to have a different government."[32]

Therein lay the problem. While containment neared the point of total collapse, the administration had no appetite for bearing the costs and consequences of a full-scale invasion and occupation of Iraq to overthrow Saddam. Furthermore, at the same time the United States was containing Iraq, it was also trying to contain Iran—and it had to be careful not to take action against Iraq that might empower its neighbor.

So the Clinton administration crafted a policy that tried to have it both ways: continuing to contain Iraq with sanctions and military pressure through the no-fly zones and a sizable force presence deployed throughout the Gulf, while devising ways to undermine Saddam's power through covert means and support of the Iraqi opposition. In effect, the United States conducted a low-level war against Iraq. Iraqi air defenses would routinely track U.S. fighter patrols with their radar, providing the pretext for retaliation. American jet fighters fired more than 1,000 missiles against some 300 Iraqi targets (three times as many as were attacked during Desert Fox) during the first eight months of 1999 alone, and the administration appointed a senior official to help work with Iraqi exiles, such as Chalabi. This policy, known as "containment-plus," unfolded largely out of the public eye and with little debate (in part because in the years after the Gulf War, America did not suffer a single combat casualty in Iraq). It was a way of buying time in the hopes that different circumstances might allow for more decisive action.[33]

Those Clinton officials who contemplated ways to undermine Saddam knew they could go only so far. Regime change remained the official policy, as well as the law of the land as codified by the Iraq Liberation Act. But the administration's approach to Saddam ended up as a policy described by one official as "one yes and two nos": yes, they would seek regime change; no, they would not try to walk back the policy; but no, they would not get into another war in the Gulf. Or as Clinton's deputy national security adviser, James Steinberg, admits, "We wandered around on Iraq. We had a reasonably prudent policy. The politics made our rhetoric more robust, but we did not contemplate using force to change the regime."[34]

Top officials believed their approach had a short shelf life, but in their remaining time in office, other priorities, such as ending repression in Kosovo, negotiating peace between Israelis and Palestinians, and fighting al-Qaeda, took precedence. The president did not want an Iraq strategy that would threaten every other policy initiative, blowing the circuits with America's allies and others around the world. As Albright remembered, "Clinton recognized, as did I, that the mixture of sanctions, containment, Iraqi defiance, and our own uncertainty about Saddam's weapons couldn't go on indefinitely."[35]

"The Clinton administration was just looking to play defense on Iraq," explained Kenneth Pollack, the National Security Council staff member assigned to work on that country. In the administration's waning days, Pollack's boss, Berger, told him that while they would not solve the Iraq problem, they "had a responsibility to leave the next administration with a viable Iraq policy, not a mess. It would be up to that administration to decide what to do."[36]

FOR CLINTON'S Republican opponents, as well as those hawks inside the government, Desert Fox's end left an alarming void in American policy. For them, "containment-plus" was nothing more than an ugly punt—a policy of not having a policy. They saw it as the worst of all worlds: Saddam kept his hold on power, and for the first time since 1991, he could do whatever he wanted out from under the watchful eyes of U.N. inspections. As Kagan wrote in the *Weekly Standard* after Desert Fox, "The bombing proved, if further proof were needed, that the administration has no strategy either for 'containing' Saddam or removing him."[37] Critics such as Perle thundered that it would leave to the next administration a legacy of weakness and vacillation: "pinprick military strikes that served principally to bolster the myth of Saddam's invincibility; endless negotiations aimed at restoring United Nations inspections on terms acceptable to Saddam and his friends on the Security Council; and a willingness to accept Saddam's rule in Iraq which has demoralized his opponents and undermined resistance in the region."[38]

Working with these outside agitators, some Republican leaders in Congress and hawkish Democrats such as Connecticut Senator Joseph Lieberman tried to push the administration to take a tougher line. They wanted Clinton to do more to supply Iraqi opposition figures or make new demands on Saddam. But inside the White House, there simply wasn't the will to go any further. What to do about Iraq illustrated an important cleavage in the debate about the nature of American power and the boundaries of what it could achieve. For many conservatives, U.S. power was not something to husband; it had to be used. But liberals were more mindful of limits. "Clinton was genuinely worried about biological and nuclear weapons," Gingrich reflects, but "he also had a real sense of the limitations of American power."[39]

Clinton and his team agreed that Iraq remained very dangerous. Yet they thought the bombing had sufficiently set back its weapons capabilities. And for them, part of being the indispensable nation meant having patience, using American influence to rebuild an international consensus behind a policy. "We knew we would have to deal with Saddam Hussein," recalls Leon Fuerth, a top aide to the vice president whom many expected would have been national security adviser in a Gore administration. "We knew we couldn't coexist with him, but we needed to give him enough rope to hang himself."[40] Few Clintonites were eager to pursue a risky policy unilaterally with little chance of success—especially given the price they would pay in terms of other priorities. Considering the choices they faced, a policy of purposeful drift seemed better than the alternatives. That decision in hindsight seems particularly wise, now that Americans have found catastrophe in Iraq.

Although Saddam was a tyrant, the Clinton administration contemplated military action against him only to uphold the no-fly zones and to contain his ambition to build weapons of mass destruction. They had no intention of using force to bring freedom to Iraq. In the Balkans, however, Clinton and his advisers had developed an appetite to use American power to confront dictators and protect suffering populations. They had saved the Bosnian Muslims in 1995, and only three years later, they were contemplating military action to save yet another ethnic minority from the wrath of Serb leader Slobodan Milosevic.

A Postscript

No discussion of America's approach to Iraq during these years is complete without addressing what we all now know: When the United States invaded Iraq in 2003, it found no weapons of mass destruction. From the immediate days after Desert Storm, through the Clinton years, into the George W. Bush administration, and during the lead-up to invasion in 2003, the premise of U.S. policy—that Saddam's ambitions to build WMD could not be stopped—was wrong. All the assumptions made, claims asserted, and dangers voiced about the extent of Iraq's weapons programs were incorrect.[41]

Since 2003, the discussion about what the United States knew about Iraq's weapons programs has been dominated by assertions of crass partisanship and dark conspiracies, assuming the policy was based on a bed of lies knowingly told by American policy-makers to fulfill some other, usually nefarious agenda. Given that the truth inside Iraq turned out to be so different from what was being described, many believe the only explanation is a web of deception. To be sure, many of the claims made about Iraq—especially those made by the second Bush administration—were grossly exaggerated and irresponsibly stripped of any uncertainties. But the extent of the intelligence failure, of course, is far more worrisome.

The U.S. intelligence community (and, to be fair, every major intelligence service in the world) and the policy-makers it served had been duped by Saddam for over a decade on an issue that is para-

The end of an era: U.S. President George H. W. Bush and Soviet President Mikhail Gorbachev sign an agreement during their final Washington summit in 1990. For decades, superpower summits had been defining moments. A year and a half later, the Soviet Union was gone.

June 8, 1991: General Norman Schwarzkopf salutes George H. W. Bush at the Gulf War victory parade. Hundreds of thousands of people jammed Washington's streets to celebrate the returning troops and, Bush hoped, a new world order.

After his November 1992 election defeat, President George H. W. Bush plans for military intervention in Somalia with his top aides, including, from left, National Security Adviser Brent Scowcroft, Defense Secretary Dick Cheney, Vice President Dan Quayle, and General Colin Powell. By the time Bush left office, over 20,000 U.S. troops would be on the ground pursuing a humanitarian mission his successor would inherit.

President Bill Clinton agonizes over a decision with Defense Secretary Les Aspin and Secretary of State Warren Christopher. During the 1992 presidential campaign Clinton's mantra had been "it's the economy, stupid," but once in office he had to deal with a series of foreign policy problems that engulfed the first year of his presidency.

March 12, 1993: President Clinton addresses the sailors and pilots of the USS *Theodore Roosevelt*. Clinton's first visit to a warship at sea was dominated by media accounts of his troubles as commander-in-chief—whether because of his lack of experience or uproar over his policy toward gays in the military—embedding a perception of presidential weakness.

After the Gulf War, the U.S. continued to use its military power to punish Saddam Hussein. On June 26, 1993, Clinton ordered missile strikes against Iraq in retaliation for its attempt to assassinate George H. W. Bush. Here the president prepares to announce his decision to the nation, while his political adviser George Stephanopoulos looks on.   RIGHT   Pat Buchanan and Ross Perot. Both men shaped the politics of the 1992 campaign—Buchanan by wounding Bush in the Republican primaries, and Perot by winning 19 percent of the vote in the general election—and they remained influential voices on global trade, especially by opposing NAFTA.

Anthony Lake hoped the end of the Cold War would enable Democrats to reunify on foreign policy, and he sought to devise a new strategy to replace containment. As Clinton's first national security adviser, he used a September 21, 1993, speech at Johns Hopkins to outline a doctrine of "democratic enlargement." The phrase never caught on.

The first crisis of the twenty-first century. President Clinton and his advisers meet with top Congressional leaders at the White House to discuss the controversial proposal to help stabilize Mexico's economy with billions of U.S. dollars. From left, Warren Christopher, House Speaker Newt Gingrich, Clinton, Senate Republican Leader Robert Dole, Treasury Secretary Robert Rubin, and his deputy Larry Summers. Foreground from left, House Democratic Leader Dick Gephardt, Vice President Al Gore, and Senate Democratic Leader Tom Daschle.

Francis Fukuyama and Robert Kagan. These two thinkers influenced the foreign policy debates among conservatives: Fukuyama by describing an "end of history" and Kagan by joining with William Kristol to call for a "neo-Reaganite" foreign policy.

Bill Clinton and Al Gore waged fierce battles with the Republicans over foreign policy, but often found common ground with their two principal political adversaries, Bob Dole and Newt Gingrich. Here the four seal an agreement in the Oval Office.

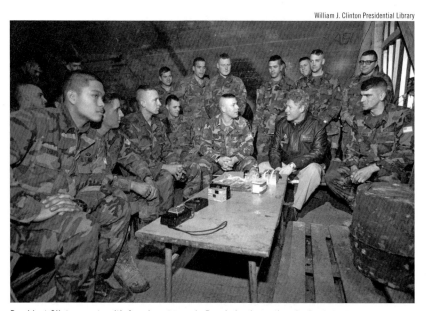

President Clinton meets with American troops in Bosnia implementing the Dayton peace agreement. Despite his early stumbles, Clinton's interventions in the Balkans helped instill confidence about his leadership and strengthen relations with the military. Yet critics decried such policies as "social work."

After his 1997 election, British Prime Minister Tony Blair became President Clinton's closest international ally—some in Britain were already calling him America's "poodle." Shown here in the Oval Office, the two leaders advocated for using force in the Balkans, punishing Iraq's Saddam Hussein, and working to revitalize progressive governance with a global "Third Way."

In December 1998, the U.S. conducted four days of airstrikes against Iraq in Operation Desert Fox. Announcing the end of the campaign, Clinton and his national security team explained the ongoing threat from Iraq. "So long as Saddam remains in power he will remain a threat to his people, the region, and the world," Clinton said. From left, Chief of Staff John Podesta, Secretary of State Madeleine Albright, Al Gore, Secretary of Defense William Cohen, Joint Chiefs Chairman Hugh Shelton, and National Security Adviser Sandy Berger.

Just three months after the attacks on Iraq, the U.S. and its NATO allies launch a massive air campaign to end Slobodan Milosevic's repression in Kosovo. As Clinton and his top aides discussed military strategy in the Oval Office, concerns about America's "hyperpower" grew abroad.

Jesse Helms visits the United Nations Security Council. Despite hopes that the United Nations would play a more important role after the Cold War, by the end of the 1990s the institution was politically tainted and financially on life-support as the U.S. withheld millions in dues. Senator Helms (left) forged an unlikely alliance with U.N. Ambassador Richard Holbrooke (right) to help put the U.S.-U.N. relationship on solid footing.

Dick Cheney at the 2000 Republican National Convention. The former defense secretary had excoriated fellow Republicans in 1993 for failing to give prominence to foreign policy, and he retreated from politics when his message went unheeded. In 2000 he was back as George W. Bush's vice-presidential nominee, promising the military that "help is on the way."

George W. Bush and Al Gore debate at Wake Forest University. In the most detailed foreign policy discussion of the 2000 campaign, Bush argued that the U.S. needed to be a "humble" nation while Gore asserted that the country should have "a sense of mission about the world." Both men accused the other of being stuck in the Cold War.

President-elect George W. Bush and outgoing President Clinton share a light moment during their December 2000 meeting in the Oval Office. They discussed a range of foreign policy issues. "One of the great regrets of my presidency is that I didn't get him [Osama bin Laden] for you, because I tried," Clinton told Bush.

September 12, 2001: The War on Terror begins. President Bush plans the response to the 9/11 attacks with his war cabinet. From left, Defense Secretary Donald Rumsfeld, Secretary of State Colin Powell, Vice President Dick Cheney, Joint Chiefs Chairman Hugh Shelton. Back row, from left, national security aide Stephen Hadley, Cheney adviser Scooter Libby, Rumsfeld deputy Paul Wolfowitz, Powell deputy Richard Armitage, White House adviser Karen Hughes, General Richard Myers, and White House spokesman Ari Fleischer.

mount to the future of America's security: the spread of weapons of mass destruction. This is not just the responsibility of a single administration or a small group of individuals from either side of the political aisle; it represents a systemic failure of the entire American national security community on an issue that has dominated its attention since the end of the Cold War.

Usually intelligence failures are ones of omission—failing to forecast that an adversary will do something, such as when the Japanese attacked Pearl Harbor, when Iraq invaded Kuwait, or when al-Qaeda launched the 9/11 attacks. Concerns about Iraq were reinforced when inspectors discovered after the Gulf War that Saddam's weapons programs had been far more advanced than anyone had thought. The fact that such revelations came from defectors or involuntary inspections only added to the suspicion that the Iraqi government had something to hide (in fact, up until the 2003 war, Saddam's own henchmen thought Iraq had such capabilities). So the intelligence failure in Iraq was one of commission—concerned that they would be proved wrong, for twelve years the intelligence community and policy-makers always thought the worst and never adequately probed their assumptions. Not once did they thoroughly investigate whether Saddam had unilaterally destroyed his weapons stocks in 1991 and was simply trying to dupe the international community to preserve his hold on power and keep his enemies guessing.[42]

Throughout their years in office, senior Clinton officials based their claims on a stream of intelligence reports detailing the Iraqi menace. Heavily researched assessments, backed by what were judged to be solid sources, painted a picture of a grave and growing threat. Their titles, including one from 1997, "Iraqi Biological Weapons Program: Well Positioned for the Future," or two from 2000, "Iraq: Steadily Pursuing WMD Capabilities" and "Iraq: Rebuilding a Chemical Weapons Production Capability," conveyed the seriousness of the danger.[43] According to CIA Director George Tenet, the information from these reports later became the spine for the influential October 2002 National Intelligence Estimate in the lead-up to the 2003 war.[44]

Some officials recall having reasons to second-guess what they were reading and hearing. "Up until Desert Fox, I believed that [Saddam] had WMD," says Anthony Zinni, the Marine general who commanded the air assault and who emerged as a leading skeptic of calls to overthrow the Iraqi government. "Then Clinton said we would bomb the WMD sites. I asked the intelligence community for the targets, but they couldn't give me any. Nothing they gave me was definitively a WMD target. They were all dual-use. That's when my doubts began."[45] But since the evidence of weapons development seemed so overwhelming, these suspicions never became more than quiet qualms. Because the Iraqi leader kicked out U.N. inspectors in 1998, American officials assumed he was hiding something. And even if Saddam's capabilities weren't as advanced as suspected, few doubted that he had every intention to develop WMD if given the chance.

Today, Republicans use this fact to defend themselves against the criticisms of how they justified the Iraq War. "If you go back and look at what Clinton had been saying and you took it seriously," Gingrich says, "it makes George W. Bush look a lot more rational."[46] To be sure, from 1991 to 2003, there was a large degree of consensus across the political spectrum, among policy experts and intelligence officials, that Iraq possessed weapons of mass destruction and was determined to develop more. But there were significant differences over the degree of the threat—meaning, how much time the United States had before Iraq posed an imminent danger—as well as over the means of dealing with it. And there were profound disagreements about how the United States should approach any military campaign and what it should expect if it occupied the country. On this last point, the intelligence community's estimates have proven to be tragically prescient.[47]

FROM THE DAY Saddam's army rumbled into Kuwait in August 1990, through the present, the history of America's tangle with Iraq represents both the soaring hopes and tragic flaws in the debate about new global threats and the ideas about U.S. power after the Cold War. The success of Operation Desert Storm in 1991 generated optimism for a "new world order" shaped around cooperation among major countries and a revitalized United Nations. Yet the way the war ended—with Saddam still in power but constrained by a range of U.N. Security Council resolutions—set the seeds for more than a decade of tension and conflict. Remembering the past, historians will ponder this story's lessons for decades. But as Americans imagine the future, they will grapple with the war's consequences for generations.

CHAPTER EIGHT

Liberal Bombs, Conservative Shields

I T HAD BEEN a bad weekend. As Bill Clinton's senior national security team shuffled into the Oval Office for a Monday morning meeting—the day before April Fools' Day, 1999—the nervous looks on their faces said it all.

American and European warplanes were again waging war. For four days, they had been conducting an around-the-clock attack on the police and military forces of Slobodan Milosevic's Serbia, trying to halt a ruthless assault against ethnic Albanian men, women, and children inside the Serb province of Kosovo. Having tussled with Milosevic through the years, and after watching him fold during the Dayton negotiations over Bosnia, Clinton's advisers thought the Serb leader would back down after a few days of intense bombing. But instead of surrendering, Milosevic escalated the conflict, accelerating his efforts to force hundreds of thousands of people from their homes and even shooting down a U.S. F-117 stealth aircraft, one of the military's most sophisticated planes. Clinton and his team had planned for a quick campaign, like the attack on Iraq three months earlier in Operation Desert Fox. Yet now they faced a war with no end in sight.

In past situations when the use of military force did not go as expected—in Somalia, in the first Haiti intervention, in Bosnia, and even at times in Iraq—the president responded with outrage, anxiety, and blame. But this time, rather than worrying about the costs to his political prospects and complaining about being ill-served—which his aides were bracing for—Clinton greeted his team with a pep talk, displaying a kind of steely confidence his top advisers weren't expecting. "Guys, let's not lose sight of why we did this," he said. "Let's not forget what prompted us to do this and who is responsible."

For days the administration had been roundly criticized and second-guessed by politicians on both sides of Capitol Hill and in the media for its conduct of the campaign. Some thought the administration was not doing enough (by refusing to prepare for a ground invasion), while others believed the bombing had already done too much damage (especially in the harm it had inflicted on Serb civilians). Clinton told his aides he was willing to take the political hit, arguing that this was what presidential capital was for. Perhaps because he had been impeached and put on trial by the Senate just weeks earlier over his affair with Monica Lewinsky (he had been acquitted by the Senate on February 12), Clinton had a degree of resolve about the political risks he was running. What more could his opponents do to him? He reminded the group that they had a plan and said they needed to be patient and stick to it. "It's my war, and we're going to see it through to the end," Clinton reassured them.[1]

THE KOSOVO CONFLICT was not something Clinton had inherited or stumbled into. It was a campaign he had led from the start to stand up to one of the world's most troubling dictators, Milosevic, and end the repression of the country's minority Albanian population. The Serb leader had emerged as a kind of European version of Saddam Hussein, a strongman who ruthlessly clung to power and who stoked regional instability. For more than a year U.S. and European envoys had tried using diplomacy to influence Milosevic, yet eventually they concluded that only force would work. Like the American air strikes against Iraq, the attacks on Kosovo split and incapacitated the U.N. Security Council, making many around the world nervous about the untethered use of U.S. power. However, instead of going it alone, Clinton now led the eighteen other countries in NATO to prosecute the war. During the Cold War, NATO had stood ready to combat an assault by the Soviet Union. Now, a decade after the fall of the Berlin Wall, NATO was going into battle for the first time—and not because an enemy had attacked its members.

Kosovo was a tiny, impoverished Balkan province tucked away in a far corner of southeast Europe, so its security was hardly a vital U.S. national interest. Milosevic had been a destabilizing presence for years, but he was not supporting terrorist operations against America or its allies, seeking to acquire weapons of mass destruction, or sitting on huge oil reserves. Using military force to stop his behavior was clearly a war of choice. Yet Clinton and most of his European counterparts believed that stopping Serbia's violent tyranny over its own minority citizens, the Albanian Kosovars, would not only help ensure a more peaceful continent but also establish an important—and to some, controversial—precedent for the future. These leaders were rewriting the rules for how the international community would respond to a government that refused to stop repressing its own people. They had not stepped in to prevent genocide in Rwanda; this time they would seize the opportunity to right a new wrong.

During the second week of April 1999, Clinton described the importance of this effort at a public forum in the White House's East Room, featuring remarks by Nobel laureate and Holocaust survivor Elie Wiesel. This was one of a series of open meetings to discuss ideas and events as the world approached the millennium, and the occasion found Clinton in a reflective mood. After Wiesel's speech on "the perils of indifference," in which he praised the action against the "crimes against humanity" in Kosovo, Clinton took the floor to comment. Asking the audience to think about Wiesel's message, the president explained his actions in Kosovo in terms of the current historical moment and the sweep of a globalizing world. "At the end of the twentieth century," he said, "it seems to me we face a great battle of the forces of integration against the forces of disintegration; of globalism versus tribalism; of oppression against empowerment. And this phenomenal explosion of technology might be the servant of either side, or both." Given this struggle, Clinton argued that the indispensable nation must help lead the world to address what he described as the "central irony of our time"—that as people came together in so many ways, they were still endangered by a combination of two elemental traits: ethnic hatred and widespread indifference.

As the president explained, "Most of us have this vision of a twenty-first-century world with the triumph of peace and prosperity and personal freedom; with the respect for the integrity of ethnic, racial, and religious minorities; within a framework of shared values, shared power, shared plenty; making common cause against disease and environmental degradation across national lines, against terror, organized crime, weapons of mass destruction. This vision, ironically, is threatened by the oldest demon of human society—our vulnerability to hatred of the other.

"In the face of that," Clinton continued, "we cannot be indifferent, at home or abroad. That is why we are in Kosovo."[2]

FOR ELEVEN WEEKS, American and European jets bombed Serb targets, loosening Milosevic's hold on power and eventually forcing him into submission. The physical costs were significant. Although Milosevic had planned his ethnic cleansing campaign months earlier, the bombing unleashed a rampage by Serb forces against the Kosovars, killing an estimated 10,000 and creating nearly one million refugees. Meanwhile, the attack did considerable damage to civilian infrastructure and buildings throughout Serbia.

Yet this seventy-eight-day bombing campaign, during which nearly 27,000 missiles and bombs were dropped on Serb forces, brought new opportunities for Kosovo. It provided the chance for Kosovars to live without fear of Serb oppression under the protection of NATO and the United Nations (although they were left with a political status that remained unresolved until Kosovo's independence in 2008). Further, the war turned out to be a transformative event for Clinton's national security policy and America's role in the world. Clinton's decision to act in Kosovo—and the means he chose—reverberated in the conduct of American foreign policy and the debate about the use of U.S. military force inside both political parties in the years to come.

To the president and his team, Kosovo showed the importance of using power to stand on principle, working with America's closest allies through NATO to help shape a new international order. Yet abroad, while Milosevic had few friends, American actions stoked worries among allies and adversaries alike about the overwhelming nature of American capabilities, becoming another example of what the French called U.S. "hyperpower." And to the administration's critics on both sides of the political aisle at home, the fight about Kosovo was a warning. For those liberals and conservatives worried about the overextension of American power or the perception of being a global bully, Kosovo was an example of misguided militarism.

Meanwhile, for those who believed in an even more robust U.S. role in the world, the way the war was fought proved troubling. America relied on a multilateral alliance and restricted itself to using air power, believing the insertion of ground troops and risk of casualties would be too politically sensitive and would jeopardize the international consensus. Those who supported the war but criticized the way it was fought feared that the United States would continue to impose restraints on itself in future interventions to keep its allies on board.

The First "Humanitarian War"

Chronologically, Kosovo was the last American-led conflict of the twentieth century. But its supporters believed it could exemplify a new twenty-first-century American way of war: using airpower alone to pummel an adversary into surrendering without suffering a single American casualty from enemy attack (a first for U.S. forces in sustained combat). Significantly, it also marked the first time an alliance of nineteen countries had used its collective military might not to roll back an invasion, thwart an imminent threat, or respond to an attack, but for purposes described as "humanitarian"—to end a sovereign government's repression of its own citizens.[3] NATO had used air strikes in Bosnia to force the Serbs to the negotiating table, but the bombing over Kosovo was the alliance's first real war. Its advocates hoped it would serve as a model for future conflicts.

KOSOVO'S STATUS within Serbia had been contested for decades, and it had long been one of the most dangerous tinderboxes in all of Europe. Since 1989, Milosevic had used alleged discrimination against the minority Serbs in Kosovo as justification for harsher crack-downs, denying the Albanians political and economic rights. Throughout the 1990s, Washington policy-makers worried about the ramifications of an outbreak of violence in Kosovo, believing it would spark a regional conflagration. The Clinton administration followed a policy first presented as a warning to Milosevic on Christmas Day 1992, conveyed in a letter to him from outgoing President George H. W. Bush: The United States stood ready to respond militarily if the Serbs initiated an armed conflict in Kosovo. So while the Clintonites relied mainly on diplomacy to ease the tensions between the Serb government in Belgrade and the Albanians in Kosovo, they did so with this "Christmas warning" in their pocket.

The Serbs had left Kosovo mostly alone while the conflict in neighboring Bosnia exploded. But after Bosnia achieved peace in the mid-1990s, the Kosovars began pushing for greater autonomy and independence, and Milosevic used Serb police and military forces to suppress his opponents. As tensions escalated in 1998, the United States and its European allies stepped up their efforts to increase the pressure on Milosevic, seeking to force him and the Kosovars to the bargaining table.

This culminated in February 1999, when Madeleine Albright and her European counterparts tried to forge an agreement through Dayton-style negotiations held in Rambouillet, France. The peace talks collapsed several weeks later after the Serbs refused to submit to a NATO-led peacekeeping force in Kosovo, arguing that foreign troops in their country would violate their sovereignty. As Milosevic's forces massed near Kosovo in late March, conflict seemed imminent.

Clinton dispatched envoy Richard Holbrooke to deliver a final ultimatum, but the Serb leader refused to budge. (Holbrooke recalls that Milosevic believed the attacks would be limited and short, like Desert Fox.) When Clinton met with his foreign policy team to discuss the options, they knew they could not back down. "Look, let's remember that the purpose of using force is to stop Milosevic-style thuggery once and for all," Albright told her colleagues, arguing that they needed not simply to end the bloodshed but also to send a message to other dictators who might have similar designs. "There is no guarantee that it will succeed, but the alternatives are worse."[4]

When the bombing began in late March, Clinton and his top advisers believed they were defending the principle that a country's government had to be held responsible for how it treated its own citizens. This idea proved controversial at home and abroad, as some saw it as a challenge to the very foundation of traditional international politics: the respect for state sovereignty. The concept that outside powers might together decide to use force to strip a state of its right to govern had started to take shape in 1991, when U.S. forces occupied northern Iraq and established a no-fly zone to protect the Kurds. It had evolved further in 1994 when American diplomatic and military action removed the military junta in Haiti and restored to power the democratically elected president. As Strobe Talbott argued later, "The sovereignty of individual governments is not absolute; a national government that systematically and massively abuses its own citizens . . . is subject to either being put out of business or having its authority suspended in that area of the country where it is running amok."[5]

AMERICANS were not alone in embracing this bold idea, which later became known as the "responsibility to protect." Importantly, in the case of Kosovo, several of Washington's closest European partners supported it, too. Bernard Kouchner, founder of Médecins Sans Frontières and later French foreign minister, had developed the notion of a "droit d'ingerence," or right to intervene. Many of

Europe's leaders had come of age as activists in the political left during the 1960s and 1970s, often decrying the use of force in the context of the Cold War's battles. But now they argued that the world could not look away from repression and human rights violations (especially when they were taking place inside Europe) and that those with the power to stop this also had the responsibility to act. Significantly, several of these onetime leftist revolutionaries and Vietnam War opponents, including German Foreign Minister Joschka Fischer and NATO Secretary General Javier Solana, emerged as leading advocates for intervention.[6]

Yet by far the most influential European advocate for strong action and the person most capable and confident in laying out the rationale for the war was British Prime Minister Tony Blair. Since taking office in 1997, Blair had forged a close relationship with Clinton. As two leaders of the center-left, they shared similar visions of their generation's challenges in the globalizing world and the changing role of progressive governance—or what they called the Third Way. Blair believed deeply in the importance of America's global role, considering it one of his country's most important responsibilities to remain close to the United States, serving as a bridge to Europe and the rest of the world and, at times, working to help shape its behavior as the sole superpower. This approach was not always popular at home, and during Kosovo the British press began to mock Blair as an "American poodle."[7]

At the time, and for years afterward, Blair often served as a more articulate and convincing proponent of U.S. actions than American leaders (often to their great chagrin). A month into the Kosovo campaign, the prime minister delivered a speech in Chicago outlining a new "doctrine of international community" that called for a broader definition of security and a radical overhaul of international institutions, such as the United Nations.[8]

In the sweeping address, which Blair wrote mostly himself, he elaborated on the argument that the international community had a responsibility to act in Kosovo, framing the rationale as defense of liberal values. In the post–Cold War environment, he explained that "our actions are guided more by a more subtle blend of mutual

self-interest and moral purpose in defending the values we cherish."
He called for a "new framework" for global action and said the most
"pressing foreign policy problem" facing the West was how to identify the circumstances in which it should get involved in other people's conflicts, and how such actions would earn legitimacy in the
eyes of the world. Blair was careful to argue that he did not mean that
the United States and its allies should seek to solve every problem or
always intervene. "We would not want to jettison [noninterference]
too readily," he said. But he did sketch a broad framework for greater
global responsibility and strong activism, one he would continue to
promote. As one of the prime minister's leading biographers argued
later, this speech proved to be "an important precursor to Blair's
response to the events of September 11, 2001."[9]

ALTHOUGH THE Clinton team largely agreed with Blair's assessment,
some of them chafed at his efforts to outline these ideas so forcefully.
In part, they weren't thrilled with the perception of being upstaged
by the British prime minister. Clinton was outraged by press accounts
contrasting his wobbly leadership with Blair's steadfast resolve
(reports he thought the British were encouraging). According to a top
Blair aide, at one point Clinton angrily told the prime minister that he
"knew what was going on, it was deliberate, and it had to stop."[10] But
aside from wanting to share credit, Clinton's team was also uncomfortable with Blair's efforts to try to rationalize their actions in Kosovo
as part of some new, overarching doctrine. Although the president
continued his prosecution of the air campaign, he was less sure about
articulating a bold new rationalization for the use of force. Senior
Clinton officials constantly rebuffed efforts to develop a doctrine
(referred to inside the administration pejoratively as the D-word)—
perhaps reflecting the frustrations of the first term in trying to come
up with a catchy new concept to explain the world.

"I am quite distrustful of doctrines," former National Security
Adviser Sandy Berger explains. "They usually emerge from a particular set of circumstances and you get into trouble when you try to

apply them to others." After seven years in office, many of Clinton's advisers had come to believe that actions mattered more than words, a view formed by their previous efforts to articulate bold visions (such as democratic enlargement) while the facts on the ground presented them with tough problems (as in Somalia and Bosnia). "We tried to establish common law rather than canon law," Berger says. "We set out to build a new role for the U.S. in the world by experience rather than doctrine."[11]

In some ways, this approach made sense. The Clinton team wanted to allay other countries' concerns about unrestrained American power as well as reduce domestic pressures against intervention, so chest-thumping rhetoric seemed ill-advised. But by staying away from any public discussion of doctrine, the administration also sent a mixed signal about its intentions, creating confusion and fueling the perception that its policies were ad hoc and lacked a deeper conceptual rationale.

SUCH CRITICISMS were especially strong among those strange bedfellows with whom the administration found itself aligned during Kosovo. At home, the arguments made by Clinton, Albright, and others about the dangers of not standing up to Milosevic were echoed by the small band of thinkers at the Project for a New American Century and by politicians such as Arizona Senator John McCain and former Senator Bob Dole. As they had before on Bosnia, these conservative interventionists supported the administration's use of force, and for months they steadily pursued a public campaign to demand action (including in op-eds and paid newspaper advertisements, cosigned by figures including Zbigniew Brzezinski, Richard Perle, Elliott Abrams, and Jeane Kirkpatrick).[12] If anything, they argued that Clinton should have gone further sooner, using American ground forces and making Milosevic's overthrow an explicit goal of U.S. policy.

But unlike in the Iraq debate the year before, when PNAC and its allies had taken aim mainly at Clinton, the targets of their efforts now were their fellow conservatives and Republicans in Congress. In some ways, this was a return to PNAC's original mission of reversing the isolationist drift on the political right. The arguments over Kosovo ignited the most heated debate among conservatives since the end of the Cold War about the use of force and the purpose of America's global power.

Fighting against those interventionists were Republicans, mainly on Capitol Hill, who warned of the Kosovo "quagmire" and argued that the American military should not be used for "humanitarian" purposes. Writing in the *Weekly Standard*, Robert Kagan and William Kristol described these conservatives as "a rather motley combination of neo-isolationists who simply don't believe the United States should much concern itself with overseas matters not directly threatening the American homeland; of Clinton despisers who don't trust the administration to do any serious thing seriously . . . and of ultrasophisticated 'realist' intellectuals who have divined that America has no interest in the Balkans and who claim that to combat Milosevic's aggression and brutality is merely to indulge in softheaded liberal internationalism."[13]

In several key votes in the Senate and House during the war, a majority of Republicans opposed the use of U.S. ground troops in Kosovo and sought to end the air campaign. These conservatives were careful to describe Kosovo as a "Clinton-Gore War," making clear that they did not support the effort and distancing themselves from its consequences, good or bad. Their views were more reminiscent of Pat Buchanan, who, not surprisingly, was a strident opponent of the war and asserted that "the Serbs had always been our friends." They also evoked the language of the anti-war left; Republican Senate Majority Leader Trent Lott actually implored Clinton to "give peace a chance."[14]

For Republican politicians such as McCain and Senators Richard Lugar and Chuck Hagel (who also supported the Kosovo intervention), the dominance of the anti-interventionist right posed tremendous dangers for the future of conservatism. "I am concerned by what I see as a growing isolationism in the Republican Party," McCain said, explaining that this was fueled in large part by his Republican colleagues' hatred of Clinton but also their declining interest in the world abroad and scant background in national security issues. "Republicans need to stand for something more than predicting, hoping for, and exulting in Clinton's failures," Kristol and Kagan wrote in a May 1999 *Weekly Standard* column. "After all, it's going to be hard to outflank the Democrats on the side of timidity and weakness, although some McGovern Republicans are trying mightily."[15]

Such arguments hardly won them friends within the Republican establishment. Nor did their unabashed praise for Clinton once Milosevic capitulated and the war ended. Kristol and Kagan congratulated the administration and a "small but stalwart" group of Republicans on the victory and asserted that this "might prove to be the most important U.S. foreign policy achievement since the Gulf War." Like the Clinton team, they argued that Milosevic's defeat sent a clear message to other would-be aggressors that the United States and its allies could and would wield their might to punish bad behavior. And it exemplified the purpose of America's power: to serve higher ideals and values. "At the very least, [Kosovo] demonstrated, once again, that American power . . . is a potent force for international peace, stability, and human decency," Kristol and Kagan wrote.[16]

Significantly, Clinton described Kosovo's outcome in much the same way. In a speech during a visit with thousands of Kosovar refugees a few weeks after the war, he said, "We're proud of what we did because we think it's what America stands for, that no one ever, ever should be punished and discriminated against or killed and uprooted because of their religion or ethnic heritage." With such words Clinton reached back to the views more reminiscent of the tough liberalism that had emerged after World War II and that saw American power as both "great" and "good," giving the United States a moral responsibility to act. Such pride was further vindicated a year later, when Milosevic was overthrown by his domestic democratic opponents, arrested, and sent to stand trial for war crimes at The Hague. (He died in prison there in 2006.) Yet even when asked directly by journalists, Clinton still resisted describing such arguments as a doctrine, leading his critics to charge that "in Washington, they still don't actually know what they're doing—even when they do it right."[17]

The Chains of Command

But *was* Kosovo done right? Despite accomplishing its core objective of ending Milosevic's tyranny over the Kosovar minority, the war was derided as "winning ugly," as the title of one book put it. The bombing campaign took longer than expected, the humanitarian costs were significant, and huge tensions emerged between the American military leaders in Europe and those in Washington.[18]

Conducting the air campaign through NATO brought common purpose and legitimacy to the effort. The United States was acting not alone, but with its closest partners, even if the technologically superior American military provided the bulk of the airpower. Standing up to Milosevic was considered critical to maintaining NATO's credibility five decades after its founding. It was the first real test of the "new" alliance Clinton had wanted to create through enlargement, although NATO's new members—Poland, Hungary, and the Czech Republic, which formally joined just before the war began—worried about the new commitments they had assumed. Albright recalled at the beginning of 1999 that Kosovo "was emerging as a key test of American leadership and of the relevance and effectiveness of NATO. The alliance was due to celebrate its fiftieth anniversary in April. If my fears proved correct, that event would coincide with the spectacle of another humanitarian disaster in the Balkans. And we would look like fools for proclaiming the alliance's readiness for the twenty-first century when we were unable to cope with a conflict that began in the fourteenth."[19]

This reasoning struck many as circular: that NATO had to bomb to prove that it would bomb.[20] Also, decisions on everything from timing to targets were harder to make through an alliance than if the United States had been operating alone, because consensus needed to be reached among nineteen allies. The need to maintain NATO unity shaped the course and conduct of the campaign, which proved immensely frustrating for American military commanders. Although the American forces dominated with their stealth aircraft, precision-guided bombs, and cruise missiles, each decision required painstaking negotiation. The United States gained legitimacy by operating through NATO's time-consuming deliberative process, but that cost it somewhat in terms of military efficacy.

NO INDIVIDUAL understood the military challenges in the Balkans better than Army General Wesley Clark, who along with his four stars wore two hats, as head of U.S. forces in Europe and as NATO's commander. Tightly wound, whip-smart, and very competitive, Clark was in many ways the perfect person to lead the campaign against Milosevic. For years he had been deeply involved in Balkan issues; as the chief military official at the Dayton talks on Bosnia, he had met with Milosevic many times and believed he knew what made the Serb leader tick. He was also very close to the senior civilian leaders inside the Clinton administration, especially Albright and Holbrooke. Clark was an activist general who believed in the assertive use of American military power—he had been advocating for the use of force against Milosevic for months. And as a former Rhodes scholar from Arkansas, he had a special affinity with the commander-in-chief that did not go unnoticed throughout the military ranks.

Yet this did not enable Clark just to do what he wanted. Throughout the campaign, he found himself caught in a double bind: At every step of the operation, he had to negotiate decisions with the eighteen other allies at NATO headquarters in Belgium as well as with his superiors at the Pentagon. This often meant that some aspects of the war plans were ill-prepared (such as when the campaign began with too few targets and not enough planes available to conduct the bombing runs) and that decisions to correct them took too long to make.

Perhaps the most controversial decision that Clark and his civilian bosses struggled over was whether to use ground forces. From the beginning of the campaign, Clinton had made clear his intention not to put boots on the ground, believing that the American people would not accept many casualties for a cause that was secondary at best to U.S. national security. This decision "was purely politics," Clark reflects. "Clinton wanted to avoid a huge political problem." The president's closest advisers do not deny this, defending the decision as the right one given the circumstances. Berger argues that "if we had not taken ground troops off the table, we'd have had a fight here and in NATO. But it was also a better strategy. The object of war is to win with the least number of casualties."[21]

This is especially true when the purpose of war is "humanitarian." On the first night of bombing, when Clinton explained in a national address that American ground troops would not be part of the campaign, his words conveyed the self-imposed limits of U.S. power: Kosovo's fate was important enough to go to war for, but not so valuable that the lives of U.S. ground troops should be risked. The military campaign was aimed to achieve bold ends (halting Milosevic's repression) with limited means (no ground troops).

As historian David Halberstam described it, the president's pledge "summed up with surprising accuracy all the contradictions and the ambivalence of America as a post–Cold War superpower."[22] Because Milosevic was not an existential threat and Kosovo itself was not vital to America, the Clinton team felt impelled to conduct the war with as few risks and costs as possible. The conflict would be limited in scope and duration, conducted from the air, and even then the planes would fly at a safe altitude of 15,000 feet. The White House believed such restraint was needed to maintain public support inside the United States and Europe. Kosovo was fought as a war of limited liability, where the use of force would be carefully calibrated to the narrow interests at stake. Critics derided this as intervention "on the cheap," or a "virtual war," a conflict in which precision-guided weapons fired from high above allowed the American people to remain far removed from the costs and pain.[23]

In purely military terms, restricting the way the war was fought made it harder to win. Without ground forces, NATO could do little to stop Milosevic's rampage against Kosovar civilians that triggered a massive refugee crisis. And as the bombing extended from days to weeks to months, it started to look as though the Serb leader would outlast the alliance, forcing it either to escalate with ground forces or to back down. Officials on both sides of the Atlantic began to contemplate the idea that NATO might actually lose. The confidence that Clinton had shown at the beginning of the campaign began to give way to desperate anxiety. In the end, Milosevic caved only after NATO began to prepare for a land invasion (encouraged mainly by Blair and despite Clinton's reluctance) and brought the Russians into the negotiations to help convince the Serb leader that he needed to accept the terms offered him.

Some military generals, such as Clark and Air Force four-star General Joseph Ralston, the Joint Chiefs' number two during Kosovo, believed in the benefits of fighting through an alliance. "Is it hard?" Ralston asks. "Hell, yes! But at the end of the day, what worked in getting Milosevic to back down was that the alliance stuck together." Yet as Ralston admits, for many of America's top military leaders, the lessons of Kosovo were clear: Future wars should be fought in a way that reduced the necessity for seeking consensus with allies. Some viewed the U.S. military's exasperation with alliance politics as evidence of a "Kosovo syndrome," expecting the United States to enter any multilateral operations with greater skepticism, or simply seek to avoid them altogether. This proved to be the case the next time the United States launched a major military campaign, after the 9/11 attacks.[24]

THE PENTAGON'S frustration over Kosovo revealed itself in the fate chosen for the war's commander, Clark. Like U.S. generals Colin Powell and Norman Schwarzkopf during the Gulf War, Clark had become the face of Americans in battle. As the country's most visible military leader, he earned popularity that he sought to translate into a run for president in 2004. Clark's strong advocacy had proven critically important to giving the administration the confidence it needed to launch the air campaign and was invaluable in making the public case for holding firm to achieve the war's aims.

But that was exactly what got him in trouble with his own superiors. Clark constantly butted heads with the Pentagon's leadership, especially with Secretary of Defense William Cohen and Army General Henry "Hugh" Shelton, the chairman of the Joint Chiefs. They grew impatient with Clark's requests for more firepower (including Apache attack helicopters and troops) and his defense of the complex and frustrating NATO decision-making process that he faithfully tried to maneuver. They also resented his frequent contacts with civilian officials (and policy allies) in the White House and State Department, which they saw as circumventing the chain of command. Some of these civilian officials recalled that Clark's Pentagon colleagues simply hated him.

Clark's style could be brusque and demanding. But this tension was about more than personality differences. It reflected unresolved conflicts inside the Pentagon about the use of American military power. Clark was ready to take greater risks, while his superiors were more cautious. Cohen (the only high-level Republican appointee inside the Clinton administration) was said to have come to "rue the day" he had recommended putting Clark in charge of NATO, and the laconic Shelton quickly tired of Clark's restless activism.[25] So when they got their chance, they relieved Clark of duty, forcing him out of his command at NATO (and replacing him with Ralston). Instead of a hero's welcome, he got early retirement.

The Hyperpower Looms

The debate about Kosovo's lessons for future military actions was part of a broader discussion: what the conflict's legacy would be for America's role in the world. Despite the confident gloss with which the Clinton team and those few conservative advocates outside government painted Kosovo's outcome, others saw a very different picture. At home and abroad, the war deepened fears that the United States had become too powerful for its own good. However benign its intentions, the United States seemed imperialistic, provoking a dangerous global backlash. Scholars such as Samuel

Huntington and Garry Wills insisted that Washington's actions were stoking anti-American sentiments around the world.[26] Such concerns were especially acute among political liberals, for whom the Clinton administration's intervention in Kosovo caused a deep rupture. Although the fights inside conservatism between inter-ventionists and neo-isolationists tended to draw more attention, the differences exposed between the camps on the political left were no less important.

Kosovo was a triumph of the "liberal hawks," those foreign policy intellectuals and progressive politicians who believed U.S. military power should be used to uphold moral values and defend human rights. Many liberals who had cut their teeth by opposing the Viet-nam War, American interventions in Latin America in the 1980s, and the 1991 Gulf War emerged as leading proponents of confronting Milosevic. They had been horrified by the West's inaction in Bosnia and Rwanda. In some ways, this showed that liberalism was returning to its hawkish roots in the early Cold War, when America's global role was defined by individuals such as Dean Acheson and John Kennedy. For the first time since Lyndon Johnson left office in 1969, a Demo-cratic president was at war. After years of being on the defensive in debates over national security, now liberals were the ones demon-strating leadership. Journalist George Packer wrote, "For lifelong doves, the first sip of this drink called humanitarian intervention car-ried a special thrill."[27]

Democratic House Whip David Bonior was not afraid to stand up to Clinton when he believed progressive causes were on the line, as he proved during the intense debates over trade. Nor was he typically an advocate for military force. As one of the most liberal members of Congress, the Michigan congressman had been a key Democratic Party leader opposing military action against Iraq in 1991. Yet he was a longtime champion of intervening to protect the Kosovars in the face of Milosevic's aggression. "There are times that we have to use force," he said later, "and Kosovo was one of them." To these liberals, the "never again" argument proved to be a powerful justification. Or as Maxine Waters, a solidly liberal Democratic representative from southern California, argued at the time: "I am not a hawk, not by any stretch of the imagination. . . . However, I vowed that I would never again remain silent in the face of genocide."[28]

FOR THE MORE THAN 1,000 people crammed inside the Leo Baeck Temple in Waters's hometown of Los Angeles, the Clinton administration's military campaign in Kosovo represented something very different. During a five-hour "teach-in" in May 1999 to discuss the war, the crowd of peace activists, progressive journalists, and intellectuals railed against the killing of innocents inside Serbia and what they saw as rampant American militarism. Perhaps few noticed that the man for whom the temple was named, Rabbi Leo Baeck, had helped protect Jews in Nazi Germany and had been deported to the Theresienstadt concentration camp during World War II.

In many respects, the event was reminiscent of a Vietnam-era protest, from the rhetoric to the people on the stage. Tom Hayden, one of the icons of the 1960s anti-war movement who had become a California state senator, decried the "evil" aspects of the Clinton administration's "spin doctors" who were working to "demonize the Serbs, minimize the news of civilian casualties, sanitize the ground troops as only peacekeepers, and hypnotize us into a ground war." The Reverend Jesse Jackson, the civil rights leader who a month earlier had traveled to Serbia during the bombing to try to negotiate peace with Milosevic, urged a search for common ground. Perhaps the most acerbic presentation came from Arianna Huffington, then a conservative commentator but who refashioned herself a few years later as a progressive doyenne. Describing Berger and Albright as dwarves, Huffington asserted that "the NATO commanders and our American leaders are in a kind of autoerotic fantasy world where there is absolute detachment between reality and the world they live in." The crowd roared.[29]

Such outrage drew attention, but it hardly represented widespread domestic opposition to the war. There was no protest against Kosovo on the scale of that mustered against Vietnam or even the Persian Gulf War. For the most part Clinton maintained popular support, although the public's confidence in his handling of the conflict dwindled as the bombing campaign raged on.[30]

The angry discontent about Kosovo that surfaced reflected deep disagreements within the political left about the exercise of U.S. military power specifically and the direction of foreign policy generally. To some degree, the war's opposition showed the enduring, yet relatively small, presence of an anti-war left, many of whom agreed with the arguments of their counterparts on the right. There were predictable criticisms from those such as Noam Chomsky, who decried the U.S. "contempt . . . for the framework of world order," and filmmaker Michael Moore, who complained that "for this 'antiwar' president to order such a misguided, ruthless—and, yes, cowardly—attack from the air is a disappointment of massive proportions."[31]

The fact that a Democrat was in the White House left these voices somewhat muted, but not silent. For those who had opposed Clinton's other military interventions, none of which had involved sustained combat for more than a few days, Kosovo was even harder to take because it lasted nearly three months. Given this, the costs of the air war were more apparent. Although few defended Milosevic's actions, many expressed anger that NATO had punished the Serb people by knocking out power grids and bombing bridges.[32]

Anti-war liberals were also unhappy with the way the Clinton administration had gotten into war, expressing worries about the domestic precedent and the international backlash it would create. As he had done five years earlier in Haiti, Clinton did not seek prior congressional authorization for the war because he wanted to protect the powers of the presidency and worried about Republican opposition. That led some to claim that the war was not subject to a proper public debate. But after the impeachment struggle and the raucous disaster of the Ohio State town hall meeting on Iraq the year before, the administration had not been looking for opportunities to engage its domestic critics in advance of another military intervention.

Clinton also sought to reduce the largest potential global constraints. Although Kosovo was NATO's first war, the Clinton administration purposely avoided seeking U.N. Security Council authorization because of opposition from Russia and China. For the Clinton team, bypassing the United Nations proved that the Security Council did not have a veto over NATO's, and by extension America's, actions. But for domestic opponents on the left and for many leaders abroad, this set the dangerous precedent of a lone superpower thumbing its nose at international law. After the war, a U.N. commission led by former South African president Nelson Mandela concluded that NATO's actions were "illegal but legitimate."[33] Even those who believed the cause was just (including the U.N. secretary general) maintained that the initiation of international conflict should be formally authorized by the Security Council to conform to international law.

The editors of *The Nation*, a flagship opinion journal of the intellectual left, warned after the war ended that the victory was Pyrrhic because "it fueled anti-American anger in Russia, China, and other countries, with negative consequences for disarmament, economic reform, and democratization." In an April 1999 column, the magazine's editors argued that the administration's actions had "once again degraded the U.N.'s authority and marginalized Security Council members Russia and China as actors on the diplomatic stage." This intervention, they continued, "has established new parameters for the United States and NATO to make war without any of the checks and balances provided by U.S. law, international agreements, or even the *realpolitik* of the Security Council."[34] Less than three years later, many of these critics drew a direct line between Clinton's handling of Kosovo and the way the George W. Bush administration approached the world after the 9/11 attacks.

IT WAS NOT as though the Clinton team failed to understand or worry about the global consequences of its handling of the crisis. The greatest mistake of the military campaign, when American planes accidentally bombed the Chinese embassy in Belgrade after erroneous intelligence reported that it was a Serb ministry building, did enormous damage to relations with Beijing. The Chinese ambassador to the United States, Li Zhaoxing, declared on the ABC News program

This Week that the bombing was a "horrifying atrocity, something rarely seen in the entire history of the worst diplomacy." At one of the many protests that sprung up in Beijing, a senior Chinese official remarked, "You were the ideal for so many of us. And now your stupid bombs have killed our people. This could set us back years. This is a perfect justification for slowing reforms, for closing political debate. And it's really your fault."[35]

Meanwhile, the Kremlin's leaders were furious about NATO's air campaign. As Serb allies, they were angry that the administration had neutered their U.N. Security Council veto by bypassing the organization. Russian Foreign Minister Igor Ivanov said NATO's bombing campaign was the worst aggression in Europe since the Second World War. The pro-Western former Russian Prime Minister Yegor Gaidar commented to Deputy Secretary Talbott, "Oh, Strobe, if only you knew what a disaster this war is for those of us in Russia who want for our country what you want."[36]

Moscow officials also worried that the rationale for Kosovo—confronting a regime over its treatment of its own population—could be too easily applied other places, including in Russia itself. (At the time, Russia was engaged in a brutal campaign against the breakaway region of Chechnya.) The Kosovo war threatened to undo all Clinton had accomplished in strengthening ties with America's Cold War adversary. It was a challenging time for the usually close Clinton-Yeltsin relationship. Talbott described Russia's anger as creating the "most severe, dangerous, and consequential crisis in U.S.-Russian relations of the post–Cold War period."[37]

To contain the damage with Russia, the Clinton team worked hard to bring along Yeltsin as a partner to try to end the war, seeking Moscow's help in the negotiations with Milosevic. Yeltsin appointed former Prime Minister Viktor Chernomyrdin to work with Talbott and European Union envoy Martti Ahtisaari to pursue a diplomatic track while the air war continued. Faced with this unified front, Milosevic agreed to the terms of surrender. There were, unfortunately, some harrowing moments in relations with Moscow at the end of the war, such as when a small group of Russian forces left their peacekeeping duties in neighboring Bosnia to lay claim to a key airfield in Kosovo. They eventually backed down in the face of NATO demands, but not before some in the West worried that they were witnessing the outbreak of World War III.

Others thought that, despite the tensions, Kosovo demonstrated the strength of the U.S.-Russian relationship. After all, faced with the choice, Moscow helped Washington end the war rather than helping Milosevic prolong it. Yet Kosovo also proved to the Russians how weak they had become in Europe during the 1990s. The Kremlin could do little to stop the United States or NATO from acting against a Russian ally. After Yeltsin stepped down from office at the end of 1999, the new president, Vladimir Putin, sought to reassert Russia's traditional place in world affairs as a country to be reckoned with.

THE ANXIETIES the conflict produced among many of America's closest friends, including the NATO partners alongside whom it had fought, were also a big concern. Many Europeans complained about the heavy-handed way Washington drove events, and they watched the U.S. military's technological superiority with worried awe. If their own capabilities were so clearly outmatched, they wondered how they could work together with the United States as partners. The Clinton team was unapologetic about its performance but recognized that any boasting could prove counterproductive. "It is possible to fight a war with nineteen nations. It is impossible without intense American leadership at every level," Berger argued. "I never have bought the 'indispensable nation' thing; it has always bothered me because it sounds a little too triumphalist, but when it comes to something like this, America has to lead."[38]

Still, Clinton and his top advisers wondered about how to defend against the backlash that bold U.S. leadership could provoke. In less than six months, the United States had used force against two countries, Iraq and Serbia, with help from a few allies but over the objections of many others. Although it had worked through NATO, it had come under criticism for being arrogant. And after first trying to work through the Security Council to resolve the problems, it had abandoned the United Nations altogether. Washington officials heard the criticisms and worried about the impact. They read the reports that at least two-thirds of the world's people saw the United States as the single greatest external threat.[39] Speculating about how other countries might act to contain American power, senior officials contemplated what more they could do to prevent the United States from being seen, as Berger lamented at the time, as "the biggest rogue state in the world."

The administration set out to understand better the growing anti-American sentiment. That summer, just weeks after the war ended, the State Department initiated a secret effort to assess the implications of Kosovo. In an "action request" cable, it asked each American ambassador worldwide to report home on the wide range of issues the conflict raised in his or her locale.[40]

The cable posed thoughtful and probing questions that revealed the deep sense of concern about the global reaction to the exercise of American power. It asked whether Kosovo was viewed as a just cause for the use of force, or one that only fueled concerns about American hegemony. Were other countries worried that the United States or NATO would now feel free to act militarily against other "Kosovos"? Would ethnic minorities elsewhere be more ambitious in seeking recognition, thinking "the U.S. or NATO would run to the rescue"? Or, by showing the difficulty in taking joint action in response to a country's internal ethnic tensions, did the war "perversely give a measure of comfort to repressive regimes"? In terms of military strategy, Washington wanted to know, would Kosovo actually stoke weapons proliferation, prompting states to seek "advanced arms to guarantee that they don't become like Serbia, remaining defenseless against the U.S."? And from the perspective of America's friends, did Kosovo engender reassurance or raise concerns? "Are our allies confident in U.S. leadership or concerned that they will be dragged into dubious adventures?"

Such introspection is uncommon in American diplomacy. But this effort reflected the unusual moment in which U.S. policy-makers found themselves. The responses to these questions revealed few surprises:

concerns about American power had existed before Kosovo, but after the war, they exploded. The psychology behind this reaction was complex, influenced not just by military concerns but by the American face of globalization. This was especially true in Europe, where worries about specific U.S. policies—on Kosovo, Iraq, trade, or soon, missile defense—were morphing into anti-Americanism in general.

Just a few years earlier, while Bosnia burned, most European leaders were criticizing the United States for showing too little leadership. Now they were upset that the Clinton administration was asserting too much. To address this, the Clinton team did not seek to scale back its ambitions or withdraw from what it believed were America's global responsibilities. But it still needed to find a way to marry its unsurpassed capabilities and unmatched ambitions with a sense of legitimacy; to find the right balance between exercising its unique power and working with the international community to avoid the counterpunches that many experts predicted were coming. The United States had to show that it sought to achieve a greater global good. "What we need is a policy of strategic reassurance," one official said after Kosovo, "a way of demonstrating that not only is this power benign, but that it isn't a zero-sum game."[41]

In the summer of 1999, Americans were just starting to grapple with how the United States could maintain its power and leadership in world affairs while at the same time reassure other nations about its benevolent intentions. But as the domestic debate shifted from how the United States could foster global cooperation to protect innocents to one about how it should deal with global threats such as enemy missiles tipped with weapons of mass destruction—and what needed to be done to make the United States invulnerable to them—the rest of the world's concerns intensified.

The Shield Showdown

Among conservatives, the debate about Kosovo had exposed an important divide over humanitarian intervention. But it also masked a strong consensus that had coalesced at the exact same time around an old issue: missile defense. The subject offered familiar terrain. Although Republicans could not solve their differences about when and how the United States should use force in ethnic conflicts, they could agree that America had to do more to combat the threat from rogue states, such as Iran, Iraq, and North Korea.

A few days before American and NATO planes began bombing Serbia in March 1999, the U.S. Congress overwhelmingly passed Republican-proposed legislation that called for the deployment of a national missile defense "as soon as technologically possible." Clinton had vetoed similar measures in the past, but this one passed with a veto-proof majority. For the Clinton team, the consequences were far-reaching.

Missile defense dominated the national security agenda during Clinton's remaining time in office, shaped the domestic political debate, and aggravated the broader concerns about America's role in the world. Talbott, who wrote several books on the arms control battles of the 1970s and 1980s and was one of Clinton's top advisers on missile defense, explained that with this act, "the administration was in more danger than ever of losing control over a key feature of defense and foreign policy."[42]

This was a remarkable turnabout on an issue that many thought had been consigned to irrelevance with the collapse of the Soviet Union. Since Ronald Reagan first proposed his Star Wars defense program in the early 1980s, shielding the United States from enemy missiles was one of the great Republican dreams. The idea was deceptively simple: The United States should use its superior technology to develop a way to shoot down an enemy's nuclear missiles, thus eliminating a major threat. But the tantalizing promise of instant security opened up a complicated array of diplomatic and political dilemmas, from Russian sensitivities about how this would affect their interests to the costs and feasibility of building such a system. It also raised the specter of a U.S. withdrawal from a 1972 agreement signed by Richard Nixon, the Anti-Ballistic Missile (ABM) Treaty, which essentially codified a suicide pact between the superpowers. By explicitly limiting the building of these kinds of defenses, the agreement aimed to make it impossible for either side to survive a nuclear strike, thus reducing the possibility that nuclear weapons would ever be launched. Although some found this grim deal abhorrent, presidents of both parties (including Reagan) had adhered to the ABM Treaty for more than a quarter-century.

The controversy generated by missile defense extended far beyond the arcane debates about nuclear strategy, arms control treaties, and ballistics technology. For its advocates, the idea of protecting the American homeland from missile attacks was a moral cause tantamount to religious conviction. For the skeptics, the notion was divorced from reality, whether in terms of technological feasibility, acceptable political costs, or, after the Cold War, the actual threat.

Missile defense had become a central battleground for conservatives and liberals in the debate about what needed to be done to enhance U.S. security—and the struggle over accuracy and bias in the U.S. intelligence community's assessment of threats. One's position illustrated how one looked at the world and the role of American power. The topic had become a "proxy between the political left and right, a kind of litmus test for how to keep America militarily strong and secure," explained Bradley Graham, a journalist and author of a leading book on missile defense. Both sides found it a convenient way to draw a clear dividing line between their views. The question, Graham argued, was "whether, in broad terms, the defense of the nation is better served by arms advances or arms control, by military buildups or diplomatic building blocks, by unilateral initiatives or compromise accords."[43]

THIS DEBATE went into hibernation during the years immediately after 11/9. When the Soviet Union broke into pieces, so did the whole premise upon which Reagan's original idea was based. By the time Clinton came into office, missile defense was no longer a pressing concern for most Americans. Clinton's first defense secretary, Les Aspin, had fiercely opposed national missile defense while in Congress, and within four months of taking office he declared the "end of the Star Wars era." The Democrats had always been skeptical of the cost, feasibility, and legality of such a program, and steered their efforts toward relatively modest research and development as well as a program of theater missile defense, which would protect American troops in the field. As long as the threat to homeland security seemed nonexistent, there was little public or political pressure on the administration to do more.

Throughout the early 1990s, some Republicans had tried to keep the flame burning, believing the threat from enemy missiles had, if anything, become worse. In the same celebrated article in which he coined the term "unipolar moment," Charles Krauthammer declared that the post–Cold War era would be better described as the "era of weapons of mass destruction," because the development and delivery of such weapons "will constitute the greatest single threat to world security for the rest of our lives." To deal with this threat, he argued that the United States must deny others the technological know-how to develop such weapons, threaten military strikes against those close to acquiring such capabilities, and develop missile defense against, in his words, "those weapons that do escape Western control or preemption." Although this gloomy vision failed to persuade many at the time because the country was in no mood to talk about WMD and military preemption, its audience grew larger as the decade wore on.[44]

During Clinton's first term, such ideas continued to attract a small but staunch group of supporters, most of whom resided in right-leaning think tanks. They worked with Republican staffers on Capitol Hill to agitate for more funding. They had prevailed on Newt Gingrich to include missile defense as one of the few national security planks in the 1994 Contract with America and then worked with the new Republican majority in Congress to write legislation— which Clinton vetoed—mandating that a system be deployed within eight years.

Sensing a political opportunity to make Clinton look weak, in 1996 the Republican majority backed a "Defend America" bill by Gingrich and presidential hopeful Bob Dole, once again seeking to mandate the deployment of missile defense. When Dole emerged as the Republican nominee, he continued to champion the idea. It had vast support in the conservative media, exemplified by a special editorial section published that summer in the *Wall Street Journal*, as well as explicitly partisan outlets. The focus on threats gave conservatives a set of issues to coalesce around, as they tried to bring unity to a movement that had been fractured since the end of the Cold War. "A consensus started to form about the threat from rogue states and the WMD," recalls John Bolton, leader of the GOP's National Policy Forum. "And so the focus turned toward undoing Cold War legacies like the ABM Treaty."[45]

But Dole's enthusiasm appeared perfunctory, as though he talked about missile defense only because it was something all Republicans could agree on. Missile defense appealed to the more isolationist wing of the party because it protected the homeland; the realist internationalists could see the practicality of hedging against a turn for the worse in Russia or the threat from North Korea, Iran, and Iraq; and the interventionists believed that a missile shield was less about defense than offense because it would enable America to project its power around the world without the threat of being deterred by an adversary.[46] As Jeane Kirkpatrick admitted at the time, Dole's support for missile defense did not reflect his particular passion. "He's really reflecting a widespread, deeply felt concern in the Republican community," she said. "It's the defense issue on which there is the greatest conviction among those Republicans who think about national security matters." Or, as Clinton later observed, supporting missile defense is "part of the theology of being a Republican."[47]

Dole's ambivalence aside, there were several reasons why missile defense failed to garner support during the campaign. The first was cost. Independent estimates showed that even a modest missile defense system had a price tag of more than $60 billion—too high for many Republican deficit hawks who wanted to cut government spending. The second was technology. It was unclear whether the United States could muster the capability to deploy a reliable system that could, in effect, hit a bullet with a bullet. But the third and most consequential reason missile defense could not get off the ground was the absence of a sense of threat. To most people, while the world certainly seemed more confusing and remained dangerous, the likelihood of getting hit by an enemy missile anytime in the near future seemed too remote to justify the cost.[48]

SUCH COMPLACENCY enraged the conservative missile defense crowd. They saw senior Clinton administration officials and Democrats in Congress ignoring a clear and present danger from regimes such as Iran and North Korea. And worse, they believed such denial was aided and abetted by the CIA and the intelligence community. The focus of their ire was a 1995 National Intelligence Estimate (NIE)—the intelligence community's most authoritative assessment of a future threat—whose conclusion undercut their arguments. It judged that no country other than the existing nuclear powers could develop a missile capability that would endanger the continental United States for at least fifteen years. That meant that the decisions about national missile defense could be kicked down the road.

Republicans in Congress and conservative national security experts were aghast. They believed that the assessment was deeply flawed in every way: It disregarded the potential missile threat to two states, Alaska and Hawaii; it dismissed the assistance that powers like Russia and China could give to Iran, Iraq, or North Korea; and it seemed too confident in America's ability to understand fully how far along homegrown programs in such countries would be. Conservatives screamed that the intelligence community was bending to pressure from the Clinton team, which wanted to weaken the rationale for missile defense. They decried the "politicization" of intelligence, claiming that the administration was willfully ignoring information about the threat, suppressing those experts with dissenting opinions, cherry-picking information that would confirm its views, or conspiring with its cronies in the intelligence community to cook the books.[49]

In response to these charges, the Republican Congress mandated two reviews of the intelligence community's work, enlisting the help of two deans of the Republican national security establishment, both of whom would return to government in key roles during the next presidency. The first review, headed by former CIA Director Robert Gates, found no evidence of political influence and endorsed the bottom-line assessment of the threat. (In fact, Gates asserted that the NIE's conclusions could have been even stronger.) The second, conducted by a nine-man commission chaired by Donald Rumsfeld and including Paul Wolfowitz and former Clinton CIA Director James Woolsey (who after leaving the administration became one of Clinton's biggest critics), reached a far darker conclusion.[50]

As a former congressman, White House chief of staff, and secretary of defense, Rumsfeld was already a legend inside the Beltway. Exceedingly confident and irascible, he tackled the job with enthusiasm. He had been out of the Washington limelight since the 1970s (although he had toyed with a presidential run in 1988) and was determined that this would not be a sleepy commission of high-level has-beens that would issue a forgettable report. Rumsfeld wanted to give a complete, top-to-bottom review of all the information the intelligence community had regarding the missile threat and demanded of CIA Director George Tenet that no piece of data be kept from this group.[51]

The report the Rumsfeld commission released in the summer of 1998 was a stark repudiation of the CIA's work. It called into question both the collection and analysis of information and described the missile threat as "broader, more mature, and evolving more rapidly" than previous intelligence estimates had stressed. The threat could come soon after the year 2000. The group's assessment did not offer any new evidence for this conclusion but instead chided intelligence analysts for underestimating the likelihood that states such as North Korea and Iran were benefiting from outside assistance. Although the commission stayed focused on the threat and did not address any remedies (one commissioner explained that they carefully stayed neutral on what to do), the conclusion was clearly a boon to missile defense hard-liners. Gingrich called it "the most important warning about our national security system since the end of the Cold War," while Bolton remembers it as a "galvanizing event."[52]

It was also a devastating blow to the intelligence community. Since the end of the Cold War, the CIA had been squeezed between budget cuts justified by the Soviet Union's collapse and increasing demands on its abilities to understand new threats. Now came claims—which were soon cemented in the minds of conservatives— that the intelligence community was either incompetent or willfully distorting analysis to satisfy its political overseers.

Rumsfeld learned a number of lessons during the process, especially concerning the CIA's ability to understand complex threats such as missile technologies and weapons of mass destruction. He found many of the intelligence analysts he encountered overly defensive and unwilling to think imaginatively. Throughout his long career, he had made a habit of writing down his favorite aphorisms about politics, bureaucracy, and leadership, and collecting them in a binder titled "Rumsfeld's Rules," which got passed around Washington like underground dissident literature in the old Soviet Union. During his commission's deliberations, one of Rumsfeld's fellow members uttered a quip about the intelligence business that he found worth remembering: The absence of evidence is not the same as the evidence of absence. Five years later, after he had returned to the Pentagon for an unprecedented second stint as secretary of defense, Rumsfeld dusted off the phrase to defend claims about Iraq's weapons programs during the buildup to war.

THE CLINTON administration initially considered the Rumsfeld commission's assertions to be little more than hard-liner grandstanding. But events soon made them impossible to ignore. In one of the odd coincidences of history, just a few weeks after the commission released its July 1998 report, North Korea test-fired a missile, the Taepodong I, that traveled farther than any launched from a third-world country before. The fact that the details of the launch (including the way the North Koreans had engineered their rocket to give it more distance) surprised the CIA seemed to confirm everything the Republicans were claiming about the intelligence community's shortcomings. The missile threat could not be dismissed as some-thing driven only by partisanship. North Korea's test, combined with increasing concerns about Iraq's WMD programs, forced the adminis-tration to give missile defense a second look. With the Republicans in an uproar and congressional Democrats increasingly nervous about opposing legislation on missile defense, Clinton and his top advisers began to consider options for building a system.[53]

At the end of 1998 and beginning of 1999—the same time Clinton was entering the thicket of impeachment, confronting Saddam, and grappling with the possibility of using force to end Milosevic's repression of Kosovo—the administration began to increase funding for missile defense and to plan for deployment. In the summer of 1999, after he signed the congressional legislation on pursuing mis-sile defense, the president decided on the specifications of the sys-tem to be built, but he delayed making a formal decision on construction for another year. In the meantime, the military contin-ued to test the system to make it workable, and Americans started negotiations with the Russians on amending the ABM Treaty. They also had to assuage the concerns of their European partners, whose nerves were already frayed by Kosovo.

This agenda posed political dangers both at home and abroad. As Talbott described it, "If we said that we were committed to preserv-ing the ABM Treaty without regard to its constraints on national mis-sile defense, we'd spend the rest of the administration in what would likely be a losing fight with Congress. . . . If, on the other hand, we acceded to congressional pressure and decided to pursue national missile defense without regard to its implications for the ABM Treaty, we'd have a blowup with the Russians—and very likely a split with our allies, who tended to see national missile defense as a return to the concept of Fortress America and an abandonment of thirty years of strategic arms control."[54]

AMERICA HAD flexed its muscles in Kosovo and debated the virtues of ballistic missile defense. Liberals showed a willingness to use force for moral purposes; conservatives focused on building a shield against rogue states. But both sides were addressing the same questions: How should America use its power, and against what threats? For some, it was tempting to think the indispensable nation was also the independent nation: The United States might be needed by others, but it did not need others for its own security. Given America's overwhelming technological superiority, economic prowess, and global influence, why would it?

But the search for independence in a globalizing world was fruitless. Far-away financial crises affected Americans who had invested their savings in pension funds with growing shares in emerging markets. And a new scale of transnational threat was emerging—from disease to organized crime to terrorism—that no one country could handle on its own. America might be indispensable, but it was not invulnerable. The country's leaders and citizens were slowly learning that their vulnerabilities came not just from traditional threats, but from individuals who could wield tremendous power, be they bond traders in silk suits or terrorists wearing bomb belts.

CHAPTER NINE

New World Disorder

I N FEBRUARY 1999, as the Clinton administration was heading into its public showdown with Slobodan Milosevic over Kosovo, a heated debate unfolded in secret among the administration's top counterterrorism experts. The CIA had Osama bin Laden in its crosshairs. The Saudi-born leader of the terrorist network al-Qaeda was on a hunting trip near Kandahar in Afghanistan with members of the royal family of the United Arab Emirates. Six months earlier, the Clinton administration had launched a volley of cruise missiles against al-Qaeda training camps in Afghanistan because it believed bin Laden was there. Having missed him then, the Pentagon kept submarines off the Pakistani coast loaded with cruise missiles targeted on the terrorist leader's likeliest whereabouts.

Clinton had issued an order to kill bin Laden, but to get him the timing had to be perfect. Transmitting the intelligence about his location to top counterterrorism officials, gathering the administration's foreign policy advisers to help the president decide a course of action, and relaying the order to submarines on the other side of the world to launch their weapons took as long as six hours. Even if everything in Washington went right, success was hardly guaranteed: Any attempted strike against bin Laden ran the risk not only of missing him but also of killing innocent civilians.

Michael Scheuer, the intense intelligence analyst who had spent two years tracking bin Laden for the CIA, believed they had located the al-Qaeda leader. Scheuer took the case to CIA Director George Tenet and the Clinton administration's top counterterrorism official, Richard Clarke. Tenet and Clarke worried that the evidence was insufficient and feared killing a number of UAE princes in an unsuccessful effort to get their target. Soon they found out that bin Laden had moved on, and they suspended the planning for the strike. The terrorist mastermind remained at large.[1]

Looking back, Tenet admitted that such fire drills exposed a weakness in the efforts to eliminate bin Laden. "Instead of considering alternatives to the less-than-ideal cruise missile attacks," he wrote in his memoirs, "policy-makers seemed to want to have things both ways: They wanted to hit bin Laden but without endangering U.S. troops or putting at significant risk our diplomatic relations." This meant that time and again, while most of the American public remained oblivious to the threat bin Laden posed, senior officials scrambled any time an opportunity arose to strike. "We were constantly ginning up attack plans and making last-minute decisions about whether some snippet of information we had just obtained was good enough to launch missiles," Tenet explained. "Bin Laden might have been spotted again, and I had to make a recommendation on the spot—do we launch or not? That's no way to do business."[2]

THE SAME MONTH that America's senior national security officials were privately debating a military strike to kill a terrorist leader in Afghanistan, *Time* magazine featured three American economic officials on its cover. The lead story fawned over Alan Greenspan, chairman of the Federal Reserve Board, Robert Rubin, secretary of the U.S. Treasury, and Lawrence Summers, Rubin's deputy, for their role in managing the response to the financial crises that had shaken economies from Thailand and South Korea to Russia and Brazil during the previous two years. The headline heralded these three men as the "Committee to Save the World." When asked later whether such a breathless moniker was correct, even Newt Gingrich grudgingly acknowledged the accomplishment. "I'm not saying we were on the edge of a Great Depression," he said, "[but] we could have been on the edge of a very serious, long tummy ache. They deserve a fair amount of credit. As a team, they were remarkably effective."[3]

Not everyone agreed. Hans Tietmeyer, president of the German Bundesbank, complained that his warnings about Mexico's precarious position during the peso meltdown five years earlier and the speed with which a crisis in Thailand in 1997 could spread around the world went unheeded by the Americans. Some blamed the Treasury Department and global financial institutions such as the International Monetary Fund (IMF) for prescribing policies to emerging market economies that created the vulnerabilities in the first place, leaving millions of people in those places impoverished. Still others argued that Rubin, a hugely successful former Wall Street trader, had bailed out troubled economies to save the investments of his friends in New York and ignored the problem of moral hazard: If traders knew that bad investments would be saved by Washington, then they had no reason not to throw money around the world promiscuously in their search for easy economic gains. Jagdish Bhagwati, a widely respected Columbia University economist, concluded that the three officials "really blew it. In fact, it is not unfair to say that Rubin and Summers may well have presided over the largest man-made disaster in the world economy since [the] Smoot-Hawley [tariffs of the 1930s]."[4]

Whether the critics were correct that Rubin and his colleagues had caused the economic disaster, or whether *Time* was right that they had saved the world, there was no denying that these unelected American officials were shaping the globalization debate and over-seeing an important shift in U.S. foreign policy. The Treasury Department, working with the IMF, the World Bank, and the Federal Reserve, was a force to be reckoned with alongside the State and Defense Departments in the formulation of the country's global agenda. Throughout the Cold War, the diplomats at the State Department and the military planners at the Pentagon dominated. Now, on many of the most important global issues, those traditional shapers of American foreign policy were left to defer to the people with experience in global markets.

When Rubin or Summers argued for a particular course of action in a roomful of foreign policy officials, the national security specialists lacked the economic expertise to challenge them effectively. This gave Treasury officials tremendous confidence not only in waging internal fights, but also in dealing with counterparts abroad. "There was a high degree of deference to Bob [Rubin], including by the president," says top trade negotiator Charlene Barshefsky. Nearly a decade later, a framed copy of the *Time* magazine cover still adorns the wall of Rubin's midtown Manhattan office. As the former treasury secretary confidently reflects, "Our team was equipped to deal with issues nobody else was."[5]

AN ELUSIVE Saudi financier was training a network of terrorists in Afghanistan. A financial crisis that started in a small country in one part of the world soon engulfed the global economy. While many in the national security community remained focused on the threat from Iraq, the escalating crisis in Kosovo, or the need for missile defense, Islamic extremism and international economic flows were changing the global chessboard. These were, as Benjamin Barber's influential 1995 book explained, the twin challenges of jihad and McWorld.[6] Yet America's foreign policy establishment was just beginning to comprehend the transformative impact of these two forces.

Clinton understood their importance as much as anyone, seeing the issues as two sides of the coin of globalization. He devoured Barber's book and talked about its ideas frequently. "In the aftermath of the Cold War, every good thing has an explosive underbelly," he said to his advisers during a White House meeting. "We're fighting a rear-guard action between the forces of integration and disintegration." Although Clinton spent much of his presidency extolling the possibilities of the spread of information and technology around the world for boosting the economy and tying people closer together, he also saw the problems such changes would bring. "You can't have an integrated world without being vulnerable to organized assholes," his aides recalled him saying. "It's an open, free, interchanging place—but a lot of bad shit crosses borders now."[7]

The Incredible Shrinking Globe

In the 1990s, as countries around the world moved to shed authoritarian rule of one sort or another and began to open themselves to the global economy, the perceived trend toward American-style liberalism seemed inevitable. From the moment they entered office, Clinton officials had pushed hard to encourage these "emerging" democracies—such as Russia, Poland, Chile, South Africa—to open their markets as rapidly as possible. They believed that states with open economies would benefit from the huge trade and investment flows, as would the American banks and brokerage firms that invested in them, and local democracy would flourish through the exchange.

In retrospect, official Washington recognized belatedly that not enough attention was paid to the underlying political and economic structures of countries that were opening up their markets to short-term capital flows. Money might pour in, but when investors got nervous about an economy's strength or a country's political stability, they could pull out their cash with incredible speed. Clinton's commerce secretary and first trade envoy, Mickey Kantor, said the lack of strong banking and legal foundations in some emerging markets meant the American promotion of liberalization was like "building a skyscraper with no foundation." Even Rubin admits that although "economic openness is positive, there should have been more emphasis on the structural underpinning for that."[8]

Many middle-class Americans had only a vague idea that their pension and mutual funds were tied so closely to the fate of developing nations. Although these investments made dramatic income growth possible, they linked the global economy more than ever before. In 1980, less than 1 percent of American pension fund assets were invested abroad; that figure climbed to 17 percent by 1997. In the mid-1990s, investors purchased $50 billion in stocks and bonds in emerging markets, while banks funneled $76 billion more. Global foreign exchange markets were seeing $1.5 trillion a day change hands.[9] Asia was a particularly appealing target of these financial flows; Clinton described the region as going from the Cold War's "dominoes" to globalization's "dynamos."

AMERICANS REMAINED uneasy about globalization. Despite a domestic economy that was humming along at record pace, and more and more Americans investing their money overseas, the fears of dislocation and vulnerability proved strong. Conservatives and liberals worried about the loss of jobs during the 1993 NAFTA debate and feared the erosion of American sovereignty when Congress approved the creation of the World Trade Organization the following year. The vast majority of Americans opposed bailing out Mexico when that country faced economic disaster in early 1995.

Two years later, the United States faced a global economic crisis that Clinton called the worst in half a century. What made it particularly frightening was that although it started so far away, its shock waves were felt everywhere. The trouble began across the Pacific Ocean, in the small Southeast Asian country of Thailand. The Thai currency, the baht, was under increasing pressure from currency traders betting that the government could not maintain its value. These traders were a new breed of international actor. They made money not by trading goods or profiting from the rise and fall of stock prices, but by betting on the changing value of currencies.

If a country facing economic trouble pegged its currency to the value of the U.S. dollar to reassure foreign investors, as was the case in Mexico in the mid-1990s and Thailand in 1997, speculators would sell the currency with the belief that the government could not afford to spend its foreign reserves to maintain the currency's value. Generally, governments would try to defend the value of their currencies rather than allow them to float freely on the open market. Why? Because both the state and private companies borrowed heavily during good economic times, and a decline in value of their home currency would lead to the threat of default on the dollar-denominated loans they had taken on, thereby ensuring that further investment would dry up and throw millions out of work.

In July 1997, Thailand's foreign reserves were nearly gone. It could no longer prop up the value of the baht and had to let its currency float—disconnecting it from the fixed exchange rate pegged to the U.S. dollar and sending its value into free fall. One of Asia's fastest growing economies hit the skids. The Thai experience made investors nervous about the prospects for other emerging markets in the region, increasing the pressure on the currencies of the Philippines, Malaysia, and Indonesia—which soon faced their own crises. Analysts dubbed the economic downturn the "Asian flu," which spread with alarming speed.

Despite the potential for significant economic distress in the region, the American government remained on the sidelines. Thailand wasn't Mexico, a large next-door neighbor that might flood the United States with immigrants and create a serious security concern. Laura Tyson, a senior economic adviser to Clinton, later recalled that they "chose not to intervene in Thailand, thinking it was not going to spill over." She asked, "Why would it?"[10] Rubin still argues that even in hindsight, the odds that the crisis would cause global markets to roil were low.[11]

IF THE THAI CRISIS had been contained, the U.S. decision not to offer a bailout package would have been uncontroversial (although officials at the National Security Council, State Department, and Pentagon were furious that Thailand, an American military ally, did not receive any support). At the time, the administration believed international financial institutions had sufficient resources to help Thailand and that the drama unfolding twelve time zones away would remain isolated.

Later that fall, however, the South Korean economy began to crumble. South Korea was the eleventh-largest economy in the world, and a major security partner of the United States, which had 37,000 troops stationed in the country. As had Mexico and Thailand,

South Korea faced the prospect of depleting its remaining foreign currency reserves by the end of 1997. U.S. Treasury officials feared that if a major economy like Korea's went into default, investors worldwide would pull back their money. Countries would begin to impose protections against the outside world, just as they had in the early 1930s, fueling the Great Depression. The IMF put together the biggest bailout package in its history, $57 billion dollars, but investors were not reassured and believed they should get their money out of Korea before they lost it. The indispensable nation could no longer stand aside. Rubin worked the phones to convince global bankers to roll over their debts—that is, to replace debts due for payment with new debt rather than demand their money. The bankers reluctantly agreed, allowing the situation to stabilize. Otherwise, the Korean economy would have collapsed.

EVEN AFTER Asia regained its footing, emerging market economies in other parts of the world came under pressure from nervous investors and currency speculators. A year after the Thailand crisis, Russia defaulted on its debt owed to external creditors. Those who had placed their money there paid the price. One major American hedge fund, Long-Term Capital Management (LTCM), found itself in danger of bankruptcy. By this time, Treasury officials and Greenspan at the Federal Reserve Board feared that the collapse of a major hedge fund would spark a larger crisis in the American stock market. The Fed arranged for a group of major financial institutions to bail out LTCM and began cutting interest rates to keep the American economy churning forward.

Although many millions of people around the world—in Thailand, South Korea, Russia, and later Brazil—suffered greatly from the economic crises shaking their national economies, officials at Treasury and the Federal Reserve breathed a sigh of relief. A 1930s-style global meltdown had been averted. The world economy stayed afloat. And before long, countries such as Russia and South Korea were experiencing renewed economic growth.

Yet Clinton and his advisers worried about how close to disaster the global economy had come. They understood economic interdependence intellectually, but it was sobering to watch the world's markets nearly collapse so quickly. To Rubin, "what happened to the world economy during that period—and perhaps more important, what didn't happen—leaves us with a sense not only of how much damage was done but how close we came to even greater calamity."[12]

Critics charged that Rubin and his colleagues had engaged in ad hoc crisis management instead of developing a comprehensive strategy to manage the global economy. George W. Bush's first treasury secretary, Paul O'Neill, denigrated the Clinton team as "firemen" who showed up whenever a crisis broke out rather than creating an environment that would prevent the crises from starting.[13] O'Neill and others believed such "bailouts" insulated investors from their losses and planted the seeds of future problems. The same seat-of-their-pants policy-making critique had dogged Clinton's national security officials for years. Rather than develop a strategic doctrine to prevent economic crises in the post–Cold War world, the Clinton team seemed only to be able to react to events—although no one, including O'Neill, had figured out how to shape them instead.

Searching for a Third Way

More important, such global financial disruptions fueled public anxieties that were never far from the surface. Although the American economy seemed as strong as ever, there was growing unease among American investors and workers about the future. Author Walter Russell Mead wryly noted that given the booming economy of the 1990s, "one might have expected American parents to be naming their children Nafta and Gatt rather than participating in protest marches against international trade agreements."[14] Although unemployment was down and the stock market was up, workers faced a decline in real wages, a rise in health care costs, and the prospect of continued outsourcing of jobs to developing nations.

Rubin recalls that Clinton mused to him as early as 1994 that as

Americans grappled with the changes brought by a transforming global economy, they wanted John Wayne to ride up on a white horse with a simple answer. Although the global economy's complexities were tough to explain, Rubin admits that the administration should have done more to make the case for embracing globalization. During the debate over NAFTA, he reflects, top Clinton officials should have launched a major program "to educate the American people on globalization, trade, and foreign aid."[15] In the administration's view, globalization was inevitable, jobs that were being lost weren't going to come back, and the remedies being proposed—stricter labor rules and tougher environmental standards in other nations—were politically important but would have little impact. The president spoke often about job retraining programs, but that didn't mollify those who were growing increasingly nervous.

Clinton saw that the political, social, and economic problems arising from the new global economy were not unique to the United States. Other countries, especially democratic governments in Europe, faced similar challenges. Many of these countries were led by individuals who, like Clinton, were center-left progressives, came of age in the 1960s and 1970s, and ascended to leadership in the 1990s. They worked to find a middle course between the laissez-faire, market-centered policies of the political right and the statist, protectionist policies of the left. To do so, they championed a political movement they called the Third Way. Clinton's point man for the effort, Sidney Blumenthal, described it as "a belief in the necessity of a new social contract for the new global economy—and for an informal network working constantly toward its framing." For an American president, this was a different way to approach world politics. The Third Way was less a traditional internationalist vision in which states interacted with each other than a globalist one that said because borders matter less, everyone faces similar challenges in managing globalization.[16]

Working with Britain's Tony Blair and German Chancellor Gerhard Schroeder, Clinton arranged a series of summits among world leaders, leading intellectuals, and policy experts to discuss not just the foreign policy challenges globalization posed, but also how countries could respond to the domestic pressures. The purveyors of the Third Way embraced many ideas on the right—such as a reliance on markets, encouragement of private entrepreneurship, and fiscal discipline—as they sought to provide opportunities for those who were suffering most from the changes in the global economy. Particularly through education and job retraining, they hoped to enable individuals to reap the fruits of economic expansion. These summits took place during 1999 and 2000 in Florence, the English countryside, Berlin, and New York City and were a remarkable example of global cooperation and collaboration. They showed Clinton at the apex of his international influence.[17]

CLINTON'S EFFORT to develop a global Third Way was a direct continuation of the New Democrat ideas for modernizing progressive politics he had championed in his first run for president in 1992. He even used his old organization, the Democratic Leadership Council, to help arrange the summits. But by the end of the decade, this centrist agenda was even more controversial among American liberals, and Clinton found himself confronting skeptics who were angrier, more creative, and far better organized.

In 1999, once again seeking to lead the global effort to break down barriers in international trade, the president called for a new round of negotiations in the World Trade Organization (WTO). Instead of choosing a remote location, where officials would have been secluded from the public, Clinton chose the bustling city of Seattle, Washington, home of Starbucks and Microsoft. Not only did thousands of delegates from 134 nations seeking to build greater global consensus around free trade fly to the Northwest, so did thousands of protestors.

Like many on the far right concerned about America's ability to maintain its sovereignty in a world of proliferating international institutions, the administration's opponents on the left believed the World Trade Organization had empowered a corporate-dominated, unaccountable international bureaucracy to legislate health, environmental, and safety standards. Among those leading the charge against the WTO was Lori Wallach, the fiery and unrelenting leader of Global Trade Watch, a group founded in 1995 under the umbrella of Ralph Nader's consumer advocacy organization, Public Citizen. Wallach believed Clinton and his economic team had moved the country backward by turning the old General Agreement on Tariffs and Trade (GATT) into a full-fledged institution, the WTO. The GATT, she says, dealt with traditional trade matters such as tariffs and quotas on goods. "If you couldn't drop the thing on your foot, it wasn't covered by GATT," Wallach says. But the negotiations that established the WTO, she believes, were "a very quiet slow motion coup d'état on democratic governance." Wallach and her allies had lost the battles in 1993 and 1994 that established NAFTA and the WTO, and they had learned their lesson. They spent several years building grassroots organizations in congressional districts around the country that could, in her words, "run some people out of town."[18]

Clinton had always argued that the United States should promote free trade but do so in ways that did not unduly harm workers or the environment. Critics on the left, however, considered his words insufficient or insincere. When the president called for a new round of WTO talks to push for further liberalization in services and agriculture, Wallach seized the moment. She and her friends booked hundreds of hotel rooms in Seattle to ensure they and their supporters could have their voices heard.[19]

THE PROTESTORS came from all over the world. A motley bunch, they included members of church groups, labor organizations, the Sierra Club, and Friends of the Earth. The protests began before dawn on November 29, 1999, when five activists from the Rainforest Action Network climbed a 170-foot construction crane and held up banners reading DEMOCRACY and WTO with arrows going in opposite directions. By noon, more than 3,000 people marched along Fifth Avenue downtown. Nearly 250 of them wore turtle suits to protest WTO action against a U.S. law prohibiting importation of shrimp from countries that didn't protect sea turtles. Later that afternoon, 5,000 people marched through the rain shouting, "We're all wet, cancel the debt." Meanwhile, Teamsters President James P. Hoffa led a group of 600 steelworkers in the chant: "Hell, no, WTO."[20]

On the second day of the WTO meeting, the protests turned nasty. As 25,000 union members protested peacefully, a group of anarchists broke windows at the Bank of America, Banana Republic, FAO Schwartz, and the Warner Bros. Studio Store. Approximately 200 people took hammers to the windows of Nordstrom, Niketown, and Planet Hollywood. Riot police intervened. With the streets full of broken glass and tear gas, the delegates to the meeting suddenly found themselves in something that looked like a conflict zone. Bodyguards told Secretary of State Madeleine Albright and U.S. Trade Representative Barshefsky to stay in their hotel rooms (Albright later snuck into the talks in the back of an ambulance). It proved impossible to hold serious negotiations, and as the protestors hoped, a new round of global trade talks collapsed.

Summers, who had succeeded Rubin as secretary of treasury, had no patience for the activists. "I find them very sad because it seems to me that there's an enormous amount of very valuable moral energy that is being very, very badly misplaced," he said later. "People in many, many poor countries produce goods under conditions that are revolting and would be unacceptable to citizens in the United States. On the other hand, they chose those conditions because they represent the best available alternative." Summers, a Harvard academic steeped in the theories of economic globalization, argued that the protestors simply didn't understand the value of free trade. "It seems to me that for us to seek to take away that best available alternative by not liberalizing trade, by not being willing to accept imports, by not opening markets, seems to take on an enormous moral burden of denying poor people the choices that they would prefer to make," he said. "There are children who are working in textile businesses in Asia who would be prostitutes on the streets if they did not have those jobs."[21]

Clinton understood Summers's intellectual argument but, as a politician often admired (and derided) for "feeling the pain" of others, he showed more empathy. As he traveled to Seattle, he was asked if he regretted choosing that city as the site for the meeting. "What I regret is not that there are protestors there," he said. "I have supported the right of people whose interests represent labor unions, who represent environmental groups, people who represent the poorer countries of the world coming and expressing their opinions. And I've repeatedly said I thought the WTO process was too closed. . . . What I regret is that a small number of people have done nonpeaceful things and have tried to block access and prevent meetings." Otherwise, he added, the protests "would be a positive." [22]

When Clinton addressed the WTO delegates at the Four Seasons Hotel, he reiterated that he was in tune with those who marched outside. Instead of seeking to forge consensus, Clinton demanded that developing countries increase labor standards or face tough trade sanctions. Business leaders and European officials were angry at the president, believing he had caved in to political pressure and sabotaged the talks. Although Clinton was careful to decry the street violence, he did not back down. "I'm glad the others showed up," he said, "because they represent millions of people who are now asking questions about whether this enterprise in fact will take us all where we want to go. . . . For fifty years, trade decisions were largely the province of trade ministers, heads of government, and business interests. But now what all those people in the street tell us is that they would also like to be heard. And they're not so sure that this deal is working for them." Clinton added, "I would like to say, first of all, I think we need to do a better job of making the basic case." [23]

It was an astonishing admission for a president nearing the end of his second term. Clinton had been giving speeches on globalization since he announced his candidacy for president eight years earlier. He was working hard to build momentum behind a global Third Way. But by the end of 1999, Clinton's political position on these issues had weakened, and he was already thinking about the next election. His vice president and heir apparent, Al Gore, felt the heat from the base of the Democratic Party as he began his run for the White

House. Labor unions were unhappy with Gore for championing NAFTA and the WTO at the start of the Clinton years; environmentalists were angry that the vice president had not prevailed on the administration to do more about the pernicious effects of climate change. In his remarks in Seattle, Clinton was trying to help Gore. But it was too little, too late for increasingly angry liberal interest groups. Author John Harris explained, "On this issue, at least, his efforts to remake the Democratic Party had fallen short."[24] Actually, for Clinton and the Democrats, it would prove worse. Enough of these people abandoned Gore for Nader in the 2000 election to tip the balance to George W. Bush.

THE ASIAN economic flu and trade were just the latest American worries about the global economy. At the end of the 1980s, Americans were anxious about Germany and Japan. In 1993, they were worried about job losses to Mexico. By the end of the decade, they feared China, whose economic and political influence was growing at an incredible pace.

Clinton's policies toward the Asian giant evolved considerably during his presidency. He entered office promising to get tough. In 1994, he decided that despite his earlier rhetoric, he was not going to hold America's trade relationship with China hostage to that country's human rights policies. Next he barreled into a military showdown with China to deter its threats against Taiwan. By the latter part of his presidency, he had settled on a course of "engagement," which included deepening diplomatic contacts between Washington and Beijing and pursuing greater trade and regional cooperation. A turning point in this effort was Clinton's nine-day trip to China in 1998—the first visit by an American president since the Tiananmen Square massacre nearly a decade earlier.

But Clinton's approach to China continued to arouse considerable political controversy. Republicans claimed that now Clinton was the one turning a blind eye to Chinese malfeasance. They seized on allegations that the Chinese had tried to influence the 1996 election by donating money to Democrats (which proved to be true) and then opened a major congressional investigation into why the administration had allowed two large defense firms to sell satellites to China. Conservatives growled that China was an adversary, not, as Clinton called it, a "strategic partner," and argued that the administration was allowing the Chinese menace to grow worse. Through such "outright appeasement," a vocal critic asserted, "the United States has actually helped create a new superpower threat."[25] This confrontational argument gathered steam as the turn of the century approached and became a Republican theme during the 2000 presidential campaign.

Meanwhile, among liberals, Clinton faced charges that he was ignoring China's abuse of human rights, its low-wage production, and its abysmal environmental record—and selling out to American business interests. Despite such pressures, Clinton maintained his belief that the only way to manage China's rise in a globalizing world was to bring it politically and economically into the American-led international order. As his presidency wound down, Clinton saw this as a central part of his legacy. The strategy suffered setbacks, from the hot political rhetoric at home to huge mistakes, such as the U.S. bombing of the Chinese embassy in downtown Belgrade. With that in mind, during Clinton's final year in office he set out to accomplish one last goal: to grant China Permanent Normal Trade Relations (PNTR) status with the United States and thereby pave the way for Beijing's entry into the WTO. With this act, he hoped that his goal of bringing China out of its post-Tiananmen isolation would be complete.[26]

Once again he needed the support of Congress. The effort to pass PNTR, however, was hobbled by the president's larger inability to articulate effectively his message on globalization. As with NAFTA nearly seven years before, Republican leaders promised to get him half the votes he needed (and since they held the majority in Congress, that was easier), but they demanded that he pull along his own party. To do so, Clinton could not rely on touting the economic benefits of trade with Asia's growing giant. Rather, he used the national security argument that it was better to pull China into globalization's tent than to leave it frustrated on the outside.

To get the trade deal through Congress, Clinton held hundreds of meetings with members at the White House, including many in the private residence, and he enlisted every cabinet official to help. He again called on former presidents and secretaries of state to voice their support and rallied the business community. Senate Majority Leader Trent Lott told Barshefsky in early March, "I am not going to stick my neck out . . . if you all are not going to get into a war-room status."[27] So Clinton treated PNTR as a battle that had to be won, and he was successful. Although the debate was intense and often bitter, the legislation passed by comfortable margins.

But Clinton's victory came at a price. The deal shaped the American debate on China, keeping the accord mired in controversy and suspicion. Just as NAFTA and the WTO had left unions and environmentalists fuming, so did PNTR. Coming on the heels of the breakdown in Seattle, it was a rebuke to the antitrade crowd. Once again, the left could argue that the administration should have stood up for stronger labor and environmental standards in pursuing global trade, and the right could unfurl charges of appeasement.

Al-Qaeda Rises

The downsides of globalization were not confined to market fluctuations and the outsourcing of American jobs to low-wage countries such as China. The new openness meant that diseases could make their way around the globe more easily, organized crime syndicates could operate worldwide, and money laundering and the drug trade could flourish. So could terrorist organizations.

To Clinton, this was the "explosive underbelly" of the new world. In a speech at a 1999 Third Way summit in Florence, the president said that in the twenty-first century, the "biggest problems to our security and to this whole form of governance will probably come not from rogue states or from . . . governments, but from the enemies of nation-states, from terrorists and drug runners." The threat posed by such groups was new and complex. Clinton predicted they would "use the same things that are fueling our prosperity—open borders, the Internet, the miniaturization of all sophisticated technology—which will manifest itself in smaller and more powerful and more dangerous weapons." Global teamwork would be needed, he argued, "to deal with the enemies of the nation-state if we expect progressive governments to succeed."[28]

ALL THIS WAS happening at the very moment the government institutions established to help policy-makers understand threats—the CIA and the rest of America's intelligence community—were experiencing the most severe crisis in their fifty-year history. The CIA was a product of the Cold War; for many, the most vivid (and popular) depictions of the superpower struggle came in the spy-versus-spy tales by writers such as John Le Carré and Tom Clancy. The resulting Hollywood thrillers always made the agency appear more capable than it really was. So when the Soviet Union collapsed, the intelligence world, like the military, found its budget slashed and its mission questioned. The massive resources that had gone into fighting the Soviets suddenly seemed irrelevant. James Woolsey, Clinton's first CIA director, explains, "Some saw the tools of intelligence as only about stealing secrets and, therefore, not very useful for understanding new threats."[29]

During the 1990s, demands on the CIA didn't go down, they went up, and in ways for which the agency was unprepared and underfunded. "It didn't look like we were searching for a new mission," says John McLaughlin, a longtime intelligence analyst who rose to be the agency's number two during the late 1990s and into the George W. Bush administration. "We were overwhelmed with new taskings and new questions that no one had ever asked before."[30] Rather than just focus most of their resources on one major mission—understanding the capabilities and intentions of the Soviet Union—they now were called upon to help interpret a dizzying array of challenges: from global diseases, the deteriorating environment, and WMD proliferation to understanding sensitive trade negotiations with allies such as Japan and the rise of new terrorist groups. "The trouble is there's too much to do," argued John Deutch, Clinton's second CIA director.[31]

The agency's morale plummeted further when a huge scandal exposed one of its top agents, Aldrich Ames, as a spy for Moscow; Ames had given the KGB the names of hundreds of American operatives. The CIA also suffered from a lack of leadership. Starting with the Cold War's end, the agency had five directors in six years. In January 1997, Clinton nominated Tony Lake to be CIA director, but Lake withdrew his nomination after running into fierce opposition from Republicans; Clinton then turned to Tenet.

By then, the CIA was in a state of collapse. Its relations with Capitol Hill became poisonous, as Congress launched numerous investigations for alleged CIA wrongdoing and criticized the agency for failing to understand emerging threats. The agency lost nearly 20 percent of its senior analysts and top operatives, leaving it without the kinds of expertise it needed. Barely anyone in the agency could speak Serbo-Croatian or the Creole dialect of Haiti, let alone Farsi or Arabic. "We were nearly bankrupt," Tenet reflected. The agency, he explained, had no "coherent, integrated, and measurable long-range plan." The result was a perfect storm: a global landscape that was becoming more complex, information that was becoming more available through the explosion of the Internet, and round-the-clock news that increased demands from officials, with a spy agency that had fewer resources, inadequate expertise, and an unfocused mission. As McLaughlin puts it, "We went from Chapter 11 to 9/11."[32]

FOR YEARS, public opinion polls had shown that Americans were worried about terrorism, and particularly about the growing threat of Islamic extremism. In 1983, they were horrified by the bombing of the Marine barracks in Lebanon. In 1993, only a month after Clinton took office, followers of Egyptian cleric Umar Abd al-Rahman detonated a car bomb in an underground garage at the World Trade Center. In 1996, a massive bomb blew up outside the U.S. military's Khobar Towers housing complex near Dhahran, Saudi Arabia.

U.S. and Saudi intelligence pointed to the Iranian-supported terrorist group Hezbollah as the culprit behind the Khobar Towers attack (only later did the 9/11 Commission and others raise the possibility of al-Qaeda involvement), and the Pentagon developed plans to strike military targets in Iran. Although the Tehran regime was a major sponsor of terrorism through groups such as Hezbollah and Hamas, White House national security officials came to worry most about the rise of al-Qaeda. In June 1995, Clinton issued a secret order, known as Presidential Decision Directive (PDD) 39, which called on the United States to "deter" and "defeat" terrorist attacks, delineating the responsibilities of different government agencies to do so. He also embarked on a sustained public effort to explain the looming dangers—an effort that grew in intensity. As Sandy Berger later explained, by mid-decade bin Laden "was on the radar screen; in 1998 he was the radar screen."[33]

In April 1996, nearly a year after the tragic bombing in Oklahoma City perpetrated by homegrown terrorists (although in the moments after that attack, many had assumed it had been orchestrated from abroad), Clinton spoke at the University of Central Oklahoma. Delivering a message to the young people in his audience, he said, "The world we're moving toward is going to offer you more opportunities to succeed, if you have a good education, than any generation of Americans has ever known. But the same forces that offer you those opportunities to succeed offer people opportunities to commit terrorist acts." Therefore, he admonished, "we must be more vigilant, more active, more determined than ever before." In a remarkably prescient moment, Clinton asked his audience to imagine that 3,000 people had been killed in the Oklahoma City bombings. That kind of loss, he said, "can paralyze a country. It can take its heart out. It can take its confidence away."[34]

A few months later, the president spoke just blocks from the

White House at The George Washington University, where he noted that his administration had prevented attacks on the United Nations and the Holland Tunnel in New York City and had foiled a plot to bring down American planes flying over the Pacific Ocean. Still, he maintained, "I want to make it clear to the American people that while we can defeat terrorists, it will be a long time before we defeat terrorism."[35]

EVENTS PROVED that statement true. In February 1998, bin Laden delivered one of his famous fatwas, this time calling on Muslims to kill Americans anywhere they could, whether innocent civilians or not. Clinton in May issued two new PDDs on counterterrorism and named Clarke the national coordinator for security, infrastructure protection, and counterterrorism. On August 7, al-Qaeda carried out simultaneous attacks against the American embassies in Kenya and Tanzania, killing more than 200 people, including twelve Americans.

These attacks sparked greater focus on Afghanistan, bin Laden's headquarters. Less than two decades earlier, Afghanistan had been a major preoccupation of the United States in the proxy battle with the Soviets. American intelligence agents provided training and arms to Afghan freedom fighters, known as the Mujahedeen. As the Red Army withdrew in defeat during the late 1980s, Washington's attention turned elsewhere.

While policy-makers in the Bush and Clinton administrations struggled with the end of the Cold War's consequences in Europe, Afghanistan festered in a civil war. The conflict was eventually won by the Taliban, which established a hard-line Islamic regime that provided a haven for terrorists. Inside the American government, Afghanistan became a bureaucratic backwater; even for South Asia regional specialists, the main focus was on India and Pakistan. Milton Bearden, the CIA's chief of station in neighboring Pakistan at the time, told author Steve Coll two months after 9/11, "Did we really give a shit about the long-term future of Nangarhar (a province in eastern Afghanistan bordering Pakistan)? Maybe not. As it turned out, guess what? We didn't." Yet some of those Islamic freedom fighters, led by bin Laden, sought to translate their victory over the Soviets into momentum for further jihad. The result was al-Qaeda.[36]

AMERICAN INTELLIGENCE officials had been trying to devise ways to capture bin Laden but could never reach consensus on the plan or timing. The simultaneous embassy bombings warranted a more forceful response. On August 20, Clinton retaliated, after receiving information that bin Laden had gathered terrorist operatives at training camps in Afghanistan to plan future attacks. The president ordered a cruise missile strike on the camps and on a pharmaceutical factory in Sudan that was allegedly producing chemical weapons for terrorist use.

Explaining the rationale for the attack, Clinton laid out the litany of bin Laden's nefarious work. By now, U.S. intelligence believed al-Qaeda had helped train the Somali militias that had killed international peacekeepers in 1993, including the American rangers in Mogadishu. The president also reported that al-Qaeda operatives had tried to kill the pope and the president of Egypt, sought to crash six American 747s over the Pacific, and bombed the embassies in Africa. "Afghanistan and Sudan have been warned for years to stop harboring and supporting these terrorist groups," the president declared in his speech to the nation. "But countries that persistently host terrorists have no right to be safe havens." He added, "This will be a long, ongoing struggle between freedom and fanaticism, between the rule of law and terrorism."[37] A headline in the *International Herald Tribune* on August 22, 1998, announced, U.S. ON ALERT, PREPARING FOR 'WAR' ON TERROR.[38]

But the country was hardly thinking about war. The embassy bombings were overshadowed by the bigger story consuming the nation's political debate. The day before the embassy attacks, Monica Lewinsky testified before a grand jury about her relationship with the president. At that moment, Washington officials were whipsawed between the tawdry and the tragic. Clinton wrote later that while on vacation that month in Martha's Vineyard, "I spent the first couple of days alternating between begging for forgiveness [from my family] and planning the strikes on al-Qaeda."[39]

Given that the retaliatory strikes occurred at the same time the Lewinsky scandal was unfolding, some were suspicious. At a Pentagon briefing, a reporter asked if Americans were witnessing a "wag the dog" moment. Secretary of Defense William Cohen swiftly responded, "The only motivation driving this action today was our absolute obligation to protect the American people from terrorist activities." (Once again, Clinton officials later admitted how important it was that the lone Republican in the cabinet could rebut these charges.) Some important leaders in Congress agreed, with Gingrich saying questions about motivation were "sick" and adding, "I don't think people should think about that at all. This is real."[40]

But not everyone was willing to give the president the benefit of the doubt. Republican Senator Dan Coats, a member of the Armed Services Committee, declared, "While there is clearly much more we need to learn about this attack and why it was ordered today, given the president's personal difficulties this week, it is legitimate to question the timing of this action."[41] The larger problem for Clinton was that even those who supported the attacks had to defend him against the "wag the dog" charge, thereby perpetuating it. Rather than serving as the first in a series of attacks against al-Qaeda, the August 20 strikes were Clinton's last. The president's political weakness certainly played a role in the minimal response to a growing problem.

Rhetorically, however, Clinton continued to press the case that the threat was serious. He used his annual address to the United Nations in September 1998 to tell the world that "all nations must put the fight against terrorism at the top of our agenda." But as he ruefully reflected, "While I was speaking to the U.N. about terrorism, all the television networks were showing the videotape of my grand jury testimony."[42]

YEARS LATER, when asked about the difficulties in conveying a sense of urgency to the public, Berger got up quickly from his chair, walked over to a shelf in his downtown Washington office, and pulled out a thick binder of the administration's public remarks on the growing danger posed by terrorism. "From 1998 on, we saw this as the dominant threat we faced," Berger said, but "people weren't listening." He admits that the Lewinsky scandal and impeachment "did make it harder to get the message across."[43] His deputy, James Steinberg, adds, with frustration in his voice, "Inside the White House, you feel like you are communicating. But people didn't get enough. We should have talked to more people on the outside about what was being heard. Maybe we could have broken through. But people had such strong views about Clinton; people didn't see his core message because of his style."[44]

In December 1998, Tenet wrote an internal memo in which he declared, "We are at war." And Clinton later recalled thinking about bin Laden, "I wanted to see him dead." But the administration did not make war the organizing concept for a new American global strategy to diminish al-Qaeda's capabilities. To do so would have been "difficult because a government that had never viewed terrorism as a first-tier threat had neither the organization nor the laws to deal with it that way," recalled two top Clinton counterterrorism officials. U.S. agencies responsible for what after 9/11 became known as homeland security were woefully unprepared for such a fight. There was a lack of actionable intelligence on bin Laden's whereabouts, a dismissive view of his training camps as good bombing targets—and the president continued to be distracted by impeachment.[45]

There was no broad strategic framework in which to fit a discussion about a sustained campaign against Afghanistan. There was instead political pressure to deal with Iraq's Saddam Hussein. And liberal hawks were trying to make a statement about the use of force to save lives in Kosovo. Attacking a new type of enemy was a different matter. Despite the belief at the top levels of the administration that the United States was at war after 1998, and despite the concerns the American public had in general about terrorism, the Clinton administration did not pursue a strategy commensurate with the language it was using internally.

Former Indiana Congressman Lee Hamilton, who cochaired the

9/11 Commission, offers the verdict that speeches are not a sufficient indicator of a policy. "If there's anything a member of Congress knows," Hamilton says, "it's what's important to a president, because when a president is interested in something, he's got the full White House steam and the full bureaucracy up there on the Hill. When he's not interested in something, you know that. Terrorism is in that category. If you asked Clinton officials, they would say, 'Terrorism is a big issue.' But the fact of the matter was, they did not attach a high priority to it."[46] Former Nebraska Senator Bob Kerrey, a Clinton opponent during the 1992 campaign and another 9/11 Commission member, expressed outrage at the claim that the Clinton team had made the best possible case. Kerrey said that if the administration had put into its intelligence estimates what it then knew about al-Qaeda's role in the death of the American servicemen who were dragged through the streets of Somalia in 1993, Congress and thus the public might have been more receptive to doing something more meaningful against the organization.[47]

What the Clinton team did or didn't do to fight al-Qaeda—and who stood in the way—remains hotly disputed. Counterterrorism officials, including Clarke and two members of his staff, Daniel Benjamin and Steven Simon, have written books describing how frustrated they were with a bureaucracy that did not take the threat seriously enough, with an FBI and CIA that were fighting jurisdictional turf wars, and with a Pentagon that did not want to provide serious plans for knocking out al-Qaeda's infrastructure in Afghanistan.

But General Anthony Zinni, the Marine commander in charge of U.S. forces in the Middle East, brushes back the criticism: "As far as missing opportunities to strike, that's just Richard Clarke bullshit. It was right to fire the TLAMs [Tomahawk land attack missiles] into Afghanistan with information that he might be there. We had to take the TLAM shot. But that was a stupid target in Khartoum. We shot the pharmaceutical factory and all we did was spread aspirin all over Khartoum. They wanted me to shoot Kandahar when bin Laden might or might not be there and there would be 1,500 casualties. I refused. I told [Secretary of Defense] Cohen, if you order me to do it, I'll have to resign."[48] Steinberg adds, "We had no actionable intelligence. The only thing we could have done was invade. We debated paramilitary operations. We weren't going to do another Desert One [Jimmy Carter's failed operation to free the hostages in Iran in 1980]. It would have been irresponsible."[49]

To convince Americans that major military action against Afghanistan was necessary to ward off a terrorist attack, the president would have had to exert serious leadership. The 9/11 Commission reported that "every official we questioned about the possibility of an invasion of Afghanistan said that it was almost unthinkable, absent a provocation like 9/11."[50] And of course, even major military action against Afghanistan after 2001 did not lead to the capture of bin Laden. It would have taken the best of circumstances—including greater presidential credibility with the military—for Clinton to garner the domestic and international support needed for a policy to match the private rhetoric within the White House about being at war.

Galvanizing an administration and Congress for a remote war requires sustained effort and ample reserves of political capital. The U.S. government had its most actionable intelligence on bin Laden's whereabouts in May 1999, at the same time the president was deliberating the introduction of ground troops into Kosovo. More significant, the Lewinsky scandal and subsequent impeachment hearings severely damaged the president. White House officials have always maintained that the president continued to focus on his business. As former Chief of Staff John Podesta says, administration officials "took a deep breath and kept to their knitting." Hamilton disagrees. "Monica Lewinsky was a huge diversion. [Clinton] wouldn't have been human if it wasn't a diversion."[51] And if it was not a distraction for the president or his top aides, it was for the press and the public. Warnings about a growing threat fell on distracted ears.

BUT WAS "war" even the best way to think about a confrontation with al-Qaeda? A year after the August 1998 cruise missile strikes, a debate played out in the pages of the *Washington Post* regarding how best to combat the growing terrorist threat. Paul Bremer, ambassador at large for counterterrorism in the Reagan administration who later gained notoriety for his role in postwar Iraq after the 2003 invasion, applauded Clinton for the military attacks on al-Qaeda. "The strikes," wrote Bremer, "dispel the impression of recent years that attacks on Americans—whether in Somalia, Saudi Arabia, or Pakistan—remain unanswered. And they come as a welcome application of unilateral American force after years of dependence on desultory multilateralism."

Unfortunately, Bremer asserted, the United States was engaged in a "long struggle," because after being attacked, bin Laden would retaliate. Bremer's conclusion was grim. "This struggle has no clear end point," he explained. "We will never 'win' the war against terrorism." America had to find a strategy that could "keep bin Laden off balance" and utilize its resources to assassinate him.[52]

But others believed that the best approach would be one that focused on root causes. Charles William Maynes, a widely respected foreign policy expert who served for many years as editor of the magazine *Foreign Policy*, wrote in response that Bremer was dangerously mistaken. The Israelis had tried such a strategy against the Palestinians, the British against the Irish Republican movement. Fighting dirty, Maynes opined, merely increased the number of terrorists. The only way to deal with the problem was to present a smaller target in the Middle East, recognize why terrorists were motivated against the United States, and enlist the support of other states. It was clear, Maynes wrote, that America's presence in Saudi Arabia was a major problem, that the United States needed Pakistan to help address the threats emanating from Afghanistan, and that progress was necessary in the Middle East peace process.[53]

Unfortunately, this debate over how best to combat terrorism got little attention at the time. Two years later, it could not have been more important.

MEANWHILE, Clinton was trying a mix of the two strategies: disrupting terrorist financing and hoping for intelligence that might allow him to take out bin Laden while at the same time pursuing peace in the Middle East. In his first year as president, Clinton had brought Palestinian leader Yasir Arafat and Israeli Prime Minister Yitzhak Rabin together for their famous handshake. That moment initiated a major American push to get a peace deal, a process in which for seven years the United States played the key role as broker. Clinton had some success negotiating interim agreements, but in the final summer of his presidency, he wanted to push for a full settlement. Bringing Arafat and the new Israeli premier, Ehud Barak, together at Camp David, Clinton believed a comprehensive deal would redound to America's advantage throughout the region.

In July 2000, discussions began at the president's retreat in Maryland. For two weeks, Clinton engaged in intense negotiations with his counterparts over the status of Jerusalem, security for the two states, the Palestinian claims of a "right of return" for those who fled their homes after the creation of the state of Israel in 1948, and the final borders of Israel and Palestine. He invested enormous personal energy and political capital, but the effort was in vain.[54]

Then, despite the violent Palestinian uprising that broke out in September, Clinton tried one last effort. In late December, after the Supreme Court declared George W. Bush president, Clinton brought the parties to the White House, putting on the table his latest ideas on land swaps and the division of Jerusalem. The Israelis agreed to the deal's terms, but Arafat refused to go along. Clinton had tried to achieve historic peace in the Middle East rather than devote his final months in office either to the North Korean nuclear program or to a serious plan to capture or kill bin Laden.[55] He felt it was a gamble worth taking, but he could not convince Arafat to make peace.

CLINTON'S EFFORT to forge a Middle East peace agreement had no impact on al-Qaeda's determination to kill Americans. On October 12, 2000, weeks before the American presidential election, a bomb tore through the USS *Cole*, stationed in Yemen, killing seventeen American sailors and injuring scores more. By the end of the year, the United States had corroborated intelligence that this was an al-Qaeda operation, but there still was not enough evidence pointing to bin Laden as the mastermind. Military planners prepared for more sustained attacks, but Clinton decided that absent definitive proof, he was not going to launch a war against the Taliban and bin Laden in Afghanistan.[56]

McLaughlin says the Clinton team deserves "a lot of credit for taking the terrorist problem seriously. Berger was seized with the issue. In the fall of 2000, he asked [the CIA] for a blue-sky proposal: How would you destroy these people if you were unconstrained by resources? Over Christmas, I was on my secure fax in my basement, going back and forth with [senior counterterrorism official] Cofer Black to finish the memo and give it to Berger. But they ran out of time." (Interestingly, Berger told the 9/11 Commission he never saw the memo or was briefed on it.)[57]

Although Clinton understood the ominous danger al-Qaeda posed, and its enormous potential to do harm, he was not able to formulate an effective strategy in response. The government bureaucracy proved too resistant, the public's attention too fleeting. The 9/11 Commission called it a failure of policy and imagination. Finally, Clinton's personal foibles hindered his capabilities at precisely the moment he needed Americans to hear his warning about the growing threat. Clarke wrote in his memoirs of those years that "because Clinton was criticized as a Vietnam War opponent without a military record, he was limited in his ability to direct the military to engage in anti-terrorist commando operations they did not want to conduct. He had tried that in Somalia [in 1993], and the military had made mistakes and blamed him. In the absence of a bigger provocation from al-Qaeda to silence his critics, Clinton thought he could do no more."[58]

Conservatives and "Globaloney"

Terrorism was a quintessential global threat, yet the only institution with worldwide reach, the United Nations, proved largely feckless to deal with it. Part of the problem was that the United Nations itself was rife with internal divisions. The U.N. General Assembly adopted numerous resolutions condemning terrorism, and the Security Council threatened sanctions against any country that harbored bin Laden. Twelve treaties called various terrorist acts illegal, such as hijacking and kidnapping. Since 1996, an Ad Hoc Committee on Measures to Eliminate Terrorism had been meeting at the United Nations, but its members could not even come up with a common definition of terrorism. Islamic states refused to name as terrorism the killing of non-combatants during "wars of national liberation," as the Palestinians considered their struggle against Israel.[59]

Yet another part of the problem was that at the end of the 1990s, the U.S. relationship with the United Nations was in tatters. The days of a Republican U.S. president declaring the institution the heart of a "new world order" seemed like ancient history; by 1999, the U.S. ambassador to the United Nations, Richard Holbrooke, was arguing that the United Nations needed to be saved from growing irrelevance. For Clinton and his top advisers, the United Nations proved extremely disappointing. They constantly fought to maintain Security Council unity on the sanctions against Iraq, and in Kosovo they had acted without explicit Security Council authorization because they knew they would not get it. Most conservatives, especially Republicans in Congress who worried about limits on American power and the dissolution of U.S. sovereignty, viewed the United Nations as outright dangerous.

The Contract Republicans considered the United Nations the bastion of "globalism"—one that could endanger American soldiers on misguided peacekeeping missions and might allow U.S. territories to be gobbled up by designating them U.N. "World Heritage Sites." These conservatives sought to choke the United Nations off by restricting the amount of money the United States could pay to the institution in annual dues. By the late 1990s, the country with the world's largest economy owed the United Nations nearly $1 billion, and the Republican Congress would let the United States pay off its debt only if the institution undertook a series of tough reforms. This standoff compounded the discomfort many other countries had with the United States, fueling the perception of American heavy-handedness, arrogance, and unilateralism.

Into this breach leaped one of Washington's most unlikely pairs: Holbrooke, the tenacious diplomat, and Jesse Helms, the elderly ultraconservative North Carolina senator who was the powerful chairman of the Senate Foreign Relations Committee. Ever since his success in forging the Dayton Accords, Holbrooke had been looking for his next act. He had narrowly missed being named as Clinton's second-term secretary of state (losing to a well-orchestrated campaign by Albright and her supporters), and since then he had taken on a series of special-envoy assignments in the Balkans. When Clinton chose him to become U.N. ambassador, many expected Holbrooke to become a formidable player inside the administration's bureaucratic battles on a range of issues. (Under Clinton, the U.N. ambassador was also a member of the president's cabinet and had a seat at the table along with the secretaries of state and defense.) But instead he poured his considerable energies into solving one of the more vexing—and, most assumed, thankless—tasks he inherited: getting the U.S.-U.N. relationship back on track.

To do so Holbrooke had to forge a close partnership with Helms, a courtly man who counted himself as one of the United Nations' staunchest foes. The North Carolinian represented a strand of conservatism that was more nationalist than isolationist. He believed the United States had to remain engaged in the world but rejected the idea that it needed the blessing of institutions such as the United Nations to make its actions legitimate. Despite what many believed about Helms, he did not want to destroy the United Nations but instead believed it should have a more limited role in world affairs. Holbrooke understood this important distinction and sought to build an alliance with Helms to reform the institution, and in the process, strengthen the U.S. relationship with it.

Holbrooke pulled out all the stops to accomplish this feat: He spent countless hours bargaining with Helms's colleagues on Capitol Hill and heaped charm on the chairman himself. The highlight of this effort came in January 2000, when Holbrooke arranged for Helms to address the Security Council in person. Speaking before a packed chamber and with the Security Council ambassadors seated around its famous horseshoe-shaped table, the senator chided the United Nations for violating the "sanctity" of sovereignty and for trying to create a "new international order." Yet he also said he wanted to "extend the hand of friendship" and find a way "to do everything we can to achieve peace in the world."

Although he administered some tough medicine, the other ambassadors took Helms's appearance as a sign of respect and willingness to cut a deal. As U.N. Secretary General Kofi Annan put it, the visit "sent a message that the U.S. is part of the organization, and we should work together." Helms's speech was front-page news. He was so proud of it that he later published the text in full as an appendix in his memoirs. The museum at the Jesse Helms Center in Wingate, North Carolina, features an exhibit re-creating his U.N. visit, including a mock Security Council chamber. The center's home page prominently displays a quote by Democratic Senator Joseph Biden: "Just as only Nixon could go to China, only Helms could fix the U.N."[60]

By the end of the year, just weeks before Clinton left office, Holbrooke prevailed upon all U.N. member states to agree unanimously to make most of the proposed reforms to satisfy Helms and allow the United States to begin repaying the money it owed. Not since the United States had mobilized the Persian Gulf War coalition had it managed such a victory at the United Nations. For a moment, it looked as though the dark chapter in U.S.-U.N. relations was coming to an end and that perhaps a revitalized United Nations could help the United States deal with global challenges such as terrorism. But those hopes were quickly dashed during the George W. Bush years.

AT THE SAME TIME Helms was trying to make peace with the United Nations, *Commentary* magazine invited authors from various points on the conservative spectrum to take part in a symposium titled "American Power—For What?"[61] Similar debates had played out in conservative journals after the fall of the Berlin Wall more than a decade

earlier. Now in January 2000, a who's who of past and future conservative foreign policy thinkers and officials, including Elliott Abrams,
Paul Wolfowitz, Jeane Kirkpatrick, Zalmay Khalilzad, Robert Kagan,
William Kristol, and Francis Fukuyama, were once again debating
when to use force and when to work through multilateral institutions,
discussing the major threats facing the United States and pondering
the country's purpose.

What's instructive is that after all that had occurred in the decade
since 11/9, only one contributor discussed globalization. And only
one mentioned terrorism as a major threat facing the United States.
He was a Democrat and former Clinton Pentagon and intelligence
official invited to join his more conservative colleagues.

The essays were solicited to respond to a *Commentary* article by
Norman Podhoretz, one of the intellectual godfathers of the neoconservative movement.[62] Podhoretz noted that mainstream conservatives opposed interventions in the Balkans in the 1990s as not in
America's national interest and seemed to be leaning toward isolationism. He also marveled that rather than turning inward, Clinton
had engaged in the use of military force in numerous locales around
the world. Conservatives and liberals, Podhoretz wrote, had shifted
positions dramatically since the end of the Cold War.

One group, he suggested, had maintained its consistency: neoconservatives. Writing in *Commentary*, the *Weekly Standard*, and *National
Review*, they had come back from the dead, pushing what Kristol and
Kagan had dubbed a neo-Reaganite foreign policy: arguing against
deep cuts in the defense budget, warning about the potential threat
that China might pose, and urging that the United States seek to
remove both Milosevic and Saddam from power. Podhoretz wanted
to make clear that neoconservatives, while on the same side as
"humanitarian" liberals in Kosovo, were concerned not just about
values, but about values *and* interests.

Podhoretz did not discuss the ways in which globalization had
dramatically changed the speed with which financial crises in one
part of the world affected another; nor did he engage the issue of how

America's military and intelligence services might need to be restructured to deal with terrorist networks. Only defense spending, China, and dictators had his attention—not jihad or McWorld.

When most of Podhoretz's conservative colleagues assessed his essay the following month, they also failed to address the new challenges facing the United States. They had long sneered at the Clinton administration's emphasis on globalization as "globaloney," believing that issues such as the environment, disease, and nonstate threats were second-tier concerns. They believed hostile states were the most pressing threats. Abrams said the key question in international relations was whether the United States would preserve its dominant position, the same question the 1992 Defense Planning Guidance had addressed. William F. Buckley Jr. asked, "What are we going to do about Taiwan?" Kirkpatrick wrote that "missile defense is the most salient issue."[63]

There was some back-and-forth over the need for a new doctrine to guide America. Columnist Charles Krauthammer suggested that a theory of prudent and selective intervention made sense, since "superpowers don't do windows." But Johns Hopkins University professor Eliot Cohen sounded a cautionary note about the continuing search for a new doctrine. The world was too messy, he argued, and "pragmatic skill, not ideological clarity, is what the times call for."[64]

Fukuyama, who had jump-started the post–Cold War debate eleven years earlier with his article on the end of history, pointed out the obvious, foreshadowing his future split with many of his conservative colleagues. "A final gap in Podhoretz's account," Fukuyama wrote, "is his silence on the subject of globalization. Twenty-five years ago, when I was studying international politics in graduate school, high politics revolved around nuclear alerts and Henry Kissinger's shuttlings to the Middle East. Today, high politics is . . . jetting off to Seoul or Jakarta to arrange a bailout." Then he added insult to injury. "Save for [Patrick] Buchanan . . . none of the [conservative] figures mentioned in Podhoretz's article has tried to come to terms with the global economy or has anything particularly interesting to say about it."[65]

It was left to Harvard University professor Joseph Nye, a Democrat who had served in the Clinton administration at the Pentagon and National Intelligence Council, to bring home further the reality of the year 2000. Nye managed to combine both a judicious notion of American power and a succinct definition of the core threats facing the country. "Preventing attacks on the United States by countries or terrorists; preventing the emergence of hostile hegemons in Asia or Europe; preventing the emergence of dangerous situations on our borders—these deserve priority because they threaten our survival," he suggested.[66]

During the Cold War, conservatives prided themselves on knowing one big thing: the need to combat the Soviet Union. A decade later, they were fixated on which countries now posed the biggest threats to America and believed Democrats too hobbled by perpetual weakness to respond. But other states weren't the only danger.

WHILE CONSERVATIVES were debating on the pages of *Commentary* and Helms was speaking at the United Nations, Clinton prepared for his last State of the Union Address. Standing before Congress in late January 2000, Clinton declared, "We are fortunate to be alive at this moment in history. Never before has our nation enjoyed, at once, so much prosperity and social progress with so little internal crisis and so few external threats." He recalled that eight years earlier, "Our nation was gripped by economic distress, social decline, and political gridlock." But he warned, "I predict to you, when most of us are long gone but some time in the next ten to twenty years, the major security threat this country will face will come from the enemies of the nation-state, the narcotraffickers and the terrorists and the organized criminals who will be organized together, working together, with increasing access to ever more sophisticated chemical and biological weapons."

The country would have to face that threat much sooner than Clinton predicted. And sadly, as the campaign to succeed him heated up, there was no evidence that those advising the Republican nominee, Texas Governor George W. Bush, saw nonstate threats anywhere on their radar screens. They viewed China as the most serious threat and missile defense as the top priority. These Republican advisers almost willfully refused to recognize the changes wrought by globalization in the years since they had last served in government. The campaign touched on many issues, but, unfortunately, the need to confront the new world disorder was not one of them.

CHAPTER TEN

The End of the Modern Interwar Years

IT WAS THE KIND of debate George W. Bush wanted. Seated at a crescent-shaped table inside Wait Chapel on the leafy campus of Wake Forest University in Winston-Salem, North Carolina, the two presidential candidates dueled before an audience of 1,000 people, while millions watched on television at home. The Texas governor and his aides believed the relaxed setting would help demonstrate his confident command of the issues, especially when contrasted with the man sitting across from him, the stiff and sometimes over-bearing vice president of the United States, Al Gore.

The North Carolina venue had a special meaning for the Bush family: It was the same lighted stage where, in 1988, George H. W. Bush had debated Michael Dukakis on his way to succeeding Ronald Reagan as president. Although no one knew so at the time, it was the last presidential campaign of the Cold War, when foreign policy reigned as a decisive issue in American politics. Back then, the discussion was dominated by such questions as whether to trust the Soviets and which new nuclear weapons systems should be deployed. Throughout that debate, George H. W. Bush sought to project strength, promising a bold policy and charging that his oppo-nent would accept limits on American power and concede U.S. weakness.

When Bush's eldest son returned to Wait Chapel on a fall day twelve years later, during the first campaign of the twenty-first century, foreign policy was no longer a major priority. Both candidates had given their obligatory thoughtful speeches and assembled their respective teams of policy experts, but they had not engaged each other directly. So when the conversation turned to what the United States now should do with its overwhelming power around the globe, the differences between the two men proved revealing. In many ways, the candidates had reversed roles: The Democrat was the interventionist hawk, sketching a daring vision for asserting American influence, while the Republican candidate espoused views that during the Cold War would have been thought of as liberal, worrying about the global ripple effects American actions might create.

George W. Bush got the opening question of the night. The debate moderator, Jim Lehrer of PBS, asked if he had formed any "guiding principles" for the exercise of U.S. power. Throughout the campaign, Bush had been dogged by questions about his lack of overseas experience and doubts about his ability to be commander-in-chief—impressions not helped by his frequent malapropisms (such as referring to Greeks as "Grecians" or Kosovars as "Kosovians") and his struggle to name the leaders of Pakistan, South Korea, and India during a television interview. But he had been studying hard and listening to his team of experienced advisers, led by his vice presidential nominee, Dick Cheney, whom he had coaxed away from Texas to return to politics. Bush's demeanor now seemed more relaxed and less tentative. The ideas he expressed, however, were modest.

"The first question is what's in the best interest of the United States?" Bush replied to Lehrer. "What's in the best interests of our people? When it comes to foreign policy, that will be my guiding question." Bush made clear he would not be as interventionist as Bill Clinton had been. He then went on to explain that given America's extraordinary power, it had to tailor its goals and project its strength with humility, lest it overextend its power and spark a global backlash. "If we're an arrogant nation, they'll resent us. If we're a humble nation, but strong, they'll welcome us ... one way for us being viewed as the 'ugly American' is for us to go around the world saying, 'We do it this way; so should you.'"

Gore did not dispute the importance of being humble. Indeed, given his performance during his first debate with Bush the week before—in which he wore too much rouge stage makeup and seemed dismissive and impatient, punctuating his responses with audible sighs—his whole strategy that night was about projecting humility. But the vice president offered a more expansive, interventionist vision of America's global role, one that reflected the confidence generated by the Clinton administration's success in using force in the Balkans.

"I see it as a question of values," he said. "I think that we also have to have a sense of mission in the world. We have to protect our capacity to push forward what America is all about." For Gore, this included using military power to stop genocide and to help stabilize war-torn countries, which since Somalia, Republicans (and now Bush on the campaign trail) had derided as nation-building. He turned and told Bush directly that such interventions "can bring into play a fundamental strategic interest because I think it's based on our values. Now, have I got that wrong?"

Bush was hardly a dove in terms of using force, but he expressed worries about promising too much, which could tarnish America's prestige or hamper its ability to pursue other goals. "We can't be all things to all people," he responded, "and I think that's where maybe the vice president and I begin to have some differences. I am worried about overcommitting our military around the world." He outlined a limited mission for military power, asking, "I mean, are we going to have a kind of nation-building corps in America? Absolutely not. Our military is meant to fight and win war."

The argument that Democrats were untrustworthy leaders of the military was a theme Republicans had emphasized since Clinton's 1993 efforts to allow gays to serve and his failure in Somalia. Bush stood squarely in that tradition, characterizing the Clinton administration's use of force as promiscuous and costly for military readiness. The only area where Bush tried to take a more hawkish posture concerned Iraq, and even there he mainly criticized Clinton and Gore for allowing the international coalition against Saddam Hussein to weaken. Harkening back to his father's diplomatic successes, Bush promised to "rebuild" the alliance against Iraq.

Gore did not back down—after all, he had years of foreign policy experience. He reminded the audience that he had been one of the few Democrats to support the 1991 Persian Gulf War and had always advocated a hard line against Saddam inside the Clinton administration. Gore explained that now he wanted to "go further," maintaining the sanctions on Iraq while giving "robust support to the groups that are trying to overthrow Saddam Hussein." On the larger question of America's global role, Gore tried to paint Bush's criticism as nothing more than warmed-over isolationism, while couching his own views squarely in the tradition of the country's post–World War II engagement.

"This is an absolutely unique period in world history," Gore concluded, "and we have a fundamental choice to make. Are we going to step up to the plate as a nation the way we did after World War II, the way that generation of heroes said okay, the United States is going to be the leader? [The] world benefited tremendously from the courage that they showed in those postwar years. I think that in the aftermath of the Cold War, it's time for us to do something very similar."[1]

AFTER THE DEBATE ended and the hordes of partisan spinners descended to claim victory for their side, many commentators pointed out that Bush and Gore had worked hard to avoid the acrimony that characterized their first encounter. The *New York Times* editorialized that they were like "two students taking a makeup exam." During the debate Bush joked that it seemed like a "love fest."[2] Indeed, in the forty-five minutes that they had discussed the U.S. role in the world, both candidates agreed on a lot of the specifics: They supported American involvement in the Middle East peace process, NATO's enlargement, the intervention to end Slobodan Milosevic's repression in Kosovo, and the decision not to get involved in Rwanda.

But beneath this general consensus lay two very different foreign policy approaches. Bush's was dedicated to protecting core interests. He argued that the United States should be careful where it employed force but free of international restraints when it chose to do so. He criticized Clinton's use of the military for "humanitarian" reasons and stressed that the United States should act humbly. Gore's conveyed a broader definition of U.S. interests and the need for its leadership in the transforming world, emphasizing the importance of working to spread liberal values and leading an international "community." These views reflected the lessons that the candidates, and their cadres of policy advisers, had learned in the decade since the Berlin Wall fell.

In the years to come, many commentators would ponder the journey Bush and Gore traveled after this debate—wondering how Bush squared his admonition to be "humble" with his policies as president, and asking why Gore abandoned his hawkish rhetoric about American intervention to emerge as a leading opponent of the 2003 Iraq War. The answers lie inside the intense debates that still roiled within both political parties about America's role in the world and that prompted their standard-bearers' respective transformations.

Legacies and Futures

The 2000 election was supposed to be a coronation for Gore. He had served loyally under Clinton and had emerged as the most powerful vice president to that point in American history. The economy was booming, the federal budget produced a surplus, and the Republican Party failed to impeach the president. Yet as the campaign began, Gore appeared stuck in first gear, offering a jumble of policy ideas that lacked an overarching theme, and he faced a surprisingly strong primary challenge from one of his former colleagues in the Senate, New Jersey's Bill Bradley.

Gore's biggest dilemma was his enormously complex relationship with Clinton. It had started with so much promise. When Clinton had picked Gore to be his vice presidential running mate in 1992, the image of such accomplished, young, moderate, Southern Democrats symbolized for many a changing of the generational guard after the Cold War. Throughout the administration, Gore was the president's most influential foreign policy adviser. The vice president had spent years earnestly studying national security affairs as a member of Congress, and unlike the president, he did not have to develop a comfort level with the issues. As a self-described "hard-liner," Gore almost always played the role of house hawk inside the Clinton team's debates, whether it was arguing for the use of force in Bosnia and Kosovo, pushing for the Mexican financial bailout, or stiffening Clinton's spine to stay strong in the confrontation with Saddam. In all of these cases, Gore's advocacy proved decisive.[3]

Despite their political partnership, the two men never became close friends, and as the 2000 campaign heated up, their relationship grew strained and awkward. Like every incumbent vice president running for the highest office, Gore struggled to move out of the president's shadow while at the same time extolling the administration's accomplishments. This proved particularly tricky in the wake of impeachment; the president's behavior repulsed Gore, and the vice president was deeply worried about its impact on his electoral fortunes. Concerned about what he called "Clinton fatigue," Gore distanced himself from the president. That decision angered Clinton, opened a breach between their staffs (Clinton loyalists sometimes referred to Gore's team derisively as "Goreniks"), and produced a clash in Democratic political circles.[4]

Yet together Clinton and Gore were the principal architects of the robust approach to the world that had come to dominate the thinking inside the Democratic establishment. They had become confident evangelists about the challenges and opportunities of the globalizing world, and what those meant for America's economy and security. For years, Gore had focused on transnational threats, such as climate change (George H. W. Bush once ridiculed him as "ozone man") and the spread of weapons of mass destruction. As Clinton neared the end of his second term, Gore focused more and more on the possibilities of global governance and continued the effort to forge a Third Way.

Gore's campaign did not intend to embark on a new foreign policy course. "The objective was not trying to divorce Gore from the previous eight years," the vice president's longtime national security adviser, Leon Fuerth, explains. "The question was what to build on, which was less well-advanced."[5] Tethered together by their ideas, the president and vice president had different yet potentially reinforcing goals: Gore needed to articulate a compelling path for the future, while Clinton set out to cement a legacy.

CLINTON APPROACHED his final months in office with the desperate fervor of someone who didn't want his time to run out. And there was no greater evidence of his evolution into a foreign policy president than the bold global agenda he set out to pursue during his last year: trying to broker peace between Israel and the Palestinians, pushing for a diplomatic breakthrough with North Korea, solidifying his international economic platform, and maintaining a punishing pace of overseas meetings and travel (including a historic visit to Vietnam). "He's come to love the puzzle of geopolitics," one of his cabinet members remarked at the time, as the president discovered that the gamesmanship, horse-trading, sense of timing, and skilled handling of people required in domestic politics were essential to success on the international stage as well. He had also come to believe, Sandy Berger said, that no other country had the "muscle, the diplomatic skill, or the trust to mediate disputes, nudge opposing sides to the negotiating table, or . . . enforce the terms of an agreement."[6]

For his first few years in the White House, Clinton had been roundly criticized for lacking ambitious global goals and not being involved enough in the inner workings of foreign policy. But by the end of his second term, his critics complained that the president was trying too hard and getting too involved and, as a result, frittering away the leverage that comes with more selective presidential engagement.[7]

Clinton wanted to do more than solve problems; he also sought to develop a convincing framework for America's global leadership that could be embraced by those both abroad and at home. He set out to use his remaining days in the bully pulpit to articulate his case. Clinton worried that many close allies feared the rise of U.S. power and "unilateralism"—which some in the State Department referred to as the "hegemony problem"—especially in the wake of Kosovo and Operation Desert Fox in Iraq. And he seethed at the criticisms from respected internationalists such as Brent Scowcroft, who argued that "we've lost the sense of what we're really good at: getting people to join us. . . . We don't consult, we don't ask ahead of time. We behave to much of the world like a latter-day colonial power."[8]

In 1993 Clinton had been pilloried for stooping to contemplate the limits of America's will and capabilities, and now he was being blamed for using U.S. power too much. This was particularly true among many of America's best friends in Europe, where the administration had produced its greatest diplomatic and military successes. Clinton wanted to make clear that a strong United States needed strong allies. This was the core message of his June 2000 speech in Aachen, Germany, where he became the first U.S. president to receive the Charlemagne Prize, the highest European honor bestowed on a leader whose efforts have helped advance European unity. The occasion itself illustrated Clinton's dominance of the world stage—the only other Americans to receive the award were General George C. Marshall and Henry Kissinger.

Speaking to his European audience, Clinton addressed the hegemony concern head-on.[9] "There is a perception in Europe that America's power—military, economic, cultural—is at times too overbearing," he said. "Perhaps our role in NATO's air campaign in Kosovo accentuated such fears." He did not deny the frictions across the Atlantic but reminded his audience that such tensions had always existed: "We've always had our differences," he explained, "and being human and imperfect, we always will." But given the range of global challenges, the president argued that America and Europe had no choice but to cooperate closely because no single nation, even one as powerful as the United States, could handle these problems alone.

To Clinton, globalization ended the zero-sum game that had defined the Cold War, in which one country's gain was another's loss. Now the world was interdependent, and countries had to find ways to cooperate. (This was the core argument of Robert Wright's book *Nonzero*, which Clinton read and often mentioned in his public speeches as dovetailing with his own philosophy.) "If we're going to win the fight against terrorism, organized crime, the spread of weapons of mass destruction," the president said in a rising peroration, "if we want to promote ethnic, religious, and racial tolerance; if we want to combat global warming and environmental degradation, fight infectious disease, ease poverty, and close the digital divide— clearly, we must do these things together."

Immediately after the speech in Germany, some of Clinton's aides were struck by how melancholy he seemed. Perhaps his brooding was simply the recognition that his ride as president would soon end. But maybe it was also a symptom of his worries about how quickly all he had accomplished could unravel. Alongside his efforts to assuage European concerns about American power, Clinton undertook the equally important task of ensuring U.S. domestic support for an ambitious foreign policy. Although Clinton had long since abandoned the search for a new catchword to rival "containment," he remained frustrated by his inability to communicate what such dramatic global changes meant for America and the world. As Strobe Talbott remembered, "He never felt that he had quite found the right words to explain what he was trying to do in his foreign policy and why it deserved the support of the American people."[10] Clinton needed to articulate his policies not just in the heart of Europe, but in America's heartland as well.

In December 2000, with the election to succeed him still in doubt a month after the polls closed and just six weeks before he was to leave office, Clinton traveled to the only state he had yet to visit as president, Nebraska, to address a college audience in a speech titled "Foreign Policy in a Global Age."[11] As a valedictory, he tried one last time to lay out his vision for America's role in the world. But rather than attempt to capture the era in a memorable phrase, Clinton covered as many topics as he could think of. It was as if, now that his presidency was ending, he thought he should mention every global issue and every region. The speech foreshadowed the role he would assume in his hyperactive postpresidency, as a global statesman.

What was most striking was not the sweeping range of this final major foreign policy address, but rather the starting point: with an admission that in one significant way, he had failed. Despite his years of trying to explain that America needed to lead a world now condensed by the dramatic integration of societies and markets, the president ruefully admitted he had not yet succeeded. "People say I'm a pretty good talker," Clinton declared, "but I still don't think I've persuaded the American people by big majorities that you really ought to care a lot about foreign policy, about our relationship to the rest of the world, about what we're doing."

Clinton had won office eight years before precisely because most Americans, and many political elites, thought that after the Cold War, attention should turn to fixing problems at home. And in this respect, he proudly noted that the country had its lowest unemployment rate in three decades, the smallest welfare rolls in thirty-two years, the lowest crime rate in twenty-seven years, the highest home ownership in American history, and three consecutive years of budget surpluses.

But the president still believed he had more explaining to do. "We are all directly affected by what goes on beyond our borders," he said. Most Americans shrugged off the Asian financial crisis of the late 1990s, but Clinton appreciated how intertwined the United States had become with emerging economies around the world. While Americans were distracted by the impeachment scandal, Clinton had become seized by the tremendous danger posed by Osama bin Laden. "The train of globalization cannot be reversed," he told his young Nebraska audience, returning to a metaphor he often used to describe the forces reshaping global politics. "But it has more than one possible destination." To stay on the right track, he argued, "America must lead."

*

ALTHOUGH CLINTON himself believed he had fallen short in convincing the American people of the need for sustained global engagement, his leadership had fundamentally reshaped the foreign policy debate inside the Democratic Party. He had helped Democrats convert their sense of drift after the Cold War into a conviction that they understood better than their Republican opponents did how to tackle the complex economic and security challenges of globalization and how the military could be used to help solve problems. His fellow Democrats embraced Clinton's belief in the importance of standing up for liberal values around the world.

Gore's candidacy signified the consolidation of these views among Democrats. His worldview—a strong defense, a higher priority on the environment in national security, a vigorous U.S. role to solve global problems, and a hard-line approach toward dictators—had become the center of gravity among liberal foreign policy elites. Even conservative commentators appreciated the transformation. "The McGovern wing of the party is clearly in retreat," William Kristol remarked at the time.[12]

Gore's choice of Connecticut Senator Joseph Lieberman to be his vice presidential running mate was symbolic of this change. As a staunch pro-defense liberal, Lieberman was heralded as the epitome of the traditional Democratic neoconservative in the mold of Scoop Jackson, with whom he shared not just hawkish views on military issues but concern for the environment. With his deep convictions about civil rights, economic justice, and the spread of democracy globally, Lieberman's views were also reminiscent of Hubert Humphrey's.

Like Gore, Lieberman supported the 1991 Gulf War and was an outspoken advocate of confronting Saddam (he had proposed the Iraq Liberation Act) and early intervention in the Balkans. And like Gore, the Connecticut senator believed the United States needed to assume an activist global agenda based on defending values, or what they called a strategy of "forward engagement." On foreign policy, there was little to indicate that a Gore administration would have scaled back the Clinton agenda. If anything, with Lieberman as vice president and advisers such as Richard Holbrooke in key positions, it probably would have been even more forthright in the use of American power.[13]

Yet the kinds of policies that Gore and Lieberman advocated were not top issues for many Americans, most of whom still paid little attention to foreign affairs. "Even in our increasingly interdependent world," Gore lamented to reporters during the campaign, "foreign policy is still usually not on the front burner for most people."[14] And even for those engaged in the debate about America's global role, the Gore-Lieberman worldview drew opposition, not just among Republicans, but also among those on the political left who believed the Democratic Party was leaving them behind.

THE RUMBLING on the left was evident during the Democratic primaries. Gore's opponent, Bradley, carved out a strong stance against the interventionism of the Clinton years. Throughout his three terms in the Senate, the former professional basketball star earned a reputation as a serious thinker and dedicated internationalist, and for a time, many believed he could pose a serious threat to Gore. He became a darling among many progressive elites in cities and on college campuses who liked his anti-establishment message but were reassured by his Washington experience. In the fall of 1999, polls showed him running in a dead heat with Gore in crucial primary states such as New Hampshire.

Although foreign policy never became a centerpiece of Bradley's campaign, he tapped into worries about the overextension of American power. "We cannot give an open-ended humanitarian commitment to the world," he argued, stressing that the United States "has been spread very thin over a wide territory." Bradley did not deny the interconnectedness (or inevitability) of globalization—if anything, the former Rhodes scholar proved Gore's equal when it came to thinking conceptually about the future, proclaiming his campaign as one of "big ideas." Bradley decried Clinton for mismanaging American engagement, especially when it came to the use of force. "We have been inconsistent about when we would act and when we should stand aside," he said.[15]

Such assertions were similar to those hurled at Clinton and Gore from the Republican presidential candidates and their allies in Congress, so much so that even some of the Clinton administration's harshest neoconservative critics (who had also had their share of tangles with the Contract Republicans) rose to Gore's defense. Robert Kagan argued that Bradley wanted "to wrap overseas intervention around Al Gore's neck in the same way that Republicans in Congress have wanted to wrap it around President Clinton's neck."[16] Bradley argued that unless the United States convinced its allies and organizations such as the United Nations to share the burden, it would squander its power. Thus Bradley echoed the arguments about the limits of American capabilities that State Department official Peter Tarnoff had promulgated back in the spring of 1993 to much jeering from the foreign policy establishment. Bradley understood the changing world much as Clinton and Gore did, but the senator differed greatly on what to do about it. Whereas Clinton and Gore sought to call on America to step up its engagement, Bradley advocated stepping back.

GORE MADE quick work of Bradley once the primaries began. Yet the vice president could not extinguish the opposition he faced on the left. In June 2000, consumer advocate Ralph Nader received the Green Party's nomination for president. The Greens had never played a large or particularly serious role in American politics, yet that year, by putting Nader on the ballot, the party had a major impact on the race.

Nader's fringe candidacy would have been little more than a small and inconsequential historical footnote had the 2000 election not been so close. His ideas never came close to attracting wide support. He never gained the kind of following Ross Perot had attracted in 1992. Instead, the Green Party helped stir up rage and discontent with Clinton, Gore, and the entire Democratic establishment. "The 1990s were a lost decade," Nader now recalls. "It didn't take too much prescience to see that the end of the Cold War was a great opportunity to do things like reduce the defense budget, but Clinton and Gore squandered it."[17]

Nader rode this leftist backlash by espousing an anti-corporate, anti-interventionist approach to the world and railing against free trade. He became a kind of Pied Piper for disaffected progressives, channeling the anger against the Democratic foreign policy that had exploded at the Ohio State University town hall meeting on Iraq in 1998 and in Seattle's streets the following year. In this sense, Nader's influence on the Democrats in 2000 was similar to Pat Buchanan's impact on the Republicans eight years earlier—he became an important irritant that pulled the Democrats to the extreme. In fact, Buchanan and Nader shared similar views on foreign policy. During the NAFTA fight seven years earlier, the two had held a press conference to rally the opposition, and they respected one another. "There's no doubt that Nader and I agreed on a lot," Buchanan reflects. "The anti-interventionist conservatives are on the same line as the anti-interventionists on the left."[18]

As the campaign wore on, Nader concentrated his attacks not on Bush, but on Gore and the Democratic Party, arguing that a Gore loss was a win. Nader saw scant difference between the two main candidates: They were "Tweedledee and Tweedledum." He elaborates that "the Democratic Party has become very good at electing very bad Republicans." When asked at the time if he worried that his candidacy might siphon off just enough votes for the Republicans to win, Nader replied that Democrats "need a cold shower for at least four years."[19]

Of course, after Nader garnered nearly 3 percent of the popular vote nationwide—including 100,000 votes in Florida, where Gore lost to Bush by less than 1,000—an ice-cold shower is exactly what Democrats, and Nader's supporters, got. Although Nader faded from the national scene and returned to his roots as an advocacy vagabond, many of the ideas championed by his campaign—skepticism of the

Democratic political establishment, deep anger with Clinton and Gore's economic and trade policies, concern about the exercise of America's global power, and above all opposition to the use of military force and penchant for intervention—lived on, gathering strength through the partisan blogosphere and proving to be a formidable force on the political left and within Democratic Party politics during the first decade of the twenty-first century.

"Help Is on the Way"

If Lieberman's addition to the 2000 Democratic ticket underscored Gore's commitment to an activist foreign policy, Bush's selection of Cheney also sent an unambiguous message about the Republican ticket's approach to the world. Some of Bush's top political aides feared that by choosing one of the most prominent figures from his father's administration, the Texas governor would seem too defensive about his weaknesses, reinforcing the impression that he needed a babysitter in the Oval Office. Although Bush proved to be far less callow than people presumed, there's no question that he sought to use Cheney's experience to reassure voters about his readiness to be commander-in-chief, especially when waging a campaign against a sitting vice president. But Bush also wanted the former defense secretary by his side to suggest that a Republican administration would restore the past glory days.[20]

Although Cheney was the senior player in the candidate's orbit, the other advisers assembled to support Bush reinforced the same sense of competence. The campaign's foreign policy team, known infamously as the Vulcans and headed by Condoleezza Rice and Paul Wolfowitz, was made up of well-respected and experienced national security hands who served in the George H. W. Bush administration and spent the 1990s agitating from the outside. When joined by Colin Powell, who never got too involved in the campaign but supported Bush, they were a formidable group. Throughout Washington's power corridors, the Bush team exuded confidence and certainty; because of their involvement with the dramatic events surrounding the end of the Cold War, they had a mystique that even Democrats admired. These advisers conceived of themselves as the professionals who had defeated the Soviet Union and believed they needed to return to Washington to bring back normality. Their sense of purpose was summed up by the slogan Cheney often used on the campaign trail: "Help is on the way."[21]

DURING THE 2000 presidential race, Bush's national security goals were far from transformational. The most striking aspect of Bush's global agenda is how utterly conventional it was, even by the standards of the foreign policy debate among conservatives at that time. It had none of the interventionist neoconservative aspirations about using American power to promote liberal ideals, to defend people who were suffering at the hands of repressive regimes, or perhaps even to topple dictators. If anything, Bush's limited global agenda had more in common with the ideas of congressional Republicans. That's why so many neoconservatives ended up backing Arizona Senator John McCain and his more ambitious ideas in the Republican primaries.[22]

Moreover, the kinds of global challenges that Clinton talked about constantly as his term wound down—economic globalization, disease pandemics, and the rise of nonstate actors—were hardly mentioned by Bush or his top aides. Like many conservatives, they belittled such "globaloney" talk. They believed U.S. foreign policy had to return to its focus on relationships with major countries, state-based threats, and a clear sense of America's national interests. In a widely read *Foreign Affairs* essay that many interpreted as a road map for Bush's foreign policy, Rice claimed the Clinton administration had allowed the national interest to be "replaced with 'humanitarian interests' or the interests of the 'international community,'" and that its "pursuit of, at best, illusory 'norms' of international behavior have become an epidemic."[23]

Rice also asserted that the great failure of the Clinton years was the inability of the president and his team to develop a strategy for dealing with the world. Instead, she wrote, "every issue has been taken on its own terms—crisis by crisis, day by day." Later in the campaign, Rice was asked by TV host Charlie Rose what she saw as the strongest indictment of the Clinton foreign policy. "I think," she replied, "absence of focus and a kind of inconsistency."[24] Clinton's fruitless search for a single overarching theme to explain his foreign policy was now at the heart of the Republican criticism.

Bush and his advisers argued that the Democrats made matters even worse by veering from crisis to crisis on the back of the U.S. military. The Bush bench had deep experience in the defense world, and military power was the main preoccupation of their approach toward foreign policy. They viewed the Clinton defense record as one of unmitigated disaster: The Democratic president had overused and under-resourced the armed forces, sending them on missions for which they were inadequately trained and which lay outside the scope of the national interest. And worse, Bush's advisers believed that through a combination of mismanagement, disrespect, and neglect, the Clinton administration had weakened civil-military relations. On the campaign trail, Cheney portrayed his return to public life as a personal cause to repair the damage done to the military.[25]

In many respects, such arguments were a continuation of the debate that had begun during the 1992 campaign and had been part of the 1996 contest, about Clinton's fitness to be commander-in-chief. The Republican establishment had recoiled at the idea of a former McGovernite in that role, and the early missteps over gays in the military, the episodes of military disrespect for Clinton, and the Somalia and Haiti disasters had done nothing but compound the problem. "They just never saw me as a legitimate person," Clinton later said about his opponents.[26]

In his major defense policy speech of the campaign, Bush told an audience at the Citadel, the military academy in South Carolina, that the Clinton administration's handling of the military was "ungrateful, it is unwise and it is unacceptable." The Democrats, Bush argued, wanted to have things both ways: "to command great forces, without supporting them. To launch today's new causes, with little thought of tomorrow's consequences."[27] A week before the election, the Republican nominee flatly declared, "The next president will inherit a military in decline."[28]

AT THE CORE of this debate were questions of mission and resources: What was the military's proper role in American national security policy when the country was at peace? How much should taxpayers spend on it? After the Cold War, politicians on both sides of the aisle believed, correctly, that the United States could spend less money on the military and embraced the idea of the "peace dividend." George H. W. Bush had begun the drawdown after the collapse of the Soviet empire, cutting the defense budget and reducing the number of active-duty troops. In a long-planned speech in Aspen, Colorado, delivered the day after Saddam invaded Kuwait in August 1990, Bush calculated that "by 1995 our security needs can be met by an active force 25 percent smaller than today's. America's armed forces will be at their lowest level since the year 1950."[29] Clinton sustained these reductions and went further in some areas, such as cutting military personnel, but overall his administration's defense spending was barely less than what the senior Bush had projected. In fact, by the end of the decade the defense budget had increased. In 1999 the Pentagon received its biggest financial boost since the end of the Cold War.[30] Yet Republicans howled at Clinton's defense budgets, arguing that he was slowly draining America's military might.

To a certain extent, such complaints reflected the fact that many conservatives still could not see beyond the caricature they had developed about Democratic weakness after Vietnam. But more than that, the criticisms represented the fundamental disagreement about what kind of global power the United States should be. One group of critics—mainly Republicans in Congress—argued that while the resource levels were reasonable, sending the military on nation-building missions was not. They were angry that U.S. troops remained in Bosnia and Kosovo without a clear exit strategy. Another group of critics—including many conservative defense intellectuals and neoconservatives—believed that the problem was not too many missions, but too few resources. They argued that the United States needed to embrace both a strategy and budget that reflected its global responsibilities and, some asserted unapologetically, its empire.[31]

Bush never tried to reconcile these views during the 2000 campaign. Instead he borrowed ideas from both sides, outlining a defense policy that was simultaneously limited and expansive: He decried the use of the military for nation-building, because it both exceeded the scope of U.S. interests and inflicted wear and tear on American troops. And he called for greater defense spending on a new generation of weapons to ensure that the military could meet modern-day threats, such as that posed by a rising China.

DEMOCRATS PUSHED back hard against this line of attack, particularly the use of the armed forces in humanitarian interventions and nation-building. They argued that U.S. interests included addressing challenges posed by weak states and that the military had a vital role to play. "It's not a new mission," Gore insisted on the campaign trail, arguing that such undertakings had roots in the post–World War II policies that had helped rebuild Europe and Japan. But he also clearly outlined his differences with Republicans, saying in a speech at West Point, "In the global age, peacekeeping takes on new importance and, along with war-fighting, is a critical mission of the armed forces of the United States." Democrats rejected Bush's assertion that they had allowed the military to atrophy during the 1990s and pointed to their efforts to modernize U.S. forces through innovations in airpower technology (such as the precision-guided weaponry honed in battle in the Balkans and Iraq) as well as efforts to make the Army lighter and more agile. Such arguments gained credibility after 2001, as the military performed brilliantly on the battlefields of Afghanistan and Iraq.[32]

Although Bush's claims about Clinton's military mismanagement were exaggerated, the defense legacy of the 1990s was problematic.

The Democrats defended nation-building, but they remained worried about the costs, particularly casualties. The Black Hawk Down disaster in Somalia had taught military mission planners and their political overseers a powerful lesson about the limits of intervention. General Hugh Shelton, Clinton's last Joint Chiefs chairman, described the need to meet the "Dover test" for committing American troops: "When the bodies are brought back, will we still feel it is in U.S. interests?"[33] The result was a policy that ducked the question by emphasizing force protection above all else. To reduce risks, U.S. troops on missions such as those in the Balkans stayed hunkered down in massive bases while the military brass resisted dangerous assignments, including arresting war criminals. They organized their planning around how quickly the United States could get out, or the exit strategy, instead of how to produce stability.

Moreover, because nation-building was still taboo within the highest echelons of the U.S. military, controversial in the foreign policy community, and a political hot button, little effort was made to develop the kinds of skills and permanent institutional capacity required for such operations. To be sure, military planners and operators drew lessons from each mission—in Somalia, Haiti, Bosnia, Kosovo. But they viewed each as unique and not instructive for overall military readiness. Thus, when the United States faced massive nation-building efforts in Afghanistan and Iraq after 9/11, it lacked many of the civilian and military capabilities needed to do the job and scrambled to develop them. One consequence of a smaller overall military force was that many military tasks were outsourced to private contractors, who often operated outside the bounds of proper accountability.[34]

ALTHOUGH MILITARY troop numbers were declining, U.S. military leaders in key regions increased their own visibility by taking more prominent roles in trying to influence events—they became superdiplomats or proconsuls. As journalist Dana Priest observed, "On

Clinton's watch the military slowly, without public scrutiny or debate, came to surpass its civilian leaders in resources and influence around the world." In some respects this was a strategic choice, as the Clinton team pushed military leaders to adopt a higher diplomatic profile as part of a new post–Cold War military mission to "shape" regional environments. Clinton's most successful defense secretary, William Perry, saw this as an important component of a "preventive defense" strategy.[35]

But asking the military to take on such roles was also a matter of necessity. As a Republican-controlled Congress made deep cuts in budgets for the State Department and foreign aid agencies, it was natural to seek the military's help in managing world affairs. "In many ways, these military leaders became the embodiment of American foreign policy during that time," says General Joseph Ralston, the Joint Chiefs' second in command at the end of the 1990s. Some military commanders leapt at the chance, believing that their civilian counterparts were not doing enough to structure a new order. "They didn't have a clear picture of what to do," says Marine General Anthony Zinni, who emerged as one of the more prominent diplomat-generals of this era. "So they said, 'Let's give the military folks the lead.' They weren't hung up on the military staying in the military lane, the civilians staying in the civilian lane. They were envious of our resources, but they didn't hold it against us."[36]

Nevertheless, there is truth in Republican assertions about the festering distrust between the uniformed military and the Clinton administration's civilian leaders. Clinton and many of his top advisers did establish strong relationships with those military generals, including Zinni, Ralston, and Wesley Clark, who were willing to think creatively about the use of American power and were not averse to missions to help weak states. These generals argue that the Clinton team and the senior military leadership developed a strong level of trust. "The common perception of a barrier between senior Clinton administration officials and the senior military leaders is totally false," Ralston asserts emphatically. "The Clinton administration wasn't unfriendly to the military," Zinni says. "I didn't vote for him either time"—and in fact endorsed Bush in the 2000 election—"but I thought he was great. He listened, and he delegated."[37]

Yet these commanders proved to be lonely military voices, as many of their colleagues, especially those down the chain of command, approached the Clinton team with a healthy dose of skepticism and, in some cases, barely contained hostility. Zinni admits the relationship "got off track" with the early battles over the "don't ask, don't tell" policy and the disrespect many in the military perceived from the Clinton White House, while Ralston explains that the "myth" of poor civil-military relations endured in the field.

It didn't help that Republicans sought to gain advantage by deliberately fanning such tensions. According to Clark, one way conservatives worked to "get revenge" on the Democrats for winning the presidency in 1992 was by "stoking military anxieties" over issues such as gays in the military and nation-building. The result was a divide between the civilians and the military that was as much about personalities and culture as it was about policy differences. It reinforced the belief that Republicans were the natural overseers of the military. According to polls taken in the mid-1990s, two-thirds of senior military officers said they were Republicans—and only 3 percent said they were "somewhat liberal." There was no more powerful illustration of this than the fact that when Gore finally conceded the election to Bush in December 2000, the Pentagon's hallways echoed with the sounds of cheering.[38]

America Invulnerable

Restoring faith in the military was one of Bush's foreign policy goals; the other was to reduce U.S. vulnerability to outside threats, the most ominous being enemy missiles. Bush embraced the Rumsfeld commission's assessment of the missile threat, pledging a "full-scale effort" to deploy a missile defense system that worked. Few were surprised that Bush made missile defense one of the central planks of his national security agenda—it would have been shocking had he chosen not to. Missile defense was the single most dominant national security issue conservatives championed throughout the 1990s. It featured in the Contract with America's national security plank and was a foreign policy centerpiece of Bob Dole's 1996 campaign.

The issue was a perfect fit for the Republicans' argument that Democrats had endangered America by ignoring gathering threats. And it reinforced Republicans' view of themselves as clear-eyed guardians of America's national security. "National security policy is about protecting the country from threats," says Douglas Feith, the Pentagon's top policy official during Bush's first term. "So when you ask yourself what needs to be done to protect the country . . . ballistic missiles are at the top of the list. There was an awareness that North Korea, Iran, and Iraq were all working on missile systems." The notion that the United States knew about such threats and was not doing more to address them alarmed Bush. "He was just fascinated with the fact of this vulnerability," Rice explained, "and appalled by it."[39]

Bush framed the case for missile defense as part of the post–Cold War reality. He saw it as a way to maintain freedom of action; an America protected could not be blackmailed. Moreover, he argued that since Russia was no longer America's enemy, it didn't make any sense to rely on the nuclear balance of terror. Failing to build a missile defense system out of adherence to outdated arms control agreements did nothing more than perpetuate Cold War thinking, Bush believed. When Gore said, "The ABM Treaty is the cornerstone of strategic stability in our relationship with Russia," conservatives could only shake their heads at what sounded like détente thinking from the 1970s. "Legacies like ABM prevented us from dealing with new threats," John Bolton asserts. "We wanted to eliminate the last vestiges of the Cold War paradigm."[40]

Yet Bush's opponents argued that his obsession with missile defense in fact proved that he was the one who could not move on. Gore charged at the time that Bush was actually the one "stuck in a Cold War mindset."[41] Gore supported missile defense but wanted to ensure that building a system would do as little damage to the U.S.-Russian relationship as possible. Conservatives could insist that the

United States and Russia were no longer enemies, but Moscow still wanted to preserve the ABM Treaty, threatening to break out of other arms control agreements if Washington made any move unilaterally. Democrats charged that instead of trying to work with Russia to develop missile defense in a way that maintained the integrity of these arms control agreements, the Republicans were determined to pursue their ideological agenda no matter the costs. So both sides used the legacy of the Cold War, and their different interpretations of the new reality, to paint the other's position on missile defense as out-dated and dangerous.

As THE CANDIDATES argued about missile defense, Clinton still had not decided on his own position. Bush and his advisers were deeply dismayed, believing that the White House was driven more by poli-tics (to ward off congressional pressure and to protect Gore during the campaign) than by a conviction about what was best for the country.

Beginning in the summer of 1999, the Clinton team attempted a delicate dance, working with the Russians and European allies to negotiate an acceptable change in the ABM Treaty to allow missile defense to go forward, while at the same time continuing to test a possible system. One of the central arguments the Clinton team made to the Russians was that cutting a deal then would likely be better than anything they could hope for from Clinton's successor. "We tried to get them to look at the choice they faced in terms of the devil they knew versus the one they didn't," wrote Talbott, Clinton's chief Russia negotiator. "The devil they didn't know was that the next president—regardless of whether it was Al Gore or George Bush—would, at a minimum, build the system we were proposing and . . . have to withdraw from the ABM Treaty."[42]

After a year, the Clinton team had made little progress on either track. The Russians weren't budging. President Vladimir Putin was not persuaded that he should cut a deal with a president about to leave office, and the missile tests weren't succeeding. By the fall of 2000, just as the presidential campaign entered its final stretch, Clinton announced that he would not make a decision on deploying missile defense, thereby deferring to his successor to decide what to do.

BUSH'S APPROACH to missile defense, and his conviction that the United States could not be tied down by the ABM Treaty, fit neatly into his larger foreign policy strategy. He believed that to ensure invulnerability, the United States must shed any artificial constraints on protecting the country's interests, be they international treaties and agreements or alliances that could hinder America's freedom of action. Bush and his advisers were not uniformly opposed to treaties or alliances (although some of his aides were more skeptical than others), but they saw them as tools that should be discarded if they proved a hindrance.

In tone and prescription, this outlook reflected the ideas articulated in the Pentagon's 1992 Defense Planning Guidance, which argued that the United States would have to rely more on "coalitions of the willing" and "should be postured to act independently." The expectation was that countries would go their own way after the Cold War and that it would be harder to forge international consensus. To a certain extent, this had turned out to be true. Some of Bush's top advisers argued that the Clinton administration ended up following these ideas, if not embracing them outright, although it would have been politically incorrect for the White House to admit it. Those who once criticized the Defense Planning Guidance, Wolfowitz charged, "nevertheless seem very comfortable with *Pax Americana*." After all, when the United States and its European allies could not get U.N. Security Council approval to act in Kosovo, they used NATO to go to war, and the United States and Britain were virtually alone in containing Saddam's Iraq nearly a decade after the first Persian Gulf War ended.[43]

Although the Clinton team had promoted the notion that the United States was indispensable, and as such must be willing to act alone, they also believed that alliances, treaties, and agreements could be much more than simple tools to augment American power;

they could help create a shared set of norms that shaped state behavior. To Bush and his advisers, such thinking showed that the Democrats had it exactly backward: The pursuit of cooperation had become an end in itself. The Bush team would not seek what Rice described as "symbolic agreements of questionable value," believing such efforts created false hope. U.S. allies and enemies alike would be influenced only by the example of raw American power, not some words earnestly written on a piece of paper. Rice and her colleagues believed the benefits of ensuring U.S. freedom of action far outweighed the costs in terms of America's global popularity.[44]

Loosening the constraints on American power was not the same as boldly using that power to remake the world. During the campaign, Bush's vision was more nationalist than neoconservative. Both perspectives embraced the idea of removing outside limits on American power, but they differed on what to do with that power. Unlike the neoconservatives, Bush promised to replace grandiose goals with the more basic objective of protecting security. His admonitions for the United States to be a "humble" power reflected a more limited sense of American interests, and a rejection of what he considered Clinton's preachy talk about U.S. leadership.[45]

This perspective was not new in American history. The critique aimed at Clinton and Gore was similar to that made nearly half a century earlier, when Dwight Eisenhower claimed that Harry Truman also talked too loudly about world leadership. "A platoon leader doesn't get his platoon to go that way by getting up and saying, 'I am smarter, I am bigger, I am stronger, I am the leader,'" the retired general and Allied commander argued in language that Bush echoed in his 2000 debate with Gore. "He gets them to go with him because they want to do it for him, because they believe in him."[46] Bush believed he would be the same kind of leader, projecting "purpose without arrogance," as described in his first inaugural address. But the paradox was that by seeking to limit the constraints on American power, Bush fed the impression among America's allies of exactly the opposite: arrogance without purpose.

History "Begins"

Despite the bitterness of the 2000 presidential campaign, made worse by its protracted and contested end, many hoped the transition from Clinton to Bush would go smoothly.

The handoff started with promise. Just a few days before Christmas, the president and president-elect sat down together in the Oval Office for the traditional private meeting. Obviously Bush was not the man Clinton had hoped to greet, but Clinton poured on the charm nonetheless. The men talked for two hours about a range of topics, from politics and life in the White House to the art of public speaking. Yet as Bush listened politely, most of what Clinton wanted to discuss was America's role in the world.

Clinton rattled on about a range of international problems, from the faltering Middle East peace process and the tensions between India and Pakistan, to the challenge of a nuclear North Korea. But among his lingering frustrations, Clinton admitted, was that two of the world's most dangerous individuals, bin Laden and Saddam, were still huge threats to the United States. "One of the great regrets of my presidency is that I didn't get him [bin Laden] for you, because I tried to," Clinton said. And as for Saddam, the outgoing president warned that "he's going to cause you a world of problems."[47]

In his final days in office, Clinton did try to solve some big challenges before Bush inherited them. Clinton made a last-ditch effort on a peace agreement between Israel and the Palestinians, and he considered traveling to Pyongyang to negotiate a deal with North Korea. But the number of foreign policy initiatives he conducted during the transition was fewer—and less open-ended—than those Bush's father had pursued. In the three months between Clinton's election in November 1992 and his inauguration in January 1993, George H. W. Bush had sent troops to Somalia, bombed Iraq, issued a warning to Serbia over Kosovo, tried to finalize the Uruguay Round of trade talks, and signed the START II treaty, NAFTA, and a chemical weapons treaty.[48] Because of the electoral recount, Clinton's transition out of office was far shorter, and he left his successor a relatively free hand.

*

THE OPENING MONTHS of George W. Bush's presidency brought both continuity and discord. As the Democrats left office, some of them hoped that despite the natural inclination for any new administration to distinguish itself from its predecessor, Bush would quickly accept reality and build a policy that looked a lot like Clinton's. They took confidence in the fact that many of the new president's appointments—starting with Powell as secretary of state—were familiar faces and serious heavyweights from the last Bush administration, which they respected for its commitment to internationalism and its willingness to work with allies. "I thought the 2001 team would be the best one I'd ever seen," recalls Les Gelb, then the president of the Council on Foreign Relations and a close friend to many of the outgoing Clinton officials. "They had unbelievable standing with the foreign policy community, the press, and the public."[49]

In fact, this was exactly the way some of Bush's top appointees saw themselves, especially those around Powell who had never really participated in the partisan wars of the 1990s. Although they believed themselves to be more competent than the team they were replacing, they did not set out to reverse every Clinton policy as a matter of principle. Even years later, they still labor to stress the continuities between the two administrations. "There was no stunning change from Clinton to Bush," asserts Powell's State Department deputy and longtime ally Richard Armitage. There might have been a change of approach on issues such as the future of the ABM Treaty, he explains, "but other than that we didn't have major differences."[50] To some extent this proved true, as the Bush administration kept in place many of the most controversial Clinton policies—such as the containment of Iraq and the deployment of U.S. troops to keep the peace in Bosnia and Kosovo—despite the desire by some to overturn them.

But Bush himself seemed more driven by an "Anything But Clinton," or "ABC," policy. He and his White House advisers prided themselves on proving there was a new team in charge, distancing the administration from Clinton's diplomatic efforts to negotiate a deal between Israel and the Palestinians and to pursue talks with

North Korea. They declared the Kyoto environmental treaty "dead," pledged opposition to the International Criminal Court, and began the process of withdrawing from the ABM Treaty. They also halted the Clinton team's efforts to put the U.S. relationship with the United Nations on solid ground. Inside the White House, even uttering the name Clinton was frowned upon; it was euphemistically called the "C-word."

Such moves sent an unambiguous message about the new administration's go-it-alone style and hands-off approach to peace negotiations.[51] Conservative commentator Charles Krauthammer heralded this as the "new unilateralism" and applauded Bush for seeking to "strengthen American power and unashamedly deploy it on behalf of self-defined global ends. . . . After a decade of Prometheus playing pygmy, the first task of the new administration is precisely to reassert American freedom of action."[52] Such moves were also an early sign that officials such as Powell, who tended to seek international consensus and stress the importance of relationships, would soon find themselves out of step with their more hard-line colleagues. This divide became more apparent after the September 11, 2001, attacks. "There were people in the administration more ideological [than Powell], but they were still in their box until after 9/11," Armitage explains.[53]

This clash over policy between Powell and his team and harder-line figures such as Cheney and Donald Rumsfeld also harkens back to the waning days of George H. W. Bush's presidency, when the Defense Planning Guidance and the Eagleburger transition memo outlined two contrasting worldviews among Republicans. During their years in exile, many of these differences were subordinated by the higher cause of opposing the Democrats, but now they unfolded in the open. The factional divide had never gone away and was indeed playing out in a second Bush administration, but the George Bush of 2001 was a very different leader than the one who had left office in 1993.

*

THE BUSH TEAM wasted little time in developing policies to address the threats they believed had gathered since Republicans last held the White House. They had little of the Clinton team's optimism in their depiction of global affairs and instead projected a sense of inevitability about the growing dangers from other states. According to one Defense Department memo that circulated among Bush's most senior advisers just weeks after they took office, the recent liberalization of trade and wider availability of advanced technologies had made it easier for countries to "rapidly acquire the most destructive military technology ever devised. . . . We cannot prevent them from doing so."[54] If the United States could no longer rely on prevention through diplomacy and trade controls to prevent rivals to its hegemony from emerging, then it had to increase its military capabilities. The Bush administration soon argued that the United States had to stand ready to pursue a new strategy of preempting such threats before they could do harm.

By stressing military solutions, the new administration also tried to restore the perceived imbalance in civil-military relations. Yet they never addressed a fundamental contradiction. On the one hand, they wanted to give the troops the "help" they had promised during the campaign. But they also set out to reduce the military's influence over decisions—both inside the Pentagon and throughout the regional commands—which put them on a collision course with the uniformed leadership.

Bush's team believed Clinton's weaknesses had diminished civilian control of the military. Led by the hard-charging Rumsfeld, who came back to the Pentagon for a second tour as defense secretary, the new administration tried to wrest decision-making powers from the military brass. There was a sense that those military officers who had thrived under Clinton were tainted, or as one former senior Pentagon official put it, they were "politically correct." Zinni said that created "a strong sense of alienation between the uniformed leadership and the civilians." So instead of healing the breach they blamed Clinton for creating, the Bush team made it worse. By the end of the administration's first term in office, this new tension led to the most significant divide between the Army and its political overseers since the Vietnam War.[55]

IN THE MONTHS leading up to September 2001, neither Bush nor his most senior advisers shared the Clinton team's sense of alarm about the threat from al-Qaeda. Insider accounts by journalists such as Bob Woodward, the 9/11 Commission report, several congressional investigations, and memoirs of high-ranking officials including George Tenet and Richard Clarke describe this lack of alarm. "There was a loss of urgency," recalled Tenet, who had written the internal memorandum in December 1998 saying that the United States was at war.[56] For Bush, the sense of being at war or bin Laden being enemy number one did not become clear until after 9/11, as the president himself later admitted to Woodward. "There was a significant difference in my attitude after September 11," the president said. Until then, "I knew [bin Laden] was a menace. . . . But I didn't feel that sense of urgency, and my blood was not nearly as boiling."[57]

One part of the problem was that some in the Bush administration lumped terrorism into the category of "Clinton issues" that they believed were a sideshow to core American interests. To a certain extent this was understandable—for eight years, Clinton and his team had struggled to understand and deal with the challenges of globalization, peacekeeping, and terrorism. Yet whereas Clinton left office claiming the United States could be "threatened more by another nation's weakness than by its strength," the Republicans were far more worried about traditional threats.[58] They remained focused on familiar national security problems, such as those caused by menacing nation-states. Even after the Soviet Union collapsed, the Bush team was concerned mostly about countries that could use their resources to undermine American influence in key regions, whether Iraq in the Persian Gulf or China in Asia. The administration understood terrorism to be a problem, but only because of support countries such as Iran provided to groups including Hezbollah and Hamas, not because terrorists could harm America on their own.

The notion that nonstate actors, failed states, and civil conflicts should dominate America's attention was simply not accepted by the Bush team. They found it inconceivable that a bin Laden could threaten the mightiest power in world history. They couldn't imagine it, so they didn't prepare for it.

The tragedy for America is twofold: Although Clinton understood that globalization fueled enormous transnational security challenges, he failed to lead the country effectively to combat the growing threat posed by Islamic extremism; and even after the events of 9/11 spurred Bush to confront terrorism with a newfound urgency, he rejected globalization as a catalyst for this new unrest. When he looked for the source of trouble, he found it in Iraq.

PRIOR TO 9/11, it was unclear where exactly the Bush presidency was headed. The administration avoided a major crisis with China over the forced landing of an American spy plane, and Bush famously peered into Russian President Putin's soul and liked what he saw. Even regarding what many of Bush's advisers called the single most important piece of unfinished business—Saddam's continued rule in Iraq—the administration barely changed the Clinton policy. Some hard-liners such as Wolfowitz (who became the number-two man at the Pentagon) attempted to ratchet up the pressure on Saddam, but they were outmaneuvered by Powell and others who preferred to stick with the sanctions approach.[59]

After just a few months in office, the administration already seemed to be in trouble. Hawks outside the government complained that Bush's leadership was diminished; *Washington Post* columnist Jim Hoagland warned that the new team's Iraq policy "risks becoming a way of letting the mistakes of Bush 41 become the mistakes of Bush 43."[60] Rumsfeld ran into enormous problems at the Pentagon, where his ideas on military reform created intense opposition from the uniformed brass, who believed that fighting wars still required significant numbers of American troops and not just a reliance on smart technologies. Prominent conservatives were calling for

Rumsfeld's head, and the press speculated that he might not survive the year.[61] Powell's star had dimmed too—the person many believed would become one of the country's most powerful secretaries of state ever seemed by the end of the summer to be losing policy fights and fading from the scene. On September 10, the cover of *Time* magazine asked, "Where Have You Gone, Colin Powell?"[62] The president showed little comfort with foreign policy, and in many respects, despite the deep experience of his more seasoned advisers, his administration was crippled by internal divisions, and adrift in the world.

WHEN AL-QAEDA attacked the United States on September 11, the modern interwar years came crashing to a close. Over the course of a decade, Americans had shown little interest in national security issues. They had paid passing attention to events in places such as Somalia, Bosnia, Mexico, and Iraq. Most Americans and their leaders understood little about Islamic extremism. They were increasingly anxious about trade, and by 2000, even white-collar workers—accountants, radiologists, and computer engineers—feared losing jobs to workers overseas. But for the most part, Americans had ignored foreign policy since the Soviet Union had collapsed.

Not anymore. Americans wanted leadership, and when Bush grabbed the bullhorn while standing atop the rubble from the Twin Towers, he seemed to provide it. For the president and many Americans, everything changed on 9/11. But did it?

CHAPTER ELEVEN

The 11/9 World

NEARLY TWELVE HOURS after the first plane slammed into the World Trade Center, George W. Bush addressed the shocked nation and declared that America and its allies must stand together to win what he called the "war against terrorism." In an instant, it seemed that the core question raised by the fall of the Berlin Wall on 11/9—what to do with American power absent a global adversary— had been answered. The country was now at war, Bush explained, and the fight would be different. The president argued that 9/11 represented a clear break with the past; responding to Islamic extremism required a radical departure from the policies pursued by Bill Clinton and even by Bush's own father.

"This war will not be like the war against Iraq a decade ago, with a decisive liberation of territory and a swift conclusion," Bush said before a packed joint session of Congress on September 20, in one of the most emotionally charged moments of his presidency. "It will not look like the air war above Kosovo two years ago, where no ground troops were used and not a single American was lost in combat. Our response involves far more than instant retaliation and isolated strikes. Americans should not expect one battle, but a lengthy campaign, unlike any other we have ever seen."[1]

Bush followed through on that pledge, and as his presidency winds down, well over 100,000 American military men and women remain at war in Afghanistan and Iraq. Ironically, Bush adopted much of what he had derided about Clinton's policies and Al Gore's proposals during the 2000 presidential campaign. In an abrupt about-face, Bush embraced nation-building and set forth a bold global agenda for the United States—the centerpiece of which was the spread of democracy—a far cry from the restrained humility he had promised.

Bush initially led with a huge reservoir of support. Yet 9/11 created a false sense of unity, and the public became as polarized as ever. Critics at home and abroad have challenged the "war on terror" concept for U.S. foreign policy. Some of America's closest allies reject the premise that the animating feature of world politics is a war on radical Islam—Tony Blair's successor as prime minister of Britain, Gordon Brown, banished the phrase from his lexicon. At home, leading Democratic politicians in Congress and on the 2008 presidential campaign trail also criticized the concept. Retired and active-duty military leaders argue that "war on terror" is not the best way to characterize the struggle because it conveys the notion that military power alone can address the threat. Even several of Bush's former top officials, including Donald Rumsfeld and Colin Powell, have spoken out against framing the current struggle as a "war on terror." As Rumsfeld left the Pentagon in 2006, he admitted, "I don't think I would have called it a 'war on terror,'" even though he often repeated the phrase as defense secretary. And Powell says, "The 'war on terror' is a bad phrase. It's a criminal problem. This is not the Soviets coming back. . . . Let's not hyperventilate."[2]

DESPITE Bush's strident assertions, 9/11 has not provided the same clarity of purpose for U.S. foreign policy that defined the Cold War. That terrible day did change some things. It made Americans and their leaders more aware of the danger radical Islam poses and instilled a new urgency that earlier attacks—on the World Trade Center in 1993, the American embassies in Kenya and Tanzania in 1998, and the USS *Cole* in 2000—had not. It prompted the government to institute major intelligence reforms and create the Department of

Homeland Security. And it provided a rationale for a number of the Bush administration's controversial actions beyond attacking al-Qaeda in its safe haven in Afghanistan, such as overthrowing Saddam Hussein, abandoning the perceived shackles of international law and institutions, and expanding executive powers here at home. But 9/11 did not, as many have argued and still believe, change everything.

The political and strategic debates of the 1990s continue. These years proved not to be a "sabbatical" or a "holiday from history," but rather the moment during which the ideas and dynamics that characterize the current era took shape. The underlying realities of international politics—the economic, political, and security challenges created by globalization; the rise of nonstate actors; the threat of weapons of mass destruction; the dangers that emanate from weak or failing states; the possibilities and limits of international institutions; and questions about whether and how to use America's preponderant power to meet global responsibilities—are legacies of the Cold War's end. We still live in an 11/9 world.

The failure of the "war on terror" framework illustrates one of the enduring lessons of the modern interwar years: that the search for a replacement for the Cold War's doctrine of containment proved not only elusive, but because of its oversimplifications, dangerous. Since the end of the Cold War, American policy-makers and scholars have labored in vain to define the era and characterize the country's new purpose in a simple phrase. From Francis Fukuyama's "end of history" and George H. W. Bush's "new world order," to Tony Lake's "democratic enlargement" and Clinton's quest for a globalization slogan, no single expression illuminated America's purpose after the Cold War. And it was folly to believe one could.

Ironically, George Kennan himself, whom the elite tried doggedly to emulate, argued that the failure to find a single foreign policy rationale was in fact a good thing. Later in his life, Kennan regretted having simplified the world through the goal of containment and believed it had led to disastrous consequences for American policy. During a private dinner discussion with several top Clinton officials in the mid-1990s, the ninety-year-old former diplomat implored them to abandon the effort to come up with a simple word or phrase. Instead, he advised them to embrace the world's complexities and compose "a thoughtful paragraph or more, rather than trying to come up with a bumper sticker."[3]

IN ONE RESPECT, however, the 1990s were indeed a "holiday": The end of the Cold War made many Americans and their leaders believe the world had become more benign and, therefore, of less concern. The three presidential campaigns of that era—in 1992, 1996, and 2000—spent little time on foreign policy issues. The mainstream media closed overseas bureaus and reduced the newsprint and air-time spent on events abroad. Instead of looking outward, Americans looked in—obsessed with oddities such as the O. J. Simpson trial and hopes fueled by the booming stock market. In many respects, these years were self-indulgent ones. David Halberstam called them "a time of trivial pursuits."[4]

This is not to say that the American people are "inherently isola-tionist," as Clinton once argued to his aides early in his presidency. For years public opinion polls have shown that Americans are willing to engage the world and to work with other nations. Yet this international-ism is often diluted by apathy, meaning any push for bold action or sus-tained engagement must come from leaders, not from the masses.[5]

CLINTON GREATLY expanded the foreign policy agenda, working to make more central such issues as trade and currency stabilization, ter-rorism and genocide, weapons proliferation, global disease, and the environment. But these efforts to broaden the country's focus beyond traditional national security threats unfolded against the backdrop of dwindling resources. There was a sense that Americans deserved a "peace dividend" after the Cold War—a view shared by both Repub-licans and Democrats. In fact, after the 1994 ascendance of the Con-tract Republicans in Congress, getting money for foreign affairs became an even harder struggle.

Because of this mismatch between ambitious ends and meager means, Clinton was belittled for pursuing "hegemony on the cheap."[6] Throughout the 2000 presidential campaign, Bush tried to capitalize on this critique. But he did so by restricting the definition of foreign policy interests to more traditional threats while promising to boost the resources devoted to national security, especially the military. During his presidency, however, the gap between American foreign policy objectives and the resources available has only grown larger—with the military overstretched and the budget deficit climbing.

Throughout the 1990s, both conservatives and liberals worried about how much could be demanded from the American people. More than anything else in foreign policy, Republicans and Democrats argued over the proper use of American military force, believing that Americans were unwilling to risk casualties. After 11/9, debates about the limits of America's will, its patience, and its responsibilities to help solve global challenges were never resolved. These questions seemed to be answered in the months after 9/11, when the American people and their leaders stood ready to sacrifice to vanquish their enemies. But that moment was squandered, and such questions continue to animate the current struggle over the course and content of American foreign policy.

The sense of limits is far more acute than it was during the 1990s. Even though the United States did not always appear to have a clear sense of purpose, because of its sheer power it enjoyed tremendous freedom of action. Although policy-makers and pundits debated when, where, and how America could act, there was rarely much doubt about whether it was capable of doing so. That was true whether responding to genocide in the Balkans or intervening to stabilize currencies in Mexico or Asia.

Many feared that America's preeminence could be fleeting. The Dick Cheney advisers who crafted the 1992 Defense Planning Guidance hoped to forestall decline with a strategy to prevent other states from rising to challenge American power in regions across the globe. Others believed that America could not remain supreme indefinitely:

Clinton said after his presidency that the most "important thing is to create a world we would like to live in when we are no longer the world's only superpower," to prepare for "a time when we would have to share the stage."[7] Nearly two decades after 11/9, the United States does find itself facing a world that is harder to manage, and in which its preeminence in many areas is under assault. In the waning days of the George H. W. Bush administration, the architects of the Defense Planning Guidance tried to create a strategy to sustain American dominance. Yet the policies they pursued during the George W. Bush administration—particularly the war in Iraq—have made that objective all the more difficult to achieve.[8]

Liberal Legacies

Both political parties are still engaged in debates that emerged in the 1990s. In the first decade of the twenty-first century, Democrats remain divided over America's role in the world. On the surface, these disputes play out in disagreements over how to respond to Republican policies—and whether since 9/11 Democrats should have been cooperating with Bush where possible or instead opposing him outright. But at a deeper level, the political left is still debating how to marry progressive policies with American power. The themes of this debate are familiar—they concern the core of Clinton's foreign policy: democracy promotion, economic integration through open trade, and the use of American power, including its military might, to uphold human rights.

Take, for example, democracy promotion, which has been at the heart of liberal internationalism since the days of Woodrow Wilson. During the 1992 presidential campaign, Clinton used the issue to challenge George H. W. Bush as a status quo president, try to reunify Democrats around a high ideal, and perhaps draw back those neoconservatives who had left the party in the 1970s. Then in office Clinton's administration articulated democratic enlargement as a strategic objective. Although the label hardly stuck, it informed policies such as expanding NATO and bringing peace to the Balkans. The administration's 1996 National Security Strategy used the words "democracy" and "democratic" more than 130 times. So after 9/11, when George W. Bush began to articulate his own goals of promoting democracy to combat extremism, many Democrats gave their enthusiastic support. As Clinton recalled later, "I think we needed a little missionary zeal."[9]

However, as democracy promotion became associated with the war in Iraq and with Bush's perceived ambitions to remake the Middle East by force, it became increasingly difficult for Democrats to lend their support. Liberal leaders complain that by acting as though he invented the idea of promoting democracy, Bush made it politically radioactive at home and abroad. Now Democratic politicians run from the issue. Public opinion polls show that far fewer Democrats than Republicans believe the United States should help establish democracy in other countries. "They picked up a lot of things we were doing and pushed them to their exponential degree," Madeleine Albright says of Bush and his team. "They give democracy a bad name."[10] Given this, liberals are asking what place democracy should have in American foreign policy after Bush.

THE 11/9 to 9/11 era also fundamentally shaped liberals' debates about America's role in the global economy. Clinton entered the White House arguing that the domestic and foreign economies were inseparable. During his presidency he elevated economic policy to be a coequal of foreign policy, pursued trade agreements, and intervened to stabilize global markets. His "theory of the case" was for the United States to pursue greater integration in the global economy in response to the technological revolution while not losing sight of the dangers it unleashed. From a political perspective, this was an unusual direction for a Democratic president to take, as he faced strong crosswinds from the party's traditional constituencies.

Clinton did enjoy a significant degree of success. In fact, some argue that his efforts to pass NAFTA and the agreement establishing the World Trade Organization are his most important legacies. Author Robert Wright asserted that the president's greatest achievement was steering the Democratic Party toward combining support for free trade with progressive principles. Just four days before Clinton left office in 2001, Wright wrote in the *New York Times*, "From the beginning, [Clinton's] embrace of technological change and of economic engagement with the world reflected his longstanding credentials as a New Democrat and, in a vaguer sense, his instinctive optimism and inclusiveness." What Clinton did, Wright explained, was save "the Democratic Party from an increasingly marginal existence as the anti-globalization party, a party that denies the world's destiny rather than shape it, a party faithful to its ideals but unable to realize them."[11]

But Clinton wondered whether his success would last. Even before he left office, he knew his global trade policy foes remained powerful. "I have not so far created a consensus within my own party . . . for the view of trade which I hold," he admitted.[12] Since 2001, a minority of Democrats has continued to support his centrist, pro-trade positions. "The problem with trade is that the beneficiaries don't feel it," Robert Rubin observes. "If people understood their interests as consumers, we'd have different politics." On the 2008 campaign trail, protectionism resurged, and Democratic candidates sounded more like Ross Perot than Clinton. Even Hillary Clinton adopted rhetoric skeptical of free trade, including criticism of NAFTA. The Democratic Party appears to be retreating from Clinton's free trade legacy and is still groping for a unified stance on the issue.[13]

"Clinton's contribution was to elevate trade as a strategic component, not a strategic stepchild of a vibrant international policy," says Charlene Barshefsky. "The contribution was substantive, not political."[14]

LIBERALS HAVE also not come to agreement on the question that generates the most heat: when and how the United States should go to war. For Democrats, one of the hopes after 11/9 was that the post-Vietnam divisions within the party could be put aside for good. The Cold War's end brought the expectation that military power would be less important and, therefore, armed intervention less frequent.

In fact the opposite happened: From 1989 to 2001, the United States averaged one large-scale military intervention every eighteen months, a rate greater than ever before and more than that of any other country at the time.[15] Many now argue that the United States erred by *not* using greater force in Rwanda in 1994 or against al-Qaeda before 9/11. In this sense, Clinton's policies and the George W. Bush administration's ideas about using military power to defend values overlap more than many Americans have perceived, or partisans on both sides care to admit.

Unlike tough decisions on economic policy, using force never came easy to Clinton. His early years as president were marred by uncertain leadership. Loud voices on the left and the right criticized him for losing control of the situation in Somalia and failing to intervene earlier in the Balkans. But by the mid-1990s Clinton and his advisers had found their comfort zone, coalescing around the limited use of force, which they employed first in Haiti and Bosnia and later in Iraq and Kosovo. They turned on its head the usual liberal debate about using military power. Instead of placing the burden of proof on those calling for intervention, they put it onto those who advocated doing nothing in the face of violence. "Inaction has consequences," says Richard Holbrooke.[16] Although that approach met resistance from some on the left—voiced loudly during the late 1990s at the Ohio State University town hall meeting and the protests over Kosovo—the liberal foreign policy establishment agreed. Many Democrats returned to this use-of-force rationale in supporting the Bush administration's post–9/11 policies.

These "liberal hawks"—the policy-makers and intellectuals who championed humanitarian intervention as part of what writer George Packer called the "Bosnia consensus"—did not necessarily agree with the way Bush implemented his decision to invade Afghanistan and Iraq. But they did not always dispute the underlying premises.[17] In the 1990s, they came to believe in the threat posed by failed states and rogue regimes. In fact, some former Clinton officials argue that Bush made his case more difficult by trying so hard to distinguish what he was doing from the approaches he inherited from Clinton.

"The cases of Iraq and Afghanistan were complicated by the Bush administration's reluctance to cast its own policies in terms of continuity with its predecessors," Strobe Talbott observed. Once weapons of mass destruction were not found in Iraq, Bush invoked the same justification that Clinton had used for threatening and using military force in Haiti and Kosovo: regime-change in the defense of democracy and human rights.[18]

Today few Democratic politicians would think it wise to stress the continuities between Clinton and Bush (yet more Democrats are willing to emphasize the similarities between Clinton and George H. W. Bush in terms of their pragmatism and effective management of allies). Some on the left accuse Clinton Democrats of being barely distinguishable from Republicans.[19] Given the consequences of the Iraq War, a number of liberal thinkers and activists, especially many of those writing in the blogosphere, are trying to make liberal hawks an endangered species. To a certain extent, they are succeeding. The influence of policy organizations that asserted hawkish positions during the Clinton years, including the Democratic Leadership Council, has waned. And those Democratic politicians who argued most forcefully for taking strong stands and using force on moral grounds are out of favor.

There is no more vivid example of the political price to be paid than the remarkable turn in the career of Senator Joseph Lieberman. In 2000, he was just a few hundred Florida votes away from being elected vice president. Six years later, he lost the Connecticut Democratic primary to an opponent who ran on an anti-war platform, with vigorous support from liberal activists and online financial contributions. Lieberman left the party and was reelected to the U.S. Senate as an Independent. He complained that "the Democratic foreign policy worldview has become defined by the same reflexive, blind opposition to the president that defined Republicans in the 1990s."[20] In 2008, the former Democrat endorsed Republican John McCain for president.

Although liberal hawks are now stigmatized among a wide swath of the partisan left, their underlying policy argument about the use of U.S. political, economic, and if necessary military power still maintains significant support among foreign policy veterans from the Clinton administration. Why? Because the global problems Clinton confronted during his presidency—genocide, ethnic conflict, the security threats emanating from weak or failed states, and the limits of international cooperation—have not disappeared. If anything, awareness of these dangers has grown. A new Democratic administration might assert such interests with more humility (ironically, heeding Bush's advice from the 2000 campaign) as well as work harder to create greater international support behind its actions, but Democrats are not likely to abandon them. For the moment the liberal political pendulum has stopped swinging in the interventionist direction, but how far it travels the other way remains to be seen.[21]

Conservatives' Conundrums

On the political right, partisans are similarly refighting the philosophical battles that began during the modern interwar years. The Cold War's end sparked a crisis in conservatism that continues unresolved. For four decades, distrust of the Soviet Union was the glue that held the political right together. In the wake of 11/9, Republicans divided among Pat Buchanan's isolationism, the anti-Clinton nationalism of the Contract Republicans, the realist pragmatism of establishment stalwarts such as James Baker and Brent Scowcroft, and the diminishing attraction of neoconservative idealism (which by the mid-1990s was assumed dead). Then came 9/11, and conservatives seized on Islamic terrorism as the new communism: an existential threat to the United States that unified a diverse party and dominated American political debate.

How long will Republicans continue to base their foreign policy on a sense of threat? Fear can be a powerful motivator. When thinkers such as William Kristol and Robert Kagan first pushed the idea of a neo-Reaganite foreign policy in the mid-1990s, their tone was optimistic, even inspirational. They called on Americans to embrace a new project for national greatness. Their arguments gained little traction among Republicans until later in the decade, when interventionist conservatives began to emphasize growing threats posed by enemy missiles and rogue states Iraq and China.

Bush did not campaign for president in 2000 as a neoconservative, but after 9/11, he adopted the core tenets. This perspective gave Bush a sense of gravitas and mission that his presidency had been lacking. Kagan explained that during the 1990s, he and his small band of colleagues kept "alive a certain way of looking at American foreign policy at a time when it was pretty unpopular" and that after 9/11, it became a "ready-made approach to the world." Embracing such ideas, Bush outlined a bold interventionist policy that emphasized the spread of democracy, and for some time he was backed by a remarkably strong conservative consensus.[22]

But that support has dwindled dramatically. Frustrations with the Bush administration's policies in Iraq and questions about its competence are only intensifying. The 1990s fault lines on the right are reemerging. More conservatives find themselves questioning the wisdom of Bush's aspiration to promote democracy and his pursuit of nation-building and are urging a return to a policy based more on interests than values. Many of Bush's harshest critics now come not just from the left but also from the right (including former members of his administration, such as controversial U.N. Ambassador John Bolton). There is growing concern about the rising costs of an American empire. "We are a culturally imperial society but not a politically imperial one," Newt Gingrich observes. "We have no interest in running the planet, we just want to shape it."[23]

As CONSERVATIVES debate America's global goals, they also still grapple with how best to pursue them and what, if anything, is necessary to legitimize American actions. George H. W. Bush hoped the United States could exercise its influence through the international institutions whose potential was hobbled by the Cold War rivalry. He and his top advisers cared about legitimacy and believed that it had to be earned. They skillfully used U.N. support to fight the Persian Gulf War and were willing to impose some constraints on American behavior to keep others by their side. Yet conservatives as a whole rejected that approach, and Republicans spent the 1990s criticizing Democrats for allowing the United Nations to dictate American interests and restrict the country's freedom of action.

This was a caricature of the Clinton administration's approach, but the critique stuck. After early stumbles, the Clinton team embraced the idea of the United States as an indispensable nation to push back against the political impulse toward disengagement. They resisted the argument being made by some conservatives that the United States should just become a "normal country" and learned through experience that solving global problems is impossible without strong American leadership. Embracing the mantra of "together if we can and alone if we must," the Clinton administration set out to reform the United Nations and to try to make it as effective as possible.

Although George W. Bush and his advisers shared the idea of the United States as the indispensable nation (they were always careful, however, to distinguish themselves from their predecessors and would not use the same words), they were largely unconcerned about whether the rest of the world joined them. The cumulative result is that in the years after 11/9, there has been a steady rise in discomfort with U.S. power around the world and deeper worries about Washington's intentions. These concerns predated Bush, but his policies have made international anxieties far worse.

This debate is often characterized as pitting unilateralism against multilateralism, but it is far more complicated than that. Clinton was not afraid to act unilaterally when he believed it in the U.S. interest to do so, and in recent years Bush has embraced some of the multilateral policies he once derided (two prominent examples are the diplomatic efforts to curb Iran's and North Korea's nuclear ambitions). During the modern interwar years, Republicans and Democrats tussled over how America's actions would gain legitimacy in the eyes of the world or whether it already had enough to do what it wanted. Liberals tended to favor cooperation—both to maximize legitimacy and spread the costs—while conservatives were more focused on maintaining America's freedom of action and preserving its power.

*

THESE FIGHTS were about more than policy. They were about the very nature of global politics. Conservatives never favored Clinton's embrace of globalization—they never shared the idea, as Clinton did, that the world was no longer zero-sum. If Clinton saw the world as one of "us and them," believing that nations had to find a way to work together to address common problems, conservatives generally see things as "us versus them."[24] They argue that what is good for the United States is good for the world, whereas liberals believe that what is good for the world is good for the United States.[25]

Conservatives are still struggling with the concept of globalization, especially as it concerns the role of economics in foreign policy. "Being out of power for eight years had consequences for the Republicans," Fukuyama says. "They didn't understand that international politics had shifted."[26] They saw 9/11 as the beginning of a new era, but in reality the attacks simply forced them to recognize the one they were already living in.

Republican political elites showed little interest in globalization during the 1990s, believing it secondary to America's core national interests. Many conservatives seemed even to find it politically incorrect to utter the word. They saw such issues as the soft stuff, not the essence of power politics. Or worse, they considered globalization a code word for eroding American independence. The relative low profile that economic officials had during the George W. Bush presidency stands in stark contrast to the Clinton years. The Republicans did not seek to promote a global economic vicar in the style of Rubin or Lawrence Summers; their "committee to save the world" was far different—composed of traditional national security and military officials.

THROUGHOUT THE 11/9 to 9/11 era, Republicans were skeptical of globalization and divided over how America should act as a global power, but their national security barons basked in their reputation as masters of the substance and politics of global affairs. This special aura of superiority and credibility created by their management of the Cold War's end shaped the foreign policy debate during the 1990s. Democrats in office felt defensive as Republicans hurled criticisms from the outside. Those who entered the Bush administration in 2001 were widely seen as the "A team" by the public, the press, and even by many leading Democrats. Cheney, Rumsfeld, Powell, Condoleezza Rice, and Paul Wolfowitz, among others, were a group as experienced and talented as any incoming administration could have hoped to assemble.

This in part explains their knee-jerk impulse to reverse many of the things they inherited from Clinton in 2001. It also is a reason for the contempt many of them showed for the intelligence professionals' assessments during the early Bush years. They simply believed that they understood international politics better and had a clearer vision of reality. But now this conservative generation—like the liberal "best and the brightest" generation in the 1960s—is widely discredited. Their image of competence has been shattered and their ideas questioned. They returned to many of the Clinton policies they once rejected and had to be rescued by career government officials or those from the George H. W. Bush administration (such as James Baker and Robert Gates) they once shunned.

The collapse of the conservative foreign policy establishment will influence foreign policy debates within the Republican Party—and between conservatives and liberals—for years to come. Since Vietnam, the Democrats have faced skepticism that they could manage national security. Clinton was elected in 1992 only because that concern was less salient, and his first years in office did little to abate the perception of weakness. Now the tables have turned, and it's the Republicans who find themselves facing deep doubts about whether they are capable stewards of the country's national security.

The Third Iraq Hand-Off

In one significant respect, we have come full circle. Whereas America's struggle with one country—the Soviet Union—defined the Cold War, its tangle with another country—Iraq—is emblematic of the conundrums it has faced since the Cold War's end. A little over a year after the Berlin Wall fell, the United States led a grand U.N. coalition to reverse Iraqi aggression, and George H. W. Bush spoke of his tremendous optimism about American leadership and the potential of the post–Cold War international system. Bush could thwart Iraqi occupation of another country, but he feared American occupation of Iraq and left Saddam defeated but not vanquished. Throughout the 1990s, the United States struggled to keep its U.N. Security Council partners united in keeping sanctions on the Iraqi regime. A decade in which Iraq never had full control over its territory yet resisted the demands of the international community demonstrated the limits of the United Nations' ability to serve as diplomatic enforcer. Clinton contained Iraq, but he left the White House saying that "one of his two or three greatest regrets" was that he had never found the right answer for the challenge the country posed.[27]

At the turn of the century, most everyone following the events in the Middle East believed that Iraq was a ticking time bomb and feared that U.S. policy had no real direction. Conservatives heaped scorn on Clinton's "cynical" strategy to keep Iraq out of the news and defer any tough decisions to his successor.[28] Then after 9/11 George W. Bush thought he had found the answer by deposing Saddam. But he simply learned the hard way a lesson he should have drawn from the 1990s—it's easy for the most powerful nation to employ military force; it's a lot more difficult to rebuild another country.

George H. W. Bush left Iraq unresolved for Clinton; Clinton handed off the Iraq question for his successor to deal with; and so it is again. George W. Bush will leave it to the next American president to figure out how to produce a stable Iraq, and what level of military, economic, and political engagement is necessary to fulfill American interests. Of course, because of Bush 43's many mistakes, Iraq in 2009 poses challenges of a far greater magnitude than those faced in 1993 or 2001.

As a consequence of the war, many Americans are pessimistic about the power of their country to be a force for global good—and again wonder whether the costs of leadership are worth it. Years after 9/11, Americans suffer from the same contradictory impulses that dominated the 1990s: They are not eager to hear a call for new global missions—especially military ones—but they know that without American leadership, it will be impossible to solve global problems.

*

WHEN FUTURE historians reflect on the ideas and debates that shaped American foreign policy in the twenty-first century, they must start by looking back at the years from 11/9 to 9/11. This follows a pattern similar to previous eras in American history, beginning with the country's founding.

The events and politics of the 1790s established the foundation for the evolution of the U.S. foreign policy in the 1800s. In many respects, that century began in 1789, with the presidency of George Washington, who famously gave a farewell address conveying his prescriptions for his country's future. Washington's injunction to concentrate on strengthening fledgling democratic institutions while avoiding being drawn into European conflicts was central to how Americans thought about their country's place in the world throughout the next century. The young republic expanded across the continent and declared that the western hemisphere was off-limits to European powers, while avoiding broader involvement in world affairs.

One hundred years later, the last decade of the nineteenth century set the United States on a course that one historian describes as its "rush to superpowerdom." The ideas, policies, and events that defined the 1890s—imperial expansion, the rise of naval power, and the 1898 war with Spain—shaped the history of the twentieth century, when the United States proved it had the military prowess, economic might, and domestic political will to play a major role on the global stage. The next one hundred years were the "American Century."[29]

Once again, the last decade of the previous century has set America on its course in the new one. The 1990s were a defining moment for U.S. politics and foreign policy. These years were the beginning of an age when American power was both unsurpassed and questioned. Although 9/11 awakened many Americans to the dangers they face, unlike Pearl Harbor, it has not changed everything. As the country grapples with the complexities of the twenty-first century, struggling to find the right balance between its capabilities, responsibilities, and ambitions in a globalizing world, the lessons and legacies of the years from 11/9 to 9/11 will endure.

From 11/9 to 9/11: A Chronology

November 29   After months of intense American diplomacy, the U.N. Security Council passes Resolution 678, giving Iraq until January 15, 1991, to comply with U.N. demands.

Winter   Writing in *Foreign Affairs*, Charles Krauthammer declares a "unipolar moment."

1991

January 17   After Saddam Hussein defies the U.N.-imposed deadline, the United States and coalition forces launch an air campaign against Iraq in Operation Desert Storm.

February 27   Following a 100-hour ground campaign, Iraq retreats from Kuwait and Bush declares a cease-fire.

April 8   Baker visits the Iraq-Turkey border, where he sees thousands of Kurdish refugees who have fled Saddam. "We've got to do something and do it now," he says to Bush afterward.

April 16   American military forces help establish safe havens in northern Iraq to protect the Kurds in Operation Provide Comfort.

June 8   Thousands of Gulf War veterans parade in a massive victory celebration in Washington. "There is a new and wonderful feeling in America," Bush says.

June 25   Slovenia and Croatia declare independence from Yugoslavia, and a civil war erupts.

August 19   Soviet hard-liners try to overthrow President Mikhail Gorbachev in a coup, and the Soviet Union begins to unravel.

December 12   In a foreign policy address at Georgetown University, Arkansas Governor Bill Clinton criticizes Bush and says that Americans must elect "not the last president of the twentieth century, but the first president of the twenty-first century."

December 25   The Soviet Union dissolves, replaced by Russia and fourteen other newly independent states.

1992

February 19   Pat Buchanan scores big against Bush in New Hampshire's presidential primary, shocking the incumbent.

February 20   Appearing on CNN's *Larry King Live*, Texas businessman Ross Perot announces that he intends to run for president as an independent. By summer, he leads the polls.

March 8   The first drafts of the Pentagon's Defense Planning Guidance are published in the *New York Times*, sparking a fierce debate.

April 5   Bosnia-Herzegovina declares independence from Yugoslavia.

October 2   In a speech in Milwaukee, Wisconsin, Clinton derides Bush's "ambivalence about supporting democracy." Around that time, many prominent neoconservatives endorse Clinton for president.

November 3   Clinton is elected the forty-second president with 43 percent of the vote.

December 4   In a nationwide address from the Oval Office, Bush announces a U.S. military intervention in Somalia to provide humanitarian assistance.

December 25   Bush sends a "Christmas warning" to Slobodan Milosevic that the United States is prepared to respond militarily if Serbs initiate armed conflict in Kosovo.

1993

Early January   In a transition memo to incoming Secretary of State Warren Christopher, Lawrence Eagleburger observes that the chaotic new world almost makes one "nostalgic for the familiar discipline and order of the Cold War." Around that time, the Pentagon releases its strategy paper, which is the revised version of the controversial Defense Planning Guidance.

January 18   Just days before he leaves office, Bush launches cruise missile attacks on Iraq in response to Saddam's thwarting of U.N. weapons inspections and violations of the no-fly zone. Clinton says, "I fully support President Bush's action."

January 20   Clinton inaugurated.

February 26   Followers of radical Egyptian cleric Umar Abd al-Rahman explode a car bomb underneath the World Trade Center.

March 12   Clinton pays his first visit to a Navy aircraft carrier, and press reports are full of stories illustrating his troubles with the military.

June 27   After an Iraqi plot to assassinate former President Bush during a Kuwait visit is foiled, Clinton launches cruise missiles at targets in Baghdad.

July 19   Clinton announces "don't ask, don't tell" policy on gays in the military, quieting the controversy that had engulfed his first months in office.

Summer   *Foreign Affairs* publishes Samuel Huntington's article describing a looming "clash of civilizations."

September 13   Israeli Prime Minister Yitzhak Rabin and Palestinian leader Yasir Arafat shake hands at a signing ceremony on the White House lawn.

September 14   Clinton, flanked at the White House by Gerald Ford, Jimmy Carter, and Bush, pushes for the North American Free Trade Agreement (NAFTA).

September 21   National Security Adviser Anthony Lake delivers a speech outlining a strategy of "democratic enlargement."

October 3   The Black Hawk Down battle in Mogadishu, Somalia, kills eighteen Americans; Boris Yeltsin launches a military assault on the Russian parliament.

October 11   The USS *Harlan County* is prevented from docking in Haiti by an angry band of thugs screaming, "Somalia! Somalia!"

November 9   Al Gore and Perot debate NAFTA on *Larry King Live.*

November 17   NAFTA passes the House 234–200, but only 102 Democrats vote in favor.

December 8   Former Secretary of Defense Dick Cheney delivers a speech at the American Enterprise Institute. Decrying the lack of attention to foreign policy, he says, "Republicans bear part of the responsibility for this state of affairs."

December 15   In a move widely seen as a consequence of the Clinton administration's missteps, Defense Secretary Les Aspin resigns.

1994

February   The *Atlantic Monthly* publishes Robert Kaplan's "Coming Anarchy," describing the new world disorder. Clinton distributes copies to his senior advisers.

April 6 Rwandan genocide begins, and the United States declines to intervene after the previous year's debacle in Somalia.

June 17 Carter meets with North Korean leader Kim Il Sung to freeze North Korea's nuclear program, defusing the possibility of U.S. military attacks.

July 31 The U.N. Security Council passes unanimous resolution authorizing "all necessary means" to restore Haitian President Jean-Bertrand Aristide to power.

September 19 With American warplanes en route to the Caribbean, Carter, Colin Powell, and Sam Nunn broker a deal with Haiti's military junta, paving the way for Aristide's return. More than 20,000 U.S. troops go to Haiti to implement the agreement.

September 27 More than 350 Republican candidates for Congress sign the Contract with America on the steps of the U.S. Capitol, pledging, "If we break this contract, throw us out."

October Saddam demands that the United Nations lift sanctions and deploys 80,000 soldiers near the Kuwait border; Clinton sends 50,000 troops to the region to deter an attack.

November 9 Republicans win back both houses of Congress for the first time since the Dwight Eisenhower administration; Newt Gingrich announces, "I am very prepared to cooperate with the Clinton administration. I am not prepared to compromise."

December Treasury official Lawrence Summers interrupts incoming Secretary Robert Rubin's vacation to tell him the Mexican peso is in trouble.

1995

January 1 World Trade Organization (WTO) is established, replacing General Agreement on Tariffs and Trade, enraging those on both the left and right.

January 12 Former Secretary of State Baker testifies before the House International Relations Committee and tells his listeners, "Attempts at congressional micromanagement of foreign policy were a bad idea when the Democrats were in control and they remain a bad idea today."

January 21   Clinton signs Presidential Decision Directive (PDD) 39 outlining federal agencies' responsibilities in response to an act of
terrorism.

February 21   The United States begins disbursing billions of dollars in loans
to stabilize the Mexican peso.

May 9   Clinton goes to Moscow for the World War II fiftieth anniversary summit; the following month, Russia joins NATO's Partnership for Peace program.

July   A National Intelligence Estimate finds that no country other
than the existing nuclear powers could develop a missile capability that would endanger the continental United States for at
least fifteen years. This conclusion is criticized by conservatives.

July 11   Bosnian Serb forces begin to massacre thousands of Muslims
in Srebrenica, the largest mass killings in Europe since World
War II.

August 30   NATO, which never used military force during the Cold
War, launches air strikes against Bosnian Serb military targets, as an intense American diplomatic effort to negotiate
peace begins.

November 21   After three weeks of round-the-clock talks in Dayton, Ohio,
negotiators reach an agreement to end the war in Bosnia. A few
weeks later, 20,000 U.S. troops enter Bosnia as part of a NATO
force.

1996

January   *Foreign Affairs* publishes Michael Mandelbaum's "Foreign Policy as Social Work," an indictment of Clinton's foreign policy
from a former campaign adviser.

February 20   Buchanan wins the New Hampshire Republican primary, calling
it "a victory for the good men and women of middle America."

March   Clinton orders aircraft carrier battle groups near the Taiwan
strait, the largest American naval armada deployed to Southeast Asia since Vietnam.

June 25   A truck bomb explodes outside the Khobar Towers military
housing complex in Saudi Arabia, killing nineteen American
military personnel.

July 3   Yeltsin is reelected as president of Russia over communist
              challenger Gennady Zyuganov.

August 29   Speaking before the Democratic National Convention,
              Clinton says the United States is the "world's indispensable
              nation."

September 3   Clinton orders a cruise missile strike against Iraq in response to
              Saddam's attacks against the Kurds.

November 5   Clinton wins reelection over Republican Bob Dole.

November 19   The United States denies U.N. Secretary General Boutros
              Boutros-Ghali a second term, the first time a secretary general
              has not been reappointed.

1997 ───

May 2   Tony Blair becomes the first Labour prime minister of Great
              Britain in eighteen years and immediately forges a close rela-
              tionship with Clinton.

June 3   The Project for a New American Century (PNAC) is launched,
              providing a new forum for conservative interventionists.

July 8   At a summit in Madrid, NATO formally invites former Warsaw
              Pact nations Poland, Hungary, and the Czech Republic to join
              the alliance.

July   An East Asian financial crisis begins in Thailand and soon
              spreads across the region; America chooses not to intervene di-
              rectly until later in the year when the Korean economy goes
              into a tailspin.

November 9   The *Washington Post* publishes Paul Wolfowitz and Zalmay
              Khalilzad's op-ed, titled WE MUST LEAD THE WAY IN
              DEPOSING SADDAM.

November 16   To illustrate the threat posed by Iraq's suspected weapons
              programs, Secretary of Defense William Cohen holds up a
              five-pound bag of sugar on ABC's *This Week* and says an equiv-
              alent amount of anthrax could destroy half of Washington's
              population.

1998 ──

January 26 PNAC releases its first letter to the Clinton administration on Iraq, calling containment "dangerously inadequate."

February 17 Clinton delivers a speech on Iraq at the Pentagon, detailing the case against Saddam and the "predators of the twenty-first century."

February 18 A town hall meeting on Iraq with Clinton's national security team at Ohio State University erupts in jeers and catcalls.

May 22 Clinton releases two new PDDs on counterterrorism, highlighting the growing threat of unconventional attacks and launching an effort to protect critical infrastructure.

June 25 Clinton begins a nine-day visit to China, the first by an American president since the 1989 Tiananmen Square massacre.

July A congressionally mandated commission chaired by Donald Rumsfeld repudiates the 1995 National Intelligence Estimate report on the missile threat.

August 7 Al-Qaeda carries out attacks against American embassies in Kenya and Tanzania, leaving 258 people dead and more than 5,000 injured.

August 17 Clinton testifies before a grand jury about the Monica Lewinsky affair.

August 20 In response to the embassy bombings, the United States launches cruise missiles against terrorist training camps in Afghanistan and a pharmaceutical factory in Sudan.

August 22 A headline in the *International Herald Tribune* reads, U.S. ON ALERT, PREPARING FOR "WAR" ON TERROR.

August 31 North Korea test fires a Taepodong I missile, raising concerns about the missile threat and renewing the missile defense debate.

September 21 Meeting in New York, Clinton and Blair convene the first Third Way summit with the leaders of Italy and Bulgaria to discuss the future of progressive governance.

October 31 Clinton signs the Iraq Liberation Act, making regime change formal American policy and authorizing $100 million to support the Iraqi opposition.

December 16   After Saddam denies U.N. weapons inspectors access to sites, the United States and United Kingdom launch a sustained air campaign against Iraq, known as Operation Desert Fox. When the air strikes end, Clinton says that "so long as Saddam remains in power he will remain a threat to his people, the region, and the world."

December 19   Clinton is impeached by the House of Representatives.

1999

February 12   After a trial in the U.S. Senate, Clinton is found not guilty.

February   The CIA receives intelligence of Osama bin Laden's whereabouts in Afghanistan. After intense deliberation, the Clinton administration decides against a strike.

February 15   *Time* magazine describes Federal Reserve Chairman Alan Greenspan, Rubin, and Summers as the "Committee to Save the World" for their role in responding to the Asian financial crisis.

February 23   After more than two weeks of talks in Rambouillet, France, Madeleine Albright and her European counterparts fail to forge a Dayton-style agreement on Kosovo.

March 24   NATO air strikes begin against Serbia to stop ethnic cleansing in Kosovo.

April 24   In an effort to explain what NATO is doing in Kosovo, Blair delivers a speech outlining a new "doctrine of international community," calling for a broader definition of security and a radical overhaul of international institutions, such as the United Nations.

May 7   U.S. warplanes mistakenly bomb the Chinese embassy in downtown Belgrade, leading to widespread anti-American protests in China.

May 23   Liberal activists, journalists, and intellectuals gather to protest the Kosovo War at a "teach-in" at Leo Baeck Temple in Los Angeles.

June 3   Milosevic agrees to end the conflict in Kosovo. Several thousand American troops deploy there as part of a NATO force to keep the peace.

June 26   The State Department asks all American ambassadors to assess perceptions of the United States abroad in light of Kosovo, asking whether the war fueled concerns about American "hegemony."

July 22   Clinton signs the National Missile Defense Act, mandating that a missile defense system be deployed as soon as technologically possible.

September 23   During a speech at the Citadel, Texas Governor George W. Bush criticizes the Clinton administration's military policies as "ungrateful, unwise, and unacceptable."

November 29–30   Thousands of protestors take to the streets in Seattle, Washington, against the WTO. Clinton offers sympathy for their concerns about global trade while decrying the violence that erupted.

December 31   Yeltsin resigns as president of Russia, installing Vladimir Putin as the interim leader.

2000 ———————————————————————————

January 20   Republican Senator Jesse Helms of North Carolina addresses the U.N. Security Council, saying, "A United Nations that seeks to impose its presumed authority on the American people without their consent begs for confrontation, and, I want to be candid, eventual U.S. withdrawal."

March 26   Putin is elected president of Russia; at his inauguration, he calls for "a free, prosperous, strong, civilized, proud Russia."

July 11   Clinton begins intensive, but ultimately unsuccessful, discussions at Camp David with Israeli Prime Minister Ehud Barak and Palestinian leader Yasir Arafat.

August 2   Speaking before the Republican National Convention in Philadelphia, vice presidential nominee Cheney promises the U.S. military that "help is on the way."

September 1   Clinton announces that he will defer to his successor a decision on deploying missile defense.

September 19   Congress grants China Permanent Normal Trade Relations status with the United States, paving the way for China to join the WTO.

October 11   George W. Bush and Gore debate at Wake Forest University; Bush calls for less global intervention, saying, "If we're an arrogant nation, they'll resent us." Gore responds, "I think we also have to have a sense of mission in the world."

October 12   Al-Qaeda operatives bomb the USS *Cole* in Yemen, killing seventeen sailors.

November 7   The U.S. presidential election fails to produce a clear winner.

December 8   Clinton gives his "Foreign Policy in a Global Age" address in Nebraska and says, "I still don't think I've persuaded the American people by big majorities that you really ought to care a lot about foreign policy."

December 13   After the U.S. Supreme Court rules to stop the Florida recount, Gore concedes the 2000 presidential election to Bush.

December 19   Meeting with President-elect Bush in the Oval Office, Clinton warns of the al-Qaeda threat and tells his successor, "One of the great regrets of my presidency is that I didn't get [bin Laden] for you, because I tried to."

2001 ───

January 20   Bush takes the oath of office.

March 29   Bush declares that the United States will abandon Kyoto protocol on global climate change, putting him at odds with European allies.

April 1   An American EP-3 plane crashes into a Chinese fighter jet, creating an international crisis.

June 16   Bush meets with Putin at a summit in Slovenia and declares that he "was able to get a sense of his soul."

August 6   While on vacation at his Texas ranch, Bush receives a Presidential Daily Briefing titled "Bin Laden determined to strike in U.S."

September 10   *Time* magazine's cover asks, "Where have you gone, Colin Powell?"

September 11   Nineteen members of the terrorist organization al-Qaeda hijack four airplanes in the United States, crashing into the World Trade Center towers, the Pentagon, and an empty field in Pennsylvania. In a nationwide address that evening, Bush pledges to conduct a war against terrorism.

September 20   Speaking before a joint session of Congress, Bush says that "our response involves far more than instant retaliation and isolated strikes. Americans should not expect one battle, but a lengthy campaign, unlike any other we have ever seen."

Notes

Preface

1. James Atlas, "Name that Era: Pinpointing a Moment on the Map of History," *New York Times*, March 19, 1995.

2. The latter referred to Senator Phil Gramm, Republican senator from Texas.

3. Sarah Boxer, "Names for an Era: No Time Like the Present to Leave Something for Posterity," *New York Times*, April 2, 1995.

4. See these essays and those by other authors in *Foreign Policy*, Summer 2000.

5. Interview with Gerson.

6. George Will, "U.S. Faces New Reality," *Chicago Sun-Times*, September 12, 2001; and Frank Rich, "The Day Before Tuesday," *New York Times*, September 15, 2001.

7. Thomas Friedman, *The World Is Flat* (New York: Farrar, Straus and Giroux, 2005), pp. 441–442.

8. Paul Kennedy, *The Rise and Fall of the Great Powers* (New York: Random House, 1987).

9. Richard Haass, *The Reluctant Sheriff* (Washington, DC: Brookings Institution Press, 1997), p. 21.

10. See Warren I. Cohen, *Empire Without Tears: America's Foreign Relations 1921–33* (New York: McGraw-Hill, 1987).

Chapter One: The Lone Superpower, Adrift

1. George Bush and Brent Scowcroft, *A World Transformed* (New York: Knopf, 1998), p. 150.

2. Remarks and a Question-and-Answer Session with Reporters on the Relaxation of East German Border Controls, Public Papers of President

George H. W. Bush, November 9, 1989. See http://bushlibrary.tamu.edu/ research/public_papers.php?id=1174&year=1989&month=11.

3. Barry Schweid, "Caution Marks U.S. Policy: Democrats Call for Dramatic Moves," Associated Press, November 13, 1989; Donald M. Rothberg, "European Turmoil May Mean Political Turmoil for U.S. Politicians," Associated Press, December 7, 1989; Stephen Chapman, "Who Is to Blame for the West's Stunning Triumph?" *Chicago Tribune*, November 16, 1989.

4. CNN Cold War Series, Episode 24. See www.cnn.com/SPECIALS/cold .war/episodes/24/.

5. This was the title of their joint memoir.

6. Soviet Union–United States Joint Statement on the Persian Gulf Crisis, September 9, 1990, Papers of the President, Administration of George Bush, 1990, p. 1344.

7. James A. Baker III, *The Politics of Diplomacy: Revolution, War, and Peace, 1989–1992* (New York: G. P. Putnam's Sons, 1995), p. 16.

8. Baker, *The Politics of Diplomacy*, pp. 430–435; Christian Alfonsi, *Circle in the Sand: Why We Went Back to Iraq* (New York: Doubleday, 2006), pp. 218–234; and Thomas E. Ricks, *Fiasco: The American Military Adventure in Iraq* (New York: Penguin Press, 2006), pp. 8–9.

9. Zinni quoted in Dana Priest, *The Mission: Waging War and Keeping Peace with America's Military* (New York: W. W. Norton, 2003), p. 65.

10. The inscriptions at the memorial are listed at www.nps.gov/fdrm/ memorial/inscript.htm.

11. Quote from John Bolton, *Surrender Is Not an Option: Defending America at the United Nations and Abroad* (New York: Threshold Editions, 2007), p. 33.

12. George H. W. Bush, Address Before a Joint Session of the Congress on the Persian Gulf Crisis and the Federal Budget Deficit, September 11, 1990. See http://bushlibrary.tamu.edu/research/public_papers.php?id=2217 &year=1990&month=9.

13. Bush, Address Before a Joint Session of the Congress on the Cessation of the Persian Gulf Conflict, March 6, 1991. See http://bushlibrary.tamu.edu/ research/public_papers.php?id=2767&year=1991&month=3.

14. Interview with Richard Haass.

15. Quoted in the National Security Council Project, Oral History Roundtables, The Bush Administration National Security Council, April 29, 1999, Ivo H. Daalder and I. M. Destler, moderators, p. 29. See www.cissm.umd. edu/papers/files/bush.pdf.

16. Interview with Scowcroft.

17. Remarks and a Question-and-Answer Session with Reporters in Aspen, Colorado, Following a Meeting with Prime Minister Margaret Thatcher of

the United Kingdom, August 2, 1990. See http://bushlibrary.tamu.edu/
research/public_papers.php?id=2124&year=1990&month=8.

18. Baker, *The Politics of Diplomacy*, p. 304.

19. Ibid., pp. 321–322.

20. Interview with Scowcroft; George H. W. Bush, "Why We Are in the Gulf,"
Newsweek, November 26, 1990.

21. Interview with Colin Powell.

22. Charles Krauthammer, "The Unipolar Moment," *Foreign Affairs*, Winter
1990/1991, p. 33.

23. Alfonsi, *Circle in the Sand*, pp. 170–190.

24. Bush quote from James T. Patterson, *Restless Giant: The United States from
Watergate to Bush v. Gore* (New York: Oxford University Press USA, 2005),
p. 236; Powell quote from Alfonsi, *Circle in the Sand*, p. 324.

25. Cheney interview with David Brinkley, on ABC's *This Week with David
Brinkley*, April 7, 1991.

26. Cheney interview by the Brian Lapping Associates television series *The
Washington Version*, December 4, 1991. We thank the Trustees of the Liddell
Hart Centre for Military Archives and Brook Lapping Productions Limited
for the use of this quotation from a transcript for the television series, made
for the BBC and the Discovery Channel.

27. Interview with Scowcroft.

28. Bush and Scowcroft, *A World Transformed*, pp. 489–491.

29. Alfonsi, *Circle in the Sand*, pp. 213–214.

30. Bush and Scowcroft, *A World Transformed*, p. 487.

31. The National Security Council Project, Oral History Roundtables, The
Bush Administration National Security Council, April 29, 1999, Ivo H.
Daalder and I. M. Destler, moderators, p. 24. See www.cissm.umd.edu/
papers/files/bush.pdf.

32. Quoted in David Frum, "The Anti-Communists Won't Concede Victory,"
Wall Street Journal, May 1, 1990, p. A18; and Ralph Z. Hallow, "Neoconservatives' 'Peace Dividend' Is Internal Strife," *Washington Times*, April 30,
1990.

33. E. J. Dionne Jr., "Cold Warrior Meltdown; Anti-Communist Group
Claims Victory and Quits," *Washington Post*, December 19, 1990, C1.

34. From the *National Interest*, Fall 1990: Irving Kristol, "Defining Our
National Interest," pp. 16–25; Nathan Glazer, "A Time for Modesty,"
pp. 31–35; Jeane Kirkpatrick, "A Normal Country in a Normal Time,"
pp. 40–44.

35. James Atlas, "What Is Fukuyama Saying? And to Whom Is He Saying It?"
New York Times Magazine, October 22, 1989, pp. 38, 42; also see Jacob

Heilbrunn, *They Knew They Were Right: The Rise of the Neocons* (New York: Doubleday, 2008), pp. 195–197.

36. "Profile: Don't Let the Bogeyman Get You, George," *Independent* (London), December 14, 1991, p. 16; see also "Pat Buchanan," *West's Encyclopedia of American Law,* Gale Group Inc., 1998.

37. Interview with Buchanan.

38. Patrick Buchanan, "America First—and Second, and Third," *National Interest,* Spring 1990, pp. 79, 82.

39. For example, see Patrick Buchanan, *A Republic, Not an Empire: Reclaiming America's Destiny* (Washington, DC: Regnery, 1999).

40. Interview with Buchanan.

41. Patrick Buchanan, "Crackup of the Conservatives," *Washington Times,* May 1, 1991, G2.

42. Frances Fitzgerald, *Way Out There in the Blue: Reagan, Star Wars, and the End of the Cold War* (New York: Simon & Schuster, 2000), pp. 75–76.

43. Charles Krauthammer, "The Lonely Superpower," *New Republic,* July 29, 1991, p. 23.

44. Mary Jordan, "Victory Party Storms into Town," *Washington Post,* June 7, 1991, p. A1; Jordan, "800,000 Jam D.C. for Tribute to Troops," *Washington Post,* June 9, 1991, p. A1.

45. Krauthammer, "The Lonely Superpower," p. 24.

46. Memorandum from Fred Steeper to Robert Teeter, "1992 Presidential Campaign: The Churchill Parallel," published in Peter Goldman, et al., *Quest for the Presidency 1992* (College Station: Texas A&M Press, 1994), p. 621.

47. E. J. Dionne Jr., *Why Americans Hate Politics* (New York: Simon & Schuster, 1991), p. 319.

Chapter Two: Democrats Unite

1. Thomas L. Friedman, "Clinton Uses Loose Circle of Advisers," *New York Times,* March 28, 1992.

2. Interview with Lake.

3. Clifford Krauss, "Only Stormin' Norman's Sacred at Press Gridiron," *New York Times,* March 25, 1991.

4. Michael Beschloss and Strobe Talbott, *At the Highest Levels* (New York: Little, Brown, 1993), p. 434.

5. "What Foreign Policy?" *New Republic,* September 30, 1991, p. 6.

6. Interview with Will Marshall; and Kenneth Baer, *Reinventing Democrats: The Politics of Liberalism from Reagan to Clinton* (Lawrence: University of Kansas Press, 2000).

7. Memo to Governor Clinton from Sandy [Berger], Tony [Lake], Nancy [Soderberg], August 22, 1992, Anthony Lake Papers, Manuscript Division, Library of Congress, Washington, D.C., Box 10, Folder 10. For more on making democracy promotion the central goal of U.S. foreign policy, see Will Marshall, *Mandate for Change* (New York: Berkley Publishing, 1993), p. 297.

8. See E. J. Dionne Jr., *Why Americans Hate Politics*, pp. 55–57; and Fred Barnes, "They're Back!" *New Republic*, August 3, 1992.

9. Interviews with Fukuyama and Weber.

10. Interview with Ross.

11. Interview with Lake; and see also Jacob Heilbrunn, *They Knew They Were Right: The Rise of the Neocons* (New York: Doubleday, 2008), pp. 142–143.

12. Memorandum from Stuart E. Eizenstat to Mickey Kantor, George Stephanopoulos, Bruce Reed, Tony Lake, Sandy Berger, and Michael Mandelbaum, "Winning Back the Neoconservatives," July 30, 1992, in Lake Papers, Box 10, Folder 10.

13. Interviews with Woolsey and Brzezinski; see also Cathryn Donohoe, "Defection of the Neocons," *Washington Times*, October 27, 1992.

14. "Bill Clinton and the Vietnam War," Lake Papers, Box 11, Folder 3.

15. Morton Kondracke, "Pennsylvania Avenue," *Roll Call*, August 6, 1992; also see Heilbrunn, *They Knew They Were Right*, pp. 206–207.

16. Bill Clinton, "A New Covenant for American Security," remarks to students at Georgetown University, December 12, 1991.

17. Text of Clinton Speech on Foreign Affairs, Los Angeles World Affairs Council, U.S. Newswire, August 13, 1992.

18. Quoted in R. W. Apple Jr., "White House Race Is Recast: No Kremlin to Run Against," *New York Times*, February 6, 1992.

19. Buchanan speech to the Los Angeles World Affairs Council, U.S. Newswire, May 19, 1992.

20. Ross Perot, *United We Stand: How We Can Take Back Our Country* (New York: Hyperion, 1992), p.103; see also Gerald Seib, "Perot's Plan to Charge Allies for Their Defense Is Fuzzy on the Facts, but Politically on Target," *Wall Street Journal*, June 16, 1992, p. A14.

21. Memo from Berger, Lake, and Soderberg to Clinton, August 22, 1992, Lake papers, Box 10, Folder 10.

22. "Excerpts from Pentagon's Plan: 'Prevent the Re-Emergence of a New Rival,'" *New York Times*, March 8, 1992, p. 14; see also Patrick E. Tyler, "U.S. Strategy Plan Calls for Insuring No Rivals Develop," *New York Times*, March 8, 1992, p. 1.

23. Patrick E. Tyler, "Lone Superpower Plan: Ammunition for Critics," *New York Times*, March 10, 1992, p. A12; Tyler, "Senior U.S. Officials Assail Lone-Superpower Policy," *New York Times*, March 11, 1992, p. A6.
24. Interview with Scowcroft.
25. Patrick E. Tyler, "Pentagon Drops Goal of Blocking New Superpowers," *New York Times*, May 24, 1992, p. 1.
26. "Pax Cheney," *Wall Street Journal*, June 2, 1992, p. A1.
27. Interview with Edelman.
28. Zbigniew Brzezinski, *Second Chance: Three Presidents and the Crisis of American Superpower* (New York: Basic Books, 2007), p. 68.
29. James Mann, *Rise of the Vulcans: The History of Bush's War Cabinet* (New York: Viking, 2004), p. 199.
30. Dick Cheney, "Defense Strategy for the 1990s: The Regional Defense Strategy," Pentagon, January 1993, see www.informationclearinghouse.info/pdf/naarpr_Defense.pdf.
31. The authors were shown a copy of this memo during the research for this book and have submitted a Freedom of Information Act request for its full declassification.
32. For example, in the mid-1990s, the DPG's principal drafter, Zalmay Khalilzad, published several articles that carried forward its main conclusions. See Khalilzad, *From Containment to Global Leadership? America & the World after the Cold War* (Santa Monica: RAND, 1995); and "Losing the Moment? The United States and the World after the Cold War," *Washington Quarterly*, Spring 1995.

Chapter Three: Wrong Foot Forward

1. Interview with Scowcroft.
2. Jon Western, "Sources of Humanitarian Intervention: Beliefs, Information, and Advocacy in the U.S. Decisions on Somalia and Bosnia," *International Security* 27, no. 1 (July/August 1999), available at www.mtholyoke.edu/acad/intrel/western1.htm.
3. Quote from Strobe Talbott, *The Great Experiment* (New York: Simon & Schuster, 2007), p. 257.
4. Clinton quote from Thomas Friedman, "Clinton Backs Raid but Muses about New Start," *New York Times*, January 14, 1993; interview with Berger; and Nancy Soderberg, *The Superpower Myth: The Use and Misuse of American Might* (New York: Wiley and Sons), pp. 36–37.
5. Interview with Albright; and Madeleine Albright, *Madam Secretary* (New York: Miramax Books, 2005), p. 141.

6. Louis J. Klarevas, "Trends: The United States Peace Operation in Somalia," *Public Opinion Quarterly* 64 (Winter 2000), p. 529.

7. Interview with Lee Hamilton; and see David Halberstam, *War in a Time of Peace* (New York: Simon & Schuster, 2001), p. 168.

8. Quoted in Bill Clinton, *My Life* (New York: Knopf, 2004), p. 502.

9. Colin Powell, *My American Journey* (New York: Ballantine, 1995), p. 560.

10. George Stephanopoulos, *All Too Human: A Political Education* (New York: Little, Brown, 2000), p. 157.

11. Powell, *My American Journey*, p. 556; Elizabeth Drew, *On the Edge: The Clinton Presidency* (New York: Simon & Schuster, 1994), pp. 47–48.

12. Interview with Podesta.

13. Eric Schmitt with Thomas Friedman, "Clinton and Powell Discover That They Need Each Other," *New York Times*, June 4, 1993.

14. See Barton Gellman, "Warship Gives Clinton a Not-So-Hail to the Chief," *Washington Post*, March 13, 1993; and Thomas Friedman and Maureen Dowd, "White House Memo: Amid Setbacks, Clinton Team Seeks to Shake Off the Blues," *New York Times*, April 25, 1993.

15. See Karen DeYoung, *Soldier: The Life of Colin Powell* (New York: Knopf, 2006), pp. 233–234.

16. Powell, *My American Journey*, p. 560; and Albright quote from David J. Rothkopf, *Running the World: The Inside Story of the National Security Council and the Architects of American Power* (New York: PublicAffairs, 2005), p. 322.

17. Stephanopoulos, *All Too Human*, p. 132.

18. Drew, *On the Edge*, pp. 47–48.

19. Quotes from Douglas Brinkley, "Democratic Enlargement: The Clinton Doctrine," *Foreign Policy*, Spring 1997, p. 113.

20. Daniel Williams and John M. Goshko, "Reduced U.S. World Role Outlined but Soon Altered," *Washington Post*, May 26, 1993.

21. For criticism, see "The Clinton Foreign Policy, 1977–81, 1993–97," *Washington Times* editorial, May 27, 1993; for Vance's speech, see "Vance Asks Realism in U.S. Rights Policy," *New York Times*, May 1, 1977.

22. See Brinkley, "Democratic Enlargement," p. 114.

23. Samuel Huntington, "The Clash of Civilizations," *Foreign Affairs*, Summer 1993, pp. 22–49.

24. Interview with Lake.

25. Quote from Jason DeParle, "The Man Inside Bill Clinton's Foreign Policy," *New York Times Magazine*, August 20, 1995.

26. Interviews with Lake, Rosner, and Gingrich.

27. Soderberg memo to Lake, September 20, 1993, Anthony Lake Papers, Manuscript Division, Library of Congress, Box 51, Folder 4.

28. Anthony Lake, "From Containment to Enlargement," speech delivered at

Johns Hopkins University School of Advanced International Studies, September 21, 1993, available at www.mtholyoke.edu/acad/intrel/lakedoc.html.

29. Bill Clinton, "Reforming the United Nations," September 27, 1993, New York. Reprinted in *Vital Speeches of the Day* 60, no. 1 (October 15, 1993), pp. 9–13.

30. Interview with Albright.

31. Drew, *On the Edge*, p. 324.

32. Safire, "On Language," *New York Times Magazine*, October 10, 1993.

33. Interview with Rosner.

34. Jacob Heilbrunn, "Lake Inferior," *New Republic*, September 20, 1993, pp. 29–35.

35. Interview with Kissinger. For Kennan quote, see John Lewis Gaddis, "Was the Truman Doctrine a Real Turning Point?" *Foreign Affairs*, January 1974, p. 398.

36. Interviews with Benjamin, Boorstin.

37. Interview with Rosner.

38. Drew, *On the Edge*, p. 239.

39. Lake Papers, Box 43, Folder 9.

40. See *The 9/11 Commission Report* (New York: W. W. Norton, 2004), p. 60.

41. Madeleine Albright, "Yes, There Is a Reason to Be in Somalia," *New York Times*, August 10, 1993, p. A19.

42. Charles Krauthammer, "The Immaculate Intervention," *Time*, July 26, 1993, p. 78.

43. Soderberg, *The Superpower Myth*, p. 38.

44. Clinton, "Reforming the United Nations."

45. Quoted in Stephanopoulos, *All Too Human*, p. 214.

46. Sidney Blumenthal, *The Clinton Wars* (New York: Farrar, Straus and Giroux, 2003), p. 60.

47. Clifford Krauss, "The Somalia Mission: White House Tries to Calm Congress," *New York Times*, October 6, 1993.

48. Interview with Gingrich.

49. Oakley, quoted in Association for Diplomatic Studies Oral History Collection, available at http://library.georgetown.edu/dept/speccoll/diplo.htm.

50. Klarevas, "Trends: The United States Peace Operation in Somalia," p. 540.

51. Jim Hoagland, "Flaws and Fissures in Foreign Policy," *Washington Post*, October 31, 1993, p. C7.

52. Quote from Joe Klein, "Eight Years," *New Yorker*, October 16 and 23, 2000, p. 200; see also James T. Patterson, *Restless Giant: The United States from Watergate to Bush v. Gore* (New York: Oxford University Press USA, 2005), pp. 338–339.

53. See interview with Bill Clinton, "His Side of the Story," *Time*, June 28, 2004; and Clinton, *My Life*, pp. 552, 554.

54. "Interview of the President by Joe Klein," Office of the Press Secretary, White House, July 5, 2000.

55. Lake Papers, Box 62, Folder 2.

56. Lake interview in *PBS Frontline: The Clinton Years*, available at www.pbs.org/wgbh/pages/frontline/shows/clinton/interviews/lake.html.

57. Thomas L. Friedman, "Clinton's Foreign Policy: Top Adviser Speaks Up," *New York Times*, October 31, 1993, Section 1, p. 8.

58. Lake Papers, Box 48, Folder 2.

59. Drew, *On the Edge*, p. 336.

60. Quoted in Stephanopoulos, *All Too Human*, p. 214.

61. Interview with Powell.

62. See Richard Holbrooke, *To End a War* (New York: Random House, 1998), p. 217; and Halberstam, *War in a Time of Peace*, p. 265.

Chapter Four: Contract and Crisis

1. Quoted in Thomas Friedman, "A Broken Truce: Clinton vs. Bush in Global Policy," *New York Times*, October 17, 1993.

2. Speech by Dick Cheney, "Getting Our Priorities Right," Francis Boyer Lecture, American Enterprise Institute, December 8, 1993; also see Lloyd Grove, "A Running Room–Only Affair; GOP Luminaries Pack Ex-Pentagon Chief's Speech," *Washington Post*, December 9, 1993.

3. Quoted in Richard L. Berke, "Cheney Won't Run in '96; Kemp Likely to Follow Suit," *New York Times*, January 4, 1995.

4. Memorandum to Republican leaders from Frank Luntz, "Public Reaction to 'the Contract,'" September 2, 1994, reprinted in Major Garrett, *The Enduring Revolution: How the Contract with America Continues to Shape the Nation* (New York: Three Rivers Press, 2005), appendix.

5. Interview with Gingrich.

6. Quoted in Garrett, *The Enduring Revolution*, p. 156.

7. Interview with Gingrich.

8. Quotes from Samantha Power, *"A Problem from Hell": America and the Age of Genocide* (New York: Basic Books, 2002), pp. 334, 370; and Derek Chollet, "The Age of Genocide," *Policy Review*, August/September 2002, pp. 87–91.

9. See James Traub, *The Best Intentions: Kofi Annan and the U.N. in the Era of American World Power* (New York: Farrar, Straus and Giroux, 2006), p. 39.

10. Bill Clinton, *My Life* (New York: Knopf, 2004), p. 593.

11. See Joel S. Wit, Daniel B. Poneman, and Robert L. Gallucci, *Going Critical:*

The First North Korean Nuclear Crisis (Washington, DC: Brookings Institution Press, 2004), pp. 210–226; Ashton Carter and William Perry, *Preventive Defense: A New Security Strategy for America* (Washington, DC: Brookings Institution Press, 1999), pp. 123–124; and John F. Harris, *The Survivor: Bill Clinton in the White House* (New York: Random House, 2005), pp. 128–132.

12. See Harris, *The Survivor*, pp. 137–138; David Halberstam, *War in a Time of Peace* (New York: Simon & Schuster, 2001), pp. 278–282; and George Stephanopoulos, *All Too Human: A Political Education* (New York: Little, Brown, 2000), pp. 305–308.

13. Harris, *The Survivor*, p. 139.

14. History Makers Series, Former Secretary of Defense William J. Perry, Federal News Service, June 7, 2007; and Harris, *The Survivor*, pp. 140–141.

15. See Joe Klein, "The Politics of Promiscuity," *Newsweek*, May 9, 1994; Gerald Ford quote from Thomas M. DeFrank, *Write It When I'm Gone* (New York: Putnam, 2007), p. 122.

16. See Robert Kagan, "A Retreat from Power?" *Commentary*, July 1995, p. 20.

17. Details of this meeting are drawn from Strobe Talbott, *The Great Experiment: The Story of Ancient Empires, Modern States, and the Quest for a Global Nation* (New York: Simon & Schuster, 2008), pp. 327–328; Strobe Talbott, *The Russia Hand: A Memoir of Presidential Diplomacy* (New York: Random House, 2002), pp. 133–134; and conversations with several of the participants.

18. Robert Kaplan, "The Coming Anarchy," *Atlantic*, February 1994.

19. Clinton quote from "Advancing a Vision of Sustainable Development," statement by Bill Clinton before the National Academy of Sciences, U.S. Department of State Dispatch, July 18, 1994.

20. Rosner had left the White House staff earlier that year and was now working at the Carnegie Endowment for International Peace, a Washington think tank. See his article "Is Chaos America's Real Enemy? The Foreign Policy Idea Splitting Clinton's Team," *Washington Post*, August 14, 1994.

21. Speech by Bill Clinton, 49th Session of the U.N. General Assembly, September 26, 1994, available at www.clintonfoundation.org/legacy/092694 -speech-by-president-address-to-un-general-assembly.htm.

22. Quote from Arthur Schlesinger Jr., *Journals, 1952–2000* (New York: Penguin, 2007).

23. See John Goshko, "Neoconservative Democrats Complain of Big Chill," *Washington Post*, March 15, 1993; and Joshua Muravchik, "Lament of a Clinton Supporter," *Commentary*, August 1993, p. 17.

24. Interview with Frum.

25. Interviews with Kagan and Schmitt; also see George Packer, *The Assassins' Gate* (New York: Farrar, Straus and Giroux, 2005), pp. 17–22.

26. Robert Kagan, "The Case for Global Activism," *Commentary*, September 1994.

27. Fukuyama letter to the editor, *Commentary*, December 1994, p. 8.

28. Wolfowitz letter to the editor, *Commentary*, December 1994, p. 15.

29. In the mid-1990s, polls showed that the public wanted to work through the United Nations and supported U.N. peacekeeping operations (as long as they were succeeding). In March 1994, 89 percent of respondents to a CBS/*New York Times* poll agreed with the statement "It is important for the United States to cooperate with other countries by working through the United Nations." Two years later, a poll conducted by the Program on International Policy Attitudes (PIPA) found that 79 percent agreed and only 18 percent disagreed with the statement that "because the world is so interconnected today, the United States should participate in U.N. efforts to maintain peace, protect human rights, and promote economic development. Such efforts serve U.S. interests because they help create a more stable world that is less apt to have wars and is more conducive to trade and other U.S. interests." See Steven Kull and I. M. Destler, *Misreading the Public: The Myth of a New Isolationism* (Washington, DC: Brookings Institution Press, 1999), pp. 68–69.

30. In April 1987, when asked, "What do you think is the most important problem facing this country today?" 22 percent of respondents cited international issues. That number dropped to 10 percent in February 1989, fell to 6 percent in May 1990, and stayed below 6 percent through 1996. In addition, when asked the two most important criteria for voting for president, 33 percent had cited international issues in 1980, a number that dropped to 24 percent in 1984 and 1988 and only 8 percent in 1992 and 1996. See Kull and Destler, *Misreading the Public*, pp. 22–23.

31. Steven Kull and his PIPA colleagues explored this gap by interviewing members of the policy elite, including members of Congress and their staff, and even soliciting their help in designing poll questions. Three-quarters of the elite surveyed believed Americans wanted to disengage from the world, but polls showed that the trend lines since the fall of the Berlin Wall had stayed steady, with two-thirds of respondents in polls saying that the United States should remain an active participant in world affairs. See Steven Kull and Clay Ramsay, "Challenging U.S. Policymakers' Image of an Isolationist Public," *International Studies Perspectives*, April 2000, pp. 105–117.

32. Robert Kagan, letter to the editor, *Commentary*, December 1994, p. 18.

33. Norman Podhoretz, "Neoconservatism: A Eulogy," *Commentary*, March 1996, p. 24; John B. Judis, "Trotskyism to Anachronism: The Neoconservative Revolution," *Foreign Affairs*, July/August 1995, pp. 128–129.

34. Dale Russakoff, "Gingrich Lobs a Few More Bombs," *Washington Post*, November 10, 1994; Ed Gillespie and Bob Schellas, eds., *Contract with America: The Bold Plan by Rep. Newt Gingrich, Rep. Dick Armey, and the House Republicans to Change the Nation* (New York: Times Books, 1994), p. 186.

35. Interview with Perry.

36. Interview with Gingrich.

37. Interview with Weber.

38. Hearings before the Committee on International Relations, House of Representatives, 104th Congress, First Session, January 12, 19, and 26 (U.S. GPO, 1995), p. 4; see also Maureen Dowd, "Baker Basks in House, and Warns on Meddling," *New York Times*, January 13, 1995.

39. Madeleine Albright, *Madam Secretary* (New York: Miramax Books, 2005), p. 175.

40. Interview with Perry.

Chapter Five: Turning Point

1. Michael Mandelbaum, "Bill Clinton and the Draft," *New York Times*, February 12, 1992.

2. See Thomas Friedman, "Clinton Uses Loose Circle of Advisers," *New York Times*, March 28, 1992.

3. Michael Mandelbaum, "Foreign Policy as Social Work," *Foreign Affairs*, January/February 1996.

4. Quoted in Steven Erlanger and David Sanger, "On World Stage, Many Lessons for Clinton," *New York Times*, July 29, 1996.

5. John Mearsheimer, "Why We Will Soon Miss the Cold War," *Atlantic*, August 1990.

6. President Bill Clinton remarks at the Brandenburg Gate, July 12, 1994, available at www.millercenter.virginia.edu/scripps/digitalarchive/speeches/spe_1994_0612_clinton.

7. Quotes from James M. Goldgeier and Michael McFaul, *Power and Purpose: U.S. Policy toward Russia after the Cold War* (Washington, DC: Brookings Institution Press, 2003), pp. 28, 32, 54.

8. Marvin Kalb, *The Nixon Memo: Political Respectability, Russia, and the Press* (Chicago: University of Chicago Press, 1994), pp. 217–218, 220; Monica Crowley, *Nixon Off the Record* (New York: Random House, 1996), p. 73.

9. Strobe Talbott, *The Russia Hand: A Memoir of Presidential Diplomacy* (New York: Random House, 2002), pp. 42–43.

10. "Remarks by the President in Live Telecast to Russian People," White House press release, January 14, 1994.

11. Goldgeier and McFaul, *Power and Purpose*, p. 93.

12. Talbott, *The Russia Hand*, p. 185.

13. George F. Kennan, "A Fateful Error," *New York Times*, February 5, 1997, p. A23.

14. James M. Goldgeier, *Not Whether but When: The U.S. Decision to Enlarge NATO* (Washington, DC: Brookings Institution Press, 1999), p. 141.

15. See his comments in History Makers Series, Federal News Service, June 7, 2007, available at www.cfr.org/publication/13564/history_makers_series. html?breadcrumb=%2Feducators%2Fmultimedia%3Fgroupby%3D1%26pa ge%3D1.

16. Interview with Talbott.

17. Kaplan later regretted that the book—which he described as "an idiosyncratic travel book"—became associated with Clinton's inaction in Bosnia. "That policymakers, indeed a president, might rely on such a book in reaching a momentous military decision would be frightening. My personal suspicion is that back in 1993 . . . Clinton had so little resolve that he was casting around for an excuse not to act," he wrote. See Robert Kaplan, *Balkan Ghosts*, rev. ed. (New York: Picador, 2005), pp. x–xi.

18. Craig R. Whitney, "Europe's Call: Lead On, U.S.," *New York Times*, May 7, 1993; and Craig R. Whitney, "NATO's Leadership Gap: Washington's Seeming Confusion on Bosnia Throws Alliance into Crisis of Relevance," *New York Times*, May 29, 1993.

19. See *The 9/11 Commission Report* (New York: W. W. Norton, 2004), p. 155.

20. The following paragraphs draw upon Derek Chollet, *The Road to the Dayton Accords* (New York: Palgrave Macmillan, 2005); "Dayton at 10: A View from Washington," *Internationale Politik*, Winter 2004/2005.

21. Interview with Feith.

22. See Holbrooke, *To End a War*, pp. 253–254; and Alan Weisman, *Prince of Darkness: Richard Perle* (New York: Union Square, 2007), pp. 130–133.

23. See Stephen Sestanovich, "American Maximalism," *National Interest*, Spring 2005.

24. John F. Harris, *The Survivor: Bill Clinton in the White House* (New York: Random House, 2005), p. 321.

25. Quote from Sean Wilentz, "Bill Clinton," *Rolling Stone*, November 15, 2007, p. 183; see also Bill Clinton, *My Life* (New York: Knopf, 2004), pp. 20–21.

26. Quote from Chollet, *The Road to the Dayton Accords*, p. 132.

27. Richard Haass, *The Reluctant Sheriff: The United States after the Cold War* (Washington, DC: Brookings Institution Press, 1998).

28. Memorandum from Warren Christopher to Clinton, "Night Note from

Brussels," December 7, 1995 (document declassified by the Department of State in response to a Freedom of Information Act request by the authors).

29. Quote from Chollet, *The Road to the Dayton Accords*, p. 128.

30. Quotes from Holbrooke, *To End a War*, p. 364.

31. Interview with Nash.

32. See Traub, *The Best Intentions: Kofi Annan and the U.N. in the Era of American World Power* (New York: Farrar, Straus and Giroux, 2006), pp. 66–67.

33. Carl Bildt, *Peace Journey: The Struggle for Peace in Bosnia* (London: Weidenfeld & Nicolson, 1998), p. 387.

34. Patrick Tyler, *A Great Wall* (New York: PublicAffairs, 1999), p. 412; James Mann, *About Face* (New York: Vintage Books, 1998), pp. 290–314.

35. Dana Priest and Judith Havemann, "Second Group of U.S. Ships Sent to Taiwan," *Washington Post*, March 11, 1996, p. A1; see also Robert S. Ross, "The 1995–96 Taiwan Strait Confrontation: Coercion, Credibility, and Use of Force," *International Security* 25, no. 2 (Fall 2000), pp. 87–123.

36. Tyler, *A Great Wall*, pp. 21–43; Mann, *About Face*, pp. 315–338.

37. See Mann, *About Face*, p. 338.

38. Quote from Michael Dobbs, "For Some, Clinton Foreign Policy Portrait Still Awaits Final Brush Strokes," *Washington Post*, December 24, 1995.

39. Bob Woodward, *The Choice* (New York: Simon & Schuster, 1996), pp. 328–330.

40. Chollet, *The Road to the Dayton Accords*, p. 37.

41. Interview with Buchanan.

42. See Alessandra Stanley, "From Japan to Britain, Foreign Leaders and Press Look Askance at Buchanan Fever," *New York Times*, February 28, 1996; Frum, *Dead Right* (New York: Basic Books, 1994), pp. 124–158.

43. Nina Easton, *Gang of Five* (New York: Simon & Schuster, 2000); Francis Fukuyama, *America at the Crossroads* (New Haven: Yale University Press, 2006), pp. 42–43; and Jacob Heilbrunn, *They Knew They Were Right: The Rise of the Neocons* (New York: Doubleday, 2008), pp. 213–214.

44. PBS's Frontline, "The War Behind Closed Doors," available at http://www.pbs.org/wgbh/pages/frontline/shows/iraq/interviews/kristol.html.

45. William Kristol and Robert Kagan, "Toward a Neo-Reaganite Foreign Policy," *Foreign Affairs*, July/August 1996.

46. Kim R. Holmes and John Hillen, "Misreading Reagan's Legacy: A Truly Conservative Foreign Policy," *Foreign Affairs*, September/October 1996.

47. See Jonathan Clarke, "Gone to the Lake: Republicans and Foreign Policy," *National Interest*, Summer 1996.

48. See Adam Nagourney, "Dole Advisors Attack Clinton's Foreign Policy," *New York Times*, October 1, 1996; Katharine Q. Seelye, "Dole Attacks Clin-

ton Asia Policy although He Supports Part of It," *New York Times*, May 10, 1996.

49. Interview with Kemp. On the Dole 1996 speech, see Seelye, "Dole Attacks Clinton Asia Policy."

50. See Evan Thomas, ed., *Back from the Dead: How Clinton Survived the Republican Revolution* (New York: The Atlantic Monthly Press, 1997), p. 153.

51. Ibid., p. 189.

52. See William Kristol and Robert Kagan, "The New Isolationist?" *New York Times*, October 14, 1996.

Chapter Six: The Indispensable Nation in a Globalizing World

1. Colin Powell, *My American Journey* (New York: Ballantine, 1995), p. 561.

2. Quote from Elaine Sciolino, "Madeleine Albright's Audition," *New York Times Magazine*, September 22, 1996; see also Madeleine Albright, *Madam Secretary* (New York: Miramax Books, 2005), p. 182.

3. According to Blumenthal, he had mentioned the phrase first to Jamie Rubin, a close Albright aide who was then the foreign policy coordinator for Clinton's 1996 reelection campaign. See Blumenthal, *The Clinton Wars* (New York: Farrar, Straus and Giroux, 2003), p. 155.

4. Interview with Albright; see Albright, *Madam Secretary*, p. 506.

5. Two packets of transition memos were prepared for Albright when she became secretary of state: "Secret/NODIS Looking Ahead Memoranda, November 1996" and "Key Issues Papers for Secretary of State-designate Madeleine Albright, December 1996." Both sets of documents have been declassified. We are grateful to Bob Wampler at the National Security Archive for obtaining these materials using the Freedom of Information Act.

6. See memorandum to the secretary from Winston Lord, "Asia and the Pacific: Looking Ahead," November 7, 1996; "U.S.-Iran Relations," key issue paper for Albright, December 4, 1996; "U.S.–Saudi Arabian Relations," key issue paper for Albright, December 6, 1996; "U.S.-Russian Nuclear Issues," key issue paper for Albright, December 6, 1996; and memorandum to the secretary from Jeffrey Davidow, "ARA: Looking Ahead," November 6, 1996.

7. Memorandum to the secretary from Barbara Larkin, "Congressional Relations: Looking Ahead," December 6, 1996; and memorandum to the secretary from Princeton Lyman, "Looking Ahead," December 6, 1996.

8. See memorandum to the secretary from Alan Larson, "Looking Ahead: International Economic Policy," December 2, 1996.

9. Interview with Steinberg.

10. Interview with Kantor.

11. Interview with Medish.

12. See Robert Reich, *The Work of Nations* (New York: Vintage Books, 1991), p. 3; and Bob Woodward, *The Agenda* (New York: Simon & Schuster, 1994), pp. 3–5.

13. On the 1920s, see Warren I. Cohen, *Empire Without Tears: America's Foreign Relations 1921–33* (New York: McGraw-Hill, 1987), pp. 18–44.

14. Alan Greenspan, *The Age of Turbulence* (New York: Penguin Press, 2007), p. 12.

15. Thomas Friedman, *The Lexus and the Olive Tree* (New York: Anchor Books, 2000), p. 7; and Blumenthal, *The Clinton Wars*, p. 652.

16. Quoted in Steven Erlanger and David Sanger, "On the World Stage, Many Lessons for Clinton," *New York Times*, July 29, 1996.

17. Interview with Kantor; Warren Christopher, *In the Stream of History: Shaping Foreign Policy for a New Era* (Stanford, CA: Stanford University Press, 1998), p. 106.

18. Henry Kissinger, "NAFTA: Clinton's Defining Task," *Washington Post*, July 20, 1993; Paul Krugman, "The Uncomfortable Truth about NAFTA," *Foreign Affairs*, November/December 1993, p. 19.

19. Interview with Bonior; David S. Cloud, "As NAFTA Countdown Begins, Wheeling, Dealing Intensifies," *Congressional Quarterly Report*, November 13, 1993, p. 3104–3106.

20. Patrick J. Buchanan, "Gergenizing the GOP," *Pittsburgh Post-Gazette*, September 13, 1993.

21. "Remarks by President Clinton, President Bush, President Carter, President Ford, and Vice President Gore in Signing of NAFTA Side Agreements," White House, Office of the Press Secretary, September 14, 1993.

22. Michael Kranish and John Aloysius Farrell, "Gore, Perot Jab Hard on Merits of NAFTA," *Boston Globe*, November 10, 1993.

23. David Gergen, *Eyewitness to Power* (New York: Simon & Schuster, 2000), pp. 284–285.

24. Cheney, quoted in *Commanding Heights: The Battle for the World Economy*, available at www.pbs.org/wgbh/commandingheights/; interviews with Gingrich and Bonior.

25. Bill Clinton, *My Life* (New York: Knopf, 2004), p. 557.

26. Tamer Malley and Patrick Woodall, "The Clinton Record on Trade Vote Deal Making: High Infidelity," *Public Citizen*, May 2005.

27. Interview with Bonior.

28. Interview with Barshefsky; Blumenthal, *The Clinton Wars*, p. 309.

29. Interview with Nader.

30. See the Congressional Record, Uruguay Round Agreements Act, U.S. Senate, November 30, 1994; also "Ralph Nader: Conservatively Speaking," in *American Conservative*, June 21, 2004, at www.amconmag.com/2004_06_21/ cover.html; Katie Kerwin, "Brown Is Champ of GATT 'Quiz Show,'" *Rocky Mountain News*, November 29, 1994.

31. Robert Rubin, *In an Uncertain World: Tough Choices from Wall Street to Washington* (New York: Random House, 2003) p. 5.

32. Interview with Rubin.

33. Rubin, *In an Uncertain World*, pp. 3, 12.

34. Greenspan, *The Age of Turbulence*, p. 158.

35. John F. Harris, *The Survivor: Bill Clinton in the White House* (New York: Random House, 2005), p. 159.

36. Clinton, *My Life*, p. 643.

37. Gingrich, quoted in *Commanding Heights*.

38. Interview with Berger.

39. Rubin, *In an Uncertain World*, pp. 28–30.

40. Rubin, *In an Uncertain World*, pp. 28–30.

41. Rubin, *In an Uncertain World*, pp. 31–34; Thomas L. Friedman, "In My Next Column," *New York Times*, May 24, 1995; interview with Daschle.

42. Quoted in Erlanger and Sanger, "On the World Stage, Many Lessons for Clinton."

43. Robert Reich, *The Work of Nations: Preparing Ourselves for 21st Century Capitalism* (New York: Vintage Books, 1991), p. 323.

44. See Harris, *The Survivor*, pp. 204–205; Blumenthal, *The Clinton Wars*, pp. 312–314.

45. Interviews with Weber and Frum.

46. Details on PNAC from interviews with Fukuyama, Kagan, Schmitt, Weber, and Bruce Jackson.

47. See Richard L. Berke, "G.O.P. Hope New Group Can Attract Support from Outsiders," *New York Times*, November 15, 1993; and Leslie Wayne and Christopher Drew, "G.O.P. Tool to Revive Party Instead Results in Scrutiny," *New York Times*, June 2, 1997.

48. Haley Barbour, *Agenda for America: A Republican Direction for the Future* (Washington, DC: Regnery, 1996).

49. Interviews with Bolton and Schmitt.

50. Interview with Schmitt.

51. See James Walsh, "America the Brazen," *Time* (Europe ed.), August 4, 1997; Albright, *Madam Secretary*, p. 506.

Chapter Seven: "Remembering the Past and Imagining the Future"

1. Kenneth Pollack, *The Threatening Storm: The Case for Invading Iraq* (New York: Random House, 2002), pp. 58–63.

2. Quoted in Christian Alfonsi, *Circle in the Sand: Why We Went Back to Iraq* (New York: Doubleday, 2006), p. 316.

3. Pollack, *The Threatening Storm*, pp. 58–59; Alfonsi, *Circle in the Sand*, pp. 305–307.

4. Thomas Friedman, "Clinton Backs Raid but Muses about a New Start," *New York Times*, January 14, 1993; and "Clinton Affirms U.S. Policy on Iraq," *New York Times*, January 15, 1993; and George Stephanopoulos, *All Too Human: A Political Education* (New York: Little, Brown, 2000), pp. 156–159.

5. Thomas Friedman, "U.S. Leads Further Attacks on Iraqi Antiaircraft Sites," *New York Times*, January 19, 1993.

6. Bill Clinton, *My Life* (New York: Knopf, 2004), p. 526.

7. Interview with Albright.

8. Pollack, *The Threatening Storm*, pp. 69–70, 76; Alfonsi, *Circle in the Sand*, pp. 343–345.

9. Alfonsi, *Circle in the Sand*, pp. 353–354; Dan Benjamin and Steven Simon, *The Sacred Age of Terror* (New York: Random House, 2002), pp. 140–142; Zbigniew Brzezinski, *Second Chance: Three Presidents and the Crisis of American Superpower* (New York: Basic Books, 2007), p. 65.

10. Pollack, *The Threatening Storm*, pp. 80–83; Alfonsi, *Circle in the Sand*, pp. 355–356.

11. Evan Thomas, ed. *Back from the Dead: How Clinton Survived the Republican Revolution* (New York: Atlantic Monthly Press, 1997), p. 1.

12. Quoted in Adam Nagourney, "Muting His Criticism of Clinton, Dole Backs Troops in Iraq Raid," *New York Times*, September 4, 1996.

13. Brent Scowcroft, "Why We Stopped the Gulf War," *Newsweek*, September 23, 1996, p. 37.

14. Paul Wolfowitz, "Clinton's Bay of Pigs," *Wall Street Journal*, September 27, 1993; and Alfonsi, *Circle in the Sand*, pp. 357–360.

15. See memorandum from Bob Pelletreau to the secretary, "The Middle East—Looking Ahead," November 8, 1996; and "Iraq," key issue papers for Secretary of State–designate Albright, December 1996.

16. Transcript of William Cohen interview on *This Week with Sam Donaldson and Cokie Roberts*, ABC News, November 16, 1997.

17. Zalmay Khalilzad and Paul Wolfowitz, "We Must Lead the Way in Deposing Saddam," *Washington Post*, November 9, 1997; and Alfonsi, *Circle in the Sand*, pp. 364–365.

18. See James Mann, *Rise of the Vulcans: The History of Bush's War Cabinet* (New York: Viking Adult, 2004), pp. 236–237; and Thomas E. Ricks, *Fiasco: The American Military Adventure in Iraq* (New York: Penguin Press, 2006), pp. 15–18.

19. Jane Mayer, "The Manipulator," *New Yorker*, June 7, 2004.

20. See James Bennet, "Clinton Describes Goals for a Strike on Iraqi Arsenals," *New York Times*, February 18, 1998.

21. Text of Clinton statement on Iraq, February 17, 1998 (available at www.cnn.com/ALLPOLITICS/1998/02/17/transcripts/clinton.iraq/).

22. For the transcript of this event, see www.cnn.com/WORLD/9802/18/town.meeting.folo/.

23. Barton Gellman, "Top Advisers Shouted Down at 'Town Meeting' on Iraq," *Washington Post*, February 19, 1998, p. A1.

24. Details on this episode from interviews with Albright, Berger, and Zinni; Madeleine Albright, *Madam Secretary* (New York: Miramax Books, 2005), pp. 282–283; and Steven Erlanger, "Top Clinton Aides Find Doubt on Iraq at Campus in Ohio," *New York Times*, February 19, 1998.

25. Writing in the *Washington Post*, Kristol and Kagan argued that "Unless we are willing to live in a world where everyone has to 'do business' with Saddam and his weapons of mass destruction, we need to be willing to use U.S. air power and ground troops to get rid of him." See "A 'Great Victory' for Saddam," *Washington Post*, February 26, 1998. See May 29, 1998, PNAC letter to Gingrich and Lott (available at www.newamericancentury.org/iraqletter1998.htm). For Lugar quotes, see Mark Lagon, PNAC Memorandum to Opinion Leaders on Iraq, November 13, 1998, available at www.newamericancentury.org/iraq–101398.htm.

26. See Pollack, *The Threatening Storm*, pp. 91–92; and Albright, *Madam Secretary*, pp. 285–286.

27. Quotes from Bob Woodward, *Shadow: Five Presidents and the Legacy of Watergate* (New York: Simon & Schuster, 1999), p. 493.

28. www.cnn.com/ALLPOLITICS/stories/1998/12/16/congresstional.react.02/.

29. Interview with Gingrich.

30. Interview with Ralston.

31. Clinton, *My Life*, p. 834.

32. Speech by National Security Adviser Samuel Berger, Stanford University, December 8, 1998; and Clinton Remarks on Iraq, USIA Washington File, December 19, 1998.

33. In the decade after Desert Storm in 1991, U.S. aircraft had been shot at or threatened more than 1,000 times by Iraqi air defenses and retaliated with hundreds of missiles and bombs. According to the U.S. Air Force, nearly

ten times more combat sorties were flown over Iraq in these "peacekeeping" operations than in Desert Storm. See John A. Tirpak, "Legacy of the Air Blockades," *Air Force Magazine* (February 2003); and Thomas E. Ricks, "Containing Iraq: A Forgotten War," *Washington Post*, October 25, 2000.

34. Interview with Steinberg.

35. Albright, *Madam Secretary*, p. 287. See also Steven Lee Myers, "In Intense but Little-Noticed Fight, Allies Have Bombed Iraq All Year," *New York Times*, August 13, 1999.

36. Pollack, *The Threatening Storm*, p. 102.

37. Robert Kagan, "Saddam Wins—Again," *Weekly Standard*, January 4/January 11, 1999.

38. Richard Perle, "Iraq: Saddam Unbound," in William Kristol and Robert Kagan, eds., *Present Dangers: Crisis and Opportunity in American Foreign and Defense Policy* (New York: Encounter Books, 2000), p. 100.

39. Interview with Gingrich.

40. Interview with Fuerth.

41. For exhaustive details on the intelligence failure in Iraq, see Chapter 1 of the Report of the Commission on the Intelligence Capabilities of the United States Regarding Weapons of Mass Destruction (the "Silberman-Robb Report"), March 31, 2005 (available at www.wmd.gov/report/chapter1_fm.pdf). Also see Tim Weiner, *Legacy of Ashes: The History of the CIA* (New York: Doubleday, 2007), pp. 488–489.

42. See Robert Jervis, "Reports, Politics, and Intelligence Failures: The Case of Iraq," *Journal of Strategic Studies*, February 2006.

43. For the titles of these reports, see Silberman-Robb Report, Chapter 1, footnotes 23, 230, and 436.

44. George Tenet, *At the Center of the Storm: My Years at the CIA* (New York: HarperCollins, 2007), p. 325.

45. Interview with Zinni.

46. Interview with Gingrich.

47. See Paul Pillar, "Intelligence, Policy, and the War in Iraq," *Foreign Affairs*, March/April 2006; and Pillar, "The Right Stuff," *National Interest*, September/October 2007.

Chapter Eight: Liberal Bombs, Conservative Shields

1. Details of this meeting are from interviews with several officials present, and John F. Harris, *The Survivor: Bill Clinton in the White House* (New York: Random House, 2005), p. 368; Sidney Blumenthal, *The Clinton Wars* (New York: Farrar, Straus and Giroux, 2003), p. 639; and John M. Broder, "In Grim Week, Pep Talk from the President," *New York Times*, April 1, 1999.

2. See "Millennium Evening with Elie Wiesel," White House press release, April 12, 1999; and Blumenthal, *The Clinton Wars*, pp. 642–643.

3. See Strobe Talbott's foreword in John Norris, *Collision Course: NATO, Russia, and Kosovo* (Westport, CT: Praeger, 2005), p. ix.

4. Interview with Richard Holbrooke; Madeleine Albright, *Madam Secretary* (New York: Miramax Books, 2005), p. 406.

5. Talbott foreword in Norris, *Collision Course*, p. x.

6. See Paul Berman, *Power and the Idealists* (Brooklyn, NY: Soft Skull Press, 2005).

7. See Alastair Campbell, *The Blair Years: The Alastair Campbell Diaries* (New York: Knopf, 2007), p. 408.

8. See "Prime Minister's Speech: Doctrine of International Community at the Economic Club, Chicago," April 24, 1999, available at www.globalpolicy.org/globaliz/politics/blair.htm.

9. Philip Stephens, *Tony Blair: A Biography* (New York: Viking, 2004), pp. 163–164.

10. Campbell, *The Blair Years*, p. 393.

11. Interview with Berger.

12. For example, see these two paid advertisements that appeared in the *New York Times*, both cosponsored by PNAC along with several other humanitarian groups, such as the International Crisis Group and Balkan Action Council: "Mr. President, Milosevic Is the Problem," September 20, 1998, and "NATO Must Act in Kosovo," January 29, 1999.

13. Robert Kagan and William Kristol, "The National Interest," *Weekly Standard*, April 26, 1999.

14. Interview with Buchanan; and see Jacob Heilbrunn, "Full Retreat," *New Republic*, April 19, 1999; Lott quote from James Kitfield, "The Folk Who Live on the Hill," *National Interest*, Winter 1999/2000.

15. McCain quote from Kitfield; see William Kristol and Robert Kagan, "All Necessary Force," *Weekly Standard*, May 3, 1999; and Robert Kagan, "Kosovo and the Echoes of Isolationism," *New York Times*, March 24, 1999.

16. William Kristol and Robert Kagan, "Victory," *Weekly Standard*, June 14, 1999.

17. Clinton quote from Blumenthal, *The Clinton Wars*, p. 651; and "The Clinton Doctrine," *Weekly Standard*, July 5/12, 1999; see also Robert Kagan, "When America Blinked," *New Republic*, December 3, 2001.

18. Ivo Daalder and Michael O'Hanlon, *Winning Ugly* (Washington, DC: Brookings Institution Press, 2000).

19. Albright, *Madam Secretary*, p. 391.

20. Michael Ignatieff, "Chains of Command," *New York Review of Books*, July 19, 2001.

21. Interviews with Clark and Berger.

22. David Halberstam, *War in a Time of Peace: Bush, Clinton, and the Generals* (New York: Scribner, 2001), p. 424.

23. See Stephen Biddle, "The New Way of War?" *Foreign Affairs*, May/June 2002; Michael Mandelbaum, "A Perfect Failure," *Foreign Affairs*, September/October 1999; Charles Krauthammer, "The Short, Unhappy Life of Humanitarian War," *National Interest*, Fall 1999; and Michael Ignatieff, *Virtual War: Kosovo and Beyond* (New York: Metropolitan Books, 2000).

24. Interview with Ralston; and see James Mann, *Rise of the Vulcans: The History of Bush's War Cabinet* (New York: Viking Adult, 2004), pp. 304–305.

25. Halberstam, *War in a Time of Peace*, p. 456.

26. Samuel Huntington, "The Lonely Superpower," *Foreign Affairs*, March/April 1999; and Garry Wills, "Bully of the Free World," *Foreign Affairs*, March/April 1999.

27. George Packer, *The Assassins' Gate* (New York: Farrar, Straus and Giroux, 2005), p. 34; see also Peter Beinart, *The Good Fight* (New York: HarperCollins, 2006), pp. 84–85; and Stephen Holmes, "The War of the Liberals," *The Nation*, November 14, 2005.

28. Interview with Bonior; Waters quote from Paul Starobin, "The Liberal Hawk Soars," *National Journal*, May 15, 1999. See also Adam Wolfson, "Humanitarian Hawks? Why Kosovo but not Kuwait," *Policy Review*, December 1999/January 2000.

29. See "Kosovo Teach-in," *The Nation*, June 10, 1999.

30. Harris, *The Survivor*, p. 373.

31. See Noam Chomsky, *The New Military Humanism: The Lessons of Kosovo* (Monroe, ME: Common Courage Press, 1999); and Michael Moore, "The Bombing of Kosovo," April 15, 1999 (available at www.michaelmoore.com/words/message/index.php?messageDate=1999-04-15).

32. For example, see Dennis Kucinich, "Why Is Belgrade a Target?" *New York Times*, April 9, 1999; "Stop the War Now," *The Nation*, May 24, 1999; and Benjamin Schwarz, "Left-Right Bedfellows," *The Nation*, June 28, 1999.

33. For the full text of the report by the Independent International Commission on Kosovo, see www.reliefweb.int/library/documents/thekosovoreport.htm.

34. "Dark Victory," *The Nation*, June 28, 1999; and "Destroying Kosovo," *The Nation*, April 19, 1999; see also Beinart, *The Good Fight*, pp. 86–87.

35. John Pomfret and Michael Laris, "Thousands Vent Anger in China's Cities," *Washington Post*, May 9, 1999; Jane Perlez, "China Suspends Some Ties as Bombing Adds Strains to Already Tense Relations," *New York Times*, May 10, 1999.

36. James M. Goldgeier and Michael McFaul, *Power and Purpose: U.S. Policy to-*

ward Russia after the Cold War (Washington, DC: Brookings Institution Press, 2003), pp. 248, 253.

37. Strobe Talbott, *The Russia Hand: A Memoir of Presidential Diplomacy* (New York: Random House, 2002), p. 297.

38. Quoted in Norris, *Collision Course*, p. 294.

39. Huntington, "The Lonely Superpower," *Foreign Affairs*, March/April 1999, pp. 42–43.

40. This request was conveyed in a U.S. State Department cable, now declassified: "Consequences and Implications of Kosovo: Request for Input," State 120220, June 26, 1999.

41. Quote from David Sanger, "Agony of Victory; America Finds It's Lonely at the Top," *New York Times*, July 18, 1999; see also Suzanne Daley, "Europe's Dim View of U.S. Is Evolving into Frank Hostility," *New York Times*, April 9, 2000.

42. Talbott, *The Russia Hand*, p. 379.

43. Bradley Graham, *Hit to Kill: The New Battle over Shielding America from Missile Attack* (New York: PublicAffairs, 2001), p. xxxi.

44. Charles Krauthammer, "The Unipolar Moment," *Foreign Affairs*, America and the World 1990/91, pp. 31–32.

45. Interview with Bolton.

46. See Lawrence Kaplan, "Offensive Line," *New Republic*, March 12, 2001.

47. Kirkpatrick quoted in Frances Fitzgerald, *Way Out There in the Blue: Reagan, Star Wars, and the End of the Cold War* (New York: Simon & Schuster, 2000), p. 493; Clinton quoted in Graham, *Hit to Kill*, p. 381.

48. See Joseph Cirincione, "Why the Right Lost the Missile Defense Debate," *Foreign Policy*, Spring 1997.

49. See Graham, *Hit to Kill*, pp. 32–33. The "politicization" claim is made explicitly by conservative missile defense expert William Schneider, in his chapter "Weapons Proliferation and Missile Defense: The Strategic Case," in William Kristol and Robert Kagan, eds., *Present Dangers: Crisis and Opportunity in American Foreign and Defense Policy* (New York: Encounter Books, 2000), pp. 278–279.

50. Fred Kaplan, *Daydream Believers* (New York: Wiley, 2008), pp. 98-99.

51. Details of the Rumsfeld commission's work is from Graham, *Hit to Kill*, pp. 30–51; and Richard L. Garwin, "What We Did," *Bulletin of the Atomic Scientists*, November/December 1998; Kaplan, *Daydream Believers*, pp. 100–103.

52. Gingrich quoted in Mann, *Rise of the Vulcans*, p. 241; interview with Bolton. See also Jacob Heilbrunn, "Playing Defense," *New Republic*, August 17/24, 1998.

53. See Mark Thompson, "Star Wars: The Sequel," *Time*, February 22, 1999.

54. Talbott, *The Russia Hand*, p. 380.

Chapter Nine: New World Disorder

1. The story of the decision not to strike the hunting party in February 1999 is told in Lawrence Wright, *The Looming Tower: Al-Qaeda and the Road to 9/11* (New York: Knopf, 2006), pp. 329–30; Richard A. Clarke, *Against All Enemies: Inside America's War on Terror* (New York: Free Press, 2004), pp. 199–200; *9/11 Commission Report* (New York: W. W. Norton, 2004), p. 138.

2. George Tenet, *At the Center of the Storm: My Years at the CIA* (New York: HarperCollins, 2007), pp. 123–124.

3. Gingrich quoted in *Commanding Heights: The Battle for the World Economy*. These and the other *Commanding Heights* interviews cited in this chapter are available at www.pbs.org/wgbh/commandingheights/lo/index.html.

4. Jagdish Bhagwati, *The Wind of the Hundred Days: How Washington Mismanaged Globalization* (Cambridge, MA: MIT Press, 2000), p. 57.

5. Interviews with Barshefsky and Rubin.

6. Benjamin R. Barber, *Jihad vs. McWorld* (New York: Times Books, 1995); and Benjamin R. Barber, *The Truth of Power: Intellectual Affairs in the Clinton White House* (New York: W. W. Norton, 2001), pp. 239–262.

7. Interviews with several former Clinton officials.

8. Kantor quoted in Nicholas D. Kristof with David E. Sanger, "How U.S. Wooed Asia to Let Cash Flow In," *New York Times*, February 16, 1999; interview with Rubin.

9. Nicholas D. Kristof with Edward Wyatt, "Who Went Under in the World's Sea of Cash," *New York Times*, February 15, 1999.

10. Tyson quoted in *Commanding Heights*.

11. Interview with Rubin.

12. Robert E. Rubin, *In an Uncertain World* (New York: Random House, 2003), p. 213.

13. See, e.g., David Ignatius, "O'Neill Formula: Aid to Brazil but No Open Hand," *International Herald Tribune*, July 25, 2001.

14. Walter Russell Mead, *Special Providence: American Foreign Policy and How It Changed the World* (New York: Routledge, 2002), p. 272.

15. Interview with Rubin.

16. Sidney Blumenthal, *The Clinton Wars* (New York: Farrar, Straus and Giroux, 2003), p. 668; Joe Klein, "Eight Years," *New Yorker*, October 16 and 23, 2000, pp. 200–201.

17. See John Judis, *The Folly of Empire* (New York: Scribner, 2004), pp. 160–162.

18. Interview with Wallach.

19. "Lori's War," an interview in *Foreign Policy* 118, Spring 2000, p. 49.

20. See the time line put together by the University of Washington at

http://depts.washington.edu/wtohist/day1.htm; also Scott Sunde, "It's Protest City—and Get Ready for the Big One Today," *Seattle Post-Intelligencer,* November 30, 1999.

21. Summers quoted in *Commanding Heights.*

22. Telephone interview with Michael Paulson of the *Seattle Post-Intelligencer* from San Francisco, California, November 30, 1999, *Weekly Compilation of Presidential Documents* 35, no. 48, available at www.gpoaccess.gov/wcomp/index.html.

23. White House, Office of the Press Secretary, December 1, 1999, Four Seasons Hotel, Seattle, Washington.

24. John F. Harris, *The Survivor: Bill Clinton in the White House* (New York: Random House, 2005), p. 394.

25. Bill Gertz, *The China Threat: How the People's Republic Targets America* (Washington, DC: Regnery, 2002), p. xi; see also James Mann, *Rise of the Vulcans: The History of Bush's War Cabinet* (New York: Viking Adult, 2004), pp. 242–243; and Mann, *About Face: A History of America's Curious Relationship with China, from Nixon to Clinton* (New York: Knopf, 1998), pp. 349–367.

26. For background on the PNTR effort, see Robert L. Suettinger, *Beyond Tiananmen: The Politics of U.S.-China Relations 1989–2000,* (Washington, DC: Brookings Institution Press, 2003), pp. 392–399.

27. Lori Nitschke and Miles A. Pomper, "Urgent Push for China Trade Bill Now Likely to Start in Senate," *CQ Weekly,* March 11, 2000.

28. Quote from Blumenthal, *The Clinton Wars,* p. 671.

29. Interview with Woolsey.

30. Interview with McLaughlin.

31. See Tim Weiner, *Legacy of Ashes: The History of the CIA* (New York: Doubleday, 2007), p. 456. As one Clinton official put it in the mid-1990s, the CIA's efforts to help American officials at global trade talks was "the World Series—the arms control talks of a new age." See David E. Sanger and Tim Weiner, "Emerging Role of the CIA: Economic Spy," *New York Times,* October 15, 1995.

32. Interview with McLaughlin; Tenet quotes from Weiner, *Legacy of Ashes,* p. 467; Tenet, *At the Center of the Storm,* p. 16; and *9/11 Commission Report,* p. 91.

33. *9/11 Commission Report,* p. 101; Amy B. Zegart, *Spying Blind: The CIA, the FBI, and the Origins of 9/11* (Princeton, NJ: Princeton University Press, 2007), p. 24.

34. Bill Clinton, "Clinton Remarks at the University of Central Oklahoma," Edmond, Oklahoma, April 5, 1996, in Public Papers of the Presidents, William J. Clinton, 1996, vol. 1, pp. 549–553.

35. Bill Clinton, "Remarks on International Security Issues at George Washington University," Washington, DC, August 5, 1996, Public Papers of the Presidents, William J. Clinton, 1996, vol. 2, pp. 1255–1260.

36. Steve Coll, *Ghost Wars: The Secret History of the CIA, Afghanistan, and bin Laden, from the Soviet Invasion to September 10, 2001* (New York: Penguin Books, 2004), p. 173; *9/11 Commission Report*, pp. 55–67; 109–110.

37. Bill Clinton, "Clinton Address to the Nation on Military Action against Terrorist Sites in Afghanistan and Sudan," August 20, 1998, Public Papers of the Presidents, William J. Clinton, 1998, vol. 2, pp. 1460–1462.

38. The IHT article is at www.iht.com/articles/1998/08/22/terr.t_0.php.

39. Bill Clinton, *My Life* (New York: Knopf, 2004), p. 803.

40. Cohen and Gingrich quotes at www.cnn.com/ALLPOLITICS/1998/08/20/strike.react/.

41. Coats quote at www.cnn.com/ALLPOLITICS/1998/08/20/strike.react/.

42. Bill Clinton, "Clinton Remarks to the 53rd Session of the United Nations General Assembly in New York City," September 21, 1998, Public Papers of the Presidents, William J. Clinton, 1998, vol. 2, pp. 1629–1633; Clinton, *My Life*, p. 812.

43. Interview with Berger.

44. Interview with Steinberg.

45. Daniel Benjamin and Steven Simon, *The Age of Sacred Terror* (New York: Random House, 2002), p. 221; Roberto Suro, "U.S. Lacking in Terrorism Defenses; Study Cites a Need to Share Intelligence," *Washington Post*, April 24, 1998; Clinton quote from Philip Shenon, *The Commission* (New York: Twelve, 2008), p. 305.

46. Interview with Hamilton.

47. Zegart, *Spying Blind*, pp. 86, 235.

48. Interview with Zinni.

49. Interview with Steinberg.

50. *9/11 Commission Report*, p. 137.

51. Interviews with Podesta and Hamilton.

52. L. Paul Bremer III, "Fight Plan for a Dirty War," *Washington Post*, August 24, 1999.

53. Charles William Maynes, "Fighting Dirty Won't Work," *Washington Post*, August 31, 1999.

54. The best account of the negotiations is Dennis Ross, *The Missing Peace: The Inside Story of the Fight for Middle East Peace* (New York: Farrar, Straus and Giroux, 2004).

55. Clinton, *My Life*, p. 929.

56. See Clinton, *My Life*, p. 925. The 9/11 Commission reported that Clinton had told them the same thing. See *9/11 Commission Report*, p. 193.

57. Interview with McLaughlin; *9/11 Commission Report*, p. 197.

58. Clarke, *Against All Enemies*, pp. 201–202, 225.

59. See Barbara Crossette, "U.N. Council in Rare Accord: Fight Terrorism," *New York Times*, October 20, 1999; and James Traub, *The Best Intentions: Kofi Annan and the U.N. in the Era of American World Power* (New York: Farrar, Straus and Giroux, 2006), p. 168.

60. See Traub, *The Best Intentions*, pp. 140–141; Jesse Helms, *Here's Where I Stand* (New York: Random House, 2005); and Suzanne Nossel, "Retail Diplomacy," *National Interest*, Winter 2001/2002. The Helms center's Web page is www.jessehelmscenter.org.

61. "American Power—For What?" *Commentary*, January 2000.

62. Norman Podhoretz, "Strange Bedfellows: A Guide to the New Foreign Policy Debates," *Commentary*, December 1999, pp. 19–31.

63. "American Power—For What?" pp. 21–23, 34.

64. Ibid., pp. 25, 34.

65. Ibid., p. 26.

66. Ibid., p. 42.

Chapter Ten: The End of the Modern Interwar Years

1. For transcript of the debate, see www.debates.org/pages/trans2000b.html. See also Frank Bruni, "Rivals Massage Their Images in Conversational Exchange," *New York Times*, October 12, 2000; David Sanger, "A Delicate Dance of the Interventionist and the Reluctant Internationalist," *New York Times*, October 12, 2000; and James Traub, "The Bush Years; W.'s World," *New York Times Magazine*, January 14, 2001.

2. "The 'Makeup' Debate," *New York Times*, October 12, 2000.

3. See Karen Tumulty, "The Secret Passion of Al Gore," *Time*, May 17, 1999.

4. See John F. Harris, *The Survivor: Bill Clinton in the White House* (New York: Random House, 2005), pp. 384–390; and John Harris and Ceci Connolly, "Gore Agenda's Delicate Balance," *Washington Post*, October 31, 1999.

5. Interview with Fuerth.

6. Quote from David Sanger, "Clinton's Final Chapter: Single-Minded, Full Steam Run at a Global Agenda," *New York Times*, January 3, 2000; Sandy Berger speech, "The Price of American Leadership," White House, Office of the Press Secretary, May 1, 1998.

7. For an example of the criticism he received, see Robert Kagan, "The Clinton Legacy Abroad," *Weekly Standard*, January 15, 2001.

8. Quote from Tyler Marshall and Jim Mann, "Goodwill Toward U.S. Is Dwindling Globally," *Los Angeles Times*, March 26, 2000.

9.   See "Speech by President upon Being Presented the Charlemagne Prize 2000," White House, June 2, 2000 (available at www.clintonpresidential center.org/legacy/060200-speech-by-president-on-international-charle magne-prize.htm).

10. Strobe Talbott, *The Great Experiment: The Story of Ancient Empires, Modern States, and the Quest for a Global Nation* (New York: Simon & Schuster, 2008), p. 325.

11. Remarks by the president, "A Foreign Policy for the Global Age," address to the University of Nebraska at Kearney, Cushing Health and Sports Center, December 8, 2000, available at www.fas.org/news/usa/2000/ usa-001208zws.htm.

12. Quote from Lawrence F. Kaplan, "Trading Places," *New Republic*, October 23, 2000.

13. At the time, commentators like Robert Kagan speculated that Lieberman's addition to the ticket could be "Gore's way of recapturing the mantle of Harry Truman and Scoop Jackson and fulfilling the promise of muscular moralism abroad that Clinton, ever preoccupied with his political fortunes at home, consistently betrayed. Maybe it means Gore wants a tougher policy on Iraq and in the Balkans. Maybe Lieberman's selection means that a Gore foreign policy really would be different from a Clinton foreign policy." See Kagan, "Lieberman Dissents," *Washington Post*, August 13, 2000.

14. Quote from David E. Sanger and Katharine Q. Seelye, "Gore Defends Civilian Uses of Military," *New York Times*, October 5, 2000.

15. See Mike Allen, "U.S. Spread Too Thin, Bradley Says," *Washington Post*, November 30, 1999; and David Chen, "Bradley Turns to Foreign Policy in a Detour from Traditional Campaigning," *New York Times*, March 4, 2000.

16. Quoted in Allen, "U.S. Spread Too Thin, Bradley Says."

17. Interview with Nader.

18. Interview with Buchanan.

19. Interview with Nader; and Robert Kuttner, "Ralph Nader: A Conversation," *American Prospect*, July 19–July 3, 2000; Scot Lehigh, "If Nader Had Been There Here's What He (Probably) Would Have Said," *Boston Globe*, October 8, 2000; and Eric Alterman, "Bush or Gore: Does It Matter?" *The Nation*, October 16, 2000.

20. According to author Robert Draper, Bush's top political adviser, Karl Rove, was one of those who argued against Cheney being picked as vice president. As Draper describes it, Cheney was "old and bald and Beltway and ideologically retro, a political Jurassic Park." See Draper, *Dead Certain: The Presidency of George W. Bush* (New York: Free Press, 2007), p. 90.

21. James Mann, *Rise of the Vulcans: The History of Bush's War Cabinet* (New York: Viking, 2004), pp. 256–257.

22. See John B. Judis, "Neo-McCain," *New Republic*, October 16, 2006.

23. Condoleezza Rice, "Promoting the National Interest," *Foreign Affairs*, January/February 2000, pp. 47–48.

24. Rice appearance on the *Charlie Rose Show*, October 12, 2000.

25. See Michael Cooper, "Clinton Handled Military Poorly, Cheney Contends," *New York Times*, August 31, 2000. Cheney had been making similar arguments for years. In a 1993 interview, just months after he had left office as secretary of defense, Cheney had argued that "the Clinton administration is seriously undermining the quality and morale of our armed forces. There is now the distinct possibility that the next time we have to use the force, the military won't be able to perform as it should because of the way it's being treated under the Clinton administration." See Adam Meyerson, "Calm after Desert Storm," *Policy Review*, Summer 1993.

26. "Interview of the President by Joe Klein," White House, Office of the Press Secretary, July 5, 2000, available at http://clinton6.nara.gov/2000/10/2000-10-10-interview-of-the-president-by-joe-klein-of-the-new-yorker.html.

27. George W. Bush, "A Period of Consequences," speech at the Citadel, South Carolina, September 23, 1999, available at www.citadel.edu/pao/addresses/pres_bush.html.

28. Bush speech in Grand Rapids, Michigan, November 3, 2000, available at http://transcripts.cnn.com/TRANSCRIPTS/0011/03/se.04.html.

29. George H. W. Bush, remarks at the Aspen Institute Symposium in Aspen, Colorado, August 2, 1990 (available at http://bushlibrary.tamu.edu/research/public_papers.php?id=2128&year=1990&month=8.

30. For example, Clinton's 1996 defense budget was $266 billion, only $30 billion less than what George H. W. Bush had spent in 1992. See Tim Weiner, "Clinton as Military Leader: Tough On-the-Job Training," *New York Times*, October 28, 1996; Elizabeth Becker, "Cohen's Top Feat May Be Monetary, Not Military," *New York Times*, November 14, 1999.

31. For the latter argument, Donald Kagan and Frederick W. Kagan, *While America Sleeps* (New York: St. Martin's Press, 2000) pp. 300–320; Frederick W. Kagan, *Finding the Target* (New York: Encounter Books, 2006), pp. 144–198; and Eliot Cohen, "Calling Mr. X," *New Republic*, January 19, 1998.

32. Gore at the U.S. Military Academy Commencement, West Point, May 27, 2000; quote on new missions from Sanger and Seelye, "Gore Defends Civilian Uses of Military." For an assessment of the innovations of the Clinton-era military, see Michael O'Hanlon, "Clinton's Strong Defense Legacy," *Foreign Affairs*, November/December 2003.

33. "Dover" refers to the U.S. air base in Delaware where the flag-draped caskets carrying U.S. soldiers killed in action are returned home. For Shelton

quote, see Michael C. Desch, "Bush and the Generals," *Foreign Affairs,* May/June 2007.

34. P. W. Singer, *Corporate Warriors: The Rise of the Privatized Military Industry* (Ithaca, NY: Cornell University Press, 2003); Deborah Avant, *A Market for Force: The Consequences of Privatizing Security* (New York: Cambridge University Press, 2005).

35. Dana Priest, *The Mission: Waging War and Keeping Peace with America's Military* (New York: W. W. Norton, 2003), p. 42; and Ashton Carter and William Perry, *Preventive Defense* (Washington, DC: Brookings Institution Press, 1999).

36. Interviews with Ralston and Zinni; see also Priest, *The Mission,* p. 104.

37. Interviews with Ralston and Zinni.

38. Interviews with Ralston, Zinni, and Clark. Polling results from Thomas E. Ricks, "Military Is Becoming More Conservative, Study Says," *Wall Street Journal,* November 11, 1997. For an account of the cheering in the Pentagon on the day Gore conceded to Bush, see Kurt Campbell and Michael O'Hanlon, *Hard Power: The New Politics of National Security* (New York: Basic Books, 2006), p. xi.

39. Interview with Feith; Rice quote from Bradley Graham, *Hit to Kill: The New Battle over Shielding America from Missile Attack* (New York: PublicAffairs, 2001), pp. 342–343.

40. Interview with Bolton; Gore speech at West Point, May 27, 2000.

41. Quote from David E. Sanger, "Rivals Differ on U.S. Role in the World," *New York Times,* October 30, 2000.

42. Strobe Talbott, *The Russia Hand: A Memoir of Presidential Diplomacy* (New York: Random House, 2002), pp. 382–383.

43. For DPG quotes, see Patrick E. Tyler, "U.S. Strategy Plan Calls for Insuring No Rivals Develop," *New York Times,* March 8, 1992; Wolfowitz made this argument in his essay "Statesmanship in the New Century," in William Kristol and Robert Kagan, eds., *Present Dangers: Crisis and Opportunity in American Foreign and Defense Policy* (New York: Encounter Books, 2000), pp. 309–310.

44. See Rice, "Promoting the National Interest," p. 48. For an excellent assessment of Bush's worldview, see Ivo H. Daalder and James M. Lindsay, *America Unbound: The Bush Revolution in Foreign Policy* (Washington, DC: Brookings Institution Press, 2003), pp. 46–47.

45. Daalder and Lindsay, *America Unbound,* pp. 15–16.

46. Quote from John Lewis Gaddis, *Strategies of Containment,* rev. ed. (New York: Oxford University Press, 2005), p. 128.

47. For details of this meeting, see Talbott, *The Great Experiment,* p. 347;

Draper, *Dead Certain*, pp. 91–92; Bill Clinton, *My Life* (New York: Knopf, 2004), pp. 935–936; and *9/11 Commission Report* (New York: W. W. Norton, 2004), p. 199.

48. See comments by Ivo Daalder at "Assessing the Bush Foreign Policy Tradition" panel, American Enterprise Institute, Washington, DC, April 18, 2001.

49. Interview with Gelb.

50. Interview with Armitage. Talbott recalls thinking that because of Powell's national popularity and standing as one of the country's most decorated soldiers, as secretary of state he seemed "particularly well suited" to counterbalance the more ideologically driven members of the Bush team. See Talbott, *The Great Experiment*, p. 372.

51. See Alan Sipress, "Bush Retreats from U.S. Role as Peace Broker," *Washington Post*, March 17, 2001.

52. Charles Krauthammer, "The New Unilateralism," *Washington Post*, June 8, 2001; also see Daalder and Lindsay, *America Unbound*, pp. 65–67.

53. Interview with Armitage.

54. Excerpts of this early 2001 memo, "Talking Points, FY01 and FY02–07 Budget Issues," are printed in Ron Suskind, *The Price of Loyalty* (New York: Simon & Schuster, 2004), pp. 76–77.

55. See Desch, "Bush and the Generals"; Zinni quote from Thomas E. Ricks, "For Rumsfeld, Many Roadblocks," *Washington Post*, August 7, 2001.

56. Tenet, *At the Center of the Storm*, p. 139.

57. Quote from Bob Woodward, *Bush at War* (New York: Simon & Schuster, 2002), p. 39.

58. "Interview of the President by Joe Klein," White House, Office of the Press Secretary, August 15, 2000.

59. See Thomas E. Ricks, *Fiasco: The American Military Adventure in Iraq* (New York: Penguin Press, 2006), pp. 26–28.

60. Jim Hoagland, "Policy Wars over Iraq," *Washington Post*, April 7, 2001.

61. See Mann, *Rise of the Vulcans*, pp. 290–291; and Robert Kagan, "Indefensible Defense Budget," *Washington Post*, July 20, 2001.

62. See Johanna McGreary, "Odd Man Out," *Time*, September 10, 2001, available at www.time.com/time/magazine/article/0,9171,173441-4,00.html.

Chapter Eleven: The 11/9 World

1. See George W. Bush, "Address to a Joint Session of Congress and the American People," September 20, 2001, available at www.whitehouse.gov/news/releases/2001/09/20010920-8.html.

2. Quotes from "Transcript of Donald Rumsfeld interview with Cal Thomas," available at www.townhall.com/Columnists/CalThomas/2006/12/11/donald_rumfeld_w_cal_thomas_transcript?page=1, and interview with Powell.

3. Quoted in Strobe Talbott, *The Russia Hand: A Memoir of Presidential Diplomacy* (New York: Random House, 2002), p. 134; and interviews with several officials present.

4. David Halberstam, *War in a Time of Peace: Bush, Clinton, and the Generals* (New York: Scribner, 2001), p. 500.

5. See James Lindsay, "The New Apathy," *Foreign Affairs*, September/October 2000.

6. Josef Joffe, "Clinton's Policy: Purpose, Policy, and Weltanschauung," *Washington Quarterly*, Winter 2001, p. 146.

7. "His Side of the Story," *Time*, June 28, 2004; Strobe Talbott, *The Great Experiment: The Story of Ancient Empires, Modern States, and the Quest for a Global Nation* (New York: Simon & Schuster, 2008), p. 329.

8. See Richard Haass, "The New Middle East," *Foreign Affairs*, November/December 2006.

9. "His Side of the Story," *Time*, June 28, 2004; and for more on the legacy of democracy promotion in U.S. foreign policy, see G. John Ikenberry, "Why Export Democracy? The 'Hidden Grand Strategy' of American Foreign Policy," *The Wilson Quarterly*, Spring 1999.

10. Interview with Albright; see also Ronald D. Asmus, "The Democrats' Democracy Problem," *Washington Post*, July 17, 2007.

11. Robert Wright, "Clinton's One Big Idea," *New York Times*, January 16, 2001.

12. "Interview of the President by Joe Klein," White House, Office of the Press Secretary, July 5, 2000, available at www.clintonpresidentialcenter.org/legacy/081500-president-interviewed-by-joe-klein-new-yorker.htm.

13. Interview with Rubin. See also Nicholas D. Kristoff, "The New Democratic Scapegoat," *New York Times*, July 26, 2007.

14. Interview with Barshefsky.

15. The interventions are Panama (1989), Somalia (1992–1993), Haiti (1994), Bosnia (1995), Kosovo (1999), Afghanistan (2001), and Iraq (1991, 1998). See Ivo Daalder and Robert Kagan, "America and the Use of Force: Sources of Legitimacy," in Derek Chollet, Tod Lindberg, and David Shorr, eds., *Bridging the Foreign Policy Divide* (New York: Routledge, 2008), pp. 7–8.

16. Interview with Holbrooke; see also Laura Secor, "The Giant in the House," in George Packer, ed., *The Fight Is for Democracy* (New York: HarperCollins, 2003), p. 61.

17. George Packer, "The Liberal Quandary Over Iraq," *New York Times Magazine*, December 8, 2002.

18. See Strobe Talbott, "Foreword," in John Norris, *Collision Course* (Westport, CT: Praeger, 2005), pp. xi–xii.

19. For example, see Tony Smith, "It's Uphill for the Democrats," *Washington Post*, March 11, 2007; Tony Judt, "From Military Disaster to Moral High Ground," *New York Times*, October 7, 2007; and David Rieff, "Without Exception," *World Affairs*, Winter 2008.

20. Joseph Lieberman, "The Politics of National Security," November, 9, 2007, speech delivered at Johns Hopkins University.

21. See James P. Rubin, "Get Serious," *New Republic*, November 19, 1997.

22. Kagan quoted in Packer, *The Assassins' Gate* (New York: Farrar, Straus and Giroux, 2005), p. 38; and see also Corey Robin, "Conservatives after the Cold War," *Boston Review*, February/March 2004.

23. Interview with Gingrich. Also see Richard Lowry, "The 'To Hell with Them' Hawks, *National Review*, March 27, 2006; Joshua Kurlantzick, "after the Bush Doctrine," *New Republic*, February 13, 2006; and Michael Abramowitz, "Conservative Anger Grows over Bush Foreign Policy," *Washington Post*, July 19, 2006.

24. This is the core argument of J. Peter Scoblic in his book *U.S. vs. Them: How Conservatism Has Undermined America's Security* (New York: Viking, 2008).

25. Richard Betts, U.S. National Security Strategy: Lenses and Landmarks, paper presented for the launch conference of the Princeton Project, November 2004, p. 7.

26. Interview with Fukuyama.

27. Quoted in Talbott, *The Great Experiment*, p. 347.

28. See Robert Kagan, "The Clinton Legacy Abroad," *Weekly Standard*, January 15, 2001.

29. See Walter LaFeber, *The American Age* (New York, W. W. Norton, 1989), pp. 148–180; Warren Zimmerman, *First Great Triumph* (New York: Farrar, Straus and Giroux, 2002); and Robert Kagan, *Dangerous Nation* (New York: Knopf, 2006).

Bibliography

9/11 Commission. *The 9/11 Commission Report: Final Report of the National Commission on Terrorist Attacks upon the United States.* New York: W. W. Norton, 2004.

Albright, Madeleine. *Madam Secretary.* New York: Miramax Books, 2003.

Alfonsi, Christian. *Circle in the Sand: Why We Went Back to Iraq.* New York: Doubleday, 2006.

Allen, Frederick Lewis. *Only Yesterday: An Informal History of the 1920s.* New York: Harper and Brothers, 1931.

Asmus, Ronald D. *Opening NATO's Door: How the Alliance Remade Itself for a New Era.* New York: Columbia University Press, 2002.

Avant, Deborah D. *The Market for Force: The Consequences of Privatizing Security.* Cambridge, UK: Cambridge University Press, 2005.

Bacevich, Andrew J., and Eliot A. Cohen, eds. *War Over Kosovo: Politics and Strategy in a Global Age.* New York: Columbia University Press, 2001.

Baer, Kenneth. *Reinventing Democrats: The Politics of Liberalism from Reagan to Clinton.* Lawrence: University of Kansas Press, 2000.

Bai, Matt. *The Argument: Billionaires, Bloggers, and the Battle to Remake Democratic Politics.* New York: Penguin Press, 2007.

Baker III, James A., with Thomas M. DeFrank. *The Politics of Diplomacy: Revolution, War, and Peace, 1989–1992.* New York: G. P. Putnam's Sons, 1995.

Barber, Benjamin R. *Jihad vs. McWorld.* New York: Times Books, 1995.

_____. *The Truth of Power: Intellectual Affairs in the Clinton White House.* New York: W. W. Norton, 2001.

Barbour, Haley. *Agenda for America: A Republican Direction for the Future.* Washington, DC: Regnery Press, 1996.

Beinart, Peter. *The Good Fight: Why Liberals—and Only Liberals—Can Win the War on Terror and Make America Great Again*. New York: HarperCollins, 2006.

Benjamin, Daniel, and Steven Simon. *The Age of Sacred Terror*. New York: Random House, 2002.

Berman, Paul. *Power and the Idealists, or, The Passion of Joschka Fischer and Its Aftermath*. Brooklyn: Soft Skull Press, 2005.

Beschloss, Michael, and Strobe Talbott. *At the Highest Levels: The Inside Story of the End of the Cold War*. Boston: Little, Brown, 1993.

Bhagwati, Jagdish. *The Wind of the Hundred Days: How Washington Mismanaged Globalization*. Cambridge, MA: MIT Press, 2000.

Bildt, Carl. *Peace Journey: The Struggle for Peace in Bosnia*. London: Weidenfeld & Nicolson, 1998.

Blumenthal, Sidney. *The Clinton Wars*. New York: Farrar, Straus and Giroux, 2003.

Bolton, John. *Surrender Is Not an Option: Defending America at the United Nations and Abroad*. New York: Threshold Editions, 2007.

Brownstein, Ronald. *The Second Civil War: How Extreme Partisanship Has Paralyzed Washington and Polarized America*. New York: Penguin Press, 2007.

Brzezinski, Zbigniew. *Second Chance: Three Presidents and the Crisis of American Superpower*. New York: Basic Books, 2007.

Buchanan, Patrick. *A Republic, Not an Empire: Reclaiming America's Destiny*. Washington, DC: Regnery, 1999.

Bumiller, Elisabeth. *Condoleezza Rice: An American Life*. New York: Random House, 2007.

Bush, George H. W., and Brent Scowcroft. *A World Transformed*. New York: Knopf, 1998.

Campbell, Alastair. *The Blair Years: The Alastair Campbell Diaries*. New York: Knopf, 2007.

Campbell, Kurt M., and Michael E. O'Hanlon. *Hard Power: The New Politics of National Security*. New York: Basic Books, 2006.

Carter, Ashton, and William Perry. *Preventive Defense: A New Security Strategy for America*. Washington, DC: Brookings Institution Press, 1999.

Chollet, Derek. *The Road to the Dayton Accords: A Study of American Statecraft*. New York: Palgrave Macmillan, 2005.

Chollet, Derek, Tod Lindberg, and David Shorr, coeds. *Bridging the Foreign Policy Divide*. New York: Routledge, 2008.

Chomsky, Noam. *The New Military Humanism: The Lessons of Kosovo*. Monroe, ME: Common Courage Press, 1999.

Christopher, Warren. *In the Stream of History: Shaping Foreign Policy for a New Era.* Stanford, CA: Stanford University Press, 1998.

_____. *Chances of a Lifetime.* New York: Scribner, 2001.

Clark, Wesley K. *Waging Modern War.* New York: PublicAffairs, 2001.

Clarke, Richard. *Against All Enemies: Inside America's War on Terror.* New York: Free Press, 2004.

Clinton, Bill. *My Life.* New York: Knopf, 2004.

Cohen, Warren I. *Empire Without Tears: America's Foreign Relations 1921–33.* New York: McGraw-Hill, 1987.

_____. *America's Failing Empire: U.S. Foreign Relations Since the Cold War.* Malden, MA: Blackwell, 2005.

Coll, Steve. *Ghost Wars: The Secret History of the CIA, Afghanistan, and bin Laden, from the Soviet Invasion to September 10, 2001.* New York: Penguin Press, 2004.

Cooper, Robert. *The Breaking of Nations: Order and Chaos in the Twenty-First Century.* New York: Atlantic Monthly Press, 2003.

Critchlow, Donald T. *The Conservative Ascendancy: How the GOP Right Made Political History.* Cambridge, MA: Harvard University Press, 2007.

Crowley, Monica. *Nixon Off the Record.* New York: Random House, 1996.

Daalder, Ivo, and James M. Lindsay. *America Unbound: The Bush Revolution in Foreign Policy.* Washington, DC: Brookings Institution Press, 2003.

Daalder, Ivo, and Michael O'Hanlon. *Winning Ugly.* Washington, DC: Brookings Institution Press, 2000.

DeFrank, Thomas M. *Write It When I'm Gone.* New York: Putnam, 2007.

DeYoung, Karen. *Soldier: The Life of Colin Powell.* New York: Knopf, 2006.

Dionne, E. J. *Why Americans Hate Politics.* New York: Simon & Schuster, 1991.

Draper, Robert. *Dead Certain: The Presidency of George W. Bush.* New York: Free Press, 2007.

Drew, Elizabeth. *On the Edge: The Clinton Presidency.* New York: Simon & Schuster, 1994.

_____. *Showdown: The Struggle Between the Gingrich Congress and the Clinton White House.* New York: Simon & Schuster, 1996.

Dueck, Colin. *Reluctant Crusaders: Power, Culture, and Change in American Grand Strategy.* Princeton, NJ: Princeton University Press, 2006.

Dunn, Charles W., ed. *The Future of Conservatism: Conflict and Consensus in the Post-Reagan Era.* Wilmington, DE: ISI Books, 2007.

Easton, Nina. *Gang of Five: Leaders at the Center of the Conservative Crusade.* New York: Simon & Schuster, 2000.

Ferguson, Niall. *Colossus: The Price of America's Empire.* New York: Penguin Press, 2004.

Fitzgerald, Frances. *Way Out There in the Blue: Reagan, Star Wars, and the End of the Cold War.* New York: Simon & Schuster, 2000.

Frankel, Jeffrey, and Peter Orszag, eds. *American Economic Policy in the 1990s.* Cambridge, MA: MIT Press, 2002.

Friedman, Thomas L. *The Lexus and the Olive Tree.* New York: Anchor Books, 2000.

_____. *The World Is Flat: A Brief History of the Twenty-First Century.* New York: Farrar, Straus and Giroux, 2005.

Frum, David. *Dead Right.* New York: Basic Books, 1994.

_____. *The Right Man: An Inside Account of the Surprising Presidency of George W. Bush.* New York: Weidenfeld & Nicolson, 2003.

Fukuyama, Francis. *The End of History and the Last Man.* New York: Free Press, 1992.

_____. *America at the Crossroads: Democracy, Power, and the Neoconservative Legacy.* New Haven, CT: Yale University Press, 2006.

Gaddis, John Lewis. *Surprise, Security, and the American Experience.* Cambridge, MA: Harvard University Press, 2004.

_____. *Strategies of Containment: A Critical Appraisal of American National Security Policy during the Cold War.* New York: Oxford University Press, 2005.

Gallucci, Robert L., Joel S. Wit, and Daniel B. Poneman. *Going Critical: The First North Korean Nuclear Crisis.* Washington, DC: Brookings Institution Press, 2004.

Garrett, Major. *The Enduring Revolution: How the Contract with America Continues to Shape the Nation.* New York: Three Rivers Press, 2005.

Gergen, David. *Eyewitness to Power: The Essence of Leadership, Nixon to Clinton.* New York: Simon & Schuster, 2000.

Gertz, Bill. *The China Threat: How the People's Republic Targets America.* Washington, DC: Regnery, 2000.

Gillespie, Ed, and Bob Schellas, eds. *Contract with America: The Bold Plan by Rep. Newt Gingrich, Rep. Dick Armey, and the House Republicans to Change the Nation.* New York: Times Books, 1994.

Goldgeier, James M. *Not Whether but When: The U.S. Decision to Enlarge NATO.* Washington, DC: Brookings Institution Press, 1999.

Goldgeier, James M., and Michael McFaul. *Power and Purpose: U.S. Policy toward Russia after the Cold War.* Washington, DC: Brookings Institution Press, 2003.

Goldman, Peter, Andrew Murr, and Tom Mathews. *Quest for the Presidency 1992.* College Station: Texas A&M Press, 1994.

Gordon, Michael R., and General Bernard E. Trainor. *Cobra II: The Inside Story of the Invasion and Occupation of Iraq*. New York: Pantheon, 2006.

Graham, Bradley. *Hit to Kill: The New Battle over Shielding America from Missile Attack*. New York: PublicAffairs, 2001.

Greenspan, Alan. *The Age of Turbulence: Adventures in a New World*. New York: Penguin Press, 2007.

Haass, Richard. *The Reluctant Sheriff: The United States After the Cold War*. Washington, DC: Brookings Institution Press, 1998.

_____. *The Opportunity: America's Moment to Alter History's Course*. New York: PublicAffairs, 2005.

Halberstam, David. *War in a Time of Peace: Bush, Clinton, and the Generals*. New York: Scribner, 2001.

Halper, Stefan, and Jonathan Clarke. *America Alone: The Neoconservatives and the Global Order*. Cambridge, UK: Cambridge University Press, 2004.

Hamilton, Nigel. *Bill Clinton: Mastering the Presidency*. New York: PublicAffairs, 2007.

Harris, John F. *The Survivor: Bill Clinton in the White House*. New York: Random House, 2005.

Heilbrunn, Jacob. *They Knew They Were Right: The Rise of the Neocons*. New York: Doubleday, 2008.

Helms, Jesse. *Here's Where I Stand*. New York: Random House, 2005.

Hertzberg, Hendrik. *Politics: Observations & Arguments 1966–2004*. New York: Penguin Press, 2004.

Hirsh, Michael. *At War with Ourselves: Why America Is Squandering Its Chance to Build a Better World*. Oxford, UK: Oxford University Press, 2003.

Holbrooke, Richard. *To End a War*. New York: Random House, 1998.

Hunt, Michael H. *The American Ascendancy: How the United States Gained and Wielded Global Dominance*. Chapel Hill: University of North Carolina Press, 2007.

Hyland, William G. *Clinton's World: Remaking American Foreign Policy*. Westport, CT: Praeger, 1999.

Huntington, Samuel P. *The Clash of Civilizations and the Remaking of World Order*. New York: Simon & Schuster, 1996.

Ignatieff, Michael. *Virtual War: Kosovo and Beyond*. New York: Metropolitan Books, 2000.

Ikenberry, John. *After Victory: Institutions, Strategic Restraint, and the Rebuilding of Order after Major Wars*. Princeton, NJ: Princeton University Press, 2001.

Johnson, Haynes. *The Best of Times: America in the Clinton Years*. New York: Harcourt, 2001.

Judis, John B. *The Folly of Empire: What George W. Bush Could Learn from Theodore Roosevelt and Woodrow Wilson*. New York: Scribner, 2004.

Judt, Tony. *Postwar: A History of Europe Since 1945*. New York: Penguin Press, 2005.

Kagan, Donald, and Frederick W. Kagan. *While America Sleeps: Self-Delusion, Military Weakness, and the Threat to Peace Today*. New York: St. Martin's Press, 2000.

Kagan, Frederick W. *Finding the Target: The Transformation of American Military Policy*. New York: Encounter Books, 2006.

Kagan, Robert. *Of Paradise and Power*. New York: Knopf, 2003.

_____. *Dangerous Nation*. New York: Knopf, 2006.

Kagan, Robert, and William Kristol, eds. *Present Dangers: Crisis and Opportunity in American Foreign and Defense Policy*. San Francisco: Encounter Books, 2000.

Kalb, Marvin. *The Nixon Memo: Political Respectability, Russia, and the Press*. Chicago: University of Chicago Press, 1994.

Kaplan, Fred. *Daydream Believers: How a Few Grand Ideas Wrecked American Power*. New York: Wiley, 2008.

Kaplan, Lawrence F., and William Kristol. *The War Over Iraq*. San Francisco: Encounter Books, 2003.

Kaplan, Robert D. *Balkan Ghosts: A Journey Through History*. New York: St. Martin's Press, 1993.

_____. *The Coming Anarchy: Shattering the Dreams of the Post–Cold War*. New York: Random House, 2000.

Kennedy, Paul. *The Rise and Fall of the Great Powers: Economic Change and Military Conflict from 1500 to 2000*. New York: Vintage Books, 2005.

Khalilzad, Zalmay. *From Containment to Global Leadership? America & the World after the Cold War*. Santa Monica, CA: RAND, 1995.

Kirkpatrick, Jeane J. *Making War to Keep Peace*. New York: HarperCollins, 2007.

Kissinger, Henry. *Diplomacy*. New York: Simon & Schuster, 1994.

_____. *Does America Need a Foreign Policy? Toward a Diplomacy for the 21st Century*. New York: Simon & Schuster, 2001.

Kull, Steven and I. M. Destler. *Misreading the Public: The Myth of a New Isolationism*. Washington, DC: Brookings Institution Press, 1999.

LaFeber, Walter. *The American Age*. New York: W. W. Norton, 1989.

Lake, Anthony. *Six Nightmares: Real Threats in a Dangerous World and How America Can Meet Them*. New York: Little, Brown, 2000.

Leffler, Melvyn P. *For the Soul of Mankind: The United States, the Soviet Union, and the Cold War*. New York: Hill and Wang, 2007.

Lieber, Robert, Kenneth A. Oye, and Donald Rothchild, eds. *Eagle in a New World: American Grand Strategy in the Post–Cold War Era*. New York: HarperCollins, 1992.

Lind, Michael. *The American Way of Strategy: U.S. Foreign Policy and the American Way of Life*. Oxford, UK: Oxford University Press, 2006.

Lippman, Thomas W. *Madeleine Albright and the New American Diplomacy*. Boulder, CO: Westview, 2000.

Litwak, Robert. *Regime Change: U.S. Strategy through the Prism of 9/11*. Washington, DC: Woodrow Wilson Center, 2007.

Lowry, Rich. *Legacy: Paying the Price for the Clinton Years*. Washington, DC: Regnery, 2003.

Mann, James. *About Face: A History of America's Curious Relationship with China, from Nixon to Clinton*. New York: Vintage Books, 1998.

_____. *Rise of the Vulcans: The History of Bush's War Cabinet*. New York: Viking, 2004.

Marshall, Will, and Martin Schram, eds. *Mandate for Change*. New York: Berkley Publishing, 1993.

McDougall, Walter. *Promised Land, Crusader State: The American Encounter with the World Since 1776*. Boston: Houghton Mifflin, 1997.

Mead, Walter Russell. *Special Providence: American Foreign Policy and How It Changed the World*. New York: Routledge, 2002.

Naftali, Timothy. *Blind Spot: The Secret History of American Counterterrorism*. New York: Basic Books, 2006.

Ninkovich, Frank. *The Wilsonian Century: U.S. Foreign Policy Since 1900*. Chicago: University of Chicago Press, 1999.

Norris, John. *Collision Course: NATO, Russia, and Kosovo*. Westport, CT: Praeger, 2005.

Nye, Joseph S. Jr. *Bound to Lead: The Changing Nature of American Power*. New York: Basic Books, 1990.

Packer, George. *The Assassins' Gate*. New York: Farrar, Straus and Giroux, 2005.

_____, ed. *The Fight Is for Democracy*. New York: HarperCollins, 2003.

Patterson, James T. *Restless Giant: The United States from Watergate to Bush v. Gore*. New York: Oxford University Press USA, 2005.

Perot, Ross. *United We Stand: How We Can Take Back Our Country*. New York: Hyperion, 1992.

Pollack, Kenneth. *The Threatening Storm: The Case for Invading Iraq*. New York: Random House, 2002.

Powell, Colin. *My American Journey*. New York: Ballantine, 1995.

Power, Samantha. *A Problem from Hell: America and the Age of Genocide*. New York: Basic Books, 2002.

Priest, Dana. *The Mission: Waging War and Keeping Peace with America's Military*. New York: W. W. Norton, 2003.

Reich, Robert. *The Work of Nations: Preparing Ourselves for 21st Century Capitalism*. New York: Knopf/Vintage Books, 1991.

_____. *Locked in the Cabinet*. New York: Knopf, 1997.

Ricks, Thomas E. *Fiasco: The American Military Adventure in Iraq*. New York: Penguin Press, 2006.

Robin, Corey. *Fear: The History of a Political Idea*. Oxford, UK: Oxford University Press, 2004.

Ross, Dennis. *The Missing Peace: The Inside Story of the Fight for Middle East Peace*. New York: Farrar, Straus and Giroux, 2004.

_____. *Statecraft: And How to Restore America's Standing in the World*. New York: Farrar, Straus and Giroux, 2007.

Rothkopf, David J. *Running the World: The Inside Story of the National Security Council and the Architects of American Power*. New York: PublicAffairs, 2005.

Rubin, Robert E., and Jacob Weisberg. *In an Uncertain World: Tough Choices from Wall Street to Washington*. New York: Random House, 2003.

Schlesinger, Arthur M. Jr. *Journals 1952–2000*. New York: Penguin Press, 2007.

Scoblic, J. Peter. *U.S. vs. Them: How Conservatism Has Undermined America's Security*. New York: Viking, 2008.

Shenon, Philip. *The Commission: The Uncensored History of the 9/11 Investigation*. New York: Twelve, 2008.

Singer, P. W. *Corporate Warriors: The Rise of the Privatized Military Industry*. Ithaca, NY: Cornell University Press, 2003.

Smith, Sally Bedell. *For Love of Politics: Bill and Hillary Clinton, the White House Years*. New York: Random House, 2007.

Soderberg, Nancy. *The Superpower Myth: The Use and Misuse of American Might*. Hoboken, NJ: Wiley and Sons, 2005.

Stephanopoulos, George. *All Too Human: A Political Education*. New York: Little, Brown, 2000.

Stephens, Philip. *Tony Blair: The Making of a World Leader*. New York: Viking, 2004.

Suettinger, Robert L. *Beyond Tiananmen: The Politics of U.S.-China Relations 1989–2000*. Washington, DC: Brookings Institution Press, 2003.

Suskind, Ron. *The Price of Loyalty*. New York: Simon & Schuster, 2004.

Talbott, Strobe. *The Russia Hand: A Memoir of Presidential Diplomacy*. New York: Random House, 2002.

_____. *The Great Experiment: The Story of Ancient Empires, Modern States, and the Quest for a Global Nation*. New York: Simon & Schuster, 2008.

Tenet, George. *At the Center of the Storm: My Years at the CIA*. New York: Harper-Collins, 2007.

Tetlock, Philip. *Expert Political Judgment: How Good Is It? How Can We Know?* Princeton, NJ: Princeton University Press, 2006.

Thomas, Evan, ed. *Back from the Dead: How Clinton Survived the Republican Revolution*. New York: Atlantic Monthly Press, 1997.

Traub, James. *The Best Intentions: Kofi Annan and the U.N. in the Era of American World Power*. New York: Farrar, Straus and Giroux, 2006.

Tucker, Robert W. *The Purposes of American Power: An Essay on National Security*. New York: Praeger, 1981.

Tyler, Patrick. *A Great Wall: Six Presidents and China: An Investigative History*. New York: PublicAffairs, 1999.

Waldman, Michael. *POTUS Speaks: Finding the Words that Defined the Clinton Presidency*. New York: Simon & Schuster, 2000.

Walker, Martin. *The President We Deserve: Bill Clinton, His Rise, Falls, and Comebacks*. New York: Crown, 1996.

Weiner, Tim. *Legacy of Ashes: The History of the CIA*. New York: Doubleday, 2007.

Weisberg, Jacob. *The Bush Tragedy*. New York: Random House, 2008.

Weisman, Alan. *Prince of Darkness: Richard Perle*. New York: Union Square Press, 2007.

Western, Jon. *Selling Intervention and War: The Presidency, the Media, and the American Public*. Baltimore, MD: Johns Hopkins University Press, 2005.

Wit, Joel S., Daniel B. Poneman, and Robert L. Gallucci. *Going Critical: The First North Korean Nuclear Crisis*. Washington, DC: Brookings Institution Press, 2004.

Woodward, Bob. *The Agenda: Inside the Clinton White House*. New York: Simon & Schuster, 1994.

_____. *The Choice*. New York: Simon & Schuster, 1996.

_____. *Shadow: Five Presidents and the Legacy of Watergate*. Simon & Schuster, 1999.

_____. *Bush at War*. New York: Simon & Schuster, 2003.

Wright, Robert. *Nonzero: The Logic of Human Destiny.* New York: Pantheon, 2000.

Wright, Lawrence. *The Looming Tower: Al-Qaeda and the Road to 9/11.* New York: Knopf, 2006.

Zegart, Amy. *Spying Blind: The CIA, the FBI, and the Origins of 9/11.* Princeton, NJ: Princeton University Press, 2007.

Zimmermann, Warren. *First Great Triumph: How Five Great Americans Made Their Country a World Power.* New York: Farrar, Straus and Giroux, 2002.

Zinni, Tony, and Tony Koltz. *The Battle for Peace: A Frontline Vision of America's Power and Purpose.* New York: Palgrave Macmillan, 2006.

Acknowledgments

Writing this book would have been impossible without help and support from many others, to whom we are deeply grateful.

This is a book about history, politics, and ideas, but it is also about people. So our thanks must begin by acknowledging the many individuals who generously shared with us their time and insights in conversations about the events and debates described in these pages. These include: Madeleine Albright, Bill Antholis, Richard Armitage, Charlene Barshefsky, Peter Bass, Daniel Benjamin, Sandy Berger, Steve Biegun, Tom Blanton, John Bolton, Bob Boorstin, David Bonior, Lael Brainard, Zbigniew Brzezinski, Patrick Buchanan, Andrei Cherny, Warren Christopher, Wesley Clark, Eliot Cohen, Tom Daschle, Tom Donilon, Eric Edelman, Douglas Feith, Michele Flournoy, David Frum, Leon Fuerth, Francis Fukuyama, Timothy Geithner, Les Gelb, Carl Gershman, Michael Gerson, Newt Gingrich, Richard Haass, Lee Hamilton, Richard Holbrooke, Rick Inderfurth, Bruce Jackson, Robert Kagan, Arnold Kanter, Mickey Kantor, Jack Kemp, Henry Kissinger, William Kristol, Steve Kull, Tony Lake, David Lipton, Jim Mann, Will Marshall, Jessica Mathews, Denis McDonough, John McLaughlin, Mark Medish, Ralph Nader, Moises Naim, William Nash, Bill Perry, Tom Pickering, John Podesta, Colin Powell, Joseph Ralston, Jeremy Rosner, Dennis Ross, David Rothkopf, Jamie Rubin, Robert Rubin, AnnaLee Saxenian, Peter Scher, Gary Schmitt, Brent Scowcroft, Liz Sherwood-Randall, Walt

Slocombe, Jim Steinberg, Strobe Talbott, Peter Tarnoff, Patrick Tyler, Lori Wallach, Vin Weber, Peter Wehner, James Woolsey, and Anthony Zinni. Several others prefer to remain anonymous, but we wish to thank them as well.

In addition, we benefited greatly from talking over ideas (and quandaries) with good friends and colleagues who have thought a lot about the events we describe and readily bestowed frank opinions and stunningly good advice. We learned much from Warren Bass, Bennett Freeman, John Judis, Peter Scoblic, Mike Signer, and Ray Takeyh.

We are also grateful to several individuals and institutions for their generous support, whether that meant indulging our frequent disappearances to write or providing quiet refuge for us to do so. Derek Chollet thanks his colleagues at the Center for a New American Security, particularly Kurt Campbell, Michele Flournoy, Jim Miller, and Tiffany Sirc, for all of their encouragement, good humor, unstinting support, and friendship. Kurt Campbell deserves special mention for going so far beyond the call of duty, not only by reading a rough manuscript and for providing so many good comments and astute suggestions, but for securing a writing office at the Aspen Institute. Thanks also go to Jonathon Price for helping to ensure such a congenial place for several months of work at Aspen. Jim Goldgeier is grateful to Prosser Gifford and Carolyn Brown at the John W. Kluge Center at the Library of Congress, Robert Litwak and Sam Wells at the Woodrow Wilson International Center for Scholars, and Richard Haass, Jim Lindsay, and Gary Samore at the Council on Foreign Relations for providing not only financial support but wonderful intellectual environments in which to research and write. He also thanks Chris Deering, chair of the department of political science at The George Washington University, for allowing (and even encouraging) an extended leave to work on the book, and the European Commission and Hal Wolman and Garry Young of the George Washington Institute for Public Policy for the financial support they provided.

Brenna Anatone, Amanda Beck, Erica De Bruin, Timothy Gowa, Joe McReynolds, Parke Nicholson, Katy Robinette, and Tiffany Sirc provided terrific research assistance, tracking down facts, batting around ideas, and reading drafts with skill and cheer. Catherine Nielsen of the National Security Archive has our deepest thanks for her help in filing Freedom of Information Act requests, which elicited important declassified documents. And we appreciate Tony Lake's allowing us access to his unclassified papers, which are deposited in the Manuscript Division of the Library of Congress.

A number of friends, colleagues, and mentors took time out of their busy schedules to read the draft manuscript, offering invaluable critiques as well as saving us from embarrassing mistakes. We thank Bob Art, Peter Beinart, Shawn Brimley, Price Floyd, Richard Haass, Richard Holbrooke, Robert Kagan, Keir Lieber, Tod Lindberg, Jim Lindsay, and Strobe Talbott for their wise suggestions, which have improved the book exponentially. Nonetheless, any remaining mistakes and the opinions expressed here are our own. We also received valuable feedback on some of our ideas from those who attended talks at Stanford University's Institute for International Studies, the Library of Congress, and a meeting of the junior staff of the Council on Foreign Relations.

Our agent, Larry Weissman, believed in the project from the beginning and helped shepherd us through the long process from ill-formed idea to finished book. We are delighted that he helped us forge a partnership with PublicAffairs and its wonderful editorial director, Clive Priddle, who has been a constant source of encouragement and sound judgment. We also thank the rest of PublicAffairs's talented team, including Annie Lenth, Niki Papadopoulos, Melissa Raymond, and Tessa Shanks, as well as our copy editor, Antoinette Smith, for bringing this book to life.

Finally, we could not have persevered without the loving support and patience of our families. Heather Hostetter and Kathy Goldgeier read this manuscript at a critical stage, and they have given us so much, both editorially and emotionally. We could not have done this without them. Lucas Chollet Hostetter and Jeffrey and Brian Goldgeier tolerated our absences and preoccupations but also reminded us of what is most important.

Index

DEREK CHOLLET is a senior fellow at the Center for a New American Security in Washington, D.C., where he also teaches at Georgetown University's Security Studies Program. He served in the State Department during the Clinton administration, as foreign policy adviser to former U.S. Senator John Edwards, and assisted former U.S. Secretaries of State James A. Baker III and Warren Christopher with their memoirs. He has written or coedited three books on American foreign policy, and his articles have appeared in the *Washington Post*, *Financial Times*, *Los Angeles Times*, *Washington Monthly*, and numerous other publications.

JAMES GOLDGEIER is a professor of political science and international affairs at The George Washington University and a senior fellow at the Council on Foreign Relations. He has authored or coauthored three books on foreign policy, and his articles have appeared in publications including *Foreign Affairs*, *Foreign Policy*, the *National Interest*, the *Washington Post*, *Financial Times*, and the *Weekly Standard*. He has held fellowships at Stanford University, the Brookings Institution, the Library of Congress, and the Woodrow Wilson Center and has served at the State Department and on the National Security Council staff.

PublicAffairs is a publishing house founded in 1997. It is a tribute to the standards, values, and flair of three persons who have served as mentors to countless reporters, writers, editors, and book people of all kinds, including me.

I. F. STONE, proprietor of *I. F. Stone's Weekly*, combined a commitment to the First Amendment with entrepreneurial zeal and reporting skill and became one of the great independent journalists in American history. At the age of eighty, Izzy published *The Trial of Socrates*, which was a national bestseller. He wrote the book after he taught himself ancient Greek.

BENJAMIN C. BRADLEE was for nearly thirty years the charismatic editorial leader of *The Washington Post*. It was Ben who gave the *Post* the range and courage to pursue such historic issues as Watergate. He supported his reporters with a tenacity that made them fearless and it is no accident that so many became authors of influential, best-selling books.

ROBERT L. BERNSTEIN, the chief executive of Random House for more than a quarter century, guided one of the nation's premier publishing houses. Bob was personally responsible for many books of political dissent and argument that challenged tyranny around the globe. He is also the founder and longtime chair of Human Rights Watch, one of the most respected human rights organizations in the world.

. . .

For fifty years, the banner of Public Affairs Press was carried by its owner Morris B. Schnapper, who published Gandhi, Nasser, Toynbee, Truman, and about 1,500 other authors. In 1983, Schnapper was described by *The Washington Post* as "a redoubtable gadfly." His legacy will endure in the books to come.

Peter Osnos, *Founder and Editor-at-Large*

A WILD CARDS MOSAIC NOVEL

SUICIDE KINGS

Edited by
George R. R. Martin

Assisted by
Melinda M. Snodgrass

And written by

Daniel Abraham | *S. L. Farrell*
Victor Milán | *Melinda M. Snodgrass*
Caroline Spector | *Ian Tregillis*

A TOM DOHERTY ASSOCIATES BOOK
New York

SUICIDE KINGS

Map by Jon Lansberg

A Tor Book
Published by Tom Doherty Associates, LLC
175 Fifth Avenue
New York, NY 10010

www.tor-forge.com

Tor® is a registered trademark of Tom Doherty Associates, LLC.

Library of Congress Cataloging-in-Publication Data

Suicide kings : a wild cards mosaic novel / edited by George R. R. Martin ; assisted by Melinda M. Snodgrass ; and written by Daniel Abraham . . . [et al.].—1st ed.
    p. cm.
  "A Tom Doherty Associates book."
  ISBN 978-0-7653-1783-4
 I. Martin, George R. R.   II. Snodgrass, Melinda M., 1951–   III. Abraham, Daniel.
  PS648.S3S85 2009
  813'.54—dc22

                                                              2009034715

First Edition: December 2009

Printed in the United States of America

0 9 8 7 6 5 4 3 2 1

for Wanda June Alexander
and all the English teachers everywhere

without you, there would be no readers

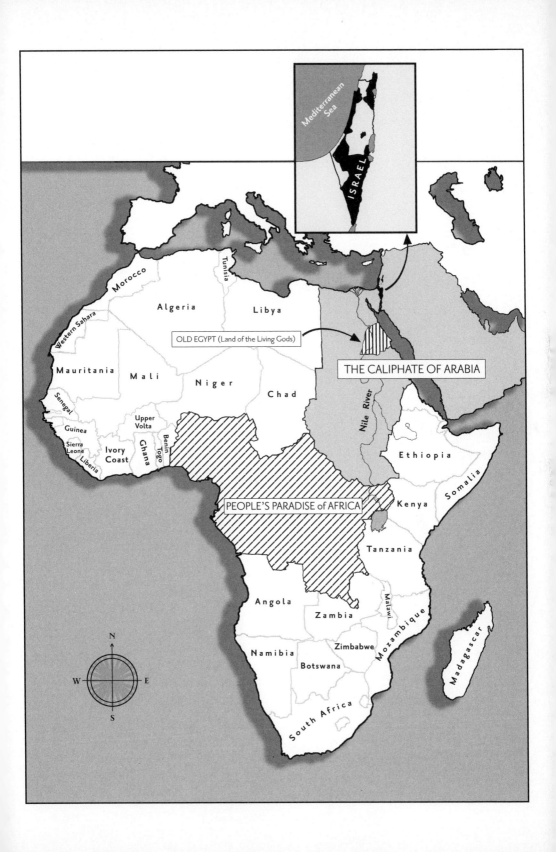

SUICIDE KINGS

Thursday, November 26

THANKSGIVING DAY

Guit District
The Sudd, Sudan
The Caliphate of Arabia

FROM WAY UP HERE it was all so clear.

Over here on the left were the Simba Brigades, the armed forces of the People's Paradise of Africa. They had foolishly deployed in an area, a couple square miles in extent, which were among the very few in the southern Sudanese papyrus swamp called the Sudd. They had armor, glittering dully in the sullen southern Sudan morning sun, dug in by bulldozers and concealed in clumps of brush and stands of trees: mostly Indian Vijayanta tanks and British-made Nigerian Mark IIIs, which were almost the same thing. They were enhanced unevenly by upgrades provided by the PPA's Chinese patrons.

Dug in alongside them were armored cars, light tanks, and several thousand mechanized infantry. They were long-term veterans of the war that had liberated and unified Central Africa, leavened by Nigerians trained to a fare-thee-well. Advised by Indian army officers, they had made a stab at catching their enemies debarking from the evanescent and nameless tributary or strand of the Nile onto ground where they could maneuver. Now with small arms and rockets they fought a desperate battle against superior numbers of Caliphate tanks and men.

Tank main guns cracked like thunder. Rockets sprang away, drawing lines of cottony white smoke behind them that settled and dissipated slowly in air so humid and heavy the flying man almost felt he could walk on it. Vehicles blossomed in sudden fire, the ripples of their fatal detonations propagating outward, the shock waves punching at the bare pale skin of the man's face. On columns of black smoke and red fire the smell of fuel combusting mounted upward, momentarily overcoming the hot reek of vegetation rotting in the endless swamps, the acrid stink of spent propellant giving way to the deceptive barbecue aroma of burning human flesh.

Up here was too high to hear the screams. Not that they carried far under the colossal head-crushing din of modern war.

The Caliphate forces rolled forward from barges guarded by Russian-made armored riverboats flying green banners that stirred like the shit-brown surface of the river in a sluggish breeze. Their fighting vehicles were mostly Russian made. Flat T-72s and a few more modern T-90s led the wave. Following came Echelons of BMP-2 and -3 personnel carriers with 30-millimeter machine cannon snarling from their turrets and laser-guided antitank missiles leaping away from rails mounted on the low turrets.

After the PPA's initial shatter of success, superior Caliphate numbers began to tell. Betrayed by their own fire, defending tanks and rocket nests were rapidly destroyed in turn. Adopting the classic Muslim crescent fighting formation, the attacking armor winged out to either side to envelop their foes. Then their infantry could dismount from the BMPs and dig them out and kill them. Despite spiking casualties the PPA's camouflage-clad black veterans held tenaciously and fought.

Up above the world so high, skimming in and out of a cloud in the sky, the man didn't much care if he was seen or not. It would be better if he wasn't, of course; it'd make for a better surprise. Not that *surprise* mattered. Not in the military sense. The people like ants down there on the green and murk-brown ground couldn't change what was about to happen.

But nobody looked. In a world where flying humans weren't unknown, they still weren't anything anybody, y'know, expected to *see*.

A roaring filled the sky, growing in the north. He heard it even above the anvils-of-the-gods racket of modern war. Looking around, the flying man saw two spots appear in the blue sky, just above the flat swamp horizon.

"My turn," he told the wind aloud. He dove.

They flashed past on his right: two Russian-made ground-attack SU-25s, as squat and unlovely as their NATO nickname of "Frogfoot." The PPA fighters, always deficient in combat aircraft—expensive to buy, crew, and maintain—had little answer except man-portable surface-to-air missiles, already arcing up from below and already chasing the dazzling foolish fires of the flares the Caliph's pilots seeded behind them. Even a single pair of attack planes, with Gatling cannon, antitank rockets, and armor-piercing bombs, could torch tanks like a kid with a magnifying glass plus ants.

Except just before they passed him by the man flung his right arm out. A white beam flashed from his palm that made the flares look dim. It punched a neat hole through both aircraft.

They stumbled in yellow flames as fuel and munitions blew up, and fell like disgraced stars.

It was a Sign. A beat after the planes exploded a darkness came upon the land. Like a wave it mounted and rolled forward, across the overmatched PPA defenses toward the triumphantly advancing Muslim army.

The flying man laughed again. He imagined the green-flagged enemy below: confidence faltering, turning quickly to sheer existential terror. It must seem to them that their Allah had forsaken them in spades.

But the liberators hadn't won the battle. Not yet. Their night-vision gear was as helpless in this unnatural Dark as the Caliphate's. All the enemy need do was roll forward blind and they'd smash the defenders to jam in their holes. *Time for Leucrotta to do his thing.* And, of course, the flying man, who swatted multimillion-dollar aircraft like mosquitoes.

It was good to be an ace. And more: an ace with nearly the powers of a god. A god of retribution. A god of Revolution.

He was the *Radical*. And it was cool to be him.

Into the Darkness he dropped. It clutched him like the fingers of a man drowned in some cold ocean, enwrapped him in fog blacker than a banker's heart. But he could see: the girl had touched his eyes with her cool slim fingers. It was like threaded twilight that leached away all colors. To announce his advent he loosed a sunbeam, another. Two of the leading T-90s flared up in response. The turret of one rose up ten feet on a geyser of white fire as its ammo stores exploded. The massive turret dropped back, not entirely in place, so that the red glare of the hell unleashed within shown clearly even to eyes blinded by the Dark.

The Caliphate tankers were totally freaking. Most had stopped when they quit being able to see outside their armored monstrosities. Others continued to plunge on, crashing into each other or crushing smaller AFVs like roaches. A T-72 fired its main gun, torching a brother tank forty feet ahead.

Despite the poison smoke that threatened to choke him, Tom threw back his golden head and laughed.

In terror Arab and Sudanese troops began to spill out of their personnel carriers. Some fell as more Caliphate gunners panicked and cut loose with machine guns. More tanks shot blindly. Others flared up like monster firework fountains.

Rockets buzzed past from behind him. The Darkness had walked among the front-line antitank pits and picked tanks and anointed their crews, too. They could see to slaughter blind foes.

Tom looked back toward the PPA lines. Through the murk surged a big four-footed form, a slope-backed high-shouldered avalanche of spotted fur and massive muscles. Saliva streamed from huge black jaws. It was a spotted hyena, *Crocuta crocuta*. But not a normal animal: a giant, four feet high at the shoulders and four hundred pounds easy. It was a were, a shape-shifter. The third ace the PPA had brought to the battle.

Behind it ran a dozen naked men. Even as Tom watched, their dark, sweat-glistening bodies began to flow and change. They became leopards, four melanistic, the rest tawny and spotted.

No aces, these. The innermost circle of the mystic Leopard Society, who had in horrific secret rituals accepted the bite of Alicia Nshombo. Even their fellow Leopard Men—the PPA's shock troops and secret police—feared them.

The snarl of a twelve-cylinder diesel filled Tom's ears, driving out even the near continuous explosions. He sprang upward. For a moment he hung in orbit. The stars shone down. He lingered a heartbeat, enough to feel the sting of the naked sun and the pressing of his eyeballs and blood outward against the vacuum. He didn't explode in vacuum: no one did. It was just a single atmosphere's difference in pressure: deal.

Then he was back, hovering two meters above a T-90 whose driver had decided or been ordered to charge straight ahead toward the infidels, in hopes of escaping the blackness, or at least getting to grips with the foe. Heat belching from the topside vents of the 1,100-horsepower engine enveloped him like dragon's breath. He dropped to the deck behind the turret.

Squatting, Tom gripped. Grunting, he stood. He deadlifted the heavy turret right out of its ring. Spinning in place, he hurled it like a colossal discus toward a nearby T-72. It struck the side of its turret. A violent white flash momentarily obscured both as ammo stowed in both turrets went off.

Tom dropped to the ground on the first tank's far side. Still massive despite the loss of turret and gun, it heeled perceptibly toward him as the blast fronts from multiple explosions slammed into it. High-velocity fragments cracked like bullets overhead.

The driver's hatch fell open with a ring as the last remaining crewman sought to abandon ship. Suddenly a giant bristling shape hunched on the truncated tank's low-sloped bow armor plate. Sensing danger the driver, half out of his hatch, froze.

Then he screamed as Leucrotta's immense jaws slammed shut with a terrible crunch, biting the driver's face off the front of his skull.

Tom took in the situation. The whole Caliphate armored force milled in utter confusion. At least the parts that weren't burning. Leucrotta and the were-leopards ran freely and killed dismounted soldiers like rabbits. The Darkness-touched PPA gunners continued to pour fire and steel into their enemies. The whole Muslim army was finished as a coherent force; it was now a stampede seeking in all directions for an exit.

All that remained was to slaughter everything in reach. Tom Weathers *really liked* that part.

Jackson Square
New Orleans, Louisiana

MICHELLE IS LYING ON a beach letting the sun bake her.

The outline of a boy blocks out the sun. "Who are you?" she asks.

He opens his mouth, but words don't come out. Light and fire spew forth.

Michelle wants to run away, but she knows she can't escape. Fire and light and power surge into her. Her body expands, opening to the overwhelming force. The power goes on and on and then the weight is crushing her, bearing her down into the ground. The earth groans beneath her. And the power inside her is thick, overwhelming, brutal. It's running through her veins. It wants out.

It wants to bubble.

Just as she feels the bubbles start to flow, she hears Juliet.

"I don't know how much longer I can do this," Juliet says. She's sitting on the edge of the bed petting a small rabbit.

When did we end up in bed? Michelle wonders. *And where did the bunny come from?*

"Ink, you don't have to fucking be here all the time," says Joey. Joey is sitting on the other side of Michelle. A cold worm burrows into her stomach. Does Juliet know about that night with Joey in the hurricane?

"What else can I do?" A tear rolls down Juliet's cheek and Michelle reaches out to wipe it away. But her hand comes in contact not with Juliet's warm face, but with cold, rubbery flesh.

She jerks her hand back, but it connects with more dead skin.

"Jesus," she says. But Jesus isn't here. It's just her alone.

It's dark, but not impenetrable darkness. She's lying inside a tangle of corpses piled up on one another.

Is this another Behatu camp nightmare? But it doesn't feel right. The colors are wrong. The light is off. And, it smells. It smells like rotting flesh. She's never had a sense of smell in a dream before.

Michelle tries to turn over, but she can't feel her legs. Her arms are useless weight, too. The light filtering through the dead limbs around her is greenish. And the air is thick and humid.

Panic begins to crawl into her throat. She's alive, but no one knows it. No one knows she's here. "Help me!" she screams.

"You know, we're her parents, and if we say she's dead, she's dead." Mommy? What was she doing here?

"You people are even worse than Michelle said you were." What was Ink saying? Now they were all sitting on the bed in Juliet and Michelle's apartment. The sheets were a pretty floral pattern that Michelle bought because Ink liked flowers.

"I don't care if you and Michelle are involved in some sickening relationship," Daddy said. "We have rights."

"The fuck you do," said Hoodoo Mama.

Oh, God, Michelle thought. *Joey will kill them.*

"Best as I can tell, you fuckers have no cocksucking rights regarding Bubbles here 't'all. Selfish pieces of sticky brown . . ."

"Joey!" Ink again.

"My goodness," her mother says. How could her mother's voice send a knife of pain through Michelle while at the same time she still wanted to curl up in her mother's arms?

But her mother is gone now. Michelle is back in the pile of bodies. Down in the twilight of dead flesh.

"Help me," she whispers.

A spider slides down a fine silk filament and dangles in front of her. It puts its front legs under its chin and studies her. Then it points up.

Michelle rolls awkwardly onto her back to look in the direction its foot is pointing.

Peering over the edge of the pit is a leopard. Its eyes glow phosphorescent yellow. Cold sweat breaks out on Michelle's brow. Her fear is coppery in her mouth. Another leopard joins the first. Soon the entire edge of the pit is rimmed with them.

The leopards exchange glances, occasionally yawning, revealing sharp, ivory-colored teeth. Then they begin to growl. Low guttural sounds like they're talking to each other.

Her heart is pounding. They must know she's down here. They must know she's alive. They must smell the fear on her. She can smell it herself now, along with the heavy feral odor of the cats. Tears burn her eyes. She tries to blink them away, but they slip out and slide down her cheeks, leaving an itchy trail.

What the hell? Michelle thinks. *I'm the Amazing Bubbles. I don't lie in a pit crying because some damn leopards are looking at me like I'm lunch. They can't do anything to me.*

And she tries to bubble, but she can't. *No hands*, she thinks. *If I had hands, I could bubble.*

"You're not so fucking special, Michelle," Joey says. "And zombies are not disgusting."

Michelle looks down at herself. She's turned a greyish color and her clothes are in tatters. Black mold is growing on her skin. She holds her hand up in front of her face. At least now she has a hand. Bones peek out between the rotted parts of her fingers.

"This is so wrong," she says.

Barataria Basin
New Orleans, Louisiana

JERUSHA CARTER GAZED OUT over a mile-wide expanse of open water. White egrets floated overhead like quick, noisy clouds; blue herons waded in the nearby shallows, and an alligator's tail sluiced through the brackish water not far from her boat.

The scene wasn't entirely idyllic; the sun was merciless, drawing wet circles under her armpits and beading her forehead. Midges, mosquitoes, and huge black flies tormented her. The muck had managed to overtop her high boots and slither down both legs. A storm front was coming in from the Gulf: thunderheads white above and slate grey below piled on the horizon, and the mutter of distant thunder grumbled in the afternoon heat.

The Barataria Basin was a marsh south of the city of New Orleans, one of the several such natural buffers for the city and St. Bernard Parish in the event of a hurricane. It was Jerusha's job to help restore it. Once, she'd been told, before the levees had been built, this entire area had been marshland, not a lake. Since the 1930s, the area around New Orleans had lost two thousand square miles of coastal wetlands. According to the experts who had briefed Jerusha, for every 2.7 miles of wetland, hurricane storm surge could be reduced by one foot. Therefore, to protect the city from future disasters, it was vital that the wetlands be restored.

That was backbreaking, hard work. Silt had to be hauled in to be dumped in the open water to make it shallow enough to allow the plants that had once flourished here to grow again. Jerusha's part came when the silt had been dumped and the margins of the lake were ready to be replanted. There, her wild card gift could make short work of what would otherwise take months or years.

Yesterday, it had been bulwhip; today Jerusha was spreading cordgrass— Spartina spartinae, specifically, Gulf cordgrass, with its ability to grow rapidly and to thrive in water of varying salinity. Without Jerusha, teams of volunteers would have been brought in to plant mats of seedlings in the mud and silt, which in time would grow into dense, tough plants high enough to hide a person entirely.

Today was also Thanksgiving. There were no teams out here today. Jerusha was working alone. Everyone else had somewhere to go, somewhere to be: with family, with friends. She tried not to think about that, tried to forget the frozen Swanson turkey dinner waiting for her back at the empty apartment or the call to her parents she'd make while she was eating, listening to their voices and their good wishes and the laughter of their friends in the background, which would only make her feel more alone. Jerusha's seed belt was full of cordgrass seed, and it needed to be planted. Today.

She stepped out into the knee-deep muck of newly dumped silt, her boots squelching loudly as the mud sucked at them. She plunged her hand into one of the pouches on her belt and tossed handfuls of the tiny seeds onto the ground in a wide arc in front of her. She closed her eyes momentarily: she could feel the seeds and the pulsing of nascent life within them.

She drew on the wild card power within her, Gardener's power, funneling it from her mind into the seeds. She could feel them responding: growing and bursting, tiny coils of green springing from them, roots digging into the soft mud, tender shoots reaching for the sun. She led the cordgrass, feeding the power slowly and carefully.

She *was* the cordgrass, taking in the nutrients of sun and water and earth and using it, her cells bursting and growing at an impossible rate, forming and re-forming, new shoots birthing every second. She could see the grass rising in front of her, writhing and twisting, a year's growth taking place in a few moments. As the grass lifted higher, Jerusha laughed, a throaty sound that held a deep, strange satisfaction. There were a few people who might recognize that laugh—it was the same laugh she sometimes gave, involuntarily, in the midst of sex: a vocal, joyous call that came from her core.

Gardening as orgasm.

The cordgrass lifted, writhing and twisting—and atop a cluster of stalks a few feet away something floppy and brown was snagged, bending the grass under its weight.

She let the power fall from her. She felt her shoulders sag: using the ability the wild card had given her always tired her. Usually, after a day out here, she would go back to her apartment and just fall into bed to sleep twelve hours or more. That was most of her days: wake up early, come out here and spread seeds to restore the marshland until near sundown, then back to the city for a quick bite in a restaurant or in her apartment (but alone, always alone), then sleep. Rinse and repeat. Over and over.

Jerusha waded through the mud to the new cordgrass. She pulled the sopping wet piece of felt from the stalks. It took a moment for Jerusha to unfold it and see that it was a hat—a battered, moldy, and filthy fedora, the lining torn and mostly missing, the band gone entirely. A mussel shell clung stubbornly to the fabric; it reeked of the swamp.

She shook her head: *Another fedora. We've sent Cameo at least a dozen hats we've found out here, hoping it was the one she lost.* The only way to know for certain was to send this one to her also: a Thanksgiving present. She'd do that when she got back.

Jerusha sighed, glancing at the sun and the clouds. The storm was rolling in. It was time to head back unless she wanted to be caught in the weather, which would only make an already miserable Thanksgiving more miserable.

Holding the sodden hat by the brim, she made her way back to where she'd tied up her boat.

The Winslow Household
Boston, Massachusetts

"**SON OF A *BITCH*!** I can't believe he dropped that pass!"

Noel Matthews was jerked back to his surroundings by the shout from his father-in-law. *He* couldn't believe he was sitting in front of an entertainment center that looked like it should be the command deck of an aircraft carrier while his American in-laws watched football and shouted at the bigscreen television.

Of course it wasn't really football. It was that turgidly slow American game where extremely large men dressed in padding and tight pants jumped on each other and patted each other's asses. For a country that was so uptight about fags this seemed an odd sport to be the national pasttime.

Noel reached for his bourbon and soda, and groaned faintly as he shifted on the couch to reach the glass. It felt like a cannonball had replaced his gut, and he surreptitiously undid the button on his slacks. It was Thanksgiving—that peculiar American holiday that seemed to be a celebration of gluttony and taking advantage of the Indians.

But there had been no choice. He and Niobe were living in New York because of fertility treatments at the Jokertown Clinic. Her parents were close by in Massachusetts. And Niobe was determined to show off her famous and successful husband to the old money society that had shunned her when her wild card expressed and she became a joker. Noel had consented to be displayed like a prize Scottish salmon because they had treated Niobe so shabbily, and gloating was a perfectly acceptable response.

Murmuring about "needing the lavatory," Noel made his escape from the company of men to go in search of his wife. In the kitchen he discovered hired help busily washing up the dishes and packaging the leftovers into plastic containers. Noel was rich now, but he hadn't been raised rich. They had lived modestly on his mother's salary as a Cambridge professor. In his house there was no hired help.

He paused in the hallway and listened. The soprano piping of women's voices in the living room vied with the basso shouts and bellows from the den. As he walked down the long hall, past a rather impressive modern art collection, he buttoned his pants and suit coat.

The living room was done in shades of gold and green, and a fire in the large marble hearth made the room seem cozy and warm. Outside, the big pines in the front yard groaned in the wind. It would snow by morning. Thank God they had a way home from this circle of family hell even if they closed the airport.

Arranging his features into a pleasant smile, he approached the women seated on sofas surrounding a low table that held a silver tea and coffee set. The scent added to the feeling of conviviality, as did the staccato of conversation. He was pleased to see that Niobe was chattering with the best of them, and that her chic equaled or excelled the other women.

It was amazing what a year of contentment—and the tender care of hairdressers in New York, spas on the Dead Sea, and couture in Paris—had done for her hair, skin, and wardrobe. The only jarring note was the thick tail that wrapped around his darling's feet. At least the laser treatments had removed the bristles.

Their eyes met, and Noel was pleased to see the triumph brimming in hers. He came around behind the sofa, leaned down, kissed her on the cheek, and made a single white rose appear. Niobe blushed, and he was pleased to see her cousin Phoebe look down and frown into her tea. The woman had spent the afternoon placing her fingertips on his forearm, leaning forward so her breasts would be displayed, and generally making a fool of herself.

"You're not watching?" his mother-in-law said.

"Forgive me, but they're fools. They're watching large men grunting and falling down in the mud. I, however, am no fool. I would rather spend my time with the ladies."

Their laughter fell like ice around him. Niobe wasn't laughing. He knew her husky little chuckle. She was looking at him, wide-eyed and questioning. He gave her a reassuring smile.

He studied his mother-in-law's profile, and briefly regretted he'd abandoned his previous profession. If ever a person deserved killing it was Rachel Winslow. When Niobe's wild card had turned, she had tried to pass her off as a cousin's child, and when Niobe had been driven to attempt suicide her parents had sent her away to a facility where she was treated like a cross between a lab rat and a sex toy.

His wife handed him a cup of tea. The china was so thin and fragile that it felt like a cricket's wing in his hand. He looked down and realized she'd already doctored it with a dollop of cream. It squeezed his heart to know that there was someone in the world who knew how he took his tea, and liked his eggs, the temperature of his bathwater. And he returned the favor. They were bonded physically, emotionally, and mentally, and she had helped to close the hole in his heart left after the death of his father a little over a year ago.

He settled onto the sofa next to Niobe and sipped his tea. Noel found himself reaching for one of the cheese crackers. God knew he wasn't hungry, but nerves made him want to do something with his hands, and he wasn't allowed to smoke in his in-laws' house. He was saved from more calories when he felt the cell phone in his left pocket begin to vibrate.

He set aside his cup, pulled out the phone, murmured an apology, and retreated to stand by the window. The caller ID offered only UNKNOWN CALLER, but he recognized the foreign exchange number—*Baghdad!*

He knew a lot of people in Baghdad, but they only knew his identity as the Muslim ace, Bahir. Only one person knew that Noel was Bahir—his onetime Cambridge housemate, now head of the Caliphate and implacable enemy, Prince Siraj of Jordan.

This was a clean phone. The fact that Siraj had the number meant the Caliphate's intelligence services had been working overtime. Looking for him and finding him. Tension buzzed along every nerve as Noel considered his options.

Better to know what he's up to. Noel answered the phone.

"I didn't know if you'd take the call," came that familiar baritone.

"I almost didn't." Silence stretched between them. Noel pulled out his cigarette case.

Finally Siraj spoke. "I need your help. Will you come to Baghdad, now?" Anxiety roughened his fruity BBC vowels.

It was the last thing Noel had expected. He fumbled out a cigarette and thrust it between his lips. "Ah, well . . . let me see . . . the last time we met you had your guards shoot me. The time before that you had me thrown into an Egyptian prison. I think I'll skip the third time. It might be the charm for you."

"I give you my word I won't make a move against you. I really do need your help."

Siraj suddenly sounded very young, like the friend who'd gotten into trouble with a professor's daughter and come to Noel for help, or the friend who'd loaned him the money to pay off his gambling debts when Noel had become fascinated with the ponies in his sophomore year.

But there was no place for sentimentality. "Why?"

"Half of my armor's been destroyed in the Sudd. This is my last army, Noel, and it's all that stands between the Caliphate and the People's Paradise of Africa. And you in the West do not want Nshombo and Tom Weathers controlling the oil. Trust me."

"Well, that really is the crux of the problem. I *don't* trust you. Sorry about your army, but I'm out of the game. For good. Just an average citizen now. Lovely talking to you." Noel hung up the phone, and rejoined Niobe.

She looked up at him, and he was struck again by her beautiful green eyes. "Was that Kevin?" she said, referring to his agent.

"Yes," Noel lied.

"You have a cigarette *in your mouth!*" his tanned and brittle mother-in-law said, forcing the words past clenched teeth.

"Yes, but it's not lit. I'll go outside and rectify that."

Stellar
Manhattan, New York

WALLY TUGGED ON THE collar of his tuxedo. The tailor had insisted the tux fit him perfectly. As perfectly as anything could fit a man with iron skin and rivets, anyway. But it sure didn't feel right.

He stopped fiddling with the bow tie. He didn't know how to tie it; it would be embarrassing if he had to ask a waiter to help him fix it.

The elevator glided to a stop. It jounced slightly as Wally stepped out.

"Hey, Rusty! Get over here, you."

Ana Cortez stood outside Stellar with a phone to her ear. It looked like she had stepped outside to take a call. She smiled and waved to Wally as he clanked out of the elevator lobby.

His footwear, like his tuxedo, had been specially tailored for him. The fancy Italian shoes looked nice, but they were pretty flimsy; they did little to lessen the pounding of iron feet on a marble floor. Wally would have preferred a less formal Thanksgiving.

Back home, denim overalls and work boots were perfectly acceptable holiday attire. He'd considered going home to Minnesota for the holiday, but in spite of the growing loneliness and homesickness that hovered over him like a cloud these days, he'd decided against it. Every visit home felt more awkward than the last one.

It wasn't that he didn't want to see Mom, Dad, and Pete. He missed them pretty bad. More than anything he wanted to go back home to the days before *American Hero*. He wanted to spend one more Saturday afternoon watching TV with his brother, while their dad snored in his easy chair.

Thing was, Pete had never traveled farther from home than Duluth. His folks had been born and raised on the Iron Range. It was their whole world. Sometimes Wally wished he could go back to being that way, too.

His family imagined Wally's life was glamorous. Exciting. Full of adventure. And it made them so happy, thinking that. The last time he went home, he thought his folks were going to burst with pride. Wally Gunderson, the hero. Wally Gunderson, international traveler. Wally Gunderson, troubleshooter for the United Nations. Pete always questioned him about the places he visited for the Committee, all the people he worked with, all the good deeds he'd done.

Every visit, it got harder and harder to tell them what they wanted to hear. To avoid telling them about the boredom, the loneliness, the dread and fear he felt every time the Committee sent him someplace new, the sense of confusion about what he was doing and why he was doing it, the sense that he'd stopped being heroic a long time ago.

Wally hadn't spent much time at home after his trip to the Caliphate.

"Rusty's here," Ana said into her phone. She cupped her hand over it. "Kate says hi."

"Howdy, Ana. Howdy, Kate."

Into the phone, Ana said, "He says howdy back . . . uh-huh . . . uh-huh." She laughed. "I doubt it . . . I should go. Happy Thanksgiving to you, too. Call me later and we'll compare notes." Ana shut her phone with a snap. "I'm glad to see you. You look good."

"You too, Ana." Her dress looked expensive. It even matched the blue in her earrings.

She reached up to give him a quick hug. Wally dwarfed her. "Gosh," he said. He returned the hug, gently.

He looked into the restaurant, where white-coated waiters carried trays, pitchers, and bottles between the tables. They looked like photo-negatives of Wally, except not as large. Inside, the clink of cutlery chirped through the murmur of conversation. Unfamiliar faces, unfamiliar voices. A sad feeling crept over Wally.

He went inside with Ana. The maître d' greeted them. He didn't bother to ask if they were on the guest list; everybody knew Rustbelt and Earth Witch, two of the Committee's founding members. He paused in the act of ushering them toward the hors d'oeuvres when he noted the gouges Wally's heels left in the floor. The pencil-thin mustache quivered on his lip. He sniffed. But he didn't raise a fuss. His establishment was full of aces.

Not that Wally knew many of them. The Committee wasn't like it had been in the beginning. It was much bigger nowadays. Which was good, really, since it was becoming more international. No longer just a bunch of kids from some dumb TV show. It felt more professional, but also more sterile. He'd met a few of the newer members in passing at other Committee functions—Garou, Noppera-bo, the Strangelets. One of the new guys, Glassteel, nodded companionably at Wally as he passed; they'd worked together in Haiti. They made a pretty okay team, though Wally had liked working with DB the best, and DB was gone now.

Most of the guests had congregated around the long tables where the appetizers had been laid out, near the windows overlooking the Manhattan skyline. Wally munched on miniature hot dogs bathed in fancy ketchup while eavesdropping, trying to find a conversation he could join. The battle in the Sudd dominated most of the conversations. Wally had seen a blurb about it on one of those big stock-ticker things in Times Square during the cab ride to the Empire State Building.

"The PPA has overstretched itself," declared Snowblind in her elegant French-Canadian accent. If silk could talk, thought Wally, it would sound like Snowblind. "There's no need for the Committee to involve itself. Once the Caliphate regroups, this will be over quickly."

Brave Hawk shook his head. "Not if Ra gets involved. Old Egypt doesn't have much use for the Caliphate."

Wally didn't have much of a head for political discussions, and truth be told he wasn't all that keen on Brave Hawk anyway. So he wandered farther down the table, where the hors d'oeuvres included grapes, smelly cheese, and pear slices marinated in port wine. Those were pretty good.

Tinker and Burrowing Owl argued about the World Court. The pending war crimes trials of Captain Flint and the Highwayman were almost as divisive an issue as the fighting in Sudan. Burrowing Owl thought it was a meaningless show trial; Tinker thought both men deserved to be tried before the world. "Oy, Rusty," said Tinker. "What do you think?"

Wally shrugged. "Um . . ." What *did* he think? "I think they did a real bad thing, killing all those folks. But I think they did an even worse thing by making that poor little boy do it."

Burrowing Owl frowned. "Yes, but what about sovereignty and jurisdiction?"

Wally sighed, wishing it was time to sit down and eat.

Jerusha Carter's Apartment
Garden District
New Orleans, Louisiana

HER CELL PHONE CHIRPED before the bell on the microwave went off. That puzzled her, since it was an hour earlier where her parents were, and they would usually still be sitting at the Thanksgiving table at this point. She picked up the cell from the entrance-hall table, glancing at the number on the front.

It wasn't her parents; it was Juliet Summers. *Ink.* Strange. She knew Ink, of course, but they certainly weren't close.

"Hey," she answered. "Ink. What's up?"

"Jerusha? I need your help." There was someone shouting, no, *cursing* in the background. A woman. "That's Joey. Those scumbag LaFleurs convinced a judge to give them that court order. They're gonna pull the plug on Michelle."

Jerusha was shocked. Michelle Pond—the Amazing Bubbles—had been lying comatose in Jackson Square for more than a year, since the day she saved New Orleans from destruction by absorbing the blast of a nuclear explosion. For the past six months, her estranged parents had been fighting in court to obtain a court order allowing them to terminate their daughter's nutrition and hydration.

Jerusha could not believe they had actually won. "If they do this, what do the doctors say will happen to Bubbles?"

"No one's certain," said Ink, "but their best guess is that given the massive amounts of nutrients that Michelle has been consuming every hour, and with a body as dense and heavy as hers, the results would be very quick. Her bodily processes could begin to deteriorate almost immediately—increased heart rate, blood pressure, organ failure. Death in no more than three hours, maybe sooner." Ink sighed. "Or maybe she'll just starve to death."

On Thanksgiving. The LaFleurs had a ghastly sense of irony, Jerusha thought. "What can I do?" She was no lawyer. The Committee had no legal standing within the United States.

"You can help me stop Joey," Ink replied. "She's gone crazy. She's pulled up every halfway fresh corpse in the city, and some that aren't so fresh. She says she's going to kill the LaFleurs as soon as they show their faces in Jackson Square."

Hoodoo Mama. I should have known. Joey Hebert had been born angry, as far as she could tell, and being turned down by the Committee had not improved her disposition.

"She won't listen to me," Ink was saying, "and you're the only one in New Orleans who might have the power to stop her before someone gets hurt. But you gotta get down there quick. You hear me?"

The shouting in the background continued. *Joey,* Jerusha realized. Then Ink was yelling back. "*Damn it,* Joey. Calm down, girl. You're gonna bust an artery."

The phone went dead. "Ink?" Jerusha said.

Nothing.

She flipped the phone shut. The microwave bell rang in the kitchen. She could smell the turkey.

Jerusha put her phone in the pocket of her jeans and grabbed her keys.

The Clarke Household
Barlow's Landing, Massachusetts

"I SEE," MARGARET TIPTON-CLARKE said, in a voice that meant she didn't see at all. "So you're . . . dead?"

Jonathan Tipton-Clarke, or Jonathan Hive, but most often Bugsy, had known that bringing his girlfriend to Thanksgiving dinner was going to be tricky. He hadn't appreciated the full depth of the issue. His mother kept asking difficult questions. His older brother Robert and sister-in-law Norma were scowling over their plates of cranberry sauce and turkey like sour-faced bookends without the books. The twin sisters were grinning with near cannibalistic delight. It just wasn't going to be a good night.

Ellen was very pretty—thin, blond, dressed in a dark charcoal item that clung in all the right places without seeming slutty. It, like all of Ellen's best dresses, had been designed especially for her by the ghost of Coco Chanel. The cameo she wore at her neck looked like it had been picked to go with the outfit more than the other way around. Just to look at her, she fit perfectly with the Tipton-Clarke family decor. Classy, expensive without having neon "nouveau riche" on her forehead. The earring was maybe a little bit off, but that was really nonoptional.

True, she was almost two decades older than Jonathan, which would have been a little weird all on its own. More the issue was that she wasn't exactly his girlfriend. She was the ace who could channel the spirits of the dead. The dead like his girlfriend.

Aliyah didn't wear Ellen with quite the same style that Ellen wore the dress.

"Yeah," she said, using Ellen's mouth. "I . . . I died back when the Caliphate army was attacking the jokers in Egypt, right before they formed the Committee? If you read about it, they might have called me Simoon. That was my ace name on *American Hero*. There was an ace on the other side called the Righteous Djinn? In Egypt, I mean. Not on the show."

When Aliyah got nervous, she ran her sentences together and everything she said turned into a question. When Jonathan got nervous, bits of his body broke off as small, green, wasplike insects, so it was hard to really fault her. He took a bite of stuffing. It was a little on the salty side, as usual, but if he kept his mouth full he wouldn't have to talk to anyone. That seemed the best strategy.

"That must have been terrible for you, dear," his mother said.

"Oh, I don't remember it," Aliyah said. "I wasn't wearing my earring. At the time. I mean, I was a sandstorm when it happened, so it's not like I had any clothes on."

One of the twins, Charlotte he thought, leaned forward on her elbows. Her smile was vulpine. "That's just *fascinating*," she said.

"Well, Ellen can only pull me back from the last time I was wearing my earring."

"No," Charlotte (or maybe Denise) said. "I mean you fought *naked?*"

Aliyah blushed and stammered, her hands moving like they weren't sure where they were supposed to be. With a small internal sigh, Jonathan decided it was time to go ahead and lose his temper. "She was a sandstorm," he said. "Big whirly scour-your-flesh-to-the-bone sandstorm. The kind that could kill you."

Charlotte's smile turned to him. There was a little victory in it. *I could kill you, too*, he thought, and Charlotte yelped and slapped her thigh. She pulled up a small, acid-green body with crumpled wings.

"Oops," Bugsy said. "Sorry."

"You act like you can't control those things," Charlotte said. Or maybe Denise. "You aren't fooling anyone."

"Is it possible," Bugsy's older brother said in a strangled voice, "to have a simple, calm, normal family meal without going into detail about the naked dead women with whom my brother is sleeping?"

"Spirit of the season," Jonathan said. "I mean, unless there's something *else* to be thankful for."

"Excuse me," Aliyah said, stood up, and walked unsteadily from the room.

"So, Robert," Jonathan said. "Have you and Norma gotten knocked up yet, or have the doctors decided there's no lead in the old Wooster pencil after all?"

"That is none of your—"

"Oh, Robert, he didn't mean anything by—" their mother said.

"*Norma!*" Denise (or maybe Charlotte) said. "I've been so worried but I didn't dare—"

With his brother's penis squarely on the chopping block, Jonathan pushed his plate aside and followed Ellen to the den. The room glowed in the festal candlelight. Two wide sofas in leather the color of chocolate seemed cozy, looking out through the glass-wall picture window at the angry Atlantic Ocean. Ellen sat on one, legs tucked up under her. He could tell by the way she held herself that the earring wasn't in.

"I told you so," he said.

"You really did," Ellen said. "I'm sorry I didn't believe you."

"The nice thing about Jerry Springer is that you get to throw chairs. I never get to throw chairs."

"And your mother," Ellen said. "She's the worst of all."

"There is that Demon-Queen-Directing-Her-Monstrous-Horde quality to her. It was more fun when Aunt Ida was still around. She was *much* worse."

"Aliyah felt awful. I told her I'd apologize for her."

"For getting beaten up by my family? Doesn't that usually go the other way?"

"It usually does," Ellen said coolly.

Before Jonathan could think of a good answer, his cell phone started the ring tone he'd set aside for the United Nations. Committee business calling. He dug it out of his jacket pocket, held up a single finger to Ellen, and said hello.

"Bugsy! I hope I'm not interrupting," Lohengrin said.

"Not at all," Jonathan said. "What's up?"

Ellen rose, shaking her head slightly, and headed back toward the ongoing train wreck of the Tipton-Clarke Thanksgiving. Jonathan put one hand over his ear to block out the voices.

"Can you come to New York?" Lohengrin asked. "There's something we need to discuss. An assignment."

Jonathan nodded. Truth to tell, it was moments like these that made working with the United Nations fun. "You bet, buddy. I'll be there with bells on," he said. Then, "You know, I could probably have fit about three more b's in that if I tried. Betcha buddy, I'll be by with bells on my—"

"Jonathan? Are you okay?"

"I may be a wee teensy drunk," Jonathan said. "Or I might hate my family. Hard to tell the difference. I'll be in New York tomorrow. Don't worry."

Lohengrin dropped the line, and Jonathan put his cell phone away. The voices in the dining room had changed. With a sick curiosity, he made his way back to the table.

"You *always* did that, Maggie, ever since you were a little girl," Ellen said, pointing an antique silver butter knife in his mother's direction. "Salt, salt, salt. You'd think God never gave you taste buds."

His mother's cheeks had flushed and her lips pressed white and bloodless. Ellen turned to consider Jonathan, except whoever she was, it wasn't Ellen. The familiar eyes surveyed him slowly. She snorted.

"Aunt Ida?" he said.

"I like this Ellen of yours, Johnny," Ida said. "I'm surprised she puts up with you. Sit, sit, sit. I feel like I'm at the bottom of a well with you just looming there."

"How did—?" he began as he sat.

Ida held up the silverware. "I always said this set was mine, and now I've proven it, haven't I? Robert, dear? Pass the potatoes, and let's see if she's oversalted them, too. Maggie, stop looking at me like that. I was right, you were wrong, and no one is in the least surprised. Thanksgiving is a time for family. *Try* not to ruin it."

Stellar
Manhattan, New York

"ANA?" WALLY WHISPERED. "CAN I sit with you?"

"Sure."

Wally followed her through a maze of round tables draped in billowing tablecloths. The lights were set low; candlelight and the glow from the skyline glinted on wineglasses and silverware. He nodded or waved at the few folks he recognized.

Ana led him to a table near the middle of the room. Wally's own chair creaked precariously. He sat between Ana and the Llama. They'd never worked together, but Wally had met the South American ace at other Committee events. Wally always thought he looked a little like a giraffe, what with his long neck and all, but never mentioned it. "Hey, how ya doin', fella? Happy Thanksgiving."

"Hi," said the Llama, chewing on something. That seemed strange, since the waiters hadn't brought any food out yet. They didn't even have bread on the table.

The Llama seemed distracted. Wally realized he was busy glaring across the room at the Lama.

Wally turned to Ana. "So how's Kate these days?"

"Good, I guess. She's glad to be back in school, but it's probably kinda weird. I think she misses us. She doesn't miss this stuff, though." She pointed to the cyan United Nations banner hanging over the head table where Lohengrin, Babel, and a few others sat.

"Yeah." The Committee had lost much of its allure for Wally over the past couple of years. For some reason he kept sticking with it, even though he'd found better ways to make a difference in people's lives. A *real* difference. Plus, these shindigs weren't the same without the old crew.

As if reading Wally's mind, Ana asked, "Do you still keep in touch with DB?"

"Sure do." They'd gone to war together, Wally and the rock star. Twice. They'd been through a lot.

He looked around the room. Except for Ana, none of the people he knew best were around. In addition to Kate and DB, Wally missed Michelle, who was still down in New Orleans and apparently not doing too good. King Cobalt, his first friend from *American Hero*, had died in Egypt. So had Simoon, who had been pretty nice to Wally.

Except that she wasn't entirely dead, not all the time, anyway. Bugsy and Simoon were going out, which Wally couldn't begin to understand. All he knew was that Bugsy spent most of his time these days with Cameo, who had joined the Committee last year in New Orleans, before she lost her old-time hat. They were having their own Thanksgiving.

Thanksgiving was a time to be with family. But what family? More and more, his visits home to Minnesota made him feel lonely and isolated. He thought he'd found a family, of sorts, with the Committee. And that had even been true for a short time. But he didn't feel at home with the Committee any longer. And so Wally had tried to help other families, on his own, but now even that seemed to be going away.

A little cheer went up throughout the room when a stream of servers emerged from the kitchen. They brought out turkey, chicken, goose, sweet potatoes, mashed potatoes, stuffing, three kinds of gravy, cranberries, corn bread, spinach salad, fruit salad, and pumpkin, pecan, apple, and cherry pie. They even brought out a turducken. Wally wouldn't have known what that was if he hadn't heard Holy Roller and Toad Man discussing it once, back before the big preacher had left the Committee to return to his church in Mississippi. Wally missed him.

He couldn't imagine anybody eating so much food. And that made him think of Lucien, his little pen pal. A single table here probably held more food than his entire family saw in a month.

"You're looking glum," said Ana.

"Just missing folks, I guess."

"Yeah," she said.

"Like, see, I got these pen pals. It happened because I saw a commercial late at night during a Frankie Yankovic marathon. You know, for one of those setups where you send in a few dollars to help out a kid somewhere?"

Ana smiled. She took a drumstick from the platter at the center of the table. "That's great, Rusty."

"Well, I got a few of them. But this one kid, his name's Lucien, and me and he got to be pretty good friends, writing letters back and forth. But his last letter said—"

Babel started tapping her wineglass with a butter knife. It chimed through the dining room.

Lohengrin stood. He waited for a hush to fall over the room before speaking. The kitchen clamor ebbed and flowed as servers passed through double doors to the dining room.

"*Ja, ja.* Welcome. My friends, we are the United Nations Committee for Extraordinary Interventions." Polite applause. "Today we gather to celebrate our achievements and be thankful for the opportunities we've been given. And the world has much to be thankful for since our inception, no?" His laughter actually sounded like ho-ho-ho. Like Santa Claus, if Santa wore magical armor. Before meeting Lohengrin, Wally had never known anybody who laughed like that for real.

If Lucien and his family had much to be thankful for, it had nothing to do with the Committee. In fact, it seemed to be the only thing Rusty had done in the past couple of years that actually improved somebody's life. But it didn't even begin to make up for what he and DB had done in Iraq.

The German ace droned on and on, peppering his remarks with references to "my predecessor," as though there had been some kind of special ceremony to transfer the reins of power when he took over the Committee. Everybody knew that John Fortune had bowed out quietly but quickly after becoming a nat for the second time. Rumor had it he was traveling the world, though to what end, nobody could say.

But thinking about John Fortune and his travels gave Wally an idea.

Jackson Square
New Orleans, Louisiana

THE MOOD WAS UGLY in Jackson Square. The triple spires of St. Louis Cathedral glistened in their spotlights; nearby, Andrew Jackson waved his hat atop his rearing horse. That was normal enough, but as Jerusha approached, she realized that the crowd ahead of her was . . . wrong. The stench of death hung around them, and their faces were stiff and unresponsive.

Zombies.

There were at least a couple dozen, more than she'd seen Hoodoo Mama raise up for a long time. At least with Thanksgiving the usual crowds in Jackson Square were sparse, though there were still enough onlookers watching from a wary distance to make Jerusha nervous.

Joey and Juliet were standing at the makeshift wooden "shrine" that enclosed Bubbles, its planks adorned with ribbons and handwritten testimonials. The thick pipes of Michelle's feeding tubes stabbed into the white cloth that covered her body, which had sunk so deeply into the soft ground that pumps had to remove the water that would otherwise have flooded the depression. Jerusha could hear Joey shouting into the night. "Fuck them. Goddamn leeches. They stole her fucking money. Now they want to kill her, too? Well, *fuck* that."

Ink was standing next to Joey, an arm around her, her voice so quiet that Jerusha couldn't hear it. Whatever she was saying, Joey didn't like it. Her zombies muttered and groaned. "I ain't gonna let that that cocksucker of a father and her cunt mother screw Michelle again. I ain't." Her lips were pressed into a tight line. A hardness came over her thin face. She ran a hand through the tangled shock of brown hair, ruffling the bright red streak. "I'll fucking rip them both into a hundred fucking pieces. I swear."

"Ink, Joey," Jerusha said loudly, skirting the edge of the zombie crowd. "Listen, you can't . . ."

She stopped at the sound of sirens, cutting through the low whine of the pumps driving Michelle's feeding tubes. Along Decatur Street, a small motorcade pulled into the square, pulling up on the far side of Bubbles's shrine, near a large grey electrical box. Jerusha plunged a hand into the open zipper of the pouch at her waist, fingering the seeds inside.

NOLA SWAT police officers piled out of the first three black vans, their faces masked by riot helmets, armed with what looked to be shotguns. Ira and Sharon LaFleur emerged from a limousine, accompanied by another phalanx of policemen.

Jerusha had always pictured them as villains, monsters who would steal money from their child. She'd expected their sins to be written on their faces, but they weren't. Ira was balding and overweight, looking pudgy and ineffectual; Sharon's face was drawn and haggard and thin, but the lines were those of a model: like her daughter's face, what Bubbles might look like in another quarter century. They looked *ordinary*.

"*Motherfuckers!*" Hoodoo Mama shrieked, and her zombies howled with her. Ink had both arms around Joey, clinging to her desperately. Joey pointed at the LaFleurs. "You miserable cocksuckers! You stay the fuck away from her, you hear me!"

Sharon LaFleur looked at them, hand over mouth. The zombies started to shamble toward them. The cops shuffled nervously, weapons up and ready. "Joey, you can't!" Jerusha shouted.

Joey shook her head. "You kill her," she screamed at the LaFleurs, "and I'll just raise her up again. She'll be the biggest fucking zombie in the whole goddamn world. You hear me, you cocksuckers?"

Ira LaFleur nodded to the officers nearest the grey box, which now had a panel open. The low whine of the pumps driving Bubbles's feeding tubes suddenly vanished. The silence was more terrible than any sound could have been.

The zombies screamed as one, wordless. They advanced.

"Damn it." Jerusha pulled her hand from the pouch, fisted around the contents there. She flung them wide. As soon as the seeds hit the ground, they were rising, a wriggling carpet of vines that tore through the pavement of Jackson Square. Kudzu. Jerusha guided the growth in her mind, snarling the vines around the zombies' legs, bodies, and arms, encasing them in living green chains. She coiled them around Joey and Ink for good measure. Hoodoo Mama glared at her, cursing wildly.

The SWAT officers were piling back into the vans, hustling the LaFleurs back to their limo. With a scream of sirens, the cars backed away and sped off again.

"*Stop them!*" Joey screeched. Spittle was flying from her mouth. "God damn it, Gardener, you're a fucker just like them. Just like them. You're letting them kill her."

Jerusha had no answer. "I'm sorry," she told them.

"Fuck you're sorry," said Hoodoo Mama. "And fuck you, too, cunt. You better hope that Bubbles doesn't die. 'Cause if she does, you're next."

Stellar

Manhattan, New York

AFTER THE MEAL—AFTER the clink of silverware and the random chorus of burps and satisfied *mmmmm*'s died down, after the last slice of

pumpkin pie had been tucked away (Wally had two pieces), when most of
the conversation in the room was a hushed murmur as people slipped col-
lectively into a digestive stupor—Wally excused himself and went over to
Lohengrin's table.

Klaus was deep in conversation with Babel when Wally clanked up to their
table. They must have been discussing something pretty intense because it
took them a few seconds to notice Wally. He caught something about New
Orleans, Sudan, and the Caliphate before they tapered off to look up at him.
Babel grinned. "Happy Thanksgiving, Rustbelt."

Wally said, "Thanks. Um, you, too." He didn't know her very well, but she
made him uncomfortable. He remembered how she'd sabotaged DB when he
split with the Committee, and wondered if she'd do the same thing to him,
since he and DB were friends.

Lohengrin yawned. Two empty wine bottles rattled on the table when he
stretched his legs. He motioned for Wally to sit and join them. "A good
feast, *ja?*"

"Oh, you bet," said Wally, taking a chair. "I like them sweet potatoes
with the marshmallows on top. Real tasty." He nodded, and patted his
stomach. His cummerbund muted, ever so slightly, the *clang* of iron against
iron. "Hey, I have a question."

Lohengrin sat a little straighter. "What troubles you, my mighty friend?"

"Well, see, I was wondering if we'd be doing anything in Africa sometime soon. I mean, you know, the Committee."

Babel assumed the tone that people did so frequently around Wally. The
tone that spoke volumes about what they thought of him and his faculties.
"Well, Rustbelt, it's a very complicated situation. The Committee's involvement with Noel Matthews in New Orleans put us on precarious footing
with Tom Weathers, and by extension the Nshombos."

"Oh, sure. Sure. But I didn't mean about any of that. It's just, see, I have
this pen pal. My friend Lucien. He and his family live up in the Congo there-
abouts."

Babel cocked an eyebrow. "Pen pal?"

"I sponsor him. I send a few dollars every month and it pays for his school
and medicine and stuff."

"Ah." Lohengrin nodded. He approved of noble causes.

"Anyway, his last letter kind of worried me. He was real excited because
he'd been chosen to attend a brand-new school. But he said that the soldiers who picked him told him he wouldn't be allowed to write to me no

more. And that when Sister Julie tried to stop them from taking the last bunch of kids to the school—Sister Julie is a nun in his village, you see—well, he said they hurt her. And I thought, that doesn't sound right. I mean, what the heck kind of school has soldiers? So I figured, maybe the next time I go somewhere, you could send me to Congo and I could check in on him."

Babel said, "I don't think that's a good idea, Rustbelt. There's no telling how Weathers and the PPA would react if they believed the Committee was encroaching on their territory."

"But I wouldn't be, not really. I'd just be visiting Lucien and making sure the little guy is okay."

Again, that tone. "Yes, certainly. You know that, and we know that, but the Nshombos would never believe it. And, let's face it, you aren't inconspicuous. They'd know you were there. Ostensibly on Committee business."

Lohengrin yawned again. "Frau Baden is correct that the situation is complicated. We must be careful with the Nshombos." Wally slumped in his chair. "But," Lohengrin continued, solemnly putting a hand on Wally's shoulder, "your cause is just. I promise to do what I can to help your missing friend."

"Well, gosh. That's swell, Lohengrin." Wally practically leaped out of his chair, grinning. The Committee would help him go find Lucien! "I can't wait."

"Yes. I believe that if I ask him, Jayewardene will make careful inquiries through diplomatic channels."

Inquiries? Oh. Wally tried to hide his disappointment. "Right. That'll be a big help, no doubt. I sure do appreciate it."

He returned to his table, just long enough to say good night to Ana; the Llama had already left. Wally didn't much feel like hopping in a taxi when he got down to the street, so he started walking in the general direction of Jokertown.

A thin dusting of snow covered the sidewalks. It fell in large flakes that drifted slowly to the ground like cotton. The clouds overhead and the snow underfoot reflected the soft glow of the city in all its colors, making everything look like a Christmas tree decoration.

Back home, Wally and his brother Pete used to make snow forts during Christmas vacation. He remembered countless snowball fights on winter mornings, too, waiting for the school bus. Lucien had loved hearing about stuff like that; to him, snow was the white stuff on distant mountains. Wally had secretly hoped he'd get to take him to the mountains someday, so he could see the snow firsthand.

But Lohengrin and Babel had been pretty clear. If he wanted to go to Africa, he'd have to go privately.

The Winslow Household
Boston, Massachusetts

THEY FINISHED OFF THE evening playing bridge and eating another round of pie before retiring to Niobe's old bedroom. Niobe found this embarrassing and Noel found it charming. He investigated her bookcase filled with a collection of late Victorian and early twentieth-century children's books—*The Bird's Christmas Carol*, *The Secret Garden*, *The Little Princess*, *Little Lord Fauntleroy*. He rooted through the closet and discovered a stuffed animal collection (now consigned to the top shelf), and picked out a few choice specimens to take home to New York. *For our baby*, he thought, but neither of them gave voice to that. This was the fourth try, and they were both too superstitious to invoke the child out loud lest it lead to another miscarriage.

Noel read aloud from *Fauntleroy* until Niobe's eyelids dropped and her breathing slowed. "He had a cruel tongue and a bitter nature, and he took pleasure in sneering at people and making them feel uncomfortable. . . ." Noel's voice died away. He slowly slipped his arm from beneath her, snapped off the light, and settled down to sleep.

It took a long time because he kept replaying the conversation with Siraj, and wondering what it all meant.

Rusty's Hotel Room
Jokertown
Manhattan, New York

"UM, HI? DB?"

The phone receiver compressed the noise of a raucous party into a dull roar. "What? Who is this?"

"It's me, Wally."

A long pause. "Ollie?" DB sounded distracted. Then, more muffled, he shouted, "Hey! Leave that fucker for me!" This was followed by peals of high-pitched laughter. Wally had looked online; it was a little after eleven in Mumbai.

"No, *Wally*. You know, Rustbelt?"

Another pause. Then: "Rusty! How the hell are ya? Great to hear ya. Hey, guys, it's Rusty!"

This provoked a chorus of greetings from the other members of Joker Plague.

"Same to you, fella. Look, I was wondering—"

"You need tickets to the show? No problem! You've got a permanent backstage pass, you know that." Something shattered, followed by more groupie laughter. Bottom shouted something that Rusty couldn't quite make out. "Wait. You're in India?"

"What? No. But I was wondering, since your tour is winding up soon—"

"—Yeah, one more month, then we're back in the States. God damn it, S'Live, I told you to leave it—"

"—if you'd wanna go to the Congo—"

"—bongo drums? We don't play much world music—"

"—no, I said Congo, like the country—"

"—country? Yeah, I hate that shit, too. What the hell is that? Hey, Rusty, I gotta go, I think I smell smoke. Take care of yourself, pal!" *Click.*

Well, cripes. Wally had figured that if anybody would join him on a trip to Africa, it would be Drummer Boy. They'd been comrades in arms (and arms, and arms) more than once. But it seemed that DB was busy with his old life.

Wally thought about other folks he knew. Kate was real nice, but it sounded from Ana like she'd had enough of traveling for a while. He would have asked Ana, too, but she'd told him the Committee was sending her to China. The government there had specifically requested Ana's consultations on a series of giant dams they were building.

He toyed with the idea of contacting Jamal Norwood. Stuntman had probably learned a whole lot about finding missing people while working for SCARE. Plus, he was real tough. And he sorta owed Wally for all that stuff he said back on *American Hero*. But Jamal would never agree to help him. Plus, Wally didn't want to travel with somebody who disliked him so much. Even he could foresee an awkward and unpleasant conversation.

One more name sprang to mind: Jerusha Carter. Gardener's ace couldn't be better suited to traveling through Africa. She was perfect for the trip in just about every way. He even knew her, a little bit.

It took some calling around to other Committee members before he got

Jerusha's cell number. Wally reclined on the bed in his hotel room. The mattress groaned; somewhere halfway across the country, a telephone rang.

"Hello?" A weary voice, thick with fatigue. Behind it, what sounded like voices raised in quiet song, like they were singing hymns or something. Not like in church, though. It sounded more like a vigil.

"Um, hi. Jerusha?"

"Yes." Her voice got distant, and the background noise got louder, as if she was holding the phone away from her face to look at the caller ID. "Who is this?"

"It's me, Wally. Gunderson. You know, Rustbelt? We worked together when the Committee sent us to Timor."

"Oh, *Wally*. I thought I recognized your voice." A pause. "What's up?"

"I was wondering—um, are you okay? You sound real tired. No offense or anything."

"Uh . . . it's been a tough few days down here. Did you hear about Michelle? Her parents?"

"Yeah. It's a bad deal." The thought of Bubbles helpless like that—at the mercy of others—made him think of Lucien, and brought on another pang of anxiety.

"Really bad." Jerusha sighed, loudly. "Anyway. What's up?"

Wally didn't know the best way to broach the subject. He plunged ahead: "Do you wanna go to Africa with me?"

"Why is Lohengrin sending you to Africa?"

"He's not," said Wally.

Another pause. "Huh?"

Wally explained the situation.

"So . . . you want me to go to the PPA to help you find your pen pal?"

"Yep. Well, no, I mean, I thought we'd go to the Congo, where Lucien's from."

Jerusha said, "That's *in* the PPA."

"Oh."

"Ugh, Wally . . ." Wally recognized that tone. It was the sound of somebody cradling her head in her hands. "Say. Why did you ask me?"

Oops. "Well, you're real smart. And you know about jungles and stuff. And you're, um . . ."

"I'm what?"

"Black."

"Uh-huh." Jerusha's tone here was a little harder to read. Maybe he shouldn't have said that. "Look. What you're trying to do is very sweet. But I think you're biting off more than you can chew. Even with that giant jaw of yours. Besides, I have my hands full down here."

"What if I came and helped out?"

"That's nice of you, but it wouldn't change my answer."

"Oh."

"Sorry, Wally. Don't do anything rash, okay?"

"You bet."

Wally stared at the ceiling. *That's in the PPA.* He hadn't put that together before. He knew a little about the PPA; that whole mess down in New Orleans, Bubbles and all, was tied up with the PPA. He knew that much. But until she'd said it, he hadn't associated Tom Weathers and Dr. Nshombo and the PPA with Lucien's Congo.

All the more reason to go to Africa, and the sooner the better. All the more reason to find a traveling companion. But the more he thought about it, the more Jerusha seemed the best choice.

Friday,
November 27

The Winslow Household
Boston, Massachusetts

A LEGACY OF NOEL'S previous profession was an inability to sleep any deeper than a doze. He awakened when the mattress shifted as Niobe left the bed. Cold grey dawn seeped around the edges of the blue velvet drapes, and Noel could hear snow pecking at the windows. He snuggled deeper under the down comforter, and was headed back to sleep when a tiny whimper of fear from the bathroom sent him leaping out of bed. "Niobe!"

At the same moment she called out, "Noel!" The panic in her voice squeezed his heart.

He ran to the bathroom, the legs of his pajamas whipping at his ankles. She was sitting on the toilet with her arms wrapped around her stomach. He dropped to his knees in front of her.

"I'm cramping."

"Bad?" he asked.

"Not as bad as last time," she replied through white lips.

Oddly she was staring at a point where the tile met the porcelain side of the bathtub rather than at him. Noel had a sudden memory as they had stood on the rocky beach of a distant Scottish island, and she had told him how she had tried to cut off the damning mark of her jokerdom, and win back her parents' love. He glanced at the thick white scars that twisted across her tail. She had nearly bled to death in the bathroom of her family home. Noel realized this was the room. *And that bitch put us in here.* He again felt that shaking desire to kill his mother-in-law. "I'm taking you to the clinic."

"We can't just run off," Niobe called out as he ran back into the bedroom. "They'll be so angry."

"Watch me. And fuck them."

Noel pulled her long, fur-lined suede coat and his overcoat out of the closet. He returned to Niobe, got slippers on her feet, and tucked her into her coat. The hood framed her face. She looked like a figure on a Russian icon box. He slipped on his own slippers and guided her back into the bedroom.

He pulled back the blinds so he could map the sun's progress. *Come on, come on!* They couldn't lose another. Niobe couldn't take much more. He wasn't sure he could, either.

It was another four minutes before he could make the transformation to Bahir. The pajamas cut into his crotch, and the overcoat strained across Bahir's broad chest. It didn't matter. He would transform back once they reached the Jokertown Clinic.

Jackson Square
New Orleans, Louisiana

MICHELLE OPENED HER EYES.

Juliet, Joey, her mother and father, and a couple of people dressed in hospital scrubs were ringed around her. Her throat was raw, like when she had strep throat. She tried to speak, but she had no voice.

"She's alive!" Juliet said.

"You don't know that," snapped Michelle's mother.

"It could be a reaction to the feeding tube being pulled," said the woman in baby-blue scrubs.

Michelle tried to look around, but she couldn't move her head much. Behind her mother, there was a table crammed with flowers and candles. The floor under the table was thick with store-bought bouquets. She looked up. The ceiling was bare plywood and had water stains.

A TV hung from the far corner with the sound turned off. It was tuned to a news channel, and there were bulletins scrolling across the bottom of the screen. She caught the last bit of one story: ". . . and the latest contestant voted off Season Three of *American Hero* is . . ."

She blinked. It couldn't be Season Three. They hadn't even finished Season Two. She was supposed to do a guest shot on Season Two.

She looked down at herself.

She was huge. Bigger than huge. Enormous. Bigger. Humongous. What was bigger than humongous? She didn't even look like a girl anymore. They had draped something over her. A parachute maybe? She could feel the rolls of fat that rippled down her front. It was impossible for her to be this big.

It came back to her then. A spinning golden necklace. Drake grabbing his chest. His eyes. His eyes were white and glowed and burned. She had embraced him and—

No. No. No. No. NO!

Blythe van Rennsaeler
Memorial Clinic, Jokertown
Manhattan, New York

THE DARKNESS AND THE cold lasted the briefest second, and then they were standing just outside the emergency room of the Jokertown Clinic. Noel willed his body to shift back into his normal form. It felt like the muscles were crawling across his bones, and there was an ache in the bones themselves as he was returned to his normal height.

Niobe had already gone in ahead of him, and was talking to the joker receptionist. The clinic was relatively quiet at 7:00 A.M. There was only a wino sleeping in a corner and a joker mother clutching her four-year-old as he alternated between sobs and hacking coughs.

Niobe gazed at the little fellow with naked longing in her green eyes. Unlike his mother, he was completely normal though to Noel's mind the green snot crusting his upper lip and his beet-red face made him a more unlovely sight than her.

The receptionist made a call, and he and Niobe settled into chairs to wait. A television hung on the wall was set to MSNBC. Noel's attention was caught by the heading—THE SUDD. A helicopter shot was panning across an expanse of reeds and water. On bits of dry ground that humped like the backs of prehistoric water beasts hiding in the swamp, destroyed tanks belched smoke into the air. Bodies, doll-like at this height, floated in pools and bled onto the ground.

Noel read the scrolling subtitles. *The Sudanese government had voted to join with the Caliphate. Dr. Nshombo, leader of the People's Paradise of Africa, has charged the Sudanese with genocide against the non-Muslim black tribesmen of the south, and moved into the Sudan to protect them. Clearly a major battle between PPA and Caliphate forces has occurred.*

Noel turned away from the lure of the flicking box. It wasn't his problem. He was done with political games on a world stage. A pox on both of them.

But there was no way that Prince Siraj could be compared to the madman who led the armies of the PPA. Siraj was a cunning politician, and killed when expedient. Dr. Nshombo was a cold ideological killer. Tom Weathers was just a killer. *And they all hate you. Why not take one of them off the table? Make Siraj an ally rather than an enemy? You were close friends once.*

Because I don't know if I can trust him now. Those boys of Cambridge are dead, Noel replied to that part of himself that sometimes missed the excitement of the game and that sense of serving a greater cause.

Fifteen minutes later the centaur doctor came clattering through the door. Dr. Finn took Niobe's wrist in his hand, feeling for her pulse. "Worse or better?"

"Better," she said.

"That's good."

"If . . . if something were to go wrong . . . I won't try again. I can't watch any more of my children die."

Niobe wasn't just talking about the miscarriages. She was thinking of the hundreds of "kids" born from her ace power. Her "tail" was actually an ovipositor. Within minutes of sex, two to five eggs would move through the tail, be laid, and hatch into tiny children. They were usually aces, and their powers seemed to be linked to Niobe's needs at a given moment.

They were the primary reason she had been able to escape from a secure facility and help free the young boy whose nuclear ace had endangered them all. But these children only lived for a few hours or a few days. Their homes were filled with photographs of the kids. Niobe grieved for every one of them. The last four had been Noel's. He grieved for them.

One of the reasons Niobe—or Genetrix as they had called her at BICC— had been studied was her ability to reverse the wild card odds. Instead of

ninety percent black queens, her clutches were ninety percent aces. She and
Noel had hoped that those odds would continue when they tried to conceive a normal baby.

Unfortunately that hadn't been the case.

Like every other ace and joker/ace trying to have a baby, they had the
same devastating odds of a black queen. Add to that the fact that Noel was a
hermaphrodite and functionally sterile, and the odds of Niobe every achieving her dream of motherhood seemed remote . . . until they came to the
Jokertown Clinic, where more authorities on the wild card practiced than
in any other place in the world. Dr. Clara van Rennsaeler had designed an
ingenious plan of treatment, which her husband Dr. Bradley Finn was
implementing.

First he pumped Niobe full of hormones so her ovaries produced multiple eggs. Then Finn had combined the nucleus from one of Niobe's wild
card ovipositor eggs with Noel's barely mobile sperm and a real egg from her
womb. By Noel's count they'd discarded forty-three zygotes. Sad little crea-
tures who had begun and ended their lives in petri dishes when they turned
out to be black queens or jokers. Four had been viable, but they'd lost three
to miscarriages.

And now this one. They knew the sex—male. They knew he would be an
ace. Finn told them that if they reached sixteen weeks they were home free.
But now . . .

"Let's see what we've got." The centaur doctor led them out of the waiting room and into the examination room. Noel waited just beyond the
screening curtains while Finn and a female nurse examined Niobe. A few
moments later the steel rings chattered as Finn pulled back the curtain.

Niobe was beaming.

"We're good," the joker doctor said. "Thirteen weeks and counting.
We're not going to lose this little guy." He made it sound like a vow.

Noel stepped up to the bed, and was surprised when Niobe took his
hand and pulled him down. "Sit down before you fall down," she said.

Noel realized that relief had left him limp. "What caused the cramping?"

"Just a little gas," Finn replied.

Niobe hung her head, taking refuge behind her mane of chestnut hair.
"I'm sorry."

"No problem. I understand why you're jumpy as a cat," Finn said.

"Can you blame us?" Noel snapped. Niobe shushed him, and stroked
her hand down his arm.

"No, of course not. Not after three miscarriages," Finn soothed. "But we're in good shape."

Noel looked at his wife's wan face, and suddenly hugged her tight.

Finn cleared his throat. "I know you don't want to take anything," he said. "But I can prescribe a mild sedative."

Niobe was already shaking her head.

"Just to take the edge off."

A more emphatic shake.

Finn sighed. "All right." He tapped Noel on the shoulder. "Take her home and keep her happy, okay?"

Noel nodded, and acknowledged to himself that going off to Baghdad would definitely not keep her happy.

Louis B. Armstrong
International Airport
New Orleans, Louisiana

THE FIRST THING WALLY noticed as he tromped down the jetway was the smell.

New Orleans smelled different from Manhattan. It didn't smell like sidewalk garbage and truck exhaust; it smelled, faintly, of earth and water. There was humidity in the air, too, which along with the wet smell reminded him of summers at the lake cabin, back home in Minnesota. It had been that way the first time he came here, too, back when Bubbles saved the city.

Thinking about Michelle saddened him. Part of him had never wanted to come back here, and part of him felt badly for not visiting Michelle.

He waited in the airport, watching people buff the floors for an hour, before calling Jerusha. He figured she might not be that happy to hear from him again, and that would only be worse if he woke her up. Was she an early riser? They hadn't shared a tent in Timor, like he and DB had done a number of times, so he had no idea. DB snored.

"Hello?" Her voice didn't sound gravelly, like most people when awakened by the phone. *Whew.*

"Jerusha? This is Wally."

"Oh, hey, Wally. Look, I hope you're not upset about yesterday—"

"Nah, I understand. I did sorta spring the whole thing on you outta the blue."

"Well, yeah. I'm glad you understand."

"Sure. But hey, can I show you something? It'll be real quick, I promise." Farther down the terminal, a buzzer launched into a series of short, loud bursts. A baggage carousel creaked to life.

Jerusha heard it, too. "Where are you right now?"

"I'm at the airport. I caught a flight."

"Wally . . ." She was doing it again—cradling her head. He could tell.

He said, "It won't take long."

A sigh. And then: "I don't know why, but I spent a lot of time yesterday thinking about your trip. So, I do have some advice for you."

Wally sat up straighter. "Wow! That's great!" His voice echoed through the carousels. A few heads turned among the people waiting for their bags to come tumbling down the conveyor belt. "Um, where should I meet ya?"

"I'm with Michelle right now, in Jackson Square. Any taxi driver can take you here."

Wally thanked her and rang off. He hiked his backpack over his shoulder and tromped off in search of a taxi stand.

As often happened when Wally used a taxi, the driver heard his accent and immediately assumed Wally was an easy way to make a few extra bucks. Wally's taxi drivers tended to take long, circuitous routes that ran up the meter. Usually he didn't mind; he liked seeing the sights in unfamiliar places. He'd been here before, so he got impatient when the driver tried pointing out some of the sights in the French Quarter. But the driver waived the fare when he learned that Wally knew Michelle.

Jackson Square was a little different than he'd last seen it. For one thing, it looked like they'd had a pretty bad kudzu infestation not too long ago. Most of it had been cut away, but he could see tendrils here and there on the sides of booths and poking up through cracks in the pavement. *Weird.*

But the main change was the wooden enclosure beneath the statue in the center of the square. It was covered with flowers, candles, cards, and home-made signs. Prayers and thank yous. The flowers and signs fluttered in the breeze; Wally caught a whiff of magnolias. The wind rattled the slats of the shrine where a pair of nails had come loose. Wally peered through the gap. He glimpsed something pale. It took a few seconds before he realized that he was staring at the white cloth draped over Michelle's body. That made him want to cry.

Wally strolled around the shrine, reading signs and cards until he found the entrance. A cop waved him through the gate. Jerusha must have told her he was coming.

If the tiny glimpse he'd had of Michelle from outside made him feel sad, what he saw inside made him feel rotten. Her body—she wasn't recognizable, but who else would it be?—quivered beneath bolts of cloth, like the biggest dress he'd ever seen. She smelled . . . not good. A water pump hummed to itself, sucking away the water that continually seeped into Michelle's crater.

There were bundles of pipes, too, draped across her. Feeding tubes, he realized. They were still. Silent.

"Hey, Wally. Over here." Jerusha waved at him from halfway around the enclosure.

Wally waved back. He trotted over to her, his iron feet echoing on what had once been a sidewalk and was now the floor of Michelle's shrine. "Holy cripes," he said. "Poor Michelle. How is she?"

Jerusha frowned at him. "She's still alive, if that's what you mean. But she's still unresponsive, too."

"I wish there was something we could do," he said.

"I like to think that deep down she knows we're here."

Huh. "Hey, Michelle," he said. "Hang in there."

Jerusha looked at him sideways, a funny look in her eye. "Come on. Let's get something to eat," she said.

She led him across Decatur Street, to a place called Café du Monde. It smelled like chicory and fresh doughnuts. They took a seat outside, at a small round table that gave them a clear view of Michelle's enclosure. There wasn't room for his legs under their table, so he sat sideways. Wally ordered hot chocolate and a plate of fancy French doughnuts heaped with powdered sugar. Jerusha got coffee.

"Okay," she said, after they'd settled in. "What's so important you had to fly all the way down here to show me?"

Powdered sugar from Wally's lips snowed into his backpack as he fumbled with the zipper. He pulled out the three-ring binder where he kept the letters from his pen pals. Wally chanted off their names as he flipped through the binder. "Marcel, Antoinette, Nicolas . . ." He found the first page of Lucien's section, and held it out to Jerusha. "This is my friend Lucien," he said. In the photo, a little boy treated the camera to a wide, gap-toothed grin. He wore a brown-and-white-striped T-shirt that was easily three sizes too big for him. He had knobby knees, and his shaved head made his ears look ridiculously large. He was giving the camera a thumbs-up.

Jerusha looked at the photo. She asked, "Did you put this binder together just for the purpose of coming down here and showing it to me?" She sounded surprised, but not in a bad way. Almost like he'd done something good but he didn't know what. If anything, she'd sounded a little bit annoyed when he'd said he was in town.

"Nah. I didn't want to lose any letters." Wally turned the page. "This is the first one I received from Lucien." Like the photo, he kept the letter in a laminated sheet protector. He mentally recited the letter while Jerusha read the scrawly handwriting. *Dear Wally, My name is Lucien I am ate years old. I live in Kalemie . . .*

Quietly, almost to herself, Jerusha said, "Huh. Smart kid." She asked, "When did you start doing all this?"

"A while back. After me and DB went to the Caliphate."

A memory grabbed him. Instead of sitting in a café, he was on the deck of an aircraft carrier, drinking beer with DB while the sun set over the Persian Gulf.

Hey, Rusty.

Bad deal, huh.

Yeah. The fucking worst.

Kids. I don't want to fight kids.

None of us should have had to.

Jerusha's voice brought him back to the present. "Okay, I'll bite. Can I see the last letter he sent?"

Wally found the page for her. Jerusha read it, looking thoughtful.

"So, what are you thinkin'?" he asked.

"So, what are you thinkin'?" Rusty—Wally—asked.

Jerusha had never seen the Café du Monde so quiet and empty, especially this early in the morning. People were drifting in from the street to buy their paper bags of beignets and café au lait. A few of the other tables were occupied, but no one sat near them. Perhaps it was Wally's bulk and his appearance. Certainly it wasn't Jerusha—she wondered how many of the patrons recognized her at all, an ordinary-looking black woman except for the belt with many pouches around her waist. The flashes of tourist cameras were constant, though, and the staff kept eyeing their table uneasily.

What are *you thinking?*

Now that she'd listened to Wally, now that she'd seen his binder, she wasn't quite so certain anymore. She'd come here with the intention of giving Wally a firm "no" and trying to talk him out of this entirely. Now . . .

The picture of Lucien stared up at her. She could see the scratches on the plastic sheet protector from Wally's metal fingers; there were a *lot* of scratches. He pawed through that binder frequently, then. And his mouth had been moving as she had read the boy's poorly scrawled letter—he'd obviously memorized it.

Wally's simple tenderness and compassion made her want to hug him. She just wasn't sure it made her want to go with him.

Jerusha sipped at her coffee. The cup rattled on the table as she set it down. "I've been looking at maps, and I called Babel and talked to her a bit after your phone call." Jerusha saw the hope rising in Wally's eyes with her statement, and she frowned in an effort to quash it. *You're not doing this. You're not.* "Wally, she's really not happy with the idea of you going to Africa, and she's doubly not happy with you taking another Committee member with you. . . ." Jerusha paused, wondering if she really wanted to say the next words. "*If* I did this," she said, with heavy emphasis on the first word and a long pause after the phrase, "or no matter *who* ends up going with you, Wally, I agree with Babel that you don't want to go directly into the PPA. What looks best to me would be flying into Tanzania and crossing over Lake Tanganyika, especially since you say that Lucien's in Kalemie, right on the lake."

The hope in Wally's face was now transcendent and obvious. "So . . . you're coming with me?"

Sure. I'm black, aren't I? she wanted to retort angrily, but she only shook her head. "I still have work here. All the marshlands that need to be reclaimed before the next big storm hits here . . ." *Alone. Out in the swamp. Alone.*

Wally looked down at the table, dusted with the remnants of beignets. "I guess you make the plants grow a lot faster . . ." She saw him start to rise, his shoulders lifting. "Well, thanks for looking at those maps. That will help." His face scrunched up stiffly, the stiff iron skin over his eyes furrowing. "So where's this Tanzania place?"

Jerusha sighed. "Tanzania is . . ." she began. Stopped. *He won't last five minutes out there on his own.* She realized that somewhere in the midst of this, she'd made the decision. *What's here for you? You've nothing. No friends, just Committee work. And when Michelle dies, now you'll get the blame for that, not the Committee. You have a chance to save a life. . . .*

"Oh, hell," she said. "I'll show you on a map on the way over."

Jackson Square
New Orleans, Louisiana

MICHELLE REACHES A HAND out in front of her face. Five fingers. *That's good.* She pulls her legs up to her chest, reaches down, feels her feet. "That's better," she says. Even though she's in the pit again, she's happy about her feet and hands being back.

The spider pops down in front of her, points up to the edge of the pit. "Yeah, leopards, I know. I'm really the wrong person to try and scare with kitties."

The spider grabs Michelle's hair. Its body lengthens and grows and the four middle legs shrink into its torso. The mandibles slide back into its head and the eight eyes move toward each other until there are only two.

Sitting on Michelle's lap is a little girl, maybe eight or nine. She wears a threadbare dress. The pattern is faded, and in the dim light of the pit it's a mottled grey. The girl places her hand over Michelle's mouth, then leans forward and whispers in her ear.

Michelle whispers back, "I can't understand you."

The girl pulls away from her, and a tear slides down her cheek. Michelle reaches up and wipes it away. "I'm sorry," she says.

The girl puts her hands on either side of Michelle's temples. The girl shuts her eyes and suddenly Michelle is slammed by a barrage of images.

Trees limbs whip her face as she runs. Vines grab at her legs, but she can't stop. She can hear her own harsh breathing. Are they closer now? Close enough that they can reach out and . . . a claw rips open her back.

She shrieks. Warm blood wells up and burns. She trips and begins to fall.

Wait a minute, Michelle thinks. *Claws don't do anything to me.* She reaches up and gently pulls the girl's hands away.

The girl gazes at Michelle with such longing and pain it makes her want to cry. Michelle reaches out and touches her own hands to the girl's temples, imagines pointing at herself, whispers, "Michelle."

An image blossoms in Michelle's mind. It's the girl in her lap, but now she's wearing a pale blue checkered dress. Her hair is plaited with a pretty pink headband. The girl points to herself and says, *"Adesina."*

United Nations
Manhattan, New York

THE UNITED NATIONS PERCHED at the edge of Manhattan like the guest at a party who really needs to leave now, but has just one more very important thing to say.

Bugsy showed his ID to the guards at the front who all knew him anyway, and took the brushed steel elevator up to the seventh floor. In the brief time that the Committee had existed, they had commandeered much more space than Bugsy would have expected the international bureaucracy to permit. Having a lot of superhuman powers probably helped with that.

Lohengrin's office was on the western side, its windows facing out toward the skyscraper mosh pit of uptown. The hallways were filled with people in thousand-dollar suits looking harried. He nodded at the people who nodded to him and ignored the ones that didn't.

It was getting harder and harder to keep track of who exactly was with the Committee. It seemed like every time he turned around, it was *Let me introduce Glassteel. He can shatter anything made from hard metal. Or Noppera-bo here can mimic anyone's appearance.* Then Bugsy would shake hands (with Noppera-bo it had been particularly creepy since she'd taken on his face as soon as their fingers touched), exchange some pleasantries, and scurry off to someplace he could add their names into his database. Even so, he forgot the newbies more often than he remembered them.

Lohengrin, at least, was familiar. The long, blond hair actually looked really good with a dark grey power suit. Maybe a little tired around the eyes, but that went with the suit, too.

Bugsy closed the office door behind him and plopped down on the couch while the Teutonic God finished his phone call. "No," he said. "I have nothing to do with the prosecution on a day-to-day basis. You'll have to call the World Court. At the Hague." He put down the handset with a sigh.

"Highwayman's lawyers still giving you shit?" Bugsy asked.

"Captain Flint today," Lohengrin said. *CAHptain flEHnt*. No one could do round vowel sounds like the Germans. Except maybe the Austrians. And the Dutch. "There was a time, my friend, that I believed this would be fulfilling work. There are weeks I spend fighting and fighting and fighting and at the end, I think I might just as well have stayed at home."

It had been a long time since they'd gotten drunk and burned Peregrine's house down. There weren't many people Bugsy had actually known that long. Not that were still alive, anyway.

"Brokering world peace keeping you busy," he said, his tone making it an offer of sympathy.

"Water rights. Human rights abuses. The slave trade. I come in every morning, and I find something new and terrible. And every afternoon, I find why we can do nothing direct. Nothing final. I am becoming tired," Lohengrin said, then sighed. "What do you know about the Sudd?"

"Their second album sucked."

Someone in the next office ran their shredder for a second. "You don't know what I'm talking about, do you?" Lohengrin said.

"Yeah, not really. No."

Lohengrin nodded like he'd just won a bet with himself and leaned forward over his desk. "The Muslim government of the Sudan has taken steps to join their nation to the Caliphate."

"Ah," Bugsy said. "That's a bad thing."

"No," Lohengrin said. "That's the background."

"That's not the problem?"

"No."

"Ok-ay."

"The People's Paradise of Africa," Lohengrin said, "under the leadership of Dr. Kitengi Nshombo, has accused Khartoum of enacting a policy of genocide against the black tribal population of the south and west Sudan."

"Got it. Genocide. Problem."

"No," Lohengrin said.

"Genocide not a problem?"

"Genocide isn't happening. It is an excuse. The PPA has manufactured evidence and generated propaganda to make a case for the invasion of the Sudan. Its forces are making incursions across the border, and the Caliphate has mobilized to defend Sudanese national territory. Yesterday there was a battle in the Sudd. A terrible battle."

"And that's the problem, right?"

"Yes," Lohengrin said. "In the bigger picture, that is the problem. But it gets worse. The PPA forces are being led by Tom Weathers. The Radical."

Bugsy sat up straighter. "Hold it," he said. "Same guy who tried to set off Little Fat Boy and nuke New Orleans last year?"

"Same guy, *ja*."

"I don't like him much, you know. He tried to kill me. I mean, I don't like the Caliphate much either. They tried to kill me too."

"Tom Weathers tried to kill many hundreds of thousands of people," Lohengrin said.

"Yeah. And I was one of them."

"The PPA has been a destabilizing influence for years. Now they have begun to use aces to further their own political agenda."

The silence was a hum of climate-controlled heating and the distant ringing of phones. Lohengrin looked serious and waited for Bugsy to work through the implications.

"World war," Bugsy said. "Only fought with aces. Meaning probably the Committee."

"And a great many dead people," Lohengrin said.

"What about getting Little Fat Boy back in play? A fourteen-year-old nuke with a personal grudge against Weathers should rein the PPA in, right?"

"*Ra,*" Lohengrin said. "His name is Ra now, and no. So long as Old Egypt is not attacked, the Living Gods are determined to stay out of the conflict."

"How very Swiss of them."

"There is a further problem with Tom Weathers. We've always known that Weathers had more powers than most aces. Insubstantiality. Strength. Ultraflight. Heat beams. We know he was involved in the battle in part because these powers were in play. But other powers have been reported as well. The wave of darkness? The terrible mauling of the bodies?"

"You think he's like the Djinn?" Bugsy said, sitting forward on the couch. Nothing took the humor out of a situation like the Djinn. "You think Weathers is picking up new powers."

"I do not know," Lohengrin said. "New powers. Or new allies. We know little about the man himself. Where he comes from, how he drew the wild card, what his weaknesses might be. What exactly his powers are. That is what I want you to uncover, Jonathan. Tom Weathers is likely the most powerful ace in the world, he is starting a war, and I know nothing substantial about him."

"And so," Bugsy said, "who the fuck is the Radical?"

Unnamed Island
Aegean Sea, Greece

"DADDY!"

The woman who came flying at him across rocky soil tufted with pale green grass was tall and slender. Despite the fact her handsome face was clearly middle-aged, it showed few lines. Her hair, long and blond, had begun by slowly evident degrees to turn to silver. Yet her manner was that of a seven-year-old girl.

A very happy one. She caught him in a hug that for all his superhuman strength still almost overbalanced him. She was just four inches shorter than his six-two.

He kissed her. "Sprout. Hey, sweetie." He tousled the long straight hair. "I missed you."

"I missed you, too. Can we go to the park soon?"

"Aye, that's a good idea," said Mrs. Clark, emerging from the modest field-stone cottage behind her. "It's not fit for her to spend all her days cooped up here alone, with no one for company but an iPod and a dried-up old biddy like me."

"I wouldn't call you dried up, Mrs. Clark," he said, past the woman's cheek, wet with happy tears.

"You'd not dare."

"You got that right."

This was true. The caretaker was a middle-aged to elderly New Zealander, half Maori with a crisp Scots brogue. Her coloration and build were those of a brick wall; her tight bun of curly hair was nearly the same hue. Sprout loved her. She treated Sprout with patient cheerful firmness and took absolutely not ounce one of shit from anybody else. Not even Tom.

Which was fine. It was what he paid her for. Fantastically well, he vaguely gathered. Unlike most of the self-proclaimed socialist revolutionaries he met, Tom had no interest in money whatsoever; it was one of the reasons he always wound up getting pissed off at the posers, and then there was trouble. Dr. Nshombo—more often Alicia—always gave him whatever he asked for. Most, in fact, went toward keeping his daughter well cared for and as happy as possible in a succession of the remotest locations Earth provided.

It was the only way he knew of keeping her safe from that teleporting puke. Until he hunted him down and killed him, of course.

"I could use a day's shopping as well, I admit," Mrs. Clark said. "Time to myself and a few necessities for the child and me. Maybe tomorrow, Mr. L?"

She didn't even try to pronounce the name he gave her, which was Karl Liebknecht. Among the things he paid her so well for was not to wonder about such things as why his daughter sometimes called herself by the last name Weathers, and other times Meadows. Or why the daughter looked older than her father. Her main concern was that there was no funny business between her employer and her charge. Once he had convinced her of that, she was content to live in isolation with her charge, so long as she got the occasional day off in civilization. And in between had a sufficient supply of mystery novels.

"Tomorrow?" his daughter said, blue eyes shining eagerly. "You promise?"

He nodded. "I promise."

Sprout hugged him fiercely. "I wish I could stay with you, Daddy."

"Someday you can, sweetie. Someday. But I got some things to *take care of* first."

Noel Matthews's Apartment
Manhattan, New York

NIOBE WAS SLEEPING, WORN-OUT by the emotional upheaval of the past few hours. Noel wandered around the apartment they had rented while they underwent the fertility treatments. It had come furnished with sofas and chairs designed more for magazine covers than the human body. They had tried to personalize an impersonal space by putting up lots of framed photos—most of them of Niobe's "children"—the little aces who had lived and died like mayflies. Noel found the pictures depressing, but they were important to Niobe so he never said a word. His own efforts had consisted of leaving magazines piled on the glass coffee table and used teacups on the side tables. Niobe had also crocheted an afghan to throw across the black leather and chrome sofa.

Three more weeks and we can really go home. Noel entered the kitchen and set about brewing a pot of tea. He realized he was hungry and set out a muffin. His back felt tight. He hadn't worked out in weeks and hadn't attended a karate class in months. The fact that he had been complacent suddenly alarmed him, and he decided to get back to the gym.

He snapped on the TV in the kitchen, headed to CNBC for the latest financial news, and found himself passing through CNN. He caught a quick flash of the Presidential Palace in Baghdad and a grim-faced Prince Siraj surrounded by security rushing up the steps. Siraj looked old. Shockingly old.

I need your help. . . . I really do need your help.

His old friend's words echoed filled with sadness, reproach, and might-have-beens.

Noel pulled out his phone and dialed. "What exactly do you want me to do?" he said.

Jackson Square
New Orleans, Louisiana

MICHELLE WAS IN THAT strange room again. Juliet and Joey were there. But her mother and father were gone now.

Her throat was still brutally raw. She could barely swallow, much less try to speak. Her arms and legs were as useless as her throat.

And the power was like napalm in her veins. *Drake*, she thought. *Oh, God, Drake. What happened? Did I kill him? Did Sekhmet kill him? Tom Weathers? Was that wound from the medallion worse than it seemed? And how am I not dead? How are we all not dead?*

"Wha . . ." Her voice was a rusty hinge. Her throat felt as if it were being stabbed by a knife when she swallowed.

Juliet started crying, and Michelle wanted to comfort her. To tell her it was all right. Whatever had happened to Michelle had clearly hurt Juliet. Juliet didn't even have any tats scrolling across her body.

Michelle closed her eyes. Maybe if she went back to sleep, she'd wake up later and everything would be all right.

◆

Saturday, November 28

Presidential Palace
Baghdad, Iraq
The Caliphate of Arabia

THE SCENT OF DUST, dried lemons, and saffron seemed to pierce not only his sinuses, but his heart.

Noel staggered, and rested his hand against the stone wall. It was hot to the touch. He drew in another deep breath and more scents were added—kerosene from countless cookstoves, the wet smell of donkey, incense from the nearby mosque. The sun beat down on his head and warmed his shoulders. He could almost feel the cold fogs of New York and England leaching from his pores. *Yes,* he thought somewhat ruefully as he stepped out of the alley, the hem of his robe brushing at his heels. *I am one of those desert-loving Englishmen.*

The music of spoken Arabic fell like glittering notes all around him, but the point of the conversations were dark and somber. Too many fathers, brothers, husbands, and sons had marched off to the Sudd, and too few had been heard from again. Speculation ran wild in the streets.

As he walked by the palace he kept touching the dark glasses that disguised his swirling golden eyes, and he kept the tail of his *keffiyeh* across his face. Not that he expected to be recognized. When he'd developed his new male avatar he had made certain that Etienne was clean-shaven. But golden eyes were always going to be a problem.

Noel knew this city almost as well as he knew London. He had lived a second life here as Bahir, the Sword of Allah, the Caliph's ace assassin. He had even taken a wife, whom he'd put aside for barrenness last year. It had been entirely his fault. He was a hermaphrodite, and basically sterile. It hadn't been easy for Finn to find a few viable sperm. Luckily the little fellows hadn't had to make their way upstream all on their own.

What would have happened if he and Gamal had undergone the fertility treatments? But thank God they hadn't. She had been just another pawn as he served as an agent for the British Secret Service. That was another life, a life he'd left behind.

Except here he was, armed with three pistols and four knives and scouting out the lay of the land. He had told Siraj he would come. He had even told him when, but Noel wouldn't keep that appointment. He would arrive earlier, at a time of his choosing. A time when every good Muslim would be at prayer.

The call from the minarets began. Achingly beautiful, it was an echo across the centuries. Noel reflected that the Catholic Church should never have abandoned the Latin Mass. They had lost that link to history.

The streets emptied. Noel ducked behind a parked truck, stared narrowly at the palace, pictured Siraj's office, and teleported. There was the faintest *pop* as his arriving body displaced air. The man kneeling on his prayer rug, forehead pressed to the floor, didn't react.

Noel studied Siraj's vulnerable back. It would be so easy to remove this threat forever. One shot. Done.

But was Siraj actually the worst of his problems? Tom Weathers was a far more dangerous enemy, and Siraj and Weathers were locked in a bitter war. *The enemy of my enemy.*

Noel pulled out a pistol, moved quickly to Siraj's side, and joined him on the floor, while at the same time pressing the barrel of the gun into the other man's side.

Siraj gasped. His expression was both angry and amused. After a moment he looked back down at the floor and resumed his prayers. Noel joined in. They finished, and both pushed up until they were sitting on their heels.

Siraj looked again at the gun. "Are you going to kill me?"

"Not today."

"That's probably wise. You see, I've prepared a number of packets with information regarding England's crack assassin and his family connections."

At this oblique reference to Niobe, fury seemed to claw across the inside of Noel's skull. His finger began to tighten on the trigger.

Siraj sensed Noel's rage for he added quickly, "And if I die by assassination those packets will be sent. To the World Court, to the press . . ." He paused for maximum effect. "To Tom Weathers."

Noel forced himself to relax.

"That's better. Would you like a drink?" Siraj moved to a table and lifted a carafe out of an ice bucket.

"What is it?" Noel asked.

"Fruit juice."

"Still being a good Muslim, I see."

The sigh seemed to shake the prince's body. "On days like this, it isn't easy." Siraj set the carafe back into the ice. He paced the office, clasping and unclasping his hands. "What happened to the boys of Cambridge?"

"They grew up." Noel paused. "And discovered the world was complicated."

"We thought we could save it."

"Yes . . . well . . . my goals are more modest now."

"Yes, I heard you got married. Congratulations."

"Thank you."

"A very different look," Siraj said. "How do you do it?"

He seemed reluctant to get to the point. Noel was willing to wait for a little while. He had told Niobe he was going to England to talk with his manager. "Simple redistribution of mass," he answered. "Etienne is taller and thinner than Bahir. Losing the beard and mustache is easy." Noel touched the frame of his dark glasses. "The eyes are harder. They never change."

Siraj walked behind his desk, randomly moved a few papers, turned, and gazed out the window. The hands clasped behind his back were still writhing as if he were choking something.

"So, what do you want?" Noel finally asked.

"I need to see what happened. I need you to take me to the Sudd."

"You don't have a helicopter?"

"You're more subtle than a helicopter," came the dry reply. "Why are you so reluctant? This is a small thing when compared to the actions you took to put me here."

Noel briefly closed his eyes and remembered the night of chaos and death when he'd killed the Nur, clearing the way for Siraj to take control of the Caliphate. He was supposed to have been a compliant puppet for Britain's ambitions.

It hadn't worked out that way.

"That was another life. I'm different now. I'm married. I'm going to be a father. I do my shows. I don't concern myself with politics."

Noel felt a blaze of anger when Siraj's lips curled into a smile. "You must be bored stiff," the prince said, and Noel's anger was swept away by a sudden cascade of laughter.

Suddenly they were whooping, struggling to catch their breaths. Siraj wiped away tears of laughter. "Well?" he asked.

"Oh, all right. One last adventure before staid middle age overtakes me. But remember, I can still kill you."

"And I can still ruin you."

Jackson Square
New Orleans, Louisiana

A FLASH OF FIRE. The smell of bacon.

Not bacon—searing flesh. And it isn't fire, either. It's raw power right before it transforms into something else—something more specific.

And now there's a bunny.

"Fuck the damn bunny."

Michelle doesn't need to look to know who it is.

"Hey there, Joey," she says. "Are we going to have zombies, too? 'Cause you know I love me some zombies."

Hoodoo Mama crouches down in front of her. "This is no way to run a fucking railroad, Bubbles. Cocksuckers out here want you gone, baby, gone. You can't stay like this."

Michelle can't look at Joey. Not after what they did.

"What? After we fucked?" Joey says. A group of zombies appears behind her. *Damn it,* Michelle thinks. *It's my dream and there are still zombies.*

"Shit, Bubbles, if you get like this every time you tear off a piece . . ."

"Okay, that is so not what happened!" Michelle yells. But she remembers what went on between them and feels ashamed and aroused.

"Don't you understand?" Michelle wails. "I betrayed Juliet. Why did I do that? And I'm now the size of a elephant and, apparently, too large to move or be moved. Oh, and if I'm not mistaken, I think I have the power of a nuclear explosion in me."

The zombies vanish. Joey stands alone on a blighted landscape. She's frail, tiny, and anyone could hurt her.

Then Michelle is back in the pit. Adesina is there. Her face is obscured by her hair come undone from its braids. She isn't wearing the faded dress anymore. Her body is barely covered by rags.

"Adesina," she says softly. Michelle crawls to her. She tries not to think about the corpses. She brushes the hair from Adesina's face. A dark bruise swells on the girl's left cheek. There are half-healed cuts on her chin and on her forehead.

"Why are you in my dreams?" she asks. Michelle puts her hands on Adesina's temples. She allows images to flow through her mind, trying to connect.

Adesina pulls away. It hurts. Dreams aren't supposed to hurt. Nothing hurts Michelle. And dreams don't smell. And there is a definite lack of bunnies here. *If there aren't bunnies, then this isn't a dream. But if this isn't a dream, then what is it?*

There are bodies piled up in the pit. They're in different stages of decomposition. And it reeks. A stench so bad she can barely keep from gagging.

"Adesina, are you really down here?"

And as she says it, a shriek explodes in her mind and Michelle runs to the only place far enough away that she can't hear it anymore.

The Sudd, Sudan
The Caliphate of Arabia

THE SUDD WAS A stinking swamp.

The bloated bodies, already rotting in the sun, didn't help. Siraj gasped, gagged, dug a handkerchief out of his pocket, but the rising vomit couldn't be stopped. He turned aside and puked. The bile and chunks pattered in the standing water. A breeze hissed through the papyrus, carrying away the scent of vomit, but bringing more stench of death and blood, overlaid with cordite and gunpowder. Smells Noel knew well.

They picked their way through the reeds and papyrus, seeking reasonably dry ground. Bodies floated in the waters to either side. There were more on the solid ground. Noel paused over one corpse. The man's face was gone. He squatted down, and inspected the raw wound at the top of the corpse's skull and beneath his jaw. "No bullet did that," Siraj said.

"No. His face has been bitten off." Noel pointed at the raw edges. "Those are teeth marks." He stood and looked around. Now that he knew what to look for he saw many more faceless corpses.

"What does that?" Siraj asked.

"Probably not your average soldier in the Simba Brigade."

They broke through the reeds to a relatively open, dry patch of ground. Ruined tanks sat smoldering like Easter Island monuments to some forgotten war god. Several of the tanks were tossed aside, as if a giant's child had thrown them in a fit of massive pique.

"I think we can safely assume that Tom Weathers was here." Noel scanned the tank graveyard and spotted a human figure leaning against the shattered treads of one reasonably intact tank.

He and Siraj ran to the man. His face was smoke-blackened, and blood had turned his shirt into caked armor. He was in his early forties, and he recognized Siraj. "Mr. President. I'm sorry." He coughed, a wet sound that Noel didn't like. "We were winning. We outnumbered the Simbas. But then a darkness came. Unnatural, horrible. Our troops were blind, but somehow the blacks could see. They massacred us. There was something else in the darkness. Not human. A demon." His head lolled forward onto his chest.

"Those are not among Weathers's known powers," Noel mused.

"We need to get this man to a hospital," Siraj snapped.

"We'll drop him in Cairo on our way to Paris."

"Why are we going to Paris?" Siraj slid his arm beneath the soldier's. He gave a grunt as he lifted him.

"Because you need a drink," Noel said.

Offices of *Aces* Magazine
Manhattan, New York

"THIS," BUGSY SAID TO himself, "is why print media is dead."

The offices of *Aces* magazine had once been in the hippest, happeningest part of Manhattan. They hadn't moved, but the neighborhood had changed.

The tides of years had eroded all the cool out from under the fashion and finance, leaving the streets decent but unexceptional, and tacitly on its way down. Like the magazine.

Bugsy leaned against the door, squinting through thick security glass into the darkness beyond. He'd only met Digger Downs a few times before during Bugsy's somewhat foreshortened run on *American Hero*. It seemed like a lifetime ago. Three years, it had been. The guy had seemed sort of an asshole, as much as you could tell when he was at the big desk and you were singing your heart out to make your big break in showbiz. But he'd been picked by the Hollywood types for exactly the reason Bugsy was there now. He was old school. He knew where the bodies were buried. In a lot of ways, Digger Downs was the history of the wild card.

But the history of the wild card clearly didn't work weekends. So screw it.

Bugsy shrugged his laptop case back up onto his shoulder and checked the time on his phone: 2:30. Still at least three hours before Ellen would be back at her place. He had some time to kill, and there were about half a billion Starbucks to choose from within an eight-block radius. He picked the third one he came to because it had the FREE WIRELESS sign up in the window and the barista smiled at him when he paused outside the window.

Double-shot tall dry cappuccino firmly in hand, he staked out a tall chair by the front window that afforded a view of the street, popped open the laptop, quietly cursed Windows Vista again, rebooted the laptop, and spent fifteen minutes checking e-mail and catching up on a couple news blogs. He cracked his knuckles and the joints in his neck, then pulled up Google and dug through the largest single machine ever built by humanity for traces of the Radical.

Wikipedia gave a decent overview. Tom Weathers, the Radical, had first appeared in China in 1993. That was actually a lot more recent than he'd thought. He followed some of the reference links at the bottom of the entry.

As long as the fascists, the capitalists, and the willing collaborators hold the reigns of power, it is the duty of the people to oppose them. When the last landlord in the world is strangled with the intestines of the last banker, the work of peace can begin. Until that, any discussion of peace is treason against the people.

Bugsy figured the guy probably meant "reins," but whatever. He read on for another few sentences, muttered "yadda yadda blah blah blah" under his breath, and went to a different site. There were a long series of small wars, guerrilla resistances, police actions, and freedom-fighting brotherhoods that Weathers had gotten himself involved in over the years. Burma, Indonesia, Colombia, Turkmenistan, Afghanistan . . . Yadda yadda blah blah blah.

A wild cards discussion board had a thread on him. It hadn't been updated in a couple of years, but the archived conversation painted the same picture. The Radical was against the Man in all His forms, fighting for whomever he was fighting for and against whatever he decided was fascist or oppressive. He had a bunch of powers, real charisma, and a bad habit of deciding his allies weren't politically pure enough. There were half a dozen sites that sold T-shirts with his face, many with slogans in alphabets Bugsy didn't recognize right off.

"Need anything?" the barista asked. She was maybe twenty-two, blond, with the black tips of a tattoo sneaking out from her shirt near her collarbone.

"Freedom from the oppressors," he said cheerfully.

"Word," she replied in the whitest, most middle-class voice imaginable.

It would have been funnier if Bugsy hadn't thought the Radical would have killed both of them, just for joking about it.

The willing collaborators. It sounded like a garage band.

Tuileries Garden
Paris, France

"IF WEATHERS DOESN'T HAVE these powers, then what killed my soldiers?" Siraj gripped the stem of his champagne glass like a man hugging a life preserver.

"Other aces. *Aces* plural." Noel sipped his Hendricks gin martini and savored the cool/hot smoothness on the back of his tongue.

Siraj knocked back his champagne in a single gulp and waved his glass at a passing waiter. He got the usual Gallic sniff, frown, and shrug, but the man did head toward the bar. Noel looked out the window at the Tuileries Garden across the street. He had wanted to sit outside, but the late November rain made that impossible. The furled umbrellas in the metal tables looked like hunched, skeletal men in dripping coats.

"Then the PPA has multiple aces." Siraj's voice was heavy with despair.

"How can that be? The release of the virus was localized over New York. The preponderance of aces has always been in America. I had one . . . Bahir . . . you. Now I have none. Unless . . . ?" The implicit question hung in the air between.

Noel held up a restraining hand. "Oh, no, no, no, no. Weathers has sworn to kill Bahir."

"I've got to have aces. If the PPA is recruiting them, then so can I."

There was something about that that struck Noel as wrong. He contemplated Tom Weathers—charismatic, arrogant, impatient, always questioning the purity of one's commitment to The Movement. "I can't imagine Weathers ever accepting a mercenary ace into his army."

"You've now taken two contradictory positions," Siraj snapped. "Which is it?"

"Oh, they're using aces. The question is where they came from." Noel remembered Weathers's dossier. The man had been thrown out of every revolutionary movement prior to the PPA because the other members always turned against him. The glimmering of an idea began to coalesce.

Siraj was speaking again. "Look, if you won't fight for me will you at least help me recruit some aces? You have contacts from the Silver Helix."

Noel gave an emphatic head shake. "If you field your own aces, Weathers will move directly on Baghdad. I have a better idea. One relying more on cunning, guile, and manipulation rather than brute force. The things at which I excel—"

"Yes, yes, yes, you're a genius. Move on."

"Remove the Nshombos. The PPA will collapse. The armies will pull back from the Sudan to join in the inevitable power struggle—"

"Which Weathers will win."

"No, he has neither the personality or the force of character to hold it together. And he's a white man. There are too many colonial memories to allow that to happen."

"Yes, there are a lot of colonial memories." Siraj smiled thinly. "So you're going to kill the Nshombos."

"That seems very crude. The last thing you want is to make a tin-pot dictator a martyr. It may come to that, but let's try something more elegant and subtle first."

"I suppose you use those same terms when referring to me," Siraj said, and again smiled thinly.

"Oh, no, you're not a *tin-pot* dictator." Noel's smile matched Siraj's in thinness. "I know you actually want to help your people. I respected you for that, and that's one of the reasons we selected you to replace the Nur."

"Please, spare me your smug British approval." The waiter returned with a bottle of champagne and an ice bucket. Siraj poured himself another glass. "I want this done by the end of the year. If it isn't, I'll release my little dossier on you to the World Court, the press, and Tom Weathers."

There were times when remonstrating was pointless. This was one of them. Noel shrugged. "All right, but we need to postpone the march of the PPA on Baghdad. Let's buy some time."

"And how would you suggest I do that?"

"Ask Dr. Nshombo for a peace conference. If Nshombo refuses he'll look like the aggressor. All these dictators like to think of themselves as the hero of their own three-penny opera. He won't want the bad press."

Siraj took another long swallow of champagne. "And if I involve the UN it will only add to the pressure on Nshombo to accept."

"It will take time to arrange the conference, and you can spool out the talks for weeks, if necessary."

"Five, to be precise." Siraj filled up Noel's empty martini glass with champagne. Their eyes met over the rim of their glasses and Noel saw no warmth in Siraj's.

His old housemate would follow through on the threat.

Jackson Square
New Orleans, Louisiana

MICHELLE HAD BEEN AWAKE for several hours when Juliet and Joey showed up. The security guard let the girls in, and when the door opened Michelle could smell the olive trees, the heavy scent of the Mississippi, and beignets cooking at Café du Monde.

"Oh, honey," Juliet said. "You're awake again!"

Michelle opened her mouth, but only managed a hoarse croak. She swallowed and said, "Oil can."

"Oil can?" Juliet asked.

"Fuck all. It's a stupid joke, Ink," Hoodoo Mama said. "'Member? *Wizard of* Fucking *Oz*? She needs some water."

"Of course," Juliet said. "You had that tube down your throat for so long." She hurried out, then came back a moment later with a cup and a straw. Michelle drank and she felt as if there wasn't enough water in the world to quench her thirst.

"Don't drink too much, baby," Juliet said. "The doctor said it could make you sick."

Michelle dropped the straw. "I'm almost indestructible," she said. "I doubt a little water will hurt me."

Adesina hasn't had water in God-only-knows how long, Michelle thought. *She was just a little girl. Even a few days without water could . . .* Michelle felt something warm and wet drop onto her cheek. Juliet was crying.

"Oh, God, Juliet . . . don't."

Juliet just cried harder. Michelle glanced at Hoodoo Mama—she felt guilty doing so with Juliet's hot tears dropping on her. She shoved her guilt away and a stab of anger rose up in her.

It was Tom Weathers's fault that she was here and that she couldn't bubble even though she'd spent the last couple of hours trying to. There was this insane power in her and she couldn't figure out how to get rid of it.

And that scared her so much she thought she might lose her mind. And then none of it mattered because Adesina was still stuck in that pit and Michelle couldn't help her as long as she was trapped in her fat.

Another of Juliet's tears fell on Michelle's head and brought her back to New Orleans. The last time she had seen Juliet, she'd gone corporate for her job with Billy Ray. Now her hair was short and spiky again. But her tats weren't the pretty Mayan ones she'd favored in her punk days. Now they were black and tribal and aggressive.

And then Michelle noticed that Joey and Juliet were dressed alike: both of them wore Joker Plague T-shirts and ratty jeans. What had happened to change Juliet back into a punk chick, and what had made Joey a fan of Joker Plague? Michelle knew the signs of girls who had hung out too long together. They'd gone all hive-mind. "What's happening, Joey?" she asked. It was getting easier to talk. "Where am I? This is still New Orleans, isn't it?"

"Jackson Fucking Square," said Joey. "After you ate that fucking nuke you got really big and really, really, really, really heavy. The cocksuckers couldn't move you, so, for a while, they just put up a tent around you."

Michelle shook her head. Or at least she tried to. "How long have I been here?"

"A year and change."

Michelle was staggered. *A year. A year. A YEAR?* She was cold, then hot, and then cold again. Her hands started shaking. How was she even alive after a year?

"I know it sounds like a long time . . ." Juliet said.

Joey interrupted her. "You just missed Thanksgiving. The city erected this temple thing over you after they couldn't keep the tourists and grateful citizens away from your massive ass. You're a cocksucking saint to most of the dumbasses on this planet. Except your shit-stain parents, who got you taken off life support so they could get their hands on your money again.

"Oh, and fuck me sideways, but Tiffani's been coming down here every chance she gets to read to you all night long. She told us you weren't dead. Fuck me if she wasn't right about that one."

Michelle tried to take a deep breath, but it didn't work. It felt like someone had punched her in the gut. Except that *that* usually felt pretty good. This felt horrible. Her parents had tried to kill her.

"You okay, Michelle?" Juliet asked. "You're looking pale. Should we get the doctor?"

Joey threw up her arms. "Jesus H. Motherfucking Christ on a pogo stick, Ink. She's not dying. She just heard that her dick-lickin' parents tried to kill her to get at her money. No one would take that good."

Michelle closed her eyes. She wanted to throw up. She wanted to run away. She wanted to scream. She wanted to cry. Was she just going to be some kind of freak for the rest of her life? A mound of flesh with so much power inside her that it hurt?

Tears stung her eyes. She hoped that Juliet wouldn't notice. She hated being this repulsive and she hated being so helpless.

♥

Sunday,
November 29

Paraguaçu River
Bahia State, Brazil

BIG CROCS SWAM THE muddy river around him. As the dolphin slid through the water with near effortless undulations of his sleek and powerful body, driven by his tail flukes, he sensed them with sonic sprays emitted from his jaw, processing the echoes with the liquid mass that gave the distinctive bulge to his forehead.

He felt no fear. For he was the baddest motherfucker in the Paraguaçu River. A dolphin had a rostrum—a beak—capable of killing great white sharks. What were overgrown aquatic river lizards to him?

The warm fresh water had a land taste, an oleaginous feel. He reveled in it anyway. Almost reluctantly, he steered toward the island.

As he began to break water he saw the hut waiting among mangroves, the woman on its porch, as blurs in sundry shades. Greater detail emerged as he approached, but what were mere eyes, especially in the desiccating air, against the sensory richness of sound in water?

On his last arcing lunge he left the river's embrace completely. The sandy silt of the bottom caressed his belly when he splashed down. It took an effort of will to will the change. When he emerged from the water, dripping water from his leanly muscled, naked bipedal form, he was Tom Weathers again.

"Hoo," he said, shaking water from his golden hair. "And to think that just a moment ago I was thinking of this air as *dry. There's* a perspective change." To his human nostrils the air smelled so ripely of tannin-rich water and wet-leaved mangrove forest it almost made his head swim.

The woman laughed. His human eyes made her out clearly. Forty-something or not, a naked Sun Hei-lian was well worth seeing. "I can never get over that particular power of yours," she called as he trudged up the gravel-paved trail from the water's edge to the rough plank steps with the slanting late-afternoon spring sun stinging his skin from upriver. "How'd you ever get the ability to do something like that?"

The question made his nut-sac tense up as if to crawl back in his belly. "There's no limit to what the power of world revolution can do," he said. "You should know that, *Shang Xiao.*"

It meant "Colonel." The world at large knew Hei-lian as an intrepid trouble telejournalist for Chinese Central Television's English-language news service. The intelligence community knew her as a top agent of China's well-feared Ministry of State Security: the Guojia Anquan Bu, or Guoanbu for short. Beijing had set her to seduce the PPA's superpotent and mercurial Western ace.

She'd succeeded so well she was now the People's Republic's chief advisor to its ally Nshombo, the hard-core male chauvinism of her communist gerontocrat bosses notwithstanding. And in the process she'd fallen in love with her chief subject.

"If you say so," she said.

As he clomped up the steps beneath the thatch overhang of the roof she handed him an open bottle of almost self-luminous green fluid. It chilled his palm, meaning it came straight from the cooler they'd brought with them from Salvador, capital of Brazil's Bahia state, about thirty miles downstream where the river emptied into the Atlantic. The little shack had no electricity or running water or any modern conveniences.

Which didn't seem to impair its popularity as a weekend retreat for urban *baianos*; getting it hadn't been easy. Especially since Tom couldn't exactly flash his ace powers to impress the booking agent. This was supposed to be a *hideout*, after all: he never spent the night in the same place twice running. That running-dog teleport Bahir was still on his case, too, and he had to sleep sometime.

More and more he was growing reluctant to let himself sleep at all, for reasons having nothing to do with the golden-eyed Arab ace.

Tom twisted off the cap and took a hit. The coolness suffusing outward from his throat was welcome relief after walking a mere thirty feet. Although it was "cool" only by comparison to the mind-blowing tropic heat.

Holding a half-full beer, Hei-lian leaned against the side of the doorway, an oblong cut through warped wood to the darkness of the interior. Her long black hair was pulled back in a ponytail. Her skin, normally ivory tinged pink, glowed gold in the angled light.

She wasn't his usual type. He'd be the first to admit that. It wasn't that he went for the big-boobed blond cheerleader types, especially not with augments out to *here*: fake tits symbolized capitalism's obsession with conspicuous consumption. But he usually did like his women fuller-figured.

Not to mention *younger*. Sun Hei-lian wore her years lightly, although he knew they'd been spent in hard service. She kept herself in remarkable shape, gymnast shape, martial-artist shape. She'd been taught *taijiquan* and internal martial arts by her Daoist-priest father, and more violent applications by her employers.

She claimed he made her feel years younger. She'd laughed more in the last year, she said, their year together, than in her entire life previously. As serious as she still normally was, he believed that.

She was the most beautiful woman he'd ever met, not despite her years but because of them. And she was *smart,* fierce smart, a trait he respected. More than a skilled, and now passionate, lover, Hei-lian was something the Radical had never known in his brief years of freedom: a confidante.

"You seem thoughtful, lover," Sun said.

He turned and leaned on the rail. Sun-heated wood stung his arms. "I miss Sprout," he said softly. "I miss being able to have her with me."

"You could've brought her along."

"Would you be running around like that?"

"Of course not," Sun said in mock outrage. "Not in front of a *child*." She came up to put her chin on his shoulder and tousle his hair. He felt the heat and yielding firmness of her body on his back and buttocks, skin on skin, the slight rasp of her bush. Unlike a lot of chicks these days she didn't shave her pussy. Her pubic hair was on the sparse and wispy side anyway.

As sunset approached, vast flocks of scarlet ibises, pink-pale from their season in the north and long flight back to southern summer, fell on sandbanks and overgrown islands and the dense *mangal* on either bank like cotton-candy rain, to feed on mangrove crabs among the tough, gnarly roots knuckling down into black water. Their cries bubbled into a sky being overtaken by bands of orange and yellow.

With a sloshing of syrupy water a crocodile, what the locals called a *jacaré*, emerged from the water by the little dock. No boat was tied there now: no need for one. The *jacaré* was a big fucker, maybe twelve feet long. It dragged itself up by the gravel path and stared insolently at the humans from gelatinous armor-lidded eyes, as if laying claim on them for supper.

Tom pointed. A pencil of fire stabbed from his finger and crisped a tuft of grass a couple of inches in front of the croc's sharp snout. Moisture in plant and mud flashed to steam, scorching the animal's nose and shooting grains of dirt against it. Opening its yellow-pink mouth to roar surprise, displaying impressive teeth, the beast wigwagged its fat tail hastily backward into the water and was gone.

"Arrogant prick," Tom said. He raised the finger and blew away imaginary gunsmoke.

Hei-lian laughed. "That's more like it. I was wondering why you brought us here to this rustic tropic paradise for the night. Other than the usual security considerations, of course. I didn't think you went in much for that whole hippie back-to-nature thing."

Supernova anger burst inside him. He spun. Hei-lian leapt back like a startled cat. "What the fuck is that supposed to mean?" he shouted in her face. "What the *fuck*?"

There was more surprise than fear in those wide black eyes. But there still was fear. Colonel Sun, consecrated to service of Guoanbu and country since prepubescence, survivor of decades of full-contact play in some of the world's most blood-soaked open sores, did not scare easily.

But Tom was the most powerful ace on Earth, except maybe for Ra. He swatted fifty-ton main battle tanks like bugs. She knew far too well what he could do with *her*. "Nothing," she said. She managed to keep her voice almost steady. "I was just making a joke. Trying. Failing."

The stricken look on her face stabbed through him like that Kalashnikov slug through the back. He let out a big breath. The anger had already vanished, as quickly as it had lit. It left behind a kind of clammy, shaky emptiness.

"I'm sorry, man," he mumbled. "Didn't mean to rattle you like that." *You got to* maintain, *man,* he told himself. *You can find another woman. But there's way more at stake here than that.* More than he dared let anyone suspect. Not Hei-lian. Not even Sprout. More than he cared to let himself think about. *Everything.*

Shaking his head, he turned back to the rail and the river and the gathering birds and evening. "I'm just a little uptight these days."

She was back, pressed against him, stroking him soothingly. Mingling sweat made a slick membrane between them. He respected the nerve it took her to approach him.

"The Sudan?" she said.

"Yeah," he said, leaning heavily on the rail. "Wrong war, wrong place, wrong time." Tom picked up the soda, now past tepid to near hot, chugged half of it. He wished he dared let himself have even one beer to take the edge off. But he didn't. Hadn't in the almost decade and a half since he'd . . . come into his own. Nor had he gotten stoned. He couldn't allow himself to alter his brain chemistry. "Nshombo's always been hung up on Muslims, especially Arabs. He remembers it was always the Arabs who encouraged the slave trade, thinks they mean to bring all that back." He shrugged. "Shit. They even might. In South Sudan we found some local Muslims—they call themselves Arabs, even though they don't look any different from their neighbors—keeping animist tribesmen as slaves. We gave the slave owners to their own slaves. Perfect propaganda by deed. This Caliph's just a puppet, and Siraj is a Western wannabe. I'm cool with putting him up against the wall. But in ten years. Maybe five. When we've shown the world the revolution works, made this place the People's Paradise in reality as it is in name. It's too early. Way too fucking early." Tom turned away to lean on the rail. "And Alicia's pet aces . . . they're too big a risk. Look at what happened with the last one."

"Dolores." She laid a hand cool on his shoulder. "Butcher Dagon killed her."

Tom turned away. "Alicia's first success story, and look how that turned out." The sun poured in crosswise beneath the thatch awning as it sank toward the *mangal* and the big river's origin in the Chapada Diamantina in the middle of Bahia state. The light had softened, lost some of its sting. But the air stayed still and hot, the humidity thick enough to swim in. The bugs, ever-present, had gone from busy to frenetic.

Tom blew out his lips in a sigh and turned to Sun with a lopsided grin. "What say we go inside and get, you know, horizontal?"

Jackson Square
New Orleans, Louisiana

AND THEN SHE'S BACK in the pit.

Adesina is crouched down. Her hair has come undone from its braids and is a tangled cloud around her face. She looks feral.

Michelle glances around. *Corpses. Check. Leopards. Check. Adesina. Check. No bunnies. Check.*

She closes her eyes hard and wills herself back to New Orleans.

Juliet and Joey were staring at her. "What was that you were saying?" Juliet asked.

"I wasn't saying anything," Michelle replied.

"Hell you weren't," Joey said. "That was some fucked-up shit, Bubbles. You were talkin' in tongues."

Michelle wanted to shake her head, but she only managed to move it a little. "No. That was Adesina."

Ink and Hoodoo Mama glanced at each other.

"Hey!" Michelle exclaimed. "I saw that!"

Juliet stroked Michelle's forehead. "Sweetie, you've been in a coma for a year. You're probably tired."

"I am *not* tired," Michelle snapped. "Hello? *Coma?* I am plenty rested. And I've been having these weird dreams that I'm pretty sure aren't dreams. No bunnies." Michelle glowered up at them. "You can stop with the looking. I can *see* the two of you."

But then they weren't looking at each other. They were staring at her. Any other time she might have laughed at the expressions on their faces. "What the hell? I swear I didn't fart."

Juliet pointed at Michelle. "You're bubbling."

Michelle looked down at her hand. A large bubble was forming on it. It glistened, iridescent and beautiful, and it felt as if it could go on for days.

She released the bubble, and it drifted up to the ceiling. Then her hand was shaking and she thought she would lose control. A horrible nausea flowed through her again. And then the power was tearing at her. Fire in her veins. But she could *bubble*.

Somewhere Over the Atlantic Ocean

FROM NEW ORLEANS THEY flew to New York. From New York they'd fly to Rome. There they would transfer to a smaller plane bound for Addis Ababa, where they would board an even smaller plane bound for Dar es Salaam.

Wally shook the foil packet the flight attendant had handed him a couple of hours earlier. He leaned across the aisle (Wally needed an aisle seat; people complained about sharing an armrest with a metal guy) and said, over the rumble of the engines, "Want my peanuts?"

Jerusha shook her head, still studying the maps spread over her tray table. She'd been studying them since they left New York. She studied a lot. "No, thanks."

It was dark in the cabin. The flight attendants had dimmed the lights, to help people sleep away the time zones. Wally had traveled a lot since joining the Committee, but he still hadn't learned how to sleep on an airplane.

He yawned; his jaw hinges creaked. Wally stretched until the metal in his seat groaned. He made another attempt to focus on the guidebooks they'd purchased, but they were full of stuff he didn't understand. He figured it would all make more sense once he got there.

The in-flight movie looked good; it even had a couple folks laughing. But the headphones didn't fit him.

"Hey, Jerusha?"

"Uh-huh?"

"What do you think we'll find over there? In Congo?"

In a stage whisper, Jerusha said, "The horror. The horror." She grinned, as if she'd just made a joke.

Wally stared at her.

"Maybe we'll find an ivory dealer."

Wally shook his head, slowly.

"Joseph Conrad? *Heart of Darkness*?"

Wally shrugged.

"It's a book."

"Oh. I don't read much." He shrugged, but inwardly he cringed. This was the sort of admission that attracted cutting remarks the way magnets attracted iron filings. He braced himself for the inevitable sneer.

But something strange happened: she shrugged, too. "You're not missing anything. I had to read it in high school. Royally hated it, too."

"We had to read *The Great Gatsby*. That's the longest book I've ever read. I had to ask Mr. Schwandt for an extra week, but I finished it."

"Good for you." Weird—it sounded like she meant it. No sarcasm. "Oh, I know. Do you see many movies?"

"Oh, sure. Lots."

"Ever see *Apocalypse Now*? It's based on *Heart of Darkness*."

"Yeah, I saw that one. I liked it pretty good when I saw it." Thinking about war movies reminded him of what he'd seen and done in the past couple of years. More quietly, he said, "I don't think I'd like it so much now."

Wally was quiet for a long time. When he looked up again, he found Jerusha still looking at him.

"Wally? How many kids do you sponsor?"

"Seven. Counting Lucien." Again, that pang of worry. "We're gonna find him, right?"

"You know what I think? I think we'll get all the way over there, and find out that Lucien is a little boy."

"What does that mean?"

"It means he's a kid. Kids are forgetful. They play and make up games and forget to do the things their parents tell them. That's what kids are supposed to do."

"I never thought about it like that. I hope so."

In a lighter tone, Jerusha asked, "So. How's it coming with those guidebooks?"

"Oh, good. Real good." She looked at the unopened books on his tray table, then cocked an eyebrow at him.

Wally's sigh sounded like the release valve on an overheated boiler. "I don't read much," he confessed.

"Did you do any preparation at all for this trip before you called me?"

"Well, I have all of Lucien's letters. And on Saturdays back home my brother and I used to watch those old Tarzan movies on TV. I've probably seen them all."

"Tarzan." Jerusha rubbed her eyes. "Great."

"I can even do a pretty good Tarzan yell."

Quickly she said, "Please don't."

"You're not mad, are ya?"

"I'm not mad at *you*, Wally. I'm mad at . . ." She gave him a wan little smile. "I'm just a little tired, that's all. I haven't slept since yesterday."

Wally didn't know what to say, so he said, "Thanks."

He picked up a guidebook. And when he woke up, they were in Rome.

Headquarters of Silver Helix
London, England

NOEL SAT ON THE floor of the file room, sucking on a Tootsie Roll Pop (part of the leftover Halloween candy stash, another peculiar American custom) and reading through the agency's files on the Nshombos. He had quit the Silver Helix last year, and he and the organization had a fragile peace.

Noel's statements to the Hague had led to the arrest of John Bruckner, aka the Highwayman, and Brigadier Kenneth Foxworthy, aka Captain Flint, for war crimes. A year ago, Flint and Bruckner had broken into his parents' house, killed the ace "kids" Noel had sired with Niobe, and kidnapped an American boy whose uncontrolled nuclear power had governments all over the world trying to kill him or control him. Bruckner had delivered Drake to Nigeria, to stop the advance of the PPA army into that oil-rich nation. Thousands had died in the detonation, and ultimately Nigeria had fallen to the PPA anyway.

Foxworthy and Bruckner were now in custody in Holland. Bruckner was gobbling about how he was "just following orders," but Flint had fallen on his sword for crown and country by taking all the blame. The Silver Helix knew that Noel had a huge file about the assassinations he had undertaken on behalf of the British government just waiting to be released if they made any move against him. Noel didn't see why the "MAD" agreement couldn't be extended to making use of the resources of the Silver Helix.

He scanned quickly through the pages, searching for something he could use to discredit the brother and sister. The brother was an abstemious man— no mistresses, no drugs, no alcohol. The sister was more sybaritic—she overindulged in food and sex. It was believed she slept with most of the men recruited into her Leopard Society. But she wasn't the head of the state— exposing her excesses would do little.

Noel flipped up another page. The heading on the one below read ASSETS. The Nshombos had three Swiss bank accounts—one guess who had two and who had one—but the numbers were unknown. In addition to the palace in Kongoville there was an apartment in Paris and a home on the Dalmatian coast. There was a yacht. A line caught his eye. *The national treasury appears to consist of a mixture of gold bullion, platinum bars, and uncut diamonds held in the Central Bank of the Congo.*

Suddenly the door opened.

Noel cursed himself for being so focused on his reading that he had missed the approaching footsteps. He glanced at his watch: 4:42 P.M. Outside, the winter sun was dropping into the fogs and fumes of Old London Town. But it wasn't full night yet, and Noel was trapped in his real body and unable to teleport. The headshrinkers with the Silver Helix had never been able to help him overcome his psychological glitch so Noel himself could teleport like his avatars.

He reached under his jacket for his pistol. He really didn't want to shoot one of his former comrades, so he just rested his hand on the butt.

"Noel, what the hell are you doing here, man?"

It was Devlin Pear, aka Ha'Penny. Since Noel was seated on the floor they were actually nose to nose. Dev was a midget. He could get smaller, a lot smaller.

Noel held up the file. "Just a bit of intel."

"You can't do this. Lady Margaret's on the desk tonight. She'd have your balls if she knew you were here."

And that was most certainly true. Lady Margaret, aka Titania, had nursed a desperate crush on the former head of the Silver Helix for years. Now Captain Flint was awaiting his war crimes trial, and Noel had put him there. "Well then, don't tell her."

"I've got to. You can't just pop in here—"

Noel laid a hand on the file. "Look, I'm doing God's work. Or at least England's, which is almost the same thing." He gave Dev a smile, but the little ace continued to look worried. "I'm looking for a way to remove the Nshombos that won't have Western fingerprints on it. That can only help British interests in the area, right?"

"Why would you do that? You left the service."

"I don't give a tinker's damn about the Silver Helix, but I'm still an Englishman. I just wanted some information."

"That's really all you want?"

"I swear."

"All right, but don't do this again." The little ace hesitated. "Call me instead."

They shook hands, Noel put away the files, stood, and checked his watch. It was still three minutes until full night.

"Wish you hadn't left us," Devlin said.

"I had to. I didn't like what I'd become."

Ha'Penny considered Noel's role in the Silver Helix—assassin—and nodded slowly. "I can see that."

It was time. Noel made the transition to Lilith. "The PPA's the danger, Dev," she said. "I just want to help." And she teleported away.

Monday,
November 30

Paraguaçu River
Bahia State, Brazil

HIS EYES SNAPPED OPEN to darkness.

The humid air remained hot long after midnight. Sweat rolled ticklingly into armpits that felt at once familiar and utterly alien. Insects buzzed like power-saw choirs. Poison-arrow frogs trilled to advertise their killer beauty. The river sighed and gurgled through the mangrove roots. The smell of the water, like strong tea and death, overwhelmed even the smell of sweat-soaked bedding.

Starlight through the open window confirmed his memory, still vague with transition, that the blur beside him was the sleeping face of Sun Heilian. Details of her incredibly fine features resolved slowly as his mind and vision focused. The lines that living left in her face somehow made her even more beautiful to Mark Meadows's eyes.

Good thing she's close, he thought. He'd always been nearsighted. And for the last fourteen years he had seen through eagle-perfect eyes.

It took him three breaths to dare to try to move his eyeballs. There was little left to see: the bed, the rough room with its few and deliberately raw furnishings of wood and coarse rope, the Coleman lantern they'd brought from Salvador, now dark. And the rest of the woman herself, pale and slender and exquisite.

That was a favor, anyway. If as much torment as pleasure. He knew that body's every contour. Yet she had never known his touch. Only the touch of this body he inhabited. *Isn't that just my luck?* he thought. *I fall in love with a lethal lady Chinese spy. And she falls in love with the evil alter ego who's taken over my body. Perfect.*

It wasn't the first time he'd made himself a fool for love. His obsession with his first love, Sunflower, had led him into the obsessive quest that resulted in his body being usurped by the Radical. Long after the love he'd felt for her had ended in divorce, acrimony, and Sprout.

Sprout—it was Hei-lian's treatment of Mark's daughter that made him fall in love with her. She had begun with coldness, almost loathing. Now she showed every sign of loving her. It was as if Sprout had awakened a capacity for kindness in a woman who had lived virtually her entire life professionally coldhearted.

Hei-lian possessed a razor-keen intellect and a will so fierce it had forced her hidebound bosses to acknowledge her excellence. Years of witnessing—and yes, no doubt working—brutality had never crushed her spirit. Yet it was her unexpected capacity for *warmth* that won him.

I love you, he wanted to tell her. *I know the Radical's seductive power. Far too well. And it's a lie.*

He ached to warn her. Warn the world. *The man you think you love is changing into something that* isn't human. *If he isn't stopped he'll destroy everything. He—*

Mark felt himself swirl away from the world, down into old accustomed darkness. He uttered a vast and desolate cry that his throat could never voice.

"Aaaahh!"

The scream snapped Tom awake and upright. Sweat soaked his hair and face and body as if a tropical downpour had busted loose inside the cabin. The rough canvas covering of the bed under his butt was a mess, more sodden than the relentless heat could account for.

Fingers trailed down his arm. "Are you all right?" Hei-lian asked, sitting up beside him.

He drew in a huge breath and palmed hair back from his forehead so it would stop stinging his eyes with sweat.

"Yeah," he said hoarsely. "Just a nightmare."

Ellen Allworth's Apartment
Manhattan, New York

IT WAS STILL DARK outside when Bugsy woke up. The alarm clock blazed 6:22 in numbers of fire. He groaned and rolled to his side, pulling the covers with him. The woman beside him made an impatient sound and pulled the blankets back. He sat up, watching her sleep in the dim light filtering in from the window.

She was beautiful, especially when she was asleep and wasn't Ellen or Aliyah. Her naked body was familiar now. Known territory, and still fascinating. The way her small breasts rose and fell with her breath. The nameless fold where her thigh stopped being thigh and turned into body. The mole on her spine. When she wasn't anyone and her face went slack like that, she looked young. She looked his age. He sighed.

The room still smelled like sex and liquor. His head hurt a little, but not enough to bother with. The soft buzz of a few stray wasps made a white noise that seemed like silence. Still, he gathered them up, folding the insects back into himself. She slept better when it was quiet.

He rose, showered, nuked some scrambled eggs and coffee. The apartment was like a really high-class junk shop or a really cheap museum. All around him were artifacts of other people's lives. The cameo that Ellen wore and sometimes channeled her mother with. The pen that brought back a dead investment banker that she used when she was planning out her budget. A pair of scissors. A pair of glasses. A hundred dead people, all of them there for Ellen when and if she needed them. He was dating a republic.

When he snuck back into the bedroom to get some real clothes, her eyes were open. Until she moved, he didn't know which one she was.

"Aliyah," he said. "You sleep okay?"

She nodded gently.

"Ellen?"

"Still asleep," Aliyah said, touching the earring gently. "It's kind of weird, not having her back there. I guess I'm really used to it now, huh?"

"Yeah," he said.

"It means I'm real, though," Aliyah said. "I mean if I can be here when she's not, that means I'm really me and not just . . . I don't know. An echo. I'm not just her wild card if I'm awake and she's asleep. I'm not just a *dream.*"

"That's what it means," he agreed, because it was what she needed to hear.

She lay back with an exhalation, watching the ceiling go from black to grey, grey to blue, blue to white. On his way back toward the kitchen, he caught himself humming something. Louis Armstrong was in his head.

Say nighty-night and kiss me
Just hold me tight and tell me you'll miss me
While I'm alone and blue as can be
Dream a little dream of me

He stopped humming.

The FedEx guy came while Ellen and Aliyah were in the shower. Bugsy signed for the box and dropped it on the counter, then picked it up and checked the return address. New Orleans. Jerusha Carter, his old teammate from Team Hearts. Somehow invoking hearts seemed like an omen, but he couldn't say whether it was good or bad. Probably it was just the hangover talking.

Ellen walked in from the back, still toweling off her short hair. "Who was it?" she asked.

"Christmas in November," he said, nodding to the package. Ellen picked it up, turned it over, then got a steak knife out of the drawer and slit the tape. Something in bubble wrap, and a note. "What is it?" Bugsy asked.

"Another hat," Ellen said with a sigh that meant another lottery ticket. Another chance that maybe this was the one she'd lost. Nick. Will-o'-Wisp. Her lost love, carried away by the wild winds of New Orleans. In the year since she'd lost him, they'd gotten hundreds, and not just fedoras. Baseball caps. Kangols. Two leather ten-gallon cowboy hats. A straw porkpie.

Ellen tore the bubble wrap open with her fingers, the popping sound like distant gunfire. The thing nestled in its center was a nasty green-brown, smelled of rot and river water, and had once been a fedora. "Hey," Bugsy said. "That one even looks kind of like—"

She had already scooped the hat up, cramming it over her still wet hair. Her body went still. Bugsy held his breath, and Nick opened her eyes for her.

Well, Bugsy thought, *fuck me sideways. Things just got more complicated again.*

"What happened?" Nick asked.

"You blew off in a hurricane. Ellen'll fill you in on the details," Bugsy said. "I'd hang out, but I've got a thing I've got to get to. Anyway, you two lovebirds probably want to catch up, right?"

Nick looked stunned, his attention focused inward, where Ellen was probably talking with him. *Another dead guy in the house.* When Bugsy slipped out the front door, there were tears in her eyes, and he couldn't tell if they were Nick's or Ellen's.

His three-way was a foursome again. Being in love with dead people was probably the only thing he and Ellen really had in common. Nick was going to be some hard explaining come Christmas dinner with the Tipton-Clarkes.

The offices of *Aces* magazine were open when he got there. He waited in the lobby drinking stale coffee from a paper cup until Digger Downs came out, shook his hand, and led him to the back office. "Sorry to keep you waiting," Digger said. "We're just about to put this issue to bed. You still doing any writing?"

"Not much," Bugsy said, with a little twinge of longing. A phantom itch on an amputated career. "Saving it up for the memoir, I guess."

Digger chuckled, gestured to a chair, and leaned against his desk, arms folded. He looked older, up close. More wrinkles around the eyes, more white in the hair.

"What can I do for you?" he asked.

"I'm doing some background work on the Radical. When he first came on the scene. Who his friends are."

"Should any of them still be alive," Downs said.

"That's the guy I'm talking about," Bugsy said. "I have him first showing up in China in 1993, but he's clearly a westerner since—"

"Sixty-nine."

Bugsy tilted his head.

"Nineteen sixty-nine," Downs said. "San Francisco. Right after they shot those kids at Kent State. The Radical was in the People's Park riot when the Lizard King fought Hardhat."

"Ah. Was T. T. even alive in the sixties?" Bugsy said.

"Who?"

"Todd Taszycki. Hardhat."

"No no no," Digger Downs said. "Not that one. There was another guy who used that name back then. Very blue-collar. Didn't have much use for the hippies."

"So when you say the Lizard King," Bugsy said, "you mean Thomas Marion Douglas? Lead singer for Destiny?"

"I sure do," Downs said. "The Holy Trinity. Jimi, Janis, and the Lizard King. He was . . . he was amazing. I saw him in concert once. When he died, we really lost someone. That was a little before your time, though."

"*Ninety-four* was before my time," Bugsy said. "Sixty-nine was the end of the Napoleonic wars. What was Weathers doing in San Francisco in the sixties? And where was he for those twenty-five years in the middle?"

"Got me," Digger said.

Jackson Square
New Orleans, Louisiana

"AND HOW DO YOU feel today, Miss Pond?"

Michelle opened one eye. A middle-aged woman wearing hospital scrubs was standing over her. "Like someone I don't know just woke me up." Her voice was still rough. And she was thirsty. Really thirsty. "Can you get me something to drink?"

"I imagine so. I'm Mary. I'm supposed to check your vitals."

"I'm not dead."

"That's pretty clear." The woman moved out of her line of sight. Michelle wanted to crank her head around, but the fat made it impossible. When Mary walked back into Michelle's sight, she had an Aquafina bottle in her hand. The water was sweet and cold, and Michelle drank almost the full bottle before gasping for breath.

Then Michelle became aware of a noise. It sounded like a flock of birds, but she'd never seen big flocks of birds in Jackson Square. "What's making that sound?"

"That? Oh, that's the faithful talking, honey."

"The faithful?"

As she pulled a stethoscope from her bag, Mary nodded. "They're the bunch of folks who've been bringing you these flowers, praying over you, making you the focus of their lives."

Michelle tried to move her leg, but couldn't. It pissed her off to no end. "That's insane."

Mary shrugged and stuck the stethoscope in her ears. "Honey, you'd be amazed. And, just to be fair, you did prevent a lot of them from dying horribly."

"I was trying to save my friends."

Mary put her hand on Michelle's wrist and popped the business end of the stethoscope onto Michelle's chest. "Doesn't matter why you did it. Just matters that you did. Now be quiet for a minute."

Michelle ignored Mary as she poked around. There wouldn't be any blood drawn. Needles broke when they came in contact with her skin. That had been happening ever since her card had turned.

"Everything sounds good," Mary said. "Same as it has for the last year."

Michelle wasn't listening to her. Her attention was focused on the TV. The volume was still turned off, but there were images of herself flashing behind the blond anchor. One showed her at the height of her modeling career. Then there were publicity shots from *American Hero*. And finally there were pictures of her lying in Jackson Square after . . . after.

Michelle had grown to love her fat. It was power and control, and it meant nothing could hurt her. But seeing herself . . . Bile rose in her throat. The whole world had seen her like *that*.

Her body was a distorted mass. Rolls and rolls of fat rippled across each other. The cement under her had shattered. Most of her body was naked. Her pale flesh mortified by the summer sun. And everyone had seen it. Hot tears stung in her eyes.

"Oh, damn it, honey," said Mary. "They should have turned that off." She walked to the set and punched the red button.

"Why are they showing that now?" Michelle asked.

"Because you're awake now. You didn't die when they took you off life support. You're a miracle."

"I'm not a miracle. I've got a virus that changed me. It could have happened to anyone. Are people really that thick?"

"Would you like to meet them?" Mary asked.

"Oh, yeah, 'cause I'm definitely at my best," said Michelle. "I love the idea of loads of strangers looking at me gape-mouthed while thinking I rescued them." She shut her eyes. Why was she being such a bitch? "I'm sorry."

"It's okay, honey," Mary said, puttering around the room throwing dead flowers out and putting the empty vases in a box. "I imagine it's something of a shock. Losing a year. That thing with your parents. And finding yourself, well . . . different."

It was impossible for Michelle not to giggle. *Different*. Yeah, she was different all right.

Noel Matthews's Apartment
Manhattan, New York

"THOSE ARE ZLOTYS. WHAT are you doing with zlotys? You don't have a show in Poland."

He'd heard the phone ring, and thought Niobe was safely ensconced in a conversation, so he'd pulled out the zlotys and began preparing for his fast trip to Poland. Now, busted, Noel tried to scrabble the bills, and—more incriminating—a passport photo of his new male avatar form, under a book, but it was way, way too late.

Niobe stood in the door of the bedroom he'd turned into an office. The desk was littered with decks of cards, linked metal rings, scarves, handcuffs, and padlocks. In a cage by the window a pair of doves billed and cooed, heads bobbing in that particularly silly fashion unique to doves. The tools of his trade.

Right now the doves' soft calls didn't seem to be having a soothing effect on Niobe. Her thick tail was lashing, hitting the floor with heavy thumps as she stared at him with a look that was two parts angry and one part worry.

"It's nothing," Noel mumbled. "I didn't want to worry you. In your condi—"

"Do not patronize me! I am not made of glass. I escaped from a federal facility and managed to elude every ace the government sent."

"Well, I helped a little," he protested.

"Granted, but either we're a team or I'm out of here."

And even just the threat made his heart stutter. He gave her the truth. "There's a man in Warsaw who makes the best forged papers in the business."

"And why do you need forged papers?"

"It's a little thing I'm doing for Siraj."

Niobe folded her arms across her chest. "Are you going to be in danger?"

"A little. But I'm always in danger. From my former associates . . ."

"And Tom Weathers."

"Him, too."

"And once you have these papers what are you going to do with them?"

"Travel with them."

"Where?" Noel squinted, pulled at his lower lip. Niobe stormed forward until she stood right in front of him. "I will not be treated like a goddamn mushroom!"

"Are we having our first fight?" Noel asked lightly.

"You only wish. If you think this is me angry . . . well, you've got a lot to learn. Now where are you going?"

"Kongoville."

"The place where Tom Weathers lives. The man who vowed to kill you."

"Well, he vowed to kill Bahir."

"And if he kills Bahir, won't *you be dead, too?*"

And suddenly Noel had to acknowledge that that loose feeling in the depths of his bowels was fear. He stood up, wrapped his arms around Niobe, and buried his face against her shoulder. The tension in her shoulders dissolved as she stroked his hair.

"The PPA is dangerous, viciously dangerous," Noel murmured into her hair.

"Oh, my dearest, don't do this. Let somebody else handle the PPA. The Silver Helix, SCARE, the Committee . . ."

Noel smiled down into her face. "Those idiots? You eluded SCARE, I ran rings around the Committee, and the Silver Helix is hamstrung with Flint and John facing trial. It has to be me."

Her hand went to her belly, fingers spread protectively. "Don't you dare get killed."

"And have you really angry with me? Not a chance." Her mouth tasted so sweet and he wished he didn't have to leave.

She broke the embrace and asked, "Do you have time to take me to New Orleans?"

"Why on Earth do you want to go to New Orleans?"

"Bubbles has woken from her coma." Niobe's eyes were glowing. "She's my friend and I want to see her." She touched her stomach again. "And I want to tell her about the baby."

"I thought we were keeping it secret until . . . we were sure. . . ."

"Not from my closest friends."

Noel sighed, and while Niobe went off to change into something cooler he phoned Bazyli to tell him he'd be delayed.

♠

Tuesday, December 1

Mwalimu J. K. Nyerere
International Airport
Dar es Salaam, Tanzania

DAR ES SALAAM. THE name translated as "safe harbor"—at least, that's what the guidebooks Jerusha had read claimed. Jerusha hoped they were right.

They flew into Mwalimu J. K. Nyerere International Airport. An aide from the American Embassy was there waiting for them—that was certainly the Committee's doing—and he walked them through Customs. Jerusha didn't attract much notice as they walked through the airport, but Wally certainly did. She saw people pointing and whispering, heard them chattering and calling to each other. A crowd followed at a judicious distance as the aide shepherded them from the airport lobby and out to the waiting limo.

The heat and humidity of the outside air hit them like a physical blow as the doors opened. "Cripes," Wally said. "It's hot here."

The aide was openly grinning. "Welcome to Africa," Jerusha told Wally. "We both need to get used to it."

As they drove eastward back toward the city, she stared out from the darkly tinted windows. The area directly around the airport was dominated by industry: warehouses and businesses served by a double-lane divided highway. The landscape was rather barren: between the buildings there was bare, brown earth punctuated with scrub brush. It reminded Jerusha of the American Southwest and the parks her parents had worked, except that the Southwest was never this humid.

The driver turned north off the divided highway after a bit, though, and they were driving among houses. There were lots of kids: laughing, running after each other, huddled in groups around adults or parents, playing ball. The aide was rattling on as he had been since they'd left the airport, talking about how proud they were to be hosting two such famous *American Hero* members as the famous Rustbelt and Gardener, how they believed in good relations with the United Nations, how Ms. Baden had called the embassy herself.

Jerusha listened to him and answered with polite nods and short replies, but Wally stared out toward all those kids. She watched him watching them, as if he were looking at each face hoping to see his precious Lucien there. She wondered what he was thinking.

They drove past a winding river heading toward the sea. Here the trees were thick and dense, more like what Jerusha imagined Conrad's "Africa" might have been. They caught a glimpse of deep blue water running out to the horizon: the Zanzibar Channel. The limousine pulled onto another large divided road and continued north. Wally's eyes were closed and he was snoring softly; Jerusha envied him. The jet lag was pulling at her and she wished the aide would stop talking. She leaned her head against the window, staring out at the strange world drifting by.

Then she lifted her head again. "What is *that?*" she asked, pointing. The aide turned in his seat.

"Oh—that's a baobab tree," he said. "Lots of native tales about them. The baobabs are one of the symbols of Tanzania—of Africa in general, in fact. We have one of the oldest baobabs in Dar es Salaam on our compound grounds."

The baobab loomed in the central divider, as if a divine hand had ripped a gigantic tree from the ground and rammed it upside down back into the hole with the root system dangling from the top and overhanging both sides of the highway. The trunk was enormous and thick, furrowed with deep ridges, and green leaves fringed the branches here and there. The tree *looked* powerful and ancient, at home here like an ancient, gnarled oak might dominate a forest back in the States.

Jerusha stared at it and touched her seed pouch. "A baobab, eh?" She would remember that. "Listen," she said to the aide. "I—we—appreciate your taking us to the embassy, but it's important that we get to Lake Tanganyika as soon as possible. We're . . ." Jerusha didn't know what Barbara had told the ambassador, but it didn't seem wise to mention that they were intending to cross over into the People's Paradise. ". . . we're supposed to meet someone there. It's Committee business. We have to keep it quiet."

"Ahh." The aide pursed his lips, tapping them with a forefinger. "There's a man," he said. "A joker, Denys Finch. He's a bush pilot flying out of a little airport a few miles north of the embassy. Sometimes we have him courier for us, or take dignitaries out to the national parks or up toward Kilimanjaro."

"Could you take us to him?" Jerusha asked. Wally was still snoring. "Now?"

A shrug. "The ambassador wishes to have dinner with you, but that's not for a few hours." He tapped on the window separating their compartment from the driver and gave the man directions. Jerusha heard the word "Kawi." Then the aide turned back to her with a smile.

"We'll go there now," he said.

Jackson Square
New Orleans, Louisiana

THERE ARE MORE CORPSES in the pile this time. Adesina is curled into a fetal position on top of the pile. Michelle crawls toward her. The limbs slide as she puts her weight on them. Some of them feel squishier. She can't see the bodies clearly. All she can see is Adesina—who is still curled in a ball, but rocking back and forth. Her hand trembles as she reaches out and touches Adesina's temple. And as soon as she touches, images explode in her mind.

Adesina runs through the forest. The leopards give chase. Clothes tear on branches and thorns.

She's in a village. There are ugly little houses made of concrete blocks and corrugated tin roofs, painted in bright colors: yellow, blue, and green. Children play in the unpaved street, their feet kick up puffs of dirt that hover in the still air.

Michelle sees Adesina among them. She's wearing the same blue-and-white checkered dress. Her feet are bare. Her hair is braided, and someone has wrapped the braids around her head so they look like a crown.

The children are laughing. In the shaded doorways of the houses, women gossip while they watch the kids. It's warm and the air smells heavy with rain.

Bursting into the town come a trio of jeeps. Each has three men riding in it. The men are armed and shots ring out. The women grab the children and cover them with their bodies. Michelle wants to bubble—wants to do something to help. But she knows she would be useless. This memory is stuck in Adesina's head.

The men are dressed in green camouflage uniforms. Their heads are shaved and some of them wear leopard-skin fezzes. Machine guns are slung over their shoulders. They train the weapons on the women and children, then start shouting orders in French. Michelle understands about half of what they're saying. She tries not to feel afraid—it's difficult. She's in the well of Adesina's fear.

Michelle looks around the village, trying not to let the fear distract her. There are tires piled up at one end of the street. A couple of thick-wheeled bicycles lean against the tires. No help there.

The guns go off again. The women and children moan and cry. Michelle looks at the soldiers. Some have their guns pointed in the air. The rest have their guns trained on the villagers.

And then she knows it's time to go. It doesn't matter what happens next in the dream or vision or memory or whatever this is.

Adesina woke Michelle from her coma. And now it's time for Michelle to repay the favor. But she can't do it trapped in her fat and afraid to use her power.

Kawi
Dar es Salaam, Tanzania

"WALLY." JERUSHA NUDGED HIM. "We're here."

Wally jerked awake, and accidentally scratched the window glass with his ear. *Nuts.* He looked around, ready to apologize to that nice fella from the embassy, but he had already stepped out of the car. Jerusha looked like she was trying not to laugh. They shared a look and shrugged at each other.

Wally followed Jerusha from the cool, air-conditioned cocoon of the embassy limousine into an equatorial steam bath. He'd first felt it when they landed, but he'd been so comfortable dozing in the car that he'd almost forgotten where he was.

When he and his brother were kids, before his card turned, one of Wally's favorite things was visiting their aunt Karen and uncle Bert up in Ely, Minnesota. Bert had built a sauna into their basement. A proper sauna, lined with spruce, and an exterior door that opened just a few dozen feet from their dock. Wally loved the smell of the spruce, the tingle in his nose, the sizzle of the stones.

He and his brother used to take turns pouring water on the stones, until the sauna was so steamy it hurt to breathe. They'd stoop lower and lower as the steam rose, until it was unbearable. Then they'd dare each other to run down and dive in the lake in their skivvies. It wasn't cold at all, even in October and November, if you were fast enough. On a crisp, still night you could see the steam rising from your skin when you stepped out of the sauna.

Tanzania in December felt a little bit like that sauna. Except you couldn't control the temperature, and saying "uncle" didn't make your brother stop pouring water on the stones. Wally didn't handle humidity as well as he had before his card turned.

It was the rainy season here. The shorter of two, Jerusha said. That meant it was ninety degrees every day, with three inches of rain in both November and December.

They were parked on a patch of hard-packed red earth, along a road bounded by dense greenery on both sides. Wally made a mental note to ask Jerusha about the trees; everything was so green. Across the road, a handful of temporary huts clustered around a large, open-ended corrugated steel Quonset hut. Part wood, part metal, the huts looked like they'd gone up quickly and wouldn't be around very long. Wally could just make out an airplane in the shadows of the Quonset, and what might have been a landing strip in a clearing through the trees. They weren't too far from the ocean; Wally could smell it, on the strongest gusts. Mostly, though, he smelled humidity and what might have been the stink of burning garbage.

A trio of kids ran past them, laughing and shouting to each other. They were kicking a ball down the street. It appeared to be a crushed-up plastic water bottle wrapped with tape. Wally wondered what they were saying, if their game had any rules, and if Lucien played something similar.

"Uh, Jerusha?" said Wally. "Where's here?"

She said, "I think this is a town called Kawi. We're just a few miles north of the embassy. There's a bush pilot here who can fly us to Lake Tanganyika." Her voice dropped to a whisper. "I told him"—she nodded her head in the direction of the aide, who was knocking on a door next to the hangar across the street—"that we're on Committee business, meeting somebody at the lake. If anybody asks, I sort of implied that it's all very hush-hush. So just play along and we should be fine."

"Okeydokey. That sounds real good," he said. "Way to go, Jerusha!" He gave her a thumbs-up and a smile.

She didn't respond. Instead, she stared at his shoulder. Her eyebrows rose. "Wally? Did you know you're . . . rusting?"

Wally craned his neck to peer over his shoulder. Little splotches of orange dusted his skin. Sure, it was wet here, but he'd hoped this wouldn't have started quite so fast. "Awww, heck."

"Does that hurt?"

Huh. Nobody had ever asked him that before.

"Nah," said Wally. "Not when it's just on the surface like that." He fumbled through his pockets until he found some steel wool. A few quick rubs turned the splotches into a red dust. The slightest of breezes carried it away.

Jerusha still looked upset. She was frowning. "Does that happen a lot?"

"Sometimes. When it's humid outside."

"Humid? We're heading into the jungle. During the rainy season."

"Don't worry. I got lots of S.O.S pads with me."

Jerusha frowned, looking doubtful. She started to say something, but stopped when the sound of raised voices echoed across the street.

They turned. The aide was talking to a fellow with grey skin, dark little eyes deep in his round face, and a snout topped with a thick horn. He was a big guy, too, built like a fire hydrant. Wally remembered the Living Gods, jokers that had taken the forms of the gods of ancient Egypt. Kinda like the way Wally had grown up around open-pit iron mines and ended up with iron skin. This fella seemed to be something similar, only here in Africa his jokerism had taken the form of a rhinoceros.

The aide waved Jerusha and Wally over. They joined him. To the rhino guy, he said, "Here they are. Jerusha Carter and Wally Gunderson." To Wally and Jerusha, he said, "This is Denys Finch. He's the pilot I mentioned."

"Best pilot in the bush," said Finch.

Wally held out his hand. "Pleased to meetcha, guy."

Finch looked him up and down, his stubby little ears twitching like crazy. He did the same to Jerusha, then looked at the aide again. "Oh, no," he said. "Not this time. I've had it with your bloody tourists."

The aide looked embarrassed. "Not tourists, Mr. Finch. I told you, they're here on business for the Committee. The United Nations."

"Yeah, you and your so-called dignitaries." Finch spat in the dirt. "Comin' all the way to Tanzania, askin' me to fly them around. 'Ooh, Mr. Finch, show us Kilimanjaro. Ooh, Mr. Finch, show us the lakes, show us elephants and hippos and the real bloody Africa so we can take a few holiday snaps before going home to brag about our safari adventure.' Then it's thank-you-Mister-Finch-good-job and before you know it they're headed back to their proper Western hotels for proper Western food and proper Western air-conditioning." He spat again. "Wankers."

The embassy aide tugged at his collar, blushing. Wally understood the gist of Finch's tirade, if not every word.

"Hey, fella, we're not tourists," he said. "Not like that. Promise. We might be here awhile."

"Is that so? Then where's your kit?"

Wally frowned. "Kit?"

Finch rolled his eyes. It looked like he was mad enough to hit somebody with that sharp horn of his. Wally sidled in front of Jerusha.

"Yes, kit," said Finch. "Provisions. Gear. Tents and the rest."

"Actually," Wally said, "we were kinda hoping you'd help us with that."

Jackson Square
New Orleans, Louisiana

THE WOMAN WAS DISGUSTING, a mass of flesh draped in a light, silky material. Noel wondered if they'd used a circus tent. They had to have something covering her for modesty's sake, but it had to be light given the sultry heat.

Michelle and Niobe were deep in conversation. Ink hovered at the edges of the conversation, and the terrifying Hoodoo Mama stalked the edges like a protective rottweiler.

"We've been married almost a year, and . . . I'm pregnant," Niobe trilled. Then all of the females let out that peculiar shrill squeal reserved for news of an impending whelping. Even Noel's large, no-nonsense, horse-faced English mother had produced *the sound* when they'd relayed the news to her.

Michelle rolled her head toward him. "I didn't know you had it in you."

"I might surprise you."

"I doubt it."

"Oh, Michelle, be nice. Though we did have to try real hard," Niobe added, and Noel closed his eyes as peals of female laughter rolled past his ears. He wondered if he would have understood these tribal responses if his mother had chosen to raise him as a girl rather than a boy.

But if she had he wouldn't have Niobe, which indicated his brain wiring was male even if his parts were confused.

Michelle smiled at Niobe. "Would you get me a cup of lemonade? Ink can help you."

Both Niobe and Ink looked startled. Noel gave Michelle a cynical know-ing smile. As the two women walked away he moved in close to her. He no-ticed that she lay in a crater formed by her massive weight in the moist soil of New Orleans.

"That was a little in-artful," he said. "So, what is it you want to say to me?"

"Are you out of the spy business?"

"I left the Silver Helix, yes."

"That didn't answer the question."

"That's all the answer you're getting."

"So you *are* up to something. I thought Niobe looked worried. She's try-ing to hide it, but she's upset."

Noel found himself just glaring at the woman, hating to admit that she was perceptive.

"Tell me or I may just have to get a message to Jayewardene and the Committee."

"I'm getting very tired of being blackmailed," Noel said.

"Tough."

He hesitated, but realized he had no choice. "Very well, I'm engineering a little regime change in the Congo."

He thought he saw something flash in the back of Bubbles's eyes when he said Congo. "Oh, great, that worked out so well the last time." And her scorn and disdain drove away all thoughts about her reaction.

"If all goes well the final act will be taken by Tom Weathers," Noel gritted.

"When I hear the phrase 'all goes well' in conjunction with you I immediately get hives."

"I'd say that's the least of your problems."

Jackson Square
New Orleans, Louisiana

"OKAY, SO WHY IS it you can't stand Noel?" asked Juliet, when he and Niobe finally took their leave.

"I met enough self-aggrandizing dickweeds when I was a model," Michelle replied. "Every time Noel pops in, he spends the entire time looking down his nose at everyone."

Joey laughed. "He thinks his shit don't stink. Yeah. Not to mention he was the fucker who stole that Sprout kid and got that cocksucker Weathers all pissed off."

"People rarely change who they are at their core," Michelle said. "Sure, occasionally, someone stops doing all the crappy stuff they used to, but most folks will revert to form if given the chance. Noel's got responsibilities now. He's got a wife and a baby on the way, but he's still playing spy. The more he screws around with Tom Weathers, the more he puts himself, Niobe, and the baby in harm's way."

"He seems to make Niobe happy," said Ink.

Joey shrugged. "He knocked her up, you mean?"

"Looks like," Michelle replied. "I confess, it's giving me the hard-core willies, but it's what she wants. I don't care if they used a spatula and a turkey baster."

Juliet nodded, then changed the subject. "Have you had any more dreams?"

"They're not dreams. And yes, every night, just about. I've got to get to her . . ."

"You're assuming she's a real person."

"I know the difference between dream real and real real. These dreams about Adesina are real. They *smell*, for crying out loud. When was the last time you had a dream that smells?"

"Never. But how is she even alive if she's really in that pit?"

And how long will she stay alive? That was a question Michelle hadn't wanted to ask, even in her own thoughts.

"Time to tear the roof off the temple," she announced. "Has the square been cleared?"

"The police have it cordoned off."

"Then let's do it."

"About fucking time." Hoodoo Mama hopped up, grinning. "One roof, coming the fuck off."

Michelle smiled at Joey, but only for a second. The guilt of what they'd done still ate at her.

Then there was a loud snapping noise, like cheap firecrackers. The midnight sky appeared above her. She could see the blue-white light of the stars. There were zombies walking across the joists, some carrying plywood, others grabbing chunks of the roof and pulling it off.

Michelle told Ink and Hoodoo Mama to leave. Juliet started crying. "*Bbbbbut*, I want to be with you." Her nose was red.

Michelle wished she had a Kleenex to dry her tears. At the same time, she felt irritated with Juliet. There were worse things happening in the world.

"And I wish I had a pony," Michelle said. "But I don't know how this is going to work. I just want you safe when I start."

Joey put her arm around Juliet. "C'mon, Ink. Bubbles is a dick-flavored pain-in-the-ass, but she's right about being careful. She swallowed a nuke, remember?"

"You do know I didn't actually eat that nuke, right?"

Juliet gave Michelle a kiss on her forehead. "I love you," she whispered. A wave of stomach-churning guilt poured through Michelle as they left.

She waited until she couldn't hear them anymore. Then she waited longer. Above her she saw a sparrow fly down and perch on one of the joists.

"*Joey, get that goddamn zombie bird off my temple,*" Michelle said. The sparrow gave a nasty squeak, then flew off. Some of its moldy feathers drifted down to her.

It was time to get down to it.

For a moment, she was terrified, but then the thought of bubbling again zinged through her body. It wasn't as good as sex, but it was damn close.

Michelle flexed the fingers of her hand, and then opened them to the sky. *One first*, she thought. *See how it goes.*

Liquid heat slid down her arm into her palm. She watched as the bubble grew. It wavered slightly, and she let it go. It drifted up and bounced against the wooden beams, then rose toward the pale stars.

◆

Wednesday, December 2

President's Hotel
Dar es Salaam, Tanzania

JERUSHA WOKE IN HER room at the President's Hotel at what the room clock insisted was 5:30 A.M., but to her body felt more like the middle of the night. She could hear Wally snoring in the adjoining room like a venting steam locomotive. She lay there for several minutes trying to will herself back to sleep, but her mind was racing with all that she needed to do, with worry about the plane flight with Finch, with even more worry about how they'd cross Lake Tanganyika and what might be waiting for them in the PPA.

Judging by Wally's snoring, he was worrying about nothing at all. She envied him that.

Jerusha threw aside the covers. Twenty minutes later, she was showered and dressed and striding out the lobby doors onto the embassy campus. The American Embassy compound was a dreary fortress: a series of rectilinear concrete buildings set behind a high security wall. To Jerusha it looked more like a prison than anything else. The ambassador had told them at dinner that this was the third embassy site they'd had in Dar es Salaam, that the campus sat on the site of what had been called the Old Drive-In Cinema, and droned on how the land gave them so much more room to expand at need.

The desk clerk had told her where the baobab tree was on the grounds; she headed in that direction. Rain had soaked the grounds overnight, and the grass was steaming as the day's heat rose, but for the moment, the air was cool enough that the humidity wasn't a bother.

She found the baobab easily. Up close, the tree was even more impressive than the one she'd glimpsed on the street, and even stranger. The trunk was massive—it would have taken a dozen people holding outstretched arms to encircle it. The trunk was furrowed and dented, branching above into nearly leafless main branches that diverged quickly into a tangled maze of branches and twigs. Birds were nesting in the hollows of the tree: several burst up into the air as she stroked the trunk. She saw a lizard sliding quickly around the trunk away from her, and dark squirrels chattered angrily at her from above.

There were pods hanging down from some of the branches, and a few on the ground at Jerusha's feet. She picked one up: a gourd roughly the size and shape of a football, the outside covering leathery and hard. It was heavy in her hands.

"Monkey fruit," someone said, and Jerusha turned to see a man in the uniform of the embassy staff stepping out of an electric golf cart a few yards away, the back stuffed not with clubs but with spades and rakes and trimmers. "That's what some people call it." His voice was heavily accented with Kiswahili or one of the other local languages, a lilt that Jerusha found charming. "Baobab fruit is very nourishing. The animals love to eat it: monkeys, baboons, elephants, even antelopes. They break open the gourds to eat the fruit and the seeds are discarded or end up in their droppings, and so new baobabs come up."

"The seeds are in here?" Jerusha hefted the gourd.

The man nodded. His skin was the color of thick cocoa, but the black hair was liberally salted with grey. "You're the one grows plants?" he asked.

It was Jerusha's turn to nod. "My name's Jerusha Carter," she said. "Sometimes they call me Gardener."

"I'm Ibada. I keep the grounds for the embassy. Toss that here." He held out his hand, and Jerusha underhanded the gourd to him. He slid a long knife from a sheath in his belt and pressed the heavy blade into the gourd, splitting it open. Jerusha could see pulpy fruit inside, laced with large seeds. "The baobab is the Tree of Life in Swahili," he said as he cut the fruit open. "That one there, it's an old, old one. It's been growing since before the birth of your Christ."

Jerusha looked at the tree again, trying to imagine all that history that had passed since it first sprouted. It was impossible. "They look so . . . strange."

"One tale says that the gods gave each of the animals a seed to plant. Poor baobab was the last, and it was given to the stupid jackal, who planted the seed upside down so that the roots came out on top." He laughed, and Jerusha had to laugh with him. He was pulling seeds from the pulp, gathering them into one large palm. "Tree of life, remember? You'll find the leaves used as a vegetable. *Kuka*, they're called—my mother used to make *kuka* soup. Here, look . . ."

He handed one of the halves of the gourd to Jerusha and poked a finger into the pulp. "You know cream of tartar? That originally came from this fruit. Down in the market, you can buy dried pulp covered with sugar; it's called *bungha.* Or you can mix it with milk or porridge. Very versatile." He took the gourd from her again, took her hands, and poured a dozen of the seeds into her cupped palms. "Those—grind them down and you can use them to thicken soup, or roast them, or grind them to get oil. But I think you will use them for growing, eh?" He smiled at her.

"Thank you, Ibada," she said. The seeds were cool and wet, and she could feel the great trees inside them, waiting to spring forth. "Later," she whispered to them. She opened a pouch of her seed belt and let them fall inside. The pouch felt heavy and comforting.

"This is why you came to the tree, no?" he asked. "You could feel the call of the Great Mother in her?"

"Yes." Jerusha brushed a hand over the thick trunk. A heat seemed to answer her, welling up from the ground below. "I think I could."

"Hey, Jerusha!" The call was a loud bellow. Both of them looked back toward the buildings of the embassy. Wally was striding toward them, waving.

Ibada nodded, grinning again. "I feel that call too, sometimes. You and the metal man, you're not here just to see the animals or take pretty pictures of Kilimanjaro?"

"No."

"Then you might need the baobab," he said. "Use the seeds well, Gardener."

"I will."

Ibada lowered his head, almost as if he were bowing to her. He began walking back to the electric cart. Wally passed him with a suspicious glance. "He bothering you?"

"No. And I can take care of myself."

Wally had the grace to look abashed. "Sorry," he said. The cart whined as Ibada left with a wave. "They said the car would be ready in an hour to take us to that Finch feller. I knocked on your door to tell you, but you didn't answer. The feller at the desk said you were out here, so . . ." His voice trailed off into silence. He was looking up at the baobab behind Jerusha. "Cripes, that's one big tree," he said. There was a distinct note of awe in his voice. Somehow that made Jerusha feel better.

"Yes, it is," Jerusha told him. "C'mon, we should get ready."

Kawi Airport
Dar es Salaam, Tanzania

FINCH HAD SAID IT would take at least a couple of hours to get them properly provisioned; they wanted to leave for Lake Tanganyika in the early afternoon. He took them to a . . . well, it wasn't really a store. Not that Wally could tell. It seemed more like a depot, or small warehouse, not far from the hangar where Finch kept his plane.

A stuffy, mildewy smell wafted out of the mud-brick building when Finch unlocked the door. Wally and Jerusha followed him inside. There was no electricity; the only illumination was the mustard-colored light leaking through grimy windows, except in places where the windowpanes were broken. Rows of shelves and piles of crates filled the space. Many shelves were empty, but those that weren't amounted to lots of gear. Camping gear, by the look of it.

"Wow!" said Wally. "This is all yours?"

"Finders keepers," said Finch. "Been flying in and outta the bush for thirty years. People get lost, people leave things behind, people get one glimpse of the jungle and go screamin' back to their hotel. I find it, take it here, and then sell it to lucky blokes like you."

Jerusha said, "This stuff isn't stolen, is it?"

"Bite your tongue!" Air whooshed through the pilot's flared nostrils. "I'm an honest businessman."

Wally edged in front of Jerusha again, just in case. "Hey, she's just asking, is all."

"Just so we're clear, mate. I don't steal, but I don't run a charity here, either."

"Huh?"

Finch rolled those tiny little eyes again. "You're gonna pay for what you take, right?"

"Oh, sure, you betcha."

"Thing is," said Finch, "I'm sure the Committee is good for it, but I can't wait around six months for a check to arrive from the United States. Not many banks around here that would honor it anyway, right?" He chortled, slapped Wally on the back. Most people flinched after doing that, but not Finch; it looked like he had pretty thick skin. The *clang* echoed through the warehouse.

"Right, I guess. So, um, what does that mean?"

"It means I run an honest *cash-only* business."

Wally looked at Jerusha. She shrugged. What else could they do?

The outfitting trip turned out to be an expedition in its own right. Though she'd offended him with her question, Jerusha won a bit of grudging respect from Finch once they got down to business. She had done her homework, and had compiled a list on the way over from New York. Wally knew they were doing this on the spur of the moment, but he had no idea just how unprepared they'd been.

He'd been camping up in the Boundary Waters Canoe Area. Preparing for a trip like that was nothing compared to this.

It was one heck of a list: Packs. Safari vests (with extra pockets). Biological water filtration bottles. Chlorine tablets. Painkillers; antibiotics; antidiarrhea medicine; rehydration salts. Pocketknives; machetes, for hacking through brush; compasses; toilet paper; rope. Flashlights; electric lanterns; a handheld GPS unit. Lots of batteries. Sleeping bags. Tents.

For Jerusha they also bought insect repellent, mosquito netting, and antimalarial tablets. Wally hadn't been bitten by a bug since his card turned. Jerusha got a wide-brimmed hat, too. Sunburn wasn't much of a danger for Wally, but he bought a pith helmet for the fun of it. He'd always wanted a pith helmet, ever since watching *Tarzan the Ape Man* (the original, not the remake). It would keep the sweat and rain out of his eyes.

Finch made a big deal about footwear. It had to be comfortable, he said, but it also had to let your feet breathe. Wally decided to go barefoot. It would be more comfortable than anything else, and besides, Finch didn't have any secondhand boots or hiking sandals that wouldn't get shredded by Wally's iron feet. As long as he was extra careful about rust, going barefoot wouldn't be a problem.

Finch made an even bigger deal about the satellite phone. "Don't lose this bloody phone," he said, shaking it in their faces. "This is your lifeline to the outside world. Your cell phones will be worthless in the jungle." He gave them a long lecture explaining how to use the phone. Wally tried to follow as best he could, but he secretly hoped Jerusha was getting it.

They unrolled one sleeping bag after another, trying to find a pair that hadn't been afflicted with mildew. Finch asked Wally, "Committee does this to you a lot, does it?"

"Does what?"

"Sends you off to the arse end of the world without any provisions." Finch's ears twitched. "Seems like a bloody awful group to work for, if you ask me."

"Uh, no. I mean, it happens sometimes. But not all the time."

Jerusha chimed in. "Our trip to the lake is an emergency. There wasn't time to get properly outfitted back in the States. We had to get here as quickly as we could."

"Ah, right. Right. So you said, so you said." Finch didn't sound entirely convinced.

After two hours, they had almost everything they needed. Jerusha haggled with Finch, so in the end it cost them just under half of the cash they'd pooled.

Then it was time to leave. They bundled up their gear and followed Finch outside. Wally offered to carry Jerusha's pack for her, but she didn't seem to like that.

Finch disappeared into the hangar. Wally lingered outside with Jerusha. "I don't think he believes us," he said. "What should we do?"

Jerusha frowned. She looked tired. "What can we do? Stick to our story until he gets us to the lake."

"Oy, tin man!" Finch pointed at Wally. "Get over here. Help me push her out."

Wally set his pack down next to Jerusha. Little eddies of red earth swirled around him as he clanged over to the hangar. The dust clung to the sweat on his legs; it looked like the worst case of rust he'd ever had.

Wally had never flown in such a small airplane, even back in Egypt. He'd flown in helicopters, but those were UN things, and still larger than this plane. He cupped his hands to a window glass and peered inside. It looked like it could seat maybe four or five, or fewer with gear.

"Grab her like this," said Finch, "gently." He leaned on the diagonal strut that braced the wing to the fuselage. Looking at Wally's hands, he added, "And don't scratch her."

Together they eased the plane outside. Finch made a musky smell when he exerted himself. Wally could have moved the plane himself, but it looked kinda fragile.

Actually . . . once they got it outside, in the sunlight, it looked *really* fragile. Long cracks spiderwebbed a couple of the windows; the fuselage had silvery gouges where the white paint had been scraped away; the wings had pits and dings and one thing that looked like a homemade *patch*. And the huge landing gear appeared to be more patch than tire.

"Hey, Mr. Finch? Is this safe?"

Finch's nostrils flared again. "Tourists," he muttered.

Jackson Square
New Orleans, Louisiana

CNN WAS BROADCASTING IT live. So was every other major news outlet. Juliet told Michelle it was being streamed live on the Internet.

Michelle had been bubbling for almost twelve hours now. She was still as huge as she had been, but she could tell she was getting lighter.

The bubbles were pouring from her hands. As many bubbles as she could release. She kept them dense enough that they didn't just pop, but light enough to float away. Just making a bunch of soap bubbles wouldn't do, and every other variation she had thought of had risks. She'd tried to make the bubbles somewhat pop-able; it was impossible to have the kind of control over them that she wanted. Even now, even hours since she'd begun bubbling, the power was still clawing through her. It was exhausting trying to keep it in check.

On the TV there was a long shot of the temple with the stream of bubbles rising from it. Then there were overhead shots, but these were on a loop since they'd shut down the Louis B. Armstrong Airport and closed New Orleans to all air traffic. Now they were cutting away to viewer video.

In every frame they showed, pretty, iridescent bubbles floated and bobbed like a child's playthings. They went up, up, up and then floated here and there, carried by the prevailing winds, until they slowly started to fall back to earth.

It was raining bubbles in New Orleans.

The TV showed a long shot of a young man in front of the Super Dome, preening for the camera. "Yeah, I know she saved the city, but damn, couldn't she have done this bubble thing somewhere else?"

The camera cut to another shot. A harried-looking woman held a toddler on her hip.

"I've got babies to think about. You don't know what's in those things. Oh, they look pretty enough, but have you tried to keep a baby away from one of them? They put everything in their mouths. I saw *American Hero*. She can make those things blow up."

Michelle yelled at the TV. "*These* aren't blowing up! They're not supposed to!"

"See, that's part of your damn problem, Bubbles." Joey turned down the TV sound. "You worry about what fuckers think about you. Me? I don't care."

"Did you tell Juliet about us?" Michelle blurted. *Stupid, stupid, stupid,* she thought.

Joey gave her an annoyed look. "Fuck no. Christ on a crutch, why would I do somethin' like that?"

"I don't know. Maybe you wanted to unburden yourself. Feel less guilty."

"I don't feel guilty about nothin' I do."

"Then why didn't you tell her?"

"You know why," Joey replied. "She sat here for a *year* waiting for you to wake up. She kept your parents away long as she fucking could, considerin' she don't have no rights. And she did it expecting nothin'." Joey shook her head. "You and me, we're alike. We're used to having to look out for ourselves. Juliet, she don't know how to do that. She loves you and that means putting everything else aside to take care of you."

"I suppose you know more about my girlfriend than I do," Michelle snapped.

"Yeah, I do." Joey slouched down in her chair. Juliet had gone out for coffee and beignets and it was the first time Michelle and Joey had been alone.

"Oh, my God. You're sleeping with her!"

"Jesus, you are one crazy bitch. No, but it ain't because I didn't want to. You just don't know a thing about Ink, do you? Fuck me all to hell." Joey jumped up from her chair and grabbed her gimme cap. "I'm gonna go see if she needs some help with those doughnuts."

Michelle fumed. She wanted to run after Joey. To tell her she was wrong. That she did *so* understand Juliet. But she was still too big. And then there were those damn bubbles. They went on and on and on . . .

Jokertown
Manhattan, New York

THE FAMOUS BOWERY WILD Card Dime Museum was a short ride on the subway. Ellen spent the time looking out the windows at the speed-blurred concrete and the darkness. She had a slight smile on her face, and a sense of peace that was almost postcoital, though Bugsy knew for a fact it wasn't.

He knew what it was. "How's Nick?" he asked.

Ellen took a deep breath and let it out slowly. "The hat itself is a little the worse for wear. It's strange having him back again. I still can't quite . . ."

Ellen's voice got thick for a moment. She hadn't expected to get Nick back. He'd died before she'd met him, and with the physical locus she used to channel him gone, she'd thought he was gone again. She'd been in the middle of mourning him.

Now he was back, and she had spent most of the last day communing with him—bringing him up-to-date, sharing confidences, no doubt telling funny stories about Bugsy and Aliyah and that one time when the FedEx guy opened the apartment door when they were in flagrante in the kitchen.

There was something basically unnerving about hearing the same mouth you kissed when you were making time with your girl laughing about you in a man's voice.

The subway reached their station, and Bugsy and Cameo ascended into the light.

Jokertown made up a section of Manhattan small enough to walk across in half a morning. It was also a different world. In the pale sun of early morning, two jokers jogged slowly down the street, one half mastodon half insect, the other with the body of a beautiful woman and the head of an oversized horsefly. But they were talking about Tara Reid's latest fashion blunder, so maybe it wasn't such a different world after all.

On one of the city buses that stopped to let out its cargo of freaks and misfits, a teenage girl was weeping. The cell phone pressed to her ear let out squeaks and buzzes, making words in no known language. An old man still drunk from the previous night urinated in an alley, his penis talking in a high, gargling voice of its own about imagined sexual conquests. A bat the size of a rottweiler with the face of a twelve-year-old Chinese girl flapped desperately, trying to catch up with a distant school bus. The coffee shops filled with the morning press of men, women, and who-the-hell-knew all grabbing a cup of joe and a corn muffin on their way to work while a neon-blue man in the back booth sucked down eight breakfasts, the plates stacking up beside him higher than his head.

Bugsy and Cameo crossed in front of a slow-moving delivery truck and went into the museum. The place smelled like old french fries and mildew, but it looked like the best secondhand shop ever. Display cases were filled with oddments and curios. A waxwork Peregrine stood in the corner in the same pose and outfit as the copy of *Aces* framed behind her. The joker at the counter could have been a man or a woman. The long face was something between a melted candle and road rash. Thick, ropey arms spilled out of a Yankees jersey. "Cameo!" it said.

"Jason," Ellen said, smiling. "It's been a while. How's Annie?"

"The same," the joker said, spreading his splayed, tumor-budding hands in a gesture that meant *Women. Whatcha gonna do?* "What can we do you for today?"

"My friend here is doing some research. People's Park riot."

"The what?"

"Apparently there was a riot in People's Park in 1969," Bugsy said.

"Could have been," the joker agreed. "I was two, so chances are I wouldn't remember."

"Thomas Marion Douglas was there," Ellen said.

"The Lizard King? Oh, fuck yeah. We've got crates of stuff on him." The joker squinted, scratched himself, and nodded. "None of that's on display anymore. The whole sixties rock thing we don't put up unless there's a revival or something going on. But . . . yeah. I think we've maybe got something back in the newsreels, too."

"Anything you've got would be great," Ellen said.

The joker held up a disjointed finger. One minute. He disappeared into the shadowy back of the museum. Bugsy walked around slowly, taking in the hundreds of small items and pictures. A poster for *Golden Boy*, the movie where the ace had gotten his name back before he got tangled up with McCarthy. Weird to think it was the same guy Bugsy had seen in Hollywood two years before. He looked just the same. Still pictures from the Rox War. A cheesy pot-metal action figure of The Great and Powerful Turtle, the grooves in the top making it look like a hand grenade cut along its length.

"I love this place," Ellen said.

A dress Water Lily had worn. A copy of an arrest warrant for Fortunato. A metallic green feather off one of Dr. Tachyon's hats. A solid two dozen pictures along one wall, each of them different, and all of them Croyd Crenson. "It's a trip," Bugsy said.

The joker stepped out of the shadows and motioned them in. The dim back office was stuffed to the ceiling with cardboard boxes and piles of paper. A ten-inch color monitor perched on the desk. It showed an image of a newscaster in the pale, washed-out colors that Bugsy associated with 1970s television.

"That's the footage I was thinking about," the joker said. "I've got a wash towel from his last concert in the box there. We got it off eBay a couple years ago, so it might be bullshit, but it's the only thing I'm sure he'd have worn after the People's Park thing."

"You're great, Jason," Ellen said.

"I try," the joker said with a sloping, awkward grin.

Bugsy squatted down, found the remote, and started the video playing. There he was. Thomas Marion Douglas. He was shouting at a crowd, exhorting them. A line of National Guardsmen stood shoulder to shoulder, facing him. This was before the advent of the mirrored face guard, so Bugsy could make out the nervous expressions on the soldiers.

Something loud happened. The reporter ducked, and the camera spun. A Volkswagen Bug was in flames. The camera pulled back to an armored personnel carrier, Thomas Marion Douglas on the upper deck, twisting the barrel as if it were nothing. The Browning came off the APC, and Douglas held it up over his head, bending it almost double.

"Watch this part," the joker said. "This is great."

The Lizard King bent down and hauled someone in a uniform out of the carrier. The poor nat kicked his legs in the air, and the Lizard King went down.

"Wait!" Bugsy said, poking at the buttons on the remote. "What happened?"

The joker lifted the remote from his hands and the images streamed backward. Frame by frame, they went through it. The burning car. The broken APC. The captain plucked out like the good bits of an oyster. And then the blurred arc of something moving fast. Thomas Marion Douglas's head flew forward and to the right, and he went down like he was boneless.

The man who stood where the Lizard King had been wore work overalls and a hard hat. A long iron wrench was in his hand. The guy was huge, but seemed to be shrinking. "Go home!" the previous generation's Hardhat called. "Go home now. Is over. You must not fight no more."

It looked like the big guy was weeping. Someone shouted something Bugsy couldn't make out, and the previous Hardhat went from maudlin to enraged in under a second.

"That's not good," Jason the joker said. But just as the guy with the big wrench was about to start in on the crowd, he went down too, tripped by Thomas Marion Douglas. The Lizard King got up as Hardhat regained his feet. The picture was jumping back and forth now, the cameraman torn between a great story and the threat of becoming collateral damage. Bugsy leaned forward. The Lizard King, blood running down his forehead and into his eyes, took a solid swing straight to the ribs and went down again. Hardhat stood over him, ready to crush the man's skull. The wrench rose, and then something—a chain, maybe—wrapped around it and spun Hardhat to face a new enemy.

Tom Weathers. Bugsy stopped the frame.

He looked familiar, but not quite the same. Slender, with blond hair down to his shoulders, wearing only a pair of blue jeans and a saucer-sized peace medallion on a chain, but this was absolutely unquestionably the Radical. The man who had threatened New Orleans, who had killed enemy and ally alike for almost two decades.

But Bugsy couldn't help thinking that the Tom Weathers on the screen looked . . . not younger, precisely. Softer. Kinder. Less ravingly homicidal.

He started the tape again. Hardhat, the Radical, and the Lizard King carried on their battle until it ended with Hardhat on the ground, reduced to merely human size and weeping, the Radical and the Lizard King in a victory embrace that was almost sexual.

"That's all we've got," Jason said.

"Okay," Cameo said. "Ready to meet the Lizard King?"

Bugsy nodded. Cameo took the old grey terry-cloth hand towel from Jason the joker's outstretched hand, settled it around her neck like a prize-fighter, and closed her eyes. Bugsy could see the change almost at once. She slouched into her chair, the angle of her shoulders changing, her head slipping back on her neck like a petulant schoolboy. He knew that Thomas Marion Douglas would be the one to open her eyes.

Apparently Ellen spent the two or three silent minutes prepping the Lizard King, because he didn't seem surprised.

"I have risen, man," Tom Douglas said in a slow, theatrical drawl. "That is not dead which can eternal lie, and in strange eons, even death may die."

"Yeah, okay. So my name's Jonathan," Bugsy said. "I was wondering if you could tell me a little bit about the Radical. From the People's Park riot?"

Tom Douglas shook his head as if he expected his hair to be longer and leaned even farther back and lower in his chair. Arrogance and contempt came off him in waves. "He's still fighting the good fight, is he? Cool for him, man. He was righteous."

"How well did you know him?" Bugsy asked.

The Lizard King shook his head. The movement was languorous, as if designed to stall just for the joy of stalling. "Just that one night, man. Just that one bright, shining moment. We showed the Man that we would not be intimidated. The people would not be pushed down. We stood the National Guard and their aces on their asses, man. And afterward, it was love, sweet love until the dawn."

Bugsy blinked, mentally recalculating. "So you and the Radical were . . . ah . . . lovers?"

"That make you uptight, man?" the Lizard King asked with a smile.

"Well, not in a queers-are-yucky way. I just never really thought of Tom Weathers as a sexual object."

"Everyone was with everyone, man. No jealousy, no possessiveness, no hang-ups. We were free and wild and full of love, man. But no, Radical and me were the power and the light. People were drawn to us. There was too much of us not to share around. Radical, he spent most of his night with a chick called Saffron . . . no, no. Sunflower. That was it. Seemed really into her."

"And after that night," Bugsy said. "Did he keep hanging out with her in particular?"

"There was no after that night, man. There was that one authentic moment, and then nothing. Dude came when he was needed and vanished with the dawn."

"You never saw him again?"

"Before or since."

"Great," Bugsy said.

Thomas Marion Douglas leaned forward, shaping Ellen's face into a smoky glower that Bugsy recognized from the covers of classic rock albums. "The thing was, we weren't afraid of death, man. We *embraced* it. We became free, and everything around us was transformed by our power. After us, nothing was the same. Nothing."

"Two words," Bugsy said.

The Lizard King lifted his chin, accepting the implicit dare.

"Britney Spears," Bugsy said, and then while the Thomas Marion Douglas looked confused, he lifted the towel from Ellen's neck and returned her to herself.

"Well," she said. "That could have been more useful."

"We've got Sunflower to work with, at least."

"Couldn't have been more than eight or nine million girls called that in sixty-nine," Ellen said.

"It's something," he said. Then, looking at the limp towel in his hand, "So that guy was the edgy, dangerous sex symbol of a generation, huh?"

"Apparently so," Ellen said.

"Guess you had to be there."

Kawi Airfield
Tanzania

THE PLANE HAD CREAKED as Wally stepped aboard, the suspension visibly sagging. Jerusha eyed the rust-spotted and patched fuselage with suspicion. "How old *is* this plane?" she asked Finch.

He grinned. "Ah, this crate's as old as me, and just as mean," he said. "She's a Cessna 206, made in 1964—a good year, all around. We're both perfectly serviceable, lady, if you catch my drift." He winked one tiny eye at her, and his glance drifted down the length of her body.

"Can it carry Wally?"

"Your metal man, you mean? Sure. How much can the bloke weigh?"

She said nothing, but climbed into the plane and took one of the four seats in the cabin, in front of a pile of boxes and crates lashed in with webbing and straps. Finch climbed into the pilot's seat, and the propeller on the plane's nose spun into invisibility as the engine coughed, sputtered, and roared. They clattered down the dirt runway, bouncing as Jerusha held tightly to the seat arms. As the plane finally lifted into the air and began to climb, Jerusha could see the sapphire water of the Zanzibar Strait, and off the horizon, the distance-blued green hump of the island itself. Below, the port city spread out, revealing all of its complexity and life.

"Where's Mount Kilimanjaro?" Wally asked, shouting against the roar of the plane's engine as they lifted from the airstrip, wings dipping left as Finch set them on a westerly course. "That's in Tanzania too, right?"

Finch snorted. He pointed out the right window of the aircraft. "Kilimanjaro's that way about six hundred kilometers: north, not west."

"Nuts," Wally said. He looked disappointed.

"Maybe on the way back we can make a detour," Jerusha told him. "With Lucien."

Wally brightened a little. "That'd be swell," he said. "I hope we can."

"So do I," she told him, but the churning of her stomach belied her confidence.

As they slid westward under the high sun, the shadow of the plane below moved initially across well-greened land, but as they moved farther from the coast, the landscape below became more arid, tan earth dotted with the green of occasional stands of trees and brush, interrupted at intervals by the winding paths of streams. An hour or so into the flight, the ground began to rise and crinkle underneath them, steep green-clad mountains and deep valleys sliding underneath their wings. "Mongoro Region," Finch called out, pointing down. "Beautiful, if you like mountains."

Jerusha nodded. Staring down, she realized that it would have taken long days to cross Tanzania by car as she'd first planned, following the winding, rough roads carved into this wild land. The mountains eventually drifted off behind them, and they were flying over flat savannah plain. Finch pointed out herds of wildebeest, and buzzed low above elephants and giraffes. Wally was entranced, staring out the windows of the cabin and pointing.

In the late afternoon, Finch set the plane down near a small village. "Delivery," he said, jerking a thumb back toward the crates. "We'll be spending the night here . . ."

The village—a Masai *boma*, according to Finch—was a collection of mud-brick adobe huts. The children hung behind the adults at first, staring at Wally mostly. By the time they'd off-loaded the plane, the kids had overcome their shyness: they darted out to tap Wally's metallic skin and dart away again, coming back to hit him harder and laugh at the sound. They plucked at Jerusha's clothes too, but it was Wally who intrigued them, and

Wally seemed to enjoy their attention. He'd make false lunges toward them, roaring when they ran away shrieking and enduring their pestering. He showed them Lucien's picture, telling them (in English that they couldn't understand) how he was going to visit Lucien, who was his friend. One of them kicked a soccer ball in Wally's direction, and he booted it high and long, the children exclaiming and shouting as they ran after it.

Jerusha watched, laughing with them. She reached into her seed pack and found an orange seed; she let it drop, drawing on the life within so that in a few minutes an orange tree had bloomed, with ripe fruit hanging on the branches.

The village smelled of orange rinds that night.

Special Camp Mulele
Guit District, South Sudan
The Caliphate of Arabia

"HEY!" TOM SHOUTED. "HEY! Knock that shit off!"

The two ignored him. One was the stocky kid Leucrotta, the other the Lagos guttersnipe with the Brit accent, Charles Abidemi, the one called the Wrecker, or sometimes ASBO, after some incomprehensible Limey bullshit.

Tom already knew who started it. Poor skinny Charlie wouldn't start shit with anybody, although he might make your Austin Mini explode a one-kilogram chunk matter at a time once he got clear of you. But Leucrotta was your typical adolescent male: a dick with legs. Which, given that he was an ace, was a very dangerous dick indeed.

Tom hauled Leucrotta off by the collar of his outsized Simba Brigade camo blouse just as it quit being outsized anymore. As a giant hyena-form chest exploded all the buttons off the front and blew out the sleeves, Tom tossed the rampaging were-beast up just far enough to transfer his grip from a collar that had just turned into a ribbon to bristly scruff.

"What the hell is *wrong* with you little shits? Don't you know there's a revolution on?" Tom spoke French. After spending six or seven years in the Congo, he could speak it just about as well as he chose to. He found that *slangy* with a deliberately nasty *américain* accent usually had the best effect. It wasn't like anybody was going to mouth off to him about his bad pronunciation. Not twice.

Of course, then he had to repeat it in his native tongue. Son of an Igbo soldier who immediately abandoned his Yoruba mum in a Lagos slum, Charlie had spent most of his short, miserable life in a housing estate in a not-so-trendy part of the London suburb of Brixton, getting his narrow ass kicked by Pakistani Muslim gangs, poor white gangs, Yardie gangs, and gangs of England-born blacks who despised immigrant Africans. He understood nothing but English. When the Limeys deported them Charlie's single mother hauled him back to Lagos, which got promptly overrun by the Simba Brigades. She'd jumped at the chance to sell her troublesome son to Alicia Nshombo's recruiters for a couple hundred bucks. But *he* wasn't the fucking problem.

As if to prove the point Leucrotta snapped at Tom. Only his ace reflexes let Tom shove him out to arm's length as drooling black jaws clacked shut. They'd have taken his face off as cleanly as any sad-sack Egyptian tanker's, *Über*-ace or no. "You little *fuck*," he shouted. "Try that shit on *me?* You need to cool off, man." And he flicked the four hundred pounds of spotted furious monster a casual two hundred yards through the air with a flip of his wrist. Trailing a howl of despair, Leucrotta landed in the middle of a swamp channel with a colossal brown splash.

About half the couple dozen kids hanging around by the tents broke out clapping. Tom gave them a sour smile and stomped off to confront the supposed *authority figures* who had made themselves oh-so-scarce during the dustup.

The special-unit camp, set well apart from the rest of the PPA army in the Bahr al-Ghazal and surrounded with coils of razor tape that glittered evilly in the white-hot sun, was as depressing a patch of perpetually soggy alkali clay, barbed-wire scrub, sorry-ass grass, and hyperactive mosquitoes as Tom had encountered in all his years spent knocking around the very least desirable real estate in the whole Third World. *What the hell possessed me to take my day off in fucking Brazil, anyway?* he asked himself furiously. *Next time I'm going to goddamn Greenland.*

The adult supervisors on duty stood aside in a clump: four surly overfed Congolese nurses from the National Health Service and a pair of Leopard Men commandos in their spotted cammies. All wore web belts with Tasers and Mace prominently displayed. The commandos wore holsters with 9mm SIG P226 handguns, too.

"What the *fuck?*" Tom said, spreading his hands palm up. "That asshole Leucrotta is throwing his weight around. You can't be dumb enough not to know how that's gonna fly: either he's gonna waste somebody or somebody's gonna waste him. Either way the People's Paradise loses a valuable asset. You need to keep these kids in line. They're freaked out and pissed off. They're gonna tear each other apart without Siraj having to lift his little finger!"

"They are like animals anyway," one of the nurses said. "Let them settle their pecking order themselves."

"At least exercise some adult moral guidance," he said in exasperation. "Try persuasion. Lead by example."

"If the great leader will show us the way," the shorter of the Leopard Men, Achille, said.

Tom walked two steps back into the sun. Then he swung back around and jabbed a finger at the handlers. "All right. I'll do that. I'll do that little thing. *Hey, kids.* Listen up."

Back came Leucrotta from his bath, human, slouching, and squelching. Tom favored him with a hot blue glare.

"Got control of yourself now, Fido?"

The boy glared. "Uh-huh."

"If you *ever* pull shit like that again with me I'll take you up for a nice little visit to orbit. For about five minutes. Do you understand? Say yes."

"*Oui,*" said Leucrotta sullenly.

Tom nodded. "Smart answer. Let's hope that means you're *getting* smart." He turned to the others. They stared at him wide-eyed. He saw awe on some faces and dread on others, but no hint of hostility. That was a relief; some of them could threaten even him. *I'm Hell's scoutmaster, here*, he thought. *Fuck me.* He drew a deep breath. "All right. Just what are we doing here in the middle of the nastiest swamp God never made? Can anybody tell me that?"

"We're helping liberate the oppressed people of the South Sudan," a boy said.

"Yeah," Tom said, nodding. "That's the official line, isn't it? And hey, that's true. That is what you're doing. Don't forget it. And what else?"

"We're trying to keep from dying." The speaker was a stick-thin girl in ridiculously baggy Simba BDUs. She was about thirteen, extremely dark-skinned and threatening to become pretty one day. Her hair was cut short to her head. Despite strict embargoes on "unnecessary" personal possessions she sported a pair of huge red plastic hoop earrings and matching glasses with big round lenses.

"You show some respect to your betters, little freak," bellowed the stoutest of the Health Service matrons, a slab-faced woman with wire glasses named Monique.

Tom opened his mouth to invite Monique to butt the hell out. Before he could speak, inky Darkness began to dance around the skinny girl like black flames, then leaped suddenly toward the matron. Screeching, she turned and fled as her fellow matrons stampeded out of the way.

"Now, that wasn't nice, was it, Candace?" Tom asked.

The Darkness shot her nonexistent hips and stuck out her underlip in a cute prepubescent pout. "We're not here to be nice, *non?* And anyway, she oppresses us. Or are we not meant to share in the Liberation?"

Candace Sessou was a bright and sassy teenybopper girl from a middle-class neighborhood of the city of Kinkala, near the former Brazzaville part of Kongoville in the southwest of what had been the Republic of the Congo before Nshombo and Tom liberated it. He was constantly surprised she'd survived to make it out of the labs alive. She had a problem with authority.

So did Tom.

"You are," he told the group. "The Revolution is for everybody. It's about liberating everybody. The people of the world. The people of the South Sudan. You."

The handlers shot him barbed looks, as if he were giving the children license to eat them all alive. None of them had the guts to say anything. They were bullies, all of them. But he couldn't very well let the kid aces go all Lord of the Flies on them, either. Time to try getting their twisted little minds right.

"But the Revolution is all about discipline, too," he told the children. "About putting aside your selfish little ego trips and squabbles. See, the way the Man keeps the people down is divide and conquer. So what you need to do is pull together. Do your parts for the Revolution, for all the other kids suffering oppression around the world, and most of all, for each other. Can you dig it?"

"Yeah!" They shot to their feet, throwing their little fists up in the air on skinny arms.

"That's the spirit. That's my brothers and sisters. The Man can't stand against commitment like that. You kids will save the world!" He let them soak that up. Then he said, "Now listen up. We got a job to do. And this time you kids are gonna make all the adults in the *world* sit up and take notice."

♥

Thursday, December 3

Near Lake Tanganyika
Tanzania

THE CESSNA BOBBED AND weaved through the air, tossing them violently from side to side. Wally clenched the seat in front of him so hard that the metal frame dented. Finch grinned back at them from the pilot's seat, his stubby rhino ears twitching. Whenever he glanced at Jerusha, his gaze seemed to drift down to her chest and linger there. At least she'd worn an athletic support bra. "Bit of a rough ride, eh?" he said. "But we're almost there."

The turbulence grew brutal, and Finch paid more attention to the plane than to Jerusha. They skirted purple-grey thunderheads tossing lightning down toward the savannah and occasionally passed through rain showers. Tanzania glided slowly underneath them, and finally ahead, Jerusha could see an immense stretch of blue water. Finch spoke over a crackling radio as he circled the aircraft as they neared the lake's shore. "We're setting down there," he said, pointing to a tiny airfield.

Ten minutes later, in a cloud of brown dust, they were down and taxiing up to a long Quonset hut. Finch cut the motor—the silence was deafening, the roar still echoing in Jerusha's ears. Finch opened the doors and gestured. The air outside was sweltering and humid; she could see the orange spots beginning to dot Wally's skin again. Huge mountains loomed to the east, but Jerusha could glimpse the lake to the west, beyond the buildings of the town. "Welcome to Kasoge," Finch said.

There was a squad of a half-dozen soldiers leaning against the hut. As Jerusha stepped from the plane, they began to saunter over toward them. When Wally followed her, they stopped. One of them snapped something, and the muzzles of their rifles suddenly came up.

"Hang on now, mates," Finch called out, his hands lifted and open. Jerusha followed his example, but Wally only raised an eyebrow. Deliberately, he stepped in front of Jerusha. The gesture was touching, but it meant she couldn't see. She moved around him. Finch was talking to the soldiers in what Jerusha assumed was Kiswahili.

Their voices were loud and strident at first, and Jerusha's hand drifted to her seed belt, her fingers curling around kudzu seeds. A quick toss, and she could entangle them. . . .

She took a step to Wally's side. The soldiers were still staring at them, but their weapons had dropped back to their sides. Finch was still talking, waving his hands. "I need your passports," he said. Jerusha handed them to him.

The squad's officer glanced through the documents, finally passing them back to Finch. The soldiers went back to the hut, conversing among themselves and still watching them. "Those blokes are looking for PPA incursions, or for refugees from there," Finch told them. "I told them we'd come from Dar es Salaam, not the Congo. I told them you had no interest in the PPA. I *think* they believe me." He sniffed, the horn on his snout tossing. "So—was that true?"

Jerusha didn't answer; Wally just shrugged. If there were soldiers patrolling the shores of Tanganyika, they were going to have to be very careful. "If Wally and I would like to take a boat ride on the lake tomorrow," she said to Finch, "would you be able to negotiate that for us? We could pay you. . . ."

"Boat ride, eh?" Finch scowled, tiny ears fluttering while he fixed Wally and Jerusha with a scowl. "A nice, leisurely sightseeing ride?"

"Yep. That's right," said Wally. "Sightseeing."

Behind him, Jerusha sighed.

Finch scratched at the base of his horn with one long, blackened finger-nail. *Scritch. Scritch. Scritch.* He narrowed his little eyes, taking a long, hard look at Wally and Jerusha. He seemed to spend more time looking at Jerusha. His gaze was a little less angry when he looked at her, too; he never seemed to have much to say to Wally.

"Well, I expect that since you're just a pair of innocent tourists with no interest in the People's Paradise of Africa you'll not know that the border between Tanzania and the PPA runs straight down the middle of the lake." Finch hacked up something dark and wet. He spat it in the dirt, adding, "And you do not want to find yourselves on the wrong side of that line."

Jerusha said, quietly, "What would happen if we did? What would we find? Just out of curiosity."

"Rebels and Leopard Men. If you're lucky."

Leopard Men? Rebels? What the heck was going on over there? What the heck had happened to Lucien? Wally couldn't help it: "Holy cow! Leopard Men?" The soldiers over by the Quonset hut looked up from their private conversation. Worrying about Lucien had got him worked up; he'd asked a little more loudly than he'd intended.

"It doesn't bloody matter, does it? Since you're not going over there." Finch had a strange look in his eye, like he was saying one thing but meant something else. "All you need to know is that they'd shoot you dead the moment they noticed you." He punctuated the last with a sharp jerk of his head, pointing his horn toward the lake and, by extension, the PPA.

"Well, look, buddy, bullets don't—"

Jerusha clapped a hand on Wally's arm. "Thanks for the warning. We wouldn't want any misunderstandings." She emphasized "misunderstand-ings." Then she tugged at Wally. "We'll trust you to hire a boat for us."

Once out of earshot from Finch, Wally asked her, "What if he gets a boat that won't go across the lake?"

"I don't think that will be a problem, Wally. I think Finch had our num-ber the minute he laid eyes on us. He thinks we're on a secret mission for the Committee."

They followed the road to a narrow bend. In one direction, from where they'd walked, Finch unloaded more crates from his battered Cessna. In the other direction, around the bend, Wally got his first glimpse of the outskirts of Kasoge.

It wasn't all that different from the other villages they'd visited. The

buildings he saw were a random assortment of wood, mud-brick, and sometimes metal siding. They gave the impression of having been built, or rebuilt, from whatever was handy at the time. Wind sighed through the trees
that grasped at a bright tropical sky. It carried with it the earthy smell of
jungle, the dead-fish-and-fresh-water scent of the lakeshore, and the stink
of the garbage fires. The smoke stung Wally's eyes.

From above, in Finch's plane, Africa had seemed like a paradise that
stretched from horizon to horizon. But down on the ground, Wally noticed
different things. Like the garbage fires. People just collected their trash into
piles on the street. When the piles grew large enough, they were burned. He
figured that was because they didn't have a city dump and regular garbage
collection like back home. It made sense. They did what they could.

Still, Wally had been real disappointed when he'd discovered that the
smoke from the garbage fires obscured his view of the stars. He'd figured
that being in Africa would mean he could see all sorts of stars. And different
from the ones he knew.

For all the beauty, Africa sure wasn't a paradise. Even here, in Tanzania.
And Finch's warnings about the PPA hadn't done anything to make Wally
feel better about Lucien. He wished he could just grab a boat and get over to
Kalemie.

Wally and Jerusha stepped off the road, out of the way of a truck. When
it passed, he saw that a long board had been nailed to the back of the truck,
and several bicyclists coasted along by gripping the board. One fellow had
fixed his bike chain with lengths of wire.

They stopped at a pavilion built from irregular panels of corrugated alu-
minum fastened atop brick stanchions. Like he had at the last village, where
they'd stopped the night before, Wally drew a lot of attention. He plopped
down on a bench and zipped open his pack.

"Want a snack?"

"Yeah, actually." Jerusha looked at his pack. "What do you have in
there?"

"I brought some peanut butter. It's good on bananas."

A funny little smile blossomed on Jerusha's face. "Hold on a sec," she said.
She wandered over to a spot near the tree line, upwind of the fires. There she
dug into her pouch and dropped something on the ground. She returned to
the pavilion a few moments later, carrying a golden yellow thing a little larger
than a pear.

"What's that?"

"It's a mango." Jerusha took the knife from her sack and deftly skinned the fruit in long, wide strips.

"Oh. I've never had a mango before."

Again, that smile. She didn't look up from peeling the mango, but she said, "Yes you have. And you liked it, too."

"I have?"

"At the embassy. Remember? All the fruit on the table at breakfast?"

"I remember some pineapple and bananas, because I like those, and some orange stuff, too. It was pretty good."

"That orange stuff was a mango. And I could tell you liked it, because you ate an entire bowl of mango slices."

"Oh." Wally felt himself blushing. "You saw that?"

"Yep." After skinning the mango, she sliced it, neatly excising a large pit from the center. She dried the pit and put it in a pocket of her belt.

Childish laughter echoed across the street. A pair of kids not much older than Lucien ran down the street, trailing a homemade kite: a plastic garbage bag, two long sticks, and about a million little scraps of string tied together into one long string. The kids had two shoes between them; one wore the left shoe, the other the right.

Wally wondered if Lucien had ever flown a kite. Maybe Wally could show him.

They ate in companionable silence, watching the kids.

"Jerusha?"

"Yeah?"

Wally looked at his feet, not wanting to embarrass her. "I'm real glad you decided to come along."

Jackson Square
New Orleans, Louisiana

THERE'S A SHOT OF the French Quarter on TV. At first, it looks like there's been a freak snowstorm. But as the camera zooms in closer, you can see that there are bubbles everywhere. People are wading knee-deep through them, kicking them up in the air. Sometimes they pop and everyone laughs.

"I've never seen anything like it," the reporter says. "It's been raining bubbles here for three days now. We've been trying to talk to Michelle Pond, the Amazing Bubbles, to find out when this will end."

Michelle rolled her eyes. She'd refused interviews because she really didn't *know* how much longer it would go on. She was definitely lighter, and she thought she was getting smaller, but there was still so much energy in her. She looked up at the TV again.

The next shot was of a playground. Kids were shrieking and laughing as they slid into the masses of iridescent bubbles. They picked up bubbles and threw them at each other. Some popped immediately, but most bounced harmlessly off their targets.

Then another shower of bubbles began, and the children held out their arms and let the bubbles rain down on them.

Friday, December 4

Lake Tanganyika
Tanzania

"**CROSSING OVER INTO THE** PPA would be very unwise," Barbara Baden said, line static hissing underneath her voice. "Don't. Things are getting very dicey there. The war, the Leopard Society, Tom Weathers . . ."

"Don't worry about us," Jerusha told her, standing on the dock where the boat they'd hired was moored. Mist was rising from the lake, and the jungle around them was noisy with stirring life. "I'm just helping Wally nose around a bit."

"Good," Barbara said. "Be very careful, and stay in touch."

"Sure will," Jerusha told her and snapped the phone shut.

"Sure will what?" Wally asked. He was scrubbing furiously at his left shoulder with an S.O.S pad. Finch was a few feet away, talking to the boat's owner. Their kit sat in bundles around them, looking heavy in the dawn light, but Wally seemed barely able to stand still now that they were so close to Lucien.

Jerusha lifted a shoulder. "Nothing important." She wondered whether she should tell him what Barbara was saying about the PPA, but she was certain it wouldn't change Wally's mind. If she refused to go with him, he'd just go alone. Jerusha wasn't quite sure why, but she knew she couldn't let him do that. *He needs you, and you . . .*

Finch interrupted the thought. "Hamisi here doesn't much like the idea of going over to the PPA side of the lake," he said. "He's saying he needs another hundred dollars. For the risk."

"You already negotiated the price. We've already paid him fifty."

Finch shrugged. "Now he wants more. Or, he says, he won't do it. Can't say I blame the bloke. The PPA's not a place I want to get too near myself, with the things I've been hearing. You're lucky to have found anyone who's foolish enough to ferry you across." He waved at Hamisi, who stood watching them from where the boat was tied up. "You want to talk to him yourself?"

"I'll pay you back when we get home, Jerusha," Wally interjected. His foot was tapping on the pier, shaking the wooden planks, which already bowed under his weight.

Jerusha sighed. "Offer him another fifty," she told Finch. The man shrugged and went back to Hamisi. After a heated exchange, he came back. "Got him to agree to an additional seventy. Best I can do. Or the two of you can try to find someone else, or better yet, stay here. Your call."

Jerusha looked at Wally. "All right," she said. "Seventy."

Ten minutes later, Finch had tossed the rope from the pier into the boat where they were sitting. The boat smelled equally of old fish and grimy diesel oil; the deck was filthy and slick, the bench seats only slightly less so. Hamisi fiddled with the controls in the small cabin; the engine snorted blue exhaust and bubbles churned at the rear of the boat. "Good luck to the both of you," Finch called as the bow began to cut through the dark water of the lake. "You're going to bloody need it."

Jerusha tried to put that last bit out of her mind as she watched Finch's body dwindle into the distance and mist.

Thirty miles across—that's what Finch said it was—a trip that would take at least three hours, according to Hamisi, who didn't understand English but could converse—haltingly—in Jerusha's French. The Congo had always used French as an official, tribally neutral official language, a practice retained by the PPA, and Hamisi had originally come from the PPA, long ago. *Three hours . . .*

The lake water seemed to drift slowly past the hull as the mist lifted in the rising sun, but there was no sign of the other side of the lake. She could see other boats out on the water: schooners with white sails, distant fishing boats with their snarls of nets, pleasure craft lifting bows high out of the water. The horizon ahead of them was unbroken water seeming eternally fixed despite their own movement. The landscape was beautiful, though: the deep lake, the walls of green mountains behind them and parading off into the distance, a rain squall spreading darkness well to the north, and thunderheads looming in the distance. It reminded her of the wild beauty of Conrad's description of the Congo.

Wally didn't glance around at the scenery. He sat in the exact middle of the boat, staying very still and looking out at the water apprehensively. "Wally, you okay?"

He gave a shrug and worked his steam-shovel mouth. "All this water," he said. "Cripes, I used to love swimming, back before my card turned. But now . . ." He tapped his chest with his fist, a sound like a trash can colliding with a Dumpster. "Can't swim. Don't like water."

"It'll be over soon. Just hang on." She rubbed at the back of her neck with her hand, kneading the ache that threatened to become a headache. *And then there's the jungle, and the rains, and the rivers we'll probably have to cross there, and getting across Lake Tanganyika again afterward . . .*

After a time, Jerusha realized that she could finally see the smudge of the PPA coastline. The blue-hazed humps there crawled toward them, far too slowly for Jerusha's comfort, but reachable now. The boat puttered steadily forward, and Jerusha was beginning to think that the crossing was, despite Finch's pessimism, to be uneventful.

"Hey, what's that?" Wally said.

He was pointing northward. A black dot was slicing through the water: a patrol boat, with a white wake tracing its path. At about the same time that they noticed it, the boat shifted course toward them. Hamisi, at the wheel, cursed.

"Can't you beat them to the shore?" Wally asked hopefully. He pointed to where the trees reached the lake. Hamisi scowled. He spat a long, loud harangue in what Jerusha assumed was Kiswahili. "What'd he say?" Wally asked Jerusha. She could only shake her head.

Someone on the patrol gunboat was shouting through a megaphone in French. "Shut off your engine!"

Hamisi looked at Jerusha. She didn't know what to tell the man. The command was repeated, and this time the machine gun mounted on the craft sent a long white line spattering into the lake just ahead of them. White smoke drifted away from the muzzle, the noise echoing back at them belatedly from the shore. Hamisi slapped at the key; the engine went silent as the waves swayed the boat from side to side.

Wally grabbed at the gunwale for balance as the patrol boat circled them at twenty yards or so. "Jerusha," he said, "just stay behind me if they start firing, and I'll . . . I'll . . ."

"You'll what? Swim over to get to them?" The crestfallen apology on his face made her regret the words even as she said them. Her hands slid over her seed belt, her fingers slipping into the enclosures to touch the seeds there. Out here, there was nowhere to hide. If they wanted them dead, all they need do was pepper their sorry little craft with holes and watch them sink. They could capture them just as easily.

Jerusha had no intention of seeing what a PPA prison might be like. Wally's strength meant little here, if there was no ground on which to stand. Hamisi was already backing away from the wheel of the boat, his hands up.

"Wally," Jerusha said. "Hands up."

He looked surprised at that. "We can't just give up."

"*They* have to think we will," she told him, nodding toward the gunboat. She lifted her own hands. "Go on," she said, and reluctantly Wally raised his own huge arms; there were large orange spots on his underarms.

The gunboat circled once more, then moved in toward them. When it passed in front of Jerusha, only an arm's length from their boat, she threw the seeds in her hand and opened her mind to her wild card power.

Kudzu vines were already sprouting wildly from the seeds before they even hit the gunboat's deck and the water near the hull. Some curled rapidly around the crew members as they tried to draw guns, while others fouled the twin propellers of the craft. Jerusha could hear the groan of the patrol boat's engine as it tried to force the props to turn. Then—with a whine and a cloud of white smoke—the engine cut off entirely.

"*Hamisi!*" Jerusha shouted in French. "Let's go! *Hâte!*"

Hamisi pressed the starter and water gurgled as they started to move, slowly, along the length of the patrol boat. The crew members were shouting, tearing kudzu from around themselves. Jerusha had been unable to toss the small seeds far enough to reach the machine-gun mount—it swung around to follow them and she heard the man ratchet a slide back. She took a baobab seed from her pouch: she wasn't certain she could toss it that far. "Rusty!" she said. "Here. Throw this onto the boat."

Wally took the seed from her, tossed it high and long. The seed rang on the deck as the baobab sprouted roots and its strange crown—a dozen years' growth done in a breath. The deck plates groaned metallically as the thick roots plunged downward seeking water and earth. One branch tipped the machine gun's barrel up, and tracers laced the sky as it chattered.

Jerusha bent the tree with her mind, tilting it so that the gunboat began to lean. Water suddenly burst around the new baobab's girth. The gunboat listed over entirely in the space of a few breaths, the half-dozen crew members beginning to scream. Jerusha had the vines fling them overboard, releasing them at the same time.

"Go!" she shouted to Hamisi. *"Allez! Au rivage! Rapidement!"* She pushed him toward the cabin of their boat as the gunboat crew flailed at the water, grasping for the baobab's branches even as the gunboat turned entirely on its side, the hull now facing them. The baobab floated low in the water as Hamisi's engine coughed and roared. They moved away from the men, who were waving their arms and calling out to them.

"Good toss," Jerusha told Rusty.

He grinned. She thought that if he could have blushed, he would have. "It was nothin'," Wally said. "But cripes, that was pretty terrific, Jerusha."

She gave him a quick, fading smile. She could feel the baobab dying in the water, drowning without earth to sustain it. The crew of the gunboat was still shouting, their voices fainter now; the tree would serve as a raft until someone noticed them. *I'm sorry*, she whispered to it. *I'm sorry.* "Let's get to the shore before reinforcements show up." She stared at the slopes there, pointing to the nearest point of land. "There," she told Hamisi. "Take us there. . . ."

Jackson Square
New Orleans, Louisiana

FOR ONCE, MICHELLE ISN'T in the pit.

This is a nice looking place. But she's still afraid. *No*, Michelle thinks. *Adesina is afraid.*

There are small buildings in a circular layout. They're nicer than any of the houses in Adesina's village. These are sturdy, built from concrete blocks and are painted in bright primary colors and all the roofs are brick red. They have glass in the windows and she sees power lines running from generators to each building. There's gravel laid out on the ground so the walkways won't turn to mud when it rains. There's even a pretty painted sign: Kisa . . . something Hospital for Children. Michelle can't quite make it out.

Even though she's frightened, Adesina is awed by this place. She's never been anywhere so nice before. A woman comes out of the red building. She wears a white coat and carries a clipboard. Something about her frightens Adesina and she cowers with the other children. The woman walks by each child, pointing at each one, then gesturing to one side of the path or the other.

After the children are divided, they're taken to different buildings. Adesina goes into the green building. She likes the color green, but not today. Today she hates it. She's crying and she wants her mother and father. One of the other children pinches her and tells her to stop being such a baby. But Adesina doesn't care. She doesn't mind being a baby now.

Another woman in a white coat comes into the room. She carries a tray covered by a white cloth. Adesina cries harder, and soon all the children are crying. The woman ignores their tears.

The woman opens the door to another room and then steps inside. Before she closes the door, she makes a quick gesture to one of the children's captors. He grabs the boy who pinched Adesina and drags him inside.

One by one, the children are taken into the small back room. The children don't come out again. When Adesina's turn finally comes, she sees why. There's a door leading out the back of the building.

The woman in the white coat speaks sharply to Adesina. Michelle doesn't understand the words, but she grasps the intent. Adesina stops crying, but snuffles as she tries to contain herself.

The woman pulls the cloth back from the silver tray. There's a row of needles. Adesina doesn't know what they're for, but they look sharp and hurty. She starts crying again. The woman grabs her arm and before Adesina can squirm away, the needle sinks into her flesh.

For a moment, nothing happens. Adesina's so surprised she stops crying. Then the fire roars through her. It tears at her mind and pulls her apart. She looks down at her hands and sees that they're changing. And that's when she begins to scream. Then the world goes dark.

Khartoum, Sudan
The Caliphate of Arabia

THE LITTLE GIRL WAS unnaturally still in his arms as they hung for a breathless instant in orbit. The bandages wrapped around her wizened little body felt rough. Tom took quick stock: for once his objective was marked by a terrain feature—the confluence of the Blue Nile from Ethiopia and the White Nile from Uganda, becoming then just the plain old Nile everybody knew. Supposedly the ancients thought it looked like an elephant's trunk. How they could tell, given that the country here was every bit as stomped-down flat as the Sudd not so far south, he had no clue. But the alleged resemblance had given the place its name: *al-Khartum*, the Elephant's Trunk.

Khartoum. Capital of the former Republic of Sudan. Now just the capital of the newest province of the Caliphate.

They called the girl the Mummy, for the bandages that covered her whole little body and big head to protect her sensitive skin from the blistering African sun. The docs said she was eleven, though she was the size of a four-year-old, and a none too healthy one at that. The Simbas had found her wandering in drought-stricken northeast Uganda during that country's recent liberation.

Downward like a beam of light—

And here, see, was where the plans ran a bit off-rail. Tom and his charge found themselves on a dais decked with festive bunting in the Sudanese colors of red and black and white and the obligatory Muslim green. It stood in the courtyard of the Defense Ministry: a blinding white colonial-era wedding cake, like a smaller version of the nearby Presidential Palace, almost on the Blue Nile bank.

The courtyard, partially shaded by trees planted by those same long-gone English colonialists, was packed with martyrs of the Sudan's wars. The living ones, of course: the merely wounded, who could look forward to life on the leavings of a rat-poor state, propped on a wheeled platform that kind of replaced your legs, and in constant pain that even the rare morphine dose could never really ease.

A mustached man in an extravagantly medaled blue uniform stood behind the podium, staring at the impossible apparition of a tall Western man and a tiny girl completely swathed in bandages *right beside him.* But he wasn't

the Sudanese president, Omar Hasan Ahmad al-Bashir. And he was *supposed*
to be.

Hell knew where Bashir was. Maybe he was held up taking a call from
one of his wives (he had two). Or maybe he had just shone the vets on. They
weren't any more use to him except for PR, after all. Instead, the dude in
blue was Major General Abdel Rahim Mohammad Hussein, Sudan's Minister of Defense. He'd been accused of assorted lurid war crimes in Darfur
and South Sudan.

He'll do just fine. Tom pointed at him. "Do your thing, honey," he said.

The Mummy never spoke. Probably she only understood a little English.
But she went where she was pointed and did what she was told. Which was
all Tom needed now.

Beyond the minister was a fat man with a blue scholar's gown and a
bunch of bristling grey beard whose extravagant eyebrows were trying to crawl
up under his sacklike hat to hide. He was another prize target, the Sunni
Imam al-Bushehri of Iraq, the Caliph's advisor to the Sudanese. He promptly
hitched up his robe and ran with surprising hippo speed for the Ministry's
portico.

Tom grinned and blinked out. He was just as happy to miss the rest of
the strangled squawks and *squelching* sounds that had begun to emerge from
the Defense Minister.

Up; then back down to the camp in the Sudd.

His next passenger was a small boy, underfed-looking but otherwise a lot
more normal than the Mummy. But his eyes were spooky. Tom didn't know
his story and wasn't sure he wanted to. And he made sure to keep his parts
well clear of his mouth. Just, y'know, *in case.*

He landed on the podium again. It was the one spot in the courtyard the
guards were unlikely to spray with frantic fire from their Kalashnikovs,
packed as it was with Sudanese brass. The Minister of Defense had shrunk,
although still upright and clinging to the podium with sticklike fingers. The
Mummy had ballooned *way* out. Fortunately they had learned to wrap her
in elastic bandages, loose and with lots of give.

The imam, now—his fat ass and billowing robes were just vanishing
through the front door between two astonished-looking guards. Still clutching the boy, Tom flew right through the open doors. Fastball fast, not photon
fast. But faster than the guards could react.

The imam's slippers made soft thumping sounds on immaculately polished hardwood floors. Smelling whole *generations* of varnish Tom flashed past the wheezing man. Ten feet ahead of al-Bushehri he set the boy down.

The bearded cleric labored to a stop. "Here," Tom said in English. "There's someone I'd like you to meet. Wanjala, Imam. Imam, Wanjala."

"Go ahead and kill me, *Mokèlé-mbèmbé*," al-Bushehri said. "I die a martyr."

The Iraqi had balls of brass. Tom had to give him that. Not like it mattered. "I'm not going to kill you," Tom said as the skinny boy fixed the huge man with a feral stare, then darted toward him. "The Hunger will."

"A child? What's—*ow*! He bit me!"

"Shit happens, *effendi*. Gotta book." He grabbed Wanjala up by the back of his camouflage T-shirt—fuck knew he didn't want the kid biting *him*—and dashed past the fat man, who was clutching his soft brown hand and staring at the blood welling up from the tooth marks on the back of it.

The guards at the entrance had wheeled to aim their rifles down the echoing hall. They hesitated to shoot for fear of hitting the imam. Tom didn't hesitate. Crimson plasma jetted twice from his palm. The two guards reeled away as torches, falling in flames on the Ministry steps. Both were dead on the instant; but superheated air venting from their lungs made them scream as if they felt the fire that consumed them.

Even before Tom cleared the door he saw that confusion still reigned outside. The Mummy was almost globular now. General Hussein lay beside her like a bundle of brown sticks in a gaudy blue sack. The other Sudanese war pigs stood gaping, too confused and horror-stricken even to run the fuck away. Tom reckoned the girl had at least a few seconds' grace before anyone thought to shoot her. As soon as he got clear sky Tom was gone to orbit, swapping Wanjala for Charlie Abidemi in a single drop and grab.

This time Tom lit on the edge of the Ministry roof overlooking the courtyard o' chaos. He let Charlie drop to the hot tarred gravel beside him, then gave a quick pulse of sunbeam to the grass right in front of the first rank of martyrs, who fell out of their wheelchairs. That was tough luck; he didn't have anything against them. But he didn't hurt them, either.

Fact was, he couldn't afford to fry too many guards: all this rapid hypertripping and flying had about worn him out. He just wanted to make the guys with guns *flinch*.

They did. He turned to the boy he'd just deposited on the roof. "All right, Wrecker, start wrecking. You got two minutes. Have fun."

As a guard lined his sights up on the Mummy his Kalashnikov's receiver exploded in his face. He shrieked. There was no flash, no flame, no fragments larger than dissociated molecules. But the shock of the bonds that held all those molecules together simultaneously bursting—*that* stripped cloth, skin, and muscle from torso and arm and the front of his skull. Howling out of a red mask the guard fell over backward.

Other similar cracks rang out around the courtyard, each followed by fresh screams. Charlie Abidemi's ace only worked on inorganic matter, and had a range of only about fifty feet. But all he had to do was look at something made of stone or metal and snap his fingers, and about two pounds of it went *poof.*

Tom jumped down beside the Mummy. Smiling down at the obsidian eyes that glittered impassively from the stretched-out bandages, and trying his best to ignore the yellow pool around her feet as her kidneys desperately processed the extravagant overload of water she'd sucked into her tissues, he put an arm around her. "No offense, honey," he said, "but you're gonna be a load."

Around the corner of the building, invisible to Tom, past high white walls but clearly not from the roof, something big blew up. Like a Russian-made BTR armored car. Wrecker was definitely living up to his name.

Tom grinned. Was gone.

◆

Saturday,
December 5

Somewhere South of Kalemie, Congo
People's Paradise of Africa

IT WOULD HAVE BEEN easier to keep to the shore as they moved north, but after the run-in with the PPA gunboat, Wally suggested they stay inland so as not to be seen from the lake. Jerusha agreed. It did hide them from the lake, but since they also had to avoid the roads, it meant slow going as they trudged through a solid wall of vegetation.

Wally took the lead. He tried to hack his way through the thickest bits. It wasn't as easy as it looked in the Tarzan movies. He hadn't realized that swinging a machete took so much technique. The hardest part was turning his wrist to make another slash on the backswing. And every swing had to be coordinated with a step of just the right size, so that he didn't overextend the next swing. A few times he even managed to hit himself on the follow-through.

He made up for the lack of technique with brute strength. His knife hand went numb from the constant *smack* and vibration of mistimed or misplaced swings.

Wally ignored the growing tingle in his hand. Kalemie was so close. Just a few more miles to Lucien, and then everything would be okay.

Hack. Rip. Slash. Rip. Hack. They hadn't been going more than half an hour before his face, chest, and forearms were splattered with little bits and pieces of green vegetable matter.

Here he was, adventuring in the middle of Africa, complete with pith helmet and machete—just like the games he and his brother had played as kids. But it wasn't very fun. In fact, it wasn't fun at all.

TV couldn't convey just how wet, how humid, it was in the jungle. That wasn't counting the rain, which, as Wally had quickly learned, sometimes came down so hard and so fast that it hurt. He wondered how Jerusha put up with it. Nor did the old movies convey the sickly sweet smell of constant decay that enveloped him like a fog. Not to mention how sticky it made a guy, cutting through all these plants.

And in the movies, Tarzan always rescued his friends in the nick of time. But if Wally had learned one thing from his time with the Committee, it was that real life offered no such guarantees. *Rebels and Leopard Men . . . What happened, Lucien? What's going on at that school of yours?*

Wally glanced over his shoulder. Jerusha had fallen back a respectable distance, to avoid the rain of debris. She didn't say anything, but he wondered if it upset her that he was hurting so many plants.

He fell into a meditative rhythm, replaying the lake crossing over and over again. Wally hadn't entirely understood just how far out of his depth he was on this trip until the gunboat showed up. In fact, he wouldn't have made it that far if not for Jerusha.

Wild card powers aside, she at least could talk to folks in French. He couldn't even do that. It hadn't occurred to him that communication might be a problem; all of his foreign travel experiences had been carried out through the Committee, where he and DB were always surrounded either by translators or folks who spoke English. Plus, Lucien had pretty good English for a little guy, so Wally had figured everybody here did.

And then, when the PPA boat had shown up, Wally had done . . . nothing. He'd been no help at all. Jerusha had taken care of the whole thing in a few seconds. Even her aim was great. Almost as good as Kate's.

She didn't need his help at all. But he sure as heck needed her.

New York Public Library
Manhattan, New York

"YES! OH, YES YES yes yes yes! Fucking A, *yes!*"

The inhabitants of the reading room raised their collective heads, considered the young man capering wildly at his carrel with amusement or uneasiness or disgust, and then went back to their business. Bugsy nodded apologetically to the guard, and sat back down. "I am too cool," he said under his breath. "I am the man. Oh, yes. Oh, yes. Ain't nobody better than me."

Three huge bound volumes were stacked before him. The first was a volume of ancient arrest records dating from the end of 1970 to the beginning of seventy-one. The second were summaries of small claims court proceedings from the same period. The last, bound in black leather like an ancient grimoire, were the documents for the New York City Family Court for the eighties.

The ruling that Bugsy was poring over, that had inspired his delight, was a custody battle between one Kimberly Ann Cordayne and her estranged husband Mark Meadows. He shifted in his seat, his grin almost ached. He took a legal pad and a pen, marked DO NOT RESHELVE—I'LL BE RIGHT BACK on the top page, and laid it across the opened book. Then, just to be sure, he popped half a dozen wasps free and set up a little perimeter guard on the books before skipping out of the reading room and pulling out his cell.

Ellen wasn't answering, so he called Lohengrin's office number. The man's secretary said he wasn't in, but offered to take a message or drop Bugsy to voice mail. He opted for voice mail.

"Lohengrin!" he said, grinning. "Lohengrin, you great quasi-Nordic war god! You huge example of German technology run amok! I am the coolest guy you know. Seriously. I have plucked the Sunflower out of a haystack. Kimberly Ann Cordayne, aka Sunflower. Arrest record like a small-town phone book starting with petty crap in the late sixties and going up—I shit you not—to suspected membership in the Symbionese Liberation Army. Married some poor schlub named Mark Meadows back in seventy-five, got divorced in eighty-one. Knock-down, drag-out custody battle over a retarded kid goes through eighty-nine. Wound up with the judge ruling both parents unfit and giving the kid to the state. And the girl was named . . . wait for it . . . Sprout!

"So unless there's a bunch of other Special Olympians named Sprout born right around seventy-seven, this is the same one Tom Weathers got his panties in a bunch about last year when he tried to nuke New Orleans. Now I don't know if this Meadows creature is the bio-dad, or Sunflower was bumping uglies with the Radical all through the seventies or what, but I am on the case. *On* it.

"So . . . *yeah.*

"Um. I get anything else, I'll call you back." Bugsy dropped the connection, smiled a little less widely at the cell phone, and went back to the reading room.

The next seven hours brought little information about Sunflower Cordayne, but Mark Meadows turned out to have a fair paper trail. The implication from press clippings and court documents was that he was some kind of ace with the *nom de virus* "Cap'n Trips," but what exactly his alleged powers were was never made explicit. Instead, he ran the Cosmic Pumpkin Head Shop and Organic Deli (renamed the New Dawn Wellness Center sometime in the late eighties) on the border between Jokertown and the Village and hung out with a raft of better-known aces. Jumping Jack Flash. Moonchild. Aquarius.

When Moonchild got herself elected the president of South Vietnam, Meadows got himself named chancellor, only to bite the big burrito when the presidential palace went up in a fireball. And supposedly his daughter Sprout died with him. Right about the time Tom Weathers showed up in East Asia, kicking ass and taking names in a list that was still growing today.

Bugsy closed the books and rubbed his eyes. The windows were all dark now, and the breeze coming in from the east smelled like taxicabs and the Atlantic.

There were a number of good scenarios. Tom Weathers shows up in sixty-nine, hooks up with Sunflower. Maybe he's living underground this whole time, getting crazier and more political right along with Sunflower.

And then . . . and then something happens, and Sunflower hooks up with Cap'n Trips. Someone gets her knocked up—Meadows or Weathers—and things go south. She's locked up in a psycho ward where she might be moldering even now. Meadows gets a long, colorful career as illegal pharmacist, fugitive from the law, minor Southeast Asian politico, and dead guy.

Then the Radical comes in from the cold, with the daughter at his side. Could Tom Weathers really have been the one who killed Moonchild? It was looking more and more plausible.

Back at Ellen's place, the scent of curry and coconut milk filled the air.

Ellen was sitting on the kitchen counter, a fork in one hand, a white take-away box in the other. She raised her eyebrows in query as he dropped onto the couch. "You see the news?" she asked.

"Not the recent stuff," he said. "Something happen?"

"The Radical led a raid in Khartoum. Killed a bunch of Sudanese officials and a few delegates from the Caliphate," Ellen said. "Things are getting worse."

"Well, small victory here. Good old-fashioned legwork paid off," Bugsy said. "It was all in the stacks."

"No database?"

"Nope. Internet doesn't know everything after all."

"Good to know."

"Ellen? Look, I don't know what your plans are tonight, but . . . ?"

She looked at him, smiling softly. He felt a small biological urge. "You want to see her?" she said.

He'd actually intended to ask for Nick. The guy was an ass, but he was a damned good detective, and he'd know better than Bugsy how to track down Sunflower. On the other hand, it looked very much like an offer of sex might be accepted, and Nick and his swamp-soaked hat would be around in the morning.

"Yeah," he said. "If that's okay."

Kalemie, Congo
People's Paradise of Africa

KALEMIE WAS WORSE THAN anything Jerusha had yet witnessed.

The city had been flattened. There were ruins everywhere—a massacre had taken place here, and much of Kalemie had burned. In the pelting rain, there were sodden black timbers marking the place where houses and buildings had stood, with vines and green shoots already poking up through them. Occasionally, they had glimpsed the white curve of rib cages protruding from the rubble.

Worse were the people who had survived: emaciated and starving, lost souls with eyes peering in shock from deep in the hollows of their faces, stretching out arms with the ropes of ligaments and muscles plainly visible, their bellies distended from hunger, fly-infested open wounds on their skin.

The school where Lucien had lived hadn't been spared. Most of the tale they received from Sister Julie, whom they found trying to salvage books in the ruined main building. "They came two weeks ago now," she said in her perfect French as she nibbled at the final crumbs of the energy bar Jerusha had given her. "Leopard Men. They said Kalemie was a haven for the rebels fighting Nshombo, and they would clean it out. They took the children, and then they . . ." She stopped, her lips pressed tightly together. "They did things I will not tell you."

"Ask her about Lucien." Wally pushed the picture of the boy forward in his thick-fingered hand, tapping at it as he placed it under the nun's nose. "Ask her if she knows him."

The nun didn't understand English, but she had taken the photo from Wally's hand. "That's Lucien," she said, and the sorrow deepened in her eyes. She looked at Wally. "You were his sponsor, weren't you? They took him with the others," she told Jerusha in French. "They took them all."

"Where?" Jerusha asked. "Where did they take them?"

The nun shook her head. "Up the river. Into the jungle. To the bad place where they *change* them. Nyunzu, they say." She began to weep then, a wracking sorrow that gathered and broke, as if everything dammed inside her had suddenly broken loose.

Jerusha started toward her but Wally was faster. He took the picture of Lucien from her with surprising gentleness, then he gathered Sister Julie in his great iron arms, holding her. "It's okay now," he told her, and Jerusha could see tears in Wally's eyes. "It's okay."

It wasn't, though. Jerusha suspected that for many of those in Kalemie, it might never be. She left Wally, stepping out into the courtyard that bordered the street. The rain had dwindled to a persistent drizzle. The school was set on a slope, overlooking the curving shore of Kalemie and the rain-swept opening where the many-armed Lukuga River exited the lake on its journey into the heart of the jungle and the headwaters of the Congo River. There were people there, scavenging through the tumbled foundations of what must have once been lovely houses, soaked clothing clinging to skeletal forms. They were pulling at whatever scraps they could find—she saw a woman fling a rock eagerly at a rat, then go scrambling after it in the mud.

Jerusha heard Wally coming up alongside her, his bare feet squelching in the muck. *He'll need S.O.S pads for his feet tonight.* The thought was strange and irreverent. "I'm sorry," she told him. "I know you were hoping to find Lucien."

"I'm still going to find him."

"Wally—"

"I'm going to *find* him," Wally said firmly. "You don't have to come."

"I'll come," she told him. The words came easily, somehow, without thought. Wally said nothing for a time; like her, watching the people picking through the ruins of their city. *He needs you. And you . . . you care about him. You like him.*

"They need food." He slid the backpack from his shoulders and set it down, opening the zipper. "This stuff we brought . . ."

"Wait," Jerusha told him. "There's another way." She reached into her seed belt. There were still orange seeds, and apples, and corn. And—there, heavy and large—the baobabs.

Jerusha took a variety of seeds in her hands. She closed her eyes, feeling them, feeling the vibrancy inside. She let herself become part of them, the gift of the wild card letting her fall inside them. She tossed the seeds wide with a cry: the oranges and apples and corn, and two of the baobabs. They hit the mud, and up sprang the trees, thrusting high and branching out, the seasons passing in the blink of an eye: a momentary flowering and a fall of petals, then the fruit growing and ripening, heavy on the branches. The flurry of cornstalks were higher than Wally's head, and golden. The baobabs especially bloomed, thick, heavy presences on either side of what had once been the road, their trunks ten feet around and the pods hanging full and ripe.

The people around them were shouting and pointing. They sidled forward, shyly, whispering among themselves. "Go on," Jerusha told them. "All of this—it's for you."

They looked at her, at Wally, as if afraid that in the next instant, all of the bounty would disappear as quickly as it had come. Then the closest of them plucked an apple from a branch and bit into its firm skin. Juice sprayed, and she laughed.

And they all came running forward.

♥

Sunday,
December 6

On the Lukuga River, Congo
People's Paradise of Africa

THE RESIDENTS OF KALEMIE gave Wally and Gardener a well-used motorboat and filled the outboard engine with gasoline, but none of them would guide them, not when they realized that the two of them were intending to go to Nyunzu. There were mutterings, curse-wardings, and prayers at that statement.

Jerusha wondered if they shouldn't have taken that as a sign.

The Lukuga River, just north of Kalemie, flowed out from Lake Tanganyika, winding and turning as its slow current slid westward into the jungle. They very quickly left behind the houses that gathered on the hills near the lakeshore, and then there was no sign of humankind at all, only unbroken jungle to either side. Jerusha felt that she was truly caught in Conrad's story, drifting down the river into an emerald-shaded, hidden world where people were more intruders than conquerors.

Away from the lake, the river narrowed to the width of a football field. A few crocodiles lounged on the banks, sunning themselves and lifting great, heavy heads to watch them as they passed. Shrikes, hornbills, herons, and storks brooded in the shallows or flickered in the branches and vanished; strange and unidentifiable animals gurgled and yowled and screeched in the shadows, monkeys chased each other high in the trees, shrieking. The mosquitoes were relentless and hungry . . . though that was a problem only for Jerusha. They left Wally entirely alone.

Once they passed a pod of hippos, steering carefully away from them. The green hummocks of islands blocked their way, and the river would split abruptly into branches where they would need to decide which one to follow—they would choose the larger of two, hoping to remain in the main flow of the river. The dense foliage was made up of trees and plants that Jerusha often didn't recognize; there were no bare-branched baobabs here, not in the jungle, nor the ubiquitous acacias of the savannah. The understory of the forest canopy loomed fifty to a hundred feet up; the floor was dense with ferns, parasitical vines, and other large-leafed plants.

The air was heavy and thick; even without the rain, Jerusha's clothing was soaked within a few hours from sweat and mist and humidity. Wally's skin was almost visibly growing orange rust spots as she watched. "I'd give a thousand bucks to be in an air-conditioned room for two minutes right now," Jerusha commented.

Wally glanced at her quizzically. "I didn't think . . ." he said, then seemed to think better of continuing. His mouth clanged shut with a sound like two cast-iron skillets striking together.

Jerusha cocked her head at him. "I *really* hope that you weren't about to suggest that because I'm black and some distant generations ago my ancestors lived somewhere on this godforsaken continent, you thought I should be perfectly comfortable here."

Wally looked away, down, to the side. He didn't speak.

"I didn't think so." Jerusha pulled her sodden shirt away from her shoulders; it clung stubbornly to her skin. She smiled inwardly at Wally's discomfiture.

Every so often, a village would appear on one bank or the other, and people would stare at them as they drifted past or watch silently from their fishing craft. No one approached them, no one called out to them, no one challenged them. They only stared. Jerusha saw almost no children in those villages, and few young men: this area, from what they could see, was inhabited largely by adult women and old people.

Once, passing one of the larger settlements, they watched as a group of older men dressed in business suits and carrying briefcases walked into an open-walled grass hut as if going to a corporate meeting: the juxtaposition was startling. The men watched them too, and one of them reached into the breast pocket of his suit jacket and spoke rapidly into a cell phone, staring at them as he did so.

"Nuts," Wally muttered. "I don't like that."

Jerusha could only agree.

They continued down the river. Around noon, a swarm of bees crossed the stream just ahead of them, a thick, snarling dark arm that twisted and churned up from yet another river island and wriggled its way toward the nearest bank. Jerusha turned off the boat's motor to avoid running into the swarm. The silence was pleasant as they watched the tail of the swarm vanish into the trees.

"That was a *lot* of bees," Wally said.

Jerusha nodded. "Biggest swarm I've seen. Not even those in Yosemite . . . Umm, what's that?"

Wally's head had also swiveled at the same time. They both heard the throaty whine coming from farther down the river and growing louder. "Another boat," Jerusha whispered. Few of the boats they'd passed so far were motorized; those that were had been, like their own boat, using single-stroke gas engines. This was something far more powerful: low, growling, sinister. "Come on," she said to Wally. "Let's take the boat into the island. . . ."

They used the paddles in the boat to maneuver to the rocks at the edge of the island. Jerusha jumped out of the boat, steadying it as Wally came ashore. Wally grabbed the rope at the bow in one massive hand and dragged the boat fully ashore into the foliage. They both hunkered down near it, watching the river through the fronds. A few minutes later, the roar of the engine increased as a patrol boat similar to the one they'd encountered on the lake rounded the nearest bend. It was moving slowly upriver, and the men aboard . . .

Several of them *weren't* men; they were boys who looked to be somewhere between twelve and fifteen, holding semiautomatic weapons strapped around their necks and wearing uniforms. What chilled the blood in Jerusha's body, though, was the man standing near the boat's cabin: a tall man in a military uniform, dark aviator sunglasses over his eyes, and a leopard-skin fez on his head.

A Leopard Man. Babs had told her about Alicia Nshombo's Leopard Society. So had Finch.

"Down!" she whispered harshly to Wally as the boat slid closer to their island. Wally collapsed like a falling tower, hard and loudly. Jerusha grimaced as she pressed herself down into the weeds and rushes, her hands on her seed belt in case they were spotted. Wally had dropped to the mud and stones of the low island, but Jerusha was afraid that his color would show through. She stripped a seed pod from one of the rushes and cast the seeds around him, pulling up the fronds carefully as a screen between Wally's body and the boat, shaping the plants carefully so that their rustling movement wouldn't be noticed.

The motor roared close by. Jerusha put her head down, one hand on Wally's body and the other at her seed belt, listening for any change in the sound and ready to move. The sound grew, too close, then finally began to recede. She could hear the chattering of the child soldiers on the boat, heard the Leopard Man grunt a command. She lifted her head carefully.

The boat had passed them, continuing on upriver, the Leopard Man and the others scanning the riverbank ahead of them, their backs now to Wally and Jerusha.

They waited until the patrol boat had passed around the next bend and they could no longer hear its motor before they stood up. "I think we just got lucky," Wally said. Jerusha nodded. Wally pushed himself up. "Uh-oh," he said.

"Uh-oh?" Jerusha repeated.

Wally's hand was on the large satellite phone case on his belt. "The phone," he said. "It was underneath me . . ." He reached into the pouch and brought out an antenna trailing wires and shattered plastic. "Cripes, it's kinda broken. I'm really sorry, Jerusha. I shoulda been more careful."

He looked so sad that Jerusha couldn't do more than shake her head. "Nothing we can do about it now. Maybe we can find a landline somewhere in one of the villages, or maybe there'll be a cell tower somewhere. Right now, there are other things for us to worry about."

"There could be more boats," Rusty agreed. "So we have to leave the river now, right?"

"If we stay on the river, we know we'll get to Nyunzu," Jerusha told him. "If we try to go overland, it'll take longer and we could easily get lost, even with our GPS unit. We still have that—it's on *my* belt."

His face sagged at that, and she regretted the comment. *You don't have to be mean to him. He wouldn't have said a thing if you'd lost the GPS.* She smiled belatedly in an attempt to soften the comment; she wasn't certain that it helped.

Wally sighed. He dropped the remnants of the phone back in its pouch.

He scratched at his arm with a fingernail. Orange flakes scattered. Silently, he pushed the boat back into the brown waters of the Lukuga.

Ellen Allworth's Apartment
Manhattan, New York

NICK MOVED DIFFERENTLY THAN Ellen. Where Ellen seemed to view the world from about three degrees back, Nick leaned five degrees forward. Where she was always just a little touched by melancholy, he was all about anger.

Or maybe he wasn't. Maybe he just didn't like Bugsy.

"All right," Nick said into his telephone. "I owe you one."

"Well?" Bugsy said.

Nick hung up the phone, kicked Ellen's legs up to rest on the coffee table, and shrugged. "She was in treatment until the mid-nineties. The big reform movement that shut down all the asylums was the end of that. She was supposed to get treatment through a local clinic, but it never happened."

"So what? She just vanished into the air? Where does that leave me?"

Nick considered Bugsy with silent impatience. In Ellen's spare bedroom/office, the fax machine rang twice. Bugsy looked over his shoulder, and when he looked back, Nick was smiling.

"That," he said, "leaves you on the couch."

Bugsy struggled for a comeback as Nick rose from the couch and walked to the back of the apartment. He even walked like a guy. It was creepy.

Nick's voice came from the back, low and conversational. He laughed twice. Bugsy looked at the room. It still smelled of old curry. The earring was in the bedroom, laid gently by the book Ellen was reading before she fell asleep. He rose to his feet, paced a little, then sat down and turned on the television.

CNN was all about New Orleans. The visuals were astounding. Thousands of bright, soft-looking bubbles rising through the air, floating in the Gulf Coast breeze. Now and then, a detonation would set off a chain reaction, bright cascades of light that made the most glorious fireworks look tame. The news anchor was talking about the airspace over the city being shut down, about the travelers stuck in the city, about the cost and inconvenience. The Amazing Bubbles was coming back to life, and Bugsy found himself both surprised and delighted. All that energy floating in the Louisiana sky had once been a nuclear fireball, and now it was coming out slowly, over hours and days, as something beautiful. Mardi Gras in December. The biggest, loudest, least convenient celebration ever of the simple fact that New Orleans still lived.

He forgot the business of the Sudd and the Caliphate and angled back toward the office to get Ellen. Nick was in her chair, leaning forward, telephone handset pressed between shoulder and ear. Bugsy, his mind still on the news channel, was almost surprised to see him.

"... with the Internal Revenue Service," he said. "I'm trying to get in touch with Kimberly Ann Goodwin. Or possibly Meadows or Cordayne, the records aren't clear, but I have her social . . . oh, did she? Well, that makes sense. Do you have that? Of course."

Nick looked up. "Declared bankruptcy and changed her name five years ago," he said. "I'm getting the new . . . Hello? Yes, that's right. Thank you." Nick patted the desk, then looked up at Bugsy, miming the act of writing. Bugsy pulled a notepad and pen from the storage closet and handed them over. "All right. Great. Yeah, and do you have a good contact number for her?" Nick went silent. "You're kidding," he said. He shook his head and wrote something on the paper. "Okay. That's great. You have one, too."

Maybe Nick was trying not to look smug as he passed the notepad back. If so, it wasn't his best effort. Bugsy took the pad. Kimberly Joy Christopher, it said. Then a phone number with a 541 area code, and block letters: RISEN SAVIOR SPIRITUAL CENTER.

"She's found Jesus," Nick said. "Apparently, they're living together."

"You rock," Bugsy said, stuffing the paper into his pocket. "But come look at the news. You've got to see this."

Kongoville, Congo
People's Paradise of Africa

"WE ARE A GREAT people. A great people," the taxi driver said in rapid-fire French. "Africa held many great kingdoms long before the whites came out of their caves."

The traffic in Kongoville was manic, with three and four lanes being formed by jostling cars on a two-lane road. Cranes loomed over the city like contemplative dinosaurs. There were vast piles of rubble where shanties and older buildings had been razed in preparation for another The People—The People's Theater, The People's Hall of Justice, The People's department store, laundrette . . .

Even in early December the air-conditioning in the car was blowing full blast. Add that to the music pouring from the radio and the driver's commentary, and it was hard for Noel to gather his thoughts for his upcoming meeting with President-for-Life Dr. Nshombo. Noel wore a perfectly tailored Italian suit, an opal and diamond ring on his little finger. He didn't want Etienne Pelletier to seem *too* upscale. He hid the avatar's golden eyes behind dark glasses.

Noel found the taxi driver's assertion of lost African kingdoms both understandable and sad. He had spent a lot of time in the Middle East, and the populace there shared the same sense of racial, national, and geographic pride, completely at odds with their actual situations. In the Middle East you heard how Baghdad had streetlights when Europe was mired in the Dark Ages. In Africa it was the lost kingdoms.

They were all the dreams of conquered and economically depressed people reacting against Western might. Noel contemplated how Prince Siraj's three-hundred-dollar-a-barrel oil had almost brought Europe and America to their knees, and how the PPA's conquests in Africa were denying the West vital resources. *Payback's a bitch*, he thought.

A large stone structure caught his attention. That was new since his last visit to Kongoville. Whatever it was it shared that Albert Speer style of architecture that was favored by the good Doctor. "What's that?" Noel pointed.

The driver turned down the radio, and said quietly and respectfully, "That is the tomb of Our Lady of Pain."

Noel pulled back a cuff and glanced at his watch. He had time. "I would like to see that."

The driver pulled over and parked. Noel walked up the stone steps. They had already begun to wear. There must have been literally thousands of people through the door, he thought.

The single room was high and cavernous. High above him Noel heard the squeaking of bats that turned the tomb into a cave. The center of the room was lit by a powerful spotlight that shone down on a crystal bier. Inside lay a beautiful young woman. The embalming job had been exquisite. Her burnished black skin seemed soft and pliable, no one had forced a false smile onto her mouth, and the way her lashes brushed at her cheeks gave the impression she was only sleeping. Around her neck hung an enormous gold medal suspended by a purple velvet ribbon.

For a moment Noel reflected on this desperate need of dictatorships to worship their dead. *Lenin, Mao, this child. The English never did such a thing. No one kept Victoria on display. Even the Americans aren't so crass.*

"A people's hero," the driver murmured.

"What did she do?" Noel asked.

"She took our pain into herself and healed us." The man bowed his head.

Jackson Square
New Orleans, Louisiana

AND ON DAY FIVE, Michelle rested.

She'd been able to stand up yesterday. It felt weird and she was a little wobbly, but it wasn't impossible.

Today she was almost as thin as she'd been when she was modeling. There was still energy in her. She felt heavier, even though she looked skinny. That seemed to be the legacy of what had happened. She was heavier all the time now. With no mirror, she couldn't tell how she looked, but the jeans and T-shirt Juliet had bought for her felt like they fit.

The temple seemed sad. The flowers had dried up and Juliet and Joey had thrown them out. The girls were waiting outside for her in the soft drizzle.

Michelle knew what she had to do next.

There was a loud murmur outside. If she hadn't known better, she would have thought it was the faithful. But they had evaporated during the rain of bubbles. What awaited her outside were reporters.

Michelle let a tiny bubble form on the tip of her finger. It was hard and bright and she shot it to the night sky. It burst high above the temple—a small pop that no one would notice. Then she turned and walked out the door.

On the Lukuga River, Congo
People's Paradise of Africa

THEY WENDED THEIR WAY downriver. Every bend in the river took Wally a little closer to Nyunzu. And, he hoped, Lucien.

Now he understood what Lucien had been referring to in his last letter, about the soldiers who hurt Sister Julie. But it had been worse than he'd feared. Lucien's village, Kalemie . . . it was one of the worst things he'd ever seen, even counting all the stuff he saw and did for the Committee. He hated himself for waiting so long before he came to Africa. "Jerusha?"

"Yeah?"

"What do you think she meant, back in Kalemie? The nun, I mean. Sister Julie."

"Meant about what?"

"About them taking the kids. About changing them."

Jerusha was quiet for a long time. The boat bobbed and swayed when he glanced over his shoulder, looking for hippos and crocs. Up front, Jerusha kept one hand on the wheel and both eyes on the river, watching for the same dangers. Finally, she said, "I don't know, Wally. I wish I did."

The *putt-putt-putt* sound of their little motor echoed up and down the river, bouncing between the dense jungle to either side. Water gurgled quietly beneath the prow, where their boat gently peeled back the murky waters of the Lukuga. Not like the patrol boats. Those things cut through the water like a knife.

"That patrol boat had kids on it. Kids with guns." It reminded him of Iraq. *Kids . . . I don't want to fight kids.*

"Yeah," said Jerusha. "It did." He didn't need to look at her to know how she felt. She was sad. Wally was getting to know her moods, the nuances of her emotions, just from the tone of her voice. Somehow that felt like a small bright spot in what was otherwise turning into a pretty bad deal all around.

"Do you think that's what she meant? Turning the kids into soldiers? Like maybe they're gonna do that to Lucien?"

"I don't . . . Ouch." She slapped at her neck, then flicked a squashed bug into the river. The sharp *slap* ricocheted down the river. "I'm afraid it might, Wally."

"Me, too. I figure Nyunzu must be where they're doing it. It's where they've got Lucien at. But he'll be okay once we get there. They all will, all those kids."

"I hope you're right."

Wally fell silent, thinking. The river forked again. As always, Jerusha took the wider branch. A small island, just a sliver of brush and trees, separated them from the other branch. Wally could see the water on the other side. All around them, the jungle chattered, shrieked, and sang with life. "I'm sorry about what I said earlier. Or, I mean, you know, what I almost said."

She was silent again. This time, he knew, she was cocking an eyebrow at him. An expression halfway between bemusement and irritation. He could picture it.

"Sometimes I say dumb stuff. But I don't mean anything by it, okay?" As soon as the words came out, Wally realized this was a dumb thing to say, too. It could give her the wrong idea. Then she'd hate him, and he really, *really* didn't want Jerusha to hate him. They were partners now, and had to work together. He needed her help. But that wasn't all of it. He just . . . wanted Jerusha to like him.

"I mean, I don't always say dumb stuff. Sometimes people think . . . aw, heck. Remember that thing with me and Stuntman? Back when we were all on TV?"

Guardedly: "Yyyyyeeeeessss."

"I didn't say that stuff."

Jerusha laughed. Not a real gut-busting laugh, but it was still the most he'd heard her laugh since they started traveling together. "I know, Wally. Everybody knows it."

Wally sighed. That was a small relief. "Well, okay. That's good. I just wanted to . . ."

He trailed off again as they passed the last bit of island. The two branches of the river rejoined behind them. Neat. It reminded him of canoe camping trips, back home.

Wally turned around just in time to see the boy on the prow of the hidden patrol boat leveling his rifle. *"Get down!"* he yelled. Jerusha must have seen his expression, because she was out of the pilot's chair and diving under the gunwale almost before the warning passed his lips.

Tat-tat-tat. Tat-ping-tat. The boy squeezed off two bursts. One round *cracked* off Wally's bicep and sent up a white spray from the river. Another shattered the windscreen. "Jerusha?"

"I'm okay," she said. "I—"

But then Wally couldn't hear anything except the howl of a motor. A big motor. Jerusha reached up from her hiding spot to wrench the wheel, aiming for the riverbank.

The Leopard Man yelled something. The patrol boat roared out of its hiding spot. It streaked like an arrow toward where they would make land. More bullets whizzed past them. Wally stood. Their boat rocked precariously, but he tried his best to shield Jerusha.

Ping-ping-ping. Hailstones falling on a tin roof.

Twenty feet to shore. Ten feet.

"Jerusha, stay behind me!"

At the last second, she wrenched the wheel again and killed the motor. They swung around, keeping Wally between her and the patrol boat as they bumped up against the roots of a massive mahogany tree leaning out over the water.

Pingpingpingpingpingping.

He crossed the boat in one stride, bullets pattering harmlessly against his back, and grabbed Jerusha under the arms. "Hold on," he said. And then, as gently as he could, he hurled her into the jungle.

It nearly capsized the boat. Water slopped over the gunwales. A *crash* and an *oof!* emanated from somewhere in the brush. Wally spun to face their attackers, hoping to heck that Jerusha wasn't hurt.

The Leopard Man shouted another order. The soldier at the wheel—the only other adult on the patrol boat—gunned the engine, wedging them between Wally and the shore. Two kids stood up front, along with the Leopard Man. The driver was in the middle; another kid stood in the stern.

Wally jumped onto the prow of the other boat, to keep them from going after Jerusha. The Leopard Man scrambled backward, out of the reach of Wally's arms, yelling another order. All three kids (*they're just kids!*) opened up with their rifles. All Wally could think about through the cacophony of gunfire was putting an end to this before a deadly ricochet killed one of the kids, just like what had happened to poor King Cobalt back in Egypt.

Wally called up his wild card power and lunged forward, reaching for a rifle with both hands. The kids tried to scoot out of reach. One barrel crumpled in his fist. The second rifle he didn't quite manage to grab, but he grazed it with a finger, which was all he needed to command the iron inside the gun to disintegrate. It crumbled.

The third kid stopped firing, but the driver pulled his sidearm and extended his arm toward Wally's head.

Cripes! Don't you guys pay any attention? You could shoot one of these kids! Wally pushed the two disarmed boys into the river. It wasn't entirely safe there, but it was a lot safer than standing next to Wally while people shot at him. Then he spun, grabbed the gun in the driver's outstretched hand, and squeezed.

The driver screamed. Wally flipped him halfway across the river.

The third boy darted past him and jumped to shore, followed closely by the Leopard Man.

"Hey! Leave her alone!" Wally charged after them.

The kid hadn't gone a dozen yards when the earth under his feet erupted in a mass of vines. They enveloped him in seconds. *Right on, Jerusha!*

The Leopard Man skidded to a halt. He spun to face Wally, and melted.

No, he didn't melt. But his body flowed like soft wax, becoming low and sleek while the yellow-and-black spotted pattern on his fez oozed down, covering his body with fur.

The big cat snarled, revealing a mouthful of fangs. Muscles rippled under the fur with deadly grace as it prowled back and forth, growling. Then, like a spring uncoiling, it leapt. Fangs clicked against Wally's throat. Inch-long claws scrabbled ineffectually at his shoulders and chest. The leopard fell off him and collected itself for another try.

"Aw, come on, fella. Give it a rest, would ya?"

The leopard lunged again. Wally caught it in midair with a punch to the nose. He heard a *crack*. The big cat dropped to the earth like a sack of potatoes. It wobbled to its feet, and crawled off into the jungle, mewling.

Wally called into the jungle. "Jerusha? You okay?"

Please, please, please . . .

"I'm okay." She emerged from behind a dense screen of foliage, rubbing her armpits. "Just a little bruised."

"Oh, cripes, did I hurt you? I'm real sorry."

Jerusha shook her head. "Don't sweat it. I'm pretty sure they didn't expect you to fling me into the jungle like that." The corners of her mouth twisted into a wry half smile. "Neither did I." She touched his arm. "It was good thinking, Wally. But next time, try to give me some warning, okay?"

Wally blushed. "Okay."

She nodded toward the rustling kudzu vines where the kid from the patrol boat struggled to free himself. "Well. Let's see what he has to say, huh?"

♣

Monday, December 7

On the Lukuga River, Congo
People's Paradise of Africa

NYUNZU. NYUNZU. NYUNZU.

Wally rapped his fingers on the gunwale, wishing their boat had a larger engine, the river a stronger current. He'd already pushed the throttle as far as it could go. *Crack.* Another hairline fracture appeared in the sun-rotted wood under his hand. He stopped tapping. But he couldn't contain the anxiety; his leg bounced up and down, almost of its own accord. Soon the boat bobbed in time with the rhythm of his impatience.

"Hey, Wally." Jerusha turned. "You're gonna give me seasickness. River sickness." Her smile didn't touch her eyes. She was worried, too.

"Sorry." Wally directed his attention to the river, turning the wheel slightly to keep them in the center of a mild bend. Jerusha went back to watching for surprises: patrol boats, submerged logs, hippos, crocodiles . . .

Lucien was in Nyunzu. He had to be. That's where the PPA was taking all the children. That's what the kid they'd caught (whom *Jerusha* had caught) had said, more or less.

To change them. To turn them into soldiers. Little kids, like Lucien, given guns and taught to kill.

In the end, Jerusha had disarmed the kid she'd caught while Wally fished the other two up from the riverbank. Then they loaded up the patrol boat with a couple days' worth of food and let them go. What else could they do? They were just kids.

Motoring around the bend, they passed a crocodile sunning itself on a sandbar. Wally tensed. But the giant reptile didn't react to their presence. It just lay there with its mouth open and its eyes closed. Jerusha said that was how they sweated—they panted, like dogs. And that a logy croc was often a well-fed croc.

Half an hour later, they passed another croc. And another. "Huh." Jerusha dug out her guidebook. She flipped through it. Wally watched how the breeze from the pages lifted stray hairs from her sweat-glistened forehead. A stirring sight, but somehow comforting, too.

"Yeah, that's what I remembered." She tapped the page with her finger. "African crocodiles don't tend to congregate. Except," she added, with another tap to the page, "during mating season, or if there's food to be found. They'll travel miles if there's a good carcass to eat."

Wally watched the crocodiles warily. He kept glancing at the sandbar until it passed out of sight around another bend. So did Jerusha.

"Lots of crocs," said Wally.

"Lots of *well-fed* crocs," said Jerusha.

"Tarzan wrestled with a crocodile once. *Tarzan and His Mate.* Johnny Weissmuller and Maureen O'Sullivan."

"That was a movie."

"Yeah, but it was pretty neat. He even—"

"Wally, look out!" Jerusha dropped the book and jumped to her feet, pointing at something in the river.

Wally spun the wheel; the engine died. *Please, not a hippopotamus.* Finch had warned them about the hippos: "Roit nasty buggers. They'll flip your boat and bite your head off just for spite. Even yours, mate," he'd said, jabbing his horn in Wally's direction.

Behind him, Jerusha braced for impact. Wally clenched his eyes shut and hunched his shoulders.

Bump. Something brushed gently against the boat.

Wally opened one eye, then the other. They were still afloat. He released the breath he'd been holding. He looked at Jerusha.

She shrugged. "I saw something floating low in the water. I couldn't tell what it was. I thought it might have been a log, or an animal."

Wally could see it now, too, just a couple of feet off the side of the boat.

They must have nudged it when he turned the boat broadside. Weird. It was a piece of pale driftwood, draped in tatters of cloth.

No, not cloth. Clothes. A sun-bleached pair of cargo pants.

On a body.

United Nations
Manhattan, New York

THE ELEVATOR DOORS SNICKED open. Lohengrin stepped out. Out of his shimmering white armor he looked like a regular guy. Big and blond and good-looking, but chunkier than she remembered. *Too much time behind a desk.*

"Bubbles. It has been too long." His accent was still heavy. He pulled her into a hug, then kissed her on the cheek. "Who is this?"

Michelle introduced Joey and Juliet. Lohengrin nodded as he shook Joey's hand. "I remember this one. You raise the dead. Hoodoo Mama, *ja?*"

"Yeah. And I remember how y'all didn't like my background. Prissy mother-fuckers."

Klaus reddened. "Ah, you are so young, you do not understand. The world watches us, all the time. The Committee must be above reproach."

"I'm not that much younger than you, asshat," Joey snapped. "Reproach my ass. Don't you shine me on."

"Joey, please." Michelle wanted to throttle the brat. The last thing she needed was Hoodoo Mama screwing things up with the Committee. "I'm sorry, Klaus." Michelle slipped her arm into his and drew him away.

Lohengrin shrugged. "Things are more complicated than before, Bubbles. Jayewardene does what he can, but we must be so careful. He is waiting for you upstairs. Come."

The hallway leading to Secretary-General Jayewardene's office was lined with photographs of Committee members. Michelle smiled as she passed Jonathan Hive, Rustbelt, and Gardener, but instead of the shots she remembered of Curveball, Drummer Boy, John Fortune, and Holy Roller, there were photos of people she didn't know. It made her uncomfortable. She'd spent a lot of time walking these halls. *A year,* she thought. Still, it wasn't right that so many of her friends were gone.

Lohengrin opened the door to Jayewardene's office and then followed the girls inside.

"Michelle, my dear, it's good to see you looking so well." G. C. Jayewardene rose from his chair, came around the desk, and crossed the room to embrace her. One of the perks of his position was having the largest office in the UN building. A wall of windows faced the East River. There was enough room for a sitting area with a couple of couches and an area for Jayewardene's desk and several sleek, modern leather chairs. It was larger than most apartments on the Lower East Side.

Jayewardene was a small man, but it never seemed to bother him that Michelle towered over him. That was one of the many reasons that she'd grown so fond of him. He also had an old-fashioned, courtly side to him that she liked.

"I see you've brought Miss Summers and Miss Hebert," he said. Both girls looked surprised. And, Michelle noted, he even pronounced Joey's name right. "How are you feeling, my dear?" Jayewardene asked as he walked back to his chair.

Michelle smiled at him. "I'm certain you already know, Mr. Jayewardene. Given what happened, I'm surprisingly well."

"You know that we want you to come back to duty as soon as possible."

The door to Jayewardene's office opened. A plump, dark-haired woman came into the room carrying a folder. She was pretty enough, but something in the way she carried herself made Michelle suspect she didn't feel pretty all of the time. "Oh, Mr. Jayewardene," she said. "I didn't realize you had guests. . . ."

Jayewardene rose from his chair. "These are old friends of mine, Barbara. Have you met? This is Miss Pond, Miss Summers, and Miss Hebert. Miss Barbara Baden."

"We've met."

Michelle remembered that Barbara had only recently joined the Committee. Just before New Orleans. Her ace name was the Translator, but some called her Babel. "It's nice to see you again, Barbara," Michelle said.

Lohengrin stepped forward. "Babs is our vice chairman now, Michelle. You must know that John left us after New Orleans . . . after he lost his powers." From the way his voice softened when he said her name, Michelle had the sneaking suspicion that there was more than translating going on between Klaus and Babel.

"Are you coming back to the Committee?" Barbara asked. "We could certainly use an ace of your power."

Michelle stuck her hands in her pockets. "I don't know. I've only been awake for a week." She turned back toward Jayewardene. "I was just about to tell the secretary-general about these dreams I've been having."

"Dreams?" Babel looked incredulous.

Michelle felt another shot of annoyance. This . . . *translator* was starting to piss her off.

"Yes, dreams. They brought me out of my coma. They weren't really dreams. They were things that had really happened to this little girl. She needs me to help her."

"Telepathy?" mused Jayewardene. "It would not surprise me that such a thing had happened. Tell us of this child."

Michelle stepped back so she could see their faces. "She's in a pit of dead bodies. And she's a little girl—maybe six or seven. It's horrible."

Babel's expression was one of complete disbelief.

Michelle ignored her. "I owe this little girl. I need to find her."

Jayewardene got up and walked to one of the tall windows overlooking the harbor. "Do you have any idea where this pit is?"

"Not exactly," Michelle said, "but I think I have it narrowed down." She just wanted him to give her the damn Committee. "There were soldiers wearing uniforms and these leopard-skin fezzes. I recognized the uniforms from our training. They were Congolese. I confess, the fezzes confuse me, but it may have been part of Adesina's trauma. She's obsessed with leopards in her dreams."

"Yes," he said softly. "Leopards."

"In her dreams, she's being captured by these soldiers and taken away from her home. It's almost like she's calling me—pulling me to her."

Jayewardene turned back from the window. "Dreams can be a powerful thing, Michelle. If you are certain that you must find her, then I suppose you must go to the Congo."

Barbara blinked in surprise.

"Sir," she said. "The Amazing Bubbles is one of the best-known and best-loved aces in the world right now. After New Orleans, she's almost a legend. If she sets foot in the People's Paradise, the Radical will . . . Klaus, *talk* to her."

Lohengrin looked very unhappy. "Babs, if this child is in danger . . . what is the Committee for, if not for things like that?"

Babel threw her hands up in dismay. "She can't just go waltzing around in the PPA. Not with Rustbelt and Gardener already in Africa, doing God knows what. This could provoke Weathers to a fresh round of atrocities."

Michelle flinched when Babs said Weathers's name. It had been a long time since anyone had scared her, but Weathers had done his best to nuke New Orleans.

All she could think about was the fire running through her veins. "Mr. Jayewardene," she said. "I know it sounds stupid, but Adesina is stuck there in a pit filled with corpses. I'm going to her. With the Committee's help or without it."

"I cannot give you the Committee." Jayewardene sounded sad. "You must do what you must do, but Barbara is correct. The Nshombos keep a careful watch on who crosses their borders. These men in the leopard-skin hats that you have seen in your dream are Alicia Nshombo's secret police, the Leopard Society. They would arrest you as soon as you entered the country."

They could try, Michelle thought. She glanced at Joey and Juliet. Neither of them looked very happy. Joey was fidgeting in her chair as if she had sand in her underwear.

"Fuck it," Joey blurted out. "Are you cocksuckers deaf, or what? Didn't you hear what she said? The little fucker in her dreams is just a *kid*!"

Dr. Nshombo's Yacht
Kongoville, Congo
People's Paradise of Africa

THE RECEPTION WAS ON the Nshombo yacht. Supposedly it was "the people's yacht," but the burly Leopard Men in their leopard-skin fezzes guarded the gangway, making damn sure none of the people actually came aboard. The word in the streets was that Alicia's crack troops could actually turn into leopards, but how much of that was clever manipulation and how much was truth Noel had no way to know.

As the fiberglass gangway bowed slightly beneath his foot, Noel realized he had better prepare for the masquerade. He was entering the lion . . . leopard's . . . den, and he needed to concentrate. Monsieur Pelletier presented his invitation to a grim-faced guard, and was waved aboard.

The hip beat of a jazz quartet, the chink of ice in glasses, and the roar of conversation led him to the party. He touched his dark glasses to reassure himself that Etienne's golden eyes were obscured. He also checked his watch to verify exactly how long until sundown. He had one hour, seventeen minutes, and forty-two seconds.

Dr. Nshombo stood by the rail discussing Marxist theory with a pair of engineers from Kenya. The two men were looking longingly toward the bar and the attractive young women who wove through the crowds offering canapés and champagne off silver trays. Noel extended his hand. "Ah, Monsieur President, so kind to include me. The yacht, so *ravissant*, and the river, like a mighty heart through your great nation," he said in French. Actually he thought the Congo smelled like an open sewer as vegetation, human waste, and probably bodies provided by the ever-helpful secret police rotted in the dark waters.

The engineers made a quick and tactical retreat. Noel joined Dr. Nshombo at the rail. The spare little man with his expressionless ebony face snapped his fingers, and one of the servers hurried over. Noel accepted a flute of champagne. Nshombo waved her off—he neither smoked nor drank. Personally Noel had always preferred the whoring, boozing, gambling variety of dictator over the abstemious, self-righteous variety. The hedonists were easier to bring down.

"Monsieur Pelletier, have you located a site for your factory?" Dr. Nshombo asked.

"Not yet, sir, but I've seen several promising locations."

"You will find my people are good workers. They will build excellent cars."

"And be able to afford them with the wages they'll earn," Noel said.

He realized his error the instant the words left his lips as Nshombo's face closed into a tight, hard mask. "Are you suggesting my people do not earn a decent wage without the actions of a white man?"

"No—"

Nshombo ran over the start of Noel's apology. "Before I founded the People's Paradise of Africa, that would have been the case. Corrupt leaders working with Western flacks sucked away the fruits of their labor, but I changed that. Through me flows the wealth of a continent, and it all goes into the hands of my people."

"Yes, yes, quite. And that was what I meant to imply, but was, alas, inartful. It is due to your prescience that you are allowing me to found this Peugeot factory. Your people will benefit from your wisdom and hard work."

"Dear, Mr. Pelletier, please ignore my brother." Alicia Nshombo flowed around him like the storm bands of a hurricane. First there was the overpowering scent of her gardenia perfume, then the salty, musky scent of a heavy woman exerting herself in the stifling Congo heat. Next the folds of her brightly colored, floral print robe/muumuu/tent tangled at his legs and torso, and finally her heavy, plump arms wrapped around Noel's shoulders. "He's still thinking it's the old days when we were not treated with respect, when the Western countries viewed us as just another set of black oppressors. You are one of the first white businessmen to see the potential in the PPA."

Noel gave Alicia a small bow, and bestowed a Gallic kiss on the back of her hand. "I'm sure I'm only the first of many. Your hospitality and willingness to assist in my little venture has been overwhelming."

Noel straightened and found himself almost mesmerized by the flat stares of the three security officers who surrounded her. He considered the motorized patrols that raced through the streets near the river, the snipers positioned on the roofs of surrounding buildings, and decided that the PPA armed forces offered a great opportunity for employment and promotion.

Alicia gave him a hug that left him breathless. "You French, always so gracious. Now, please, come and meet a few more of our illustrious citizens."

Noel followed, feeling like a wood chip caught in the wake of a carrier. As they moved across the polished oak deck Alicia continued. "In a few weeks these decks will be draped with beautiful girls. I arranged with *Jalouse* for them to hold the swimsuit shoot in Kongoville aboard our yacht. You should time your return trip to coincide with that." She gave him a wink, then tucked his arm through hers and pressed it against her side. "Though why you men prefer these skinny rails . . . African men are wiser. They like a woman of substance." She leered at him.

Noel suppressed a shudder and gave her a Gallic pinch on the tips of her fingers. Alicia giggled, her breasts jiggled, and she patted Noel on the crotch. He tried to will a reaction, but even he wasn't that good an actor.

She led him up a short flight of stairs and onto a small upper deck. "So nice to watch the sunset from up here," she crooned.

"Alas, madam, I need to return to the hotel to take part in a conference call with some American backers. The Americans have no taste, but a vast amount of money."

Alicia giggled again, an incongruous sound from so large a woman.

"Alicia, you bawdy broad, there you are." The words were delivered with a boyish lilt. Noel felt his genitals trying to retreat deeper into his belly.

He turned to find Tom Weathers bounding up the stairs. He had the face of an aging model. Handsome, but his expression was too young for the wrinkles, as if he hadn't realized that time marches on, and even the golden youth must grow up.

A few steps behind him walked a middle-aged but still beautiful Chinese woman. When Noel had last seen Sun Hei-lian her face had been shiny with Lilith's juices, as Sun had eaten pussy while Tom Weathers boned her from behind. *The things I did for crown and king.* Noel knew from her dossier in the files of the Silver Helix that she was a Chinese agent, very smart and very deadly. Today she seemed oddly subdued, her head bent, eyes on the polished wood deck. Occasionally she glanced up at Tom's back, and her expression was an odd combination of fear, frustration, and grief.

So, Noel thought, *maybe this isn't just an agent running a useful asset. She might actually care for Weathers. If he cared for her she might offer a decent substitute for Sprout. Or she's an agent who knows her asset has gone rogue, and she's trying to decide how to liquidate him. Either way she might prove useful.*

Noel's attention was so tightly focused on Sun Hei-lian that he didn't notice the arc of Alicia's arms as she threw them wide to accept Weathers's embrace. One of her heavy bracelets caught Noel's sunglasses and swept them from his face. Noel spun away, covered his eyes, and bent to snatch them up.

"Oh, Monsieur Pelletier, I'm so sorry," Alicia cooed.

"Hey, man, let me help you."

Noel seized the glasses just before Weathers did, and slammed them back over his eyes. *Had he seen? Did he see? Oh, Niobe, I'm sorry.* "Cataracts," he muttered, his voice breathless with fear. "I'm trying to avoid surgery."

Suspicion melted away into concern, though Noel read it as calculated as his own performances. "Oh, man, I'm sorry. That sucks. Aren't you a little young?"

"A genetic propensity. It blinded my father," Noel lied glibly.

"Wow, sucks," Weathers repeated.

"Monsieur Pelletier, I would like to introduce our dear Tom, and his lovely lady Sun Hei-lian."

"So pleased to meet you." They shook hands, and Tom played boy games with an overly strong handshake. Noel kept his deliberately weak, quickly pulled his hand away, and gave it a surreptitious shake . . . though not *too* surreptitious. Weathers noticed, grinned, and dismissed him as a weakling, and therefore not worthy of attention. Noel turned his attention to Sun, and gave her one of Monsieur Pelletier's flourishing greetings. She didn't respond to it half as well as Alicia.

Noel decided that engaging in small talk with Tom Weathers and a Chinese agent known for her brains and deadly abilities didn't make a lot of sense. "My champagne is empty," he said. "I'll leave you all to talk."

And he hurried away down the stairs, only to stop halfway down. He kept walking in place as he tried to overhear.

A shadow fell across the hatch. Someone was coming.

It was too late to move farther down the stairs. Noel set aside his glass, and bent quickly to tie his shoe. He always wore wing tips for just this reason. Retying a shoe was always an excuse for loitering.

Sun appeared at the top of the steps and stared down at him. Noel straightened, recovered his glass, smiled, nodded at her, and continued his descent.

Manhattan, New York

THEY WERE ALL QUIET on the way back to the apartment.

They came out from the subway at Fourteenth Street, the closest stop to Michelle's apartment. The first snow of winter was falling in thick, wet, white flakes. Most of the people exiting the subway turned up their collars against the cold, hunching down in their coats.

"Snow," Joey said in an awed voice Michelle had never heard before. She held out her hand and stared at the flakes hitting her palm. "Cool. I've never seen snow before." Her face was full of wonder.

Michelle just wanted to get inside and figure out what to do next. But Juliet took her hand and that made her stop walking.

And so Michelle and Joey and Juliet stood on the sidewalk and let the snow fall on them until they were damp and cold.

♠

Tuesday,
December 8

On the Lukuga River, Congo
People's Paradise of Africa

THE BODIES IN THE river were becoming more numerous; they'd passed three of them in just the last hour, and one of the floating corpses was that of a child. Wally had stared at the bloated form, at the distorted face, trying to see if it might be Lucien. Jerusha could feel his silent anguish, and she could do nothing more than put a hand on his shoulder. "It's not him, Wally. It's not."

The worry and fear on his face was a torment to her. She found tears gathering in her own eyes as she saw the anguish in Wally's face. She hugged him, wishing there were something she could say that would comfort him, wanting to be able to reassure him that it would be all right in the end.

But she didn't believe that. She couldn't believe that. They needed help; they needed it quickly. If the babbling of the frightened child soldier they'd captured was even halfway true, then the Committee *had* to know. Now.

Jerusha hardly believed it herself: a prison where hundreds of children had been injected with the wild card virus, where hundreds more had already died in order to produce two or three aces for the PPA. The thought sickened and infuriated her. She wanted to see the place razed and burned, wanted to see the Nshombos and Tom Weathers tried and executed for what they were doing here. And Wally . . .

Poor Wally. She didn't know what to say to him. He glared downriver as if his gaze alone could drive them toward Nyunzu and his precious Lucien. All she could do was stay close to him, to stroke his shoulders, to whisper ineffective comforts that yes, they would still find Lucien alive. They would . . .

Their satellite phone was useless, and her cell didn't work—no bars, no service—and the battery was nearly dead to boot. Jerusha sighed and thrust the phone back into one of the pockets of her cargo pants. Squinting into the sunlight, she could see a village set in the hollow of the next bend.

Wally crowded into the tiny cabin of the craft as they passed the village, and Jerusha avoided looking at the people staring as they motored past, facing forward as if confident and unworried about their presence on the river.

As soon as the bend put the village out of sight, she extended a hand to help Wally clamber out again. "Put us in here, Wally," Jerusha said. "We really need to find a way to tell Lohengrin what's going on down here. Maybe there's a landline in that village I can use."

Wally's face stiffened. "That's too dangerous."

The roiling in her stomach agreed with him. "I don't see another choice. Some of these people may not like the Nshombos any more than we do; they're scared, but they might be willing to let me make a phone call."

"And what if there's a PPA fella there? It would only take one of them."

She'd been thinking the same, but she tried to shrug as nonchalantly as she could. "It's a chance we gotta take. I'm not sure we can do this alone, Wally. There's something awful going on here, something big—something Lucien looks to be caught up in."

Wally vented a breath through his nostrils. The boat puttered toward the bank and Jerusha cut the engine; Wally jumped out, knee-deep in the water, to drag the boat out of the river into the cover of leaves.

Jerusha gave him another hug. "Be right back," she said.

"I'm going with you."

She shook her head. "I'm black, remember?" she said with a brief flash of a smile. "Wally, it's one thing if a woman who looks mostly like them shows up in the village. I'm not visibly an ace and not visibly threatening. It's another thing entirely if a big guy made out of iron is with me. Then they'd *know* we're up to something." She slid a hand along his arm. She could *feel* the rust spots, like patches of dry, scaly skin. "Stay here—hey, use those S.O.S pads you brought along."

"I don't like it."

"I don't either," she admitted. "I'll tell you what: if you hear me yell, you come running, okay?"

A grimace. "Okay."

She hugged him once more, then headed back upriver along the bank, pushing through the thick vegetation toward the settlement as stealthily as she could. If anything looked wrong with the village, she promised herself, she would head immediately back to Wally and the boat.

As she approached, she could see through the fronds and leaves a cultivated field between her and the village: corn, soybeans, and other crops rising straggling from the poor jungle earth. A woman worked the field, walking along the rows with a cloth sack from which protruded a few corn husks. The woman was only a dozen feet away. Jerusha parted the leaves at the edge of the field and called out softly to the woman in French. *"Bonjour."*

The woman glanced up, startled, and backed up a few steps. "No," Jerusha called out, showing her hands. "I'm not going to hurt you. I need a telephone. A landline. Do you have one here?"

The woman glanced over her shoulder, and Jerusha looked in the same direction. A man was standing at the end of the small field nearest the village. He had a semiautomatic weapon of some sort strapped around him, though he was looking out toward the river, not toward Jerusha.

"No," the woman answered in heavily accented French, quickly and softly. Her eyes were wide and frightened. "You should go. There's nothing here. Nothing."

"I have to make a call," Jerusha persisted. "It's urgent. Please. If there's any way . . ."

"There's no phone here. What the rebels didn't destroy, the Leopard Men smashed. No phone. No electricity. Not for months." She gestured. "Go! You can't be here!"

The armed man called out to the women, though not in French—he was looking their way. Jerusha slid back toward the brush but it was already too late. He began to run toward them, bringing up the blackened muzzle of his weapon. Jerusha plunged a hand into her seed belt as the man shouted again, words that Jerusha couldn't understand. The woman screamed and flung herself to the ground.

Something dark and heavy slammed into Jerusha from behind and she went down just as the weapon loosed its deadly staccato clamor. She heard the bullets whining away, tearing harmlessly into the leaves, and ricocheting off iron. Wally was standing in front of her.

Gardener threw the seed she'd plucked from the seed belt as if it were a hand grenade: one of the remaining baobab seeds. It rolled to the ground at the attacker's feet and he glanced down, scowling as Jerusha sent her power plunging hard into the seed. It seemed to explode: roots plunging down, branches shooting skyward. One snagged the weapon and ripped it away from him as others wrapped around him. Soon he was encased in a snare of branches fifteen feet off the ground.

Wally plucked Jerusha up from the ground. The village woman lay in a fetal curl. Wally stared upward at the new baobab and its captive.

"You were supposed to stay with the boat," Jerusha told him.

Wally grinned. "Sorry."

The man shouted from his wooden cage, and people were beginning to look toward the field from the village.

"We should go, Jerusha," Wally said.

"Yeah," she told him. "I think maybe we should."

Wally turned and plunged into the jungle, tearing the foliage apart and crushing it underneath his massive feet. Jerusha followed his orange-spotted back.

People's Bank
Kongoville, Congo
People's Paradise of Africa

THE BANK HAD BEEN built during the colonial era, so it had some grace and charm as opposed to the proletariat grandeur (an oxymoron if Noel had ever heard one) of the Nshombos' People's Palace, Palace of the Arts, People's Defense Headquarters, Justice Center, etc.

His guide for the day was supposed to be the Economics Minister, but at the last minute he had been replaced with Alicia. Noel looked over at the woman as they sat in the backseat of a Mercedes limo. "What an . . . ah . . . incongruous building," he said, not wanting to call it beautiful in case the sister loved proletariat grandeur.

Alicia made a face. "I think it's beautiful. I wish we had emulated this building, but my brother has strong attitudes about Western culture. I think we should embrace all the West has to offer." And she stretched out an arm, and dragged her fingertips across the back of Noel's neck and down his arm.

Just as Lilith's sexuality could arouse men, his male avatar had the same effect on women. This was one time when Noel wished he could have appeared as a middling height, very average Englishman.

Noel leaned in close to Alicia's ear and whispered confidingly, "I too love French architecture. But then we French love many things."

Alicia turned to face him. They were only an inch apart. Every line in her body and the softness of her lips said she was waiting to be kissed. Noel knew he had to oblige her.

As he pulled back from the snog he thought, *God, I hope it doesn't go past this*. Noel knew Alicia had a taste for torture . . . no, *more* than a taste, a veritable *passion* for torture. And he also had Niobe waiting at home. He wanted to be done with killing and fucking for crown and country.

Realizing the silence was going on a little too long, Noel said, "I do hope the security has been upgraded since 1920. On your recommendation I'll be depositing a great deal of cash rather than using electronic transfers."

Alicia made a soothing gesture with her plump but perfectly manicured hands. "Not to worry. The president put in place state-of-the-art security measures."

"May I have a hint as to what they are?" Noel asked.

"I'll tell you a few, but I must keep some secrets," Alicia said with a suggestive smile.

Noel returned the smile. "Thank you, I am reassured."

The driver parked illegally in front of the bank, and they climbed out. Noel glanced back at the not-so-subtle unmarked security car that rolled slowly past them. The three men inside were so large it looked like a college prank or a clown car at the circus. Monsieur Pelletier would not notice a tail, no matter how obvious, so Noel said nothing.

The bank manager held open the etched-and-frosted glass-and-brass front doors and bowed them into the marble interior. Art Nouveau nymphs held up brass lamps, carved pediments showed a Classical Greek influence, a pair of gigantic chandeliers illuminated every corner of the lobby. Their heels rapped sharply against the marble and echoed in every corner. What with all the brass, glass, and stone, Noel expected it to be cool inside, but the moist, breathless Congo heat still held sway. The Europeans could bring their architecture, insist on their own cuisine, wear wool, corsets, and cravats, and die, but they could not defeat the jungle. Ultimately it won. It always won.

"Monsieur Pelletier is going to be building a Peugeot factory that will employ three thousand people," Alicia said to the manager. "You know how my beloved brother prefers to do business in cash, so that the Western powers cannot steal our wealth."

The manager's head bobbed up and down so energetically that all Noel could picture was the man's head set on a dashboard instead of a hula girl or a bobble-headed dog.

"I would like to see the vault, just to reassure myself," Noel said.

The manager looked to Alicia for guidance. She nodded, and he said, "But of course."

Two of the men from the car strode into the bank and began pushing patrons aside. This, as well as the slung Uzis, were so obvious that Noel felt he could comment. "There seems to be a great deal of . . . er . . . security around you. I'm concerned. Are you in danger?"

"Oh, no, no, no, monsieur. There is no problem *inside* the country." Alicia frowned. "The problem is counterrevolutionaries who seek to stop the march of our glorious country. One of these aces actually came into the country and killed our beloved Tom. Shot him dead as he stood inspiring the troops."

That wasn't actually how it had been. Bahir had unloaded a clip from a machine gun into Tom Weathers's back as he took a piss into a latrine trench. Noel put on an appropriately horrified expression. "But I met him yesterday. How did he survive?"

"Our Lady of Pain brought him back to life before she was killed by those same wicked elements."

Ah, mystery solved, Noel thought. *I'd wondered about that. But as one of those "evil elements" I know I didn't kill her, and I didn't hear of any other Western power moving against her. Interesting.* "You must be terrified for your brother," Noel said.

"I do worry, but the Leopard Men are ever vigilant. They even stand guard next to the beds while we sleep. And we change our rooms every night."

"How wise. I'm reassured." *God damn it. Paranoia makes my job so difficult.* And then, as if he'd heard Niobe's voice, Noel corrected himself. *Not my job any longer.*

Alicia gave him a secretive little smile. "And we have other . . . resources. The PPA will soon be one of the great powers in the world."

Noel slipped an arm around Alicia's waist. It was a long reach. "Oh, you intrigue me. Might I know what constitutes these resources? I might find myself wanting to make a larger investment."

Alicia bestowed a flirting tap on the cheek. "Now, now, you mustn't be too nosy. Perhaps when we know each other . . . better."

The manager led them down to the vault. The massive steel doors were rolled back, but steel bars still separated Noel from the actual vault. The two walls that weren't covered with safety deposit boxes were discolored, and there were a few evidences of actual mold where the moisture from the surrounding soil had leached through the concrete. Noel made note of steel tracks beveled into the floor, cameras that had a depressingly wide angle of coverage, and tiny nozzles mounted up near the ceiling. There was a doorway into another room, and Noel could just see steel pallets stacked to a height of about four feet and covered with tarps. It could only be one thing: the treasury of the PPA.

And only twenty feet and a vast array of security devices lay between him and it. Noel looked over at the bank manager. "You have people watching those cameras?"

"But of course."

"Would you like to see the control room, dear Etienne?" Alicia cooed.

"Yes, please."

As they headed back up the stairs the manager asked, "And when might we expect monsieur's deposit to arrive?"

"It will take me several weeks to raise that much cash, and arrange to have it safely transported to Kongoville." *And by that time I hope to have recruited help, returned, and robbed you blind.*

Risen Savior Spiritual Center
Ashland, Oregon

THE RISEN SAVIOR SPIRITUAL Center looked like a cheap community college. A neatly kept "campus" with winter-yellow grass where dirty snow hadn't melted, flagstone paths, and concrete benches built to withstand Armageddon. Bugsy guessed that if the world ended in fire, there would probably still be something more comfortable to sit on. The residential buildings were in the back. They looked less like a cloister and more like dorms.

He asked a pleasant-faced woman in a conservatively cut blue dress where he could find Kimberly Joy and was directed to the back.

The meeting room looked less like college, and more like a preschool for adults. Soft couches and cheap linoleum tables. Inexpensive butter cookies and a cheap metal samovar squatting next to a stack of foam cups and a basket of herbal teas. Low bookshelves were filled with magazines featuring pictures of a white, big-eyed Jesus or his ecstatic white followers or else books with crosses on the spines. The woman by the window looked up as he walked in.

If he hadn't spent most of the plane ride out from New York reviewing his records, he wouldn't have recognized her. The long blond hair was gone, replaced by a shoulder-length soccer mom coif. The challenging grin was a tight, nervous smile with lines around it that made her mouth seem puckered, even when it wasn't. The free-breasted hippie chick had vanished. A thick-bodied grandmother in her not-so-great Sunday best remained.

And still, knowing who she had been, he could see her in the shape of her eyes, the angle of her nose. Kimberly Ann Cordayne, or the ghost of her.

"You must be Mr. Tipton," she said.

"Tipton-Clarke," Bugsy said, "but yes, that's me. Thank you for seeing me on such short notice."

"I had to sit with the Lord," Kimberly Joy said. Her inflection meant *I had to think about it.* Bugsy had a brief, uneasy image of Jesus Christ sitting on the cheap couch and talking the decision over with her like a cut-rate therapist.

"Well," he said. "Thanks. I'm working with the United Nations," he said, then regretted saying it. Her face went cold. "Not the black helicopter, new world order part. That's a whole different division. Real jerks. I'm with the feeding the starving African babies part."

"You don't have to condescend," she said.

"Sorry."

"I'm perfectly aware of what you think of me. You think I'm an emotional cripple who's spent her whole life bouncing from one cult to another."

"Mind if I have some tea?"

She nodded toward the samovar and the cups. He was a little surprised to find his hands were shaking. He'd fought in wars before. Having a Christian lunatic call him out shouldn't have meant anything.

"May I ask you a question, Mr. Tipton-Clarke?"

"Sure."

"Have you accepted Jesus Christ as your personal lord and savior?"

"Ah. Well, not as such, no. The big guy and I haven't ever really hung out, if you see what I mean."

"You will be condemned to hellfire and damnation," she said as if she were an insurance adjuster pointing out the fine print on a policy.

"If we can, let's table that just for a second," he said. "I was wondering if I could ask you about the Radical."

"Who?"

"The Radical. He goes by Tom Weathers now. You knew him back in sixty-nine. He was at the People's Park riot. I was led to understand that you and he were . . ."

It was like a caul had formed over her eyes. A grey film that wasn't really there. "I remember," she said. "I remember him. I never knew his name. I have been lost many times in my life. Yes, I know who you mean."

"The thing is, he's turned out to be kind of a . . . well . . . crazed, homicidal, political fanatic with the blood of hundreds if not thousands of people on his hands."

She closed her eyes for a moment and sighed. When she opened them, there seemed to be even less joy in them than before. "I am sorry to hear it, but I can't say I'm surprised. We were all enchanted by Satan. I am sorry he was called to do the devil's work."

"Lot of folks are sorry about that. Seriously. I was wondering if you could tell me more about your relationship with him, and how exactly he knew Mark Meadows?"

"Mark?" She laughed. "Oh, poor Mark. Mark didn't know the Radical. Neither did I. I had no relationship with him."

"But . . ."

"I spent one night with him, and I have not seen him again. I know you can't believe this, but I had sinful encounters with many, many men when I was young."

"Oh, I believe it," Bugsy said. "I've seen pictures."

Kimberly's face showed a flickering cascade of emotions—surprise, embarrassment, pleasure—and she looked out the window. He sipped his tea. It was too hot.

"What about Mark?"

"Mark was . . . Mark was my fault. I've accepted that. He was one of the many people I led away from the path of righteousness. We were in high school together. He was brilliant. Everybody knew that. He was going to be the next Einstein. Fascinated by chemistry and physics . . . all the sciences. I met him again in New York, and he hadn't changed. He was so . . . *square*."

With the last word, the Kimberly Joy Christopher mask seemed to slip, and Kimberly Ann Cordayne peeked out from behind it. Bugsy sat across from her, leaning forward to keep from sinking irretrievably into the couch.

"He wanted so badly to be part of the scene," she said. "He wanted to be free and unfettered by all the old morality that we'd been taught. He wanted to be political. And he just *wasn't*. He wanted . . ."

She paused, her head tilted as if she were listening to someone. Jesus, maybe. "That's not fair," she said. "That's not true. He didn't want any of those things. Not really. It was just that the men I was sleeping with back then were all like that. Not just the Radical. There was Jim and Teddy and Gabriel and . . . I couldn't make a list, Mr. Tipton. But they were all the same. Young, strong, political, sure of themselves. Mark wanted to be like them."

"Because he wanted to sleep with you?" Bugsy asked.

"He was a sweet boy," she said.

Ah, Mark, you poor little geek, Bugsy thought. *You wanted to get laid, and you wound up being her best girlfriend.* "What about Sprout?" he asked.

"I came back to Mark," she said. "It was later. I'd followed my chosen path. It led to . . . very dark places. I was very, very lost back then. I was looking for the light of Christ, and Mark was the nearest thing I knew. He was a good-hearted man. So when I needed a safe haven, I found him."

"You got married," Bugsy said. "Got pregnant. Had Sprout."

"I am a sinner," she said. "I have confessed myself to the Lord, and he has forgiven me. My sins have been washed from me." She sounded angry saying it. Like she was talking him into something. Or maybe herself. Kimberly Joy squared her shoulders, her jowly chin raised in defiance if not pride.

"Okay," Bugsy said. "Good. I mean, good on you with the sin washing and all. But . . . Sprout?"

"I hated it that I'd been afflicted with a retarded child," she said. "I found the thought alone repulsive. Do you understand how far I had fallen? God sent me a little girl made from purest love, and I rejected her in my heart."

"You sure fought like hell for her when it came time for the custody battle," he said.

"I was angry," she said. "I was weak, and I hated Mark because he was capable of loving her and I wasn't. So I made myself believe that I loved her, that I needed her, and I did everything I could to take her from him. And I suppose I succeeded. I wept when they made her a ward of the state, and put me away, too. And Mark. They called Mark an unfit parent because he was involved with the drug scene. And they took her away from him, too. This was all my doing, Mr. Tipton. The drugs, my daughter, Mark's so-called friends . . ."

"What about the Radical and Sprout? Why does *he* care so much about her?"

In the silence, the small wall-mounted heater clicked. The samovar let out a small hiss. Kimberly Joy Christopher looked into his eyes with distress and confusion that told him he had reached something deep within her. When she spoke, her voice was hoarse.

"What the fuck are you talking about?" she said.

♦

Wednesday,
December 9

The Lab at Nyunzu, Congo
People's Paradise of Africa

THE CHILD SOLDIER HAD told them the landmarks to watch for. The lab at Nyunzu, he'd said, was east of the town, so they'd encounter it first.

Wally cut the engine of the boat once they sighted the rocky island the kid had described; they let the boat drift downstream with the current, staying close to the southern shore and eventually tying up well before they were in sight of the compound. They plunged into the jungle as quietly as possible with Wally leading, his powerful arms clearing the way.

It might have been an idyllic march under other circumstances. Monkeys clambered overhead, calling and scattering; bright parrots and macaws flitted from branch to branch. There were calls: grunts and hoots and gurgles that Jerusha could not identify, and unseen forms that went crashing away as they approached. There were strange plants and flowers sprouting up from the ground at their feet. It would have been fascinating, had she been able to pay attention.

But . . . there was a smell, a horrible smell drifting through the jungle, and it grew worse as they approached the lab encampment.

Wally hunkered down suddenly, gesturing at Jerusha. Crouching, she crept forward. The smell was nearly overpowering. Through the cover of huge, paddle-shaped green leaves, she could see that the area in front of them had been cleared all the way down to the river. A backhoe, its bucket and wheels mud-encrusted, sat at their left not ten feet away. There were buildings erected there, most of them open-sided.

And there, in the humid shade . . .

They were caged in small boxes, stacked two high: children, none of them more than ten or eleven. They were emaciated and fly-blown. Thin fingers gripped the wire that wrapped their wooden cells, and they were guarded by children who were not much older than them and a few adults in military uniforms.

But it was what was closer to them that was truly horrifying. Near the backhoe, the earth had been dug up and disturbed. Black and bloated flies hovered over the clods; white maggots wriggled in the soil; white-headed vultures crowded there. Here and there, horrific forms thrust out of the earth in a mockery of life: an arm, a leg, a hand with splayed fingers, to be picked at by the vultures' hooked beaks. This was a mass grave, poorly covered, and the source of the stench. Jerusha felt her stomach heave, and she forced the bile back down.

Oh, God, this is worse than we imagined. . . .

Even as they watched, a door opened in a walled building with a rusting tin roof. Two Leopard Men emerged, a man in a doctor's white lab coat, and a boy of perhaps twelve accompanying them.

The boy looked frightened and uncertain. Jerusha felt Wally start as he saw them: one of the Leopard Men was the were-leopard they'd encountered on the river, with scabbed-over cuts on his face and arms. The doctor held a tray with several hypodermic needles on it. They went to the nearest of the structures holding the caged children.

"Let *him* do it," Jerusha heard one of the Leopard Men say to the doctor in French, gesturing at the boy. "Go on," he said to the boy. "Prove your loyalty. Prove you're a man."

The boy visibly gulped and plucked one of the hypodermics from the tray. He approached the nearest cage. One of the soldiers opened the lock, pulled at the rickety door, and reached toward the young girl inside, who was crouching as far away as possible. He grasped the girl's arm and pulled her halfway from the cage. *"Allez-y,"* the Leopard Man said. "Do it."

The boy plunged the hypodermic into the girl's arm. She screamed as he pressed the plunger and yanked it out again. The soldier shoved her back in the cage and slammed the door shut again. And Wally . . .

Wally roared a wordless fury and sprang toward the Leopard Men. Vultures squawked and scattered out of his way. Jerusha didn't have time to stop his charge; in a few seconds, Wally was in the middle of a firefight and she could only respond.

Automatic weapons were chattering from all directions. She could hear bullets shrilling and tearing chunks from the leaves to either side of her; a green rain was falling all around her. Someone screamed—not Wally—and she heard the sinister, low growling of a leopard. Taking a breath, Jerusha pushed through the screen of greenery and into the clearing, trying to make sense of the chaos.

Everyone's attention seemed to be on Wally, who had closed on the Leopard Men. The doctor was running toward the lab building, his white coat flapping. The boy that had been with him was also retreating—toward the river. One of the Leopard Men was on the ground, his weapon gone to rust in his hands and his arms broken; the other had shifted to leopard form and was snarling at Wally, ready to leap. The guards were firing at him, and bullets were pinging and whining from his body, gouging shiny dings in the black iron.

Jerusha ran over the broken ground of the grave pit as the vultures scowled at her, not daring to look down and hoping that no one would see her. She plunged her hand into the seed belt, not caring what she brought out. She cast the seeds hard toward the soldiers. Green erupted around them—some were vines that she wrapped around the guards, tearing away their weapons from their grasp at the same time; a few were trees that she brought up thick between them and Wally, who had closed with the were-leopard. She half closed her eyes, trying to *be* the plants, to control as many of them at once as she could, as closely as she could. She heard the liquid snarl of a leopard.

Behind. *Behind.*

Jerusha turned even as the creature started its run toward her, lifting into the air with powerful legs, claws ready to rip and slice. She flung the seed in her hand toward it. It was a toss that would have made Curveball proud: into the beast's open mouth. She tore at the seed with her mind, with the power the wild card had given her, ripping the growth out faster than she'd ever done it before. In mid-leap, greenery erupted from the leopard's neck and mouth: even as the creature slammed into her, even as she fell and the Leopard Man rolled past her. Roots grabbed the earth and held; the leopard yowled, a terrifying scream, and the cat was suddenly a man again, writhing and tearing at the branches still growing longer and thicker, rupturing his neck and finally tearing his head entirely loose from his body. Arterial blood fountained from the body as the tree shot upward.

A mango, Jerusha realized belatedly.

Two of the buildings were on fire. Jerusha didn't know why: perhaps stray bullets or ricochets had ignited the oil and gasoline cans scattered through the compound. Yards away, Wally slammed the other were-leopard to earth and stomped on it. The crack of its spine was audible even against the gunfire.

The nearest child soldier flung his weapon to the ground and ran screaming, and suddenly they were all fleeing. Strangely, she thought she saw blood running down Wally's left leg, a long line of it, and he limped as he took a step and spun around.

Wally shouted, *"Lucien! Where are you!"* Jerusha could hear the sinister crackling of the fire, and the plaintive, alarmed shouts of the kids in their cages. Wally had already moved toward them, putting his hand on the wires and dissolving them into ruddy powder. He was pulling kids out, calling for Lucien as he did so.

Jerusha shuddered. The were-leopard's head was staring at her, caught in the fork of a mango branch nearly at eye level. Mangoes were ripening around it, and Jerusha found herself shaking.

She went to help Wally.

Michelle Pond's Apartment
Manhattan, New York

"YOU NEED TO PAY these bills," Juliet said in a reproachful voice as she shuffled the piles of mail that covered Michelle's kitchen table.

"You know, I started going through them, and I just couldn't concentrate," Michelle said. "I mean, I don't really care right now. They aren't stuck in a pit of corpses. You know?"

She felt Juliet kiss her hair. "They'll still need to be paid," she said softly.